D1507612

Australia
The East

Other Travellers' Wildlife Guides

Alaska
Belize and Northern Guatemala
Brazil: Amazon and Pantanal
Costa Rica
Ecuador and the Galápagos Islands
Hawaii
Peru
Southern Africa
Southern Mexico

Australia
The East

by Les Beletsky

Illustrated by:
Hannah Finlay (frogs, reptiles, plants)
Frank Knight (birds, mammals)
Kyoko Kurosawa (fish)
Fernanda Oyarzun (marine invertebrates)
Andy Woodham (fish)

With additional animal art by:
Priscilla Barrett (mammals)
Linda Feltner (reptiles)
Starlet Jacobs (fish)
Douglas Pratt (reptiles, birds, mammals)

Photographs by:
Les Beletsky

Contributors:
Michelle Christy
Stacey Combes
Richard Francis
Kristine French
Gerry Swan

Interlink Books

An imprint of Interlink Publishing Group, Inc.
Northampton, Massachusetts

This edition first published 2007 by

INTERLINK BOOKS
An imprint of Interlink Publishing Group, Inc.
46 Crosby Street, Northampton, Massachusetts 01060
www.interlinkbooks.com

Text copyright © 2007 Les Beletsky
Maps by Jacob Shemkovitz
Illustrations copyright © Priscilla Barrett (Plates 74d, 75c,d)
Linda Feltner (Plates 11b, 12a)
Hannah Finlay (Plates A–K, 1–10, 11a,c,d, 12d,e, 13–19)
Starlet Jacobs (Plates 83, 86, 89)
Frank Knight (Plates 20–32, 33b, c, 34–39, 40b–f, 41–57, 58b–f, 59,
60a–e, 61–73, 74a–c, 75b)
Kyoko Kurosawa (Plates 78a, 90–94, 97–102, 103b,f)
Fernanda Oyarzun (Plates 107–114)
Douglas Pratt (Plates 12b,c, 33a,d,e, 40a, 58a, 60f, 74e, 75a)
Andy Woodham (Plates 76–77, 78b–f, 79–82, 84–85, 87–88, 95–96, 103a,c–e,g, 104–106)

Library of Congress Cataloging-in-Publication Data
Beletsky, Les, 1956-
Australia : the east / Les Beletsky.-- 1st American ed.
p. cm. -- (Travellers' wildlife guides)
Includes bibliographical references and index.
ISBN 1-56656-614-2 (pbk.)
ISBN 13: 978-1-56656-614-8
1. Animals--Australia. 2. Ecotourism--Australia. I. Title. II. Series.
QL338.B45 2005
591.994--dc22

2005026656

Cover image: Eastern Grey Kangaroo (*Macropus giganteus*), Wilsons Promontory National
Park, Australia © Natphotos/Getty Images

Printed and bound in China

To request our complete 40-page full-color catalog,
please call us toll free at **1-800-238-LINK,** visit our website at
www.interlinkbooks.com, or write to
Interlink Publishing
46 Crosby Street, Northampton, MA 01060
e-mail: info@interlinkbooks.com

CONTENTS

PREFACE

This book is aimed at environmentally conscious travellers for whom some of the best parts of any trip are glimpses of animals in natural settings; at people who, when speaking of a journey, often remember days and locations by the wildlife they saw: "That was where we watched the crocodiles," and "That was the day we saw the hawk catch a snake." The purpose of the book is to enhance enjoyment of a trip and enrich wildlife sightings by providing identifying information on about 640 of eastern Australia's most frequently encountered land and ocean animals and plants, along with up-to-date information on their ecology, behavior, and conservation. With color illustrations of 90 species of amphibians and reptiles, 78 mammals, and about 230 birds, this book truly includes almost all of the vertebrate land animals that visitors are likely to encounter. Also included is information on and illustrations of 240 of the most commonly sighted sea creatures seen by divers and snorkelers at the Great Barrier Reef. The majority of international visitors to Australia are interested in its natural attractions, and so can be considered nature tourists; and it is my hope that this book will become a frequently consulted reference during many highly enjoyable trips.

The idea to write this book and some others like it grew out of my own travel experiences and frustrations. First and foremost, I found that I could not locate a single book to take along on a trip that would help me identify all the types of animals that really interested me—birds and mammals, amphibians and reptiles, and fish. There are bird field guides, which I've used, but they are often large books, featuring information on every bird species in a given country or region. If I wanted to be able to identify mammals, I needed to carry another book. For "herps"—amphibians and reptiles—another. Thus, the idea: create a single guide book that travellers could carry to help them identify and learn about the different kinds of animals they were most likely to encounter. Also, like most ecotravellers, I am concerned about the threats to many species as their natural habitats are damaged or destroyed by people; when I travelled, I wanted current information on the conservation statuses of animals that I encountered. This book provides the traveller with conservation information on Australia in general, and on many of the animal family groups pictured or discussed in the book.

A few administrative notes: Because this book has an international audience, I present measurements in both metric and English system units. By now, you might think, the scientific classification of common animals would be pretty much established and unchanging; but you would be wrong. These days, what with new molecular methods to compare species, classifications of various animal groups that were first worked out during the 1800s and early 1900s are undergoing sometimes radical changes. Many bird groups, for instance, are being rearranged after comparative studies of their DNA. The research is so new that many biologists still argue about the results. I cannot guarantee that all the classifications that I use in the book are absolutely the last word on the subject, or that I have been wholly consistent in my classifications. However, for most users of this book, such minor transgressions are probably irrelevant. Also, common English names of some animal groups, especially among fish, amphibians, and reptiles, are not universally agreed upon and vary depending on sources consulted. The names included here were in common use in Australia when this book was written.

I must acknowledge the help of a large number of people in producing this book. First, most of the information here comes from published sources, so I owe the authors of those scientific papers and books a great deal of credit (see References and Additional Reading). Many people provided information for or helped in the preparation of this book including David Pearson, who let me use some of his writing on birds and mammals; Gordon Orians, who allowed me to use some of his ideas for the close-up essay "Nectar and Nectar-eaters"; and Martha Crump, who helped with the close-up essay "Frog Population Declines." Special thanks to Gerry Swan for writing the chapter on reptiles, Michelle Christy and Gerry Swan for writing the chapter on amphibians, Richard Francis for writing the chapter on marine life, Kris French for writing the chapter on habitats and vegetation, and Stacey Combes for writing the chapter on environmental threats and conservation and for help with editing. Bill Buttemer, Lee Astheimer, and Richard Major were most helpful during my information-gathering trips in Australia. Walter Boles (birds) and Sandy Ingleby (mammals), both curators at the Australian Museum, Sydney, were extremely generous in helping me to select species for illustration, and Dennis Paulson assisted in this endeavor. Also I want to thank the artists who produced the book's wonderful illustrations, and the Burke Museum at the University of Washington for kindly allowing me access to its facilities. Please let me know of errors you find in the book, and suggestions for future editions (ECOTRAVEL8@aol.com).

Chapter 1

ECOTOURISM
AND AUSTRALIA

- *Why Visit Australia?*
- *Australian Tourism and Ecotourism*
- *Ecotourism and Its Importance*
- *How Ecotourism Helps*
- *Ecotravel Ethics*

Why Visit Australia?

In previous wildlife/travel books I've written, I've felt compelled, in the books' first paragraphs, to tell travellers why they should visit the particular countries or regions covered by the books. For Australia, there is no need for this. And although Australia now lavishly advertises itself internationally as a wonderful tourism destination, there is really no need for that, either. The reason is that, for the past 150 years and continuing right up through the present day, people with adventurous souls and those who wish to experience new and very different kinds of places eventually travel to Australia. Why? Three broad reasons—physical, biological, and cultural.

Australia is distant and huge. For most North American and European travellers, it is "about as far as you can go." A trip to this distant land is a life goal for many, on "the list" together with an East African safari and a visit to the Amazon rainforest. When asked where on Earth they would like to visit some day, many people will enumerate closer places, then state some version of "Oh, and of course, Australia." The vastness of Australia also attracts: this smallest of continents, or largest of islands (depending on your point of view), with its immense, unpopulated, internal stretches of what most would consider empty landscapes, exerts a magnetic pull on people who live in cities and towns and want to refresh themselves by wandering through open, wild spaces. Australia's sunshine, bright colors, and stunning wild scenery—rainforests and eucalypt forests in the east, desert-scapes in the "Outback"—also powerfully attract.

Biologically, Australia is absolutely unique. If Australia is a great distance physically from North America and Europe, it is an even greater "distance" zoologically. The primary attractions, of course, are its celebrity mammals, the diverse and abundant marsupials (kangaroos, wallabies, koalas, wombats, possums, gliders, bandicoots, not to mention Tasmanian Devils) and the primitive, it's-difficult-to-believe-they-still-exist, egg-laying mammals, Platypuses and Echidnas (Spiny Anteaters). But the birds are wonderful, too, and often easier to see: the parrots, including the large, amazing, and diverse cockatoos, the ostrich-like Emu and Southern Cassowary, the beautiful bowerbirds, which build elaborate stick structures to attract mates, and the megapodes, or mound-builders, which construct enormous mounds of decaying vegetation that they use to incubate their eggs. Also, huge, fascinating monitor lizards (goannas) abound (and, yes, there are also lots of snakes and crocodiles). The Great Barrier Reef—a collection of thousands of individual reefs populating northeastern Australia's continental shelf—provides easy access to an enormous, thrilling marine ecosystem. Zoological oddities include the world's largest segmented worms (the Giant Gippsland Earthworm, from southeastern Victoria), which reach lengths of more than 3 m (10 ft).

Finally, there is no denying that Australia's history and culture also encourage people to visit: the immensely old Aboriginal culture, the compelling story of the European settling of the land as a prison colony, the feeling that contemporary Australia is a vibrant, young, multicultural, live-and-let-live, progressive society with unlimited potential, and the fresh, sophisticated cities of Sydney, Melbourne, and Brisbane all contribute.

Add to the factors mentioned above the following considerations, and you quickly see why Australia is a prime ecotravel destination, one that almost always lives up to expectations and produces unforgettable trips: (1) a large number of world-class national parks (in total, more than 500 parks and nature reserves), many of them easily accessible; (2) myriad accomodations and restaurants that span the range of prices; and (3) the feeling of safety, of travelling in a relatively prosperous place that is one of the world's most solid, successful democracies.

Australian Tourism and Ecotourism

If not for the (not so minor) consideration of relatively expensive, physically stressful, 12-hour airplane flights to reach Australia, many more Americans and Europeans would visit each year (many Japanese also visit, but their flights are shorter, of course). There were recently about 4.1 million international visitors per year travelling to Australia, and, in fact, the number of international visitors has been increasing by significant amounts each year since the mid-1990s. The 2000 Olympics in Sydney, with its attendant publicity and exposure, provided an additional boost to tourism. One important distinction between visitors to many other heavily visited tourist destinations and visitors to Australia is that the majority of international travellers to Australia are definitely interested in natural attractions (i.e., attractions other than cultural ones such as cities and museums) and so can be considered nature tourists or ecotourists. Ecotourism is now popular in Australia, a main buzzword of both the domestic and international travel industries. The state of New South Wales, for instance, promotes the "national park experience" as a main tourism initiative. In fact, it is as a natural paradise—an ecotourist's dream destination—that Australia now markets itself to the rest of world, using images of the Great Barrier Reef, Ayers Rock, and Kakadu National Park. Tourism/ecotourism is the largest revenue-producing industry in many parts of the country. Australian ecotourism is discussed further in Chapter 5.

Ecotourism and Its Importance

People have always travelled. Historical reasons for travelling are many and varied: to find food, to avoid seasonally harsh conditions, to emigrate to new regions in search of more or better farming or hunting lands, to explore, and even, with the advent of leisure time, just for the heck of it (travel for leisure's sake is the definition of tourism). For many people, travelling fulfills some deep need. There's something irreplaceably satisfying about journeying to a new place: the sense of being in completely novel situations and surroundings, seeing things never before encountered, engaging in new and different activities.

During the 1970s and 1980s, however, there arose a new reason to travel, perhaps the first wholly new reason in hundreds of years: with a certain urgency, to see natural habitats and their harbored wildlife before they forever vanish from the surface of the earth. *Ecotourism*, or *ecotravel*, is travel to destinations specifically to admire and enjoy wildlife and undeveloped, relatively undisturbed natural areas and indigenous cultures. The development and increasing popularity of ecotourism is a clear outgrowth of escalating concern for conservation of the world's natural resources and biodiversity (the different types of animals, plants, and other life forms found within a region). Owing mainly to the actions of people, animal species, plant species, and wild habitats are disappearing or deteriorating at an alarming rate. Because of the increasing emphasis in schools on the importance of the natural environment and the media's continuing coverage of environmental issues, people have an enhanced appreciation of the natural world and increased awareness of global environmental problems. They also have the very human desire to want to see undisturbed habitats and wild animals before they are gone, and those with the time and resources are increasingly doing so.

But that's not the entire story. The purpose of ecotravel is actually twofold. Yes, people want to undertake exciting, challenging, educational trips to exotic locales—wet tropical forests, wind-blown deserts, high mountain passes, mid-ocean coral reefs—to enjoy the scenery, the animals, the nearby local cultures. But the second major goal of ecotourism is often as important: The travellers want to help conserve the habitats and wildlife in the very places that they visit. That is, through a portion of their tour cost and spending into the local economy of destination countries—paying for park admissions, engaging local guides, staying at local hotels, eating at local restaurants, using local transportation services, etc.—ecotourists help to preserve natural areas. Ecotourism helps because local people benefit economically by preserving habitats and wildlife for continuing use by ecotravellers as much or more than they could by "harvesting" the habitats for short-term gain. Put another way, local people can sustain themselves better economically by participating in ecotourism than by, for instance, cutting down rainforests for lumber or hunting animals for meat or the illicit exotic pet trade.

Preservation of some of the world's remaining wild areas is important for a host of reasons. Aside from moral arguments—the acknowledgment that we share the earth with millions of other species and have some obligation not to be the continuing agent of their decline and extinction—increasingly we understand that conservation is in our own best interests. The example most often cited is that botanists and pharmaceutical researchers each year discover another wonder drug or two whose base chemicals come from plants that live, for instance, only in the tropical rainforest. Fully one-fourth of all drugs sold in the US come from natural sources: plants and animals. About 50 important drugs now manufactured come from flowering plants found in rainforests, and, based on the number of plants that have yet to be cataloged and screened for their drug potential, researchers estimate that at least 300 more major drugs remain to be discovered. The implication is that if the globe's rainforests are soon destroyed, we will never discover these future wonder drugs, and so will never enjoy their benefits. Also, the developing concept of *biophilia*, if true, dictates that, for our own mental health, we need to preserve some of the wildness that remains in the world. Biophilia, the word recently coined by Harvard biologist E. O. Wilson, suggests that because people evolved amid rich and constant interactions with other species and in natural habitats, we have deeply ingrained, innate tendencies to affiliate with other species and an actual physical need to experience, at some level, natural habitats. This instinctive, emotional attachment to wildness means that if we eliminate species and habitats, we will harm ourselves because we will lose things essential to our mental well-being.

How Ecotourism Helps

To the traveller, the benefits of ecotourism are substantial (exciting, adventurous trips to stunning wild areas; viewing never-before-seen wildlife); the disadvantages are minor (sometimes less-than-deluxe transportation and accommodations that, to many ecotravellers, are actually an essential part of the experience). But what are the actual benefits of ecotourism to local economies and to helping preserve habitats and wildlife?

In theory, the pluses of ecotourism are considerable:

1   Ecotourism benefits visited sites in a number of ways. Most importantly from the visitor's point of view, ecotourism generates money locally through park admission fees, guide fees, etc., that can be used directly to manage and protect wild areas. Ecotourism allows local people to earn livings from areas they live in or near that have been set aside for ecological protection. Providing jobs and encouraging local participation is essential because people will not want to protect the sites, and may even be hostile toward them, if they formerly used the now protected site to support themselves (by farming or hunting, for instance) but are no longer allowed such use. Finally, most ecotourism destinations are in rural areas, regions that ordinarily would not warrant much attention, much less development money, from central governments for services such as road building and maintenance. But all governments realize that a popular tourist site is a valuable commodity, one that it is smart to cater to and protect.

2   Ecotourism benefits education and research. As people, both local and foreign, visit wild areas, they learn more about the sites—from books, from guides, from exhibits, and from their own observations. They come away with an enhanced appreciation of nature and ecology, an increased understanding of the need for preservation, and perhaps a greater likelihood to support conservation measures. Also, a percentage of ecotourist dollars are usually funneled into research in ecology and conservation, work that will in the future lead to more and better conservation solutions.

3   Ecotourism can also be an attractive development option for developing countries. Investment costs to develop small, relatively rustic ecotourist facilities are minor compared with the costs involved in trying to develop traditional tourist facilities such as modern beach resorts. Also, it has been estimated that, at least in some regions, ecotourists spend more per person in the destination countries than any other kind of tourists.

Ecotravel Ethics

A conscientious ecotraveller can take several steps to maximize his or her positive impact on visited areas. First and foremost, if travelling with a tour group, is to select an ecologically committed tour company. Basic guidelines for ecotourism have been established by various international conservation organizations. These are a set of ethics that tour operators should follow if they are truly concerned with conservation. Before committing to a tour, travellers wishing to adhere to ecotour ethics should ascertain whether tour operators conform to the guidelines (or at least to some of them), and choose a company accordingly. Some tour operators conspicuously trumpet their ecotour credentials and commitments in their brochures and sales pitches, yet a large, glossy brochure that fails to mention how a company fulfills some of the ecotour ethics may indicate an operator that is not especially environmentally concerned. Resorts, lodges, and travel agencies that specialize in ecotourism likewise can be evaluated for their dedication to eco-ethics. Some travel guide books that list tour companies provide such ratings. The International Ecotourism Society, an organization of ecotourism professionals, may also provide helpful information (US tel: 802-447-2121; e-mail: ecomail@ ecotourism.org; www.ecotourism.org).

Basic ecotour guidelines, as put forth by the United Nations Environmental Program (UNEP), the International Union for Conservation of Nature (IUCN), and the World Resources Institute (WRI), are that tours and tour operators should:

1   Provide significant benefits for local residents and involve local communities in tour planning and implementation.
2   Contribute to the sustainable management of natural resources.
3   Incorporate environmental education for tourists and residents.
4   Manage tours to minimize negative impacts on the environment and local culture.

For example, tour companies could:

1   Make contributions to the parks or areas visited; support or sponsor small, local environmental projects.
2   Provide employment to local residents as tour assistants, local guides, or local naturalists.
3   Whenever possible, use local products, transportation, food, and locally owned lodging and other services.
4   Keep tour groups small to minimize negative impacts on visited sites; educate ecotourists about local cultures as well as habitats and wildlife.
5   When possible, cooperate with researchers. For instance, Costa Rican researchers are now making good use of the elevated forest canopy walkways in

tropical forests that several ecotourism facility operators have erected on their properties for the enjoyment and education of their guests.

Committed ecotravellers can also adhere to the ecotourism ethic by patronizing lodges and tours operated by local people, by disturbing habitats and wildlife as little as possible (including fish and other coral reef wildlife, not to mention the coral reef itself!), by staying on trails, by being informed about the historical and present conservation concerns of destination countries, by respecting local cultures and rules, by declining to buy souvenirs made from threatened plants or animals, and even by actions as simple as picking up litter on trails.

Chapter 2

AUSTRALIA: GEOGRAPHY, CLIMATE, AND BIODIVERSITY

- *Geography, Topography, and Population*
- *Climate and Best Time to Visit*
- *Biodiversity*
- *The States: Geography and Features*
  Queensland
  New South Wales
  Victoria
  Tasmania

Geography, Topography, and Population

Australia lies south of Asia, with the Pacific Ocean to its east and the Indian Ocean at its west (Map 1, p. 8–9). It may be the smallest continent but it nonetheless encompasses a huge area: 7,682,300 sq km (2,966,000 sq mi), approximately the size of the 48 contiguous US states or about three-quarters of the size of Europe. Australia is about 4,000 km (2480 mi) wide (east to west), 3,200 km (1980 mi) "tall" (north to south), and has a convoluted shoreline of approximately 36,750 km (23,000 mi). The country spans more than 30 degrees of latitude, with its northern half (actually closer to 40%) located in the tropics and its southern half in the south temperate zone. Australia is divided politically into seven states: Queensland (northeast), New South Wales (southeast), Victoria (southeast), Tasmania (an island south of Victoria), South Australia (south-central), Western Australia (west), and Northern Territory (north-central; not formally considered a state). Canberra, Australia's capital, sits in its own tiny "state," the Australian Capital Territory (ACT; 2,366 sq km, 915 sq mi), which is nestled within southeastern New South Wales.

Australia holds the title of flattest continent. Most of Australia lies at elevations of less than 300 m (1,000 ft) above sea level, with much of it below 200 m (650 ft). The average elevation is about 275 m (900 ft), as compared to a worldwide average terrestrial elevation of about 700 m (2,300 ft). Most of the higher areas are

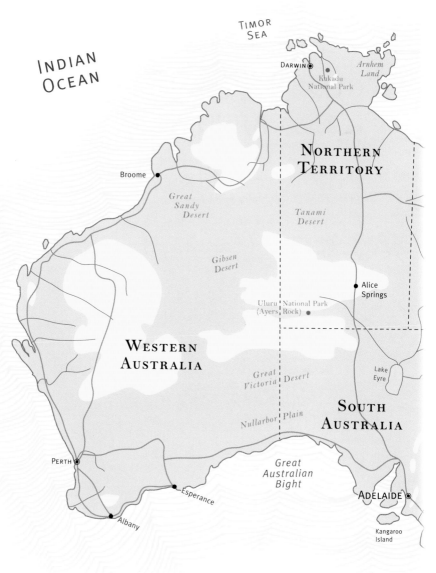

TIMOR SEA

INDIAN OCEAN

DARWIN ⊙

Arnhem Land

Kakadu National Park

NORTHERN TERRITORY

Broome ●

Great Sandy Desert

Tanami Desert

Gibsen Desert

Alice Springs ●

Uluru National Park (Ayers Rock) ●

WESTERN AUSTRALIA

Great Victoria Desert

Lake Eyre

Nullarbor Plain

SOUTH AUSTRALIA

PERTH ⊙

Esperance ●

Great Australian Bight

ADELAIDE ⊙

Albany ●

Kangaroo Island

SOUTHERN OCEAN

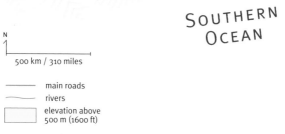

N

500 km / 310 miles

── main roads

── rivers

elevation above 500 m (1600 ft)

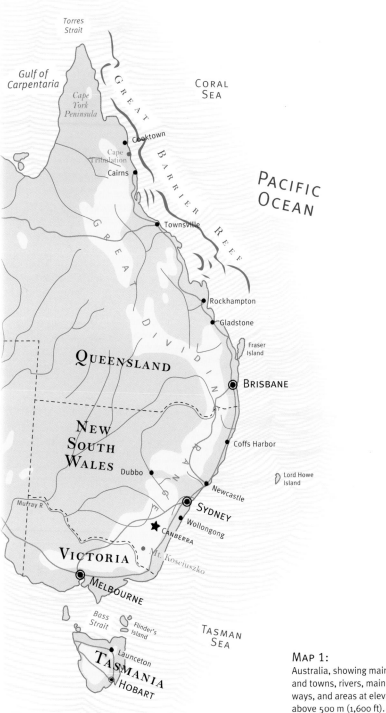

Torres Strait

Gulf of Carpentaria

CORAL SEA

Cape York Peninsula

GREAT BARRIER REEF

Cooktown
Cape Tribulation
Cairns

Townsville

PACIFIC OCEAN

GREAT DIVIDING RANGE

Rockhampton
Gladstone

Fraser Island

QUEENSLAND

BRISBANE

NEW SOUTH WALES

Coffs Harbor

Lord Howe Island

Dubbo

Newcastle

Murray R

SYDNEY
Wollongong
CANBERRA

VICTORIA

Mt. Kosciuszko

MELBOURNE

Bass Strait

Flinder's Island

TASMAN SEA

Launceton

TASMANIA

HOBART

MAP 1:
Australia, showing main cities and towns, rivers, main highways, and areas at elevations above 500 m (1,600 ft).

distributed along or near Australia's coasts. The only "real," fairly high mountains are in the Great Dividing Range, which runs parallel to the eastern coast, 50 to 400 km (30 to 250 mi) inland (Map 1, p. 9). The average elevation of the Great Dividing Range (also called the "eastern uplands," and referred to casually in the East as "the ranges") is only about 910 m (2985 ft). None of the peaks are very high. The tallest ones are concentrated where Victoria meets New South Wales, in a region known as the "Australian Alps." This is where Mt. Kosciuszko ("kozzy-osko"), Australia's highest peak (2237 m, 7339 ft), is located. Snow in Australia occurs in winter only in this region and in the mountains of Tasmania (which, geologically speaking, are a continuation of the Great Dividing Range). West of the Great Dividing Range, all the way to the Indian Ocean, Australia is mainly flat and dry with only occasional small outcroppings of higher terrain (such as Ayers Rock, and the MacDonnell Ranges near Alice Springs). Most of this land is monotonous, flat plains, barren semi-desert and grasslands used extensively for livestock grazing and, in certain areas, mining. Between the Great Dividing Range and the Pacific Ocean is a narrow, fertile strip of land on which most of Australia's people live and work. This book covers this eastern coastal strip and the Great Dividing Range; a future book will cover the remainder of the continent.

About 20 million people live in Australia, but they are far from randomly distributed over the landmass. Most, 90% or more, live along the coasts in towns and cities (which have heavy doses of suburbs), and most of these inhabit coastal regions from Melbourne to Cairns. New South Wales, which contains Australia's largest city, Sydney, has 6.5 million people (Sydney has 4 million); Victoria, with the second-largest city of Melbourne, has 4.8 million (Melbourne has 3.3 million); Queensland has 3.5 million (Brisbane, the third-largest city, has 1.6 million); and Tasmania has about a half-million people. The great arid and semi-arid inland portion of the continent, the Outback, is very sparsely populated. One obvious consequence of Australia's relatively small population (less than 10% of the US's population) is that there are many areas, indeed, entire regions, with few people and fairly wild, natural habitats. In other words, there's a lot of "the bush," as Australians tend to call all rural landscapes outside cities and towns. Some differentiate "the bush" as mainly forest and woodland habitats, and use "the Outback" to refer to the arid and semi-arid desert and grassland habitats that occupy much of the middle and western portions of the continent.

Climate and Best Time to Visit

Most of Australia (up to 85% of it) is classified as having an arid or semi-arid climate, and it is often cited as the driest continent (aside from Antarctica). Humid climates are limited to narrow coastal strips mainly in the north, east, and southeast—and it is mostly these areas that are covered in this book. On average, 37% of the Australian landmass receives less than 25 cm (10 in) of rain annually (and so, according to some classifications, could be considered "desert"); 57% receives less than 37.5 cm (15 in); and 68% receives less than 50 cm (20 in). Rainfall is highly variable in Australia, geographically (from less than 12.5 cm, 5 in, annually in the northern desert reaches of South Australia, to more than 400 cm, 155 in, in the northeastern Queensland rainforests, and about 370 cm, 145 in, in western Tasmania) and from year to year. The wet (monsoon) season in Australia's northern (tropical) regions lasts from November to April; the dry season is from April to October. Australia lies at fairly low latitudes, so winter temperatures are mild everywhere; with the exception of the highest elevations in the southeastern mountains, no part of the country experiences days during which temperatures do not rise well above freezing. On the other hand, summer midday temperatures over most of the continent can be quite high, sometimes exceeding 40° C (104° F).

You can visit Australia at any time of year and have a great trip. Most travellers try to avoid the northern part of the country (northeast Queensland, the Darwin area and Kakadu, etc.) in summer (December to February) when it is very warm and humid and rains frequently (the height of the wet season, often called "The Wet"). This is also the hottest and most uncomfortable period in Australia's center. During this time, the southern states (New South Wales, Victoria), during their warmest period of the year, are more heavily visited. During winter (June to August) the north is cooler and drier, and this is the peak visitation period for the Cairns area, the Cape York Peninsula, the Queensland coastal beaches, and Kakadu National Park. Australia's southern reaches are cooler in winter, with some very cool days in Sydney and Melbourne; at sufficiently high elevations in the Australian Alps, there is snow and skiing. This is also the best time to visit the Outback—with warm, sunny days and cool nights. Spring and autumn provide a mixture of weather types and are fine times to visit. Try to avoid periods of major school holidays, particularly mid-December through late January, when many Australians travel and hotels and transportation systems are clogged.

Biodiversity

The uniqueness of much of Australia's native flora and fauna is mainly owing to geological chance and the vagaries of continental plate tectonics. The basic story is this: Long ago, Australia was part of a huge supercontinent that covered a large portion of the southern hemisphere. *Gondwanaland*, the name we now give to this supercontinent, was formed from what are now the separate landmasses of Africa and Madagascar, India, Antarctica, New Zealand, and South America, in addition to Australia. At some point, perhaps between 40 and 50 million years ago, Australia separated from the supercontinent and began drifting northwards on its geological plate (and, in fact, it is still drifting, between 5.5 and 7 cm, 2 to 3 in, per year). Animals (and plants) in Australia when it separated, such as monotreme and marsupial mammals (whether they had first evolved in Australia or had evolved on other continents and then had spread to Australia), were stranded and, from that point to nearly the present day, were largely isolated from the rest of the terrestrial world. Over time, they changed (evolved, speciated) into the organisms that inhabit Australia today—and the fact that they had little interaction with species on other continents during their long, isolated development explains the high proportion of *endemic* species (those unique to a place) found in Australia (see Close-up, p. 110).

A common observation of newcomers to Australia is that often one does not see a great deal of biodiversity in any one habitat—for instance, the endless, repetitive eucalypt woodlands of eastern Australia, or the montonous tussock grasslands of the country's northern arid areas; but the thing to keep in mind is that most of what you DO see is novel and interesting. Australia's overall biodiversity is ample, as befits a continent whose current human occupants advertise it as a natural wonder. By some estimates, it is one of the five biologically richest countries on the planet. It has about 15,000 species of flowering plants; 210 amphibians (all frogs, no salamanders; the extremely arid climate over most of the continent explains this relative dearth of moist-skinned terrestrial vertebrates); two of the world's 22 crocodile species, about 30 turtle species, 525+ lizards, and 170+ snakes (and yes, the majority of snake species in Australia are venomous, but only a few are deadly. See p. 105). It also has about 750 bird species; and 300 terrestrial mammals, including 150 or so marsupials, 60 rodents, 70 bats, and 20 introduced species, including rabbits, rodents, foxes, cats, pigs, and deer.

The States: Geography and Features

Below are brief descriptions of the states/regions covered in this book, with information on geography and biodiversity.

Queensland

Queensland (Map 3, p. 29) is officially Australia's "Sunshine State," unofficially its "holiday" state, and for our purposes here, must be considered the main destination state for ecotravellers—its biodiversity is enormous (see below). Queensland is huge (1,727,000 sq km, 667,000 sq mi; the size of Alaska or of Spain, Germany, the UK, and France combined) and occupies the northeast section of the continent. The northern half of the state is above the Tropic of Capricorn, so it is located within the tropics; the southern half is in the temperate zone. Over all of the state, summers are hot and winters warm. Queensland can be divided into four regions, from east to west. First there is a narrow, low strip along the east coast, essentially from the border with New South Wales and Brisbane (Australia's third-largest city) in the south to Cairns and beyond in the north, with numerous beaches, bays, islands, and national parks that permit coastal access. This area includes the famed holiday spots for beaches, surfing, boating, and fishing known as the Gold Coast (a 35 km, 22 mi, strip of beaches running northward into Queensland from the New South Wales border) and Sunshine Coast (the 40 km, 25 mi, stretch from Caloundra north to Noosa Heads). Along with Queensland's coast we can include the Great Barrier Reef, one of the world's most famous diving and snorkeling venues (pp. 32; 244). The reef occurs in many separate pieces that begin off the Queensland coast near the Tropic of Capricorn, offshore from Gladstone, and then run northward for about 2,000 km (1,250 mi), all the way to the northern limit of Queensland and a bit beyond, into the Torres Strait. At its southern reaches, the reef is far from the mainland; in the north, it is quite close.

Queensland's second region, slightly inland from the coastal strip, is an area of flat, mainly agricultural districts known as "tablelands," and west of the tablelands, third, are the mountains of the Great Dividing Range. The Range runs north to south through the entire state, with its highest point at Mt. Bartle Frere (1,611 m, 5,285 ft). West of the mountains, and fourth, the land drops off to flat plains, the beginning of the Outback.

Queensland's economy, like those of the other states covered in this book, has a large cattle- and sheep-ranching component, but several grain crops are grown: Sugarcane is a dominant crop along the eastern coast, and tropical fruit, such as bananas, mangoes, and pineapples, is a major contributor. Mining is also a significant part of the economy, with copper, zinc, lead, silver, and uranium. Tourism is an important segment of the economy too; the prime tourist attractions in Queensland are the mainland coast and the Great Barrier Reef, which together attract the most visitors and account for most tourism receipts. The Cairns area and the Cape York Peninsula are also heavily visited. Cairns, a larger town on the coast in northeastern Queensland, is considered the "capital" for the northeast tourist region, the jumping-off point to explore nearby national parks, Cape York Peninsula, and parts of the Great Barrier Reef. Daintree and Cape Tribulation National Parks, north of Cairns, contain magnificent scenery, where wild rivers meander through green forests and tropical rainforest meets ocean. The Daintree River is a favorite birding location. The Atherton Tablelands, a relatively high-elevation plateau (at about 900 m, 3,000 ft) just west of Cairns, is a popular area for its small rustic towns, green scenery, mountain views, and waterfalls. The Cape York Peninsula is a predominantly wilderness area in Queensland's north that juts toward New Guinea. The peninsula, considered one of Australia's "last frontier" areas, has many national parks and is an area of tropical 4-wheel-drive adventuring. Fraser Island, near Brisbane, with rainforests, hiking trails, and great animal life, is one of Queensland's biggest eco-attractions. Beautiful Lamington National Park, in the Great Dividing Range in southeastern Queensland, is an easily reached park that draws visitors for its gorgeous subtropical rainforest scenery, hiking trails, and wonderful birdlife.

Queensland's biodiversity is unmatched in the rest of Australia. More than 2,000 species of marine fish are found off Queensland's coasts and around the Great Barrier Reef, and about 70% (175) of Australia's freshwater fish species occur in the state. Reptiles are represented by 442 species (about 140 of them endemic to the state), including 2 crocodiles and 112 snakes (22 of them being sea snakes); 6 of the world's 7 species of sea turtle breed on Queensland's coastal or island beaches. There are 120 frogs, 32 of them endemic (including the Hip Pocket Frog, in which the male shelters eggs and tadpoles in skin-folds in his groin area). Australia's richest bird fauna occurs in Queensland—about 615 native species have been observed here (about 160 of them being international migrants); included are the huge Emu and Southern Cassowary, mound-builders such as the Australian Brush-turkey and Orange-footed Scrubfowl, about 33 parrot species, and 6 bowerbirds. Queensland has 226 mammal species, including 66 bats and 28 cetacean species offshore, as well as the Dugong. The "Wet Tropics" alone (the rainforest parts of northern Queensland) support 36% of Australia's mammals, including 30% of its marsupial species, 58% of its bats, and 25% of its rodents. For questions/information about Queensland national parks and wildlife, contact: Queensland Parks and Wildlife Service of the Queensland Environmental Protection Agency, tel: (07) 3227-8186; www.epa.qld.gov.au; e-mail: nqic@epa.qld.gov.au.

New South Wales

New South Wales (Map 4, p. 37), occupying most of southeastern Australia with the shining city of Sydney on its central coast, is the "gateway" to the country for most international travellers. Although many ecotravellers arrive in Sydney and then fly to Queensland or other states to get to their final destinations, there are about 70 national parks in the state and many of them are moderately or heavily visited—especially those that ring the Sydney area. Parks such as Royal, Ku-ring-gai Chase, and Kosciuszko National Parks, as well as the Blue Mountains region, offer splendid views and outdoor activities in coastal, mountain, and forested areas. The New South Wales economy is diversified, with Australia's heaviest industrial and manufacturing centers, but agriculture has a dominant presence with cattle and sheep ranches, dairy farms, and crops such as fruit, vegetables (corn), grains (wheat), and sugarcane (in the northeast). Fishing, logging, and mining are also important.

The state (total area 801,500 sq km, 309,500 sq mi; the size of Texas or of France and the UK combined) is conveniently viewed as having four sections. A narrow, lowland strip with beaches, coastal lakes, and a host of national parks (often offering coast access) runs along the coast (which has 1,450 km, 900 mi, of shoreline); this area is more developed in the north, from Sydney toward Brisbane, and less developed in the south, from Sydney toward the Victoria border. At various distances inland from the coast, but usually about 100 km (60 mi), are the low mountains of the Great Dividing Range. Often "the mountains," or "the ranges," here consist of series of plateaus, or "tablelands." In the north, the New England tablelands average about 750 m (2,500 ft) elevation; in the center, the Blue Mountains, west of Sydney, rise to about 1,100 m (3,600 ft); and in the south, the Snowy Mountains, part of the Australian Alps (and mainly in Kosciuszko National Park), with the highest peak at Mt. Kosciuszko, rise to a bit more than 2,200 m (7,200 ft). The third part of New South Wales consists of the western slope of the Great Dividing Range, a region consisting of fertile, undulating hills, used mainly for farming and ranching; and the fourth part, where the mostly uninhabited land flattens out, is the dry western plains, the beginning of the Outback.

As for wildlife, New South Wales offers about 174 species of mammals, 474 bird species (including Emu, the mound-building Australian Brush-turkey, myriad seabirds, lyrebirds, bowerbirds, and about 30 parrot species—including 6 cockatoos), about 75 species of frogs, and 209 reptiles (including 4 monitor lizards and 15 agamid, or "dragon," lizards). For questions/information about New South Wales national parks and wildlife, contact: NSW National Parks and Wildlife Service, tel: 1300-361-967 (from inside Australia); www.npws.nsw.gov.au; e-mail: info@npws.nsw.gov.au.

Victoria

Victoria (Map 5, p. 43), Australia's smallest mainland state (227,500 sq km, 87,888 sq mi; the size of Utah or the UK), is known for its great variety of landscapes—from mountains, to tablelands, to forests (more than 25% of its area is forested) and rolling hills and woodlands, to grassy plains, to coastal dunes. The state, in the continent's southeast corner, is Australia's second largest in terms of population, and so, combined with its small area, is the country's most densely settled state; but most people live in or near urban centers—chiefly Melbourne, Geelong, and Ballarat. Victoria has three main geographic divisions: the southern coastal region, with a convoluted shoreline, beaches, and wild areas such as at Croajingolong National Park; the foothills and mountains of the southernmost portion of the Great Dividing Range, which can be considered to run east-to-west through the state; and the far west and northwest, with large areas of flat plains.

The economy of Victoria is split between agriculture (sheep and cattle ranching, wool production, dairy products), timber/forestry products, oil/gas production (in the Bass Strait), and manufacturing, including motor vehicles.

Travellers visit Victoria to undertake a large variety of activities, including hiking, whitewater rafting, hang gliding, fishing, and skiing in the high country of the Victorian Alps (the southern portion of the "Australian Alps," the south end of the Great Dividing Range); tasting the city delights of Melbourne and its surroundings; driving the Great Ocean Road (p. 45) along the coast; hiking and viewing the wonderful natural scenery at Wilsons Promontory National Park, the southernmost part of the Australian mainland; experiencing the mountains, hills, valleys, and waterfalls of Grampians National Park; and watching the "penguin parade" at Phillip Island Nature Park. Victorian wildlife includes, in addition to myriad seabirds, waterbirds, and songbirds, conspicuous populations of one of the world's largest birds, the Emu, and the world's smallest penguin, the Little Penguin. Temperate-zone Victoria also supports about 35 frog species, 6 turtles, 11 geckos, 11 agamid lizards, or "dragons," 3 monitor lizards, 19 elapid snakes, and about 100 terrestrial mammals, plus 30 seals and cetaceans in its territorial waters. For information about Victoria national parks, wildlife, and conservation, contact: Parks Victoria, tel: 13-1963 (from inside Australia); www.parkweb.vic.gov.au; e-mail: info@parks.vic.gov.au; and/or Victoria Dept. of Sustainability and Environment, www.dse.vic.gov.au; e-mail: customer.service@dse.vic.gov.au.

Tasmania

Tasmania (Map 6, p. 47), Australia's smallest state (67,800 sq km, 26,200 sq mi; about the size of West Virginia or Ireland), is a heart-shaped, mountainous, forested island located across the Bass Strait from Victoria (about 240 km, 150 mi, away). When the first Europeans reached Tasmania, it was the towering wet forests that most impressed them; one Frenchman in 1792 described "trees of an immense height and proportionate diameter, their branchless trunks covered with evergreen foliage, some looking as old as the world...." The huge trees still impress (about 40% of the island is still forested), and they are some of the most amazing sights to be seen in national parks. A lot of the island is mountainous, but few peaks rise above 1,500 m (4,900 ft); those that do are snow-covered in winter. This is Australia's rainiest state, with the western region receiving annually up to 370 cm (145 in) of rain. The major population centers are along the northern and southeastern coasts (centered around the cities of Hobart and Launceton); around these areas and filling the middle of the island are fertile agricultural regions. The remote western part of Tasmania, particularly the southwest, is sparsely populated, and national parks protect great swaths of largely inaccessible wilderness—about 25% of the island is protected public land. Logging and mining are significant parts of the island's economy, and their operations are sometimes conspicuous as you drive around. Tasmanian agriculture includes cattle and sheep ranching, dairy products, and orchard fruit, especially apples.

Visitors to Tasmania come to trek and bushwalk in alpine habitats and temperate rainforests at such wonders as Mount Field and Cradle Mountain National Parks, to see beautiful, wild, coastal panoramas such as at Freycinet National Park, and to experience the quiet, small-town charms of a largely rural state. Tasmania, being a solidly temperate-zone island with cold winters, is not as biologically diverse as the rest of eastern Australia. But it has some interesting and unique wildlife, including some that is adapted to its cold alpine and subalpine regions, and boasts 11 frog species, 3 snakes, 17 lizards, about 200 regularly occuring birds (11 endemics, including Tasmanian Native-hen, Green Rosella, Dusky Robin, Yellow-throated Honeyeater, Forty-spotted Pardalote, and Black Currawong) and 35 or so terrestrial mammals, including the endemic Tasmanian Devil. For questions/information about Tasmania national parks and wildlife, you can contact: Tasmania Parks and Wildlife Service, tel: 1300-135-513 (from inside Australia); www.parks.tas.gov.au.

Chapter 3

HABITATS AND COMMON VEGETATION

by Kristine French
School of Biological Sciences
University of Wollongong, New South Wales

- *History of the Australian Flora*
- *The Modern Australian Environment*
- *Characteristics of the Main Families of Plants*
  Myrtaceae—eucalypts, tea trees, melaleucas, and lilly-pillys
  Fabaceae—wattles and peas
  Proteaceae—banksias and grevilleas
  Epacridaceae—the heath family
- *Main Vegetation Types*
  Heaths and Shrublands
  Open Forests and Woodlands
  Closed Forest
- *Environmental Close-Up 1: Plant–Animal Interactions*

History of the Australian Flora

Initially, Australia was part of an immense continent called Gondwanaland (the Great Southern Continent) that included South America, Africa, India, Australia, and Antarctica. About 110 million years ago this continent started to break up, though Antarctica and Australia remained joined until about 40 million years ago, when Australia finally separated. During the Gondwanan period Australia experienced a warm, wet climate that saw the evolution of groups of plants such as the southern pines (*Araucaria*), southern beech (*Nothofagus*), the eucalypt and lilly-pilly family (Myrtaceae), and the banksia family (Proteaceae). The similarities between the flora of Australia, South America, and Africa are still evident today. The fact that the main Australian plant families evolved when it was still connected to other continents means that Australia does not have many unique families, but it does have many unique species.

When Australia separated from Antarctica, the strong ocean currents circled Antarctica, cutting off the transfer of warm equatorial water that previously contributed to Australia's wet climate. As a result, the Australian climate became drier, cooler, and more seasonal. As Australia moved northward under the forces of continental drift, it came under the influence of the drying subtropical atmospheric high-pressure cells. The isolation of Australia during this period resulted in the evolution of a flora adapted to this increasing aridity and more seasonal climate. This flora is unique and unusual, but derived from the initial closed forests that covered Gondwanaland. The original forest type became confined to small patches of closed forest (rainforest) along the eastern coast of the continent. As the Australian plate moved northward, there came an increasing interchange with southeast Asian ecosystems (for instance, via occasional land bridges that linked Australia with New Guinea), allowing some plants from the Indo-Malaysian region to establish in Australia. These can still be seen in the closed forests of northern Queensland.

The Modern Australian Environment

Today Australia is characterized by generally poor soils that have few nutrients and poor ability to hold water. Plant species often have adaptations to overcome this; for example, specialized roots that tap small sources of nitrogen (such as dead insects), *mycorrhizae* (fungi that aid in gathering nutrients), and efficient recycling within plants that maximizes use of rare nutrients such as phosphorus.

While the poor soils are hard for the traveller to see, the impact of fire is often spectacular and obvious in the landscape. For many vegetation types, fire is a regular occurrence, happening naturally about once every 10 to 100 years in temperate forests. Fires are less frequent in the southern areas, some only experiencing fire every century or more. The fire frequency increases toward the tropics. Plants show a range of adaptations for recovering after fire: storing seeds in the soil for many years (wattles and peas) or in woody capsules in the canopy (banksias and eucalypts), and the ability to resprout from roots or stems that have been burnt. While the species in the open forests and woodlands, shrublands, and heaths are well adapted to fire, the species in closed forests throughout Australia typically are destroyed by fire.

Characteristics of the Main Families of Plants

Travelling up Australia's eastern coast from Tasmania to Queensland, you will move from a cool climate with high winter rainfall through to a subtropical, then tropical climate with a high summer rainfall. Despite the changes in climate, you will probably be struck by two things: most of the forests are composed of similar-looking trees, eucalypts, and the understory plants are quite similar from one area to the next. Indeed, forests and woodlands throughout much of Australia have similar plant families and genera (plural of genus). However, in each area the species within those families and genera differ. There are few widespread species. So, while you may not be able to identify species of plants, you may, with a few pointers, be able to identify the family or the genus and observe different members of each family and genus as you travel along the east coast. These families are similar in heaths and shrublands as well. Four main families are described below:

Myrtaceae—eucalypts, tea trees, melaleucas and lilly-pillys

Whether in open forests and woodlands or in closed forests, the Myrtaceae (Plate A) are common plants. Where leaves are large, they have a characteristic venation (vein pattern) and the flowers have many stamens (giving them a "fluffy" appearance), often surrounding a small cup. The leaves, when crushed, give a strong scent. The species from open forests and woodlands, shrublands, and heaths have a woody capsule that usually remains on the plant. These species include the eucalypts (Plate C), tea trees (*Leptospermum*, Plate D), bottlebrushes (*Callistemon*), and paperbarks (*Melaleuca*, Plate D). In closed forests, lilly-pilly (*Acmena*, Plate H) and cherry (*Syzigium*, Plate K) are common and produce berries rather than capsules.

Fabaceae—wattles and peas

Family Fabaceae (Plate B) is always diverse in any vegetation, and often obvious during spring and in regenerating areas. All plants produce a pod (legume) enclosing the seeds. Wattles (*Acacia*, Plate B) have a very characteristic yellow inflorescence (a structure made up of several flowers), with leaves either bipinnate (a leaf made up of leaflets along stalk) or as flat phyllodes (leaf-like stems). The peas are usually small woody shrubs, with a characteristic flower shape (just like sweetpeas). Most are yellow (such as *Phyllota*, *Dillwynia* (Plate G), *Pultenaea*, and *Gompholobium*) but a few are purple (such as *Hovea* and *Hardenbergia*).

Proteaceae—banksias and grevilleas

The Proteaceae (Plate A) are usually taller shrubs or small trees that frequently have large cones remaining on the tree—that is, until a fire occurs and the seeds are released. Often these plants form the overstory in heaths and shrublands. The flower is the most characteristic feature, often in large showy inflorescences that attract birds, possums, and a range of insects. The family includes some spectacular plants, such as the Waratah (*Telopea* spp., Plate A), Silky Oak (*Grevillea robusta*), and the conspicuous banksias (*Banksia* spp., Plate E).

Epacridaceae—the heath family

The members of family Epacridaceae (Plate B) are easy to distinguish as small woody shrubs, usually less than 1 m (3.3 ft) in height. They are particularly prominent in heaths and shrublands. The leaves are always small (and spiky), heart-shaped, and clinging to the stem in abundance. The flowers, occurring on the stems, are small and tubular, often pink or white. This family is very closely related to the Ericaceae—the family of heath plants in Europe and America.

Main Vegetation Types

Heaths and Shrublands

Heaths and shrublands occur on poor soils that are particularly low in nitrogen and phosphate. These habitats lack a canopy of eucalypts and are dominated by hard-leaved shrubs. Despite the lack of overstory, these areas are usually spectacular in their diversity and are great to visit during spring and early summer, when many plants are in flower. They occur all along eastern Australia's coastal areas. Where soils are well drained, such as behind the foredune on beaches, the shrublands are dry and quite tall. Here *Banksia integrifolia* (Plate E), *Melaleuca armillaris*, and *Acacia longifolia* are common. *Westringia fruticosa* (Plate G) is often planted in coastal areas, though it is less abundant naturally. Areas that are waterlogged and swampy are often dominated by different species of paperbarks, such as *Melaleuca linariifolia* (Plate D) in NSW. Casuarinas (*Allocasuarina* and *Casuarina*) are unusual in having cylindrical braches that appear segmented. In coastal areas *Allocasuarina littoralis* (Plate D) is common. In more exposed areas where soils are shallow and waterlogged, heaths are found. These are characterized by small epacrids (for example, *Epacris impressa*, Plate F; and *Woollsia pungens*), sedges (such as *Lepidosperma laterale* and *Lepyrodia scariosa*), and lilies (Christmas bells, *Blandfordia* spp., Plate E; flax lily, *Dianella* spp.). Look out for grass trees, *Xanthorrhoea* sp. (Plate G), which only flower after fire and, like Christmas bells, are uniquely Australian.

Good representatives of these vegetation types are found in Wilsons Promontory National Park, Nadgee Nature Reserve, Jervis Bay, Royal National Park, and Myall Lakes National Park, but they are not hard to find anywhere. The introduced Bitou Bush (*Chrysanthmoides monilifera*) is a major problem of coastal heaths and shrublands. This species is unfortunately the most common plant of coastal areas from Moruya (NSW) through to southern Queensland. It has yellow daisy flowers.

Open Forests and Woodlands

Open woodlands share many species with some of the shrublands; however, they have a eucalypt canopy. Often, a couple species of eucalypts occur in any area, with different species occurring in the gullies (valleys) compared to the slopes and ridges. These trees can be sparsely distributed, allowing plenty of light to reach the ground. The understory is often dense, with a great diversity of shrubs, including many different peas, epacrids, and species from the Proteaceae. The soil is usually poor, but where the soil is richer (for example, shales), grasses tend to dominate the understory. These richer areas are usually cleared for farming. The woodlands that occur around Sydney are on poor soils but the diversity of plants is astounding. A visit to Ku-ring-gai Chase National Park or Brisbane Water National Park (near Gosford, north of Sydney) will show you some wonderful bushland dominated by the pink-orange trunks of Smooth-barked Apple (*Angophora costata*, Plate C) and the appropriately named Red Bloodwood (*Eucalyptus gummifera*, Plate C). Good examples of Spotted Gums (*Eucalyptus maculata*, Plate C) occur at Batemans Bay and near Jervis Bay.

In the foothills of the ranges, the soils become deeper. These areas support taller forests that often have more soft-leaved understory species, including ferns. The species of eucalypts change with both increasing latitude and altitude. These forests are important timber-producing habitats, and regrowth forests that are up to 80 years old are commonly seen. In Tasmania and Victoria, Mountain Ash (*Eucalyptus regnans*) produces magnificent forests and are the tallest hardwood species on Earth. Mt. Donna Buang and the Dandenongs, near Melbourne, are good places to see this tree on the mainland, but the best examples are in the mountains of Tasmania. Other ash species (*Eucalyptus sieberi* and *Eucalyptus nitens*) occur in the southern mountains of NSW and areas around Eden. Blackbutt (*Eucalyptus pilularis*) and Sydney Blue Gum (*Eucalyptus saligna*, Plate C) forests commonly occur in warmer areas throughout NSW. Good examples are found in the hills around Wauchope. There are some wonderful patches of forest here that have never been logged, particularly in Belangry State Forest near Wauchope. The forests of the far north coast of NSW are some of the world's fastest-growing and most productive forests. The forests near Buladelah, dominated by *Eucalyptus grandis*, produce the tallest forests in NSW, with these trees' trunks a spectacular white. *Eucalyptus grandis* occurs all the way through to Cairns, where forests of this species occur within the Queensland World Heritage Area (p. 30). In southeastern Queensland, some forests are dominated not by eucalypts but by a species of wattle, the Brigalow, *Acacia harpophylla*, which often grows in dense stands. In the Cape York Peninsula, open forest with a grassy understory mixes with tropical savannah.

Closed Forest

Millions of years ago, as Australia dried, closed forests became restricted to small patches along the coastal regions of eastern Australia. These forests do not have a eucalypt overstory, instead being dominated by many different species from a range of families. Most of these species are derived from plants that were around when supercontinent Gondwanaland was still intact and many ancient families still persist in these forests (for instance, Winteraceae, the pepperbush family; Eupomatiaceae, bolwarra family; and Lauraceae, laurel family). Closed forests have a dense canopy that lets little light through to the understory. Consequently, these areas, having little understory, are often easy to walk through, once the vines are negotiated.

In Tasmania and Victoria, the closed forests are cool, with a fern understory and lots of mosses and lichens. These forests are dominated by Myrtle Beech (*Nothofagus cunninghamii*, Plate H) and Southern Sassafras (*Atherosperma moschatum*). These cool forests also occur at high altitudes in NSW at Dorrigo, Werrikimbe, and Border Ranges National Parks. Warm temperate forests occur from Wollongong (NSW) north. They are dominated by Lilly-pillies (*Acmena smithii*, Plate H), Coachwood (*Ceratopetalum apetalum*, Plate H), and Sassafras (*Doryphora sassafras*, Plate H). In the subtropics, a greater diversity of trees occur, but the figs are an easy-to-recognize addition. The Giant Stinging Tree (*Dendrocnide excelsa*, Plate J), despite looking like a lush deciduous tree from the northern hemisphere, has a painful and long-lasting "bite" if you touch its large, light-green, heart-shaped leaves or stems. The Cheese Tree (*Glochidion ferdinandi*, Plate I) and the Cabbage Tree (*Livistona australis*, Plate I) are frequently encountered. There are many epiphytes (plants, such as orchids, that grow on trees) in these forests. A trip to Sea Acres in Port Macquarie is a pleasant walk through the canopy of this habitat. Mt. Warning in Queensland and the border ranges region have excellent areas of subtropical closed forest. Here the Hoop Pines (*Araucaria cunninghamii*, Plate K) and White Booyong (*Heritiera trifoliatum*, Plate J) commonly dominate the forest. And here there is the first overlap between the species that dominate the southern closed forests and those derived from the tropical Indo-Malaysian area.

In the tropical closed forests, vines, epiphytes, ferns, orchids, palms, and a host of different tree species abound. A huge diversity of species mix with Indo-Malaysian species such as lawyer vines (used for wicker baskets) and king palms (such as Bangalow Palm, *Archontophoenix cunninghamiana*, Plate J). Black Beans (*Castanospermum australe*, Plate K), Rosewoods (*Dysoxylum* spp.), and figs like the Cluster Fig (*Ficus racemosa*) commonly occur in the canopy. The Proteaceae family (Plate A) is very diverse in tropical closed forests, with 40 species endemic to the area. For example, the Firewheel Tree (*Stenocarpus sinuatus*, Plate K) produces stunning red inflorescences. The Umbrella Tree (*Schefflera actinophylla*) is also seen, particularly around Cairns and the Daintree area. The Fan Palm (*Licuala ramsayi*) is endemic to the Cairns area. The closed forests in this area have some 1,160 species of plants, including a huge diversity of the genus *Syzygium* (for example, Bumpy Satinash, *Syzygium cormiflorum*, Plate K). In far northern Queensland, in the McIlwraith and Iron ranges, closed forests occur, some dominated by Flame Trees (*Brachychiton* sp.). This area is isolated and not well described or studied but is an important area for plant biodiversity, with 16% of Australia's orchid species occurring in the area.

Environmental Close-up 1: Plant–animal Interactions

by Kristine French

Two plant–animal interactions characterize Australia. They are not unique to this continent, but their commonness is unusual. The first, pollination by birds, is usually considered a tropical phenomenon. It is completely absent from Europe, where bumblebee pollinators dominate. In Australia, there are no bumblebees, but there are at least 75 species of honeyeaters (p. 168) plus a range of primarily nectarivorous parrots (p. 150) and fruit bats (p. 229) that pollinate many plants. Over a thousand species of Australian plants are pollinated by birds, each plant producing copious quantities of nectar in large showy inflorescences (structures made up of several flowers). In shrublands and open woodlands, honeyeaters can be very common, feeding on the large inflorescences of banksias (Plate E), bottle-brushes, and the flowers of eucalypts (Plates A, C).

The second plant–animal interaction, and perhaps the more peculiar to Australia, is the role that ants play in seed dispersal. It has been estimated that more than 1,500 plant species produce seeds that are attractive to ants, most of these in the drier habitats. In closed forests, seed dispersal by birds and mammals is more common, with lots of fleshy fruit being produced. In open woodlands around Sydney, 40% of plant species produce elaiosomes (see below), more species than use any other type of dispersal mechanism. Many of these seeds are hard-coated, so the ants cannot break open the seeds to eat them. Instead, on the outside of each seed is a small, lipid-rich appendage, which is called an elaiosome (eh-LIE-OWE-some), and it is the elaiosomes that attract the ants. Ants pick up a seed, transport it back to the nest, eat the elaiosome, and discard the seed. Interestingly, for many plant species in the Fabaceae family (Plate B), the hard seed coat prevents the seed from germinating until a fire occurs and the seed is heated. It also prevents the seed from being eaten by ants. Perhaps the real value of ants carrying seeds underground is that they are protected from the very high temperatures (that can be above 5000° C) of the fire on the soil surface, and only get heated a little (to between 80° and 1000° C). This elevated temperature is required to crack the hard seed coat and allow water to enter for germination. After fire, there is often a flush of germination of species that have ant-dispersed seeds. This includes all the peas and wattles, some epacrids, grevilleas, and a number of monocotyledons. The elaiosome is easy to see if you open a pod from a pea or wattle.

The ants, of course, are very easy to see if you have a picnic. In eastern Australia, there can be more than twenty species of ants in a relatively small patch of bush, most not a nuisance and many useful as seed dispersers. The carnivorous Bull Ants (genus *Myrmecia*), which don't collect seeds, may be the only ants that you will wish to avoid.

Chapter 4

PARKS, RESERVES, AND GETTING AROUND

- *Getting Around in Australia*
  Roads and Some Great Drives
  Roadside Scenery and Wildlife
  Trails and Hiking; Hiking Pests
- *Descriptions of Parks, Reserves, and Other Eco-sites*
  Cape York Peninsula (CYP)
  Tropical Queensland (TRQ)
  Temperate Queensland (TEQ)
  New South Wales (NSW)
  Victoria (VIC)
  Tasmania (TAS)

Getting Around in Australia

Roads and Some Great Drives

Roads in eastern Australia are generally in good repair, although secondary and tertiary roads in more rural areas can be potholed. Be aware that once you are outside of the environs of Sydney, Melbourne, and Brisbane, most paved (sealed) roads are one lane in each direction and fairly narrow. Also; many roads discussed in this book are very twisty and turny; you will drive them at 40 to 70 kph (25 to 40 mph), and it will take you much longer to get from point A to point B than it looks like it will from perusing a map. For instance, don't expect any fast, straight roads in eastern Victoria and New South Wales—it often takes a good long while to get to various parks or other eco-attractions. Roads in the Blue Mountains area especially are narrow, constantly twist and turn, and can be quite steep as they climb and descend mountains. Often, in eastern Australia, there are minor paved roads that cross land that is largely agricultural; they may be touted on maps or roadsigns as "scenic" drives. These are usually farm roads that, quite often, are essentially one-lane roads with two-way traffic; be very careful and go slowly as you drive them, and watch out for potholes and large agricultural trucks (or, depending on location, logging trucks; you often don't expect such big trucks on such small roads).

Speaking of roads, below are some great ones to take for forest, mountain, or ocean scenery. All have access to trails and places to park, take in the views, and picnic: (1) in Kosciuszko National Park, New South Wales: the 70 km (40 mi) road from Khancoban to Cabramurra; (2) in New South Wales: Route 69 from Colo Heights to Bulga, along the boundary between Wollemi and Yengo National parks; (3) through Blue Mountains National Park, New South Wales: the 60 km (35 mi) from Bell (near Lithgow) to Kurrajong (near Windsor); (4) in Victoria, the Great Ocean Road west of Melbourne from Torquay to Peterborough; (5) in Queensland, north from Cairns on Route 44 to Mossman and on to Cape Tribulation; (6) in Tasmania, Route A10 from the Mount Field National Park area north to the Lake St. Claire area of Cradle Mountain National Park, then west toward Queenstown (this last portion with spectacular lookouts, such as Donaghy's Hill Wilderness Lookout, and roadside nature trails).

Roadside Scenery and Wildlife

What do you see as you drive around eastern Australia? Passing scenery is sometimes spectacular, as for the six routes listed just above. But much of the countryside is agricultural—mostly grazing lands for livestock, but also crop farms. For instance, much of the roadside scenery in the eastern halves of Victoria and New South Wales consists of cattle and sheep ranches, with views of grazing livestock (sheep are the smaller, usually dirty-brown animals; cattle are larger, and come in a variety of colors, including black and white). Typically, the scenery is endless rolling hills (Habitat Photo 14) with mostly bare pastures, and occasionally patches of trees, under which cattle and sheep shelter from hot sun. In tropical coastal areas of Queensland, cane fields predominate.

Common roadside wildlife during the daytime includes, among reptiles, goannas (very large monitor lizards) beside or crossing roads (or stubbornly blocking roads), and among mammals, various kangaroos and wallabies (sometimes lounging around roadside picnic areas) and the occasional Echidna. Birds are, of course, the most frequently seen wild roadside vertebrates. Some of the most notable, common, and obvious: in the parrot group, Sulphur-crested and Redtailed Black-cockatoos, Galahs, lorikeets and rosellas; Australian White Ibises, Masked Lapwings, and kookaburras; among the perching birds, a host of black and white birds such as Willie Wagtails, Magpie-larks, butcherbirds, currawongs, and the Australian Magpie, and, in some areas, introduced species such as Common Blackbirds, Common Mynas, and Common Starlings. At night, nocturnal marsupials, of which there are many, frequent roads, and many are killed by cars. In mornings in many areas, dead bandicoots, wallabies, and even wombats and koalas litter the roads—it's not a pretty sight, but stopping when it is safe to do so to examine these roadkills is often the only way most ecotravellers have of seeing these mammals.

Trails and Hiking; Hiking Pests

Australian parks generally each have several great trails for hiking (or, in the local language, "walking tracks" for "bushwalking"). Hiking is the same as anywhere else: bring appropriate gear such as good hiking boots, prepare for strong sun and possible rain, take along water and food, and go. If you are visiting at a time when some national park trails are crowded, an alternative is to hike on lesser-used trails in state forests. These preserves are open to commercial logging, but many serve mainly or secondarily as recreational lands. As you travel about eastern Australia, you will see signs along roadways announcing that you are entering state forest land (in New South Wales alone there are more than 3 million ha, 7.4 million ac, of such lands). Often there are trailheads along these roads with places to park or logging roads that you can follow and park alongside (but be careful of logging trucks!).

While it is true that the majority of Australia's snake species are venomous, a few quite dangerously so, most short-term visitors see very few snakes (and most that you do see are sunning themselves on or near roadways); so aside from the normal precautions of watching where you are going and not putting hands and feet into any places that you cannot see, don't worry about snakes. But in parks and along trails, there are other pests to consider. Ants are present everywhere, in large numbers (this is why populations of Echidnas, otherwise known as Spiny Anteaters, are doing so well!). Mosquitos ("mozzies") may or may not be a problem, depending on location, season, and recent amount of rain; they can be bad in tropical regions (for example, Cape York Peninsula) during and just after wet seasons. In some areas, various types of flies are a bother. Small black leeches that you find crawling on your arms and legs after brushing against trailside vegetation, are an occasional minor nuisance. Walk in the center of trails, avoid brushing vegetation, and stop occasionally to check yourself and trail buddies for leeches (the way hikers in parts of North America check themselves for ticks). In the wet tropics there are disease-carrying ticks and stinging trees (genus *Dendrocnide*) to watch out for; the trees have hairs on their heart-shaped leaves that can penetrate your skin, sometimes causing pain that can last for months. In tropical coastal regions near water (rivers, billabongs, rock pools, estuaries), you need to be alert for Saltwater (Estuarine) Crocodiles—but very few tourists are actually eaten by these fellows. (And in the ocean, off the coast or around the islands of the Great Barrier Reef, there are seasonal jellyfish, or "stingers," to worry about, not to mention sharks, venomous sea snakes, and occasional crocs. Enjoy your trip.)

Descriptions of Parks, Reserves, and Other Eco-sites

Eastern Australia has a huge number of national parks, some large and many small ones (they may be called "national," but they are actually owned and operated by the individual states). The parks and reserves described below were selected because they are the ones most often visited by ecotravellers or because they have a lot to offer; also, all (except in Cape York Peninsula) can be reached mostly on paved roads with a regular, two-wheel-drive rental sedan (roads within parks, however, are often gravel or dirt). Many other parks are in more remote areas and are often difficult to access—their roads are for four-wheel-drive vehicles only (especially in wet seasons), or they lack accessible roads. The animals profiled in the color plates are keyed to parks and reserves in the following way: the profiles list the locations (Map 2, p. 27; CYP = Cape York Peninsula, TRQ = Tropical Queensland, TEQ = Temperate Queensland, NSW = New South Wales,

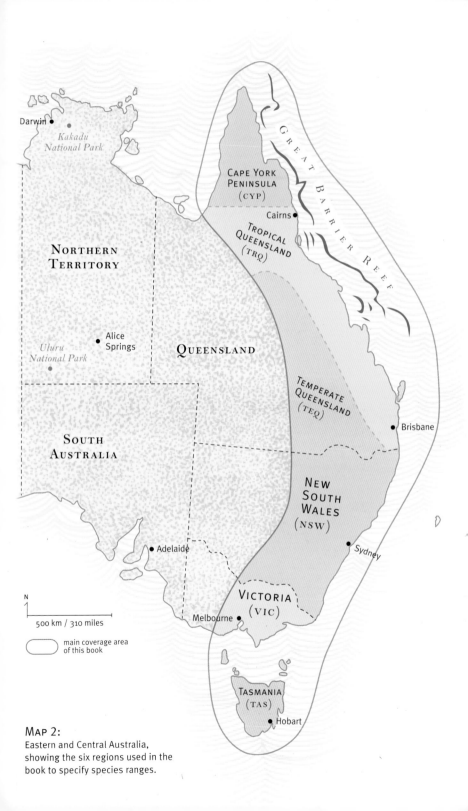

Darwin

Kakadu National Park

CAPE YORK PENINSULA (CYP)

GREAT BARRIER REEF

Cairns

TROPICAL QUEENSLAND (TRQ)

NORTHERN TERRITORY

Uluru National Park

Alice Springs

QUEENSLAND

TEMPERATE QUEENSLAND (TEQ)

Brisbane

SOUTH AUSTRALIA

NEW SOUTH WALES (NSW)

Adelaide

Sydney

VICTORIA (VIC)

Melbourne

N

500 km / 310 miles

main coverage area of this book

TASMANIA (TAS)

Hobart

MAP 2:
Eastern and Central Australia, showing the six regions used in the book to specify species ranges.

VIC = Victoria, TAS = Tasmania) in which each species is likely to be found, and the parks listed below are arranged by these locations. Park locations are shown in Maps 3 to 6, pp. 29, 37, 43, and 47. If no special information on reaching parks and on wildlife viewing is provided for a particular park, you may assume the site is fairly easy to reach and that wildlife can be seen simply by walking along trails, roads, beaches, etc. Tips on increasing the likelihood of seeing mammals, birds, reptiles, or amphibians are given in the introductions to each of those chapters.

A few helpful hints: go early! To enhance your eco-pleasure, I cannot stress this enough. Regular tourists rise at 08:00 or 09:00, have a leisurely breakfast, then head out for a day's activities. Ecotourists (this means you!), rise at 06:00 (yes, that's six in the morning) and get a two- or three-hour head start on everyone else. The earlier morning hours are better times to see wildlife, especially birds; it's of course cooler, and you avoid most other people. (In any case, you can't sleep late in Australia; the cockatoos and other parrots start squawking loudly at dawn!) In the early morning, you will often enjoy a few hours of blessed isolation, even at popular parks. Some parks, of course, are well known and heavily visited by both locals and international visitors, such as Blue Mountains National Park near Sydney and Lamington National Park near Brisbane. But others are only lightly visited and, if you are lucky, on some days you may be the only human in a park (as I appeared to be on a weekday at Barrington Tops National Park north of Sydney).

In many parks, wildlife is not obviously abundant or diverse. You can hike for hours in some habitats—such as open eucalypt woodlands—and see very little; a few songbirds perhaps, some parrots, some small trailside lizards. If you have trouble locating the animals you'd like to see, ask people—park personnel, tour guides, resort employees. One way to see more wildlife is to stay at "eco-lodges"— hotels (sometimes expensive ones), often with naturalist guides, that cater to people wanting to experience natural areas and see wildlife. A few in eastern Australia are O'Reilly's Rainforest Guesthouse (www.oreillys.com.au; e-mail: reservations @oreillys.com.au; tel: (07)-5544-0644) and Binna Burra Lodge (www.binnaburralodge.com.au; tel: (07)-5533-3622) in southeast Queensland; Kingfisher Park Lodge in Julatten, near Cairns (www.birdwatchers.com.au; e-mail: sootyowl@ bigpond.com.au; tel: (07)-4094-1263); Lotus Bird Lodge near Musgrave, Cape York Peninsula (www.cairns.aust.com/lotusbird; e-mail: lotusbird@ iig.com.au; tel: (07)-4060-3295); and Yaraandoo Environmental Interpretive Centre near New England National Park and Armidale, New South Wales (www.yaraandoo.com.au; tel: (02)-6775-9219). Guides at these lodges and rangers at national parks will sometimes organize night walks, during which nocturnal marsupials and night-active birds such as owls and frogmouths can be seen in the beams of spotlights. Finally, if you are really desperate to see wildlife, there are many roadside animal attractions that vary in quality. Some are rather nice small zoos, such as Ballarat Wildlife Park west of Melbourne, and Wild World near Cairns; others are mainly money-making and exploitive, but nonetheless popular tourist attractions, where you can see and sometimes touch a Koala or watch crocodiles eat. In fact, the largest concentrations of rental cars in the Cairns area are not at Cairns Airport but in the parking areas of roadside wildlife attractions that announce with large signs "Croc feeding at 11:00 AM and 3:00 PM."

MAP 3:
Queensland, showing main roads
and locations of parks and reserves
discussed in the text.

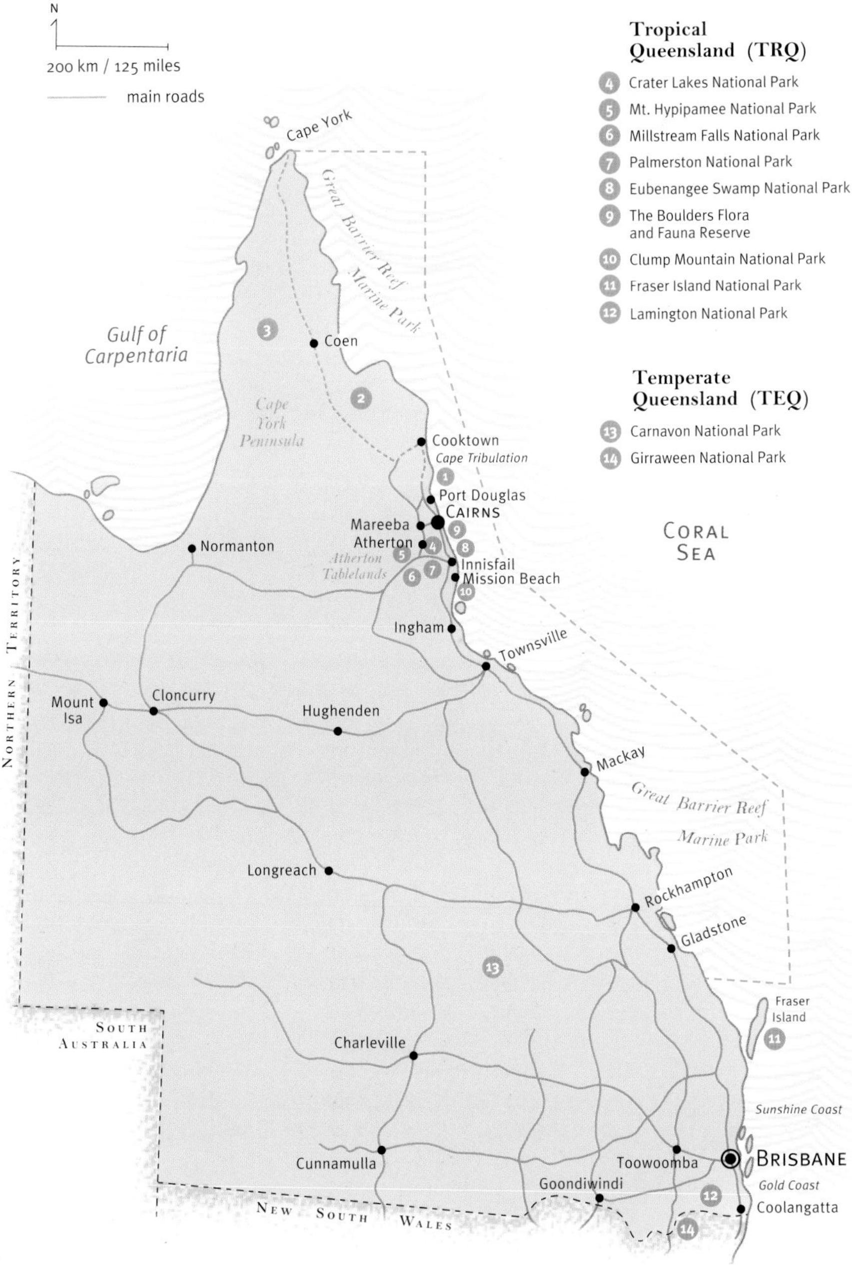

N

200 km / 125 miles

——— main roads

**Cape York
Peninsula (CYP)**

1. Daintree National Park
   and Cape Tribulation
2. Lakefield National Park
3. Mungkan Kaanju National Park

**Tropical
Queensland (TRQ)**

4. Crater Lakes National Park
5. Mt. Hypipamee National Park
6. Millstream Falls National Park
7. Palmerston National Park
8. Eubenangee Swamp National Park
9. The Boulders Flora
   and Fauna Reserve
10. Clump Mountain National Park
11. Fraser Island National Park
12. Lamington National Park

**Temperate
Queensland (TEQ)**

13. Carnavon National Park
14. Girraween National Park

Cape York

Great Barrier Reef Marine Park

Gulf of
Carpentaria

Cape York Peninsula

3 · Coen

2

Cooktown
Cape Tribulation

1
Port Douglas
CAIRNS
Mareeba 9
Atherton 4 8
Normanton 5 Innisfail
Atherton 6 7 Mission Beach
Tablelands 10

Ingham

Townsville

CORAL
SEA

NORTHERN TERRITORY

Mount
Isa Cloncurry Hughenden

Mackay

Great Barrier Reef
Marine Park

Longreach

Rockhampton

Gladstone

13

Fraser
Island
11

SOUTH
AUSTRALIA

Charleville

Sunshine Coast

Cunnamulla

Toowoomba BRISBANE

Goondiwindi *Gold Coast*
12 Coolangatta

NEW SOUTH WALES

14

Cape York Peninsula (CYP)

The Cape York Peninsula (Map 3, p. 29) has a reputation as one of Australia's last great wilderness areas, and it is a wonderful place to visit. But, as in most places worldwide, people and their developments are intruding, so this remote, beautiful region gets a bit less wild each year; visit it before the large tour buses can make it there. Many people imagine the peninsula as being covered with dense tropical rainforest. However, "classical" closed rainforest (with emergent trees more than 30 m, 100 ft, tall; locally often called "vine forest" or "gallery forest") covers only small pockets, such as the Daintree area. (The "Wet Tropics" area of Queensland, a UNESCO World Heritage Area that contains the closed rainforests tracts, stretches from just north of Townsville to just south of Cooktown.) Much of the peninsula is covered by open eucalypt forest, with trees topping out at 10 to 30 m (30 to 100 ft). Wildlife, albeit often difficult to see aside from birds, abounds in the region (the highest diversity of fauna in Australia): more than 70 species of frogs (at least 5 being rare or threatened), 160 reptiles (27 rare or threatened), about 320 birds (including marine birds off the coast; 29 rare or threatened), and 70 mammals (excluding recently introduced species; 20 rare or threatened). For access to Lakefield National Park, Mungkan Kaanju National Park, and all points north of them, a four-wheel-drive vehicle (and an adventurous spirit) is required. Few rental car companies want their precious vehicles taken to these wilderness parks—you usually need to rent from an outfit in Cairns that specializes in four-wheel-drive vehicles, get a special waiver from a "normal" rental company, or take an organized tour. If you rent, try to get a vehicle with a "snorkel"—you will be fording rivers and creeks frequently, and it is helpful to keep the air intake of your vehicle above water! Note: roadsigns in these four-wheel-drive areas are poor or non-existent.

Daintree National Park and Cape Tribulation

Daintree is the rainforest national park that most eco-visitors to the Cairns area include in their trips. Many people drive themselves from Cairns northwards along the coast, past some spectacular shoreline scenery. (Daintree can be reached easily on paved roads with a two-wheel-drive sedan; north of Daintree, four-wheel-drive is required.) Daintree National Park has two main sections. The Mossman Gorge section, which lies west of Route 44 (Captain Cook Highway), is largely inaccessible. However, one small area of it, Mossman Gorge, is easily reached via a 5 km (3 mi) road westward from the town of Mossman. It is quite popular (tour buses are common), with picnic grounds, a short nature trail, and creek access. The Cape Tribulation section is a must-see, but be warned, traffic in the area can be heavy (since the roads here were improved during the 1980s and the park and commerical tourist attractions heavily promoted thereafter, this area is now on the regular tourist circuit). A required crossing of the Daintree River on a small car ferry, sometimes with a long backlog of waiting cars, further slows things. After crossing the Daintree River, there is spectacular scenery to the left and right as you drive through rainforest on a narrow, rough, winding paved road that rises to cross coastal highlands and falls to pass gorges and river valleys. This area around the Daintree River Valley is in fact one of Australia's largest remaining intact rainforest wilderness sites. The drive is lovely—take it slow, stop at the lookouts, perhaps stay at some of the local eco-lodges, or take some of the offered boat tours of the area. (Mossman Gorge section, area: 56,500 ha, 140,000 ac.

Elevation: 40 to 1350 m, 130 to 4,400 ft. Habitats: rainforest, rivers. Cape Tribulation section, area: 17,000 ha, 42,000 ac. Elevation: sea level to 1,360 m, 4,450 ft. Habitats: rainforest, open forests and woodlands, coastal mangroves, ocean beaches, fringing coral reefs.)

There are two eco-attractions you will want to visit, both located along the main road after crossing the Daintree River. The first is the Daintree River Environmental Centre (with an admission fee), a nice place to learn about the Cape York rainforest. There is an interpretive center with charts, graphs, videos, and display organisms (beetles, butterflies), a 400 m (440 yd) boardwalked trail through the rainforest with 40 labeled sites that identify and explain tree species and forest ecology, and a 25 m (82 ft) tall multi-tiered canopy tower that lets you get up into the forest canopy for bird-watching, photos, and forest observation and contemplation. The second site is the Marrdja Botanical Walk. This trail, created by the Queensland National Parks and Wildlife Service, consists of an extensive boardwalk (800 m, 880 yd) built through beautiful, shady rainforest and mangrove forest habitats. A small population of the Southern Cassowary (Plate 20), a threatened species, lives in the Daintree region, and you need to drive slowly to make sure you do not hit one of these large, flightless birds crossing a roadway. Other dangers are Saltwater Crocodiles, stinging plants, and, in the ocean during May to October, very dangerous "stingers," or jellyfish. The Daintree rainforest also harbors a mysterious, dangerous disease, "Daintree ulcer." The disease, which does not respond to antibiotics, is in the same disease group as leprosy and tuberculosis and can be treated only by excising the surface ulcers, taking along a lot of skin and underlying tissue. Rest easy, though; tourists are never affected. It seems that long exposure is necessary for infection, and only a few local residents per year are afflicted.

Lakefield National Park

Lakefield (Habitat Photos 16, 17) is a semi-wilderness park with one long main road (dusty when dry) through it. There are a few ranger stations where you can obtain information, and primitive campgrounds, usually flat, cleared areas near water and thus crocodiles. Being a semi-wilderness park with a small budget, there's not much in the way of hiking trails. One 4.3 km (2.5 mi) trail through eucalypt woodland takes off from the main campground, Kalpowar Crossing. Otherwise, you sightsee by walking or driving the main road and the tracks to the campgrounds, or by real "bushwalking"—heading off cross-country without a trail. The scenery is wonderful, if mostly flat and monotonous in places. Agile wallabies are commonly seen, as are such birds as lorikeets and other parrots, honeyeaters, cuckoo-shrikes, kingfishers, bee-eaters, and swallows. The park protects important habitat for the endangered Golden-shouldered Parrot, a Cape York endemic. Before its designation as a park in 1979, the area consisted largely of private cattle stations, and feral cattle still roam the park (causing ecological damage). You can visit in drier months, May (sometimes still wet, flooded, and so iffy) through September or October. Bring all your food and water. (Area: 537,000 ha, 1,326,000 ac. Elevation: sea level to 230 m, 750 ft. Habitats: mostly open eucalypt woodlands, often with scattered termite mounds; patches of gallery rainforest along waterways; grasslands, plains, scrub areas; freshwater wetlands—billabongs, waterholes, rivers; plus mudflats and mangroves along coastal sections.)

Mungkan Kaanju National Park

At Mungkan Kaanju (Habitat Photo 18) are all the things (habitats, wildlife) you can see at Lakefield National Park, but here you can experience them in blessed solitude. A friend and I visited recently and, apart from a nature photographer we bumped into, we were, as far as we could determine, the only visitors to this huge park. Most individual travellers and tour groups drive north from Daintree through Cooktown, then east through Lakefield National Park, then north toward "The Top," the tip of the peninsula. But few turn off into the little-known Mungkan Kaanju National Park (formerly Archer Bend and Rokeby National Parks), 24 km (15 mi) north of Coen; it's definitely off the beaten track. A sign near the ranger station advises that the park's ranger would like it if you left him a note that you'll be camping in the park, and then again when you leave, so he knows you made it out alright. Aside from camping (and some of the camp-grounds are only tenuously laid out or marked) and bird-watching by walking the main road, a few side tracks, and along rivers, swamps, and waterholes (there really aren't any hiking trails), there's nothing to do but enjoy the peace and quiet. The largest of the cockatoos, the endangered Palm Cockatoo, which in Australia occurs only in the Cape York Peninsula, lives in the park in rain (gallery) forest along rivers. You can visit the park in drier months, May (sometimes still flooded, and so iffy) through September or October. Bring all your food and water. (Area: 457,000 ha, 1,129,000 ac. Elevation: 20 to 520 m, 65 to 1,700 ft. Habitats: mostly open eucalypt woodlands, some very savannah-like; deciduous vine thick-ets or gallery rainforest line waterways; some rainforest at higher elevations; scrub areas; freshwater wetlands—billabongs, swamps, lagoons, rivers.)

Tropical Queensland (TRQ)

Great Barrier Reef Marine Park

Parks in the tropical region of Queensland include the Great Barrier Reef Marine Park. Approximately 2,000 km (1,250 mi) long and running along the Queensland coast, this reef area is one of the world's most famous snorkeling and scuba-diving sites. The reef is at some points quite near the coast but at others up to 300 km (185 mi) away. People visit the reef for diving, snorkeling, "island-walk-ing," and sightseeing, usually by taking ferries or other boats from the mainland (from such jumping-off points as Cairns, Townsville, Mission Beach, Gladstone, and Port Douglas) for day trips ("have five hours on the reef and be back in town by dinnertime!") or for extended stays at reef island resorts. Flights (from Brisbane and Cairns, but also from smaller airports such as those at Gladstone and Townsville) to some of the larger islands (Lady Elliot Island, Hamilton Island, and Lizard Island, for instance) are also available. Great Barrier Reef natural attractions are covered in Chapter 11.

Crater Lakes National Park (Atherton Tablelands)

Located in the Atherton Tablelands tourist area southwest of Cairns (19 km, 11 mi, east of Atherton), Crater Lakes National Park protects some nice volcanic crater lakes, and the lakes are the primary attraction to most visitors. Lake Eacham and Lake Barrine are separated by only about 3 km (1.8 mi). There are nice forested trails around the lakes (for instance, the 4 km, 2.4 mi, Lake Eacham Bank Circuit Track) and some other nature trails. Lake Eacham is a good birding spot, with Brush-turkeys, Orange-footed Scrubfowl, Tooth-billed Bowerbirds, whip-birds, catbirds, and robins common. (tel: (07) 4095-3768) (Area: 960 ha, 2,370 ac. Elevation: 650 to 790 m, 2,100 to 2,600 ft. Habitats: rainforest, lakes.)

Mt. Hypipamee National Park (Atherton Tablelands)

Just off the main highway through the Atherton Tablelands, Mt. Hypipamee National Park sports two 400 m (440 yd) trails to two striking natural phenomena. Dinner Falls is a series of nice falls with an adjacent forest pathway to view it, but the main attraction is "The Crater," an impressive, huge, deep, steep-sided, water-filled hole in the ground (okay, it's a volcanic crater). It's worth seeing, and there's a viewing platform that lets you get right above the drop-off. The main habitat is wet, closed rainforest, with lots of epiphytes, tree buttresses, vines, and climbers. Brush-turkeys are common here, and the park claims to harbor seven of Australia's 24 possum species, including Striped Possum. (tel: (07) 4095-3768) (Area: 364 ha, 900 ac. Elevation: 860 to 1,070 m, 2,800 to 3,500 ft. Habitats: rainforest, open eucalypt forest, river)

Millstream Falls National Park (Atherton Tablelands)

Located along the main highway through the Atherton Tablelands, near Ravenshoe, Millstream Falls National Park is on the west slope of the tablelands, and its main attraction is its falls. There's a picnic area and a trail to the waterfalls, which are in a forest setting and are one of Australia's broadest falls. (tel: (07) 4095-3768) (Area: 372 ha, 920 ac. Elevation: 770 to 890 m, 2,500 to 2,900 ft. Habitats: open eucalypt woodlands.)

Palmerston National Park (Wooroonooran National Park)

Perhaps not technically within the Atherton Tablelands, the Palmerston section of Wooroonooran National Park is accessed via the Palmerston Highway, a main route from the tablelands to the coast. Wooroonooran itself is one of Queensland's largest rainforest parks, part of the Wet Tropics World Heritage Area, and most of it is inaccessible wilderness. Palmerston is a large fragment of upland rainforest, dense, wet, and closed-canopy, sometimes mist-shrouded, with lots of epiphytes, tree buttresses, vines, and climbers. It is considered one of the richest biological regions of Australia, having, for instance, more than 500 tree species. Eleven km (6.7 mi) of trails can be accessed from a roadside trailhead. These are beautiful graveled trails through towering tropical rainforest, past some huge trees; one trail goes to the spectacular Tchupalla Falls, with its often-circling population of swifts. Tree-kangaroos occur here, as does the Golden Bowerbird, both of which, in Australia, are restricted to this small region of tropical Queensland. If you see a sign to a "platypus viewing platform," don't sneer—many visitors catch their first glimpse of a platypus here. (tel: (07) 4064-5115) (Area: 79,500 ha, 196,000 ac. Elevation: 20 to 1,622 m, 65 to 5,322 ft at Mt. Bartle Frere). Habitats: rainforest, peaks, gorges, streams, waterfalls.)

Eubenangee Swamp National Park

Located only about 10 km (6 mi) off northern Queensland's main coastal highway, about 16 km (10 mi) north of Innisfail, this park protects the final remnant of natural wetlands between Cairns and Townsville. There is a 1.5 km (0.9 mi) trail from a parking area to a swamp lookout where waterbirds such as ducks, spoonbills, ibises, and herons can be seen. About 175 bird species have been spotted here. (tel: (07) 4067-6304) (Area: 1,720 ha, 4,250 ac. Habitats: rainforest, open eucalypt forest, wetlands.)

The Boulders Flora and Fauna Reserve

Located a few kilometers west of Babinda, this small, popular park protects an area of lowland rainforest adjacent to Wooroonooran National Park. There are picnic areas, a campground, and two trails through the forest, plus a swimming hole.

Clump Mountain National Park

This park, located not far off northern Queensland's main coastal highway, protects a fragment of coastal closed tropical rainforest on a small mountain. There's a 3.9 km (2.4 mi) uphill trail, but the park is near a popular beach region (Mission Beach, which is also a jumping-off point for boat trips to the Great Barrier Reef), so the area and the trail can be congested, and there is often car noise from nearby parking lots. Skip this park, but if you're in the area, there is adjacent state forest land with a worthwhile 5.6 km (3.4 mi) "Rainforest Walk."

Fraser Island, Great Sandy National Park

The world's largest island made of sand, and known as a sun and beach recreation area, a "beachcomber's paradise," and as an ecotravel destination, Fraser Island is one of southeastern Queensland's biggest tourism draws (so don't expect non-commercialized wilderness). The entire island, more than 120 km (74 mi) long and 14 km (8.5 mi) wide, is environmentally protected and listed as a UNESCO World Heritage Area, but a national park, Great Sandy National Park, actually occupies only the northern half. (Part of the park also occupies the mainland just south of Fraser Island, and is known either as the Cooloola section of Great Sandy National Park or as Cooloola National Park.) Fraser Island's main eco-attractions are its long white beaches, incredible sand dunes (some to an elevation of 240 m, 800 ft, above sea level), colored sand cliffs, and striking, tall rainforest. About 250 bird species have been noted on and around the island, and it is a particularly good place to see migratory shorebirds that breed in Siberia. Parrots such as lorikeets and cockatoos are common, and both Ground Parrots and Glossy Black-cockatoos, threatened or endangered in parts of their ranges, occur here. Fraser Island mammals include echidnas, bandicoots, possums, gliders, Red-legged Pademelons, Swamp Wallabies, bats, dingos, and near shore, dugongs. Most people get to Fraser Island via ferries from the Rainbow Beach and Hervey Bay areas. (tel: (07) 5486-3160, 4123-7100) (Area—entire island: 166,000 ha, 410,000 ac. Elevation: sea level to 240 m, 780 ft. Habitats: coastal rainforest, open eucalypt forest and woodlands, coastal heathland, shrubland, lakes, streams, ocean beach, and sand dunes.)

Lamington National Park

Located just a couple of hours southwest of Brisbane, Lamington National Park (Habitat Photo 13), with its wonderful forested trails over and through green mountains and valleys and its abundant wildlife, is one of the region's great natural attractions. It protects southeast Queensland's largest remaining fragment of undisturbed subtropical rainforest. This park has had a role in developing ecotourism in Australia because O'Reilly's Rainforest Guesthouse, an internationally known ecolodge, has been associated with the park for more than 85 years. The park has two access areas, Green Mountains (where there is a visitor center and where O'Reilly's is located) and Binna Burra (where there is a parks information center and where Binna Burra Mountain Lodge is located); both areas are reached on roads leading from the town of Canungra, to the north. There are more than 100 km (62 mi) of trails in and around the park. The best hike is probably along the Main Border Track between O'Reilly's (Green Mountains) and Binna Burra (23 km, 14 mi), but others, such as the Toolona Creek Circuit, are wonderful also. Lamington is known for its wildlife, especially its birds (Brush-turkeys, many parrots, and some bowerbirds, for instance, are common). The park's wildlife list includes 35 frogs, 4 turtles, 59 lizards, 31 snakes, 290 birds, and 70 mammals. The only drawback associated with Lamington is its popularity—avoid the place on weekends, when large numbers of people visit. (park tel: (07) 5544-0634; O'Reillys Guesthouse tel: 5544-0644; Binna Burra Lodge tel: 5533-3622) (Area: 20,500 ha, 50,600 ac. Elevation: 190 to 1,140 m, 620 to 3,700 ft. Habitats: subtropical rainforest, creeks, waterfalls.)

Temperate Queensland (TEQ)

Carnavon National Park
Carnavon, with a reputation for unsurpassed beauty, is located in central Queensland, in what can be considered the rolling western foothills of the Great Dividing Range. The park is located north of the town of Roma or south of Emerald, and is reached via partially paved roads. Most of the park is inaccessible wilderness. There are a few access points, but the easiest and most popular is the Carnavon Gorge area, with a visitor center and good trail access. The main trail, 9.3 km (5.5 mi) long, follows Carnavon Gorge, a 30 km (18 mi) gorge beneath towering sandstone cliffs. There is majestic scenery to gawk at, Aboriginal art on rock walls to examine, and creek pools to wade in. Local wildlife includes Green Tree Frogs, Eastern Water Dragons, and Frilled Lizards; Platypuses, Northern Quolls, Eastern Grey Kangaroos, Brush-tailed Rock-wallabies, Whiptail Wallabies, Common Brushtail Possums, and gliders; and birds such as waterbirds (ibises, herons, cormorants), cockatoos, fairy-wrens, spinebills, and honeyeaters. (tel: (07) 4982-4555) (Area: 298,000 ha, 736,000 ac. Elevation: 340 to 1,220 m, 1,100 to 4,000 ft. Habitats: open eucalypt forests and woodlands, shrublands, plains, gorge with high cliffs, rivers, creeks and pools with riparian vegetation.)

Girraween National Park
Known for its pretty granite rock formations, wildflowers, and swimming holes, Girraween National Park is located near Queensland's border with New South Wales (north of Tenterfield or south of Stanthorpe). There is a visitor center and several good trails, some with panoramic views of the area. Wildlife includes kookaburras, currawongs, rosellas and other parrots, flycatchers, honeyeaters, spinebills, robins, and firetails; and Common Wombats, Eastern Grey Kangaroos, wallabies, Common Wallaroos (or Euros), possums, and gliders. (tel: (07) 4684-5157) (Area: 11,700 ha, 29,000 ac. Elevation: 900 m, 3,000 ft. Habitats: open eucalypt forests and woodlands, rocky granite boulders and outcroppings, swamps, waterholes, creeks with pools.)

New South Wales (NSW)

Bundjalung National Park
Bundjalung (Habitat Photo 6) is a coastal park in northern New South Wales. There are three access roads from the main (Pacific) highway, but only the southernmost one, Iluka Road, is paved. Mostly a park for beach access (38 km, 24 mi, of beach that you can walk or, in some areas, four-wheel-drive on), Bundjalung also contains New South Wales's best surviving example of coastal rainforest. There's little

in the way of formal trails (one 4 km, 2.5 mi, nature walk starting at a picnic area); this is a place people come to walk on the beach, fish, surf, and canoe. But there are fire tracks that start at the sides of roads. For example, one leads off from the left side of Iluka Road (going east) just before it crosses the Esk River bridge. The track winds through coastal scrub and forest habitats, and it's a good early morning birding location (parrots, kookaburras, Noisy Miners, wattlebirds, fairy-wrens). About 200 bird species, 30 mammals, 13 amphibians, 38 reptiles, and about 800 different plants have been observed in the park. (tel: (02) 6627-0200) (Area: 20,100 ha, 49,600 ac. Elevation: sea level. Habitats: coastal rainforest, eucalypt forest and woodlands, shrublands, heathlands, swamp forest and mangroves, river, mudflats, beaches, and sand dunes.)

Dorrigo National Park

This is a great park located about 60 km (37 mi) southwest of Coffs Harbour. There are very nice rainforest trails, some to waterfalls, starting at the visitor's center ("Rainforest Centre"), which is only a few minutes from the main highway. Also near the visitor's center is a "skyway" overlook that allows you to stand above the rainforest and look out over the surrounding hills and countryside. As soon as you descend into the trails (at about 760 m, 2,500 ft, elevation), you are immersed in towering rainforest, with large buttressed trees covered in green climbers and epiphytes, and with hanging woody vines. Some portions of the trails are on elevated walkways through the forest. Because the visitor center is near a main highway, cars and trucks can sometimes be heard from portions of its trails (Wonga Walk Circuit), but there are more secluded trails deeper in the park, starting at the Never Never picnic area (reached via a partially unpaved road). The northern section of the park is less accessible, and there are trails that can be hiked over two or three days (ask at visitor center). Another possibility is to walk along a fire track road (a jeep track; sometimes called Slingsbys Trail): drive to the town of Dorrigo, then go north past Dangar Falls about 5 km to Slingsbys Road; make a right and go to the end of Slingsbys Road. You can park by the gate at the very end of the road. This fire track, through open forests and grasslands, leads to Lane's Lookout, a high lookout from an escarpment, and connects to other trails in the park. Common mammals in the park are Swamp Wallabies, Red-necked Pademelons, and possums. But the park is best as a birding location—Brush-turkeys, lyrebirds, Noisy Pittas, parrots, currawongs, catbirds, riflebirds, Satin and Regent Bowerbirds, whipbirds, and lots of honeyeaters are often seen. (tel: (02) 6657-2309) (Area: 11,900 ha, 29,400 ac. Elevation: 700 to 900 m, 2,300 to 3,000 ft. Habitats: closed-canopy rainforest, moist eucalypt forest, grasslands.)

New England National Park

Main access to New England National Park (Habitat Photo 9) is about 11 km (7 mi) up a good gravel road that leaves the main highway between Dorrigo and Armidale. The road terminates at Point Lookout at 1,563 m (5,128 ft; quite high for Australia!). This cool site, at a cliff edge, has magnificent views (considered some of the country's best) in several directions, including down the Bellinger Valley to the coast; from the lookout you look directly down upon forest more than 300 m (1,000 ft) below. Views, however, are often obscured because the place is frequently misty and dripping. Wonderful trails, such as the Lyrebird Walk/Loop, start from this site, but exercise real caution: the trails ascend and descend steeply at times, usually on wet rocks, rock "staircases," and wood stairs— it can be a bad place if your medical insurance is not fully paid up, and it's not a

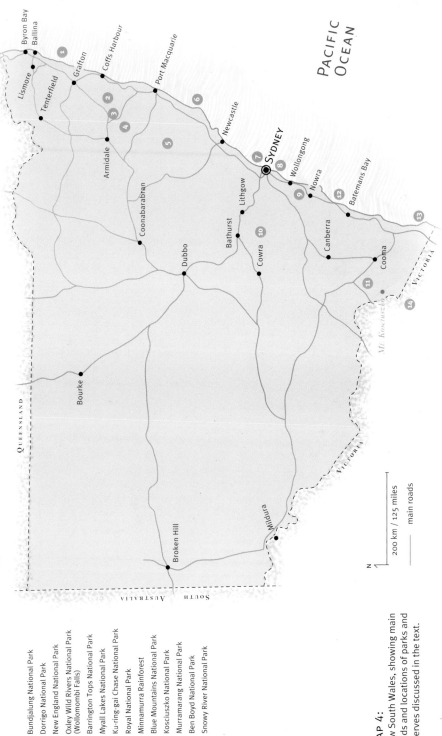

1. Bundjalung National Park
2. Dorrigo National Park
3. New England National Park
4. Oxley Wild Rivers National Park (Wollomombi Falls)
5. Barrington Tops National Park
6. Myall Lakes National Park
7. Ku-ring-gai Chase National Park
8. Royal National Park
9. Minnamurra Rainforest
10. Blue Mountains National Park
11. Kosciuszko National Park
12. Murramarang National Park
13. Ben Boyd National Park
14. Snowy River National Park

MAP 4:
New South Wales, showing main roads and locations of parks and reserves discussed in the text.

trail for young kids. Raptors, including Wedge-tailed Eagles, cruise the fields and pastures along the road into the park, and Brush-turkeys, Wonga Pigeons, cockatoos, lyrebirds, and whipbirds are often seen. Common mammals are platypuses, kangaroos, wallabies, gliders, and possums. (tel: (02) 6657-2309) (Area: 71,200 ha, 176,000 ac. Habitats: rainforest, open forest and woodland, heathland.)

Oxley Wild Rivers National Park — Wollomombi Falls

Oxley Wild Rivers National Park includes a large wilderness area and is fairly easily accessed, but most of the access points require four-wheel-drive. However, the Wollomombi Falls area of the park is just off the main highway between Coffs Harbour and Armidale (readily visited if you are traveling to Dorrigo or New England National Parks). The attraction, definitely worth a look, is a huge gorge surrounded by high cliffs and a waterfall. The falls, with a 260 m (853 ft) drop, is one of Australia's highest, but the amount of water falling varies seasonally, sometimes amounting to no more than a trickle. There are several lookouts and shorts trails along the gorge's rim. (tel: (02) 6773-7211) (Area: 120,000 ha, 296,400 ac. Elevation: 700 to 900 m, 2,300 to 3,000 ft. Habitats: open eucalypt forest, dry rainforest, shrublands, steep gorges, rivers.)

Barrington Tops National Park

Ever wanted to have a national park to yourself? On a weekday, you have that chance at Barrington Tops. On the map, the park looks to be close to the town of Singleton, which lies along a main highway, but it is actually about two hours from Singleton to the Williams River Day Use Area of the park (via the village of Dungog). (Other park access points require four-wheel-drive.) There is a parking lot here (usually with lounging wallabies), as well as a picnic area and access to the park's extensive trail network (some trails of 20 km, 12 mi, or more). Beautiful trails go through various habitats, including higher, sub-alpine regions. Trails near the Williams River area are forested, shady, dark, often wet, and sometimes muddy. Watch out—land leeches cling to trailside vegetation. At the motel in Singleton at which I spent the night prior to visiting the park, I asked the woman behind the reception desk for directions to Barrington Tops. Her immediate answer: "You don't want to go there—all those snakes!" A perfect place for me, I thought, and for you, fellow ecotraveller. But the park's snake-infested reputation was not borne out—I saw nary a one. (tel: (02) 6558-1478) (Area: 73,900 ha, 182,500 ac. Elevation: 400 to 1,577 m, 1,300 to 5,174 ft. Habitats: temperate rainforest, wet eucalypt forest, alpine woodland, grassland, swamps, six major rivers, creeks.)

Myall Lakes National Park

Myall Lakes (Habitat Photos 7, 8) is a hugely popular coastal park that most people visit for the water and beach access (during Aussie summer holidays an estimated 5,000 locals swarm the park for boating, swimming, beachfront camping, cooking, and partying). But if you're in the area anyway (along the coast, between Newcastle and Port Macquarie), and it is NOT a holiday period, then this park is a good early morning birding spot (there are no gates, so you can drive in as early as you want). Sandy trails are usually out in the open, so bring sun protection and lots of water. Trails and fire tracks are mainly flat, which is nice—a good place for a pleasant, low-exertion bush-walk. Wildlife includes Echidnas, bandicoots, Swamp and Red-necked Wallabies, possums, and gliders; waterbirds (ocean-dwelling but also in the largest coastal lake system in the state), raptors, pigeons and doves, parrots, bowerbirds, orioles, honeyeaters, wattlebirds, and robins; many geckos, skinks and other lizards, and of course snakes, including Carpet Pythons and Red-bellied Black Snakes. In addition to keeping a lookout for snakes, watch out for mosquitos and the largest horseflies you will ever encounter. (tel: (02) 4987-3108) (Area: 44,200 ha, 109,000 ac. Elevation: just above sea level. Habitats: open eucalypt forest, heathlands, beach dunes, ocean beach, lakes.)

Ku-ring-gai Chase National Park

If not preserved as a park, Ku-ring-gai Chase would simply be the name of another one of Sydney's well-to-do northern suburbs (it's located just 25 km, 15 mi, north of central Sydney). Entrance roads to the park pass through some plainly affluent neighborhoods. The park is heavily visited (more than two million visits per year), but is still a nice place with striking scenery; if you're visiting Sydney for only a brief period and want a nearby birding site, or just a beautiful park near the city to wander, Ku-ring-gai Chase will definitely suffice (avoid weekends, of course). Trails are nice but fairly tame and frequented by joggers. There are wonderful views from high spots down to the water below. There is a large enclosure near the Kalkari Visitor Centre that houses kangaroos—you can often see them near the fence. This park is better for walking and views than for wildlife. (tel: (02) 9472-8949) (Area: 14,900 ha, 36,800 ac. Habitats: temperate rainforest in some deep valleys, open eucalypt forest and woodland, heathland, mangroves, estuary.)

Royal National Park

Royal (Habitat Photos 1, 3) is the oldest national park in Australia, established in 1879, and usually considered the world's second oldest after Yellowstone. Located just south of Sydney, it now preserves some natural areas, mostly of coastal heathland and open forest, for the region's large human population. Plainly, if not a park, this area would now be a housing development known as "South Sydney Heights." Indeed, suburban sprawl has leap-frogged over the park, and continues to its south, in the Wollongong area. Even given its age and close proximity to a large city, Royal is still a nice place to visit—but it is heavily used, so wildlife is not plentiful. Still, if you are in Sydney for only a few days and need a good place to go bird-watching early in the morning, perhaps for your first exposure to Australian birds, Royal is a good destination. More than 230 bird species have been seen here. Some common mammals, most of which are only seen at dusk, night, or dawn, are Echidnas, Swamp Wallabies, Red-necked Wallabies, and ringtail and brushtail possums. There are many walking trails, including a 26 km (16 mi) trail along the coast. (tel: (02) 9542-0648 or 9542-0666) (Area: 15,000 ha, 37,000 ac. Elevation: 0 to 280 m, 920 ft. Habitats: open forest and woodland, small pockets of temperate rainforest, heathlands, cliffs, beach dunes, ocean beach and bays, swamp, lake, creeks.)

Minnamurra Rainforest

Located south of Wollongong and a bit west of the town of Jamberoo, Minnamurra Rainforest, a small part of Budderoo National Park, is a very good spot to spend a cool (shady) couple of hours, especially for families. The trail though this steep canyon patch of spectacular native temperate rainforest is fully board-walked, with small suspension bridges over creeks. The walkways are at times elevated, so you can see the middle parts of the forest, including vines, epiphytes, and tree buttresses. An additional steep, paved trail leads up to the actual Minnamurra Falls. Eastern Water Dragons are often seen in or along the river. Birds that can be seen include Superb Lyrebirds, Azure Kingfishers, Satin Bowerbirds, Pied Currawongs, whipbirds, fantails, and fairy-wrens. Mammals, if you could see them, include Echidnas, Spot-tailed Quolls, Grey-headed Flying-foxes, and Gould's Long-eared Bats. (tel: (02) 4236-0469) (Area: 400 ha, 1,000 ac. Habitats: temperate rainforest, creek/river, waterfalls.)

Blue Mountains National Park

The Blue Mountains (Habitat Photo 2) offer some of Australia's and, indeed, the world's, most magnificent mountain vistas, and so it is no surprise that Blue Mountains National Park, only 100 km (60 mi) west of Sydney, is one of New South Wales's most heavily visited natural sites. This is a "recreation and resort" area, but don't let that dissuade you from visiting; the scenery is so nice and the trails so wonderful that this park is a must-see if you're in the region. The park is easily reached; one of the region's main highways (Route 32) cuts right through it. Often, you don't realize you're in the mountains because you're on a high, flat plateau; only when you come upon steep gorges that penetrate down into the plateau—sometimes 600 m, 2,000 ft, straight down—do you appreciate your current elevation. There are roadside lookouts that afford views of stunning mountain and forest landscapes, trails along high escarpments, and others that plunge deeply into gorges through eucalypt woodlands, narrow rainforested gullies, and slot canyons. More than 110 bird species have been seen in the park, and Superb Lyrebirds, parrots, kookaburras, and honeyeaters are common. Mammals here include Echidnas, Spot-tailed Quolls, Common Wombats, Grey Kangaroos, wallabies and rock-wallabies, and wallaroos. (tel: (02) 4787-8877) (Area: 248,000 ha, 613,000 ac. Habitats: open forest and woodland, rainforest in small pockets, heathlands, swamps, rocky outcroppings, and cliffs.)

Kosciuszko National Park (and Snowy River National Park, Victoria)

Kosciuszko ("kozzy-osko") is a great place with stunning scenery (Habitat Photo 5), great views, and fantastic trails that you can walk for a half-day, a full day, or over many days. About 450 km (280 mi) from Sydney in what is known as the Australian Alps, this is the largest national park in New South Wales, and the most visited (probably because it doubles in the cold season as a ski area). There are great roads (narrow but paved) through the park, and lots of trails and fire roads lead off the roads so you can simply park and hike. A plus is that at the higher elevations it is a lot cooler during warm months of the year than it is in the surrounding lowlands. The narrow, winding, 70 km (43 mi) road within the park between Khancoban and Cabramurra is worth the drive even if you do not leave the car (but if you do, hiking along trails or fire roads into the Jagungal Wilderness area of the park is a great thing to do). Wildlife includes your standard parrots—cockatoos, rosellas, and others—as well as raptors, lyrebirds, currawongs, kookaburras, and honeyeaters; Common Wombats, kangaroos, wallabies, ring-tailed possums; and 31 reptile species. This park is listed as a UNESCO Biosphere Reserve. Across the border in Victoria, Snowy River National Park is contiguous with Kosciuszko. (tel: (02) 6076-9373) (Area: 650,000 ha, 1,605,000 ac. Elevation to 2,228 m, 8,772 ft, at Mt. Kosciuszko, Australia's highest mountain. Habitats: treeless alpine and subalpine areas, open eucalypt forest and woodland, savannah woodland, scrubland.)

Murramarang National Park

Murramarang, south of Ulladulla, is one of several coastal parks in New South

Wales (another is Jervis Bay National Park, to the north) that mainly appeal to people seeking beach access for sun and sport, but these parks also protect important coastal habitats. Murramarang, which also encompasses some offshore islands important for seabird breeding, is a place to go to walk along the beach or perhaps to follow its short trails, which follow the coast and occasionally side-step through eucalypt forest. Eastern Grey Kangaroos, Swamp Wallabies, and Red-necked wallabies are common. (tel: (02) 4423-2170) (Area: 2,170 ha, 5,360 ac. Elevation: 0 to 283 m, 930 ft. Habitats: open eucalypt forest, rainforest in small pockets, rocky headlands jutting into the sea, coastal dunes, ocean beach.)

Ben Boyd National Park
There are two sections of Ben Boyd National Park, located in the southeast corner of New South Wales. In the northern section, you drive a few minutes from the main highway to the Pinnacles Trail, a brief sandy trail through open forest to a coastal overlook (some rock formations near the surf are the "pinnacles"). In the early mornings, wallabies crash through the underbrush ahead of you as you proceed. The southern section (Habitat Photo 4) is accessible by a 15 km (9 mi) road to Boyd's Tower, an old stone structure. From this point there are magnificent coastal views, with the blue-green surf crashing far below. There is access from the parking area to a 30 km (18 mi) "coastal walk," often along the clifftops that parallel the ocean or in the forest along the clifftops. About 220 bird species have been recorded in the park. (tel: (02) 6495-5000) (Area: 10,260 ha, 25,340 ac. Elevation: sea level to 250 m, 820 ft, at Haycock Hill. Habitats: open forest and woodland, coastal heathland and shrubland, beach dunes, ocean beach.)

Victoria (VIC)

Croajingolong National Park
Croajingolong is mostly a wilderness area of forest, heathland, and ocean beaches, extending about 100 km (60 mi) along Victoria's southeast coast, bordering New South Wales. There are some great views toward the coast from high granite peaks. Only one of the access roads that head south into the park from the main highway (Princes Highway), is paved, that from Genoa. (Other roads into the park may be impassable during wet months.) This road passes through a 10 km (6 mi) slice of the park and yields access to several good trails. The best trail in this area of the park may be the long Genoa River Fire Trail, through beautiful eucalypt/pine forest. It's a good place to see a bunch of lizard species, including Lace Monitors and Eastern Water Dragons. More than 1,000 plant species have been identified in the park, and more than 275 bird species, including seabirds, sea eagles, kingfishers, and lots of parrots, have been spotted. (tel: (03) 5158-6351) (Area: 87,500 ha, 216,000 ac. Elevation: sea level to 489 m, 1,604 ft, at Genoa Peak. Habitats: eucalypt forest and woodland, temperate rainforest, heathland, rocky cliffs, estuaries, ocean beaches.)

Tarra-Bulga National Park
Tarra-Bulga (Habitat Photo 10) is a beautiful small park located about 35 km (22 mi) south of Traralgon and off the regular tourist beat. The road to the park climbs constantly (the park occupies a mountaintop) through rolling ranchlands and provides excellent views to the lowlands below. The park protects a remnant fragment of cool temperate rainforest and is known mainly for its vegetation—39 fern species,

abundant treeferns (in deep gullies), epiphyte-laden, buttressed rainforest trees, ancient Myrtle Beech trees, and towering Mountain Ash trees, to over 60 m (200 ft) high. There are some short, nice trails. Mammals include Platypuses, Echidnas, Swamp Wallabies, possums, and bats. Common birds are lyrebirds, swifts, rosellas, cockatoos, kookaburras, and whipbirds. (tel: (03) 5196-6166) (Area: 1,670 ha, 4,100 ac. Elevation: to about 600 m, 1,960 ft. Habitats: higher-elevation temperate rainforest.)

Wilsons Promontory National Park

If you're in the area, Wilsons Promontory National Park (Habitat Photo 12), or "the Prom," as locals call it, is pretty much a must-see eco-destination. The park occupies the entire peninsula, which is the southernmost tip of the Australian mainland. (The waters around the park are also protected as Wilsons Promontory National Marine Park and Preserve.) There are lots of places to stop and gawk and hike along the main road through the park; kangaroos, wallabies, and emus are common roadside attractions. The park has more than 130 km (80 mi) of trails. The 5 km (3 mi) silly-sounding Lilly Pilly Gully Nature Walk, near the end of the main road, provides a good introduction to some of the park's flora and fauna, including a nice boardwalked section of temperate rainforest. For magnificent views of the peninsula, drive up to the Telegraph Saddle parking area (sometimes closed). Just look around here or start hiking; most of the park's long hikes begin at this parking area. If you take the long walk to Sealers Cove (2.5 hours each way), you won't be disappointed. Thirty mammal species inhabit the park, including Common Wombats, Koalas, and Echidnas; about 180 bird species have been seen here. (tel: (03) 5680-9555) (Area: 53,000 ha, 131,000 ac. Elevation: sea level to 754 m, 2,475 ft, at Mt. Latrobe. Habitats: open eucalypt forest and woodland, rainforest, heathland, grassland, swamps, rocky cliffs, ocean beaches.)

Dandenong Ranges and Dandenong Ranges National Park

Dandenong Ranges is one of Victoria's most visited parks because it is set essentially in the suburbs of Melbourne and is at a higher elevation than the city, so it is cooler when Melbourne is hot. Dandenong Ranges itself is a resort area (like the Catskills, or Poconos, or Vermont, if you're familiar with the northeast US), cool and shady, with twisty-turny roads, small, rustic, funky hill towns, and fancy roadside family restaurants where city people come for Sunday brunch or long dinners on warm nights. Trails often start at roadside picnic areas and crisscross the region; there are more than 200 km (120 mi) of walking tracks. The park proper is in several pieces, with various access points; one entrance is at the village of Upper Ferntree Gully, and many trails, most of them ascending or descending fairly steeply, start nearby. The park is known for its lyrebirds, but more than 130 bird species have been spotted, along with 31 native mammals, 21 reptiles, and 9 frogs. (tel: (03) 9758-1342) (Area: 3,215 ha, 7,940 ac. Elevation: about 200 to 630 m, 650 to 2,050 ft. Habitats: eucalypt woodlands, pockets of temperate rainforest in deep valleys.)

Phillip Island Nature Park

Part of 10,000 ha (24,700 ac) Phillip Island is a protected nature park, famous for its coastline, beaches, and wildlife. The island, reachable by road (via a bridge) or ferry, is only about 130 km (80 mi) from Melbourne, and more than three million people visit annually. About 5,500 people live on the island full-time, but the big tourism draw is some of the island's other residents—Koalas, which can be seen

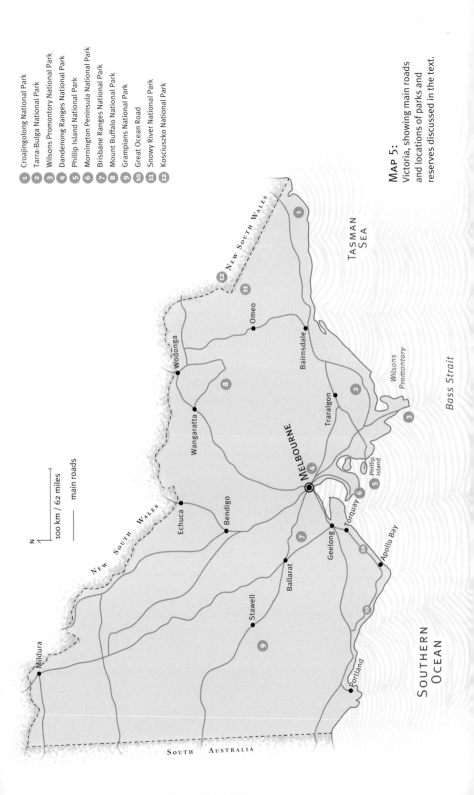

1. Croajingolong National Park
2. Tarra-Bulga National Park
3. Wilsons Promontory National Park
4. Dandenong Ranges National Park
5. Phillip Island National Park
6. Mornington Peninsula National Park
7. Brisbane Ranges National Park
8. Mount Buffalo National Park
9. Grampians National Park
10. Great Ocean Road
11. Snowy River National Park
12. Kosciuszko National Park

MAP 5:
Victoria, showing main roads and locations of parks and reserves discussed in the text.

fairly easily at various Koala reserves and at the island's Koala Conservation Centre, and penguins. The Phillip Island Penguin Parade is one of Australia's most famous tourist attractions, seen by one million visitors each year. The penguins are Little Penguins (Plate 22), the world's smallest. They feed during the day in the Bass Strait, then emerge from the ocean in early evening and waddle to their burrows in the dunes. Ridiculous numbers of tourists line up to watch the "parade," at Summerland Beach. There are about 10,000 breeding pairs of penguins in the island's population. Another attraction is a large population of fur seals (between 5,000 and 8,000 individuals) that haul out on offshore islands (especially off Point Grant, the southwest tip of Phillip Island). (tel: (03) 5956-7447) (Area: 2,850 ha, 7,040 ac. Habitats: eucalypt forest and woodlands, rocky coastline, beaches.)

Mornington Peninsula National Park

This national park south of Melbourne provides mostly coastal and beach access. One part of the park is a long, narrow 20 km (12 mi) strip along the southwestern coast of the Mornington Peninsula. Many people come to this park for picnicking, for swimming or other water sports, or for the spectacular coastal scenery. There is an extensive trail system here, including the 32 km (20 mi) Peninsula Coastal Walk, which is half along coastal clifftops and half along the beach. Some long, sandy trails follow paths between banks of high dune shrub vegetation that shade you from the sun, arriving eventually at stunning high lookouts with crashing surf far below. Albatrosses, petrels, and shearwaters are sometimes seen along the coast, as are fur seals. (tel: (03) 5984-4276) (Area: 2,686 ha, 6,635 ac. Elevation: sea level to 305 m, 1,000 ft. Habitats: open eucalypt forest and woodland, vegetated sand dunes, rocky cliffs, ocean beaches.)

Brisbane Ranges National Park

Brisbane Ranges (Habitat Photo 11) is a beautiful park just an hour or so west of Melbourne, located in an area of small mountains and rocky gullies. It has more than 20 km (12 mi) of wide, well-marked trails through striking eucalypt forest, and, on a weekday, you are unlikely to run into many other hikers. The area is famous for its wildflower displays. If you'd like to try to find a Koala in the wild, this is one of the very best places. The local population, which once had crashed to low levels, has increased with conservation measures and an infusion of "new" Koalas from the Phillip and French Island populations. Walk the trails, keep looking up into trees, and eventually you will find one (usually in a Manna Gum or Swamp Gum). Often the Koala's only response to your presence is to slowly look you over, grimace, and turn away. Watch it for a while from a distance with binoculars, then continue on your way. If you walk the trails in late morning or afternoon, the place can seem to have minimal biodiversity—but it's there, just hiding. Echidnas, Grey Kangaroos, wallabies, possums, and gliders inhabit the park, as do about 180 bird species: raptors such as Wedge-tailed Eagles and Peregrine Falcons, owls, parrots, kookaburras, woodcreepers, honeyeaters, fairywrens, bee-eaters, and lots of others. (tel: (03) 5284-1230) (Area: 7,720 ha, 19,070 ac. Elevation: about 200 to 400 m, 650 to 1,300 ft. Habitats: open eucalypt forests and woodlands.)

Mount Buffalo National Park

Visitors frequent Mount Buffalo National Park (Habitat Photo 15), located about 320 km (200 mi) northeast of Melbourne within the district known as the "Victorian Alps," for its breathtaking scenery and sweeping views, for sports recreation such as rock climbing and hang gliding, and for its 90 km (56 mi) of wonderful trails (some cross-country skiing occurs in the park as well, but Mount Buffalo is not high enough to get large amounts of snow; skiiers usually flock to higher mountains to the east such as Mount Hotham). Mount Buffalo rises steeply from surrounding plains. The park and its surroundings are gorgeous, and many local people visit to walk or hike and look at the wildlflowers, or to sit by riverside motels and fish and talk. Park entry is via the village of Porepunkah. The one main road through the park climbs steeply up the mountain. There are spots along the road to pull off and park, and many trails, short and long, lead off from the main road. Many of the trails, such as parts of "The Big Walk," emerge from under the trees to follow along high ridges, yielding sweeping views to the flatlands far below; hang gliders often appear, but they are below, not above you. Wildlife here, although not easy to see, includes Platypuses, Echidnas, and Common Wombats (all three at lower elevations), possums and gliders, including Feathertail Gliders, and wallabies; and about 130 bird species, including raptors, lyrebirds, cockatoos, currawongs, ravens, bee-eaters, wattlebirds, honeyeaters, and robins. (tel: (03) 5755-1466) (Area: 31,000 ha, 76,570 ac. Elevation: about 300 to 1,723 m, 1,000 to 5,653 ft, at The Horn. Habitats: eucalypt forest and woodlands, subalpine grassland, rocky cliffs.)

Grampians National Park

Grampians National Park, located about 250 km (155 mi) northwest of Melbourne, is not really within the scope of this book, but a lot of the wildlife discussed in these pages occurs there. The mountains of the park can be considered the westernmost fringes of the Great Dividing Range. Grampians is a large park and heavily visited. More than 160 km (100 mi) of trails wend around and through mountains, hills, and valleys, often to waterfalls or amazing rock formations. More than a third of the species of vertebrate animals that occur in Victoria are found in the park, including more than 200 birds. (tel: (03) 5556-4381) (Area: 167,000 ha, 412,000 ac. Elevation: About 200 m, 650 ft, to 1,168 m, 3,830 ft, at Mount William. Habitats: eucalypt forest and woodlands, heathland, grassland, lakes, rivers, waterfalls.)

Great Ocean Road

Located along the coast southwest of Melbourne, the Great Ocean Road is just what it says—a long drive along a section of spectacular coastline. The roadway is sometimes right along the sea (the Southern Ocean), with great views right down to the surf. The route passes through forest reserves, rolling livestock ranches, areas of wealthy cliffside ocean-view homes, and seaside tourist towns. The "Twelve Apostles" area of the shoreline (the apostles are huge stone formations that were eroded from the shore and now sit just offshore) is quite striking. Shorebirds and seabirds can be seen on the region's beaches.

Tasmania (TAS)

Tasmania is well endowed with national parks and reserves, which cover about 25% of the island state. The largest, covering 20% of Tasmania and including Cradle Mountain National Park (Tasmania's most famous park), Franklin-Gordon Wild Rivers National Park, and Southwest National Park, is the 1.38 million ha (3.4 million ac) Tasmanian Wilderness World Herritage Area. The majority of ecotourists visit the three parks listed below; most of Tasmania's other national parks are largely wilderness areas, and either difficult to access or not developed for ecotourism.

Mount Field National Park

Mount Field (Habitat Photo 22) is a stunningly beautiful place located only 90 minutes or so from Hobart. There are two main visitor areas. The Russell Falls area is the park's entrance. Russell Falls itself is a broad, cascading waterfall in the midst of tall evergreen forest just a short walk from the parking area. Further along the trail is a second waterfall, Horseshoe Falls, and then the Tall Trees Walk—a trail with wet gullies lined with prehistoric-looking treeferns and through towering eucalypt trees, some 75 to 80 m (245 to 260 ft) tall and 4 m (13 ft) in diameter (some of the world's tallest trees are here). Some trees have buttressed trunks and many are moss covered. The other visitor area is Lake Dobson (Habitat Photo 24)—it's out of the way, up a narrow, climbing 16 km (10 mi) gravel/dirt road, but definitely worth the drive. Along the way are wonderful alpine vistas of mountains and forested valleys and, near the end of the road, there is access to subalpine and alpine trails. The trails reach deep green valleys, lakes, rocky areas, and real alpine habitats with short-stature vegetation (in cold months, the area above Lake Dobson is a downhill and cross-country skiing site). Common Mount Field wildife includes Laughing Kookaburras, Pink Robins (small, black with a bright pink chest—you can't miss them!), Black Currawongs (large, crow-like Tasmanian endemics), Green Rosellas (also endemic) and some higher-elevation parrots, Platypuses, Tasmanian Pademelons, and Red-necked Wallabies. *Caution:* Weather can change fast in alpine areas; sunny and nice weather can change quickly to freezing cold when clouds and mist arrive, and it can snow almost anytime. If you walk in this region, wear hiking boots and have warm clothes with you. At Mount Field, you can get information about accessing Southwest National Park via Maydena. (tel: (03) 6288-1149) (Area: 17,000 ha, 42,000 ac. Elevation: 150 to 1,434 m, 500 to 4,700 ft. Habitats: rainforest, shrublands, alpine moorland and bogs, lakes, creeks.)

Cradle Mountain National Park

Cradle Mountain is one of Tasmania's must-see eco-attractions. There are two access points. The first, closer to Hobart and along the main A10 highway, is the Lake St. Clair area (also called Lake St. Clair National Park). There's a visitor center here, with access to trails. However, the more spectacular parts of the park are more easily accessed from the Cradle Mountain Visitor Centre at Cradle Valley in the north part of the park (several hours' driving from the Lake St. Clair area; the two access points of the park are also linked by a long trail, the Overland Track, that traverses the center of the park and takes five days or so to stroll). There are some brief nature walks to be done near the Visitor Centre. Then drive south on a gravel/dirt road 7 km (4 mi) to Dove Lake (or, alternatively, to the Cradle Valley/Waldheim parking area), where there is access to longer trails with splendid mountain scenery (including views of Mt. Ossa, Tasmania's highest peak at 1,616 m, 5,302 ft). Common wildlife includes echidnas and wallabies, and birds such as Black Currawongs, Yellow-tailed Black-cockatoos, Green Rosellas, Yellow Wattlebirds, scrubwrens, and robins. *Caution:* These mountains and Cradle Valley have a reputation for "having their own weather," which can change fast. If you walk in this region, wear hiking boots and have warm clothes with you. When you drive between the Lake St. Clair and Cradle Valley sections of Cradle Mountain National Park, you pass through Franklin-Gordon Wild Rivers National Park (park pamplet/map available at Lake St. Clair Visitor Centre). The road twists and turns through the mountains, and there are lots of nice well-marked stopping

1. Mount Field National Park
2. Cradle Mountain National Park
3. Franklin-Gordon Wild Rivers National Park
4. Freycinet National Park

Flinders Island

Cape Barren Island

Bass Strait

Robbin's Island

Burnie

Devonport

St. Helens

Launceton

St. Marys

2

Queenstown

Strahan

3

Swansea

4

1

Maria Island

Sorell

SOUTHERN OCEAN

HOBART

Port Arthur

N

50 km / 30 miles

—— main roads

Dover

Southport

South Bruny Island

TASMAN SEA

MAP 6:
Tasmania, showing main roads and locations of parks discussed in the text.

spots (for lookouts and short nature trails) along the way. An especially nice stop, which will take you about 50 minutes in total (20 minutes there, 20 return, and 10 minutes to gawk at one of the best 360-degree mountain vistas you've seen in your entire life), is the Donaghy's Hill Wilderness Lookout walk. Go in the late afternoon; the view is stunning, surely one of Australia's most beautiful spots. (tel: (03) 6492-1133 (Area: 161,000 ha, 398,000 ac. Elevation: 900 to 1,600 m, 3,000 to 5,300 ft. Habitats: rainforest, open eucalypt forest, alpine moorland, lakes, creeks.)

Freycinet National Park

Occupying a peninsula that juts out into the Tasman Sea, Freycinet National Park (Habitat Photo 23) has excellent sandy and rocky walkways through low-stature coastal open forest, along granite cliffs and peaks, and across beaches and coastal heathland. Some trails run above the ocean and bay below, with splendid coastal views, and there is a fantastic lookout high above Wineglass Bay. There are wallabies and pademelons here, and common birds include seabirds, wattlebirds, honeyeaters, and raptors. (tel: (03) 6527-0107) (Area: 13,000 ha, 32,000 ac. Elevation: sea level to 620 m, 2,030 ft. Habitats: Open forests and woodlands, scrub forest, heathland, rocky shoreline, ocean beach, lagoons.)

Chapter 5

ENVIRONMENTAL THREATS AND CONSERVATION

by Stacey Combes
Department of Integrative Biology
University of California, Berkeley

- *Environmental Threats*
  - *Biodiversity Loss*
  - *Land Clearing*
  - *Agriculture and Grazing*
  - *Logging*
  - *Introduced Species*
  - *Urban Growth*
  - *Global Warming and the Ozone Layer*
- *Conservation*
  - *Cassowary Recovery Program*
  - *National Landcare Program*
  - *Ecotourism*

Environmental Threats

Biodiversity Loss

Australia is perhaps the most unique continent on Earth, and many of its conservation problems stem from this fact. The continent itself is geologically stable—no volcanic eruptions have blanketed its surface in recent times, no glaciers or large rivers have sculpted its landscape, and no tectonic plates have crashed together to raise mountain ranges for hundreds of millions of years. Thus Australia contains some of the oldest ground surface on earth. With the exception of Antarctica, it is also the driest continent on Earth, and contains fewer sizable rivers than any other continent. Yet it experiences severe changes in sea temperature and atmospheric pressure associated with the periodic El Niño–Southern Oscillation, and suffers frequent natural hazards such as droughts, floods, fires, earthquakes, and tropical cyclones.

Australia is also one of the most biologically diverse countries in the world, due in part to its complete isolation from other land masses for more than 50 million years. By some estimates, it is home to about 7% of the Earth's species, including more than half of the world's *marsupial mammals*, as well as two species of the bizarre *monotremes* (p. 202), or egg-laying mammals, the Platypus and Short-beaked Echidna (Plate 61). Even more important than the diversity of its fauna, however, is the high degree of *endemism*, or occurrence of animals that are found nowhere else (see Close-up, p. 110). Ninety percent or more of Australia's marsupials and amphibians are endemic, as are 80% or more of its mammals, reptiles, vascular plants, and inshore, temperate-zone fishes. In fact, Australia's biological diversity places it among the "mega-diverse" countries of the world, a group of twelve countries that collectively contain 60% to 70% of the world's species. Australia is the only one of these twelve countries that has a developed, industrial economy and a relatively small population, and this places a special responsibility on Australia to conserve its biological wealth.

Yet Australia's historical and recent conservation record has not been good. A lack of understanding about the continent's unique land and animals, and the application of land management practices developed in Europe and North America, which did not work well Down Under, have led to Australia having one of the worst records of plant and animal extinctions in the world. Fully 10% of the 484 animal extinctions known to have occurred globally during the past 400 years happened in Australia. The country's record with mammals is particularly dismal. Of 69 mammal species that became extinct during the past 400 years, 19 were Australian, and during the past 200 years, about half of all mammal extinctions occurred in Australia. At least 10 of its marsupial species have become extinct, about 7% of the total number; and many others, often after undergoing drastic reductions in their ranges and numbers, are now endangered or threatened. Seven of Australia's native rodent species have also become extinct recently. In total, about 43 Australian mammal species and 50 birds are currently considered endangered or vulnerable. Two hundred vascular plant species have become extinct in Australia since 1800.

The cause of most of the Australian animal and plant extinctions has been habitat loss due to land clearing for agriculture, urban expansion, and industrial growth. The large number of extinctions currently occurring in Australia makes biodiversity loss the country's primary environmental threat.

Land Clearing

When Europeans arrived in Australia in the late 1700s, they began clearing the land of native vegetation. They planted farms and established ranches for domestic animals based on land management practices that had proven perfectly sound in Europe. Unfortunately, many of the fragile and unique aspects of Australia's ecology were not obvious, and to this day are not well understood. In addition to the loss of habitat for animals, clearing native vegetation has led to erosion and the loss of topsoil, sediment runoff into rivers and the ocean, and salinization of the land.

Because of its geological stability, Australia's soil is generally poor—only 6% of the continent contains fertile land, compared, for instance, to 20% of the United States. For millions of years, the land surface has remained exposed; rainfall has leached its nutrients, and salt has accumulated from ocean breezes and marine deposits of earlier geological periods.

Water and wind erosion occur at rates up to ten times those of new soil formation, and Australia's sizable groundwater reserves (including the Great Artesian Basin, which underlies 22% of the continent) are being depleted more quickly than they can be replenished. Yet at the same time, the water table is rising in certain areas owing to to irrigation and the replacement of deep-rooted native trees (which would normally tap into the ground water and stabilize the water table) with shallow-rooted crops. The rising water table brings even more salt to the surface of the land and results in land salinization, which decreases productivity, and in severe cases can create *salt lakes*, where nothing can grow.

Although the effects of clearing and altering the land are now well known, land clearing continues at alarming rates. Almost half of the native forests on the continent have been cleared, and vegetation in temperate zones, where agriculture and ranching are easier, have been hardest hit. While 25% of the continent's rainforests have been spared, 90% of *mallee* (arid-region scrub areas with low-growing eucalyptus plants) and temperate woodlands have been cleared, as have 99% of temperate grasslands. Rates of habitat loss on private land in Australia in the 1980s and early 1990s were similar to rates of land clearing in Thailand, Bolivia, and Zaire, and were exceeded only in Indonesia and the Brazilian Amazon.

Agriculture and Grazing

The most intensive land clearing in Australia occurs to make room for agriculture and grazing. Because of Australia's poor soil and arid climate, crops often require irrigation and the addition of large amounts of fertilizers. Irrigation water is generally salty, and raises the water table, thus compounding the problem of land salinization initiated by clearing deep-rooted trees.

In addition, the run-off of sediment, fertilizers, and animal waste from agriculture is the most serious threat to Australia's coasts and oceans. In Queensland, it has been estimated that run-off of sediments and nutrients such as nitrogen and phosphorus is now three to five times greater than it was when Europeans arrived. The extra nutrients in rivers and the ocean lead to algal blooms that are often toxic, and combine with sediments to shade seagrass beds and other important coastal communities, decreasing growth and limiting the communities' abilities to recover from storms and other disturbances.

Grazing livestock, which happens on a massive amount of Australian land, creates additional problems. Grazing can cause severe habitat modification—including the loss of understory plants and grasses, dislodging of rocks and logs, and damage to wetlands and riverbanks—that can lead to the disruption of ecological communities and species extinctions. Artificial water sources (especially wells, or "water points," drilled all over Australia's arid center) created for the introduced grazers cause further problems. Domestic livestock, as well as some native animals, aggregate around these water sources, but studies have shown that a significant proportion of some native mammals actually decrease in abundance with proximity to water sources (or to the grazing livestock around them). Thus these water sources, where they occur, are affecting the native species. They also permit some introduced species, such as hares and rabbits, to thrive in regions that otherwise might be too dry to support them.

Logging

While about 40% of Australia's forests have been completely cleared (mostly for agriculture), another 35% to 40% are affected by logging. The disturbances caused by logging include the loss of food and habitat for animals, changes in the structural and biological features of communities, alteration of natural fire cycles, and fragmentation of habitats by roads and clear-cutting (when all trees in an area are cut). In Australia, a significant additional effect of logging is the loss of hollow-bearing trees. Hollows in large, old trees provide dens, nests, and shelter for 400 species of Australian vertebrates, including possums, gliders, bats, and parrots. More than 40% of Australia's marsupials depend on tree hollows at some point in their lives, as well as 28% of amphibians and reptiles, and 17% of birds. Hollow-dependent animals play major roles in forest ecosystems, including plant pollination and the control of insect populations.

Because Australia contains no wood-drilling vertebrates, such as woodpeckers, tree hollows can take several hundred years to form by the much slower processes of decay by bacteria, fungi, and wood-eating insects.

Unfortunately, logging operations in many Australian forests occur at intervals of every 40 to 120 years, precluding new hollows from forming before trees are re-cut. However, the logging industry recognizes that nature reserves alone cannot preserve biodiversity, and that efforts must be made to maintain ecosystems in logged forests. The New South Wales National Parks and Wildlife Service is conducting research on how to maintain habitat for hollow-dependent animals in logged forests, addressing questions such as how many tree hollows must be maintained per hectare (2.5 acres), which tree species are preferable, and how the spatial arrangement of trees affects hollow-dependent fauna.

Introduced Species

Introduced species (species that are not native to a place) are surpassed only by habitat loss as a primary cause of extinctions in Australia and worldwide. Australia has proven particularly vulnerable to the effects of non-native species introductions because its native species had evolved for 50 million years in near-total isolation from other plants and animals. Introduced species now make up 10% of Australia's terrestrial vertebrate fauna, and include 26 birds, 24 mammals, 22 fishes, and at least 500 invertebrates. The effects of non-native species generally fall into three categories: predation on native species, competition with native species, and disease transmission to native species, domestic animals, or humans.

Foxes and feral cats in Australia primarily eat rabbits, which are also introduced (cats were in fact spread throughout Australia to try to control the rabbit population), but they also eat native birds, mammals, reptiles, and invertebrates. Predation by cats and foxes has been implicated in the population declines of at least 17 endangered or vulnerable vertebrate species (including quolls and the Bilby), as well as 22 other vertebrates that are considered to be at risk. In addition, feral cats are known to spread *toxoplasmosis*, a parasite that can cause anemia and severe birth defects. The parasite can be passed to native fauna, livestock, and humans, and is particularly deadly to marsupials.

Other introduced species compete with native species for food sources or nesting sites. Herbivores such as goats and rabbits compete with native herbivores; competition from goats may have led to the decline of several species of rock-wallabies. Rabbits, which now number in the hundreds of millions, have a whole range of damaging effects: they eat seedlings, preventing the regeneration of trees and shrubs, damage pastures, burrow in the soil, causing soil destabilization and erosion, and compete for food with endangered small mammals such as the Bilby and Burrowing Bettong. In addition, they provide food for introduced cats and foxes, and thus contribute to the problems caused by these predators. A great deal of effort has gone into controlling rabbit populations; viruses such as *myxomatosis* (a mosquito-borne rabbit virus) and *rabbit calcivirus* have been released, with patchy and often temporary results.

Some introduced species have had effects that were harder to foresee. Honeybees, which were introduced in the 1800s for the honey and beeswax industry, take over the tree hollows that many native vertebrates depend on and compete with native animals for nectar and pollen. The Cane Toad, which was introduced in 1935 to control populations of cane beetles, did not eat the cane beetles, but did feast on native invertebrates and small vertebrates. The toads compete with native frogs and snakes, and their skin is deadly to the native predators that consume them.

Introductions of marine species have also caused problems. At least 55 species of fish, invertebrates, and seaweeds have been released intentionally or accidentally from aquaculture sites, aquariums, or the ballast water of ships. Introduced fish can eliminate native species, and toxic dinoflagellates, tiny invertebrate organisms, have had severe impacts on the shellfish industry.

Urban Growth

Australia is one of the most urbanized nations in the world, with 88% of its 19 million people living in large cities and towns, most of which are on the coast. While urban areas occupy only 1.3% of Australia's land, urban growth has caused more extinctions of vascular plants than land clearing for agriculture or logging. The habitat modification involved with urbanization is severe and permanent, and urban sprawl increasingly consumes large areas of bushland, threatening the koala in southeast Queensland, and promoting the spread of weeds and feral animals to the bush.

While Australia's oceans and estuaries are in generally good health, those located closer to urban areas experience problems with sediment run-off and excessive nutrients from fertilizers and animal, human, and industrial waste. In addition, large areas of mangroves and salt marshes (which provide important habitat for wading birds and juvenile fishes) have been cleared or filled for development (in areas such as Moreton Bay, Queensland), and many seagrass beds, which can take centuries to recolonize, have recently died near urban areas.

Global Warming and the Ozone Layer

Unlike most industrialized nations, Australia has no serious problem with sulfur dioxide or acid rain, but it does have reason to worry about the health of its atmosphere. The hole in the ozone layer that appears over Antarctica every spring is growing larger and deeper, exposing humans and animals in Australia to harmful ultraviolet radiation. Australia takes this threat seriously, and is ahead of international targets to reduce the release of substances that deplete the ozone layer, such as chlorofluorocarbons (CFCs).

Unfortunately, Australia has not been as successful in decreasing its emission of *greenhouse gases* (carbon dioxide, carbon monoxide, and others) that lead to global warming. While Australia's emissions are low on a global scale (1% to 2% of the world total), it releases more greenhouse gases per capita than almost any other country. Much of these emissions are from the burning of fossil fuels, but about a quarter of emissions are from agricultural activities, such as burning native vegetation. Australia's rate of emissions growth is one of the highest in the world, and is expected to increase to 28% over 1990 levels by 2008, the target date for reducing emissions according to international agreements.

Air temperatures are predicted to rise by several degrees over the next century as a result of global warming, and the associated changes in water temperature, sea level, and habitat types could have significant impact on Australia. Changes in air temperature are likely to lead to changes in plant and animal distributions, as organisms adapted to cooler environments move to different latitudes or higher elevations (if they are available). The rate of change in temperature that is predicted in the next 40 years, however, will be too quick for evolutionary adaptation, and thus many organisms such as slow-growing, temperature-dependent corals may be vulnerable.

Conservation

The conservation movement has developed relatively late in Australia, and many ecologically harmful activities remain largely unregulated. Australia has participated in a number of international conferences and agreements over the last several decades, but has developed most of its significant national and state environmental legislation only in the last decade.

Nationally, Australia enacted legislation in the 1990s regarding sustainable development, conservation of biodiversity, and protection of endangered species, and set a goal to preserve 15% of each forest type that existed on the continent before 1750. Much of this legislation provides only guidelines, though. The forest proposal, which allows that preserving less than 15% of forest types is acceptable where the socio-economic impact of preservation is considered to be too great, is a case in point. Many of these commonwealth acts also suffer from a severe lack of funding. In addition, environmental laws and policies are often made at the commonwealth, state, territory, and local levels, and coordination between the participating agencies is difficult.

One exception to this, and an example of successful inter-agency coordination, is the Great Barrier Reef Marine Park Authority, in which several different agencies jointly manage the 340,000 sq km (130,000 sq mi) Great Barrier Reef Marine Park, which receives two million visitors per year. In spite of heavy visitation, Australia's oceans and coastlines are generally healthy. Large areas of Australia's oceans are protected as reserves, but very little area within these reserves is completely protected from human disturbance. For example, in 80% of the Great Barrier Reef Marine Park, all fishing and other commercial activities are permitted, including trawling and collecting, and only oil drilling and mining are prohibited. As a result, the Great Barrier Reef is not free of environmental problems; Dugongs (Plate 74) and Loggerhead Sea Turtles are endangered here, and many fish species are over-exploited by fishing industries.

Many environmental problems in Australia are exacerbated by the fact that some government agencies still see their role as promoting economic development without regard to the environmental costs. Despite the significant impacts that agriculture and grazing are known to have, these industries are among the most weakly regulated in Australia, and many environmental considerations remain foreign to farmers and ranchers. Land clearing is tolerated and even encouraged in some areas. Queensland, which contains some of the last remaining biologically rich tropical rainforests in Australia, has issued a policy and guidelines on tree clearing that first came into effect only in late 1997. But the state still issues permits to clear old growth and tropical rainforests, and has no state policy or guidelines for clearing on private land.

There is a great deal of pressure to preserve as much of the remaining native forests in Australia as possible, but the current reserve system is patchy. For example, in 1992 about 14% of remaining old growth (never-cut) forests were in reserves; this included 64% of remaining mangroves and swamps (which are difficult to access and perhaps somewhat less important ecologically), but only 5% of the economically valuable southeastern dry forests and woodlands.

Still, Australia has had great success in preserving its eleven World Heritage Sites. These are sites that have made it through the rigorous process of international screening and been determined to be of such outstanding universal value that their conservation is of concern to all people. Australia is distinguished in containing four of the seventeen sites worldwide that are listed for both natural and cultural criteria, including the Tasmania Wilderness and Kakadu National Park, and in having four sites that meet all four of the World Heritage criteria for natural sites, including the Great Barrier Reef, Tasmania Wilderness, and the Wet Tropics of Queensland.

Cassowary Recovery Program

As biodiversity loss is the most immediate and obvious threat to Australia's environment, many conservation programs focus on the recovery of a single species, such as the Dugong in the Great Barrier Reef or the Southern Cassowary in the tropical rainforests of northern Queensland. This latter rainforest area, known as the "Wet Tropics," supports large proportions of Australia's animals, including 36% of its mammal species, 50% of its birds, about 25% of its amphibians and reptiles, about 35% of its freshwater fish, and 60% of its butterflies, while taking up only a tiny fraction (about 0.1%) of the continent's area.

The Southern Cassowary (Plate 20), a very large, striking flightless bird, is considered a *keystone species* (one whose presence affects the survival of many other species) in these forests. It is the largest vertebrate in the forest, and eats the fruits of rainforest plants, passing seeds through its digestive tract intact to be distributed throughout the forest. The cassowary is the *only* disperser of more than 100 plants that produce very large fruits, and the major disperser of hundreds more, single-handedly filling the roles that numerous mammals, birds, and reptiles play in other forests. Thus, its loss could lead to the loss of several species of plants, as well as the animals associated with them.

Southern Cassowaries in Australia are found only in the tropical rainforests of northern Queensland; only two populations remain—one of about 1,500 individuals located in the Wet Tropics World Heritage Area (centered around Cairns) and another, separate population, of unknown size, in the northern part of the Cape York Peninsula. These birds are threatened by a variety of human disturbances, including habitat destruction, hunting, competition with feral pigs, predation by domestic dogs, collisions with motor vehicles, and disease.

A cassowary recovery program has been coordinated and funded by the Wet Tropics Management Authority and the Queensland Parks and Wildlife Service. The program relies on a strong foundation of community involvement, and active community groups at Mission Beach, Kuranda, and Daintree have achieved significant conservation gains in their areas. The groups have achieved results with relatively simple actions, such as placing road signs to alert drivers to the animals' presence and educating the public about how to deal with these animals, which have a generally false reputation of being aggressive toward humans. Local groups and the Cassowary Advisory Council have produced a range of brochures for local communities, including advice on dog control, planting cassowary food trees in areas where their habitat is reduced, and cassowary-friendly fencing.

National Landcare Program

Rather than preserving a single important species, the National Landcare Program seeks instead to involve rural and urban communities in improving the long-term health of Australia's land. The amazing growth of Landcare groups throughout the country demonstrates a trend of increasing community awareness and concern about environmental issues in Australia that is perhaps more important in the long run than any legislation that the commonwealth or state governments could enact.

There are now over 2,000 Landcare groups (with more than 25,000 members) throughout Australia. The first Landcare group was established in Victoria in 1986 by the Victorian government and the Victorian Farmers Federation. The emphasis was on mobilizing land owners and community members to restore rural lands by such activities as planting trees, fencing off rivers from livestock, controlling soil salinization, and saving bits of the bush. In 1988, the National Landcare Program was established to provide funding for Landcare groups and to help coordinate planning. The 1990s were declared the "decade of Landcare" and funding was given to Landcare from the newly established National Heritage Trust.

Membership in Landcare is voluntary and the agenda is set by each group, yet Landcare is slowly working its way into the culture of Australia, particularly in rural regions. In the early 1990s, surveys showed that 50% of properties in Victoria, Tasmania, and Western Australia had a Landcare member. It has also been demonstrated that a significant percentage of Landcare members adopt better land management practices than non-members.

It is not yet clear how much of an impact Landcare programs actually have on the Australian environment. The program has generated a great deal of enthusiasm for tree planting, but some argue that the activities could use more planning and coordination. Unfortunately, one of Landcare's main problems is finding enough people in rural areas with the expertise to lead groups in prioritizing agendas and planning restoration projects.

Yet Landcare groups continue to form and land management practices continue to improve gradually. The rapid growth of the National Landcare Program is attributed not only to the social aspect of the groups, but also to the fact that it has shown people that they have the capacity to deal with problems in their communities that seem too large for a single family to tackle. While it may not save keystone species or protect untouched, biologically rich ecosystems, Landcare has the potential to integrate conservation values and practices into agricultural and rural regions of Australia, where appropriate land management has proven to be so critical.

Ecotourism

The goal of ecotourism is not only to expose visitors to features of the natural environment, but also to contribute to conservation and local communities. But even the best run ecotourism programs can be potentially harmful to the animals and ecosystems that the tourists come to see. The sheer numbers of visitors coming to Australia can cause problems; from the early 1980s to the early 1990s, the number of visitors to the Great Barrier Reef more than doubled and visitors to Kakadu National Park quadrupled.

Though the effects of ecotourism on natural communities remains largely unstudied, a few problems are already apparent. For example, populations of Silver Gulls (Plate 32) that scavenge for waste around island resorts have increased 10 to 13% per year in some areas, and these gulls put pressure on other seabirds by preying on their eggs. The Cod Hole (a famous dive site northeast of Cooktown) in northern Queensland has seen an unexplained decline in the numbers and health of Potato Cod (Plate 91), which have attracted divers there for many years. Other effects are less obvious, such as changes in the migratory and nomadic behavior of lorikeets that are fed nectar by tourists.

On the other hand, genuine ecotourism does produce tangible and important benefits. In addition to providing money for conservation programs, ecotourism provides education and changes public opinion, promotes conservation-oriented land use and management, and increases support in local communities for conservation. In some cases, ecotourism provides valuable information and even manual labor through unique programs that integrate ecotourism with research and conservation efforts. Also, Aboriginal communities are beginning to benefit economically from ecotourism. For example, the community that lives around (and owns parts of) Kakadu National Park shares in park receipts, and Ayers Rock, which was officially returned to Aboriginal people in 1986, likewise generates some tourist revenue. (The Aboriginal communities also have a hand in managing these areas.)

Australia has in fact become a leader in promoting cooperation between tour operators and management agencies. In the Great Barrier Reef, visitors help monitor the coral reefs, and report rare sightings of the threatened Grey Nurse Shark. In northern Queensland, tour operators developed programs focusing on the Dwarf Minke Whale, about which little is known, and involved scientists from the beginning to share information and develop interactive activities.

Finally, the Australian ecotourism industry has developed the first National Ecotourism Accreditation Program, a voluntary program that sets standards for eco-friendly tours, attractions, and accommodations. The program rates ecotourism products on ecological sustainability, contributions to conservation and the local community, accurate marketing, and client satisfaction. This program not only encourages tour operators to adopt eco-friendly practices, but also allows visitors to identify tours and attractions that are likely to provide positive benefits to Australia's animals and environment, while minimizing the negative impacts of visitation.

Chapter 6

HOW TO USE THIS BOOK: ECOLOGY AND NATURAL HISTORY

- *What is Natural History?*
- *What is Ecology and What Are Ecological Interactions?*
- *How to Use This Book*
    Information in the Family Profiles
    Information in the Color Plate Sections

What is Natural History?

The purpose of this book is to provide ecotravellers with sufficient information to identify many common animal and plant species and to learn about them and the families to which they belong. Information on the lives of animals is generally known as *natural history*, which is usually defined as the study of animals' natural habits, including especially their ecology, distribution, classification, and behavior. This kind of information is of importance for a variety of reasons: researchers need to know natural history as background on the species they study, and wildlife managers and conservationists need natural history information because their decisions about managing animal populations must be partially based on it. More relevant for the ecotraveller, natural history is simply interesting. People who appreciate animals typically like to watch them, touch them when appropriate, and know as much about them as they can.

What is Ecology and What Are Ecological Interactions?

Ecology is the branch of the biological sciences that deals with the interactions between living things and their physical environment and with each other. *Animal ecology* is the study of the interactions of animals with each other, with plants, and with the physical environment. Broadly interpreted, these interactions take into account most everything we find fascinating about animals—what they eat, how they forage, how and when they breed, how they survive the rigors of extreme climates, why they are large or small, or dully or brightly colored, and many other facets of their lives.

An animal's life, in some ways, is the sum of its interactions with other animals—members of its own species and others—and with its environment. Of particular interest are the numerous and diverse ecological interactions that occur between different species. Most can be placed into one of several general categories, based on how two species affect each other when they interact; they can have positive, negative, or neutral (that is, no) effects on each other. The relationship terms below are used in the book to describe the natural history of various animals.

Competition is an ecological relationship in which neither of the interacting species benefit. Competition occurs when individuals of two species use the same resource—a certain type of food, nesting holes in trees, et cetera—and that resource is in insufficient supply to meet all their needs. As a result, each species is less successful than it could be if the other species were not present.

Predation is an ecological interaction in which one species, the *predator*, benefits, and the other species, the *prey*, is harmed. Most people think that a good example of a predator eating prey would be a lion eating an antelope, and they are correct; but predation also includes interactions in which the predator eats only part of its prey and the prey actually survives. Thus, some antelope eat tree leaves and branches, and so, in a way, they can be considered predators on plant prey.

Parasitism, like predation, is a relationship between two species in which one benefits and one is harmed. The difference is that in a predatory relationship, one animal kills and eats the other, but in a parasitic one, the parasite feeds slowly on the host species and usually does not kill it. There are internal parasites, such as protozoans and many kinds of worms, and external parasites, such as leeches, ticks, and mites.

Mutualisms, which include some of the most compelling of ecological relationships, are interactions in which both participants benefit. Plants and their pollinators engage in mutualistic interactions. A bee species, for instance, obtains a food resource, nectar or pollen, from a plant's flower; the plant it visits benefits because it is able to complete its reproductive cycle when the bee transports pollen to another plant. A famous case of mutualism involves several species of acacia plants and the ants that live in them: the ants obtain food (the acacias produce nectar for them) and shelter from the acacias and in return, the ants defend the plants from plant-eating insects. Sometimes the species have interacted so long that they now cannot live without each other; theirs is an *obligate* mutualism. For instance, termites cannot by themselves digest wood. Rather, it is the single-celled animals, protozoans, that live in their gut that produce the digestive enzymes that digest wood. At this point in their evolutionary histories, neither the termites nor their internal helpers can live alone.

Commensalism is a relationship in which one species benefits but the other is not affected in any way. For example, *epiphytes*, such as orchids and bromeliads, that grow on tree trunks and branches obtain from trees some shelf space to grow on, but, as far as anyone knows, neither hurt nor help the trees. A classic example of a commensal is a fish that attaches itself with a suction cup on its head to a shark, then feeds on scraps of food the shark leaves behind. Remora are commensals, not parasites—they neither harm nor help sharks, but they benefit greatly by associating with them. Cattle Egrets (Plate 25) are commensals—these birds follow cattle, eating insects and other small animals that flush from cover as the cattle move about their pastures; the cattle, as far as we know, couldn't care one way or the other (unless they are concerned about loss of dignity when the egrets perch not only near them, but *on* them).

A term many people know that covers some of these ecological interactions is *symbiosis*, which means living together. Usually this term suggests that the two interacting species do not harm one another; therefore, mutualisms and commensalisms are the symbiotic relationships discussed here.

How to Use This Book

The information on animals is divided into two sections: the plates, which include artists' color renderings of various species together with brief identifying and location information; and the family profiles, with natural history information on the families to which the pictured animals belong. The best way to identify and learn about Australian animals may be to scan the illustrations before a trip to become familiar with the kinds of animals you are likely to encounter. Then when you spot an animal, you may recognize its type or family, and can find the appropriate pictures and profiles quickly. Color drawings of common plant species are shown in Plates A to K; many of the illustrated plants are referred to in Chapter 3.

Information in the Family Profiles

Classification, Distribution, Morphology
The first paragraphs of each profile generally provide information on the family's classification (or *taxonomy*), geographic distribution, and *morphology* (shape, size, and coloring of the animals). Classification information is provided because it is how scientists separate animals into related groups and often it enhances our appreciation of animals to know these relationships. You may have been exposed to classification levels sometime during your education, but if you are a bit rusty, a quick review may help. *Kingdom* Animalia: aside from plant information, all the species detailed in the book are members of the animal kingdom. *Phylum* Chordata, *Subphylum* Vertebrata: most of the species in the book, including fish, are vertebrates, animals with backbones (exceptions are the marine *invertebrate* animals discussed in Chapter 11). *Class:* the book covers several vertebrate classes such as Amphibia (amphibians), Reptilia (reptiles), Aves (birds), and Mammalia (mammals). *Order:* each class is divided into several orders, the animals in each order sharing many characteristics. For example, one of the mammal orders is Carnivora, the carnivores, which includes mammals with teeth specialized for meat-eating—dogs, cats, bears, raccoons, weasels. *Family:* families of animals are subdivisions of each order that contain closely related species that are very similar in form, ecology, and behavior. The family Canidae, for instance, contains all the dog-like mammals—coyote, wolf, fox, dog. Animal family names end in "-dae;" subfamilies, subdivisions of families, end in "-nae." *Genus* (plural *genera*): further subdivisions; within each genus are grouped species that are very closely related—they are all considered to have evolved from a common ancestor. *Species:* the lowest classification level; all members of a species are similar enough to be able to breed and produce living, fertile offspring.

Example: Classification of the Sulphur-crested Cockatoo (Plate 36):

Kingdom: Animalia, with more than a million species
Phylum: Chordata, Subphylum Vertebrata, with about 40,000 species
Class: Aves (Birds), with about 9,700 species
Order: Psittaciformes, with about 350 species; includes parrots, cockatoos, and lories
Family: Cacatuidae, with 19 species; all the cockatoos
Genus: *Cacatua*, the largest genus of cockatoos, with 12 species
Species: *Cacatua galerita*, the Sulphur-crested Cockatoo

Some of the family profiles in the book actually cover animal orders; others describe families or subfamilies.

The distributions of species vary tremendously. Some species are found only in very limited areas, whereas others range over several continents. Distributions can be described in a number of ways. An animal or group can be said to be *Old World* or *New World;* the former refers to the regions of the globe that Europeans knew of before Columbus—Europe, Asia, Africa; and the latter refers to the Western Hemisphere—North, Central, and South America. Biogeographers—scientists who study the geographic distributions of living things—consider Australia, appropriately, to fall within the part of the world called the *Australian* region, which includes Australia, New Zealand, the New Guinea area, and oceanic islands of the Pacific; an *Australian species,* in this terminology, is one that occurs naturally in Australia, New Zealand, the New Guinea area, or on Pacific islands. The terms *tropical, temperate,* and *arctic* refer to climate regions of the Earth; the boundaries of these zones are determined by lines of latitude (and ultimately, by the position of the sun with respect to the Earth's surface). The tropics, always warm, are the regions of the world that fall within the belt from 23.5° north latitude (the Tropic of Cancer) to 23.5° south latitude (the Tropic of Capricorn). The world's temperate zones, with more seasonal climates, extend from 23.5° North and South latitude to the Arctic and Antarctic Circles, at 66.5° North and South. Arctic regions, more or less always cold, extend from 66.5° North and South to the poles. Australia straddles the Tropic of Capricorn, with its northern half in the tropics and its southern half in the south temperate zone (Map 7, p. 63).

Several terms help define a species' distribution and describe how it attained its distribution:

Range. The particular geographic area occupied by a species.

Native or Indigenous. Occurring naturally in a particular place.

Introduced. Occurring in a particular place owing to peoples' intentional or unintentional assistance with transportation, usually from one continent to another, or from a continent to an island; the opposite of native. For instance, pheasants were initially brought to North America from Europe/Asia for hunting and Europeans brought rabbits and foxes to Australia for sport. Europeans also brought House Sparrows and European Starlings to North America and Australia. Other words used somewhat interchangeably with "introduced" to describe non-native species spread by people are alien, exotic, and invader.

Endemic. A species, a genus, an entire family, etc., that is found in a particular place and nowhere else (see Close-Up, p. 110). Galapagos finches are endemic to the Galapagos Islands; Hawaiian honeycreepers are endemic to Hawaii; nearly all

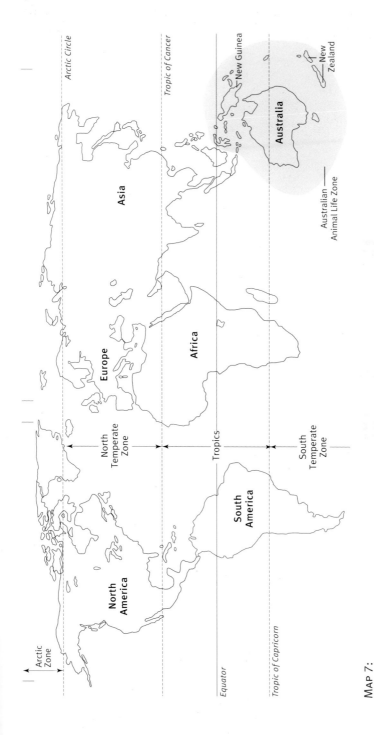

Arctic Circle

Tropic of Cancer

New Guinea

New Zealand

Australia

Asia

Australian Animal Life Zone

Europe

Africa

North Temperate Zone

Tropics

South Temperate Zone

Arctic Zone

South America

North America

Equator

Tropic of Capricorn

MAP 7:
Map of the Earth showing the position of Australia and the Australian animal life zone; Old World and New World zones; and tropical, temperate, and arctic regions.

the reptile and mammal species of Madagascar are endemics; all species are endemic to Earth (as far as we know).

Cosmopolitan. A species that is widely distributed throughout the world.

Some terms used especially for birds: A *resident* species stays in the same place all year and breeds there. A *migratory* species breeds in one location but spends the nonbreeding portion of each year elsewhere. For instance, many shorebird species breed in the north temperate or arctic zone (often in northeastern Siberia or Alaska) but spend nonbreeding months in Australia. Seabirds can often be classed as *coastal* (spending all or much of their time along mainland or island coasts); *inshore* (occurring near the seashore, usually in or over water depths of 50 m, 160 ft, or less; the terms "coastal" and "inshore" are sometimes used interchangeably); *offshore* (occurring at sea in or over water depths between 50 and 200 m, 160 and 650 ft, usually over continental shelves; these species rarely come near shore, except to nest); or *pelagic* (open ocean species that do not come near land or even continental shelves, except to nest).

Ecology and Behavior

In these sections, I describe some of what is known about the basic activities pursued by each group. Much of the information relates to when and where animals are usually active, what they eat, and how they forage.

Activity Location—*Terrestrial* animals pursue life and food on the ground. *Arboreal* animals pursue life and food in trees or shrubs. *Cursorial* refers to animals that are adapted for running along the ground. *Fossorial* animals live most of their lives in tunnels underground.

Activity Time—*Nocturnal* means active at night. *Diurnal* means active during the day. *Crepuscular* refers to animals that are active at dusk and/or dawn.

Food Preferences—Although animal species can usually be assigned to one of the feeding categories below, most eat more than one type of food. Most frugivorous birds, for instance, also nibble on the occasional insect, and carnivorous mammals occasionally eat plant materials.

> *Herbivores* are predators that prey on plants.
> *Carnivores* are predators that prey on animals.
> *Insectivores* eat insects.
> *Granivores* eat seeds.
> *Frugivores* eat fruit.
> *Nectarivores* eat nectar.
> *Piscivores* eat fish.
> *Omnivores* eat a variety of things.
> *Detritivores*, such as vultures, eat dead stuff.

Ecological Interactions

These sections describe what I think are intriguing ecological relationships. Groups that are often the subject of ecological research are the ones for which such relationships are more likely to be known.

Breeding

In these sections, I present basics on each group's breeding particulars, including type of mating system, special breeding behaviors, durations of egg incubation or *gestation* (pregnancy), as well as information on nests, eggs, and young.

Mating systems—A *monogamous* mating system is one in which one male and one female establish a pair-bond and contribute fairly evenly to each breeding effort. In *polygamous* systems, individuals of one of the sexes have more than one mate (that is, they have harems): in *polygynous* systems, one male mates with several females, and in *polyandrous* systems, one female mates with several males.

Condition of young at birth—*Altricial* young are born in a relatively undeveloped state, usually naked of fur or feathers, eyes closed, and unable to feed themselves, walk, or run from predators. *Precocial* young are born in a more developed state, eyes open, and soon able to walk and perhaps feed themselves.

Notes

These sections provide brief accounts of folklore associated with the profiled groups, and any other interesting bits of information about the profiled animals that do not fit elsewhere in the account.

Status

These sections comment on the conservation status of each group, including information on relative rarity or abundance, factors contributing to population declines, and special conservation measures that have been implemented. I use the following terms to describe degrees of threat to various species: *Endangered* species are known to be in imminent danger of extinction throughout their range, and are highly unlikely to survive unless strong conservation measures are taken; populations of endangered species generally are very small, so they are rarely seen. *Threatened* species are known to be undergoing rapid declines in the sizes of their populations; unless conservation measures are enacted, and the causes of the population decline identified and halted, these species are likely to move to endangered status in the near future. *Vulnerable to threat,* or *near-threatened*, are species that, owing to their habitat requirements or limited distributions, and based on known patterns of habitat destruction, are highly likely to be threatened in the near future. Several organizations publish lists of threatened and endangered species.

Where appropriate, I also include threat classifications from the Convention on International Trade in Endangered Species (CITES). CITES is a global cooperative agreement to protect threatened species on a worldwide scale by regulating international trade in wild animals and plants among the 140 or so participating countries. Regulated species are listed in CITES Appendices, with trade in those species being strictly regulated by required licenses and documents. CITES Appendix I lists endangered species; all trade in them is prohibited. Appendix II lists threatened/vulnerable species, those that are not yet endangered but may soon be; trade in them is strictly regulated. Appendix III lists species that are protected by laws of individual countries that have signed the CITES agreements. The International Union for Conservation of Nature (IUCN) maintains a "Red List" of threatened and endangered species that often is more broad-based and inclusive than the CITES lists. References in the book to threat classifications in individual

Australian states are taken from *CSIRO List of Australian Vertebrates: A Reference With Conservation Status*. CSIRO, the Commonwealth Scientific and Industrial Research Organization, is Australia's chief public science organization.

Information in the Color Plate Sections

Pictures. Among amphibians, reptiles, and mammals, males and females of a species usually look alike, although often there are size differences. For many species of birds, however, the sexes differ in color pattern and even anatomical features. If only one individual is pictured, you may assume that male and female of that species look alike or almost alike; when there are major sex differences, both male and female are depicted.

Name. I provide the common English name for each profiled species and the scientific, or Latin, name, as well as alternative common names, if any are frequently used. Aboriginal names often vary according to region, and are not given here.

ID. Here I provide brief descriptive information that, together with the pictures, will enable you to identify most of the animals you see. The lengths of reptiles and amphibians given in this book are *snout-vent lengths* (SVLs), the distance from the tip of the snout to the vent, unless it is mentioned that the tail is included. The *vent* is the opening on their bellies that lies approximately where the rear limbs join the body, and through which sex occurs and wastes exit. Therefore, long tails of lizards, for instance, are not included in the reported length measurements, and frogs' long legs are not included in theirs. For mammals, measurements I give are generally the lengths of the head and body, but do not include tails. For most mammals, I give approximate weights. Birds are measured from tip of bill to end of tail. For birds commonly seen flying, such as seabirds and hawks, I provide wingspan (wingtip to wingtip) measurements, if known. For the songbirds (passerine, or "perching birds;" see p. 117), I use the following measures: *large* (more than 30 cm, 12 in, long); *mid-sized* (15 or 18 cm to 30 cm, 6 or 7 to 12 in); *small* (11 to 15 cm, 4.5 to 6 in); and *very small* (less than 11 cm, 4.5 in). Lengths given for fish are *standard lengths*, the distance from the front of the mouth to the point where the tail appears to join the body; that is, tails are not included in the measurement.

Habitat/Regions. In these sections I give the habitat types in which each species occurs, symbols for the habitat types each species prefers, and the states/regions where each species may be found. The term "ranges" refers to the Great Dividing Range, the mountains that run parallel to Australia's eastern coast, 50 to 400 km (30 to 250 miles) inland.

Explanation of region symbols (see Map 2, p. 27):

CYP = The Cape York Peninsula, which is the northern tip of Queensland
TRQ = Tropical Queensland; coastal and inland northern parts of the state
TEQ = Temperate Queensland; inland southern parts of the state
NSW = New South Wales
VIC = Victoria
TAS = Tasmania

Explanation of habitat symbols:

 = Rainforest (also called closed forest, monsoon forest).

 = Open forest and woodland (includes most eucalypt forests; also called sclerophyll forest).

 = Shrubland (generally with shrubs up to 4 m, 13 ft, high).

 = Heathland (open areas of evergreen shrubs usually less than 2 m, 6.5 ft, high; occurs over some coastal lowlands and in subalpine and alpine areas).

 = Open habitats: grassland, pastures, savannah (grassland with scattered trees and shrubs), gardens, roadsides, rocky cliffs. Species found in these habitats prefer very open areas.

 = Freshwater. For species typically found in or near lakes, dams (ponds), reservoirs, streams, rivers, marshes, swamps, billabongs (stagnant pools in beds of seasonal streams).

 = Saltwater. For species usually found in or near the ocean, ocean beaches, or mangroves.

Example:

Plate 36d

Sulphur-crested Cockatoo
Cacatua galerita
ID: Large white parrot with blackish bill, conspicuous yellow crest; yellowish tinge under wings and tail; to 52 cm (20.5 in).

HABITAT: Rainforests, open forests, agricultural areas, and around human settlements; often along watercourses; usually small to large groups.

REGIONS: CYP, TRQ, TEQ, NSW, VIC, TAS

Chapter 7

AMPHIBIANS

by Michelle Christy
Colorado State University

and Gerry Swan
The Australian Museum, Sydney

- *General Characteristics and Natural History*
- *Seeing Frogs in Eastern Australia*
- *Family Profiles*
    - *1. Tree Frogs*
    - *2. Southern Frogs*
    - *3. Narrow-mouthed Frogs*
    - *4. True Frogs*
    - *5. Toads*
- *Environmental Close-Up 2: Frog Population Declines*

General Characteristics and Natural History

The word "amphibia" is derived from the Greek *amphi*, meaning "of both kinds," and *bios*, meaning "way of life." Thus amphibians can be defined as animals that characteristically inhabit two different environments, namely, water when they are eggs and tadpoles, and land during their later life stages. Although this is true of many amphibians, there are a significant number of species that do not spend any part of their life cycle in water; some never leave the safety of the treetops, while others develop in the stomach or pouches of their parent.

The first amphibians evolved toward the end of the Devonian period, between 270 and 345 million years ago. Their ancestors are thought to have originated from a group of bony fish (class Osteichthyes), probably lungfishes, and these early amphibians became the first vertebrates to colonize the Earth's land. The earliest amphibian fossils from Australia are from Queensland and date back some 50 million years. Our modern amphibians bear very little resemblance to these early ancestors.

The eggs of amphibians do not have a shell and are mainly laid in relatively fresh water. The eggs develop into distinctive larvae that use gills to breathe. The life cycle generally involves an aquatic larval stage that undergoes a process called *metamorphosis* (change in form) to become an air-breathing, land-living adult. Adult amphibians commonly have soft, wet, thin, glandular skin and quickly die if they dry out. This is why amphibians live in moist environments.

Although amphibians are a relatively small group in terms of the number of different species (they make up approximately 0.3% of the Earth's known species—totaling about 4,700), they are able to survive in almost any type of environment, from deserts to rainforests. In fact, Antarctica, with its icy dryness, is the only continent on which amphibians are not found. Where conditions are favorable, amphibians often occur in large numbers, which makes them particularly important as a food source for many other animals higher on the food chain.

There are three groups of amphibians living today:

Caecilians. Species in order Gymnophiona, the smallest group of amphibians, commonly called *caecilians* (suh-SIL-ians), are curious, limbless animals that resemble large earthworms. Their skin appears bare, but is actually made up of tiny scales that form bands or rings around the body. Although caecilians can be quite common within their range, they are often very difficult to find because they spend most of their lives underground in moist crevices, dirt, or rotting wood (and because of this lifestyle, relatively little is known about them). Caecilians, of which there are about 170 species, are found only in tropical forest areas. None are found in Australia; the closest ones are in southeast Asia.

Salamanders. The second group, order Caudata (meaning "with tails"), contains *salamanders* and *newts*. There are approximately 430 species, but none are native to Australia. These animals possess both limbs and a tail as adults, and so are lizard-like in form. The Axolotl (*Ambystoma mexicanum*), a medium-sized salamander and the only representative of this group that you may see in Australia, is not native but was brought here from the northern hemisphere for the pet trade.

Frogs and Toads. The largest group of amphibians is the *frogs* and *toads* (order Anura, meaning "without tails"), of which about 4,100 species have been described to date (and it is thought that many more species are yet to be discovered). These are the only amphibians currently found in Australia, where just over 200 species live. They differ from the other two groups in not possessing a tail as an adult. While the majority of frogs and toads are found in Africa and the Americas, Australia and the surrounding region are also significant in terms of number and diversity of species. Currently, 209 named Australian species are recognized, although it is estimated that between 20 and 40 more await description or discovery.

There has long been debate over the distinction between frogs and toads. But what, if anything, is the difference? A frog is generally thought of as being a tailless aquatic, semi-aquatic, or terrestrial amphibian that characteristically has smooth, moist skin, webbed feet, and long hind legs adapted for leaping. Technically, a toad is actually a type of frog. But the name "toad" conjures up a different image: of amphibians chiefly of family Bufonidae (which contains more than 300 species), which resemble frogs but characteristically are more terrestrial and have a broader body and rougher, drier, usually glandular skin. Historically, the difference was actually based on the anatomy of the shoulder girdles (bones) and the way in which these bones were joined at the chest. However, scientists soon discovered that there were many animals that were called frogs but that had the toad-like bone arrangement. To make matters more confusing, in Australia, where we have mostly "frogs," we have only seven species that have the frog-like shoulder girdle structure. Therefore, if we were to be accurate, the vast majority of Australian amphibians would be called toads rather than frogs! For the purposes of this book we will stick to simple definitions: Frogs are amphibians with smooth, "slimy" skin, long legs and webbed toes adapted for hopping and swimming. Toads are frogs that have large, "stubby" bodies and short legs, so they tend to walk rather than hop. They have dry, rough, warty skin, often with poison glands behind the eyes, and spend more time on the land than most other frogs.

Frogs (including toads) have large, exposed eardrums (*tympanum*) on the sides of their head. They also have at most nine vertebrae (the individual bones that make up the backbone; whereas salamanders have between 30 and 100, and caecilians up to 250). Frogs usually have moist, permeable skin, which helps them with gaseous exchange—the equivalent of breathing through their skin. Often they feel cold to the touch, partly because they are constantly moist, and partly because they are *ectothermic* (cold-blooded), regulating their body temperature by exchanging heat with their surroundings.

All frogs fertilize their eggs externally, which means the female lays her eggs, usually in water, and the male covers them with a fluid that contains sperm. The act of mating, which is when the male climbs onto the back of the female and holds on until she releases her eggs, is called *amplexus*. All male frogs vocalize, usually during the breeding season, to attract females. When a female gets close, the male ambushes her and starts to amplex. Sometimes the male gets it wrong and mistakes a male wandering by for a female and amplexes with him. Usually the ambushed male lets out a scream (a *release call*) and the original male lets him go. Males sometimes vocalize when they are defending their territories against other males, and both males and females can produce a squeal-like noise when they are caught (known as a *distress call*). These calls are produced usually by exhaling large amounts of air that frogs hold in vocal sacs under their chin. Some species can produce sound when they inhale also. As the air moves from the vocal sac to the throat, it causes the vocal chords in the throat to vibrate. The calls of each species can be quite distinctive and it is often easy to identify different types of frogs by their calls. The calls of some frogs can carry over long distances and be heard many kilometers away.

Seeing Frogs in Eastern Australia

Five families of frogs and toad are recognized in Australia. These are the *tree frogs* (Hylidae), *southern frogs* (Myobatrachinae), *narrow-mouthed frogs* (Microhylidae), *true frogs* (Ranidae) and *toads* (Bufonidae). Unfortunately, it is often difficult to separate species into their different families based on their appearance alone, and this can be very frustrating when you are trying to identify them. This task can be made a little easier by knowing that only species within the families Hylidae and Myobatrachidae are found Australia-wide; Microhylidae, Ranidae, and Bufonidae are found only in northeastern Australia and Arnhem Land (the sandstone plateau region east of Kakadu National Park, in the Northern Territory). This knowledge should make identification of frogs you see in the field a bit easier.

It is not difficult to find frogs in eastern Australia, and the east coast is home to many interesting species. Northern Queensland supports the richest variety of species because it is the only area in which representatives of all families can be found. If you were heading up north from the southern regions, it would be most valuable to travel by car; this allows you the freedom to stop wherever and whenever you like, which will increase your chance of seeing frogs. Keep an eye out for moist, wet habitats such as bogs, streams, creeks, ponds, dams, and even puddles. Many species are nocturnal, so going out at night for "spotlighting" will also help, especially if you venture out during rain. But, don't despair if you didn't bring a raincoat, because the period just after rain is also very good for finding frogs. Many frogs may be difficult to locate because of the habitat in which they live (even when they are calling). But with patience and effort, you will be surprised at what you can find.

If you are really keen, we suggest contacting a zoo or frog group (a human group of frog enthusiasts, that is) in the areas you are planning to visit. You can find the names and contact addresses of such groups on the Internet or by contacting your local natural history museum or zoo. Remember though, that all frogs you are likely to see are wild animals and don't take kindly to being handled. If you do need to handle them, be aware that many have poisonous secretions that may be harmful to you, so make sure you wash your hands after handling them. This also helps decrease the likelihood of your spreading diseases from one frog to another. Make sure your hands are wet before picking them up. Be aware: all native frogs in Australia are protected, whether they are rare or common. This means that it is illegal to collect, harass, or harm any frog you are likely to see. Please give them the respect they deserve and leave them in peace where possible.

Family Profiles

1. Tree Frogs

Worldwide, there are estimated to be more than 500 species of *tree frogs*, family Hylidae, with some 73 occurring in Australia. The *hylids* includes some of the most beautiful frogs in the world, with dazzling colors that range from bright purple, green, and orange to metallic blues and golds. The majority of species in this family are known as "tree frogs" because they live in trees or small shrubs. There are also a few members of the family that can't really climb and instead spend most of their time on the ground, in leaf litter or in low-growing vegetation.

Natural History

Ecology and Behavior

Tree frogs need to be able to climb vegetation and also perch there. To do so, they all can flatten themselves against a branch or leaf. This increases the amount of skin in contact with the tree or leaf and gives them a better grip by increasing the friction between themselves and the substrate. Try putting a tree frog on a piece of vertical glass and you can see the way the underside of the frog is almost entirely in contact with the glass (this is why some people refer to tree frogs as "magnet frogs").

The feet and toes of a tree frog are also well adapted for climbing and/or perching. They often have circular pads on the tips of their fingers that also increase the amount of contact between the skin and the substrate. A special gland found just below skin on the underside of the toe-pad secretes an adhesive material that also helps the frog to "stick." If you look closely at a tree frog's foot, you will see thin skin stretched between the toes. This webbing is used to help the frog swim more efficiently, but is equally important (at least in some species) for flight (yes, some frogs can fly!). For example, the New Guinea Tree Frog *Litoria graminea* spreads out its fingers so the hands act like little wings, enabling the animal to glide from tree to tree!

But not all hylids climb trees. The family also contains the *water-holding frogs* (genus *Cyclorama*). These frogs spend almost all of their lives underground, and only surface after rain to breed and feed. The rains penetrate the soil and allow the young frogs to emerge and disperse from their birthplace. As the name suggests, most of these species are able to survive long periods of dry conditions by storing enough water in their body; when they do so they take on a ball-like shape. Once, in the middle of central Australia's Simpson Desert, we watched, very impressed, as thousands of juvenile water-holding frogs "sprouted" from the ground when heavy rains fell.

Most hylids are insectivorous and feed on flying insects, bugs, and beetles, as well as on spiders and caterpillars. There are some species, though, such as the *bell frogs,* that will eat other frogs—including their own species! They have been known to actively hunt other frogs by listening for their advertisement calls and tracking them down.

Ecological Interactions

Many hylids have the ability to live in very close association with people, and members of this family are most often kept as pets (such as the GREEN TREE FROG, Plate 3). People who partake of an Australian Outback experience will, no doubt, happen across a frog or two in outside toilets, rainwater tanks and kitchen sinks.

Breeding

All tree frogs of the Australian region are thought to lay their eggs in water, except one New Guinea species that deposits its eggs in a sloppy jelly mass on the underside of leaves high in rainforest trees. Tree frog eggs are pigmented and are normally laid in a mass of jelly-like mucous, which is usually attached to some form of vegetation under the surface of the water. Eggs quickly develop into free-living, aquatic tadpoles. Most breed in spring (September to November), but a few are summer breeders (December to February), and even fewer breed in winter or throughout the year.

Notes

At present, Australia has the largest known tree frog, the GIANT TREE FROG (*Litoria infrafrenata*), which can grow to 14 cm (5.5 in) in length. This species lives only in remnant rainforest on the eastern coast of northern Queensland and can be difficult to find.

Tree frogs are impressive leapers and, from a standing start, can sometimes jump distances greater than fifteen times the length of their body. A person trying to leap a comparable distance (given the relative difference in head and body length between an average tree frog and an average person), would have to jump at least 10 m (30 ft).

For reasons that are unclear, some frogs have the ability to change color—not usually as dramatically or quickly as chameleons, but noticeably nevertheless. The GREEN AND GOLDEN BELL FROG (Plate 3) is a good example. We have seen many individuals sitting on reeds and sporting the most spectacular colors of lime green, metallic turquoise, and pure gold—truly an awesome sight. But the frogs can turn very dark and drab in a matter of minutes; greens become dirty olive, and gold becomes muddy bronze. The only hint of the dazzling color from moments before is a still-visible turquoise flashing on the thighs. The cause of the color change is not known for certain, but ideas are that it may be stimulated by a drop in temperature or by a change in the substrate color. If the latter is true, the color change would enable the frog to blend more into the background; that is, it would become more *cryptic*, less conspicuous to predators. More research is needed in this area.

Status

There are tree frogs in all Australian states, although many are difficult to see because they live high up in trees or in thick vegetation. Quite a few species are rare and in danger of becoming extinct. Currently, twelve species are listed by Australian authorities as vulnerable or endangered, including the Green and Golden Bell Frog. A further five species have been insufficiently studied, and their status cannot accurately be assessed.

Profiles

Striped Burrowing Frog, *Litoria alboguttata*, Plate 3b
Green and Golden Bell Frog, *Litoria aurea*, Plate 3c
Green Tree Frog, *Litoria caerulea*, Plate 3d
Blue Mountains Tree Frog, *Litoria citropa*, Plate 4a
Dainty Green Tree Frog, *Litoria gracilenta*, Plate 4b
Brown Tree Frog, *Litoria ewingi*, Plate 4c
Broad-palmed Frog, *Litoria latopalmata*, Plate 4d
Lesueur's Frog, *Litoria lesueuri*, Plate 4e
Peron's Tree Frog, *Litoria peronii*, Plate 5b

2. Southern Frogs

Southern frogs (family Myobatrachidae) are restricted to the Australian region. They are found throughout the continent, where they are represented by 117 species. *Myobatrachid* frogs vary extensively in form, ecology, and behavior. Coloring is highly variable, some having striking patches of blue, red, yellow, black, and/or white. These frogs range in size from 2 to 11.5 cm (0.8 to 4.5 in). Toes are half-webbed or mostly un-webbed. In general, any ground-dwelling frog you find in Australia (except in far northern Queensland and parts of the Northern Territory) that can burrow and does not have expanded discs on the fingers or toes is likely to be a member of this family.

Natural History

Ecology and Behavior

The ecology of myobatrachids is quite diverse. They range from large, heavily built, ground-dwelling frogs or burrowers to tiny "toadlets" that live in the moss that surrounds ponds. Several species live in very fast-flowing rivers or streams and even in and around waterfalls. Two of the 117 known Australian species are entirely aquatic, and none spend much of their life off the ground, unlike tree frogs.

Some species within the group are extremely specialized in their behavior and use of habitat, while others are able to survive practically anywhere. For example, the BAW BAW FROG (*Philoria frosti*) is restricted to subalpine and montane habitats at elevations between 1,100 and 1,560 m (3,600 and 5,100 ft). Even more restricted is its breeding habitat, which is found only along seepage lines within or on the edge of frosty hollows. In contrast, the SPOTTED MARSH FROG (Plate 2) can live virtually anywhere and takes advantage of almost any man-made modification or disturbance; this frog can be found living quite happily under a piece of discarded tin or plastic, or in manure ponds, muddy tire tracks or flooded quarries. Many species are swamp-dwellers, while others spend their lives burrowing. Members of one genus (*Pseudophryne*) even live above the snow-line in the southern alpine areas of New South Wales and Victoria, where often one or more adults are found guarding a nest.

Ecological Interactions

Some myobatrachids have the ability to survive in harmony with other animals considered quite dangerous to a defenseless, tiny frog. For example, some live in bull ant nests or share chambers with scorpions. For some reason, the ants and scorpions allow the frogs to enter the nests and live in the cool, humid galleries. This type of association is strange because a tiny frog would be an easy and tasty meal for either ants or scorpions, and also because the frogs are actually competitors with the ants and scorpions, which eat some of the same foods.

Breeding

The life cycle and breeding biology of these frogs are extremely interesting and unusual. Egg and tadpole development range from being completely aquatic to being entirely terrestrial. Some species show incredible breeding adaptations. For instance, many species spawn in water on rafts of foam that the frogs produce by secreting mucous and then whipping it, using their hind legs as beaters. Others lay their eggs on land, where the eggs lay dormant, waiting for rains to flood the area so they can develop into tadpoles. One species soaks up water from damp sand, then lays its eggs underground. The eggs later hatch into fully formed frogs. Incredibly, the male HIP POCKET FROG (Plate 1) has hip pouches in which the tadpoles metamorphose and emerge as frogs. But probably the most spectacular breeding adaptation of all involves the aquatic GASTRIC-BROODING FROG (*Rheobatrachus silus*). This species lays its eggs, then swallows them; the eggs develop in the mother's stomach before she vomits up the fully formed juvenile frogs! What has baffled scientists most is the way the frog can turn off the production of hydrochloric acid (digestive juices) when the baby frogs are in the stomach. Sadly, the species disappeared seven years after its discovery in 1973 and is now believed to be extinct.

Most species have a breeding season that lasts at least two months. Unlike many of their northern hemisphere cousins, most Australian frogs do not breed *synchronously*, that is, all at the same time. There are, however, exceptions. Some species of frogs that live in marshes have been known to act in unison, moving in groups of hundreds or thousands. We once watched more than 2,000 frogs jostle their way down a steep cliff to a creek below to breed. It was as though they were following the Pied Piper of Hamelin.

Notes

Southern frogs (family Myobatrachidae) were considered, until recently, part of a larger, very diverse family, Leptodactylidae, the species of which could be found in the Americas, southern Africa, Australia, and New Guinea. But Leptodactylidae was a kind of "biological dustbin"—many frogs that did not fit clearly and easily into other families were placed here. The Australian and New Guinean members of this large group are now placed in their own, smaller, yet still diverse group— the myobatrachids.

Some species, such as the brightly colored *toadlets* (genus *Pseudophryne*), play dead in order to avoid predation. They either lay on their backs among the leaf litter or, if caught, go limp. For some predators, eating dead animals is presumably unappetizing, so they ignore a seemingly dead frog. Once the predator has moved away, the toadlet miraculously recovers and waddles away.

It is perhaps inaccurate to describe any species of frog as "aquatic." It is true that most frogs are strongly associated with water, but very few actually spend most of their time in it. Most live around the edge and only use the water to escape predators, breed, and sometimes feed. (One of us painfully learned this lesson as a child, when pet tadpoles in a water-filled container died after changing into frogs; the young frogs, with no dry land to hang on to, drowned.) Incidentally, the possibly extinct Gastric-brooding Frog is one species that does (or *did*) spend most of its time in water, hiding among submerged rocks during daylight hours.

Status

Fifteen species within this group are listed as either vulnerable or endangered in Australia. For a further nine we have so little information that their status cannot be adequately assessed. Probably the most well known in this group is the Gastric-brooding Frog.

Profiles

Common Froglet, *Crinia signifera*, Plate 1a
Brown Toadlet, *Pseudophryne bibronii*, Plate 1b
Corroboree Frog, *Pseudophryne corroboree*, Plate 1c
Southern Toadlet, *Pseudophryne semimarmorata*, Plate 1d
Hip Pocket Frog, *Assa darlingtoni*, Plate 1e
Striped Marsh Frog, *Limnodynastes peronii*, Plate 2a
Spotted Marsh Frog, *Limnodynastes tasmaniensis*, Plate 2b
Ornate Burrowing Frog, *Limnodynastes ornatus*, Plate 2c
Eastern Banjo Frog, *Limnodynastes dumerilii*, Plate 2d
Giant Burrowing Frog, *Heleioporus australiacus*, Plate 2e
Giant Barred Frog, *Mixophyes fasciolatus*, Plate 3a

3. Narrow-mouthed Frogs

Narrow-mouthed frogs (family Microhylidae) are a large group of frogs that occur throughout the warm, temperate regions of the world. The word Microhylidae, literally translated, means "small, hylid-type frogs" (tree frogs, p. 71). But the family also includes many burrowing and ground-dwelling frogs. Although some *microhylid* species are large and very plump, most rarely reach adult size of more than 4 cm (1.5 in), and some reach only 1 cm (0.4 in). Within Australia, the family is restricted to the wet rainforests of far northeastern Queensland and the monsoonal forests of Arnhem Land (the region east of Kakadu National Park). There are presently only 19 Australian species within the family. Yet nearby in New Guinea, microhylids have really thrived and diversified, and there are now more than 90 described species there, and many more waiting to be discovered.

Natural History

Ecology and Behavior
Microhylids within Australia are partially arboreal and terrestrial in their behavior. Relatively few people see microhylids, simply because most can only be found in tropical and subtropical rainforests, usually at high altitudes. More often than not these locations are in completely inaccessible mountainous terrain. This is why so little information is available for this group of frogs. It is difficult enough to find them during the day, but it would take a pretty brave person to be willing to climb trees at night when, presumably, these frogs are most active. Microhylids and hylids (tree frogs) are often found together in the same trees.

Ecological Interactions
The identification of microhylid species is extremely difficult because of the wide variety of forms and general appearance among the frogs in the group. Much of this variation can be explained in terms of ecology and evolution. For example, one genus of these frogs contains, among others, two broadly different species. One is a slender, long-legged frog with big pads on its fingers. The other is a short, rotund frog with squat legs and no toe pads. At first you would think that the researchers who determined that these two species were closely related and classified them together did not really know what they were talking about—it seems intuitive that the species must be from different families. But when you examine them closely, there are many characteristics common to both. Further examination of their behavior shows that the skinny, long-legged frog lives in rock crevices and trees, while the large, squat frog lives on or under the ground. The characteristics common to them (such as internal structures) are the ones inherited from their long-ago ancestors and are the reason they are considered to be closely related—at the genus level. But the major outward differences in form between them occur because they have learned to live in different environments. They occupy different ecological niches; one has adapted itself, through evolution, to live in rocks and trees, the other underground.

Breeding
All species within this group lay their eggs out of water. The eggs develop on land and hatch into fully-formed frogs. No microhylid has a free-swimming tadpole

stage. Males often guard the eggs, and some New Guinean species carry the newly hatched frogs on their back to protect them.

Status

Currently there are no microhylid species listed as vulnerable or endangered in Australia. This may simply reflect the fact that little is known about species in this group, and the assurance that some species are not threatened cannot be given.

Profiles

Ornate Frog, *Cophixalus ornatus,* Plate 5c

4. True Frogs

Frogs in family Ranidae are generally referred to as *true frogs*. They are abundant in most parts of the world, and they dominate the frog fauna of Europe, Asia, and North America. In fact, true frogs, or *ranids*, include many of what most people from Europe and North America regard as typical frogs—green ones that spend a lot of their time in water. These are far from plentiful in Australia, however. In fact the family is represented by a single species, the WOOD FROG (Plate 5), which occurs only in the Cape York Peninsula area. Why is such a successful group worldwide seemingly unsuccessful in Australia, in terms of number of species and distribution? It may be that by the time ranids first entered Australia (from Indonesia via New Guinea), the other frog families (tree frogs, narrow-mouthed frogs, southern frogs) were already successfully occupying all the most obvious habitats. The ranids may have found it difficult to compete with the established groups.

Natural History

Ecology and Behavior

Apart from a few well-studied species, our knowledge of ranid habits is rather limited. Most species are good swimmers and live close to water, into which they dive when disturbed. The Wood Frog, which lives primarily in rainforests, tropical woodlands, and monsoon forests, is rather typical of ranids. It spends most of its time foraging on the ground near water, where it actively seeks out its prey.

Breeding

As with other ranids, the Wood Frog breeds in permanent, slow streams and lagoons, where it lays about 800 eggs. The eggs hatch into tadpoles, and metamorphose into frogs in as little as six weeks.

Notes

To most northern hemisphere naturalists, ranid frogs typify the general characteristics of a frog. They are the frog of choice for dissections in schools and universities. As such, ranids have been invaluable for helping us understand the finer points of frog physiology. As the subject of countless dissections and biological experiments, we have learned about frog respiratory and circulatory systems, muscle function, and vision. Scientists have studied the mechanics of movement using ranid frogs and have been able to adapt these theories to study other animals.

Ranids are also the frogs usually found gracing the jam jars and terrariums in the homes of northern hemisphere children, and the hind legs of individuals from this family can be found sautéed in a little bit of garlic butter in restaurants around the globe.

Status
The Wood Frog is relatively common within its range in northeastern Queensland.

Profile
Wood Frog, *Rana daemeli*, Plate 5a

5. Toads

True toads (family Bufonidae) can be found worldwide except in the Australian region, Polynesia, Madagascar, and polar areas. However, the CANE TOAD (Plate 5) has been introduced to Australia, where it is now abundant (and ever expanding its range) in the northeastern part of the continent. It is a big, powerful toad that grows to lengths of over 23 cm (9 in), and is one of the largest of the *bufonids*. It is native to Central and South America.

Natural History

Ecology and Behavior
The Cane Toad feeds on a wide variety of plant and animal material, including bugs, mice, and other frogs. It can tolerate dry to wet conditions and highly saline water, and will either out-compete or eat other frogs with which it comes in contact. This toad possesses a pair of prominent, wart-like, *parotoid glands* on the sides of the head that produce poisons toxic enough to kill a cat or even a crocodile. Because of these glands, the toad has no regular predators in Australia, although some animals have been reported to have found ways of successfully avoiding the poison glands. (Water Rats eat only the toad's hind legs; crocodiles wash the poison off toads before devouring them.) Owing to their potent defense, individual cane toads can survive for periods in excess of 15 years. Apparently the biggest danger to Cane Toads is their own kind—juvenile toads are in constant danger of being eaten by larger, adult toads.

Ecological Interactions
Because of the Cane Toad's prolific breeding capacity (see below) and its ability to live in virtually any environment, it has become a serious pest in Australia, particularly in areas where human density is highest. More ominously, because of the Cane Toad's presence, the future for some Australian frogs (and some other types of small animals as well) seems grim—the Cane Toad is an efficient predator. To date, there is no known way to control or stop the spread of Cane Toads in Australia.

Breeding
The Cane Toad is capable of breeding in almost any available water, from fresh to brackish. Whereas most Australian frogs breed during a relatively limited breeding season, this toad can breed in almost any month of the year. Female frogs may spawn only once during a breeding season, but female toads spawn at least twice each year. A toad can lay 10,000 to 21,000 eggs at a time, some 40,000 eggs per year. Unlike Australian frogs, toads lay their eggs in long strings that look like spaghetti. Provided there is enough food, the tadpoles develop quickly and metamorphose into small toads in one to two months.

Notes
About a hundred Cane Toads (from Hawaii, where they were also introduced) were introduced into the Northeast in 1935. The introduction was part of an experiment to control greyback and frenchi beetles, which ate sugarcane crops.

Unfortunately, not only did the toad fail in its duties to eat these cane pests, but it also proved to be an extremely adaptable invader that could out-compete its rivals for food, shelter, and breeding habitat, was resistant to parasites, and had no natural enemies. Not everyone thought the introduction of the toad was a good idea. Some Queensland residents took matters into their own hands and started killing toads whenever they were found. The state of Queensland, at one point, actually contemplated seeking official protection for this species, which has now become one of Australia's biggest pest problems.

Status

The Cane Toad is extremely common in most of eastern Queensland, and is spreading rapidly south into New South Wales and west across the Northern Territory at a rate of about 30 km (18 miles) per year. Scientists are concerned that at its current rate of invasion, unless quick action is taken, the toad may eventually occupy suitable habitat in most parts of Australia.

Profile
Cane Toad, *Bufo marinus*, Plate 5d

Environmental Close-up 2:
Frog Population Declines

by Les Beletsky

For over a decade, scientists have reported that many populations of frogs, toads, and salamanders are declining in numbers. Some populations, and in fact entire species, have disappeared entirely. Several major questions are being asked: How widespread is the problem? Are amphibian population declines a special case, happening for reasons unrelated to the general loss of biodiversity? If there is a generalized worldwide amphibian decline, what are the causes?

The available data indicate a widespread pattern of amphibian declines. There are reports from low elevations and high elevations, from Australia, the US, Central America, the Amazon Basin, the Andes, and Europe. Habitat loss almost certainly contributes to general declines in population sizes of amphibians, and in this sense, amphibian declines are part of the worldwide loss of biodiversity. But what is going on with amphibians seems to be more extreme than the declines seen in other animals. Why would amphibians be more vulnerable? One reason is that because amphibians have thin, moist skin that they use for breathing, chemical pollutants found in the water, soil, and air are able to enter their bodies easily. Secondly, many amphibians are exposed to double jeopardy: because they live both on land (usually in the adult stage) and in the water (usually the egg and larval stages), they are exposed to environmental contaminants, vagaries of the weather, and other potential factors affecting survivorship in both habitats.

So what could be causing the observed declines of amphibians? One possible cause is environmental pollution, for example *acid rain*—rain that is acidified by various atmospheric pollutants, making lake and river water more acidic. Acidic water is known to decrease fertilization success because sperm become less active and often disintegrate. The eggs that are fertilized often develop abnormally.

Another suggestion is that the increased level of ultraviolet (UV) radiation, due to the thinning of the protective atmospheric ozone layer, might be damaging. Frogs often lay their eggs in shallow water directly exposed to the sun's rays; tadpoles often seek shallow water where the temperatures are warmer; and some juvenile and adult frogs bask for warmth. Studies have shown that increased levels of UV light kill some species of frog eggs and can interact chemically with diseases and acid rain to increase amphibian mortality rates. Another possible cause is global warming. Some species of amphibians may not be able to adapt to the warmer, drier climate the world is currently experiencing. For example, drought during a severe El Niño year in 1986–1987 has been implicated in the declines and disappearances of 40% (20 of 50 species) of the frog species (including the now likely extinct Golden Toad) that lived in the vicinity of Monteverde, Costa Rica. The frogs may have died directly from dessication (drying out), or they may have been so stressed that they became more vulnerable to disease, fungus, or wind-borne environmental contaminants.

Another cause of some population declines is a parasitic chytrid fungus that has been identified from Australia, Central and South America, the US, and Europe. The fungus affects the skin, especially on the victims' bellies—the area where frogs take up water through the skin. Thus, one speculation is that the frogs are suffocating and drying out. Another possibility is that the fungus releases toxins lethal to the frogs. Scientists wonder where the killer fungus will show up next, and what is stressing amphibians to make them more vulnerable to pathogens such as fungus. They're also wondering if people (including researchers and ecotourists) could inadvertently be spreading the fungus on their shoes and boots. Perhaps non-human animals, such as insects, are spreading the fungus as well.

Not all biologists agree that amphibian declines are a phenomenon over and above the worldwide decline in biodiversity. Scientists who study natural fluctuations in size of animal populations point out that populations of many animals cycle between scarcity and abundance. Many insects are known for their wildly fluctuating population sizes. Population levels of vertebrates also fluctuate with environmental conditions such as food availability and density of prey. For example, voles and lemmings, small rodents of the arctic tundra, are well known for being at low population densities (a few per acre or hectare) for one year, and at very high densities (thousands per acre or hectare) several years later. Skeptics point out that, unless those sounding the alarm of amphibian declines can show that the declines are not part of natural cycles, it is too early to panic. They emphasize that the only way to document natural population cycles is to monitor amphibian populations during long-term field studies. Unfortunately, few such studies have been done.

Those scientists who believe that widespread amphibian declines are more than merely natural fluctuations argue that we need to act *now*. Although they agree that we need to initiate long-term studies, they believe we can't wait for the conclusions of such studies 10 or 20 years down the road before we try to reverse the situation. At that point, they argue, it will be too late to do anything but record extinctions.

The controversy will continue. The important consequence of the debate is that many investigators are working on the problem, considering many different possible causes, from climatic change to a parasitic fungus. A major problem is that even if the scientific consensus right now were that disease, fungi, pollution, climate change, increased level of UV radiation, or some combination were causing worldwide amphibian declines, at present there is neither enough interest or resources to address the problem on the massive scale required. Because amphibians and reptiles are not uniformly liked and respected, preservation efforts for these animals, except for special cases like sea turtles, will always lag behind conservation efforts made on behalf of birds and mammals. Fortunately, however, because the current conservation emphasis is on preserving entire ecosystems, rather than particular species, amphibians will benefit even if they don't have feathers or fur.

Chapter 8

REPTILES

by Gerry Swan
The Australian Museum, Sydney

- *General Characteristics and Natural History*
- *Seeing Reptiles in Australia*
- *Family Profiles*
    - *1. Crocodilians*
    - *2. Turtles*
    - *3. Geckos*
    - *4. Flap-footed Lizards (Pygopodids)*
    - *5. Monitor Lizards (Goannas)*
    - *6. Dragons (Agamids)*
    - *7. Skinks*
    - *8. Pythons—The Constrictors*
    - *9. Elapids—Venomous Snakes*
    - *10. Miscellaneous Snakes*
- *Environmental Close-up 3: Australia's Endemics: Species That Occur Nowhere Else*

General Characteristics and Natural History

With more than 800 known species from a worldwide figure of about 7,000, Australia has a reptile fauna that, in terms of numbers and diversity, provides ample opportunity for observation by those with an interest in these animals. Most reptiles are harmless to people and, if discovered going about their daily business, are worth watching. Unfortunately, to avoid predation, most reptiles are inconspicuous both in their behavior and color patterns, and often flee when alerted to people's presence; consequently it is hard to see them during a brief visit to a region. Nevertheless, some of the larger reptiles are quite conspicuous, particularly when basking on or along roads. It is a good idea to keep a careful watch for them, remembering not to get too close to any that you find.

Reptiles have been around for a long time, arising during the late Paleozoic Era, some 300 million years ago. Today, more than 7,000 species of lizards, snakes, turtles, and crocodiles inhabit most regions of the Earth, with a healthy contingent in Australia.

All reptiles have an impermeable, scaly skin that helps reduce water loss from the body. This, together with their ability to convert soluble body wastes, primarily urea, into solid uric acid, provides them with an efficient body water conservation system, enabling terrestrial reptiles to colonize arid areas successfully. Aquatic reptiles, of course, do not have the same need to conserve body water and most of them pass a liquid urine.

Having an inelastic body covering means that as it grows a reptile must shed skin as a new one forms beneath it. This process is called *sloughing*. Prior to sloughing, the skin may become milky; this is particularly noticeable in the eyes of a snake, which turn quite opaque. Sloughing is usually achieved piecemeal in lizards and it is not unusual to find individuals with pieces of old skin still adhering to various parts of the body. In snakes the skin is usually shed in one piece, with the old skin being turned inside out. A snake achieves this by rubbing its snout against a fixed object to start the peeling process. The old skin rolls back over the head and, as it catches against other objects, it is drawn back over the snake, which, by moving around, pulls itself out of the old skin.

Many lizards, particularly geckos, pygopodids, and skinks, have the ability to cast off all or part of the tail to distract the attention of a potential predator, a process known as *autotomy* (p. 101). (One local snake, the Keelback, Plate 7, also has this ability.) Another tail eventually grows to replace the lost portion but is usually quite different in color or texture and lacks the vertebral bones of the original. Occasionally, lizards are found with two or three tails. This can happen when the original tail is partially broken but does not break off; it heals, but a new tail also grows from the place where the partial break occurred.

Reptiles are *ectothermic* (cold-blooded) animals, which means that they must use an external source of heat to raise the body temperature to the preferred level for normal activities. This is usually achieved by basking in direct sunlight or by absorbing heat from a warmed surface. To lower its body temperature, or to maintain it at the preferred level, a reptile moves into the shade or alters its body posture to reduce heat uptake. This method of heat regulation, while ideal in tropical or warm parts of the world, puts reptiles at a disadvantage in cooler environments. In these regions, for at least part of the year, daytime temperatures are insufficient for the animal to raise its temperature to that required for any activity. In these circumstances reptiles typically enter an immobile period of hibernation or *torpor* (reduced metabolic activity) in a suitable shelter site.

Most reptiles lay eggs, which are deposited in crevices, burrows, cavities beneath rocks, and similar situations. In Australia, only pythons and crocodiles demonstrate any parental care of eggs after they have been laid. In some species, however, the female retains the eggs within her body until they hatch. In others, the embryos develop a placental attachment to the oviduct. These latter two modes are often found in reptiles that inhabit cooler regions.

Generally, reptiles are carnivorous and consume a wide variety of prey. Some snakes in other parts of the world feed on slugs, snails, centipedes, or insects, but very little evidence demonstrates that Australian snakes eat invertebrates. The obvious exception are the *blind snakes* of family Typhlopidae, which feed on ant and termite pupae, larvae, and eggs. Our other terrestrial snakes feed mainly on lizards, frogs, other snakes, reptile eggs, birds or mammals, all of which are swallowed whole. Snakes can go for some weeks or even months without eating. Most lizards are carnivorous but many are also partly herbivorous. Some turtles elsewhere in the world are entirely herbivorous but all Australian species are predominently carnivorous, although some eat a little aquatic vegetation and adult Green Sea Turtles (Plate 12) prefer marine grasses.

Reptile biologists usually recognize four major groups of reptiles.

The *turtles* and *tortoises* (land turtles) constitute one group, with about 260 species worldwide. Some turtles live wholly on land; the *sea turtles* live out their lives in the oceans (coming ashore only to lay eggs), but most turtles live in rivers, streams, and ponds. Turtles are easily distinguished by their unique body armor: tough plates that cover their back and belly, creating wrap-around shells into which head and limbs are retracted when danger looms.

The *crocodiles* and their relatives, large predatory carnivores that live along the shores of swamps, rivers, and estuaries, constitute a small second group of about 22 species.

The two species of *tuatara* of New Zealand are the sole survivors of the beak-headed reptiles. Though they like lizards, they differ in a number of ways. There are several skeletal differences: the tuatara have no external ears, and males do not have a penis.

Last, and currently positioned as the world's dominant reptiles, the 3,300 lizard species and 3,500 snakes comprise a fourth group (lizards and snakes have very similar skeletal traits, indicating a very close relationship).

Lizards walk on all four limbs, except for a few that are legless. Most are ground-dwelling animals, but many also climb when the need arises; a fair number spend much of their lives in trees. Almost all are capable of moving quite rapidly. Most lizards are insectivores, but some, especially larger ones, eat plants, and several prey on amphibians, other lizards, mammals, birds, and even fish. Lizards are hugely successful and are often the most abundant vertebrate animals within an area. Ecologists suspect that they owe this ecological success primarily to their ruthlessly efficient predation on insects and other small animals and to low daily energy requirements.

Lizards employ two main foraging strategies. Some lizards are *active searchers*. They move continually while looking for prey, for instance nosing about in the leaf litter of the forest floor. Others are *sit-and-wait predators*, highly camouflaged, remaining motionless on the ground or on tree trunks or branches, waiting for prey to happen by. When they see a likely meal—a caterpillar, a beetle—they reach out to snatch it if it is close enough or dart out to chase it down.

Many lizards are territorial, defending territories from other members of their species with displays, such as bobbing up and down on their front legs and raising their head crests. Lizards are especially common in deserts and semi-deserts, but they are numerous in other habitats as well. They are active primarily during the day, except for many of the gecko species, which are nocturnal.

The *flap-footed lizards*, or pygopodids, are almost entirely endemic to Australia (of the 36 species, 34 are endemic, 1 is shared with New Guinea, and another is found only there). Despite the fact that they look very much like snakes, they are closely related to the geckos and share with them a number of characteristics.

Snakes probably evolved from burrowing lizards, and all are limbless. Snakes are all carnivores, but their methods of capturing prey differ. Several groups have evolved glands that manufacture poisonous *venom* that is injected into prey through the teeth. The venom immobilizes and kills the prey, which is then swallowed whole. Other snakes pounce on and wrap themselves around their prey, constricting the prey until it suffocates. The majority of snakes are non-venomous, seizing prey with their mouths and relying on their size and strong jaws to subdue it. Snakes generally rely on vision and smell to locate prey, although members of two families have thermal sensor organs on their heads that detect the heat of prey animals.

The success of snakes in colonizing most regions is thought to be due to their ability to devour prey that is larger than their own heads (their jaw bones are highly mobile, separating partially and moving around prey as it is swallowed). This unique ability provides snakes with two great advantages over other animals: because they eat large items, they have been able to reduce the frequency with which they need to search and capture prey; owing to this, they can spend long periods hidden and secluded, safe from predators. Like lizards, snakes use either active searching or sit-and-wait foraging strategies.

Snakes are themselves prey for hawks and other predatory birds, as well as for some mammals. While many snakes are quite conspicuous against a solid color, being decorated with bold and colorful skin patterns, against their normal backdrops, such as leaf-strewn forest floor, they are highly camouflaged. They rely on their *cryptic colorations,* and sometimes on speed, to evade predators.

Mating systems and behaviors of snakes in the wild are not well known. In some, males remain in mating areas during the breeding period, where interested females tend to gather. Males may fight each other to gain the right to mate with a particular female. Male size seems to matter most in determining the outcomes of these fights. Males and females are known to engage in multiple matings with different individuals.

Seeing Reptiles in Australia

Like amphibians, many reptiles are difficult to observe. They spend most of their time concealed or still. Most do not vocalize like birds or frogs, so you cannot use sound to find them. The superb cryptic coloration of snakes, including venomous ones, makes a motionless snake a dangerous snake. Because of the difficulty people have in seeing snakes before getting very close to them, the rule for exploring an area known to harbor venomous snakes, or any area for which you are unsure, is never, *never* to place your hand or foot anywhere that you cannot see first. Do not climb rocks or trees; do not clamber over rocks where your hands or feet sink into holes or crevices; do not reach into bushes or trees. Walk carefully along trails and, although your attention understandably wanders to new sights and sounds, try to watch your feet and where you are going.

There are a few ways to view reptiles without compromising your safety. Knowing about activity periods helps. Most lizards and snakes are active during the day, but some species are active during early evening or at night. Thus, a night walk with flashlights that is organized to find amphibians might also yield some reptile sightings. Weather is also important—snakes and lizards are often more active in sunny, warm weather. If all else fails, one may look for small snakes and lizards by carefully turning over rocks, logs, or debris on the ground, although such activities are not for the faint-hearted. (And do remember to replace rocks and logs to their initial positions.)

In Australia all reptiles are protected, and in most states it is illegal to collect or to disturb a reptile. If you wish to observe reptiles with more than the chance encounter, you should contact the wildlife authorities in the relevant state or territory to clarify what you can or cannot do.

Family Profiles

1. Crocodilians

Remnants of the age when reptiles ruled the world, today's *crocodilians* (alligators, caimans, and crocodiles) when seen in the wild generally inspire awe, respect, a bit of fear, and a great deal of curiosity. Recent classification schemes include a total of 22 species, distributed over most tropical and subtropical areas of the continents. Two crocodile species are found in Australia (there are no alligators). The SALT-WATER, or ESTUARINE, CROCODILE (Plate 11), occurs in the coastal regions of northern Western Australia, the Northern Territory, and northern Queensland. This crocodile can reach lengths of almost 7 m (23 ft) but the usual range is from 3 to 5 m, 10 to 16.5 ft. The FRESHWATER CROCODILE (Plate 11), which is endemic to Australia, also occurs in northern Western Australia, the Northern Territory, and northern Queensland. This crocodile reaches a length of 3 m (10 ft).

Generally, differences in coloring are not a good way to distinguish crocodiles—most are shades of brown or olive-brown. Anatomy and location are more useful clues. The snout of the Saltwater Crocodile is broad, with raised ridges running from the front of the eye to the center of the snout. This species occupies the immediate coastal areas, including tidal and non-tidal rivers, swamps, and billabongs. It will sometimes move long distances upstream. The Freshwater Crocodile, on the other hand, has a smooth, slender snout, and is usually further inland, in the upper reaches of rivers, and inland swamps and billabongs. The two species are sometimes found in the same area, but it appears that in such circumstances the Saltwater Crocodiles displace the smaller Freshwater Crocodiles. Male crocodilians, in general, are larger than females of the same age.

Natural History

Ecology and Behavior
Although not amphibians, crocodiles are amphibious animals. They usually move slowly over land but in short bursts can cover ground rapidly. The Freshwater Crocodile, unlike most other crocodiles, can even break into a gallop when it needs to. Most of the time, however, crocodiles are in or near water. They bask for lengthy periods in the sunshine along the banks of rivers or billabongs to raise their body temperature so that they can hunt effectively. Crocodilians in the water are largely hidden, from above resembling floating logs. This unassuming appearance allows them to move close to shore and seize animals that come to the water to drink.

Crocodiles are carnivorous and are mainly active at night, when most of their feeding occurs. Still, they are opportunistic feeders and will feed during the day if a meal presents itself. Most prey is caught in the shallows at the water's edge; young crocodiles in particular will snap at anything that disturbs the water near them. Adults will wait in shallow water for suitable prey to come down to the edge but they will also spot potential prey at a distance and approach underwater until they are within striking range. The prey taken depends on age and size. Juveniles eat primarily aquatic insects and crustaceans, moving up to fish, small birds, aquatic reptiles, and small mammals as they grow.

One might guess that among such primitive reptiles, parental care would be absent—females would lay eggs, perhaps hide them, but at that point the eggs and hatchlings would be on their own. Surprisingly, however, crocodilians show varying degrees of parental care. Nests are guarded and the female often helps hatchlings free themselves from the nest and carries them to the nearest water. Females may also remain with the young for up to two years, protecting them. Crocodiles use vocal signals extensively in their behavior, presumably to communicate with one another, but their sounds have been little studied. It is known that juveniles give alarm calls when threatened, and that females respond by quickly coming to their rescue.

The sex of a crocodile is determined by the temperature at which its egg was incubated. Eggs in a nest will not all be incubating at the same temperature: those at the bottom may be cooler because it is damper, or they may be hotter because they are in the middle of rotting vegetation. Embryos incubated at high or low temperatures become females, while those incubated at mid-range temperatures become males.

All crocodiles, even those living in fresh water, have salt glands on the tongue. This enables crocodiles that live in estuarine environments to get rid of excess salt absorbed through the body or when eating. To get rid of this excess salt through the kidneys would require large amounts of fresh water, which is often not available. Instead, crocodiles excrete the salt in a highly saline solution through the glands on the tongue. Alligators and caimans do not have these glands and so are restricted to freshwater habitats.

Crocodilians are long-lived animals, many surviving more than 60 years in the wild and even over 90 years in zoos.

Ecological Interactions
Somewhat surprisingly, crocodilians are prey for a number of animals. Egg mortality is high, with only 20 to 30% of a season's eggs actually hatching. Known predators include goannas, feral pigs, and people. Aboriginal people have collected and eaten crocodile eggs for thousands of years. Young, very small crocodiles are eaten by a number of predators, including birds, freshwater turtles, fish, and larger crocodiles. Large adults probably have only one enemy—people.

Breeding
During courtship, male crocodiles often defend aquatic territories, giving displays with their tails—up-and-down and side-to-side movements—that probably serve both to defend the territory from other males and to court females. The female Saltwater Crocodile makes a nest by scraping together grass, leaves, twigs, and sand or soil into a pile near the water's edge. She then lays and buries up to 60 eggs in the pile. She remains near the nest while the eggs incubate and will defend it against intruders. Nests of the Freshwater Crocodile are a bit different. The female digs a hole in sandy soil, deposits her eggs, then covers them with sand.

Several females may use the same area to nest, so sometimes a nest of eggs will be excavated by another female as she digs her own nest. When the young are born, they call from the nest and are dug out by the female and carried to the water. Crocodile young from a brood may remain together in the nest area for weeks or even months. Breeding seasons vary, with Saltwater Crocodiles nesting during the wet season, and Freshwater Crocodiles during the dry.

Notes

Saltwater Crocodiles are known predators on people and must be regarded as dangerous. Freshwater Crocodiles are usually inoffensive and do not prey on humans. Still, they can and do bite, and can cause considerable damage to human flesh.

Owing to their predatory nature and large size, crocodilians play significant roles in the history and folklore of many cultures, going back at least to ancient Egypt, where a crocodile-headed god was known as Sebek. The Egyptians apparently welcomed crocodiles into their canals, possibly to defend against invaders. Egyptians and other African peoples may have believed that crocodiles cause blindness, probably because a disease called river blindness results from infestation with a river-borne parasitic roundworm.

The Australian Aborigines have many legends, stories, and songs about crocodiles. For some Aboriginal groups, crocodiles are held in special regard as members of their extended families. Aboriginal bark and rock paintings consistently feature crocodiles.

Status

All crocodilians are listed by the international CITES agreements, preventing or highly regulating trade in their skins or other parts, and their numbers have been steadily rising during the past 20 years. Nevertheless, most of the 22 crocodilian species remain threatened or endangered. The Saltwater Crocodile is listed in CITES Appendix II for Australia, Indonesia, and New Guinea, and listed in Appendix I for elsewhere in its range; the Freshwater Crocodile is listed in CITES Appendix II. Both species are listed by Australian conservation organizations as specially protected, vulnerable, or threatened.

Profiles

Saltwater Crocodile, *Crocodylus porosus,* Plate 11c
Freshwater Crocodile, *Crocodylus johnstoni,* Plate 11d

2. Turtles

The approximately 250 living turtle species are usually grouped into 12 families that can be divided into three types according to their typical habitats. These are the *marine* (or *sea*) *turtles,* the *freshwater turtles,* and the *land tortoises,* which are completely terrestrial. The 23 or so turtle species that occur in Australia are all marine turtles or freshwater turtles; there are no land tortoises in Australia.

Of the six species of marine turtles that occur in Australian waters, only the FLATBACK SEA TURTLE is confined to this region. The other five species, the LOGGERHEAD SEA TURTLE, GREEN SEA TURTLE (Plate 12), LEATHERY SEA TURTLE (Plate 12), HAWKSBILL SEA TURTLE (Plate 12), and PACIFIC RIDLEY SEA TURTLE are more wide-ranging, inhabiting most tropical and warm temperate seas.

There are 17 species of freshwater turtles in Australia and all except one belong to a group known as *side-necked turtles* (family Chelidae), which are so named because the neck is folded under the carapace. Within this group some have very long necks and are known as *long-necked,* or *snake-necked, turtles.* The other group is *short-necked turtles.*

Turtles all basically look alike: bodies encased in tough shells (made up of two layers, an inner layer of bone and an outer layer of scale-like plates); four limbs, sometimes modified into flippers; highly mobile necks; toothless jaws; and small tails. This body plan must be among nature's best, because it has survived unchanged for a long time; according to fossils, turtles have looked more or less the same for at least 200 million years. Enclosing the body in heavy armor above and below apparently was an early solution to the problems vertebrates faced when they first moved onto land. It provides both rigid support when outside of buoyant water and a high level of protection from drying out and from predators.

Turtles come, for the most part, in a variety of browns, blacks, and greens, with olive-greens predominating. They range in size from tiny terrapins 11.5 cm (4.5 in) long to 250 kg (550 lb) GALAPAGOS TORTOISES, and giant Leathery Sea Turtles, the largest living turtles, which can grow to nearly 2 m (6.5 ft) long, 3.6 m (12 ft) across (flipper to flipper), and which can weigh in at over 550 kg (1,200 lb). The smallest Australian freshwater turtle is the WESTERN SWAMP TURTLE at 15 cm (6 in), and the largest is the PIG-NOSED TURTLE at 60 cm (24 in).

In many turtle species, females are larger than males. Turtle sexes are sometimes distinguishable by a curved indentation in the bottom shell of the male, which fits over the female's top shell during sex.

Natural History

Ecology and Behavior

Over much of mainland Australia, most bodies of fresh water are likely to have some freshwater turtles. Some prefer the slow, deeper inland rivers, while others are found in the rapid, clear rivers on the coast. Indeed, on the east coast, each major river drainage system seems to carry its own distinct freshwater turtle.

Some freshwater turtles feed mainly on plant material while others are carnivorous, taking crustaceans, shellfish, insects, snails and any other suitably sized animals they can seize. Their extendable necks allow them to breathe while keeping their bodies submerged. These turtles feed in the water, some using the long neck to strike at prey. The BROAD-SHELLED TURTLE, for example, relies on ambush to procure its food; buried deep in debris on the river bottom, it lunges its head and neck forward to take its prey.

The Pig-nosed Turtle differs from other Australian freshwater turtles in having a shell covered with a soft, pitted skin and paddle-like limbs similar to marine turtles, rather than clawed, webbed feet. As the name suggests, it has a prominent pig-like nose. It occurs in New Guinea and in a few river systems in northern Australia, and feeds mainly on seeds, fruits, and leaves that fall into the water, although it also takes fish and shellfish. Unlike all other Australian freshwater turtles, which must twist their necks sideways to retract their heads, the Pig-nosed Turtle can pull its head straight back into its shell.

Marine turtles are large reptiles that live in the open oceans, with the result that, aside from their beach nesting habits, relatively little is known of their behavior. They are adapted to a life at sea in many ways. Their front legs have been modified into powerful oar-like flippers, which propel them through the water. They have glands to get rid of excess salt that accumulates in the body. Their shells, although they look heavy and cumbersome, are in fact light and streamlined; they are honeycombed to reduce weight. Although they need air to breathe, they can remain submerged for long periods.

At first, all sea turtles were assumed to have similar diets, probably sea plants. But some observations of natural feeding, as well as examinations of stomach contents, reveal a variety of specializations. Green Sea Turtles eat bottom-dwelling sea grasses and algae, Hawksbill Sea Turtles eat bottom sponges, and Loggerhead Sea Turtles feed predominantly on mollusks (such as snails) and crustaceans (such as crabs), and some other species eat jellyfish.

Ecological Interactions

If turtles can make it through the dangerous juvenile stage, when they are small and soft enough for a variety of predators to take them, they enjoy very high year-to-year survival—up to 80% or more of an adult population usually survives from one year to the next. But there is very high mortality in the egg and juvenile stages. Nests are not guarded, and many kinds of predators, such as foxes, pigs, water rats, goannas, and various birds dig up turtle eggs. Hatchlings are prey to just as many predators, including crocodiles, birds, eels, fish, and snakes.

An intriguing relationship between turtle reproduction and temperature nicely illustrates the intimate and sometimes puzzling connection between animals and the physical environment. For many vertebrate animals, the sex of an individual is determined by the kinds of sex chromosomes it has. In people, if each cell has an X and a Y chromosome, the person is male, and if two Xs, female. In birds, it is the opposite. But in most turtles, it is not the chromosomes that matter, but the temperature at which an egg develops. In most turtles, eggs incubated at constant temperatures above 30° C (86° F) all develop as females, whereas those incubated at 24 to 28° C (75 to 82° F) become males. At 28 to 30° C (82 to 86° F), both males and females are produced. In some species, a second temperature threshold exists—eggs that develop below 24° C (75° F) again become females. The exact way that temperature determines sex is not clear, although it is suspected that temperature directly influences a turtle's developing brain. This method of sex determination is also mysterious for the basic reason that no one quite knows why it should exist; that is, is there some advantage of this system to the animals that we as yet fail to appreciate? Or is it simply a consequence of reptile structure and function, some fundamental constraint of their biology?

Breeding

Courtship in turtles can be quite complex. In some, the male swims backwards in front of the female, stroking her face with his clawed feet. In the tortoises, courtship seems to take the form of butting and nipping. All turtles lay their eggs on land. The female digs a hole in the earth or sand, deposits the eggs into the hole, then covers them and departs. It is up to the hatchlings to dig their way out of the nest and navigate to the nearest water. Many tropical turtles breed at any time of the year.

All sea turtle species breed in much the same way. Mature males and females appear offshore during breeding periods. After mating, females alone come ashore on beaches, apparently the same ones on which they were born, to lay their eggs. Each female breeds probably every 2 to 4 years, laying from 2 to 8 clutches of eggs in a season (with each clutch laid on a different day). Usually at night, a female drags herself up the beach to a suitable spot above the high-tide line, digs a cavity for her body, and then digs a hole with her rear flippers (a half meter or more, 2 ft, deep), deposits about 100 golf ball-sized eggs, covers them with sand, tamps the sand down, and heads back to the ocean. Sometimes females emerge from the sea alone, but often there are mass emergences, with hundreds of females nesting on a beach in a single night. Eggs incubate for about two months, then hatch simultaneously. The hatchlings dig themselves out of the sand and make a dash for the water (if tiny turtles can be said to be able to "dash"). Many terrestrial and ocean predators devour the hatchlings; only between 2 and 5% survive their first few days of life. The young float on rafts of sea vegetation during their first year, feeding and growing, until they reach a size when they can, with some safety, migrate long distances through the world's oceans. When sexually mature, in various species from 7 to more than 20 years later, they undertake reverse migrations, returning to their birth sites to breed.

Notes

The Aboriginal people have long regarded turtles as desirable food. In some areas turtles are gathered in large numbers by feeling for them in the water or mud. Turtles aestivating (sleeping away prolonged periods of poor weather) beneath dried mud are also located by looking for the small breathing hole on the surface of the mud. Turtles often feature in Australian Aboriginal art; turtle shells are painted and decorated by a number of contemporary Aboriginal artists.

Some overseas turtles are quite aggressive toward people. When disturbed, the New World's SNAPPING TURTLES, which are often described by experts as "vicious," can use their large, powerful jaws to wreak considerable damage to human flesh. Australian freshwater turtles present no danger to people in the water. Some will attempt to bite if handled, so if you are unfamiliar with how to handle these animals, don't.

Status

The ecology and status of populations of most freshwater and land turtle species are still poorly known, making it difficult to determine whether population numbers are stable or declining. Sea turtle eggs are harvested for food in many parts of the world, and adults are taken for meat (only some species) and for their shells. Many adults also die accidentally in fishing nets and collisions with boats. One of the sea turtles, the Hawksbill, is the chief provider of tortoiseshell, which is carved for decorative purposes. The Hawksbill is under international protection, but some are still hunted. All sea turtles are listed as threatened or endangered (CITES Appendix I and IUCN Red List). Other than sea turtles, in Australia the MARY RIVER TURTLE, Western Swamp Turtle, and the FITZROY TURTLE are considered threatened or endangered (IUCN Red List).

Profiles

Leathery Sea Turtle, *Dermochelys coriacea,* Plate 12a
Green Sea Turtle, *Chelonia mydas,* Plate 12b
Hawksbill Sea Turtle, *Eretmochelys imbricata,* Plate 12c
Eastern Snake-necked Turtle, *Chelodina longicollis,* Plate 12d
Krefft's River Turtle, *Emydura krefftii,* Plate 12e

3. Geckos

Geckos, family Gekkonidae, with more than 900 species, occupy all continents except Antarctica, although they are most numerous in tropical and subtropical areas. In many regions, geckos have invaded houses and buildings, becoming ubiquitous adornments of walls and ceilings. Ignored by residents, these lizards move around dwellings chiefly at night, munching insects. Australia has 102 species of gecko. The largest number occur in the arid and warm temperate areas, and the numbers decrease sharply in rainforest or colder regions. None are found in Tasmania. About 45 occur within the areas covered by this book.

Characteristically, geckos:

• Are small—typically less than 10 cm (4 in) long, tail excluded; tails can double the length. (Lizards are properly measured from the tip of their snouts to their vent, the urogenital opening on their bellies, usually located somewhere near where their rear legs join their bodies. The geckos' 5 to 10 cm, 2 to 4 in, length, therefore, is their range of "SVLs," or *snout-vent lengths*.) Lizard tails frequently break off and regenerate, and these new tails usually differ markedly from the original. Gecko tails are particularly fragile. Original tails come in a variety of shapes and sizes, from short and bulbous to long and thin, with others being broad and flattened. Unlike other lizards, the tail in most geckos is quite distinguishable from the body.

• Have four well developed limbs with five digits on each limb. In addition to claws, many species have expanded toe pads for climbing or hanging upside down on ceilings. The way geckos manage these feats has engendered a number of theories over the years. These range from the ability of their claws to dig into tiny irregularities on man-made surfaces, to their large toes acting as suction cups, to an adhesive quality of friction. The real explanation appears to lie in the series of miniscule hair-like structures on the bottom of the toes, which provide attachment to walls and ceilings by something akin to surface tension—the same property that allows some insects to walk on water.

• Have small, granular, non-shiny scales that do not overlap. In some species, a number of the scales are modified to form spines or *tubercles* (knob-like projections, or bumps).

• Have skin that may be velvet-like in appearance. The belly skin is sometimes semi-transparent, with the internal organs visible.

• Have large, prominent, unblinking eyes with vertically contractile pupils. As there is no moveable eyelid, the eye is protected by a transparent scale.

• Are nocturnal.

• Are capable of vocalization in the form of barking or rasping. This is often a defense mechanism, and may be accompanied by raising the body off the ground and inflating it with air.

• Have a short, thick, fleshy tongue.

Natural History

Ecology and Behavior

Although most lizards are active during the day and inactive at night, nearly all gecko species are nocturnal. In natural settings, they are primarily ground dwellers, but, as their behavior in buildings suggests, they are also excellent climbers. Most geckos feed on arthropods, chiefly insects. In fact, it is their ravenous appetite for cockroaches and other insect undesirables that renders them welcome house-guests in many parts of the world. The *day geckos* of Madagascar and several New Zealand geckos also eat nectar and pollen. Unlike the great majority of lizards, which keep quiet, geckos at night are avid little chirpers and squeakers. They communicate with each other with loud calls—surprisingly loud for such small animals. Various species sound different; the word gecko approximates the sound of calls from some African and Asian species.

Geckos are *sit-and-wait predators;* instead of wasting energy actively searching for prey that is usually highly alert and able to flee, they sit still for long periods, waiting for unsuspecting insects to venture a bit too near, then lunge, grab, and swallow.

Geckos rely chiefly on their *cryptic coloration* and their ability to flee rapidly for escape from predators, which include snakes during the day and snakes, owls, and bats at night. When cornered, geckos give threat displays; when seized, they give loud calls to distract predators, and bite. Should the gecko be seized by its tail, it breaks off easily, allowing the gecko time to escape, albeit tail-less; tails regenerate rapidly. Some geckos when seized also secrete thick, noxious fluids from their tails, which presumably discourages some predators. Many geckos can lighten or darken their skin coloring. The primary function of such color changing is often thought to be increased camouflage—to make themselves more difficult to see against various backgrounds.

Breeding

The majority of geckos are egg-layers, but those found in New Zealand give birth to live young, as does a species from New Caledonia. Mating occurs after a round of courtship, which involves a male displaying to a female by waving his tail around, followed by some mutual nosing and nibbling. Clutches usually contain two eggs (one in some species), but a female may lay several clutches per year. There is no parental care—after eggs are deposited they and the tiny geckos that hatch from them are on their own.

Notes

The world's smallest gecko, at 1.7 cm (0.7 in), is the MONITO GECKO from the Caribbean. The smallest Australian gecko is the CLAWLESS GECKO, which grows to about 7.5 cm (3 in) including tail, while the largest is the RING-TAILED GECKO, which measures more than 30 cm (12 in) including tail.

Status

More than 10 gecko species are listed by Australian conservation organizations as rare, vulnerable to threat, or endangered. These include the LORD HOWE ISLAND SOUTHERN GECKO and the CHRISTMAS ISLAND CHAINED GECKO. Four of these are also included in the IUCN Red List.

Profiles

Marbled Southern Gecko, *Christinus marmoratus,* Plate 13a
Eastern Stone Gecko, *Diplodactylus vittatus,* Plate 13b
Bynoe's Prickly Gecko, *Heteronotia binoei,* Plate 13c
Southern Leaf-tailed Gecko, *Phyllurus platurus,* Plate 13d
Barking Gecko, *Underwoodisaurus milii,* Plate 13e

4. Flap-Footed Lizards (Pygopodids)

The *flap-footed lizards,* family Pygopodidae, are sometimes incorrectly called *legless lizards* or *snake-lizards.* There are a number of Australian skink species that are almost or completely limbless, but none have the unique hindlimb flap typical of the flap-footed lizards (and the two groups, the flap-footed lizards and the legless skinks, evolved their limbless conditions independently and are not even closely related). Flap-footed lizards, or *pygopodids* or *pygopods,* are unique to Australia and New Guinea, with 35 species known to occur in Australia and two in New Guinea, one of which is shared with Australia. About 12 species occur in the areas covered by this book.

Characteristically, these lizards:

• Are snake- or worm-like in appearance. Unfortunately, in their relations with people, they often suffer the lethal consequences of their snake-like appearance. It is difficult for people unfamiliar with reptiles to tell the difference, but when seen clearly, pygopods are recognizably distinct from snakes.

• Have no trace of any forelimbs.

• Have remnants of hindlimbs that consist, at most, of a scaly flap that is usually held against the body. In some species, the flap is not much bigger than the surrounding scales, but in others it is easily observable.

• Cast off their tail when grasped or handled roughly. The tail will regrow but regenerated tails are not the same color as the originals.

• Have original tails that range from almost as long as the body to more than three times the body length.

• Have broad, fleshy tongues with a notch at the tip.

• Can vocalize in the form of a squeak or bark.

• Range in total length from 15 to 85 cm (6 to 33 in).

Pygopods differ from snakes in that the tail is much longer and is fragile and easily cast off; their tongue is broad and fleshy, unlike that of a snake, which is long, slender, and deeply forked; and they have belly scales that are about the same size as the adjacent scales, or, if larger, are paired (unlike snakes, which have single enlarged scales across the belly). Pygopods are closely related to the geckos, with which they share the ability to vocalize and to wipe their eyes with their tongues.

Natural History

Ecology and Behavior

Flap-footed lizards appear in woodlands, shrublands, and grasslands in the arid, semi-arid, and seasonally dry parts of Australia. They are not found in cool, wet regions, nor in swamps and closed forests. The ten or so worm-like members of the group (genus *Aprasia*) are small and, because they live underground most of the time, are very rarely seen. Their bodies are the same width from the head all the way back to their rounded tail, and they have well-developed eyes. Several of these lizards have bright pink or red tails that may serve to divert a predator's attack to the tail rather than the head.

Another group, the *delmas*, are predominantly grassland dwellers. Several of these exhibit a startling method of escape that they use when disturbed. This involves "flick-leaping," in which the lizard will flick itself into the air, while at the same time propelling itself forward.

One of the most commonly encountered of the flap-footed lizards, and the most widespread, is the BURTON'S SNAKE-LIZARD (Plate 14). It comes in a wide range of colors and patterns and has a distinctive wedge-shaped head.

While most pygopods eat invertebrates such as ant and termite larvae, insects and spiders, Burton's Snake-lizard feeds on other lizards, such as geckos, dragons, and skinks, which it pounces on when they come too close. I have seen these lizards immobile at night in prickly porcupine grass clumps, waiting to snatch a gecko.

Several flap-footed lizards will mimic the behavior of an elapid snake by raising the forebody off the ground, flicking the tongue, and striking. Presumably this is sufficient to deter or at least slow down a predator so that the lizard can make its escape.

Breeding
Almost nothing is known of the courtship behavior of flap-footed lizards. All are egg-layers, and normally two elongate, parchment-shelled eggs are laid in a clutch. Instances have been observed in which several females have laid their eggs at one nest-site.

Notes
The BRONZEBACK is a flap-footed lizard that was first discovered in the 1890s and then not seen again for many decades. It was found again in 1978, when two amateur herpetologists rediscovered it. The lizard is found in the mats of leaf litter beneath trees and shrubs, and is rarely seen on the surface. Once it was known where to look for it, numerous specimens were found.

Status
Eleven of the flap-footed lizards are considered by Australian conservation organisations to be rare, vulnerable, or threatened. Six of these are also included in the IUCN Red List.

Profiles
Burton's Snake-lizard, *Lialis burtonis*, Plate 14a
Southern Scaly-foot, *Pygopus lepidopodus*, Plate 14b

5. Monitor Lizards (Goannas)

Monitor lizards, or *varanids*, are more commonly known in Australia as *goannas*. There are approximately 50 species (family Varanidae), of which 26 are found in Australia. Elsewhere they occur in Africa, the Middle East, and Asia, including southeast Asia. All are in a single genus, *Varanus*, which comes from the Arabic word "ouaran," meaning lizard.

With more than half the known varanid species occurring here, Australia can be regarded as the land of goannas. The word "goanna" is a corruption of "iguana," which is what early European settlers called them; however, iguanas are a New World family, while goannas belong to the Old World. They are more correctly called monitor lizards. There are several explanations offered for the use of the word "monitor." One suggestion is that the Arabic word "ouaran" was corrupted to the German word "warane," meaning to warn. Another explanation is that these lizards were thought to warn of the presence of crocodiles.

Varanids are found over most of mainland Australia (there are none in Tasmania), but the majority of species occur in the northern regions. Approximately 15 occur in the areas covered by this book. Goannas have successfully occupied most Australian habitats and they can be grouped into four categories: those that live mainly on the ground; those that are arboreal; those that utilize rocky outcrops; and those that are aquatic or semi-aquatic.

Characteristically goannas have:
• A long, deeply forked tongue that is constantly flicked in and out when the lizards move about.
• Powerful limbs with sharp, curved claws.
• A long, slender tail.
• A dull, loose-fitting, rough skin.
• A long, flat head and a long neck.

In Australia, monitor lizards range in size from the 25 cm (10 in) SHORT-TAILED PYGMY GOANNA to the 2.5 m (8.2 ft) PERENTIE. The largest living goanna is the KOMODO DRAGON, which is not a dragon at all; it is found on several small islands in Indonesia. However, the biggest of them all, and the largest lizard that ever lived, was *Megalania prisca*, which roamed over much of Australia up to 25,000 years ago. This goanna apparently was more than 7 m (23 ft) long and possibly weighed more than 600 kg (1,300 lb).

Natural History

Ecology and Behavior

Goannas are active diurnal lizards with good eyesight and an excellent sense of smell. All Australian goannas are carnivorous and are opportunistic feeders. Some of the smaller species use a sit-and-wait ambush strategy, but most forage actively. They will methodically move around with the tongue constantly flicking in and out, as they check out crevices, logs, holes, and any other likely places where prey may be found. Food consists of almost anything that can be caught and eaten. Invertebrates seem to form a large part of the diet, even in the larger goannas. Still, they also take small mammals, reptiles, frogs, eggs, and in some cases, carrion, and it is not uncommon to see one of the larger goannas dining off a road-killed kangaroo or other animal. One animal they have not been able to eat, unfortunately, is the introduced Cane Toad; there are reports that goannas mouthing a Cane Toad have died shortly afterward. One LACE MONITOR (Plate 14) that weighed 20 kg (44 lb) is documented with having disgorged four fox cubs, three young rabbits, and three bluetongue lizards just after being caught. Goannas themselves, depending on size, are prey to other reptiles, including larger goannas, birds, the introduced foxes, cats, and dogs.

Some of the larger goannas are known to raise themselves upon their hind legs to look about them. Presumably this gives them an added advantage while foraging. This same posture is also used occasionally when a goanna is threatened. Several of the smaller goannas have sharp, spiny scales on the tail. This is useful when the animal is in a rock crevice and a predator is trying to get it out. The spiny tail can be used to wedge the animal securely.

Breeding

Males of many goanna species engage in combat during the mating season. This takes the form of two males locking their bodies together in an upright position and endeavouring to topple the opponent. At least some species engage in courtship displays, but this has rarely been seen and documented. Females lay from 2 to 35 eggs, depending upon the species. These are deposited in a chamber under or in a log, in a burrow, or within a termite mound. The eggs take from 60 days to almost 12 months to hatch, again depending on the species. As most of these data are from captive animals, it is uncertain if the same durations apply to clutches laid in the wild. Hatchlings are very secretive and rarely seen. They are very wary and keep well under cover at the least sign of danger.

Notes

Myths about goannas in Australia abound. One that crops up regularly is that the wound from a goanna bite will break out again every year. Many species of goanna feed on carrion, and a bite from one of these will very likely set up a nasty infection if not treated properly. This is probably the origin of the myth.

Another myth that is trotted out regularly concerns the immunity of goannas to snake venom. Some goannas will attack and eat snakes, and these encounters may result in a savage battle between the two. Having killed and eaten the snake, the goanna is said to race off into the bush to eat some as-yet-unidentified plant, which is an antidote to the venom.

Folklore has it that goanna oil had almost magical properties. Apart from seeping through glass, it was purported to cure almost all known complaints. While it makes a good story, that's all it is—a story.

Goannas feature prominently in Aboriginal art, both ancient and modern. In many regions they were a staple food item and regularly dug from burrows by Aboriginal women and children.

Status

All monitor lizards are listed in the CITES Appendix II, considered vulnerable or threatened; at least four species, including Indonesia's Komodo Dragon, are endangered. Six Australian species are categorized as rare, vulnerable, or threatened by Australian conservation authorities.

Profiles

Sand Goanna, *Varanus gouldii,* Plate 14c
Lace Monitor, *Varanus varius,* Plate 14d

6. Dragons (Agamids)

The *dragon lizards* (family Agamidae), of which there are about 330 species, are found in Africa, southern Europe, Asia, and Australia. They closely resemble the *iguanid lizards* of the New World, not only in general form, but also in the diversity of habitats they occupy. The two families can be distinguished by how the teeth are fixed to the jaw and whether or not they are replaceable. About 70 species of dragons occur in Australia.

Characteristically, dragons have:

• Skin with a rough, dull appearance and often with tubercles (knob-like projections, or bumps), prickles, or spines.
• Four well-developed limbs with five digits with claws on each.
• Long hindlimbs.
• A long, tapered tail.
• A broad, fleshy tongue.

Natural History

Ecology and Behavior

Australia's dragons are active diurnal lizards that occupy a wide range of habitats, but most live in arid regions. Only two live in the moister environment of rainforests, and one occurs along creeks and rivers. The rest occupy woodlands, heath, sand dunes, rock outcrops, stony deserts, and even dry salt lakes. The EASTERN WATER DRAGON (Plate 15) is the largest of the Australian dragons, males reaching 1 m (3.3 ft) in length. They are unusual in that they inhabit watercourses, whereas most Australian dragons are found in dry areas. Males are territorial and have a territory along a creek or river in which only females can move freely (other males are aggressively confronted and ejected). In some areas these dragons will spend summer nights submerged in the water, hanging onto the bank with only their heads exposed. In such a situation a predator would find it difficult to attack, and escape into deep water is an easy option for the dragon.

The FRILLED LIZARD (Plate 15) is another large dragon. It is familiar to many people because it appears frequently on postcards and other printed material. It was also featured on the now obsolete two-cent coin. During normal activities the frill is folded back and the lizard can be quite inconspicuous on the trunk of a tree, as it merges with the bark. The frill is only used when the dragon is threatened. At such times, the dragon opens its mouth to show a wide gape, hoping to scare off the perceived threat. The action of opening the mouth causes the frill to extend; the apparent increase in size is designed to intimidate still further. Because the frill contains long, rod-like bones that connect with the jaw and tongue, the wider the mouth is opened, the more extended from the neck the frill becomes. If all else fails the Frilled Lizard can take to its hind legs and escape by running at high speed.

Australian dragons come in all shapes and sizes, and there are some quite bizarre ones. Many people have seen pictures of the THORNY DEVIL, a small dragon from central and western Australia. Despite its very spiky appearance it is quite harmless; the spines and thorns there only to protect it from predators. It has a small head and a prominent hump on the back of its neck, the purpose of which is unclear; but since it lowers its head when frightened, presenting the spiky hump to the would-be predator, the hump possibly acts as a defense mechanism. Thorny Devils have an almost mechanical, jerky gait and are slow-moving. They live entirely on small black ants and will sit by an ant trail simply eating them as they run past. They are able to drink by taking up water along capillary grooves on the skin that lead the water to the mouth. In this way they maximize water uptake from light showers or even dew.

One place where you would not expect to find any reptiles at all is on the salt-encrusted surfaces of dry inland lakes, but the small SALT LAKE DRAGON is found only at Lake Eyre and a few other lakes in South Australia. Here it burrows into the fine sand beneath the cracked salt crust. It feeds on ants, which live around the edges of the lakes, and any other insects that may get blown onto the lake surface. If the lake floods, the dragon is forced by rising waters to leave its shelter and swim to the shore, inflating itself with air in order to remain afloat. In such a hostile environment, this dragon has made a number of adaptations. It has elongated scales at the margin of the lower eyelids that form a prominent fringe and act as a protection from salt glare.

Dragons are mainly sit-and-wait predators. They eat mostly arthropods, including a high proportion of ants. In some cases the diet is exclusively ants. Many also eat some vegetable matter.

Agamid coloration varies considerably and many species are colored to match their usual background or substrate. They have good eyesight and can spot prey or predators from a distance. Males of many agamids are quite brightly colored or prominently marked, especially in comparison with the females. One assumes females have color vision and can perhaps use it to sort out competing males.

When threatened, most dragons will race off to a burrow or other retreat. However, some will remain motionless, perhaps in the belief that they are invisible, bolting for cover at the last second. Others, such as the Frilled Lizard and EASTERN BEARDED DRAGON (Plate 15), will open the mouth and display the frill or "beard," before running for cover.

Ecological Interactions
On emergence in the morning to bask in the sun and raise its body temperature, a dragon is usually dark colored. As its body temperature rises, its color lightens and brightens. To avoid overheating, dragons use a range of strategies. As well as moving into shade or shelter, they turn and face into the sun to reduce the amount of body surface exposed to sun. If the temperature gets more extreme, they will raise the body and tail off the ground and literally stand on tip-toes, to minimize contact with the hot ground.

Breeding
All dragons are egg-layers, with from 2 to 35 eggs laid in a clutch, depending on the species. Multiple clutches during a single breeding season also occur. The sex of the young for many species, but not all, is dependent upon the temperature at which the eggs are incubated (see p. 90). Typically the female will excavate a burrow, lay eggs in it, and then fill in the hole. In some species attempts are made to camouflage the site.

Notes
Several of the dragons can run on their hindlimbs only, usually when fleeing over a long distance. This has resulted in the name "bicycle lizard."

A behavior known as "arm-waving" is frequently seen in many of the dragons. This involves the foreleg being rotated rapidly, almost as if the lizard was waving goodbye. Such lizards are commonly called "ta-ta lizards," from the Australian expression for goodbye.

Status
Several dragon species are listed by various Australian conservation authorities as endangered or vulnerable, including the GRASSLANDS EARLESS DRAGON, whose decline has been linked with the replacement of native grasslands with introduced pasture grasses.

Profiles
Jacky Lizard, *Amphibolurus muricatus,* Plate 15a
Frilled Lizard, *Chlamydosaurus kingii,* Plate 15b
Eastern Water Dragon, *Physignathus lesueurii,* Plate 15c
Eastern Bearded Dragon, *Pogona barbata,* Plate 15d

7. Skinks

The *skinks* are a large family (Scincidae, with about 1,300 species) of small and medium-sized lizards with a worldwide distribution. Over the warmer parts of the globe, they occur just about everywhere. The skinks are the largest and most diverse family of lizards in Australia, with more than 370 recognized species, and it is difficult to generalize on their features. There are diurnal, nocturnal, and crepuscular species, and they may be arboreal, terrestrial, or fossorial. In size they range from a few centimeters to more than 50 cm (20 in). Most have smooth scales and a long tail that is easily cast off; some species have rough or very prickly scales. A notable area of diversity is in the number and size of the limbs (four, two or none) and the number of digits on each limb.

Characteristically, skinks:
• Are mostly active in the day, although some species are active at dusk.
• Have overlapping scales that in most species are smooth and shiny, but several have rough or spiny scales.

• Have the ability to break off all or part of the tail and regrow the discarded portion (see below).
  • Have a broad, fleshy tongue.
  • Usually have an ear opening.
  • In most cases have four well-developed limbs, each with five digits. There are, however, some groups in which the number of digits or limbs is reduced. One species has no limbs at all. Like the pygopodids (p. 93), those that have reduced limbs do not have flaps.

Natural History

Ecology and Behavior

Skinks occur almost everywhere in Australia. They may be found in suburbs, alpine peaks, deserts, rainforests, and at the edge of the ocean. The greatest diversity occurs in the hummock grasslands of the inland deserts. The majority are terrestrial, sun-loving lizards, and while some are active throughout the day, many confine their activities to a particular time of day.

Many skinks, the active running and climbing species, have well-developed limbs and digits. Also, a significant proportion of the Australian skinks that burrow or "sand swim" have reduced limbs. Propulsion in such cases is by a rapid wriggling movement of the body known as *lateral undulation*. Surprisingly, even those skinks with well-developed limbs use this method of propulsion to move through leaf litter or vegetation. One genus of Australian skinks (*Ctenotus*; Plate 16) has 95 currently recognized species. They are all active, diurnal, small to medium-sized lizards that reach their greatest diversity in the arid regions. Another interesting genus is *Lerista*, with 79 current species. These are burrowers, and between them they show just about all the possible limb reductions, from four limbs, two forelimbs and no hindlimbs, no forelimbs and two hindlimbs, to no limbs at all. The number of digits on each limb ranges from five to one.

Five species of the large *bluetongue lizards* (Plate 19) occur throughout most of Australia. So named because of their large, deep-blue tongues, they are familiar to most people and still manage to survive in suburban gardens. Most of the species eat just about anything, from snails, slugs, insects, and fruit to the food put out for the cat or dog. The most unusual of the bluetongues is the ADELAIDE PYGMY BLUETONGUE, which is only 15 cm (6 in) long. It has a very restricted range in South Australia and was thought to be extinct; none had been seen since the 1950s despite intensive searches. Then, one was found in the stomach of a brown snake in 1992 and, after many weeks of frustrating searches they were finally rediscovered—living down spider burrows!

With its large pine-cone-like scales, and short, rounded tail, the SHINGLE-BACK lizard (Plate 19; also known as the bobtail, stumpy lizard, boggi, or pinecone lizard) can scarcely be mistaken for anything else. It has a large angular head, stout body and a blue tongue. It is often encountered ambling across the road in country areas, and is unfortunately often killed by cars.

Some skinks are sit-and-wait foragers, whereas others seek their food actively. They consume many kinds of insects, which they grab, crush with their jaws or beat against the ground, then swallow whole. Many of the larger skinks include vegetable matter in their diet.

Many of the skinks are not seen unless searched for. This applies particularly to the burrowing and sand-swimming species. Still, plenty are quite visible and commonly encountered on a warm day.

Ecological Interactions

Many lizards, including the skinks, have what many might regard as a self-defeating predator-escape mechanism: They detach a large chunk of their tail, leaving it behind for the predator to attack and eat while they make their escape. This process is known as *tail autotomy*—"self removal." Owing to some special anatomical features in the tail vertebrae, the tail is only tenuously attached to the rest of the body; when the animal is grasped forcefully by its tail, the tail breaks off easily. The shed tail then wriggles vigorously for a while, diverting the predator's attention for the instant it takes the skink to find shelter. A new tail grows quickly to replace the lost one. It is not uncommon to see skinks with two or even three tails. This occurs when the tail only partially breaks and does not fall off. The regeneration process begins and a new tail starts to grow from the partial break point, while the wound heals and the original tail remains.

Is autotomy successful as a lifesaving tactic? Most evolutionary biologists would argue that of course it works—otherwise it could not have evolved to be part of lizards' present-day defensive strategy. We have hard evidence, too. For instance, some snakes that have been caught and dissected have been found to have in their stomachs nothing but skink tails! Also, a very common finding when a field biologist surveys any population of small lizards (catching as many as possible in a given area to count and examine them) is that a hefty percentage, often 50% or more, have regenerating tails; this indicates that tail autotomy is common and successful in preventing predation.

Breeding

Some skink species lay eggs and some bear live young. The live-bearing species are predominantly those from cooler climates, where the lower temperatures might threaten the young developing in eggs. By keeping the young in her body, a female can provide them with higher temperatures by basking.

In one Australian skink species some populations are egg-laying and some are live-bearing. The Southeastern Slider, *Lerista bougainvillii*, is found in the southern Australian mainland, and on the islands in Bass Strait, which separates Tasmania from the mainland. On the Bass Strait islands the young are live-born, while on the mainland most of the populations lay eggs. Interestingly, the populations on the mainland adjacent to Bass Strait lay eggs, but they hatch very quickly—within about a week or two. Several species of Australian skinks lay eggs in communal nests, and such a nest may comprise 20 to 30 eggs or even several hundred. In some instances the nests seem to be used over several years.

Notes

One Australian skink, the GRASS SKINK (Plate 18), successfully colonized the Hawaiian Islands after having arrived there in the early 1900s. It is now the most common skink in Hawaii. This skink is also now established in the northern areas of the North Island of New Zealand, after arriving in the 1960s. The same lizard and its close relative, the GARDEN SKINK (Plate 18), have been observed on a number of occasions in what can only be described as a ball of lizards. This can comprise anything up to 15 or more lizards all locked together, each grasping another with its mouth. After squirming about for some minutes they will break up and dash off. The purpose of this activity is unknown, but it does sound like fun.

Status

Nine species of Australian skink are considered threatened or endangered on the IUCN Red List. Many others are listed by Australian national or state conservation authorities as endangered, rare, or vulnerable.

Profiles

Shaded-litter Rainbow Skink, *Carlia munda*, Plate 16a
Southern Rainbow Skink, *Carlia tetradactyla*, Plate 16b
Fence Skink, *Cryptoblepharus virgatus*, Plate 16c
Robust Ctenotus, *Ctenotus robustus*, Plate 16d
Coppertail, *Ctenotus taeniolatus*, Plate 16e
Major Skink, *Egernia frerei*, Plate 17a
Cunningham's Skink, *Egernia cunninghami*, Plate 17b
Land Mullet, *Egernia major*, plate 17c
Tree Skink, *Egernia striolata*, plate 17d
White's Skink, *Egernia whitii*, Plate 17e
Warm-temperate Water Skink, *Eulamprus heatwolei*, Plate 18a
Eastern Water Skink, *Eulamprus quoyii*, plate 18b
Bar-sided Forest Skink, *Eulamprus tenuis*, Plate 18c
Grass Skink, *Lampropholis delicata*, Plate 18d
Garden Skink, *Lampropholis guichenoti*, Plate 18e
Tussock Cool Skink, *Pseudemoia entrecasteauxii*, Plate 19a
Weasel Skink, *Saproscincus mustelina*, Plate 19b
Pink-tongued Skink, *Hemisphaeriodon gerrardii*, Plate 19c
Blotched Bluetongue, *Tiliqua nigrolutea*, Plate 19d
Common Bluetongue, *Tiliqua scincoides*, Plate 19e
Shingleback, *Trachydosaurus rugosus*, Plate 19f

8. Pythons—The Constrictors

Pythons belong to the family Boidae, which has about 60 species and includes the largest living snakes, such as the anaconda of South America. The pythons (subfamily Pythoninae) are mostly in the Old World and consist entirely of egg-laying species. *Boas* (subfamily Boinae), on the other hand, are mostly New World in distribution and produce live young. There are about 24 species of pythons worldwide, of which 14 occur in Australia (with 10 endemic). Pythons occur in all mainland Australian states (there are none in Tasmania), but they are most common in the tropical north. Eleven species occur in the areas covered by this book. Australia's smallest is the PYGMY PYTHON of Western Australia, with a total length of 50 cm (20 in), while the largest snake in Australia is northern Queensland's AMETHYSTINE PYTHON (Plate 6). There are anecdotal accounts of this snake reaching 8.5 m (27.75 ft); however, the largest specimen accurately measured reached only 5.65 m (18.5 ft).

All pythons except the WOMA and BLACK-HEADED PYTHON (Plate 6) have a broad head, a relatively narrow neck, and heat-sensitive pits on their lips. The pits are capable of detecting differences in temperature and assist in locating warm-blooded prey. All pythons constrict their prey. Pythons are the only snakes to retain vestiges of hindlimbs, which take the form of spurs situated on either side of their vent (the opening on their bellies through which sex occurs and wastes exit). While all are mainly nocturnal, larger pythons are also active during the day and are often encountered basking or moving around. Although pythons are non-venomous, they have sharp, backward-curving teeth and can inflict a painful bite. Some species have a reputation for snappiness, so be cautious when observing large pythons.

Natural History

Ecology and Behavior

Pythons occupy most Australian habitats but are more common in woodlands and rocky outcrops. Some are also found in closed forest, while others live in hummock grass areas in the desert.

Pythons possess some most unusual sense organs, called *labial pits*. These are heat sensors on the lips designed to collect infra-red radiation. They are positioned on the lower lip close to the corners of the mouth, and this location, with respect to the shape of the python head, helps a snake orient itself for a strike. The pits also provide information to the snake on the angle of the heat source (prey) in relation to the pits and the direction in which the prey is moving. With these organs, a python can detect, strike, and catch prey even on the darkest night.

Pythons are generally ambush predators rather than active hunters, although a few use both strategies. They select a spot next to a trail used by other animals and lie in wait, either coiled on the ground or hanging down from a low branch. It is not unusual for a python to remain at one spot, waiting, for several days.

Pythons are non-venomous snakes that kill their prey by *constriction*, which consists of throwing tight coils of their bodies around it until it suffocates. Prey is first captured by a rapid, open-mouthed strike. Python teeth are recurved, meaning they point back into the mouth, and this helps the python to keep a grip on the struggling prey item after biting it. Having seized its prey, the python quickly coils around it and proceeds to constrict it. The coils tighten each time the prey exhales until eventually it runs out of oxygen and is asphyxiated. Contrary to popular belief, these constrictors do not actually crush their prey to a pulp—the tissues remain intact.

One desert species, the Woma, uses a different approach to conventional constriction. This species catches many of its prey within narrow burrows, where there is not enough space to loop coils of the body around the prey. Instead, the Woma uses a loop of its muscular body and pushes against the unlucky mammal so that it is squeezed and eventually suffocated between the snake and the burrow wall. This technique doesn't immobilize prey as quickly or effectively as would constriction, so many adult Woma pythons carry scars from struggling prey.

CARPET PYTHONS (Plate 6) are the most widespread group of pythons in Australia, occurring across much of the mainland. Robust snakes, they vary considerably in color and form. Carpet Pythons from the rainforests of northeastern Queensland can be a striking black or dark brown with long bold yellow stripes or blotches. The so-called Diamond Python is an often encountered Carpet Python that occurs along the east coast from northern New South Wales to Victoria; it is olive black with creamy yellow rosettes along the body. Other variations occur inland in northern and western Australia.

In some python species, male–male combat takes place at the beginning of the breeding season. Typically this involves the two males twining around each other and endeavoring to place their head over that of their rival and force it down. In other species the combat involves biting as well as gouging with their spurs. This combat is presumed to be a form of competition among males to gain access to females in reproductive condition. It seems probable that females lay down some form of scent trail, because males have been observed following exactly the trail of a female they cannot see. More than one male will follow the trail, even several days after the female has passed.

Ecological Interactions

Pythons are doubtless preyed upon by large birds of prey, crocodiles, and goannas. Some of the larger carnivorous marsupials could also make a meal of some of the smaller pythons. Feral cats, dogs, and pigs can be assumed to eat these snakes when the opportunity arises. Large goannas will harass brooding female pythons and take the eggs. Larger pythons are probably too big for predators other than people.

Breeding

All pythons lay eggs. A female builds a nest of vegetation by coiling under loose leaf litter, for example, or simply selects an appropriate, well-insulated burrow. The eggs when laid are sticky and the female pushes and arranges them into a mound that she can coil around while they incubate. She stays coiled around the eggs, not eating, and leaves only to drink or to heat up in the sun.

Although pythons are *ectothermic* (cold-blooded) like other reptiles—that is, they rely on heat from the environment to keep themselves warm—brooding female pythons actually generate heat by shivering, and this keeps the eggs at a high and stable temperature throughout development. It is very expensive in terms of the female's own energy reserves: she may lose up to half her own body weight between egg-laying and the end of incubation, and it may take her two or three years to regain enough energy reserves to breed again. When the young emerge from the eggs and disperse, the female departs to find food for herself. From birth, the hatchlings are on their own and must fend for themselves.

Notes

The GREEN TREE PYTHON, which is found in Australia and New Guinea, has an almost exact counterpart in the EMERALD TREE BOA found in South America. Coloration is almost identical in adults—emerald green with whitish markings— and the way in which they rest on a branch by draping coils evenly on each side is the same. The young in both species are not born green, but rather yellow or reddish brown. They both undergo a change to green at between six months and two years. The reason for the close similarity between these two species is suspected to be convergent evolution; that is, they converged in form and behavior because they have similar lifestyles and similar ecologies and not because they are closely related.

"Children's Python" is the name of a group of three small pythons. Contrary to popular belief, their name does not mean that they are pythons for children; it refers to an English naturalist, J. G. Children, after whom the snakes were named. Coincidentally, they are popular snakes with reptile-keepers and are a good species for young people to keep because of their small size and placid temperament. Children's pythons occur over much of Australia and are often associated with rock outcrops and caves, where they are very adept at catching bats. They climb rock faces at the entrance to caves where bats are roosting and wait there until the bats fly out in the evening. They catch bats flying past and eat them hanging in mid-air, secured to the rocks only by their tails.

Status

The Woma is considered threatened or endangered (IUCN Red List) and several other pythons are recognized as rare or endangered at the state or national level in Australia. Worldwide, all members of family Boidae (pythons and boas) are listed in the CITES Appendix II, considered vulnerable or threatened, mainly because they are frequent victims of the illicit international trade in exotic pets.

Profiles

Carpet Python, *Morelia spilota variegata*, Plate 6a
Diamond Python, *Morelia spilota spilota*, Plate 6b
Black-headed Python, *Aspidites melanocephalus*, Plate 6c
Water Python, *Liasis fuscus*, Plate 6d
Amethystine Python, *Morelia amethistina*, Plate 6e
Eastern Small-blotched Python, *Antaresia maculosus*, Plate 7a

9. Elapids—Venomous Snakes

Elapid snakes (family Elapidae) are found in most of the tropical and warmer regions of the globe and, along with such well-known Australian representatives as the TAIPAN (Plate 9), TIGER SNAKE (Plate 9) and SOUTHERN DEATH ADDER (Plate 7), include the Old World *cobras* and *mambas* and New World *coral snakes*. The family includes what are usually regarded as Earth's most dangerous snakes. There are about 250 species worldwide and they are the major group of land snakes in Australia. Out of a total of about 160 species of snakes known to occur in Australia, 92 are elapids, accounting for more than half the continent's snake fauna. So Australia certainly has its fair share of these beauties.

Elapid snakes are all venomous, although most are only mildly so and are not considered to be dangerous. Only about 20 elapids in Australia are regarded as dangerous. Most of the non-dangerous ones bite and inject venom, but their venom causes reactions in people similar to that of a bee or wasp sting, or possibly no reaction at all.

Elapid snakes are found throughout Australia. Diversity varies: while there are as few as three species in Tasmania, there are more than 20 species in northeastern Queensland. Some are specialized in their requirements but many are generalists and occupy a wide range of environments: provided there is food and shelter, they will be there. They all have fixed hollow fangs toward the front of the upper jaw, and these are connected to the venom gland by a duct.

Sea snakes are in a different family (Hydrophiidae) than elapids, but are closely related; all are venomous, some lethally so. They spend their time in the ocean, and have flattened tails that help with aquatic propulsion. About 30 species (including the two shown in Plate 11) occur off Australia's coasts, mainly in northern, tropical waters.

Natural History

Ecology and Behavior

Most Australian elapids are terrestrial, and some species are burrowing or at least semi-burrowing. A few display a tree-climbing ability, but only the three species of genus *Hoplocephalus* (including STEPHEN'S BANDED SNAKE, Plate 8) are regarded as arboreal. It seems strange that the Australian elapids have not made more use of trees—quite a number of African elapids are arboreal. The reasons for this difference are not fully understood.

The larger elapids are mainly diurnal although they become nocturnal, particularly during hot weather. In contrast, many of the smaller elapids are nocturnal and, as a consequence, not often seen. The larger elapids more likely to be seen include the *black snakes*, of which there are five species. The RED-BELLIED BLACK SNAKE (Plate 9) is the most well known, although the most widespread is the MULGA, or KING BROWN, SNAKE (Plate 9). Yes, despite its name and color, it is actually a member of the black snake group. Except for southern areas of the east coast, this species occurs over most of mainland Australia. All black snakes are heavy-bodied terrestrial snakes that flatten out their necks and hiss loudly if disturbed.

Another group commonly encountered are the fast-moving *brown snakes*, which bite readily, although their fangs are short. All have a more slender body than black snakes or *tiger snakes*. There are seven species of brown snake distributed over most areas of mainland Australia. The most widespread are the WESTERN BROWN SNAKE (Plate 8) and EASTERN BROWN SNAKE (Plate 8), which, together with the DUGITE in Western Australia, are the ones most likely to be encountered. Color is extremely variable in this group—some individuals are not even brown. They range from grey or tan through various shades of brown to black, and some have bands; the Western Brown Snake alone has nine recognized color and pattern variations. The Eastern Brown Snake is adept at concealing itself in grass clumps and will get right down into the roots, where it is almost impossible to find. Here it will remain quite still and not retaliate even if stepped on, which is probably just as well: when encountered in the open, it has a reputation for being bad-tempered.

The larger elapid snakes eat a lot of mice and rats, and in doing so they play a significant role in reducing numbers of these pests. This is one reason why larger snakes are found around houses and outbuildings: they are attracted by the various rodents that live there. The small elapids are mainly lizard- and frog-eaters but several, such as the *shovel-nosed snakes* (for example, the NARROW-BANDED SHOVEL-NOSED SNAKE), eat the eggs of other reptiles. The frog-eaters may be attracted to the frogs found in suburban fish ponds.

The majority of the elapids actively forage for prey but the Southern Death Adder is a sit-and-wait predator. It will coil up, often partially buried, and either wait for prey to approach or lure it in by twitching the tip of its tail, which is curled in front of the head. The twitching tip presumably simulates a wriggling grub or insect and attracts the interest of a bird, lizard, or mammal. Several of the smaller nocturnal elapids feed mainly on diurnal lizards, which they find at night while resting.

Breeding
Some elapid species are egg layers and some give birth to live young. Eggs are laid between November and January, while live young are born usually between December and March. Mating in most species occurs during August to November, although some of the more southern species mate in autumn (March to April), with the female carrying the sperm overwinter. No elapids are known to show any maternal care of their eggs or young, although some may stay with newly laid eggs for a few days before departing. When born, the young are just as dangerous as the adults, with complete and functional venom-injection apparatus.

Notes
Snake venom has three main functions: first, to incapacitate prey so that the snake can subdue and eat it; second, to aid digestion of the prey by breaking down the tissue; and third, as a deterrent to possible predators.

Venom is not a single substance but rather a mixture of components; it is actually modified saliva. The venom is stored in glands situated behind the eyes and is carried to the front of the head, where it enters a duct or groove in a fang and travels down to the tip. A snake can control the amount of venom that is delivered to the fangs. When biting a person, a snake sometimes injects no venom at all.

There are three general categories of toxins in snake venom. There are *neurotoxins*, which affect nerve functions, especially with respect to heart and lungs; their effect is to suffocate by causing paralysis of the diaphragm muscles. *Myotoxins*, which damage muscles and break down muscle fiber, are a second group. The last category is *hemotoxins*, which affect the blood and interfere with its clotting properties. Some hemotoxins are coagulants, which cause small blood clots to form in the veins; others are anticoagulants, which prevent clotting and cause bleeding and hemorrhages. Hemotoxins also contain components that destroy red blood cells.

The symptoms of snake-bite in humans vary considerably depending on the species, but common symptoms are headache, drowsiness, sweating, and nausea. Lymph nodes in the armpits and groin may become painful and swollen. As the venom takes effect, the symptoms will become more pronounced, with accompanying dilation of the pupils, blurred or double vision, slurred speech and difficulty in swallowing. There may also be diarrhea, blood in the urine and chest, and/or abdominal pain. The only comfort is that it takes, on average, 24 hours for death to occur.

If someone is bitten, apply immediate first aid. Do not bother about washing the site of the bite and do not cut the site. Apply a broad constrictive bandage as soon as possible, working from the site of the bite toward the heart. Most bites occur on a limb, and as much of the limb as possible should be bound. Wind the bandage firmly but not too tightly. Immobilize the limb with a splint or a sling. Keep the bitten person calm, do not administer alcohol, and keep movement to a minimum. Transport the person to the nearest hospital. Telephone the hospital in advance if possible. Do not remove the bandage or splint; this should be done under medical supervision. It is unnecessary to try to identify the snake or kill it for identification. Hospitals have test kits to determine the species of snake responsible. Anti-venom comes in two types: *monovalent*, which is for a particular species, and *polyvalent*, which can be used for all dangerous Australian snakes.

Status

A number of the smaller elapids are regarded as endangered, vulnerable, or at risk, mainly because little is known about their numbers or distributions. Six Australian elapids are listed as threatened or endangered on the IUCN Red List.

Profiles

Southern Death Adder, *Acanthophis antarcticus,* Plate 7e
Highland Copperhead, *Austrelaps ramsayi,* Plate 8a
Lowland Copperhead, *Austrelaps superbus,* Plate 8b
Western Brown Snake, *Pseudonaja nuchalis,* Plate 8c
Eastern Brown Snake, *Pseudonaja textilis,* Plate 8d
Stephen's Banded Snake, *Hoplocephalus stephensii,* Plate 8e
Black Tiger Snake, *Notechis ater,* Plate 9a
Eastern Tiger Snake, *Notechis scutatus,* Plate 9b
Taipan, *Oxyuranus scutellatus,* Plate 9c

Mulga Snake, *Pseudechis australis,* Plate 9d
Red-bellied Black Snake, *Pseudechis porphyriacus,* Plate 9e
Yellow-faced Whipsnake, *Demansia psammophis,* Plate 10a
White-lipped Snake, *Drysdalia coronoides,* Plate 10b
Marsh Snake, *Hemiaspis signata,* Plate 10c
Coral Snake, *Simoselaps australis,* Plate 10d
Bandy-bandy, *Vermicella annulata,* Plate 10e
Stokes' Sea Snake, *Astrotia stokesii,* Plate 11a
Yellow-bellied Sea Snake, *Pelamis platurus,* Plate 11b

10. Miscellaneous Snakes

Grouped together here, for convenience, are three families of snakes that, because they have few representatives in Australia or live mainly underground, are relatively infrequently seen.

File snakes (family Acrochordidae) are bizarre-looking reptiles. Totally aquatic, they have very baggy, loose-fitting skin that is coarse and file-like to the touch. There are three species, two of which occur in the northern areas of Australia (the other is Asian): the ARAFURA FILE SNAKE, which occurs in freshwater creeks and billabongs, and the LITTLE FILE SNAKE, found in coastal waters such as estuaries. Neither is venomous.

The *blind snakes* (family Typhlopidae), or *worm snakes,* as they are also known, have small, highly polished, worm-like bodies with blunt heads and short tails that end in a spine. Their eyes are reduced to dark spots and the scales are a uniform size around the body (with none enlarged on the belly, as in some other snakes). When handled, some have a tendency to emit a strong, pungent odor. There are about 40 species worldwide, of which 33 occur in Australia. There are none in Tasmania or in alpine areas.

In most of the world, *colubrids* (family Colubridae) are the most common and widespread family of snakes, with about 1,600 species in total. In Australia this is not the case because they arrived on the continent after the elapids (p. 105) became established, and there are only 10 species represented here. They only occur in northern Australia, although the distribution of a few extends down the east coast. Only two, the GREEN TREE SNAKE (Plate 7) and BROWN TREE SNAKE (Plate 7), are found as far south as Sydney.

Natural History

Ecology and Behavior
File snakes are nocturnal. The Arafura File Snake, which is confined to permanent billabongs during the tropical dry season, moves rapidly into surrounding flooded countryside during the wet season. Their baggy skin flattens out when they are swimming, allowing the snake to move more efficiently through the water. They have nostrils that are high on the snout and have valves that close when the snake is under water. Out of water, they have trouble moving around and are almost completely helpless. Unlike the paddle-like tail of the typical sea snakes (p. 105), file snakes have a grasping tail for gripping roots or snags in the water to prevent them from being carried about by the current. They eat fish, which they squeeze to death. Their rough and rasp-like skin is very useful when holding this slippery prey, giving the snake a good grip as it constricts the fish

prior to eating it. Predators of file snakes include fish, crocodiles, goannas, birds, and humans.

Blind snakes are found in both arid areas and rainforests. The largest species grow to about 60 cm (24 in) but most are much smaller. They are sometimes found in aggregations, with individuals of various sizes all knotted together. The reasons for these snake bundles are not known. It is believed that most blind snakes eat the eggs and larvae of ants, and their bodies are designed to get into these animals' nests without being eaten themselves. The smooth, hard skin leaves no room for ants or termites to take hold and each species knows what size nest to enter: small blind snakes do not go into bulldog ant nests, for example, as these ants are large enough to attack and kill them. The larger blind snakes, however, go into such nests without problem. The unpleasant odor some of these snakes give off when handled is thought to be some form of predator deterrent. They live underground most of the time but occasionally are found above ground at night, usually after rain. One elapid snake, the Bandy-bandy, feeds almost exclusively on blind snakes, which it presumably trails and catches underground.

Most Australian *colubrids* are found in or near water. One group (subfamily Homalopsinae) of four species consists of venomous, *back-fanged* water snakes that also occur in Asia and the Pacific (back-fanged snakes have enlarged, grooved, poison-conducting teeth at the rear of the mouth that are capable of injecting venom). Apart from one that is found in fresh water, they are generally found in mangroves and on coastal mudflats. They are mainly fish-eaters but one, the WHITE-BELLIED MANGROVE SNAKE, catches and eats crabs. If the crab is too big to swallow whole, the snake will pull off and eat the claws and legs before the main course.

The other group of Australian colubrids, the six species of subfamily Colubrinae, comprise one venomous back-fanged species and five non-venomous species. Most inhabit moister habitats and several are frog-eaters. For instance, the KEELBACK (Plate 7) is a non-venomous semi-aquatic frog-eater that inhabits coastal streams and marshes in northern and northeastern coastal regions, as far south as New South Wales. None of the Australian back-fanged snakes are regarded as dangerous to people, but they can and do bite.

Breeding

File snakes bear live young. Females may reproduce only once every 3 to 5 years because they need to build up reserves of energy to develop their young. Because they are slow and not very efficient fish-catchers, it often takes several years to accumulate sufficient reserves. Blind snakes are all believed to be egg laying, with eggs laid during January and February. One widespread species, known as the FLOWER POT SNAKE, which occurs in Australia only in the tropical north, appears to be *parthenogenic*; that is, a female can develop fertile eggs without their being fertilized by a male. Some colubrids (subfamily Colubrinae) are egg layers, and some (subfamily Homalopsinae) are live bearers.

Notes

The Arafura File Snake is a favorite food of local Aboriginal people, who go into billabongs and often stand waist-deep to feel about with their feet for the snakes beneath banks and logs.

The tail of a blind snake ends in a short spine, which is incorrectly thought by many people to be a stinger. It is actually used by the snake to secure a grip when it is pushing with its head through narrow underground passages.

Status

Eight blind snakes are listed by Australian conservation authorities as being of concern, mainly because they are known from only a few specimens. Similarly, two or three of the Australian colubrids are insufficiently known to be able to determine their statuses accurately.

Profiles

Blackish Blind Snake, *Ramphotyphlops nigrescens,* Plate 5e

Brown Tree Snake, *Boiga irregularis,* Plate 7b

Green Tree Snake, *Dendrelaphis punctulata,* Plate 7c

Keelback, *Tropidonophis mairii,* Plate 7d

Environmental Close-Up 3:
Australia's Endemics: Species That Occur Nowhere Else

by Les Beletsky

A few years ago I attended an international scientific conference on birds held in New Zealand. The conference, a quadrennial event, moves from continent to continent, I suspect because this permits the participants—scientific researchers who usually double as birdwatchers—to see wild birds they cannot see back home. Indeed, overheard conversations at the conference centered on two topics: the awful cafeteria food at the host university and seeing *"endemics."* People asked each other "Which endemics have you seen so far?" and "Where would I go to see this or that endemic?" They were referring to New Zealand species of birds that occur nowhere else on Earth. For many a birder, seeing such unique species is the paramount reason for visiting isolated spots of the world such as New Zealand. An organism is endemic to a place when it is found only in that place. But the size or type of place referred to is variable: a given species of frog, say, may be endemic to the Eastern Hemisphere, to a single continent such as Australia, to a small mountainous region of New South Wales, or to a speck of an island off Queenland's coast.

A species' history dictates its present distribution. When it's confined to a certain or small area, the reason is that (1) there are one or more barriers to further spread (an ocean, a mountain range, a thousand kilometers of tropical rainforest), (2) the species evolved only recently and has not yet had time to spread, or (3) the species evolved long ago, spread long ago, and now has become extinct over much of its prior range. A history of isolation also matters: the longer a group of animals and plants are isolated from their close relatives, the more time they have to evolve by themselves and to change into new, different, and unique groups. The best examples are on islands. Some islands once were attached to mainland areas but continental drift and/or changing sea levels led to their isolation in the middle of the ocean; other islands arose wholly new via volcanic activity beneath the seas. Take the island of Madagascar. Once attached to Africa and India, the organisms stranded on its shores when it became an island had probably 100 million years in isolation to develop into the highly endemic fauna and flora we see today. It's thought that about 80% of the island's plants and animals are endemic—half the bird species, about 800 butterflies, 8,000 flowering plants, and essentially all the mammals and reptiles. Most of the species of lemurs of the world—small, primitive, but cute primates—occur only on Madagascar, and an entire nature tourism industry has been built there around the idea of endemism: if you want to see wild lemurs, you must go there. Other examples of islands with high concentrations of endemic animals abound: Indonesia, where about 15% of the world's bird species occur, a quarter of them endemic; Papua New Guinea, where half the birds are endemic; the Philippines, where half the mammals are endemic.

Australia, together with Africa, Madagascar, India, Antarctica, New Zealand, and South America, was once part of a huge, southern super-continent known as *Gondwanaland*. Perhaps 40 to 50 million years ago, after India and Africa broke off, Australia separated from the super-continent and began drifting northward. Animals and plants that occupied Australia when it became a separate continent are the ancestors of most of the species that occupy present-day Australia. For tens of millions of years, these organisms were essentially isolated from the rest of the terrestrial world. They adapted to changing Australian climates and habitats (which shifted toward seasonality and aridity as the continent moved northward into lower, and so warmer, latitudes) and evolved into the highly endemic flora and fauna we see today (Table 1, below).

Not all of Australia's species, of course, are endemic, and not all are the direct descendants of the species "trapped" in Australia when it first separated from the super-continent. Some other species arrived more recently. Birds and bats fly, and thus can move over oceans from one landmass to another (and indeed, Australia shares many of its current flying animals with other countries). Various terrestrial reptiles and rodents probably first arrived in Australia from the Indonesian region

Group	Total Number of Species in World	Total Number of Species in Australia (% of world total)	Number (%) of Species Endemic to Australia
Vascular Plants	300,000	20,000 (6.7%)	about 17,000 (85%)
Insects dragonflies	1,000,000 5,000	70,000 (7%) 300 (6%)	Unknown about 220 (74%)
Freshwater Fish	10,000	200 (2%)	Unknown
Frogs	4,100	210 (5.1%)	about 195 (93%)
Reptiles	7,000	800 (11.4%)	about 720 (90%)
Birds	9,700	750 (7.7%)	about 330 (44%)
Land Mammals marsupials	4,630 255	300 (6.5%) 142 (55.7%)	240 (80%) 128 (90%)

Table 1. Australian Biodiversity and Endemism: Number of Species in Australia and Percent Endemic.

by floating in on logs or mats of vegetation, moving from island to island over thousands of years. Some rodents, for instance, based on fossil evidence, are thought to have first arrived in Australia about 15 million years ago, as Australia, drifting northward, moved closer to Indonesia. The Torres Strait, which separates Queensland's Cape York Peninsula from New Guinea, is now only about 150 km (95 miles) wide, and pocked with more than 100 scattered islands that can serve as midway points for species crossing this waterway. Furthermore, during the past few million years, and, in fact, as recently as 15,000 to 20,000 years ago, cool climates worldwide several times led to major glaciations of continents, tying up water in ice, and, as a result, lowering ocean levels. At these times, there were likely broad land bridges between Australia and New Guinea, permitting "dry" species movement and transfers. (Even today, the Torres Strait is a particularly shallow body of water.) Finally, people arrived in Australia, probably first crossing from New Guinea, 40,000 to 60,000 years ago; they likely facilitated the entry of some new plant and animal species to the continent—as they continue to do to this very day. Dingos, for instance, were brought to Australia by people perhaps 3,500 to 4,000 years ago. *Introduced* species, those which people, intentionally or not, first brought to Australia, and which are now well-established characters in Australian ecosystems, include, among mammals, many rodents (House Mice, Black and Norway Rats), Red Foxes, domestic cats, rabbits, Brown Hares, pigs, camels, deer, goats, horses, donkeys; and among birds, about 23 species, including Mallards, Common Peafowl, domestic pigeons, Red-whiskered Bulbuls, Song Thrushes, Common Blackbirds, House Sparrows, Common (European) Starlings, and Common Mynas.

A knowledge of endemism is important for ecotravellers for two main reasons, one practical, one environmental. First, like my friends the New Zealand birdwatchers, if there is a specific type of wildlife you'd like to see, you must first know where it occurs, then travel there. Madagascar for lemurs. Africa or Asia for elephants. New Zealand for Yellow-eyed Penguins. Australia for koalas, wombats, and emus. If you wanted to visit a region where you might encounter large varieties of strange, exotic wildlife, a region with a high degree of endemism would be just the ticket—such as some of the hot spots mentioned in this article. Second, species that are endemic to small areas often bear a special environmental vulnerability. Basically, when and if their numbers fall, these species or groups face a greater chance of extinction than others because they lack other places to go or other populations in far-off places that might survive. For example, if a species of bird occurs only on a single island, all of its eggs are in one basket, so to speak: if a calamity strikes there—a powerful hurricane, a volcanic eruption— the entire species could become extinct. This type of species extinction has apparently happened often on islands with birds over the past 400 years, as people colonized. People caused habitat destruction and brought animal predators that the native birds had no fear of or experience with. It's thought that about 108 bird species have become extinct in the last 400 years, 97 of them island endemics. (The problem persists: about 900 of the 9,700 living bird species are island endemics, and so continually vulnerable.) Similarly, about 75% of mammals driven to extinction recently have been island dwellers.

Knowledge of the existence and distribution of endemic species is crucial for conservation of biodiversity. If we want to preserve biodiversity, then identifying areas with unique species (endemics) and areas with large numbers of unique species (*centers of endemism*), then targeting those areas for conservation attention makes sense. We don't have to make as much of an effort to conserve species that are distributed worldwide or hemisphere-wide: their broad ranges often provide protection against quick extinction. Endemics, with their restricted distributions, are inherently more vulnerable and so deserving of immediate attention. A recent concept in conservation biology has been the idea that *hot spots*—relatively small areas of the world supporting very high numbers of endemic species—should receive priority conservation attention. Time, effort, and funds allocated in these regions will result in greater conservation of biodiversity than efforts elsewhere. For instance, it's estimated that fully 20% of the Earth's endemic plants occur over just half a percent of the world's land area: preserve just that half a percent and save fully one-fifth all of endemic plants. Some reptile and amphibian hot spots are Madagascar, certain regions of Colombia, and Atlantic coastal Brazil; chief mammal hot spots are the Philippines, Madagascar, and northern Borneo.

Two Australian regions, with their highly endemic flora and fauna, can certainly be considered hot spots of endemic biodiversity, places where investments in conservation will hopefully pay big dividends in preserving large numbers of unique species. One is the "Wet Tropics" (p. 30)—the rainforest portions of northeastern Queensland, centered around Cairns, with 13 endemic bird species and 10 endemic mammals. The other is the very southwestern corner of the country, a small bit of the huge state of Western Australia. Of the 5,470 plant species known to occur in this small region, 51% are endemic to the region (79% are endemic to a slightly larger area of southwestern Australia); and vertebrates endemic to the region include, among mammals, the Numbat (p. 198) and Honey Possum, and among birds, five parrots, including the Long-billed Black-cockatoo.

Chapter 9

BIRDS

- *Introduction*
- *General Characteristics of Birds*
- *Classification of Birds*
- *Australian Birds*
- *Seeing Birds in Australia*
- *Family Profiles*
    - *1. Seabirds I: Tube-nosed Seabirds*
    - *2. Seabirds II: Pelicans and Allies (Frigatebirds, Boobies, and Cormorants)*
    - *3. Seabirds III: Gulls, Terns, and Noddies*
    - *4. Penguins*
    - *5. Ducks, Geese, and Grebes*
    - *6. Marsh and Stream Birds*
    - *7. Herons and Egrets*
    - *8. Shorebirds (Waders)*
    - *9. Emu and Cassowaries*
    - *10. Megapodes and Quail*
    - *11. Raptors*
    - *12. Pigeons and Doves*
    - *13. Parrots*
    - *14. Cuckoos and Coucals*
    - *15. Owls*
    - *16. Nightjars and Frogmouths*
    - *17. Swifts, Swallows, and Woodswallows*
    - *18. Kingfishers, Kookaburras, Bee-eaters, and Rollers*
    - *19. Lyrebirds and Pittas*

20. *Treecreepers and Fairy-wrens*

21. *Australian Warblers (Pardalotes, Scrubwrens, Gerygones, and Thornbills)*

22. *Honeyeaters and Chats*

23. *Robins, Babblers, and Logrunners*

24. *Whipbirds, Whistlers, and Sittella*

25. *Flycatchers, Monarchs, Fantails, Magpie-larks, and Drongos*

26. *Cuckoo-shrikes, Trillers, Orioles, and Figbird*

27. *Butcherbirds, Magpies, and Currawongs*

28. *Crows, Ravens, Riflebirds (Birds of Paradise), Chough, and Apostlebird*

29. *Bowerbirds*

30. *Larks, Pipits, and Sunbirds*

31. *Estrildid Finches (Grassfinches)*

32. *Old World Warblers and White-eyes*

33. *Thrushes, Starlings, Mynas, and Bulbuls*

- *Environmental Close-Up 4: Nectar and Nectar-eaters*

Introduction

Most of the vertebrate animals one sees on a visit to just about anywhere are birds, and Australia is no exception. Regardless of how the rest of a trip's wildlife viewing progresses, birds will be seen frequently and in large numbers. Birds are, as opposed to other terrestrial vertebrates, most often active during the day, visually conspicuous and usually far from quiet as they pursue their daily activities. But why are birds so much more conspicuous than other vertebrates? The reason goes to the essential nature of birds: they fly. The ability to fly is, so far, nature's premier anti-predator escape mechanism. Animals that can fly well are relatively less prone to predation than those that cannot, and so they can be both reasonably conspicuous in their behavior and also reasonably certain of daily survival. Birds can fly quickly from dangerous situations and remain above the fray. Most flightless land vertebrates, restricted to moving on the ground or on plants, are easy prey unless they are quiet, concealed, and careful or, alternatively, very large or fierce; many smaller ones, in fact, have evolved other special defense mechanisms, such as poisons or nocturnal behavior.

A fringe benefit of birds being the most frequently encountered kind of vertebrate wildlife is that, for an ecotraveller's intents and purposes, birds are innocuous. Contrast this with too-close encounters with potentially dangerous fish (sharks), amphibians (frogs with toxic skin secretions), reptiles (venomous snakes), and mammals (bears and big cats). Moreover, birds do not always depart with all due haste after being spotted, as is the wont of most other types of vertebrates. Again, their ability to fly and thus easily evade our grasp permits many birds, when confronted with people, to behave leisurely and go about their business (albeit keeping one eye at all times on the strange-looking bipeds), allowing us extensive time to watch them. Not only are birds among the safest and easiest animals to observe; they are also among the most beautiful. Australia's birds will almost certainly provide an ecotraveller some of any trip's finest, most memorable moments.

General Characteristics of Birds

Birds are vertebrates that have feathers and can fly. They began evolving from reptiles during the Jurassic Period of the Mesozoic Era, perhaps 150 million years ago, and saw explosive development of new species during the last 50 million years or so. The development of flight is the key factor behind birds' evolution, their historical spread throughout the globe, their current ecological success, and arguably dominant position among the world's land animals. Flight, as mentioned above, is a fantastic predator evasion technique; it permits birds to move over long distances in search of particular foods or habitats, and its development opened up for vertebrate exploration and exploitation an entirely new and vast theater of operations—the atmosphere.

At first glance, birds appear to be highly variable, ranging in size and form from 135 kg (300 lb) ostriches to 4 kg (10 lb) eagles to 3 g (0.1 oz) hummingbirds. Actually, however, when compared with other types of vertebrates, birds are remarkably similar physically. Whereas mammals or reptiles can be quite diverse in form and still function as mammals or reptiles (think how different in form are lizards, snakes, and turtles), if birds are going to fly, they more or less must look like birds, and have the forms and physiologies that birds have. The most important traits for flying are: (1) feathers, which are unique to birds; (2) powerful wings, which are modified upper limbs; (3) hollow bones; (4) warm-bloodedness; and (5) efficient respiratory and circulatory systems. These characteristics combine to produce animals with two overarching traits—high power and low weight, which are the twin dictates that make for successful feathered flying machines. (Bats, the flying mammals, also follow these dictates.)

Classification of Birds

Bird classification is one of those areas of science that continually undergoes revision. Currently about 9,700 separate species are recognized. They are divided into 28 to 30 orders, depending on whose classification scheme one follows, perhaps 170 families, and about 2,040 genera. For purposes here, we can divide birds into *passerines* and *nonpasserines*. Passerine birds (order Passeriformes) are the perching birds, with feet specialized to grasp and to perch on tree branches. They are mostly the small land birds (or *songbirds*) with which we are most familiar—blackbirds, robins, wrens, finches, sparrows, etc.—and the group includes more than 50% of all bird species. The remainder of the birds—seabirds and shorebirds, ducks and geese, hawks and owls, parrots and woodpeckers, and a host of others—are divided among the other 20 or so orders.

Australian Birds

About 740 bird species (348 passerine, 390 nonpasserine) occur in Australia, perhaps 7.5% of the world's total and approximately the same number that occur in North America north of Mexico. Some 350 of these species (47%) are endemic to the Australian region (includes New Guinea and New Zealand); many of the remainder are birds that migrate or wander over long distances and many continents—such as shorebirds and seabirds. There are some well-known bird groups that are absent from Australia, including flamingos, Old World vultures, hummingbirds, woodpeckers, true wrens, nuthatches, shrikes, true finches, titmice, and buntings. (The absence of woodpeckers is interesting; Australia is the only continent, aside from Antarctica, to lack them. Woodpeckers usually make the holes in trees that they and many other animals, which usually cannot excavate holes in wood, use as breeding sites. Ten of Australia's 21 duck species and 52 of its 55 parrots nest in tree holes. Who usually creates these holes? Termites!) What kinds of birds does Australia have? Are there some special types that birdwatchers and other visitors interested in wildlife look for? I don't qualify as a fanatic birder, but I can tell you that Australia has a good many spectacular birds that will thrill the ornithologically inclined.

1. *Flightless and big*. Australia has two large flightless birds that anyone interested in birds will want to see: the Emu, Australia's answer to Africa's Ostrich and the nation's bird emblem, standing up to 2 m (6.5 ft) tall, is still common and easy to see; and the Southern Cassowary, which is a bit smaller than the Emu and more difficult to observe—it is considered a vulnerable species in Australia. About ten penguin species occur in the cold waters south of Australia, but only one, the Little Penguin, is easily seen.

2. *Mound-builders*. Australia has three species of famous mound-builders, chicken-like birds that breed by constructing sometimes enormous mounds of leaves and other vegetation, placing their eggs within the mounds, and allowing the heat generated by the rotting vegetation to incubate the eggs. Two of these species, the Australian Brush-turkey and Orange-footed Scrubfowl, occur within this book's coverage area and are common.

3. *Parrots*. Australia has about 55 species of parrots, and some of the largest and most spectacular in the world. Many are common and easy to see; indeed, it is a rare day in eastern Australia when you will not have some encounter with them. Parrots in Central and South America are usually seen only high in the treetops; in Australia, they also like treetops, but they are also seen low in shrubs and even

on the ground in urban and suburban parks, schoolyards, and backyards. Your first good looks at Crimson Rosellas, Rainbow Lorikeets, Sulfur-crested and Black-cockatoos, and even Galahs, all of which are so common that many Australians probably regard them as "trash" or "pest" birds, will truly amaze you.

4. *Bowerbirds*. Bowerbirds are medium-sized birds, some of which are spectacularly colored, that are celebrated for their courtship activities: males build "bowers"—stick structures—and sometimes decorate them with special objects (in one species, blue objects) to attract females and convince them to mate. There are only 18 species of bowerbird, 8 in Australia, and 7 occur within this book's coverage area.

5. *Birds of Paradise*. Many bird fanciers consider the birds of paradise to be the most beautiful of the world's birds. Mid-sized to largish birds, many of them are fantastically colored and males often have very long ornamental tails. There are 43 species of birds of paradise, and the four that occur in Australia (which are not among the group's most gaudy and are known as riflebirds and manucodes) occur within this book's coverage area.

6. *Honeyeaters*. An interesting facet of Australian ecology is the large number of birds (and some mammals) that feed mainly on plant nectar (see Close-up, p. 192). One group of medium-sized birds, the honeyeaters, is especially numerous in Australia and in fact, in some parks on some days, it seems as if all the birds you see are honeyeaters. There are 170 species of honeyeaters, about half of which occur in Australia.

7. *Seabirds*. A good number of seabird species that fly occur over coastal Australia, but many stay far from land and are therefore seen only during cruises and other boat trips. (Seabirds can be divided into *inshore species,* which often inhabit coastal areas; *offshore species,* which mostly stay near continents but away from coastlines, feeding on fish in the shallow waters of the continental shelves; and *pelagic species,* which frequent the open ocean except when nesting on oceanic islands.) Many of these birds come ashore only to nest, and then usually not on the mainland but on small islands often unoccupied by people. Australia has numerous representatives of three main seabird orders: Procellariiformes (p. 120), or tube-nosed seabirds, such as albatrosses and shearwaters; Pelecaniformes (p. 123), pelican relatives such as boobies, cormorants, and frigatebirds; and Charadriiformes (p. 125), including the terns, gulls, and noddies.

Ecologically, Australia's land birds are known for their sedentariness, communal breeding, and breeding season lengths. Most of Australia's birds don't make the kind of long migrations that are a regular feature of birds in North America and Europe, for instance. Only 17% of Australian birds are migratory, whereas about 70% in Europe and 55% in North America are migratory. Communal breeding, in which a group of birds (not just a single pair), usually related, contribute (eggs and/or parenting efforts) to a single nest, is considered relatively rare among the world's birds, but is fairly common in Australia—34% of Australia's land birds are communal breeders. Breeding seasons for Australia's temperate-zone birds are usually longer than those of comparably sized birds in temperate areas on other continents; incubation and fledgling periods, in particular, are often longer. Reasons for these ecological differences are not known for sure, but researchers believe that they may all relate to the Australian birds' food supplies, most of which are obtained year-round from evergreen eucalypt forests with only weak seasonal changes in availability.

In Australia, many bird species are experiencing declining population sizes because of changing land-use patterns and deforestation. The IUCN Red List for Australia includes 26 bird species that are considered near-threatened, 20 that are vulnerable, 11 that are endangered, and 2 that are critically endangered (Orange-bellied Parrot, Night Parrot).

Seeing Birds in Australia

Illustrated in the color plates are 276 of eastern Australia's most common and conspicuous birds. The best way to spot many of Australia's birds is to follow three easy steps: (1) Look for them at the correct time. Birds can be seen at any time of day, but they are often very active during early morning and late afternoon, and so can be best detected and seen during these times. (2) Be quiet as you walk along trails or roads, and stop periodically to look around carefully. Not all birds are noisy, and some, even brightly colored ones, can be quite inconspicuous when they are directly above you in a forest canopy. (3) Bring binoculars on your trip. You would be surprised at the number of people who visit parks and reserves with the purpose of viewing wildlife and don't bother to bring binoculars. They need not be an expensive pair, but binoculars are essential to bird viewing.

Emus are seen along roadsides in inland livestock grazing areas and in many other kinds of habitats; Wilsons Promontory National Park in Victoria is a good place to spot them. The Southern Cassowary can be seen fairly regularly in its redoubt, the rainforests of northeastern Queensland. And for penguin aficionados, the Little Penguin, the world's smallest, can be seen in Victoria at Phillip Island Nature Park. For forest birds, simply visit parks, walk on trails, and look around. Megapodes are very common and easy to see in some places—for instance, at Lamington National Park (also good for bowerbirds) and the Atherton Tableland parks in northern Queensland. Cockatoos and other parrots will be seen everywhere.

Many visitors to eastern Australia spend at least part of their stay in coastal areas, and these are good places to spot seabirds and shorebirds. If they are a priority for you, taking a boat trip—perhaps out to the islands of the Great Barrier Reef—is a good idea. Many seabirds, the tubenoses in particular, rarely cruise the mainland, preferring to remain out at sea or around offshore islands. Staying on one of the Reef's islands for one or more nights will be a worthwhile bird experience—especially if noddies are nesting (trees can be filled with noddy nests) or shearwaters ("muttonbirds") are present (their dawn take-offs down sloped, sandy runways are amazing to watch).

If you have trouble locating the birds you'd like to see, ask people—national park personnel, tour guides, resort employees—about good places to see them; staying at lodges that cater to ecotravellers ("ecolodges") and arrange special hikes and tours can also be of help (see p. 28).

Family Profiles

Along Australia's coasts, as along coasts almost everywhere, *seabirds*, many of them conspicuously large and abundant, reign as the dominant vertebrate animals of the land, air, and water's surface. Many Australian seabirds commonly seen by visitors from northern temperate areas are very similar to species found back home, but some are members of groups restricted to the tropics or subtropics (or, in the case of albatrosses, mostly to the southern hemisphere) and, hence, should be of eco-traveller interest. A few of these birds, such as gulls and terns, will be seen by almost everyone. As a group, seabirds are incredibly successful animals, present often at breeding and roosting colonies in enormous numbers. Their success surely is owing to their incredibly rich food resources—the fish and invertebrate animals (crabs, mollusks, insects, jellyfish) produced in the sea and on beaches and mudflats.

1. Seabirds I: Tube-nosed Seabirds

The seabird order Procellariiformes includes the *albatrosses, shearwaters, petrels,* and *storm-petrels.* All are found only in marine (sea water) habitats, and they spend their entire lives at sea (a *pelagic* existence) except for short periods of nesting on islands. They are called "tube-nosed" seabirds because their nostrils emerge through tubes on the top or sides of their distinctly hooked upper bills. Like many seabirds, they have a large gland between and above their eyes that permits them to drink seawater; it filters salt from the water and concentrates it. This highly con-centrated salt solution is excreted in drops from the base of the bill, and the nostril tubes then direct the salt drops to the end of the bill, where they can be easily dis-charged. Some of these tube-nosed seabirds, or *tubenoses*, will be seen by visitors to the Great Barrier Reef and by people who take boat trips or fishing cruises off Australia's coasts, but tubenoses are only rarely seen from the mainland.

Family Procellariidae, with an essentially worldwide oceanic distribution, has 70 species of petrels and shearwaters, about 40 of which frequent Australian waters. The two profiled species, WEDGE-TAILED and SHORT-TAILED SHEARWATERS (both Plate 23), are among the few petrels and shearweaters that breed in Australia. Family Hydrobatidae contains the 20 species of small petrels known as storm-petrels; about 5 species occur regularly in Australian waters, but only one, the WHITE-FACED STORM-PETREL, breeds in Australia. Family Diomedeidae contains the 14 albatross species distributed over the world's southern oceans and the northern Pacific; about 10 occur in Australian waters, but only one, the SHY ALBATROSS, breeds around the mainland (on islands off Tasmania).

The tubenoses include the largest and smallest seabirds. Australia's tubenoses range from the huge WANDERING ALBATROSS, about 1 m (3.3 ft) long and with a wingspan to 3.5 m, 11.5 ft (the world's largest seabird), to the small WILSON'S STORM-PETREL (Plate 23), at 15 to 19 cm (6 to 7 in) and with a wingspan of about 40 cm (16 in). Albatrosses are large, heavy birds with very long wings and long, heavy, hooked bills. Shearwaters are small to mid-sized seabirds with slender, hooked bills. Petrels comprise a large group of mid- to large-sized seabirds with long wings. Storm-petrels are small, with proportionally shorter wings and longer legs than petrels and shearwaters. Tubenoses are often dark above and lighter below, although some are all dark; coloring is limited to black, brown, grey, and white.

Natural History

Ecology and Behavior

Albatrosses feed either solitarily or in small groups, on fish, squid, and other invertebrates (crabs, krill) near the surface at night and sometimes during the day. Larger species sit on the water and seize prey in their bills; smaller, more agile species can also seize prey from the surface while flying. Also, they are not above eating garbage thrown overboard from ships, as well as floating carrion such as dead whales and seals. They often go out to sea for several days to bring food back to nestlings. Albatrosses use a type of non-flapping flight, known as *dynamic soaring*, that takes advantage of strong winds blowing across the ocean's surface. Their efficient but peculiar soaring flight takes them in huge loops from high above the ocean surface, where the wind is fastest, down toward the surface, where friction slows the wind, and then up into the faster wind again to give them lift for the next loop—a kind of roller coaster flight that requires virtually no wing flapping. Albatross wings are so long and narrow that these birds literally need wind to help them fly, and on absolutely calm days (which, luckily, are rare on the open ocean) must wait out the windless hours sitting on the sea's surface. Even taking flight for these long-winged birds is problematic: in very windy conditions, whether they are on land or the water, they need only spread their wings, and the wind moving over and under the wings provides sufficient lift to make them airborne. But in low winds, they face into the wind (like an airplane taking off) and make a take-off run; at island breeding colonies, there are often actual "runways," long, clear paths on the island's windier sides, usually on slopes, along which the large birds make their downhill take-off runs (see below).

Petrels and shearwaters are often excellent flyers, some using dynamic soaring like albatrosses, some alternating flapping flight with gliding. They feed at sea by day or by night, often in groups, on squid, fish, and crustaceans. Some (particularly some storm-petrels) pluck prey from the surface of the sea using their wings to flutter and hover, with their legs extended, just above the water. Petrels and shearwaters are sometimes solitary, but some species tend to be seen in small to large flocks; some Short-tailed Shearwater flocks number in the millions. Petrels, shearwaters, and other tubenoses are ocean wanderers, often moving over huge distances; some, such as the Short-tailed Shearwater, breed in the Australian region, then wander to the northern Pacific.

Tubenoses have perhaps the best developed sense of smell of any birds, and they use this ability to locate young and nest sites when returning from extended foraging trips and also probably to locate some types of food. Tubenoses produce a vile-smelling stomach oil that they regurgitate to feed to nestlings and to squirt at enemies. (The oil reputedly makes an excellent suntan lotion, but its smell, I'm sure, would wreak havoc on your social life.)

Breeding

Tubenoses usually breed in large, dense colonies, often but not always on small oceanic islands. Albatrosses are monogamous and most breed with the same mate for life. On their remote breeding islands they engage in elaborate courtship dances in which male and female face each other, flick their wings, bounce their heads up and down, and clack their bills together. This behavior probably strengthens the pair-bond and also coordinates hormone release and synchronizes mating readiness. Nests vary from a scrape on the bare ground to scrapes that are surrounded by vegetation, soil, and pebbles. The female lays one large egg. Male and female alternately incubate and brood the young, in shifts lasting several days to weeks. The other adult flies out to sea and searches for food. When it returns, it feeds the chick regurgitated fish, squid, and stomach oil and takes over its turn at brooding again. When the chick's demand for food becomes overwhelming, both adults leave it alone for long periods as they search great distances over the ocean for enough food. At some points in its nestling period, a young albatross can actually weigh more than its parents. After about 7 months, the chick is large enough to fledge and fly. Albatrosses take 5 to 7 years to mature, staying at sea during this period before finally returning to their birthplace to breed. Many individuals do not breed until they are 7 to 9 years old; some albatrosses in the wild live over 40 years.

Petrel and shearwater breeding is similar to that of albatrosses. Some nest in the open, with nests simply small depressions in the ground, but most are burrow or cavity nesters, nesting in a burrow they dig themselves or take over, or in a natural cavity, such as rock cavities in cliffs. The burrow or cavity is reused each year by the same pair. One large egg is incubated for 6 to 9 weeks, with both parents incubating the egg and feeding and brooding the chick. These birds probably live an average of 15 to 20 years.

Storm-petrels, hole- or burrow-nesters, breed in colonies of a few dozen pairs to tens of thousands. One large egg is incubated by both parents, in shifts lasting 3 to 7 days, for about 40 days. The chick is fed a partially digested paste of small fish and crustaceans, eventually growing to outweigh its parents. It fledges at 7 to 11 weeks old; one night it leaves the nest burrow and flies out to sea. It probably does not come back to land for 2 to 4 years, until it begins to consider its love life.

Notes

A truly amazing sight you can experience on islands off Australia's east coast: the take-off runways of Short-tailed and Wedge-tailed Shearwaters (locally called *muttonbirds* because dense breeding colonies provided large amounts of human food in the form of the birds' chicks). During breeding seasons, these birds land on islands toward evening, then waddle to their nest burrows to spend the night. At dawn, they waddle to the island's shore, mill about in a crowd on a dune above the water, then one by one run down the slope of the dune toward the water, spread their wings, and fly. Given their long, narrow wings, they usually need the take-off run, like an airplane, to create enough lift to take to the air. Many islands in the Great Barrier Reef, such as Heron Island, seasonally have muttonbirds, and off Coffs Harbour is Muttonbird Island Nature Reserve.

Petrels get their name from the Greek word "petros," which refers to the biblical disciple Peter, who tried to walk on water, just as some storm-petrels appear to be doing when feeding (they have a fluttering flight low over the water's surface, and some species even patter their feet on the surface).

Sailors have long believed albatrosses contained the souls of lost comrades, so it was considered bad luck for one's ship and shipmates to kill one. Albatrosses are highly respected birds in many cultures, perhaps owing to their amazing flight capabilities, and killing them is frowned upon. Albatrosses are sometimes called *gooney birds* because of their awkwardness moving on land and the untidiness of their take-offs and landings (crashing into beach shrubbery is a common occurrence).

Status

Because of their often highly restricted nesting sites on small islands and vulnerability during the nesting period, many species of tubenoses are at risk. Albatrosses cannot become airborne readily from land and are easy victims for humans and introduced predators. Cats and rats, for instance, if carelessly released by people, can wreak havoc on an entire island's population of petrels. Albatrosses during the 1800s and early 1900s were widely killed for their feathers, and entire breeding colonies were destroyed. Two albatrosses are endangered, the AMSTERDAM and SHORT-TAILED ALBATROSSES. Both are restricted now to single breeding colonies. The New Zealand subspecies of the ROYAL ALBATROSS is also endangered. The subspecies of Wandering Albatross that occurs in Australian waters is considered endangered in some areas. About 20 species of petrels, shearwaters, and storm-petrels worldwide are currently endangered (IUCN Red List).

Profiles

Wedge-tailed Shearwater, *Puffinus pacificus,* Plate 23a
Short-tailed Shearwater, *Puffinus tenuirostris,* Plate 23b
Wilson's Storm-Petrel, *Oceanites oceanicus,* Plate 23c

2. Seabirds II: Pelicans and Allies (Frigatebirds, Boobies, and Cormorants)

The large seabirds treated in this section are all members of order Pelecaniformes. (1) *Pelicans,* family Pelecanidae (8 species worldwide, only one in Australian waters) are fishing birds familiar to most people because of their large throat sacs, or "pouches." (2) *Boobies* and *gannets* (family Sulidae, 9 species worldwide, 5 occurring off Australian shores) are large, straight-billed seabirds known for their sprawling, densely packed breeding colonies, spots of bright coloring, and for plunging into the ocean from heights to pursue fish. They have tapered bodies, long pointed wings, long tails, long pointed bills, and, often, brightly colored feet. Gannets, mostly southern temperate-water birds, are very similar to boobies but have shorter tails. (3) *Cormorants* (family Phalacrocoracidae, with about 35 species, 5 around Australia), with long necks and long bills with hooked tips, inhabit coasts and inland waterways over much of the world, diving for and swimming after fish. (4) *Darters* (and *anhingas;* family Anhingidae, with 4 species, one in Australia), closely related to cormorants, are fresh- and brackish-water birds mostly of tropical and subtropical regions; they have long necks with long, sharply pointed bills that they use to spear fish. (5) *Frigatebirds* (family Fregatidae, 5 species with mainly tropical distributions, 3 around Australia), are very large soaring birds, black or black and white with huge pointed wings that span up to 2 m (6.5 ft) or more, and long, forked tails. Males have red throat pouches that they inflate, balloon-like, during courtship displays.

Natural History

Ecology and Behavior

Most seabirds feed mainly on fish and have developed a variety of ways to catch them. Pelicans eat fish almost exclusively. AUSTRALIAN PELICANS (Plate 23) feed as they swim along the water's surface, using the throat sac as a net to scoop up fish (to 30 cm, 1 ft, long). Captured fish are quickly swallowed because the water in the sac with the fish usually weighs enough to prohibit the bird's lifting off from the water. Often, groups of pelicans herd fish, trap them between birds, then grab. Pelicans, though ungainly looking, are nonetheless excellent flyers and can use air updrafts to soar high above in circles for hours. These are large, handsome birds; a flight of them, passing low and slow overhead on a beach, in perfect V-formation or in a single line, is a tremendous sight. Of special note is that adult pelicans are largely silent, although grunts and croaks are occasionally heard. Boobies, which also eat squid, plunge-dive from the air (from heights of up to 15 m, 50 ft, or more) or surface-dive to catch fish underwater. Sometimes they dive quite deeply, and they often take fish unawares from below as they rise toward the surface. Unlike most other birds, boobies do not have holes or nostrils at the base of the upper bill for breathing; the holes are closed over to keep seawater from rushing into their lungs as they plunge-dive.

Diving from the surface of lakes, rivers, lagoons, and coastal saltwater areas, cormorants and DARTERS (both Plate 24) pursue fish underwater, mainly using their feet for propulsion. Cormorants, which take crustaceans also, catch food in their bills; darters, which also take other aquatic animals such as small turtles, use their sharply pointed bills to spear fish. Cormorants are social birds, foraging, roosting, and nesting in groups, but darters are less social and sometimes solitary. Both cormorants and darters are known for standing on logs, trees, or other surfaces after diving and spreading their wings, presumably to dry them (they may also be warming their bodies in the sun following dives into cold water). Frigatebirds feed on the wing, soaring effortlessly sometimes for hours at a time. They swoop low to catch flying fish that leap from the water (the fish leap when they are pursued by larger predatory fish or dolphins) and also to pluck squid and jellyfish from the wavetops, but they also commonly steal food (see below). They even drink by flying low over the water's surface and sticking their long bill into the water. Although their lives are tied to the sea, frigatebirds cannot swim and rarely, if ever, enter the water voluntarily; with their very long, narrow wings, they have difficulty lifting off from the water. To rest, they land on remote islands, itself a problematic act in the high winds that are common in these places.

Ecological Interactions

Frigatebirds, large and beautiful, are a treat to watch as they glide silently along coastal areas, but they have some highly questionable habits—in fact, patterns of behavior that among humans would be indictable offenses. Frigatebirds practice *kleptoparasitism:* they "parasitize" other seabirds, such as boobies, frequently chasing them in the air until they drop recently caught fish. The frigatebird then steals the fish, catching it in mid-air as it falls. Frigatebirds are also common predators of baby sea turtles (p. 91), scooping them from beaches as the reptiles make their post-hatching dashes to the ocean.

Breeding

Pelican allies usually breed in large colonies on small oceanic islands (where there are no mammal predators) or in isolated mainland areas that are relatively free of predators. Some breed on cliffs or ledges (some boobies and cormorants), some in trees or on tops of shrubs (frigatebirds, some boobies and cormorants, darters), and some on the bare ground (pelicans, most boobies, and frigatebirds if their preferred nesting sites are unavailable). Where people have introduced small mammals such as rats, which feed on seabird eggs and nestlings, to breeding islands, reproductive success is often dramatically reduced. Most species are monogamous, mated males and females sharing in nest-building, incubation, and feeding young. High year-to-year fidelity to mates, to breeding islands, and to particular nest sites is common. AUSTRALIAN PELICANS lay 1 to 4 eggs, which are incubated for about 35 days; usually only one young is raised successfully. Booby females usually lay 1 or 2 eggs, which are incubated for about 45 days. Usually only a single chick survives to fledging age (one chick often pecks the other to death; p. 134). Cormorants and darters produce and incubate 1 to 5 eggs for about 4 weeks, and young fledge 5 to 8 weeks after hatching. Frigatebirds lay a single egg that is incubated for about 50 days; male and female take turns during incubation, taking shifts of up to 12 days. Young remain in and around the nest, dependent on the parents, for up to 6 months or more. In most seabirds, young are fed when they push their bills into their parents' throats, in effect forcing the parent to regurgitate food stored in its *crop*—an enlargement of the top portion of the esophagus. Seabirds reach sexual maturity slowly (in 2 to 5 years in boobies, 7 or more years in frigatebirds) and live long lives (frigatebirds and boobies live 20 or more years in the wild).

Notes

The term *booby* apparently arose because the nesting and roosting birds seemed so bold and fearless toward people, which was considered stupid. Actually, the fact that these birds bred on isolated islands and cliffs meant that they had few natural predators, so had never developed, or had lost, fear responses to large mammals such as people. Frigatebirds are also known as *man-of-war* birds, both names referring to warships and to the birds' kleptoparasitism; they also steal nesting materials from other birds, furthering the image of avian pirates.

Status

Most of the seabirds that occur in Australian waters, including boobies, cormorants, and frigatebirds, are quite abundant and not considered threatened. ABBOT'S BOOBY, now limited to a single, small breeding population on the Indian Ocean's Christmas Island, is endangered (CITES Appendix I, IUCN Red List). Two of the frigatebirds, the CHRISTMAS ISLAND FRIGATEBIRD (CITES Appendix I, IUCN Red List) and ASCENSION FRIGATEBIRD, are threatened or endangered.

Profiles

Lesser Frigatebird, *Fregata ariel,* Plate 23d
Australian Pelican, *Pelecanus conspicillatus,* Plate 23e
Australasian Gannet, *Morus serrator,* Plate 24a
Darter, *Anhinga melanogaster,* Plate 24b
Brown Booby, *Sula leucogaster,* Plate 24c
Great Cormorant, *Phalacrocorax carbo,* Plate 24d
Little Black Cormorant, *Phalacrocorax sulcirostris,* Plate 24e
Little Pied Cormorant, *Phalacrocorax melanoleucos,* Plate 24f

3. Seabirds III: Gulls, Terns, and Noddies

The most common and conspicuous birds over mainland seacoasts and near-shore and offshore islands almost anywhere are *gulls* and *terns*. These highly gregarious seabirds—they feed, roost, and breed in large groups—are also common in offshore waters and even, in certain species, inland. Family Laridae (about 100 species worldwide), which is allied with the shorebirds (p. 136) in order Charadriiformes, includes the gulls, terns, *noddies*, and *jaegers* (often called *skuas*). The approximately 45 species of gulls (6 species in Australia) are distributed worldwide, but they are mainly birds of cooler ocean waters, and even of inland continental areas. Few occur in the tropics or around isolated, oceanic islands. Gulls generally are large white and grey seabirds with fairly long, narrow wings, squarish tails, and sturdy, slightly hooked bills. Many have a blackish head, or *hood*, during breeding seasons. The 40 or so tern species are distributed throughout the world's oceans; about 20 species occur in and around Australia. Terns (and noddies, which are a type of tern) are often smaller and more delicate-looking than gulls. They have a slender, light build, long, pointed wings, a deeply forked tail, a slender, tapered bill, and webbed feet. They are often grey above and white below, with a blackish head during breeding. Noddies are dark birds with lighter crowns and have broader wings and tails than do other terns. Five of the seven species of jaegers, dark, gull-sized birds known for their predatory habits, and mostly birds of the polar seas, occur regularly or occasionally in Australian waters. Finally, two of the world's seven *oystercatchers* (family Haematopodidae in order Charadriiformes), also gull-like birds, occur around Australian shores. Their red bills are flattened side-to-side and used like a shucking knife to open clams and other mollusks. The PIED OYSTERCATCHER's (Plate 32) black-and-white plumage, together with its red legs and bill, makes it easy to identify.

Natural History

Ecology and Behavior

Gulls and terns feed on fish and other sealife that they snatch from shallow water, and on crabs and other invertebrates they find on mudflats and beaches, often in the intertidal zone. Also, they are not above visiting garbage dumps or following fishing boats to grab whatever goodies that fall or are thrown overboard. They also scavenge what they can, taking bird eggs and nests from seabird breeding colonies when parents are gone or inattentive. Gulls also follow tractors during plowing, grabbing whatever insects and other small animals flush from cover when the big machines go by. Many larger gulls also chase smaller gulls and terns in the air to steal food the smaller birds have caught—kleptoparasitism. Terns, which eat mainly fish, squid, and crustaceans, feed during the day but also sometimes at night (like the SOOTY TERN, Plate 33) Their main food-gathering technique is a bit messy: they spot prey near the water's surface while flying or hovering, plunge-dive into the water to grab the prey, then rapidly take off again, the prey held tightly in the bill. Some terns, such as the Sooty Tern, feed more frequently by simply flying low and slow over the water and picking prey from the water's surface. Most terns seem to fly continuously, rarely setting down on the water to rest. They are often distinguished from other seabirds by their continually flapping flight. Jaegers have a reputation of being predatory birds: in addition to catching and eating fish, they also take small seabirds and, from the land, seabird nestlings, newly hatched sea turtles, and even small rodents such as lemmings. They are also well known for their kleptoparasitism. Oystercatchers use their strong, flattened bills to pry open oysters, clams, and other bivalve mollusks, and also to pry and dismember various other marine invertebrates (gastropods, crustaceans) from rocky shorelines.

Ecological Interactions

Many gulls have a commensal relationship (p. 60) with people. They make good feeding use of human-altered landscapes and human activities, such as garbage dumps, agricultural fields, and fishing boats. Human activities have reduced the populations of many other bird groups, but people's exploitation of marine and coastal areas has, in many cases, enhanced rather than hurt seabird populations.

In fact, many gull species worldwide are almost certainly more numerous today than at any time in the past. For instance, one of the most common birds you will see around coastal cities and towns in Australia is the SILVER GULL (Plate 32), which lives largely by scavenging garbage.

Breeding

These seabirds usually breed in large colonies, often in the tens of thousands, on small islands where there are no mammal predators, or in isolated mainland areas that are also relatively free of predators. Gulls and terns usually breed on flat, open ground near the water (but some breed on cliffs, or inland in marsh areas, and noddies breed in trees, bushes, or cliffs). Most species are monogamous, mated males and females sharing in nest-building, incubation, and feeding young. Gulls and terns typically lay 1 to 3 eggs, and both sexes incubate for 21 to 30 days; young fledge after 28 to 35 days at the nest. Young are fed when they push their bill into their parent's throat, in effect forcing the parent to regurgitate food stored in its *crop*—an enlargement of the top portion of the esophagus. These seabirds reach sexual maturity slowly, often not achieving their full adult, or breeding, plumage until they are 3 to 4 years old (terns) or 4 to 5 years old (gulls).

Status

Most gulls, terns, jaegers, and oystercatchers are abundant seabirds and, as noted earlier, some species have even been able to capitalize on peoples' activities and during the past few hundred years have succeeded in expanding their numbers and breeding areas. BLACK NODDIES (Plate 33), for instance, which nest in trees, started nesting in large numbers on several small islands in the Hawaiian Island chain only during the mid-20th century, when landscape modification by the military resulted in trees growing where none had been before. A few tern species are considered vulnerable to threat or already endangered over various parts of Australia. For example, LITTLE TERNS and FAIRY TERNS are increasingly rare in southeast Australia, the declines mostly owing to people disturbing their beach nesting sites. The Fairy Tern population in Australia is estimated as only about 2,000 breeding pairs. The SOOTY OYSTERCATCHER, endemic to Australia, is not truly threatened, but is considered vulnerable in New South Wales, and its total population may number less than 5,000.

Profiles

Pied Oystercatcher, *Haematopus longirostris,* Plate 32a
Pacific Gull, *Larus pacificus,* Plate 32b
Silver Gull, *Larus novaehollandiae,* Plate 32c
Roseate Tern, *Sterna dougallii,* Plate 32d
Crested Tern, *Sterna bergii,* Plate 32e
Sooty Tern, *Sterna fuscata,* Plate 33a
Common Tern, *Sterna hirundo,* Plate 33b
Whiskered Tern, *Chlidonias hybridus,* Plate 33c
Common Noddy, *Anous stolidus,* Plate 33d
Black Noddy, *Anous minutus,* Plate 33e

4. Penguins

The 17 species of the *penguin* family (Spheniscidae) are all restricted to the southern hemisphere, with one species on the equator in the Galápagos Islands. The largest species stands 1 m (3 ft) tall and the smallest, only 40 cm (16 in). All are flightless and use their highly modified wings for propulsion underwater. These wings are unique in that, unlike in other birds, the bones are fused together and the wings cannot be folded. The feathers that cover the penguins' bodies and wings are small and dense, looking more like large scales than proper feathers. Their feet are placed far back on the body, and they have webbing between the toes and long sharp nails. The feet are used for steering and braking underwater and for clambering up steep and slippery slopes when going ashore. Most species are highly social, with great numbers of individuals foraging together at sea and breeding in colonies.

The LITTLE PENGUIN (Plate 22), endemic to Australia and New Zealand and the world's smallest of its kind (40 to 45 cm, 16 to 18 in, tall; 1 kg, 2.2 lb), is the only penguin seen regularly by travellers to Australia—because of the famous "Penguin Parade" on Victoria's Phillip Island (see p. 44). Most of the other ten penguin species that occur in Australian waters are seen only very rarely. One, the ROCKHOPPER PENGUIN, is a moderately common visitor to Australia's southern coast; it is easily distinguished from the plain black-and-white Little Penguin by its larger size, light eye-stripe, and crest.

Natural History

Ecology and Behavior
Little Penguins are not as social as some other penguins and often feed alone. They eat fish, squid, and crustaceans, all of which they capture in their strong, sharp bills after underwater pursuit. Their mouths are lined with rear-facing spines that help them hold onto and swallow slippery and wiggling prey. Although some large penguin species in the Antarctic can dive to depths of nearly 275 m (900 ft) and stay under for almost 20 minutes, the Little Penguins stay under for briefer periods and dive only to depths of about 70 m (230 ft).

Breeding
The Little Penguin is the only penguin that occurs in Australia that breeds there, on sandy or rocky islands off the southern coast. Breeding takes place at various times of year depending on location. Nests are burrows in sandy areas or in natural cracks or cavities. The eggs (1–2) are incubated by both male and female, in shifts lasting 6 hours to several days, for about 35 days. Parents return from foraging trips at dusk to feed young on shore by regurgitating food caught at sea. Young fledge and begin to care for themselves at 50 to 55 days old, and reach sexual maturity in 2 or 3 years.

Status
Most penguin species are not globally threatened, but two or three species are endangered because of their restricted ranges. For instance, the YELLOW-EYED PENGUIN, which breeds only over small areas of New Zealand, the total population of which is less than 10,000, causes concern; likewise, the HUMBOLDT PENGUIN (CITES Appendix I listed) breeds only along the coast of Peru and northern Chile, and there are probably fewer than 10,000 individuals. Although the Little Penguin is sensitive to human disturbance, its population size is estimated to be about one million.

Profile
Little Penguin, *Eudyptula minor,* Plate 22f

5. Ducks, Geese, and Grebes

Members of family Anatidae are universally recognized as ducks, geese, and swans. These 150 species or so of water-associated birds are distributed throughout the world in habitats ranging from open seas to high mountain lakes. Although an abundant, diverse group throughout most temperate regions of the globe, ducks and geese, or *waterfowl* (*wildfowl* to the British), have only limited representation in most tropical areas. About 22 species occur in Australia, essentially all of them in the covered region. Most of the 22 breed in Australia; the remainder are migratory, breeding on other continents and only passing through Australia or spending time there during nonbreeding months. Ducks, geese, and swans vary quite a bit in size and coloring, but all share the same major traits: duck bills, webbed toes, short tails, and long, slim necks. Plumage color and patterning vary, but there is a preponderance within the group of greys and browns and black and white, although many species have at least small patches of bright color. In some species males and females look alike, but in others there are many differences between the sexes.

Many ecotravellers who are not birdwatchers often ignore ducks and geese because they have similar birds in their own countries. However, Australia has some common, beautiful members of this group that you might want to take a look at, including BLACK SWANS (Plate 21; large, black with white wing tips and red bill; the only nearly all-black swan), MAGPIE GEESE (Plate 21; black and white with knobbed head and orange legs), AUSTRALIAN SHELDUCKS (Plate 21; striking black with chestnut and white patches and green on their wings), and PACIFIC BLACK DUCKS (Plate 22; dark brown, wild in most regions but tame in urban ponds). The MALLARD, naturally distributed around the northern hemisphere and probably the world's most abundant duck, has been introduced to southeastern Australia and Tasmania.

Grebes, often mistaken for small ducks, are actually members of a different family (Podicipedidae), one only very distantly related. The 20 or so grebe species are distributed nearly globally (none occur in the high Arctic or Antarctic, or on some oceanic islands). They are fully aquatic and built to dive and swim well underwater. They have short wings, very little tail, legs placed well back on their bodies, and lobed toes (but not fully webbed) that aid in propulsion underwater. Bills are usually sharp-pointed, not duck-like. Male and female grebes look alike or nearly so. Of Australia's three grebes, the AUSTRALASIAN GREBE (Plate 22), at only about 25 cm (10 in) long, is the smallest and also the most common.

Natural History

Ecology and Behavior

Ducks are birds of wetlands, spending most of their time in or near the water. Many of the typical ducks are divided into *divers* and *dabblers*. Diving ducks plunge underwater for their food; dabblers, such as Australian Shelducks, Pacific Black Ducks, Black Swans, Mallards, and *teal* (Plate 22) take food from the surface of the water or put their heads down into the water to reach food at shallow depths. Ducks mostly eat aquatic plants or small fish, but some forage on land for seeds and other plant materials. Magpie Geese, for instance, feed mainly on rushes and other plants they find growing in open areas and dried-up swamps (they probably prefer open habitats for feeding so they can constantly scan for predators, such as Dingos). Australian Shelducks, which sometimes occur in flocks of hundreds or even thousands, graze on plants both on shore and in shallow water. Pacific Black Ducks eat both plants, water plants and those growing along the water's edge, and animals, mostly aquatic insects and crustaceans. Swans forage for vegetation mainly in the water.

Breeding
Ducks place their nests on the ground in thick vegetation or in holes. Typically nests are lined with downy feathers that the female plucks from her own breast. Among many of the ducks, females perform most of the breeding duties, including incubation of the 2 to 16 eggs and shepherding and protecting the ducklings. Some of these birds, however, particularly among the geese and swans, have lifelong marriages during which male and female share equally in breeding duties. The young are *precocial*, able to run, swim, and feed themselves soon after they hatch.

Status
Most Australian ducks are abundant animals, their populations secure, but a few are currently rare, threatened, or endangered, at least in some regions. The FRECKLED DUCK, an Australian endemic, is on the IUCN Red List and is considered vulnerable over most of its range in Australia and endangered in Western Australia. The COTTON PYGMY-GOOSE is rare and possibly threatened over its Australian range in the northeast part of the country (but its range extends to other countries, as well). The Magpie Goose, still abundant in Australia's northern plains, was eliminated during the past 200 years from southern Australia, mostly owing to use of its habitat for agriculture. Its swamps were drained to make arable land, cattle destroyed more swamps and ate the goose's plant food, and farmers shot geese that ate their crops.

Profiles
Magpie Goose, *Anseranas semipalmata*, Plate 21a
Black Swan, *Cygnus atratus*, Plate 21b
Australian Shelduck, *Tadorna tadornoides*, Plate 21c
Cape Barren Goose, *Cereopsis novaehollandiae*, Plate 21d
Australian Wood Duck, *Chenonetta jubata*, Plate 21e
Plumed Whistling-duck, *Dendrocygna eytoni*, Plate 21f
Pacific Black Duck, *Anas superciliosa*, Plate 22a
Grey Teal, *Anas gracilis*, Plate 22b
Chestnut Teal, *Anas castanea*, Plate 22c
Hardhead, *Aythya australis*, Plate 22d
Australasian Grebe, *Tachybaptus novaehollandiae*, Plate 22e

6. Marsh and Stream Birds

Marsh and *stream* birds are a collection of unrelated small, medium-sized, and large birds adapted to walk, feed, and breed in swamps, marshes, wet fields, and along waterways. The chief characteristics permitting this lifestyle, for most of the smaller birds, are long legs and very long toes that distribute the birds' weight, allowing them to walk among marsh plants and across floating vegetation without sinking. A few of the species in this group (*native hens, bustards*), however, spend much or all of their time on land. Order Ciconiiformes, which also includes herons, contains the *ibises, spoonbills,* and *storks*. The 33 species of ibises and spoonbills (family Threskiornthidae), largish, long necked, heavy-billed wading birds, are globally distributed; three ibises and two spoonbill species occur in Australia. Storks (family Ciconiidae), very large wading birds (some nearly as tall as a person), occur worldwide in tropical and temperate regions; there are 17 species, but only one, the BLACK-NECKED STORK (also called Jabiru; Plate 26), occurs in Australia.

Order Gruiformes includes the *cranes, rails, coots,* and bustards. There are 15 species of cranes (family Gruidae), which occur on all continents but South America. These are large, long-necked and long-legged wading birds that stride across prairies and wetlands. Most cranes have a patch of red, naked skin on top of their head. Two species of cranes occur in Australia, but only one, the BROLGA (Plate 26), is widespread. The rails (family Rallidae) are a large group of often secretive, skulking small and medium-sized swamp and dense vegetation birds, about 130 species strong. They inhabit most parts of the world save for polar regions. Sixteen species occur in Australia, including rails, *crakes, native-hens, moorhen, swamphen,* and coots. Most of these *rallids* are shades of grey or brown, which helps them blend in with their marsh habitats, but some larger ones, such as the PURPLE SWAMPHEN (Plate 29), are brightly colored. The AUSTRALIAN BUSTARD (family Otididae; Plate 30), one of 20 or so bustards (which occur mostly over Africa) and the only one in Australia, is a large brown-and-white bird that inhabits grassland areas.

Finally, *jacanas* (jha-SAH-nahs or jah-KAH-nahs; family Jacanidae, in the same order, Charadriiformes, as the shorebirds and gulls) are small and medium-sized birds with amazingly long toes and toenails that stalk about tropical marshes throughout the world. There are 8 species; only one occurs in Australia, but it is found over most of the eastern half of the country wherever there is floating aquatic vegetation. Female jacanas are larger than males. In most species of Australian marsh and water birds, male and female look alike or nearly so.

Natural History

Ecology and Behavior

Ibises are gregarious birds that insert their long bills into the soft mud of marshes and shore areas and poke about for food—insects, snails, crabs, frogs, and tadpoles. Apparently they feed by touch, not vision; whatever the bill contacts that feels like food is grabbed and swallowed. Spoonbills, likewise, are gregarious birds that feed in marsh or shallow-water habitats. They lower their bills into the water and sweep them around, stirring up the mud, then grab fish, frogs, snails, or crustaceans that touch their bills. Storks feed by walking slowly through fields and marshy areas, looking for suitable prey, essentially anything that moves: small rodents, young birds, frogs, reptiles, fish, earthworms, mollusks, crustaceans, and insects. Food is grabbed with the tip of the bill and swallowed quickly. Storks can be found either alone or, if food is plentiful in an area, in groups. These birds are excellent flyers, often soaring high overhead for hours during hot afternoons. Some stork species are known to fly 80 km (50 mi) or more daily between roosting or nesting sites and feeding areas. Cranes, such as the Brolga, forage by walking slowly and steadily in water or on swampy ground; they eat both plant materials and small animals. Cranes, like storks, soar to great heights. They are seen both solitarily and in groups.

Rails, coots, swamphens, and moorhens stalk through marshes, swamps, grassy shores, and wet grasslands, foraging for insects, small fish and frogs, bird eggs and chicks, and berries. Many of them move with a head-bobbing walk.

Many rails are highly secretive, being heard but rarely seen moving about in marshes. Native-hens (there are only two species, both of which are Australian endemics) live in grassy and swampy areas in small groups, often near water. They eat shoots and other plant parts, insects, and snails. The TASMANIAN NATIVE-HEN (Plate 29) is flightless and runs to escape danger. Jacanas are abundant near marshes, ponds, and lakeshores. Weak flyers, they walk along, often on top of floating plants, picking up insects, snails, small frogs and fish, and some vegetable matter such as seeds. Bustards, although they can fly, and do so when necessary, are primarily *cursorial* birds—they walk and run along the ground. With their brown, grey, and white plumage patterns, they are usually well camouflaged as they move over the ground searching for seeds, invertebrates, and small vertebrates such as lizards and mice.

Breeding
Breeding in marsh and stream birds varies considerably from group to group. COMB-CRESTED JACANAS (Plate 29) are one of three or four jacana species that employ *polyandrous* breeding, the rarest type of mating system among birds. In a breeding season, a female mates with several males, and the males then carry out most of the breeding chores. Males each defend small territories of floating vegetation from other males, but each female has a larger territory that encompasses one to three male territories. Males build nests of floating, compacted aquatic vegetation. Following mating, the female lays 3 or 4 eggs in the nest, after which the male incubates them for about 28 days and then cares for (leads and protects) the chicks. Young are dependent on the father for up to 2 months. Meanwhile, the female has mated with other males on her territory and provided each with a clutch of eggs to attend. The mating system of the Tasmanian Native-hen varies from monogamy to polyandry. Often there is a breeding group of 2 males and 1 female. A woven cup of grass and reeds is placed in thick vegetation near water. Eggs (3 to 9) are incubated in turns, for 19 to 25 days, by all members of the group, sometimes including young from previous years that are assisting their parents. The precocial chicks are then cared for by the group for 6 to 8 weeks until they are independent. Brolga pairs share breeding duties. Two eggs are incubated for 4 weeks and chicks remain in the nest, a large mound of grasses and stems, for about 100 days after hatching. Ibises and spoonbills, monogamous and nesting in colonies or solitarily, make stick nests, sometimes mixed with green vegetation, in bushes and trees. The eggs (1–4) are incubated for about 3 weeks, and young fledge 4 to 7 weeks after hatching. Australian Bustards are polygamous, males giving elaborate courtship displays to attract females and convince them to mate. After mating, females depart and nest alone. The eggs (1–2) are laid on bare ground, and incubated for 3.5 weeks until hatching.

Notes
Jacanas of Australia and Africa are also known as *lily-trotters* and *lotus-birds*. The word *jacana* is from a native Brazilian name for the bird. The term "skinny as a rail" refers originally not to a railroad track but to the bird. Rails are extremely flattened from side to side so they can fit into narrow spaces—hence the saying.

Status
Most of Australia's marsh and stream birds are abundant and secure. Although not really threatened, the Black-necked Stork is considered vulnerable in New South

Wales, and the Brolga is classified as vulnerable in New South Wales and South Australia. The Australian Bustard is much less common today than in the past. A hundred years ago, groups of 50 or more bustards were common in open areas over much of the continent. Now bustards are absent from most of southern Australia, chased out of some areas by human settlement and from others by use of their grassland habitats by sheep and rabbits. Small groups of bustards are now usually seen only in drier parts of northern Australia. The species is considered endangered in New South Wales and Victoria, and vulnerable in South Australia.

Profiles

Buff-banded Rail, *Gallirallus philippensis,* Plate 29a
Purple Swamphen, *Porphyrio porphyrio,* Plate 29b
Tasmanian Native-hen, *Gallinula mortierii,* Plate 29c
Dusky Moorhen, *Gallinula tenebrosa,* Plate 29d
Eurasian Coot, *Fulica atra,* Plate 29e
Comb-crested Jacana, *Irediparra gallinacea,* Plate 29f
Australian White Ibis, *Threskiornis molucca,* Plate 26c
Royal Spoonbill, *Platalea regia,* Plate 26d
Black-necked Stork (Jabiru), *Ephippiorhynchus asiaticus,* Plate 26e
Brolga, *Grus rubicunda,* Plate 26f
Australian Bustard, *Ardeotis australis,* Plate 30b

7. Herons and Egrets

Herons and *egrets* are beautiful medium- to large-sized wading birds that enjoy broad distributions throughout temperate and tropical regions of both hemispheres. Herons and egrets, together with the similar but quite elusive wading birds called *bitterns,* constitute the heron family, Ardeidae, which includes about 60 species. (Ardeidae is included in order Ciconiiformes, along with ibises, spoonbills, and storks.) Fourteen species occur in Australia; all 14 are found in this book's coverage area. Herons frequent all sorts of aquatic habitats: along rivers and streams, in marshes and swamps, and along lake and ocean shorelines. They are, in general, highly successful birds, and some of them are among Australia's most conspicuous and commonly seen water birds. Why some in the family are called herons and some egrets, well, it's a mystery, but egrets are usually all white and tend to have longer *nuptial plumes*—special long feathers—than the darker-colored herons.

Most herons and egrets are easy to identify. They are the tallish birds standing upright and still in shallow water or along the shore, staring intently into the water. They have slender bodies, long necks (often coiled when perched or still, producing a short-necked, hunched appearance), long, pointed bills, and long legs with long toes. In Australia, birds in this group range in height from 0.3 to 1.1 m (1 to 3.6 ft). Most colorings include soft shades of grey, blue, brown, and black and white. From afar most are not striking, but close-up, many are exquisitely marked with small colored patches of facial skin or broad areas of spots or streaks; some of the bitterns (three species in Australia) in particular have strongly barred or streaked plumages. Some species during breeding seasons have a few very long feathers (nuptial plumes) trailing down their bodies from the head, neck, back, or chest. The sexes are generally alike in size and plumage, or nearly so.

Natural History

Ecology and Behavior

Herons and egrets walk about slowly and stealthily in shallow water and sometimes on land, searching for their prey, mostly small vertebrates, including fish, frogs, the occasional turtle, and small invertebrates like crabs. On land, they take mostly insects, but also other invertebrates and vertebrates such as small rodents. CATTLE EGRETS (Plate 25) have made a specialty of following grazing cattle and other large mammals, walking along and grabbing insects and small vertebrates that are flushed from their hiding places by the moving cattle. A typical pasture scene is a flock of these egrets intermixed among a cattle herd, with several of the white birds perched atop the unconcerned mammals. Many herons spend most of their foraging time as *sit-and-wait* predators, standing motionless in or adjacent to the water, waiting in ambush for unsuspecting prey to wander within striking distance. Then, in a flash, they shoot their long, pointed bills into the water to grab or spear the prey. Herons will also slowly stalk prey and, occasionally, even actively pursue it. They take anything edible that will fit into their mouths and down their throats, and then some. One particular heron that I recall grabbed a huge frog in its bill and spent half an hour trying to swallow it. Typically, the larger herons are easier to spot because they tend to stay out in the open while foraging and resting; smaller herons, easier prey for predators, tend to stay more hidden in dense vegetation in marshy areas. Most herons are day-active, but many of the subgroup known as *night herons* forage at least partly nocturnally. Most herons are social birds, roosting and breeding in colonies, but some, such as Australia's STRIATED HERON, are predominantly solitary.

Ecological Interactions

Herons and egrets often lay more eggs than the number of chicks they can feed. For instance, many lay three eggs when there is sufficient food around to feed only two chicks. This is contrary to our usual view of nature, which we regard as having adjusted animal behavior through evolution so that behaviors are finely tuned to avoid waste. Here's what biologists suspect goes on: Females lay eggs one or two days apart, and start incubating before they finish laying all their eggs. The result is that chicks hatch at intervals of one or more days, so the chicks in a single nest are different ages and different sizes. In years of food shortage, the smallest chick dies because it cannot compete for food from the parents against its larger siblings, and also because, it has been discovered, the larger siblings attack it (behavior called *siblicide*). The habit of laying more eggs than can be reared as chicks may be an insurance game evolved by the birds to maximize their number of young; in many years, true, they waste the energy they invested to produce third eggs that have little future, but if food is plentiful, all three chicks survive and prosper. Apparently, the chance to produce three surviving offspring is worth the risk of investing in three eggs even though the future of one is very uncertain.

Breeding

Most herons breed in monogamous pairs within breeding colonies of various sizes. A few species are solitary nesters and some are less monogamous than others (such as the AUSTRALASIAN BITTERN, which often appears to be polygynous). Herons are known for their elaborate courtship displays and ceremonies, which continue through pair formation and nest-building. Nests are often constructed by the female out of sticks procured and presented to her by the male (males of some species also particpate in nest-building). Nests are placed in trees or reeds or on the ground. Both sexes incubate the 3 to 7 eggs for 16 to 30 days, and both feed the chicks for 35 to 50 days before the young can leave the nest and feed themselves. The young are *altricial*—born helpless; they are raised on regurgitated food from the parents.

Notes

The story of the phoenix, a bird that dies or is burned but then rises again from the ashes, is one of the best-known bird myths of the Western world. One version, from about 2,800 years ago, has it that one phoenix arrives from Arabia every 500 years. When it is old, it builds a nest of spices in which to die. From the remains a young phoenix emerges, which carries its parent's bones to the sun. Some authorities believe that the phoenix was a heron; in fact, the Egyptian hieroglyph for the phoenix appears to be a heron or egret.

The Cattle Egret is a common, successful, medium-sized white heron that, until recently, was confined to Africa and southern Asia, where it made its living following herds of large mammals. What is so interesting about this species is that, whereas many of the animals that have recently crossed oceans and spread rapidly into new continents have done so as a result of people's intentional or unintentional machinations, these egrets did it themselves. Apparently the first ones to reach the New World were from Africa. Perhaps blown off-course by a storm, they first landed in northern South America in about 1877. Finding the New World to its liking, during the next decades the species spread far and wide, finding abundant food where tropical forests were cleared for cattle grazing. Cattle Egrets have now colonized much of northern South America, Central America, all the major Caribbean islands, and eastern and central North America as far as the southern US. Cattle Egrets first arrived in Australia in the middle part of the twentieth century, moving into northern Australia from Indonesia; some were also introduced at this time by people to other parts of Australia.

Status

A few of Australia's herons and egrets are fairly rare in some regions, but they are not considered threatened species because they are more abundant in other parts of their ranges. The Australasian Bittern, endemic to the Australia/New Zealand region and on the IUCN Red List, is considered endangered in the isolated population that occurs in southeastern Western Australia (but is not threatened within its main continental range in southeastern Australia).

Profiles

White-faced Heron, *Egretta novaehollandiae,* Plate 25a
Eastern Reef Egret, *Egretta sacra,* Plate 25b
White-necked Heron, *Ardea pacifica,* Plate 25c
Pied Heron, *Ardea picata,* Plate 25d
Cattle Egret, *Ardea ibis,* Plate 25e
Little Egret, *Egretta garzetta,* Plate 25f
Rufous Night-heron, *Nycticorax caledonicus,* Plate 26a
Great Egret, *Ardea alba,* Plate 26b

8. Shorebirds (Waders)

Spotting *shorebirds* in Australia is usually only a priority for truly committed bird-watchers. The reason for the usual lack of interest is that shorebirds are often very common, plain-looking brown birds that most people are familiar with from their beaches back home. Still, it is always a treat watching shorebirds as they forage in meadows, along streams, on mudflats, and especially on the coasts as they run along beaches, parallel to the surf, picking up food. Some of the small ones, such as *sandpipers*, as one biologist wrote, resemble amusing wind-up toys as they spend hours running up and down the beach, chasing and then being chased by the outgoing and incoming surf. Shorebirds are often conspicuous and let themselves be watched as long as the watchers maintain some distance. When in large flying groups, shorebirds such as sandpipers provide some of the most compelling sights in bird-dom, as their flocks rise from sandbar or mudflat to fly fast and low over the surf, wheeling quickly and tightly in the air as if they were a single organism, or as if each individual's nervous system was joined to the others'.

Shorebirds are traditionally placed along with the gulls in the avian order Charadriiformes. They are global in distribution and considered to be hugely successful birds—the primary reason being that the sandy beaches and mudflats on which they forage usually teem with their food. There are several families, five of which require mention. The sandpipers, family Scolopacidae, are a worldwide group of approximately 85 species. About 43 species occur in Australia, a few being around all year but most being migrants that breed on other continents and thus are seen only seasonally. SHARP-TAILED SANDPIPER, BAR-TAILED GODWIT, RED-NECKED STINT (all Plate 31) and EASTERN CURLEW (Plate 30) are all members of the sandpiper group. *Plovers* (family Charadriidae), with about 65 species (16 in Australia), likewise have a worldwide distribution. Seven species breed in Australia; the others are migrants from breeding sites elsewhere. PACIFIC GOLDEN PLOVER, RED-CAPPED PLOVER, and BLACK-FRONTED DOTTEREL (all Plate 31) are all members of this group. Another member, the MASKED LAPWING (Plate 30), brown and white with yellow face wattles, is frequently seen in suburban parks, gardens, and other open grassy areas. The broadly distributed family Recurvirostridae consists of about 13 species of *stilts* and *avocets*, three of which occur in Australia. Family Burhinidae, also widely distributed, includes nine species of *stone-curlews*, two of which occur in Australia. Last, family Glareolidae contains 17 species (2 in Australia) of mostly Old World wading birds of inland areas, known as *pratincoles* and *coursers*.

All shorebirds, regardless of size, have a characteristic "look." They are usually drably colored birds (especially during the nonbreeding months), darker above, ligher below, with long, thin legs for wading through wet meadows, mud, sand, or surf. Depending on feeding habits, bill length varies from short to very long. Most of the Australian sandpipers range from 15 to 48 cm (6 to 19 in) long. They are generally long-legged, slender birds with straight or curved bills of various lengths. Plovers, 14 to 30 cm (6 to 12 in) long, are small to medium-sized, thick-necked, round-headed shorebirds with short tails and straight, relatively thick bills. They are mostly shades of grey and brown but some have bold color patterns such as a broad white or dark band on the head or chest. Stilts and avocets, mid-sized (33 to 48 cm, 13 to 19 in), striking shorebirds, have very long legs and long, fine bills (straight in stilts, upturned in avocets). Stone-curlews are largish birds (55 cm, 22 in) with unusually large heads, big pale yellow eyes (for night vision), long yellowish green legs, and knobby, thick "knees" (actually, they correspond more to the ankle joint) that give the bird its other common name, "thick-knee." Pratincoles are brownish wading birds, about 25 cm (10 in) long, with long wings and forked tails. The sexes look alike, or nearly so, in most of the shorebirds.

Natural History

Ecology and Behavior

Shorebirds typically are open-country birds associated with coastlines and inland wetlands, grasslands, and pastures. Sandpipers and plovers are excellent flyers but they spend a lot of time on the ground foraging and resting; when chased, they often seem to prefer running to flying away. Sandpipers pick their food up off the ground or use their bills to probe for it in mud or sand; they take insects and other small invertebrates, particularly crustaceans. They will also snatch bugs from the air as they walk and from the water's surface as they wade or swim. Larger, more land-dwelling shorebirds may also eat small reptiles and amphibians, and even small rodents; some of the plovers also eat seeds (Masked Lapwings eat insects, spiders, small crustaceans, and wiggly worms). Stilts, usually in small groups, wade about in shallow fresh and salt water, using their bills to probe the mud for small insects, snails, and crustaceans. Stone-curlews, land waders, are usually gregarious, and although they fly well, tend more to walk and run. Unusual among shorebirds, they spend days quietly in a sheltered spot, such as under bushes, then become active at twilight, foraging nocturnally for invertebrates and small vertebrates.

Many shorebirds, especially among the sandpipers, establish winter *feeding territories* along stretches of beach; they use the area for feeding for a few hours or for the day, defending it aggressively from other members of their species. Many of the sandpipers and plovers are gregarious birds, often seen in large groups, especially when they are travelling. Several species make long migrations over large expanses of open ocean, a good example being the Pacific Golden Plover, a migrant that breeds in Siberia and Alaska and spends nonbreeding months (August to April) in the Australian region and some Pacific islands (including Hawaii).

Breeding

Shorebirds breed in a variety of ways. Many species breed in monogamous pairs that defend small breeding territories. Others, however practice *polyandry*, the least common type of mating system among vertebrate animals, in which some females have more than one mate in a single breeding season. This type of breeding is exemplified by some sandpipers and by other shorebirds known as *phalaropes*. In these species, the normal sex roles of breeding birds are reversed: The female establishes a territory on a lakeshore that she defends against other females. More than one male settles within the territory, either at the same time or sequentially during a breeding season. After mating, the female lays a clutch of eggs for each male. The males incubate their clutches and care for the young. Females may help care for some of the broods of young, provided that there are no more unmated males to try to attract to the territory.

Most shorebird nests are simply small depressions in the ground in which eggs are placed; some of these *scrapes* are lined with shells, pebbles, grass, or leaves. Sandpipers lay 2 to 4 eggs per clutch, which are incubated, depending on species, by the male alone, the female alone, or by both parents, for 18 to 21 days. Plovers lay 2 to 4 eggs, which are incubated by both sexes for 24 to 28 days. Stilts breed in small colonies near water. The scrape or platform of sticks, into which 4 eggs are placed, is often lined with vegetation. Both sexes incubate for 22 to 26 days. Stone-curlews, in permanent pairs, breed solitarily. Two eggs in the scrape are incubated by both sexes for 28 to 30 days. Shorebird young are *precocial*, that is, soon after they hatch they are mobile, able to run from predators and feed themselves. Parents usually stay with the young to guard them at least until they can fly, perhaps 3 to 6 weeks after hatching.

Status

None of the Australian shorebirds are endangered but a few are considered vulnerable or threatened owing to small or declining populations. The Eastern Curlew is declining in Australia and so considered vulnerable there. The BUSH STONE-CURLEW, although widespread and still numerous, is considered vulnerable in Victoria and endangered in New South Wales and South Australia. The BEACH STONE-CURLEW, a coastal species, is vulnerable in Australia because of its small (about 1,000 birds) population and because of its sensitivity to disturbance by people of its beach habitat; however, it ranges widely through the Indonesia/Malaysia region. A major goal for conservation of shorebirds is to preserve critical migratory stopover points—pieces of habitat such as coastal mudflats, sometimes fairly small, that hundreds of thousands of shorebirds settle into midway during their long migrations to stock up on food. Destruction or use of these areas for any other activity could cause huge losses to the birds' populations.

Profiles

Bush Stone-curlew, *Burhinus grallarius,* Plate 30a
Eastern Curlew, *Numenius madagascariensis,* Plate 30c
Black-winged Stilt, *Himantopus himantopus,* Plate 30d
Masked Lapwing, *Vanellus miles,* Plate 30e
Red-necked Stint, *Calidris ruficollis,* Plate 31a
Bar-tailed Godwit, *Limosa lapponica,* Plate 31b
Sharp-tailed Sandpiper, *Calidris acuminata*, Plate 31c
Pacific Golden Plover, *Pluvialis fulva,* Plate 31d
Red-capped Plover, *Charadrius ruficapillus,* Plate 31e
Black-fronted Dotterel, *Elseyornis melanops,* Plate 31f

9. Emu and Cassowaries

Most visitors to Australia, their minds tuned to kangaroos and the like, don't expect to see huge, flightless, ostrich-like birds roaming woodlands and savannah. First glimpses of EMUS (EE-mews; Plate 20), therefore, are usually surprising. These are enormous brownish or blackish birds, with pale or bluish bare skin on head and neck, that stand 1.5 to almost 2 m (5 to 6.5 ft) tall and often weigh up to 50 kg (110 lb). A second large, flightless bird, the SOUTHERN CASSOWARY (Plate 20), which occurs in Australia only in Queensland's northeastern dense tropical rainforests (where the Emu does not), is usually just a bit smaller than the Emu (but some cassowary females can be larger); it is also dark with a bare-skin head and neck, but sports an unmistakable large bony crest, or "helmet."

The Emu and Southern Cassowary are two of the world's surviving ten species of *ratites*, birds with flat, raft-like ("ratite") sternums. Other birds have sternums with deep keels, upon which the breast flight muscles attach (think of the deep keel to which attaches the main portion of white meat in chickens and turkeys). The ratites, flightless birds that run along the ground (that is, they are *cursorial*), have no need of thick, powerful flight muscles, so they have no keel. Ratite classification is controversial, with some authorities placing all living groups in a single order, Struthioniformes; others divide the ratites into Struthioniformes (the OSTRICH of Africa), Rheiformes (the two *rheas* of South America), Casuariiformes (the Emu of Australia and three species of cassowary: one in Australia and two others in the New Guinea region), and Apterygiformes (the three species of *kiwi*, endemic to New Zealand). Emus you will see if you leave Australia's cities; they are fairly common and abundant, especially in some agricultural and ranching areas; seeing Southern Cassowaries, now threatened in Australia, is more problematic.

Natural History

Ecology and Behavior

Emus, which occur over most of mainland Australia except in heavily settled or thickly forested areas, are omnivores. They eat mainly grasses and other vegetation, fruit, seeds, flowers, and insects. They are seen alone or in pairs, and also often in small groups of four to nine. A typical day in the life of emus consists of early morning foraging, then, in late morning, a slow amble toward a water source, feeding as they go. Afternoons are also spent foraging, but at a slower pace; in hot weather, parts of afternoons are spent in tree shade. Emus, which can move along at a quite respectable 48 kph (30 mph) when they are in a hurry, are considered nomadic wanderers, at least in some of their populations. They have no real territories but are very mobile, following food availability; seasonally, they tend to move out of areas that become dry (where food is less available). Populations in the western part of the country are known to move over distances of 500 km (300 miles) in a year. Emus are very curious, and sometimes approach or even follow people.

Southern Cassowaries, which are now limited in rainforest Australia to the northern Cape York Peninsula and a narrow coastal band of northeast Queensland centered around Cairns, eat mainly fruit. They eat mostly fallen tree fruit but also pull some from plants; they also take seeds, insects and other small invertebrates, and will nibble on carrion. In one study in Queensland, cassowaries ate the fruit of 75 different tree species. When wild fruit is scarce, cassowaries enter orchards and gardens to eat cultivated fruit such as bananas; citrus fruit, however, is scorned. Cassowaries may use their bony crest primarily as a shovel, to turn over soil and leaf litter on the rainforest floor in search of fallen fruit. These large birds occur singly, in pairs, or in small groups of up to six. They are fairly sedentary, not moving over long distances unless forced to by lack of food. They form territories during breeding seasons (June to October) that vary from 1 to 5 sq km (0.4 to 2 sq miles). Cassowaries can be aggressive birds, especially when breeding, and have one very long (12 cm, 5 in) sharp claw on each foot that can do considerable damage; they have been known to disembowel mid-sized mammals.

Ecological Interactions

One Aboriginal legend explains why emus cannot fly. Emu in the past was the leader of birds and a great flyer. But other birds, notably Brush-turkey, were jealous of Emu. So they tricked him into cutting off his wings by telling him that any bird could fly, but that walking, like people and like Brush-turkey, was a sign of distinction (A. W. Reed, 1998). Biologists have another explanation. They believe that ostriches, emus, cassowaries, and rheas lost their ability to fly because they followed an evolutionary pathway to become very large, which was beneficial for them; with their long legs, large mass, and sometimes aggressive natures, they could run rapidly and defend themselves. But as they evolved to be larger, flying became more and more difficult and less necessary to escape predators, and eventually it was lost. As for New Zealand's kiwis and some other flightless birds, such as some island-dwelling pigeons and rails, it is thought they may have lost the power of flight because they evolved in what were essentially predator-free zones— where large, powerful wings and energy-expensive flight were not needed.

Breeding
Emus pair in summer or fall. After mating, the female lays 5 to 20 eggs (usually seven to eleven) in a nest of twigs and crushed vegetation in a depression on the ground, then departs; she may later pair with other males. Each egg weighs up to 900 g (2 lb). The male incubates the eggs for about 2 months, leaving the nest only occasionally to forage; males can lose 15% or more of their body weight during incubation. After hatching, the male cares for the young for up to a year or more by leading them and, when they are small, brooding them at night in his feathers. Emus begin breeding at 2 years of age. Southern Cassowaries, like emus, practice a kind of successive polyandry. A female lays 3 to 5 eggs in a scrape on the ground lined with vegetation; afterwards she departs and later mates with other males. The male incubates the eggs for 50 days, then leads and broods the young for about 9 months, until they are independent.

Notes
Cassowaries are a main source of food and other materials for some of the native peoples of New Guinea. Wild birds are hunted and young ones are kept in pens and fed until they are large enough to eat. A single cassowary provides a lot of meat, feathers for decorations (headdresses and the like), sharp claws for arrow construction, and robust leg bones to make daggers and other tools. But some tribes—the Kalam people of the Schrader Mountains are one—revere and respect cassowaries as reincarnations of their ancestors and so do not hunt or kill them. Unlike emus and ostriches, cassowaries do not breed well in zoos.

Aboriginal people would sometimes use the Emu's curiosity to hunt it: they would attract a bird's attention by waving objects or flashing it with a mirror, then spear it when it approached.

Some notes from the Queensland Wildlife Parks Association Code of Practice with respect to keeping ratite birds:

> Suitable fruits and vegetables for cassowaries include apples, banana, paw-paw, pear, figs, melons, tomato, carrot, sweet potato and any other soft fruit or vegetable. The protein component of the diet can be in the form of mice, rats, insects, fish, lean meat, and mince.... A suitable diet for emus includes a mix of commercial chicken pellets, lucerne hay, chopped vegetables and greens and grains.... Rodents, day-old chicks, and insects are not essential for the well-being of emus but can be fed occasionally as a treat.

Status

Emus did well in Australia until European settlement, when they were killed with abandon by early settlers for their meat and oil (for lamps), and their eggs were collected and eaten. (They were, in fact, eliminated in Tasmania in the mid-nineteenth century.) Later, farmers killed them because the birds ate some of their crops. However, emus survived and eventually even benefited to a degree from development, because, with new sources of open water provided by farmers and ranchers (wells, irrigation canals and ponds), they could now occupy many semi-arid regions in the middle of the country that previously had been closed to them. Emus are now common animals, although they are still persecuted in agricultural areas for breaking fences and raiding crops (such as wheat). Emus are farmed in Australia and some other countries for their low-cholesterol meat, leather, oil, and feathers. I have even seen them on commercial properties in suburban southern California, where they seemed to fit in quite nicely.

The northern Cape York Peninsula population of the Southern Cassowary is considered vulnerable, and the isolated population to its south is endangered. Much of the rainforest habitat of these birds has been cleared, and the remaining birds are threatened by dogs, illegal shooting, and by feral pigs, which spread disease, destroy nests, and compete with them for fallen fruit. In addition, some cassowaries are run over by cars as they cross roads (you will see road signs in these areas asking you to drive slowly because of the presence of cassowaries). The three species of cassowaries that occur in New Guinea (includes the Southern Cassowary) are generally scarce in populated areas due to hunting, but they are not considered endangered. Emus and Southern Cassowaries are protected under Australia's 1992 Nature Conservation Act.

Profiles

Southern Cassowary, *Casuarius casuarius*, Plate 20a
Emu, *Dromaius novaehollandiae*, Plate 20b

10. Megapodes and Quail

Some of the most intriguing birds on Earth, and now a staple subject of TV nature programs, are the *megapodes*, or "mound-builders," of the Australia/New Guinea region. The plain but amazing facts are these: some of the species construct enormous mounds of soil and vegetative matter (to 11 m, 36 ft, across and 5 m, 16 ft, high), and lay their eggs in tunnels in the mounds. The heat emitted by the decaying, fermenting plant material is the main source of warmth for incubation (supplemented by the sun). Males attending the mounds apparently can regulate the temperature toward the optimum for their eggs' development by scratching more matter onto the mounds or taking some of it off. Other megapode species do not build mounds but lay their eggs in sandy soil or in holes dug on beaches, and let the sun incubate them.

The megapodes (meaning "big feet"; family Megapodiidae) are included in order Galliformes with the chickens, turkeys, pheasants, partridges, and guineafowl. Their classification is controversial, but there seem to be about nineteen living species in Australia, New Guinea, eastern Indonesia, the Philippines, and on some Pacific islands; three occur in Australia, two of them (ORANGE-FOOTED SCRUBFOWL, AUSTRALIAN BRUSH-TURKEY; both Plate 20) being common, and commonly seen, birds found within the coverage area of this book.

(The third species, the MALLEEFOWL, endemic to southern Australia, is threatened and now uncommon in many areas of its range.) Megapodes are mostly dull brownish birds with small crests, about 50 cm (20 in) long. The ones known as *brush-turkeys* are larger (to 70 cm, 28 in), black with bare heads and necks and conspicuous large, folded tails.

The BROWN QUAIL (Plate 20) is one of over 200 species in family Phasianidae, which is distributed globally and contains the pheasants, grouse, and partridges. Three quail species occur in Australia, all of them small, brown-streaked, ground-dwelling birds of grasslands and thickets. (Other Australian quail species are known as *button-quail*, but they are members of another family that is limited to Eurasia and the Australian region.)

Natural History

Ecology and Behavior

Megapodes, also known generally as mound-birds, thermometer birds, incubator birds, and, in Australia, as scrubfowl and brush-turkeys, are mostly omnivores. Orange-footed Scrubfowl and Australian Brush-turkeys are known to eat a lot of plant materials such as seeds, shoots, roots, fruit, and berries, and also small invertebrates such as insects and worms; brush-turkeys have also been recorded eating carrion. They are all ground-dwelling birds, seldom flying unless given no other choice. They are usually shy and inconspicuous, but individuals in parks and other public areas have gotten used to people and sometimes show themselves readily. Scrubfowl are usually seen in pairs (they may mate for life), which usually appear to have territories that are defended from other scrubfowl. However, each territory does not necessarily have its own breeding mound; sometimes two breeding pairs utilize the same mound in one territory. Brush-turkeys are often solitary in most of their daily activities, but when food is plentiful (such as around picnic areas and garbage dumps), groups of up to twenty or more may gather. Male brush-turkeys are strongly territorial, defending the area around their breeding mounds with aggressive displays, chasing, and deep, booming vocalizations. These birds are sedentary, the same males, for example, owning the same territories for several years. At night, groups of brush-turkeys usually roost together.

The Brown Quail is seen in pairs or in loose aggregations of up to 30 birds; they eat seeds and insects.

Breeding

Australian Brush-turkey breeding is complex. Males are polygynous and may associate simultaneously with two or more females. The females are serially polyandrous: they associate with a particular male for a few weeks, laying eggs in his mound, then move on and do the same with other males. At the start of the breeding season (May to June in southeast Queensland), the male constructs an incubation mound by scratching and kicking material from a large area of the forest floor backwards into a heap. He stops occasionally to trample on and compact the material. Leaves, twigs, sticks, moss, soil, and other components of the forest floor litter become part of the mound, which takes an average of 37 days to complete and, when finished, is 1 to 1.5 m (3.3 to 5 ft) high and up to 5 m (16 ft) across. The male spends much of each day during the breeding season constructing and then tending his mound. Eventually, by the male digging holes and manipulating the material, the mound has its finer material inside and much of its coarser material, twigs and sticks, outside. It is the fine material decomposing, especially fungi, that is the chief heat source for egg incubation.

When the mound is finished, females arrive on a male's territory, mate with him, and begin laying eggs. A female digs a hole in the mound, lays an egg, covers it, and departs. She may lay up to 16 eggs, one every 2 or 3 days (individual mounds may have up to 20 eggs, placed there by multiple females). Incubation is about 50 days, and the optimal temperature for incubation is apparently about 33 to 34°C (91 to 93°F). This is the usual temperature of the mound about 60 cm (2 ft) deep, where the eggs are. The male actually regulates the temperature of the mound, keeping it relatively constant inside for the 2 or 33 months during which eggs are incubating. He does this by thrusting his bill, and sometimes his whole head, into the mound to sense its temperature. If the temperature is too low, he adds more leaf litter, which provides more nutrients to the mound's decomposers (bacteria), which are then more active, and more heat is generated. If the temperature is too high, the male digs into the middle of the mound, mixing the material; steam rises, and the temperature declines. (In some megapodes, males appear to cool mounds by covering them with more material, which may slow the penetration of sunlight into the mound.) Egg survival can be good: in one study of 500 eggs, about 87% survived to the hatching stage. When eggs hatch, it usually takes chicks two days or so to dig themselves out of the mound. They are strongly precocial, able to run (and just about fly) and feed as soon as they emerge; there is no parental care of chicks.

Nesting in Orange-footed Scrubfowl is somewhat similar, but they are monogamous breeders. Although smaller birds than the brush-turkeys, scrubfowl mounds are often larger than the turkeys'.

Notes

One major problem for mound-building megapodes is that huge mounds of dirt and vegetation are easy to detect. In Australia, monitor lizards and foxes take advantage of this, locating mounds and excavating eggs. In New Guinea, people also get involved. Traditionally, a mound belongs to the person who finds it. He may decide to dig up all the eggs at once, or gather them slowly over a period of time to keep them fresh longer.

Brush-turkeys are doing a little too well around Brisbane, according to some homeowners. During the 1970s the birds expanded from the edges of forests and began occupying suitable habitat in city and suburban parks and residential areas. When people's gardens or compost heaps are scraped up to become part of a brush-turkey's breeding mound, the people often decide that nature is getting a bit too close to home, and that the brush-turkey in the yard might look better on the dining room table.

Status

Of the 19 or so species of megapodes, four or five species or subspecies are considered rare, vulnerable, or already endangered. The Australian Brush-turkey, endemic to eastern Australia, is secure, with a population of more than 100,000. Likewise, the Orange-footed Scrubfowl of Australia, New Guinea, and Indonesia is abundant, with a population estimated between 100,000 and a million. Australia's only other megapode, the endemic Malleefowl, is considered vulnerable on the IUCN Red List. Australia lists it as vulnerable in Victoria and endangered throughout the rest of its range in New South Wales, South Australia, and Western Australia. Its population (now estimated at less than 10,000) has been declining since the nineteenth century, caused by its low eucalypt woodland habitat being cleared and burned for agriculture and grazing, by sheep eating its food plants, and by predation on adults and eggs by foxes. There are reserves now for Malleefowl throughout its range, and fox-control programs are aimed at reducing losses due to predation.

Profiles

Orange-footed Scrubfowl, *Megapodius reinwardt*, Plate 20c
Australian Brush-turkey, *Alectura lathami*, Plate 20d
Brown Quail, *Coturnix ypsilophora*, Plate 20e

11. Raptors

Raptor is another name for *bird of prey*, birds that live by hunting, killing, and eating other animals, usually other vertebrates. When one hears the term raptor, one usually thinks of soaring *hawks* that swoop to catch rodents and of speedy, streamlined *falcons* that snatch small birds out of the air. Although these are common forms of raptors, the families of these birds are large, the members' behavior diverse. The two main raptor families are the Accipitridae, containing the hawks, *kites*, and *eagles*, and the Falconidae, containing the *true falcons* and another group, the *caracaras*, which are limited to the New World. The reasons for classifying the two raptor groups separately have to do with differences in skeletal anatomy and, hence, suspected differences in evolutionary history. (Owls, nocturnal birds of prey, can also be considered raptors.) Raptors are common and conspicuous animals over most of Australia. Many are birds of open areas, above which they soar during the day, using the currents of heated air (*thermals*) that rise from the sun-warmed ground to support and propel them as they search for meals. Raptors are found in all types of habitats, including within open forests and woodlands and even in rainforests.

The *accipitrids* are a worldwide group of about 200 species; they occur everywhere but Antarctica. Australia is home to 18 species, including, among others, six kites, three eagles, three *goshawks*, three *harriers*, and one *buzzard*; all but one breeds in Australia. *Falconids* likewise are worldwide in their distribution. There are about 60 species, six occurring in Australia, and all breed there as well. Some falcons have very broad distributions, with the PEREGRINE FALCON found almost everywhere (including Australia), that is, its distribution is *cosmopolitan*. Peregrines may have the most extensive natural distribution of any bird. The OSPREY (Plate 27), a fish-eater, occurs worldwide and is the only species in its family, Pandionidae. Its large size, black-and-white color pattern, peculiarly bowed wing profile in flight, and its obligatory association with water—coastal areas to some inland lakes and rivers—make it easy to recognize.

Raptors vary considerably in size and in patterns of their generally subdued color schemes, but all are similar in overall form—we know them when we see them. They are fierce-looking birds with strong feet; hooked, sharp claws, or *talons*; and strong, hooked, pointed bills. Accipitrids vary in size in Australia from a 30 cm long (1 ft) sparrowhawk to the 1 m long (3.3 ft) WEDGE-TAILED EAGLE (Plate 28). Females are usually larger than males, in some species noticeably so. Most raptors are variations of grey, brown, black, and white, usually with brown or black spots, streaks, or bars on various parts of their bodies. The plumages of these birds are actually quite beautiful when viewed close-up, which, unfortunately, is difficult to do. Males and females are usually alike in color pattern. Juvenile raptors often spend several years in *subadult* plumages that differ in pattern from those of adults. Many falcons can be distinguished from hawks by their long, pointed wings, which allow the rapid, acrobatic flight for which these birds are justifiably famous.

Natural History

Ecology and Behavior
Raptors are meat-eaters. Most hunt and eat live prey, although many will also regularly or opportunistically partake of carrion. They usually hunt alone, although, when mated, the mate is often close by. Kites and eagles take mainly vertebrate animals, including some larger items such as rabbits and smaller members of the kangaroo family. Prey is snatched with talons first, then killed and ripped apart with the bill. Some invertebrate prey is also taken; for instance, goshawks take a lot of insects, and the PACIFIC BAZA, a beautiful hawk with a grey, crested head and boldly brown-and-white striped chest, specializes on insects, particularly large "stick" insects.

Falcons are best known for their remarkable eyesight and fast, aerial pursuit and capture of flying birds—they are "birdhawks." Among Australia's falcons, the AUSTRALIAN HOBBY, a smaller falcon, and the Peregrine Falcon specialize at catching birds in flight. Most people are familiar with stories of peregrines diving through the atmosphere (*stooping*, defined as diving vertically from height to gain speed and force) at speeds approaching 320 kph (200 mph) to stun, grab, or knock from the sky an unsuspecting bird. But some falcons eat more rodents than birds, and some even take insects. For example, the BROWN FALCON and NANKEEN KESTREL (both Plate 28) perch on trees, rocks, or wires, or hover, scanning the ground for small vertebrates (small mammals, birds, lizards, snakes) and invertebrates. Ospreys, sometimes called "fish-eagles," eat fish; they hover momentarily over fresh or salt water, spot a likely meal, dive in feet-first and grab the fish in their talons, then fly off to a tree branch to feast.

Many raptors are territorial, a solitary individual or a breeding pair defending an area for feeding and, during the breeding season, for reproduction. Displays that advertise a territory and may be used in courtship consist of spectacular aerial twists, loops, and other acrobatic maneuvers. Although many raptors are common birds, typically they exist at relatively low densities, as is the case for all *top predators* (a predator at the pinnacle of the food chain, preyed upon by no animal). That is, there usually is only enough food to support one or two of a species in a given area. For example, a typical density for a small raptor species, perhaps one that feeds on mice and small lizards, is one individual per sq km (0.4 sq miles). A large eagle that feeds on pademelons and rabbits may be spaced so that a usual density is one individual per 100 sq km (40 sq miles).

Ecological Interactions
The hunting behavior of falcons has over evolutionary time shaped the behavior of their prey animals. Falcons hit perched or flying birds with their talons, stunning the prey and sometimes killing it outright. An individual bird caught unaware has little chance of escaping the rapid, acrobatic falcons, but birds in groups have two defenses. First, each individual in a group benefits because the group, with so many eyes and ears, is more likely to spot a falcon at a distance than is a lone individual, thus providing all in the group with opportunities to watch the predator as it approaches and so evade it. This sort of anti-predation advantage may be why some animals stay in groups. Second, some flocks of small birds, such as starlings, which usually fly in loose formations, immediately

tighten their formation upon detecting a flying falcon. The effect is to decrease the distance between each bird, so much so that a falcon flying into the group at a fast speed and trying to take an individual risks injuring itself—the "block" of starlings is almost a solid wall of bird. Biologists believe that the flock tightens when a falcon is detected because the behavior reduces the likelihood of an attack.

Breeding

Hawk, kite, and eagle nests are constructed of sticks that both sexes place in a tree or on a rock ledge. Some nests are lined with leaves. Usually only the female incubates the 1 to 6 eggs (only 1 or 2 in the larger species), for 28 to 49 days, and gives food to the nestlings. The male frets about and hunts, bringing food to the nest for the female and for her to provide to the nestlings. Both sexes feed the young when they get a bit older; they can fly at 4 to 17 weeks of age depending on species size. After fledging (at 4 to 10 weeks old, in various Australian species), the young remain with the parents for several more weeks or months until they can hunt on their own. Falcon breeding is similar. Falcons nest on cliff edges, in rock cavities, in tree hollows, or in old stick nests of other birds. Some make their own stick nest; others apparently make no construction. Incubation is from 25 to 35 days, performed only by the female in most species. In most falcons, the male hunts for and feeds the female during the egg laying, incubation, and early nestling periods. Males and females feed nestlings, which fledge after 25 to 49 days in the nest. The parents continue to feed the youngsters for several weeks after fledging until they are proficient hunters.

Notes

Large, predatory raptors have doubtless always attracted people's attention, respect, and awe. Wherever eagles occur, they are chronicled in the history of civilizations. Both the ancient Greeks and Romans associated eagles with their gods. Early Anglo-Saxons were known to hang an eagle on the gate of any city they conquered. Some Native (North) American tribes deified large hawks or eagles. Several states have used likenesses of eagles as national symbols, among them Turkey, Austria, Germany, Poland, Russia, and Mexico. Eagles are popular symbols on regal coats of arms, and one of their kind, a fierce-looking fish-eater, was chosen as the emblem of the US. The Wedge-tailed Eagle, Australia's largest raptor, figures in the cultures of many Aboriginal tribes, and its likeness is included in many cave, rock, and bark paintings that are a main part of Aboriginal religious and daily life.

Status

Most of Australia's raptor species are secure, but some are threatened by habitat destruction, and the large eagles are sometimes persecuted by farmers and ranchers, as they are everywhere, for allegedly killing livestock. The population of Wedge-tailed Eagles on Tasmania is considered endangered and recently numbered only about 100 breeding pairs. Mostly owing to habitat destruction, the RED GOSHAWK is considered endangered in Queensland, New South Wales, Western Australia, and the Northern Territory; the SQUARE-TAILED KITE is rare and vulnerable throughout Australia; and the GREY FALCON is endangered in Western Australia. Some raptors have actually increased in abundance during the past 200 years; for instance, the BLACK-SHOULDERED KITE (Plate 27) is almost certainly more numerous now than in the past, probably because one of its main snack foods, the House Mouse, is now so abundant.

Profiles

Osprey, *Pandion haliaetus*, Plate 27a
Black-shouldered Kite, *Elanus axillaris*, Plate 27b
Black Kite, *Milvus migrans*, Plate 27c
Whistling Kite, *Haliastur sphenurus*, Plate 27d
Brahminy Kite, *Haliastur indus*, Plate 27e
Brown Goshawk, *Accipiter fasciatus*, Plate 28a
White-bellied Sea-eagle, *Haliaeetus leucogaster*, Plate 28b
Wedge-tailed Eagle, *Aquila audax*, Plate 28c
Brown Falcon, *Falco berigora*, Plate 28d
Nankeen Kestrel, *Falco cenchroides*, Plate 28e

12. Pigeons and Doves

The *pigeon* family is a highly successful group, represented often in large numbers almost everywhere on dry land, except for Antarctica and some oceanic islands. Their continued ecological success must be viewed as at least somewhat surprising, because pigeons are largely defenseless creatures and quite edible, regarded as a tasty entree by human and an array of nonhuman predators. The family, Columbidae, includes approximately 290 species, about 25 of which occur in Australia (about half of them being endemic). They inhabit almost all kinds of habitats, from arid grasslands to tropical rainforests to higher-elevation mountainsides. Smaller species generally are called *doves*, larger ones pigeons, but there is a good amount of overlap in name assignments.

All pigeons are generally recognized as such by almost everyone, a legacy of people's familiarity with domestic and feral pigeons. Even small children in zoos, upon encountering an exotic, colorful dove, will determine it to be "some kind of pigeon." Pigeons worldwide vary in size from the dimensions of a sparrow or robin to those of a small turkey; Australia's range from 20 cm long (8 in) mostly ground-dwelling doves to the 50 cm (20 in) TOPKNOT PIGEON (Plate 35). Doves and pigeons are plump-looking birds with compact bodies, short necks, and small heads. Legs are usually fairly short, except in the ground-dwelling species. Bills are small, straight, and slender. Typically there is a conspicuous patch of naked skin, or *cere*, at the base of the bill, over the nostrils. The soft, dense plumages of most pigeons and doves come in understated greys and browns, although some have bold patterns of black lines or spots; many have splotches of iridescence, especially on necks and wings. But some groups, such as the *fruit-doves* (three species in Australia), which mostly occur in the Indonesia/Malaysia and Australia/New Guinea regions, are easily among the most gaily colored of birds. Green, the predominant hue of fruit-doves, obviously assists these birds with camouflage in their arboreal habitats. Some pigeons have conspicuous crests, and three Australian species are good examples: the Topknot, CRESTED (Plate 35), and SPINIFEX PIGEONS. In most Australian species, males and females are generally alike in size and color, although some females are a bit duller than the males.

Natural History

Ecology and Behavior

Most of the pigeons are at least partly arboreal, but some spend their time in and around cliffs, and still others are primarily ground-dwellers. They eat seeds, ripe and unripe fruit, berries, and the occasional insect, snail, or other small invertebrate. Even those species that spend a lot of time in trees often forage on the ground, moving along the leaf-strewn forest floor with the head-bobbing walk characteristic of their kind. Owing to their small, weak bills, they eat only what they can swallow whole; "chewing" is accomplished in the *gizzard*, a muscular portion of the stomach in which food is mashed against small pebbles that are eaten by pigeons expressly for this purpose. Fruit-doves swallow small fruits whole, and the ridged walls of their gizzards rub the skin and pulp from the fruits. Pigeons typically are strong, rapid flyers, which along with their cryptic color patterns provides their only defense against predation. Most pigeons are gregarious to some degree, staying in groups during the nonbreeding portion of the year, though some gather into large flocks. In Australia, pigeons partially fill the ground seed-eater niche that pheasants, grouse, and partridges occupy on other continents. Some Australian pigeons are nomadic, moving regularly to find available food.

Ecological Interactions

The great success of the pigeon family—a worldwide distribution, robust populations, the widespread range and enormous numbers of Rock Doves (wild, domestic pigeons)—is puzzling to ecologists. At first glance, pigeons have little to recommend them as the fierce competitors any hugely successful group needs to be. They have weak bills and therefore are rather defenseless during fights and ineffectual when trying to stave off nest predators. They are hunted by people for food. In several parts of the world they compete for seeds and fruit with parrots, birds with formidable bills, yet pigeons thrive in these regions and have spread to many more that are parrotless. To what do pigeons owe their success? First, to reproductive advantage. For birds of their size, they have relatively short incubation and nestling periods; consequently, nests are exposed to predators for relatively brief periods and, when nests fail, parents have adequate time to nest again before the season ends. Some species breed more than once per year. Also, the ability of both sexes to produce pigeon milk (see below) to feed young may be an advantage over having to forage for particular foods for the young. Second, their ability to capitalize on human alterations of the environment points to a high degree of hardiness and adaptability, valuable traits in a world in which people make changes to habitats faster than most organisms can respond with evolutionary changes of their own.

Breeding

Pigeons are monogamous breeders. Some breed solitarily, others in colonies of various sizes. Nests are shallow, open affairs of woven twigs, plant stems, and roots, placed on the ground, on rock ledges, or in forks of shrubs or trees. Reproductive duties are shared by males and females. This includes nest-building, incubating the 1 or 2 eggs, and feeding the young, which they do by regurgitating food into the nestlings' mouths. All pigeons, male and female, feed their young *pigeon milk,* a nutritious fluid produced in the *crop,* an enlargement of the esophagus used for food storage. During the first few days of life, nestlings receive 100% pigeon milk but, as they grow older, they are fed an increasing proportion of regurgitated solid food. Incubation time ranges from 11 to 28 days, depending on species size. Nestlings spend from 11 to 36 days in the nest. Parent pigeons of some species give *distraction displays* when potential predators approach their eggs or young; they feign injury as they move away from the nest, luring the predator away.

Notes

Although many pigeons today are very successful animals, some species met extinction within the recent past. There are two particularly famous cases. The DODO was a large, flightless pigeon the size of a turkey, with a large head and strong, robust bill and feet. Dodos lived until the seventeenth century on the island of Mauritius in the Indian Ocean, east of Madagascar. Reported to be clumsy and stupid (hence the expression, "dumb as a dodo"), but probably just unfamiliar with and unafraid of predatory animals such as people, they were killed in the thousands by sailors who stopped at the island to stock their ships with food. This caused population numbers to plunge; the birds were then finished off by the pigs, monkeys, and cats introduced by people to the previously predator-free island—animals that ate the Dodos' eggs and young. The only stuffed Dodo in existence was destroyed by fire in Oxford, England, in 1755.

North America's PASSENGER PIGEON, a medium-sized, long-tailed member of the family, suffered extinction because of overhunting and because of its habits of roosting, breeding, and migrating in huge flocks. People were able to kill many thousands of them at a time on the Great Plains in the central part of the US, shipping the bodies to markets and restaurants in large cities through the mid-1800s. It is estimated that when Europeans first settled in the New World, there were three billion Passenger Pigeons, a population size perhaps never equaled by any other bird, and that they may have accounted for up to 25% or more of the birds in what is now the US. It took only a bit more than 100 years to kill them all; the last one died in the Cincinnati Zoo in 1914.

Status

Most of Australia's pigeons and doves are secure, even though in the past they were hunted extensively for food and sport, and some hunting continues. Aboriginal tribes hunted pigeons, birds relatively easy to catch, with nets and clubs, and European sailors and settlers also killed pigeons for food. Habitat loss is now the main threat to Australia's pigeons and doves, especially the fruit-doves. The FLOCK BRONZEWING and SQUATTER PIGEON are considered endangered in New South Wales; their once-large populations suffered from habitat loss and introduced predators such as foxes and cats. Some Australian island subspecies of pigeons that have broader ranges elsewhere have become extinct, the victims of human settlement of the islands, hunting, and of the cats people brought along. For instance, the Lord Howe Island (east of Brisbane) form of the METALLIC PIGEON was last seen alive in 1853.

Profiles

Spotted Turtle-dove, *Streptopelia chinensis*, Plate 34a
Brown Cuckoo-dove, *Macropygia amboinensis*, Plate 34b
Emerald Dove, *Chalcophaps indica*, Plate 34c
Peaceful Dove, *Geopelia striata*, Plate 34d
Common Bronzewing, *Phaps chalcoptera*, Plate 34e
Rose-crowned Fruit-dove, *Ptilinopus regina*, Plate 35a
Crested Pigeon, *Ocyphaps lophotes*, Plate 35b
Wompoo Fruit-dove, *Ptilinopus magnificus*, Plate 35c
Pied Imperial-pigeon, *Ducula bicolor*, Plate 35d
Topknot Pigeon, *Lopholaimus antarcticus*, Plate 35e
Wonga Pigeon, *Leucosarcia melanoleuca*, Plate 35f

13. Parrots

Everyone knows *parrots* as caged pets, so discovering them for the first time in their natural surroundings is often a strange but somehow familiar experience (like a dog owner's first sighting of a wild fox or wolf): one has knowledge and expectations of the birds' behavior and antics in captivity, but how do they act in the wild? Along with a few birds famous for some highly specialized behaviors, such as the megapodes with their mound-building, Australia's parrots are probably the birds most ecotravellers in the country want to see. And because many of these birds, even some very common ones in settled areas, are large and conspicuous, almost everyone wanting to see parrots will be successful.

The 350 or so parrot species that comprise order Psittaciformes are globally distributed across the tropics, with some species extending into subtropical and even temperate zone areas. The order has a particularly diverse and abundant presence in the Australian region. For our purposes, we can separate Australia's parrots into two main groups. The *cockatoos*, family Cacatuidae, are medium- and large-sized parrots with crests that they can erect. The world's 20 species occur in the Australia/New Guinea and Indonesia regions, with 14 in Australia (11 endemic); included are cockatoos, *corellas*, the GALAH (Plate 36) and the COCKATIEL. The remaining parrots comprise family Psittacidae (the P is silent; refer to parrots as *psittacids* to impress your friends and tour guides!). About 40 species (three-quarters endemic) occur in Australia, including *rosellas*, AUSTRALIAN RINGNECK, BUDGERIGAR, and six species of *lorikeets*. The latter are a distinct subgroup of brilliantly colored parrots that eat nectar and pollen, confined to the Australia/New Guinea, Indonesia, and Pacific Island regions.

Consistent in form and appearance, all parrots are easily recognized as such. They share a group of traits that set them distinctively apart from all other birds. Their typically short neck and compact body yield a form variously described as stocky, chunky, or bulky. All possess a short, hooked bill with a hinge on the upper part that permits great mobility and leverage during feeding (one Australian species, the LONG-BILLED CORELLA, has a notably longer bill for digging up roots). Finally, their legs are short and their feet, with two toes projecting forward and two back, are adapted for powerful grasping and a high degree of dexterity—more so than any other bird. Australia's parrots range in size from large cockatoos at 64 cm (25 in) to smaller lorikeets and parrots at 14 to 16 cm (5.5 to 6.5 in). The *macaws* of Central and South America are the world's largest parrots, ranging up to 1 m (40 in) long. Cape York's PALM COCKATOO (Plate 36) is Australia's largest parrot. The basic parrot color scheme is green, but some species depart from the basic in spectacular fashion, with gaudy blues, reds, and yellows; many cockatoos are mostly all-white or black. Australia has some bedazzling species, including rosellas, such as the red and purple CRIMSON ROSELLA (Plate 38), the scarlet-headed (male) AUSTRALIAN KING-PARROT (Plate 37), and that ridiculously colorful and common inhabitant of parks and gardens, the RAINBOW LORIKEET (Plate 37). Green parrots feeding quietly amid a tree's high foliage can be difficult to see, even for experienced birdwatchers. In most Australian parrots, the sexes are very similar or identical in appearance, but some do have moderate differences.

Natural History

Ecology and Behavior

Parrots are very noisy, highly social seed- and fruit-eaters. Some species seem to give their assortment of harsh, screeching squawks during much of the day, whereas others are fairly quiet while feeding. During early mornings and late afternoons, raucous, squawking flocks of parrots characteristically take flight explosively from trees, heading in mornings for feeding areas and later for night roosts, and these are usually the best sighting times. Parrots are almost always encountered in flocks of 4 or more, and groups of more than 50 smaller parrots are common. Flocks are usually groups of mated pairs and, with brief observation of behavior, married pairs are often noticeable. Flocks move about seeking fruits and flowers in forests, parkland, and agricultural areas. In flight, parrots are easily identified by their family-specific silhouette: thick bodies and usually long tails, with short, relatively slowly beating wings. Parrots generally are not considered strong flyers, but are certainly fast over the short run. Most do not need to undertake long-distance flights; they are fairly sedentary in their habits, although some species in arid areas are somewhat nomadic, always looking for areas where recent rainfall has caused flowers to blossom and fruit to ripen. One highly unusual Australian parrot is the GROUND PARROT of southern coastal regions. By day it roosts on the ground in its wet heathland and pasture habitats; at dusk, it becomes active, using its long legs to forage on the ground for seeds and grasses.

Most parrots use their special locomotory talent to clamber methodically through trees in search of fruits and flowers, using their powerful feet to grasp branches and their bills as, essentially, a third foot. Just like caged parrots, they will hang at odd angles and even upside down, the better to reach some delicious morsel. Parrot feet also function as hands, delicately manipulating food and bringing it to the bill. Most Australian parrots are seed-eaters, but they usually also take some fruit, berries, flowers, and even insects and insect larvae to varying degrees. When they take fruit, it is often to get at the seeds within. The powerful bill slices open fruit and crushes seeds. As one bird book colorfully put it, "adapted for opening hard nuts, biting chunks out of fruit, and grinding small seeds into meal, the short, thick, hooked parrot bill combines the destructive powers of an ice pick (the sharp-pointed upper mandible), a chisel (the sharp-edged lower mandible), a file (ridged inner surface of the upper mandible), and a vise." Thick, muscular parrot tongues are also specialized for feeding, used to scoop out pulp from fruit and nectar from flowers. Some cockatoos, in addition to seeds, blossoms, and some insects, also eat roots. Paradoxically, a large parrot like the RED-TAILED BLACK-COCKATOO (Plate 36) eats mainly very small seeds it finds on the ground. Lorikeets, noisy, fast-flying, mostly forest-dwelling birds, eat nectar and pollen, and some also take fruit. To gather nectar and pollen from flowers of trees and shrubs, they have long tongues with brush-like tips. On good days a lorikeet can gather enough nectar and pollen in two to three hours to meet its daily energy requirements; this may entail visiting about 5,000 eucalypt flowers, which can be done at rates up to 35 per minute. Some other parrots, such as the SWIFT PARROT (Plate 38), also feed on nectar and pollen.

Ecological Interactions

Many fruit-eating birds are fruit seed dispersers, but apparently not parrots. Their strong bills crush seeds, and the contents are digested. For example, in one study in Central America, a parrot was examined after it fed all morning at a fig tree. It had in its digestive tract about 3,500 fig seeds, almost all of which were broken, cracked, or already partially digested. Therefore, the main ecological interaction between parrots and at least some fruit trees is that of seed predator. Because parrots eat seeds and fruit, they are attracted to farms and orchards and in some areas are considered agricultural pests. A wide range of parrots often visit *licks*, exposed earthbank or riverbank clay deposits. They eat the clay, which may help detoxify harmful compounds that are consumed in their seed and fruit diet, or may supply essential minerals that are not provided by a vegetarian diet. Australian parrots are sometimes found to have charcoal in their stomachs, which also may help detoxify harmful chemicals.

Breeding

Parrot breeding is monogamous and pairing is often for life. Most species breed in tree cavities, often in dead trees or branches high up off the ground; nests may be lined with wood chips. A few Australian species breed in tunnels that they dig in termite mounds. A female parrot lays 1 to 8 eggs (large cockatoos, usually 1 or 2), which she incubates alone for 17 to 35 days while being periodically fed regurgitated food by her mate. The helpless young of small parrots are nest-bound for 33 to 44 weeks, those of large cockatoos, 3 to 4 months. Both parents feed nestlings and fledglings.

Notes

Parrots have been captured for people's pleasure as pets for thousands of years. Greek records from 400 BCE describe parrot pets. Ancient Romans wrote of training parrots to speak and even of how they acted when drunk! The fascination stems from the birds' bright coloring, their ability to imitate human speech and other sounds, their individualistic personalities (captive parrots definitely like some people while disliking others), and their long lifespans (up to 80 years in captivity). Cockatoos especially, with their long lifespans and ability to bond with people, are kept as "companion" animals. Parrots have also been hunted and killed for food for thousands of years. Historically, people have also killed parrots to protect crops—Charles Darwin noted during his travels that in Uruguay in the early 1800s, thousands of parrots were killed to prevent crop damage. In Australia, cockatoos in particular—Galahs, Cockatiels, Red-tailed Black-cockatoos, and Western Corellas—have long been poisoned, shot, trapped, or otherwise killed or scared away from crops. SULFUR-CRESTED COCKATOOS (Plate 36), ranging broadly over eastern Australia, sometimes in large groups, are considered by many to be real pests—they damage trees in orchards and, apparently exercising their powerful bills, tear up car windshield wipers and house window moldings. The Galah ("ga-LAH"), a mid-sized pinkish parrot with grey wings, takes advantage of agriculture and artificial water supplies; with water and its seed food now available almost everywhere, Galahs occur throughout Australia in large numbers and are as much a part of the landscape as kangaroos.

Status

Worldwide, about 90 parrot species are considered vulnerable, threatened, or endangered. Many Australian parrot species still enjoy healthy populations and are frequently seen. Unfortunately, however, parrots are subject to three powerful forces that, in combination, take heavy tolls on their numbers: Parrots are primarily forest birds (often nesting only in tree hollows), and forests are increasingly under attack by farmers and developers; parrots are considered agricultural pests by farmers and orchardists owing to their seed- and fruit-eating, and are persecuted for this reason; and parrots are among the world's most popular cage birds. Among Australia's cockatoos, Cape York's Palm Cockatoo, much sought-after by the illegal cage-bird trade, is CITES Appendix I listed, but is not really considered globally threatened; it also occurs in New Guinea, where it is still hunted for food. The three most endangered Australian parrots are probably the NIGHT PARROT (a nocturnal ground-dweller similar to the Ground Parrot, mentioned earlier), which is critically endangered and was formerly thought extinct; the Ground Parrot; and the ORANGE-BELLIED PARROT, which breeds only in parts of Tasmania and which, during the 1990s, was down to a total of about 120 breeding pairs. All three species are CITES Appendix I listed. The IUCN Red List also considers the Swift Parrot, GOLDEN-SHOULDERED PARROT, and CARNABY'S BLACK-COCKATOO to be endangered.

Profiles

Red-tailed Black-cockatoo, *Calyptorhynchus banksii*, Plate 36a

Palm Cockatoo, *Probosciger aterrimus*, Plate 36b

Yellow-tailed Black-cockatoo, *Calyptorhynchus funereus*, Plate 36c

Sulphur-crested Cockatoo, *Cacatua galerita*, Plate 36d

Galah, *Cacatua roseicapilla*, Plate 36e

Gang-gang Cockatoo, *Callocephalon fimbriatum*, Plate 36f

Rainbow Lorikeet, *Trichoglossus haematodus*, Plate 37a

Scaly-breasted Lorikeet, *Trichoglossus chlorolepidotus*, Plate 37b

Musk Lorikeet, *Glossopsitta concinna*, Plate 37c

Purple-crowned Lorikeet, *Glossopsitta porphyrocephala*, Plate 37d

Australian King-parrot, *Alisterus scapularis*, Plate 37e

Crimson Rosella, *Platycercus elegans*, Plate 38a

Red-winged Parrot, *Aprosmictus erythropterus*, Plate 38b

Eastern Rosella, *Platycercus eximius*, Plate 38c

Pale-headed Rosella, *Platycercus adscitus*, Plate 38d

Swift Parrot, *Lathamus discolor*, Plate 38e

Red-rumped Parrot, *Psephotus haematonotus*, Plate 38f

14. Cuckoos and Coucals

Many of the *cuckoos* are physically rather plain but behaviorally rather extraordinary: as a group they employ some of the most bizarre breeding practices known among birds. Cuckoos and *coucals* are included in the cuckoo family Cuculidae, which, with a total of about 130 species, enjoys a worldwide distribution in temperate areas and the tropics. Thirteen species occur in Australia. Cuckoos are mainly shy, solitary birds of forests, woodlands, and dense thickets. Most cuckoos are medium-sized, slender, narrow-winged, long-tailed birds. Males and females mostly look alike, attired in plain greys, browns, and whites, often with streaked or spotted patches. Several have alternating white and black bands on their chests and/or tail undersides. They have short legs and bills that curve downwards at the end. Australia's four smallest cuckoos, all of which are metallic greenish above, are members of a group known as *bronze-cuckoos*. Australia's only coucal (one of about 30 species that occur in Africa, Indonesia, and the Pacific region) is the PHEASANT COUCAL (Plate 39), a largish, dark ground-dweller.

Natural History

Ecology and Behavior

Most of the cuckoos are arboreal and are known for their fast, graceful, undulating flight. They mainly eat insects and insect larvae, apparently having a special fondness for caterpillars. They even safely consume hairy caterpillars, which are avoided by most potential predators because they taste bad or contain sickness-causing noxious compounds. Cuckoos have been observed to snip off one end of the hairy thing, squeeze the body in the bill until the noxious entrails fall out, then swallow the harmless remainder. Larger cuckoos will also take fruit, berries, and small vertebrates. A few cuckoos, such as the Pheasant Coucal, are chiefly ground-dwellers, eating insects but also vertebrates such as mice and small lizards and snakes. These coucals, which live in dense vegetation areas, do fly, albeit not gracefully or for long distances; they prefer to run along the ground to catch food or to escape from potential predators. They are seen occasionally crossing roads and trails. Most of Australia's cuckoos are migratory, breeding during spring in the southern part of the country and then migrating to northern Australia and/or New Guinea for the nonbreeding months.

Breeding

Cuckoos are known in most parts of the world for being *brood parasites:* they build no nests of their own, and the females lay their eggs in the nests of other species. These other birds often raise the young cuckoos as their own offspring, usually to the significant detriment of their own, often smaller, young. About 50 of the 130 members of the family are brood parasites, as are almost all of Australia's (the Pheasant Coucal is not). Australia's cuckoos "parasitize" more than 100 other species. Some cuckoo species specialize in open-cup nesters, some choose to parasitize species that build domed nests. A female cuckoo lays an egg in a "host" nest usually when the host couple is absent, and she often removes a host egg before laying her own (presumably so the same number of eggs is in the nest when the hosts return). Many host species are smaller than the cuckoos that parasitize them, so some cuckoos actually lay eggs that are smaller than those of similar-sized birds, so that their eggs more closely match the size of the host's eggs. Other cuckoos lay eggs that resemble the host's eggs in shell color and patterning. All of these machinations are thought to be adaptations (changes through evolution) so that the hosts cannot recognize the cuckoo eggs and eject them (as happens in some species). When the cuckoo chick hatches, it actually tosses other eggs and the host's own chicks out of the nest by pushing them with its back; anything in the nest that is contacted is pushed out. If any host chicks are left in the nest, the cuckoo chick, usually larger, out-competes them for food brought to the nest by the host parents, and the hosts' own young often starve or are significantly weakened. Cuckoo chicks are famous for their loud, continuous begging calls and for their begging postures, both of which continually stimulate the host parents to feed them. After fledging, the cuckoos continue to call and beg, and the hosts, and sometimes other birds, keep feeding them. Because one population in these interactions benefits and one is harmed, the relationships between cuckoos and their hosts is *parasitic*—social parasitism in this case. How can brood parasitic behavior arise? Evolutionary biologists posit that one way would be if, long ago, some female cuckoos that built nests had their nests destroyed midway through their laying period. With an egg to lay but no nest in which to place it, females in this situation may have deposited the eggs in the nests of other species, which subsquently raised the cuckoo young.

Pheasant Coucals, monogamous breeders, build their own covered nest in grassy vegetation near the ground; the female lays 2 to 5 eggs, which are incubated by both sexes for 15 days. Young fledge about 2 weeks after hatching and are independent at about 40 days old.

Notes

The name cuckoo comes from the calls made by a common species in Europe, whch is also the source of the sounds for cuckoo clocks. In the realms of literature and language, the word "cuckold," of course, has a meaning that implies social amorality—obviously related to the cuckoos' reproductive habits. And the term "cuckoo" is sometimes applied to people to mean they are foolish or demented, a slang usage perhaps stemming from the birds' perceived "silliness" in always abandoning and neglecting its own young.

Status

None of Australia's cuckoos are threatened. The SHINING BRONZE-CUCKOO (Plate 39) is considered to be rare in South Australia, but is numerous and secure in other parts of its broad Australian range.

Profiles

Shining Bronze-cuckoo, *Chrysococcyx lucidus*, Plate 39a
Fan-tailed Cuckoo, *Cacomantis flabelliformis*, Plate 39b
Brush Cuckoo, *Cacomantis variolosus*, Plate 39c
Common Koel, *Eudynamys scolopacea*, Plate 39d
Channel-billed Cuckoo, *Scythrops novaehollandiae*, Plate 39e
Pheasant Coucal, *Centropus phasianinus*, Plate 39f

15. Owls

Although some *owls* are common Australian birds, they are considered here only briefly because most are active only at night and so are rarely seen. But there are a few exceptions. Most owls are members of family Strigidae, a worldwide group of about 130 species that lacks representation only in Antarctica and remote oceanic islands; the *barn owls*, with 12 species worldwide, constitute a separate family, Tytonidae. Owls are particularly diverse in the tropics and subtropics; Australia has only nine species. Most people can always identify owls because of several distinctive features. All have large heads with forward-facing eyes, small, hooked bills, plumpish bodies, and sharp, hooked claws. Most have short legs and short tails. Owls are clad mostly in mixtures of grey, brown, and black, the result being that they usually are highly camouflaged against a variety of backgrounds. They have very soft feathers. Most are medium-sized birds, but the group includes species that range in length from 15 to 75 cm (6 to 30 in); Australia's range in size from the POWERFUL OWL, at up to 65 cm (26 in), to the SOUTHERN BOOBOOK (Plate 40), at 25 to 30 cm (10 to 12 in). Males and females generally look alike, and in many species, females tend to be a bit larger. In some Australian species, however, such as in the BARKING OWL (Plate 40), males are larger.

Natural History

Ecology and Behavior

In general, owls occupy a variety of habitats: forests, clearings, fields, grasslands, deserts, mountains, and marshes. They are considered to be the nocturnal equivalents of the day-active birds of prey—the hawks, eagles, and falcons. Most owls hunt at night, taking prey such as small mammals, birds (including smaller owls), and reptiles; smaller owls specialize in insects, earthworms, and other small invertebrates. But some owls hunt at twilight (*crepuscular* activity) and sometimes during the day (the Barking Owl is Australia's least nocturnal owl, sometimes beginning to hunt before sunset). Owls hunt by sight and sound. Their vision is very good in low light, the amount given off by moonlight, for instance, and their hearing is remarkable. They can hear sounds that are much lower in sound intensity (softer) than most other birds, and their ears are positioned on their heads asymmetrically, the better for localizing sounds in space. This means that owls in the darkness can, for example, actually hear small rodents moving about on the forest floor, quickly locate the source of the sound, then swoop and grab. Additionally, owing to their soft, loose feathers, owls' flight is essentially silent, permitting prey little chance of hearing their approach. Owls swallow small prey whole, then, instead of digesting or passing the hard bits, they regurgitate bones, feathers, and fur in compact *owl pellets*. These are often found beneath trees or rocks where owls perch and they can be interesting to pull apart to see what an owl has been dining on.

Breeding

Most owls are monogamous breeders. They do not build nests themselves, but either take over nests abandoned by other birds or nest in cavities such as tree or rock holes; most Australian species nest in tree hollows. Incubation of the 1 to 8 or more eggs (often 2 to 4) is usually conducted by the female alone for 4 to 6 weeks, but she is fed by her mate. Upon hatching, the female broods the young while the male hunts and brings meals; later, young are fed by both parents. Young fledge after 5 to 10 weeks in the nest.

Notes

The forward-facing eyes of owls are a trait shared with only a few other animals: humans, most other primates, and to a degree, cats. Eyes arranged in this way allow for almost complete binocular vision (one eye sees the same thing as the other), a prerequisite for good depth perception, which, in turn, is important for quickly judging distances when catching prey. On the other hand, owl eyes cannot move much, so owls swivel their heads to look left or right. Owls have a reputation for fierce, aggressive defense of their young; many a human who ventured too near an owl nest has been attacked and had damage done!

Status

Owls in Australia are threatened primarily by the clearing of their forest habitats for agriculture. No species are endangered, but some populations on offshore islands are threatened. The Powerful Owl is considered vulnerable in Queensland and New South Wales and rare in Victoria, and the Barking Owl is vulnerable in South Australia. Because owls are cryptically colored and nocturnal, it can be difficult to correctly determine their population sizes.

Profiles

Barn Owl, *Tyto alba*, Plate 40a
Southern Boobook, *Ninox novaeseelandiae*, Plate 40b
Barking Owl, *Ninox connivens*, Plate 40c

16. Nightjars and Frogmouths

Species of birds known as *nightjars* are in the family Caprimulgidae, which has about 70 species worldwide, three in Australia. Like their closest relatives the owls, nightjars are primarily nocturnal. They have a very characteristic appearance. They have long wings, medium or long tails, and big eyes. Their small, stubby bills enclose big, wide mouths that they open in flight to scoop up flying insects. Many species have bristles around the mouth area that act as a food funnel. With their short legs and weak feet, they are poor walkers—flying is their usual mode of loco-motion. The plumage of these birds is uniformly cryptic: mottled, spotted, and barred mixtures of brown, grey, tan, and black. They often have white patches on their wings or tails that can be seen only in flight. In Australia they range in size from 26 to 37 cm (10 to 15 in) long. A separate small group (family Aegothelidae) of small nightjars, known as *owlet-nightjars,* is represented in Australia by a single species, the AUSTRALIAN OWLET-NIGHTJAR (Plate 40). Another group, the *frog-mouths* (family Podargidae), closely related to nightjars, has a total of 13 species that are distributed in southern Asia and the Australian region. Three occur in Australia, the TAWNY FROGMOUTH (Plate 40) being the only one that has a broad range. Frogmouths, so named because of their massive, broad, slightly hooked bills, are mid-sized to largish grey or brown birds that are, like owls and nightjars, nocturnal hunters.

Natural History

Ecology and Behavior
Most nightjars are night-active birds, with some becoming active at twilight (*cre-puscular* activity). They feed on flying insects, which they catch on the wing, either by forays out from a perched location or with continuous circling flight. You can see some species feeding on insects drawn to lights at night. Others you will see only as you flush them from their daytime roost on the ground or in low vegetation. Their camouflage coloring makes them difficult to see, even when you are close to them. Owlet-nightjars catch flying insects but also seize prey on the ground. Frogmouths roost by day on exposed tree banches, making use of their extremely cryptic plumage and behavior to avoid detection by predators; they perch motionless with their bills pointing upwards and strongly resemble dead branches. The resemblance is so close that sometimes you will stare through your binoculars for extended periods, trying to decide if the object you are watching is a bird or a branch. At dusk, frogmouths begin foraging by "perch-pouncing": sit-ting on various perches, detecting prey—insects and spiders, snails, small vertebrates—and then swooping and grabbing with their bill.

Breeding
Nightjars breed monogamously. No nest is built, but instead the female lays her 1 or 2 eggs on the ground in a small depression, often in leaf litter. Either the female alone or both sexes incubate the eggs for 20 to 28 days, and both parents feed the young once they hatch. The precocial young can fly at about 4 weeks old. As is typical of many ground-nesting species regardless of family, nightjars engage in *broken-wing displays* to distract predators away from the nest and young. They flop around on the ground, often with one or both wings held down as if injured, making gargling or hissing sounds, all the while moving away from the nest. Frogmouth breeding is not well understood. Nests are small platforms of twigs,

moss, and lichens built fairly high up in trees. One to 3 eggs are incubated by the female only or both sexes for about 30 days, and the young, fed by both parents, fledge at about 30 days of age.

Notes
Nightjars are sometimes also called *goatsuckers* or *nighthawks*, both of which are misleading names. At twilight, some species fly low over the ground near grazing animals, such as goats. The birds often fly right next to the mammals to catch insects being scared up as they walk through the grass. Evidently the assumption was that these birds were after the goat's milk, and a legend was born. These often pointed-winged species of birds were also mistaken for hawks flying around at dusk and at night, when accurate identification was difficult, and the name "nighthawk" has stuck ever since.

Status
None of Australia's nightjars are threatened. The MARBLED FROGMOUTH, with a small range in Australia but a larger range in the New Guinea region, is considered rare and vulnerable in New South Wales.

Profiles
Tawny Frogmouth, *Podargus strigoides*, Plate 40d
Australian Owlet-nightjar, *Aegotheles cristatus*, Plate 40e
White-throated Nightjar, *Eurostopodus mystacalis*, Plate 40f

17. Swifts, Swallows, and Woodswallows

Swifts and *swallows*, although not closely related, are remarkably similar in appearance and habit. Most famously, they pursue the same feeding technique—catching insects on the wing during long periods of sustained flight. The swallows (family Hirundinidae) are a passerine group 80 species strong, with a worldwide distribution. Six species occur regularly in Australia, but two, including the near-globally distributed BARN SWALLOW, are present only as nonbreeding migrants. Swallows, including *martins*, are small, streamlined birds, 11.5 to 20 cm (4.5 to 8 in) in length, with short necks, bills, and legs. They have long, pointed wings and forked tails, plainly adapted for sailing through the air with high maneuverability. Some are covered in shades of blue, green, or violet, but many are grey or brown; the sexes look alike. *Woodswallows*, in another passerine group (family Artamidae, which most authorities believe should also include the butcherbirds and currawongs; p. 178), somewhat resemble swallows in form and behavior. They are small birds (12 to 19 cm, 5 to 7.5 in), mostly black, brown, grey, and white, with short legs, long, pointed wings, and blunt, short tails. Their stout, slightly down-curved bill and wide gape are used to catch flying insects. Six of the ten woodswallow species occur in Australia, and the others range over southern Asia.

Swifts, although superficially resembling swallows, are actually only distantly related; they are not even classified with the passerine birds. The 80 or so species of swifts (family Apodidae) are in fact most closely related to hummingbirds. Six species are found in Australia, but only one, the WHITE-RUMPED SWIFTLET (Plate 41), breeds here. Swifts, like swallows, are slender, streamlined birds with long, pointed wings. They are 9 to 25 cm (3.5 to 10 in) long and have very short legs, short tails or long forked tails, and very small bills. Swifts' tails are stiffened to support the birds as they cling to vertical surfaces. The sexes look alike: sooty-grey or brown, with white, greyish, or reddish rumps or flanks. Many are glossily iridescent.

Natural History

Ecology and Behavior

Among the birds, swifts and swallows represent pinnacles of flying prowess and aerial insectivory. It seems as if swifts and swallows fly all day, circling low over water or land or flying in erratic patterns high overhead, snatching insects from the air. Perpetual flight was in the past so much the popular impression of swifts that it was actually thought that they never landed—that they essentially remained flying throughout most of their lives (indeed, it was long ago believed that they lacked feet; hence the family name, Apodidae, literally, *without feet*). They do land, however, although not often. When they do, they use their clawed feet and stiff tail to cling to and brace themselves against vertical structures. WHITE-THROATED NEEDLETAILS (Plate 41), for instance, are sometimes seen at night clinging high up on vegetation. Swifts almost never land on the ground, having trouble launching themselves back into the air from horizontal surfaces. A swift spends more time airborne than any other type of bird, regularly flying all night, and even copulating while in the air (a tricky affair, apparently: male and female are partially in freefall during this activity). Swifts are also aptly named, being among the fastest flyers on record, zipping along at up to 160 kph (100 mph).

Swallows also take insects on the wing as they fly back and forth over water and open areas. Some also eat berries. Not quite the terraphobes that swifts are, swallows land more often, resting usually during the hottest parts of the day. Directly after dawn, however, and at dusk, swallows are always airborne. Woodswallows are known for their habit of huddling together in small groups when perched—a common sight being four to six of them together on a dead tree branch. They fly gracefully with much gliding as they chase insects in flight.

Ecological Interactions

Because swifts and swallows depend each day on capturing enough insects, their daily habits are largely tied to the prevailing weather. Flying insects are thick in the atmosphere on warm, sunny days, but relatively scarce on cold, wet ones. Therefore, on good days, swallows and martins, for instance, can catch their fill of bugs in only a few hours of flying, virtually anywhere. But on cool, wet days, they may need to forage all day to find enough food, and they tend to do so over water or low to the ground, where under such conditions bugs are more available.

Breeding

All swallows are monogamous, many species breeding in dense colonies of several to several thousand nesting pairs. Nests are constructed of plant pieces placed in a tree cavity, burrow, or building, or, alternatively, consist of a mud cup attached to a vertical surface such as a cliff. Both sexes or the female alone incubate the 3 to 7 eggs for 13 to 16 days. Both parents feed nestlings for 18 to 28 days, until they fledge. Woodswallows also nest in colonies, with nests placed usually in trees or bushes. Two to 4 eggs go into cup nests made of twigs, grasses, and roots. Both sexes incubate for 12 to 16 days and feed the young. Swifts are monogamous and most are colonial breeders, but some species nest solitarily. The sexes share breeding chores. Nests consist of plant pieces, twigs, and feathers glued together with the birds' saliva. One to 6 eggs are incubated for 16 to 28 days, with young fledging at 25 to 65 days of age.

Notes

Swallows have a long history of association with people. The ancient Greeks believed swallows to be sacred birds probably because they nested in and flew around the great temples, and during the Roman Empire swallows were considered good luck. In the New World, owing to their insect-eating habits, they have been popular with people going back to the time of the ancient Mayan civilization. Arrival of the first migratory Barn Swallows in Europe is considered a welcoming sign of approaching spring, as is the arrival of CLIFF SWALLOWS at some of California's old Spanish missions. People's alterations of natural habitats, harmful to so many species, are often helpful to swallows, which adopt buildings, bridges, road culverts, roadbanks, and quarry walls as nesting areas. Barn swallows, common in many parts of the world, have for the most part given up nesting in anything other than human-crafted structures.

Status

None of the swifts, swallows, or woodswallows that breed or winter in Australia are threatened. A few species of swifts and swallows from Africa and Asia are known to be quite rare and are considered threatened; for some others, especially swifts, so little is known that we are uncertain of their population sizes or vulnerabilities.

Profiles

White-throated Needletail, *Hirundapus caudacutus*, Plate 41a
White-rumped Swiftlet, *Collocalia spodiopygius*, Plate 41b
Welcome Swallow, *Hirundo neoxena*, Plate 41c
White-backed Swallow, *Cheramoeca leucosternus*, Plate 41d
Fairy Martin, *Hirundo ariel*, Plate 41e
Tree Martin, *Hirundo nigricans*, Plate 41f
Dusky Woodswallow, *Artamus cyanopterus*, Plate 54e
White-breasted Woodswallow, *Artamus leucorynchus*, Plate 54f

18. Kingfishers, Kookaburras, Bee-eaters, and Rollers

Kingfishers are handsome, bright birds of rainforests and woodlands that, in some parts of the world, live chiefly by diving into fresh or salt water to catch fish. However, most of Australia's kingfishers, including the famous *kookaburras*, hunt on land. Classified with the *bee-eaters* and *rollers* in order Coraciiformes, the approximately 90 kingfisher species (family Alcedinidae) range over most of the temperate and tropical areas of the globe. Ten species, including the LAUGHING and BLUE-WINGED KOOKABURRAS (both Plate 42), occur in Australia, and they range in size from the small, fish-eating LITTLE KINGFISHER, at 12 cm (5 in), to the world's largest kingfisher, the Laughing Kookaburra, at up to 46 cm (18 in). (There are a total of four kookaburras, genus *Dacelo*, with two others in New Guinea.) Kingfishers may range in size from small to largish birds, but all are of a similar form: large heads with very long, robust, straight bills, short necks, short legs, and, for some, noticeable crests. *Paradise-kingfishers*, represented in Australia by the BUFF-BREASTED PARADISE-KINGFISHER (Plate 42), often have a few long, thin central tail feathers that stream out from the end of the tail. Kingfishers are usually quite colorful, but in Australia and some other regions, blue and white, along with chestnut-orange, tend to predominate. The bee-eater family, Meropidae (24 species total, mostly in Eurasia and Africa), comprised of smallish, slender, brightly colored birds with long, thin, down-curved bills to feed on flying bugs, has a single Australian representative, the abundant RAINBOW BEE-EATER (Plate 43). Rollers (family Coraciidae, with 12 species distributed around Eurasia, Africa, and the Pacific) are stout-bodied, colorful birds with large heads that also chase flying insects. They are called "rollers" because they roll in flight during their spectacular aerial coutship displays. Australia's single roller is known as the DOLLARBIRD (Plate 43), ostensibly owing to the large bluish white "dollar-sized" spot on each wing.

Natural History

Ecology and Behavior

Despite the name, Australian kingfishers mainly eat insects and their larvae, vertebrates such as small reptiles and mice, and, when near water, freshwater and saltwater crustaceans. Usually seen hunting alone, they perch motionless on a tree branch, fence post, or telephone wire, staring down at the ground. When they detect prey, they glide smoothly down, grab with their bill, and return to a perch to eat. Kookaburras specialize on small snakes, lizards, and rodents, but also take a lot of larger insects. (I'll never forget my day spent with an Australian research biologist, trying to catch kookaburras with traps baited with live mice.) Two Australian kingfishers are fish-eaters (that is, they are *piscivores*). They sit quietly and attentively on a low perch, such as a tree branch over the water, scanning the water below. When they locate suitable prey, they swoop and dive, plunging head first into the water to seize it. If successful, they quickly emerge from the water, return to the perch, beat the fish against the perch to stun it, then swallow it whole, head first. They will also, when they see movement below the water, hover over a particular spot before diving in.

Kingfishers fly fast and purposefully, usually in straight and level flight, from one perch to another; often they are seen only as flashes of blue darting between trees or along waterways. Kingfishers are highly territorial, aggressively defending their territories from other members of their species with noisy, chattering vocalizations, chasing, and fighting. Laughing and Blue-winged Kookaburras are ecologically very similar, have much the same diet, and where their ranges overlap (eastern Queensland), are *inter-specifically territorial*—that is, they defend territories from each other as well as from their own species. The laughing call of the Laughing Kookaburra ("koo-hoo-hoo-hoo-hoo-ha-ha-ha-HA-HA-hoo-hoo-hoo") is perhaps one of the world's most recognizable bird sounds. It is a territorial vocalization, given usually at dawn and dusk, among other times. Often, two or three birds join in, amplifying and prolonging the 5- to 8-second call. The call of the Blue-winged Kookaburra is different but also very distinctive, a maniacal, screeching "kuk-kuk-kuk-kuk" that turns into loud "ow's" and trills and then stops abruptly.

The Rainbow Bee-eater and Dollarbird both "hawk" for flying insects. They sit on exposed perches such as bare banches, then sally out to catch prey that flies by. Bee-eaters, usually gregarious, take many different insects, but usually between 60 and 90% of their prey consists of bees, wasps, and hornets. To avoid being painfully stung, they grip these insects by their abdomens and beat and rub them against a tree branch or other substrate until the venom is discharged; the bugs are then swallowed whole. The bee-eaters may also have some immunity to bee venom.

Breeding

Most kingfishers are monogamous breeders that nest in holes. Both members of the pair help defend the territory in which the nest is located, and both help dig nest burrows in earth or river banks, into termite mounds (such as in the Buff-breasted Paradise-kingfisher), or they help prepare a tree hole. Both parents incubate the two to seven eggs, up to 24 hours at a stretch, for a total of 16 to 24 days. The young are fed by both parents until they fledge at 25 to 38 days old. Fledglings continue to be fed by the parents for up to 12 weeks. Kookaburras are unusual in that the young, when old enough to be independent, sometimes do not leave their parents' territory, but remain there for up to 4 years, helping their parents defend the territory and raise more young. These "auxiliaries" sometimes comprise a third of the adults in some areas; during breeding they help incubate eggs, brood nestlings, defend nests, and feed nestlings and fledglings. Presumably, the advantage to these "helpers at the nest" is that they are assisting in raising close relatives, whose genes they share. A consequence of this family breeding system is that sometimes a single kookaburra nest is tended by 6 or 7 adult birds. Bee-eaters nest in burrows that are tunneled into sandy banks or into the ground. Both sexes contribute to nesting chores; three to seven eggs are incubated for 21 to 25 days. Like the kookaburras, bee-eaters have helpers at the nest, so there may be anywhere from two to eight adults in attendance. Monogamous Dollarbirds nest in tree holes or natural hollows.

Notes

Kingfishers are the subject of a particularly rich mythology, a sign of the bird's conspicuousness and its association with water throughout history. In some parts of the world, kingfishers are associated with the biblical Great Flood. It is said that survivors of the flood had no fire and so the kingfisher was chosen to steal fire from the gods. The bird was successful, but during the theft, burned his chest, resulting in the chestnut-orange coloring we see today in many kingfishers. According to the ancient Greeks, Zeus was jealous of Alcyone's power over the wind and waves and so killed her husband by destroying his ship with thunder and lightning. "In her grief, Alcyone threw herself into the sea to join her husband, and they both turned immediately into kingfishers. The power that sailors attributed to Alcyone was passed on to the Halcyon Bird, the kingfisher, which was credited with protecting sailors and calming storms" (D. Boag 1982). Halcyon birds were thought to nest seven days before and seven days after the winter solstice, and these days of peace and calm, necessary to rear young, were referred to as *halcyon* days.

Some kingfishers die in rather unusual ways. Among the fishing species, many youngsters apparently die during their first attempts at diving for food. Some species that nest in termite nests, such as the FOREST KINGFISHER (Plate 42), have been observed to begin opening a nest burrow by flying at the termite nest and bashing it with their heads; not surprisingly, some die during this effort.

The Laughing Kookaburra is sometimes known as the "bushman's clock" because of the reliability of its dawn calling. One Aboriginal legend is that the laughing call at dawn is "a signal for the sky people to light the great fire that illuminates and warms the Earth by day."

Bee-eaters are killed in some parts of their range, including Australia, because of their cheeky habit of perching near commercial beehives and feeding on the businesses' inventories of stinging insects.

Status

All of Australia's kingfishers are moderately to very common; none are considered threatened. Some do quite well in the vicinity of human settlements. The AZURE KINGFISHER (Plate 42) on Tasmania has a small population, lives along remote stretches of river, and is not often seen. About ten species of kingfishers worldwide currently reside on lists of vulnerable or threatened animals, the most endangered ones being from the Philippines and French Polynesia.

Profiles

Laughing Kookaburra, *Dacelo novaeguineae*, Plate 42a
Azure Kingfisher, *Alcedo azurea*, Plate 42b
Buff-breasted Paradise-kingfisher, *Tanysiptera sylvia*, Plate 42c
Forest Kingfisher, *Todiramphus macleayii*, Plate 42d
Blue-winged Kookaburra, *Dacelo leachii*, Plate 42e
Sacred Kingfisher, *Todiramphus sanctus*, Plate 42f
Dollarbird, *Eurystomus orientalis*, Plate 43a
Rainbow Bee-eater, *Merops ornatus*, Plate 43b

All of the bird families considered below are of *passerine*, or *perching*, birds, contained within order Passeriformes (p. 117).

19. Lyrebirds and Pittas

Treated here are two groups of passerine birds that are on the viewing wish lists of most birdwatchers from North America and Europe and that are frequently emphasized during ecotours and in national park literature and pamphlets. There are multiple reasons for the strong interest, but the only one shared by the two groups is that neither occurs in Europe or the New World, so both are very novel to many visitors to Australia. *Lyrebirds* (family Menuridae, with only two species) attract interest because they are endemic to Australia, occur over a fairly small area, and have spectacular long tails (resembling a Greek lyre—a musical instrument) that are used in courtship displays. They are large (pheasant- or chicken-sized; to 90 cm, 35 in), brownish, secretive, ground-dwelling forest birds with big, powerful feet. The SUPERB LYREBIRD (Plate 43) occurs in southeast Queensland, eastern New South Wales, and Victoria, and has been introduced to Tasmania; it is fairly common if sometimes difficult to see. ALBERT'S LYREBIRD is uncommon and occurs only around the eastern border region between Queensland and New South Wales. Male and female lyrebirds look much alike, but females are a bit smaller and their tails less elaborate. There are about 30 *pitta* species (family Pittidae), distributed in Africa, Asia, and the Australia/New Guinea and Pacific regions; three occur in Australia. Although pittas are, like lyrebirds, secretive ground-dwellers, have fairly small ranges in Australia, and only one, the NOISY PITTA (Plate 43), is a common bird; they are sought out for their bightly colored plumages. Pittas are stocky and smallish (16 to 20 cm, 6 to 8 in, in Australia), with stumpy tails and long legs. They have in common greenish backs and white wing patches that are seen only in flight. One species, the RED-BELLIED PITTA, which occurs in Australia only in the Cape York Peninsula, has a blue and red chest (most of the bright colors in pittas are confined to the underparts). Male and female pittas look alike.

Natural History

Ecology and Behavior

Lyrebirds forage on the forest floor either alone or in small groups. They use their large feet to dig into the earth (to 12 cm, 5 in, deep), exposing worms, spiders, insects and insect larvae, and millipedes, among other invertebrates, which they gobble up. They will also tear apart rotting wood on the forest floor to look for food. The brown lyrebirds are camouflaged on the ground and further protect themselves with their shy, secretive ways. When alarmed, they tend to run speedily away; they are weak flyers, usually managing only short, clumsy flights. They do, however, roost overnight in trees, and usually they jump up, branch by branch, to these high roosts. Lyrebirds are most famous for their courtship displays (see below) and their vocal mimicry. They sing long, loud songs that often include mimicked parts of the vocalizations of such birds as whipbirds, kookaburras, rosellas, cockatoos, currawongs, magpies, and eagles. Lyrebirds are largely sedentary, males maintaining territories of about 2.5 to 3.5 ha (6 to 9 ac) during breeding periods.

Pittas are usually seen alone or in pairs in their rainforest, tropical scrub, and mangrove habitats. They spend most of their time on the ground, so to protect themselves from predators, they are mostly shy and retiring. (Many pittas are thought to be fairly rare, but it may just be that they are hard to detect, given their secretive ways.) But they do roost in trees at night and they also fly up to high tree perches to vocalize. Pittas hop along, foraging by using their strong bills to flip, scatter, and toss leaves and other vegetation on the forest floor. They are searching for snails, insects, spiders, worms, and even crabs and small lizards. When a hard-shelled animal is caught, pittas bash them against rocks or logs to crack them open. Pittas are fairly strong fliers, and some, such as the Red-bellied Pitta, which winters in New Guinea, are migratory.

Breeding

Lyrebirds are promiscuous breeders. Males on their territories give vocal and visual displays to attract females. They strut around on the ground, on low tree branches, and, like the Superb Lyrebird, on raised earthen mounds, singing and displaying their gaudy tails. The central part of the long tail is held, spread and fan-like, over the head, and the two large, boldly patterned side feathers (*lyrates*) point out to either side. When a female approaches, the male quivers the tail feathers, and there is much jumping and circling. After mating, the female departs to nest on her own. She builds a nest of sticks, moss, bark, and rootlets on or near the ground in vegetation tangles or on earthen banks, in tree ferns, or on rock faces, among other places. One egg is incubated for about 40 days, and the nestling fledges after about 45 days in the nest. Pittas are monogamous, both sexes participating in nest construction, incubation, and feeding young. The nest is a large, loosely constructed domed structure of sticks, leaves, moss, and rootlets on or near the ground in trees, vegetation tangles, or rock cavities. Two to 7 eggs are incubated for about 2 weeks.

Notes

The Noisy Pitta has one very odd aspect to its nesting: it brings pieces of mammal droppings to its nest and places them just outside, as a "doormat"; the function of this odoriferous behavior is unknown.

Status
The two species of lyrebirds are not threatened at this time, but they are restricted to relatively small areas of moist forest that are increasingly cleared or degraded. ALBERT'S LYREBIRD is considered vulnerable in Queensland. Lyrebirds were killed in great numbers during the nineteenth century for their tail feathers. Australia's pittas are secure, but several pitta species in the New Guinea/Indonesia region are vulnerable (IUCN Red List); Thailand's endangered GURNEY'S PITTA survives now with only about 25 breeding pairs.

Profiles
Noisy Pitta, *Pitta versicolor,* Plate 43c
Superb Lyrebird, *Menura novaehollandiae*, Plate 43d

20. Treecreepers and Fairy-wrens

Detailed here are two groups of small insect-eaters, one highly camouflaged and often difficult to see, one brightly colored and sometimes easily observed. *Australian treecreepers,* family Climacteridae, are small (13 to 19 cm, 5 to 7.5 in), stocky, brownish forest birds with tan/fawn wingbars, slender, ever-so-slightly down-curved bills, and long toes and live by searching for insects on tree trunks and branches. There are only seven species, six of which are endemic to Australia and one to New Guinea. Male and female treecreepers look slightly different.

Family Maluridae contains about 28 species of small insect-eaters that mainly inhabit shrubs, thickets, and undergrowth and that are known as *fairy-wrens, emu-wrens,* and *grass-wrens*; 22 species occur in Australia and the remainder in the New Guinea region. A few species are common denizens of forest edge areas, parklands, and picnic grounds, so they are commonly seen. These birds, 14 to 22 cm (5.5 to 8.5 in) long, with small, short dark bills and long tails (half or more of each bird's total length) that are usually held stiffly upwards, often stand out because the males have patches of varying sizes of bright, iridescent blue. Some of these birds, including the male SUPERB FAIRY-WREN (Plate 44), are considered by bird-lovers to be among the world's most beautiful small birds. Females in the group are usually brownish, some having blue tails.

Natural History

Ecology and Behavior
Treecreepers hop over tree trunks and branches, using their slender bills to poke and probe for insects, especially ants. They forage in predictable patterns, spiraling up tree trunks, then flying down to the bottom of the trunk of the next tree and repeating the process, or moving along thick tree branches, from the base outwards. Some also forage on the ground. Treecreepers are sedentary birds, holding permanent territories in which they forage and breed. Fairy-wrens (and grass-wrens and emu-wrens) are also mostly sedentary. They live in highly social, communal groups, usually consisting of a dominant male and female that breed and subordinate nonbreeders that help with nesting and maintaining the year-round territory. The helpers, or "auxiliaries," are male offspring from previous nests that stay with their parents for one or more years to help out before striking out on their own. Fairy-wrens occupy all kinds of terrestrial habitats, from rainforests to desert grasslands and rocky hillsides, but they are most typical of

grassland, heath, thickets, and shrub areas. They forage on the ground and in shrubs, hopping as they search for insects to eat; grass-wrens also eat seeds.

Breeding

Most of the treecreepers, such as the BROWN TREECREEPER (Plate 43), breed in small communal groups. "Auxiliary" males, presumably related to the main breeding pair, help feed the young (and sometimes the incubating female). Both sexes build the nest, a saucer-shaped mat of leaves, bark, fur, and feathers placed in a tree hollow. Usually only the female incubates the 2 to 4 eggs, for 16 to 18 days. Young fledge when about 25 days old. The WHITE-THROATED TREECREEPER (Plate 43) is a bit different. It breeds in solitary pairs; the female builds the nest and incubates the 2 or 3 eggs for about 22 days. In fairy-wrens, the female alone usually builds the nest, a dome of vegetation in a shrub or low thicket, and incubates the 2 to 5 eggs for 13 to 16 days. The male and other members of the group help feed the young for 12 to 14 days, until fledging. Cuckoos heavily parasitize (p. 154) fairy-wren nests.

Notes

Emu-wrens were so-named because their long tail feathers are thought to be emu-like—coarse, loose, and messy; they lack the tiny hooks that, in most birds, hold the feather barbs together, forming and stiffening the feathers. Emu-wrens are usually difficult to see, and this is the main reason none are illustrated here.

Status

None of Australia's treecreepers are threatened. However, three of the six species are considered vulnerable in various Australian states owing to their dependence on forest habitats that are increasingly cleared or degraded. The Brown Treecreeper, for instance, is vulnerable in the Australian Capital Territory, and the WHITE-BROWED TREECREEPER is vulnerable in Victoria. Most of the fairy-wrens are common birds. The MALLEE EMU-WREN is endangered in South Australia and vulnerable in Victoria; more than half of its historical scrub and grassland habitat has been cleared for agriculture. The THICK-BILLED GRASS-WREN is endangered in Western Australia; many of its populations in Australia have declined precipitously during the past century.

Profiles

White-throated Treecreeper, *Cormobates leucophaeus*, Plate 43e
Brown Treecreeper, *Climacteris picumnus*, Plate 43f
Superb Fairy-wren, *Malurus cyaneus*, Plate 44a
Variegated Fairy-wren, *Malurus lamberti*, Plate 44b
Red-backed Fairy-wren, *Malurus melanocephalus*, Plate 44c

21. Australian Warblers (Pardalotes, Scrubwrens, Gerygones, and Thornbills)

Birdwatchers and other observant travellers will realize that there are large numbers of tiny birds that flit about Australian trees, shrubs, and on the ground. For good reason, these birds are treated here only lightly. Owing to their sizes, agile natures, and mostly dull plumages, they are often difficult to identify, even for journeymen birdwatchers, who sometimes despair of trying to differentiate between the various species. So for our purposes, brief descriptions of a few of the groups of these birds will suffice. When one's interest is sufficiently piqued by these tiny birds to warrant further exploration, it is time to consider oneself a birdwatcher and to invest in a professional field guide! The main family in question is Pardalotidae, which contains about 65 species distributed in Australia, New Guinea, New Zealand, and the Indonesia/Malaysia region; 47 occur in Australia. Most of these are very small birds (*pardalotes* 8 to 12 cm, 3 to 5 in; *scrubwrens* 11 to 14 cm, 4 to 5.5 in; *gerygones* 9.5 to 11.5 cm, 3.5 to 4.5 in; *thornbills* 9 to 12 cm, 3.5 to 5 in), although a few, such as the thicket-dwelling *bristlebirds*, range up to 27 cm (10.5 in). They tend to be dully, cryptically colored. Browns, olives, and greys predominate, so much so that North American birders will be tempted to lump them with the "LBJs" ("little brown jobs") or, in the local vernacular, "WLBBs," ("wretched little brown birds"). Some species usually hold their tail erect, or "cocked," like wrens, and so are called scrubwrens, *heathwrens*, or *field-wrens*; others are warbler-like in their looks and behavior, and therefore the entire group is sometimes called "Australian warblers." Pardalotes (pardl-OATS; four species total, all endemic to Australia), sometimes called *diamond birds*, are perhaps the most distinctive of the group, having very short bills and tails and being brightly patterned with patches of white, black, brown, red, and yellow. Males and females in all these groups generally look the same or almost the same.

Natural History

Ecology and Behavior

These birds inhabit mainly rainforests, open eucalypt forests, and mangroves, but some occur in heaths, shrubland, thickets, or grassland. Most species are arboreal insect-eaters, but behavior is variable; many also eat some plant materials, especially seeds. Scrubwrens feed on the ground or in lower parts of vegetation, often taking snails and crustaceans; they are seen alone, in pairs, or in small groups. Gerygones (jeh-RIG-on-eez; also known as *fairy warblers*) feed singly or in pairs on insects they find in the outer foliage of woodland trees. Thornbills, always very active, usually feed in small groups on insects and occasional seeds; some specialize on the tree canopy, some at lower levels of the forest, and some are more terrestrial feeders, foraging on fallen tree limbs and even on the ground. Pardalotes scurry about the high leaves of eucalypts, especially in trees along watercourses, searching for insects; they often hang upside down to search a leaf or grab a bug. Many of these birds are sedentary, but some, such as the pardalotes, gather into flocks after breeding and make migratory or nomadic movements.

Breeding

Most of these small, cryptically colored birds construct small dome-shaped nests of vegetation (grass, bark, stems, roots), often lined with feathers, which are placed on or in the ground, in tree cavities, or in shrubs or tree foliage. Two to 5 eggs are incubated for 12 to 21 days until hatching. Some species have been studied in detail. For instance, in the endemic WHITE-BROWED SCRUBWREN (Plate 45), clutch size is usually 3 eggs, and during the long breeding season (5 months), 2 or even 3 broods can be raised successfully. But precise breeding information is not known for several species. Most species are monogamous, but a good number are *cooperative breeders*, in which grown young from previous nests stay with their parents and help them maintain their breeding territories and feed young in subsequent nests. In many (gerygones and thornbills, for instance), the female builds the nest and incubates alone, but the male and, often, other members of the family group, help feed the young. In other groups, male and female share nesting duties more equally. Pardalotes breed in monogamous pairs or in small groups that include nest helpers. A cup or domed nest is placed in a burrow in the ground or in a tree hollow; both the male and female dig the burrow, build the nest, and usually share incubation.

Notes

The WEEBILL, tiny, yellowish, and similar in habits to thornbills and gerygones, is Australia's smallest bird (8 to 9 cm, 3 to 3.5 in).

Status

Most of the "Australian warblers" are secure, but a few species are in trouble, mostly because of habitat destruction. One of the four pardalotes, the FORTY-SPOTTED PARDALOTE, endemic to Tasmania, is now confined to small bits—peninsulas and small near-shore islands—of southeast Tasmania; it is endangered (IUCN Red List). Two of the three bristlebirds, the EASTERN and WESTERN BRISTLEBIRDS, only occur over small ranges, and are endangered (IUCN Red List for both; CITES Appendix I for Western) by vegetation clearance and by the effect of introduced plants and animals, among other reasons.

Profiles

Spotted Pardalote, *Pardalotus punctatus*, Plate 44d
Striated Pardalote, *Pardalotus striatus*, Plate 44e
White-throated Gerygone, *Gerygone olivacea*, Plate 44f
Brown Gerygone, *Gerygone mouki*, Plate 45a
Yellow-throated Scrubwren, *Sericornis citreogularis*, Plate 45b
White-browed Scrubwren, *Sericornis frontalis*, Plate 45c
Brown Thornbill, *Acanthiza pusilla*, Plate 45d
Yellow-rumped Thornbill, *Acanthiza chrysorrhoa*, Plate 45e
Yellow Thornbill, *Acanthiza nana*, Plate 45f

22. Honeyeaters and Chats

If you drive through the Australian countryside and stop at a roadside picnic area or visit a national park and walk along a trail, your attention almost certainly will be drawn eventually to an abundant group of very active, noisy, aggressive, usually plain-looking small and mid-sized birds known as *honeyeaters*. Comprising Australia's largest bird family, they are everywhere on the continent, occupying essentially all terrestrial habitats. These arboreal birds are so abundant and successful that in many woodland areas there are 10 or more species present, sometimes at densities of up to 20 individuals per species per hectare (2.5 ac). The family, Meliphagidae ("meli" means honey; "phag," means eater) contains about 170 species that are distributed mostly in the Australia/New Guinea region, but also in New Zealand and on many Pacific islands; 71 species, including five within a subgroup known as *Australian chats*, occur in Australia. The reason for this group's great success in Australia is related to its chief food source—plant nectar. These birds specialize in feeding on nectar (also taking some fruit and insects; see below), and nectar, which is mostly a sugar-water solution, is super-abundant in most habitats across Australia. (Possible reasons for this are discussed in Close-up 4, p. 192.) For instance, it is estimated that a single large eucalyptus tree can support about fifteen honeyeaters for one to two months during its peak flowering period.

Honeyeaters are small (13 to 20 cm, 5 to 8 in) or, in their most conspicuous forms, mid-sized (20 to 35 cm, 8 to 14 in), slender, streamlined birds with long, slim, down-curved bills. Most are attired in dull grey, greenish olive, or brown, often with streaks—not the most visually glamorous of birds. But many have small, contrasting patches of yellow, and one group, genus *Myzomela*, is largely red. Many, such as the *friarbirds*, have areas of bare skin on the face, and some, such as the *wattlebirds*, have hanging protuberances from the ear or eye region. In most species, males and females look alike, but females are usually smaller.

The Australian chats are small (10 to 13 cm, 4 to 5 in), brightly colored birds of open country that forage by walking along the ground, picking up seeds and insects in their straight, slim, dark bills. There are five species total, all endemic to Australia, now included in the honeyeater family; in times past they were variously placed in with the thornbills (p. 166) or given their own family.

Natural History

Ecology and Behavior
Honeyeaters are mainly birds of forests and heath areas, but some occupy more open habitats. Gregarious, pugnacious birds, they forage in flowering trees and shrubs usually in small parties. If you watch them, you can see that they often squabble over feeding areas, sometimes chasing each other and different species away from good food resources; apparently, groups in some species form feeding hierarchies, with the largest individuals at a fruiting tree having feeding precedence. Most honeyeaters have very long tongues that can be thrust deep into long, tubular flowers to collect nectar and into cracks between pieces of tree bark to gather other fluids. The tongue is tipped with a brush-like structure that soaks up nectar and other fluids like a mop; it is then "wrung-out" against the roof of the mouth. Many of these birds can flick their tongues into flowers at rates of up to ten licks per second, thus quickly emptying flowers of nectar. Probably all honeyeaters include in their diet, to varying degrees, some insects (for protein), and some take a good amount of fruit and berries (particularly the rainforest species); other sugary substances consumed are *honeydew* (a sugary solution produced by some small insects after they feed on plant juices), *manna* (sugary granules from damaged eucalypt leaves), and *lerp* (sugary coatings of some sap-sucking insects).

In some regions, honeyeaters fall into three broad groups: the chiefly *nectarivorous*, such as the wattlebirds and the BROWN (Plate 48) and NEW HOLLAND HONEYEATERS (Plate 49), feeding mainly on nectar; the *insectivorous*, such as the BELL and NOISY MINERS (Plate 47), searching tree trunks, branches, and leaves for insects as well as lerp and honeydew; and the *frugivorous*, such as the SPINY-CHEEKED and SINGING HONEYEATERS, which concentrate on fruit when it is in season. Honeyeaters are often nomadic birds, settling opportunistically in places with flowering trees and shrubs and then, when food availability declines, moving on to new areas. Many apparently only establish territories during breeding periods.

Ecological Interactions
Honeyeaters spend a large portion of their time feeding at tree and shrub flowers and, in so doing, pick up a lot of pollen on their bodies and transport it to other plants of the same species, where it falls off, thus helping plants achieve pollination. Most honeyeaters typically carry around thousands of pollen grains, from several plant species, from flower to flower. Because honeyeaters are so diverse

and abundant in Australia, it is not surprising that many Australian plants use these birds, instead of insects, as their main pollinators. Many trees have flowers with long, narrow tubes, sometimes with surrounding hairs, that prevent insects from stealing nectar, but that are perfectly structured for ease of entry by the honeyeaters' long, slender bills and tongues. Also, these flowers are often red or yellow, colors the birds see but that insects have trouble with. Estimates are that at least 1,000 Australian plants (including most of the native tree and shrub flora) are pollinated at least partially by birds. Many honeyeaters also disperse plant seeds that are in the fruits and berries they eat or that stick temporarily to their bodies and later fall off. These birds therefore help spread and maintain populations of Australian trees and shrubs.

Breeding
Honeyeater breeding is tied to food availability; most species breed from July to December when most trees and shrubs flower. Most species nest alone in monogamous pairs but some nest in colonial groups of up to 20 or more pairs. Only the female builds the nest, a rough cup made of twigs and bark that is placed in a tree/shrub fork or hung from small branches. She also is the sole incubator, for about 2 weeks, of the 1 to 2 eggs (rainforest species) or 2 to 4 eggs (woodland and open-country species). Males help feed the young, which fledge at 10 to 16 days old.

Notes
Honeyeaters that eat fruit sometimes damage orchards, and, especially in the past, some of these birds were persecuted for their actions. In coastal Queensland, the BLUE-FACED HONEYEATER (Plate 46) is known as the banana bird because it feeds on and damages bananas on banana plantations. The YELLOW WATTLEBIRD, a Tasmanian endemic and one of the largest of the honeyeaters at up to 48 cm (19 in) long and 250 g (a half-pound) in weight, was regularly shot during an annual hunting season until the early 1970s, both to cull populations to reduce orchard damage, and for eating—their fruit and nectar diets apparently make them quite delicious.

Status
Most of Australia's honeyeaters are abundant birds. A few species are rare in certain parts of their ranges and are considered vulnerable in some states because of this. Loss and degradation of their forest and woodland habitats is the chief threat to these birds, and these are the probable reasons that two Australian species are endangered (IUCN Red List), the REGENT HONEYEATER and BLACK-EARED MINER. About five members of family Meliphagidae occurred in Hawaii (US). They were striking mid-sized birds, mostly black with patches of yellow, with long tails and long down-curved bills. As of the mid-1980s, two species, the KAUAI OO and BISHOP'S OO, still lived; now all are probably extinct, victims of habitat loss and introduced diseases.

Profiles
Red Wattlebird, *Anthochaera carnunculata*, Plate 46a
Little Wattlebird, *Anthochaera chrysoptera*, Plate 46b
Noisy Friarbird, *Philemon corniculatus*, Plate 46c
Little Friarbird, *Philemon citreogularis*, Plate 46d
Blue-faced Honeyeater, *Entomyzon cyanotis*, Plate 46e

Lewin's Honeyeater, *Meliphaga lewinii*, Plate 46f
Bell Miner, *Manorina melanophrys*, Plate 47a
Noisy Miner, *Manorina melanocephala*, Plate 47b
Bridled Honeyeater, *Lichenostomus frenatus*, Plate 47c
Yellow-faced Honeyeater, *Lichenostomus chrysops*, Plate 47d
Varied Honeyeater, *Lichenostomus versicolor*, Plate 47e
White-eared Honeyeater, *Lichenostomus leucotis*, Plate 48a
Fuscous Honeyeater, *Lichenostomus fuscus*, Plate 48b
White-plumed Honeyeater, *Lichenostomus penicillatus*, Plate 48c
White-naped Honeyeater, *Melithreptus lunatus*, Plate 48d
Brown Honeyeater, *Lichmera indistincta*, Plate 48e
Eastern Spinebill, *Acanthorhynchus tenuirostris*, Plate 49a
New Holland Honeyeater, *Phylidonyris novaehollandiae*, Plate 49b
Banded Honeyeater, *Certhionyx pectoralis*, Plate 49c
Scarlet Honeyeater, *Myzomela sanguinolenta*, Plate 49d
White-fronted Chat, *Epthianura albifrons*, Plate 49e

23. Robins, Babblers, and Logrunners

Detailed here are a large group of commonly seen arboreal songbirds and two smaller groups of less frequently observed ground-dwellers. The *Australian robins* are sometimes known as Australia's "perch-and-pounce insectivores." A mid-sized group (family Petroicidae) of 45 species spread over Australia, New Guinea, New Zealand and some Pacific islands, about 20 species occur in Australia, occupying essentially all wooded habitats. These are generally small (11 to 17 cm, 4.5 to 6.5 in), plumpish birds with large, rounded heads, large eyes, squarish tails, and, in most, white wing bars. Their short dark bills are surrounded by small whiskers (*rictal bristles*) that presumably help funnel flying or running insects into the mouth. The Australian robins can be divided into several groups based on plumage color. There is a "red" group, including the FLAME ROBIN (Plate 50) and RED-CAPPED ROBIN, in which males have bright red or pinkish breasts (presumably furnishing the group name "robin," after the European red-breasted robins); a "yellow" group, including the EASTERN YELLOW and PALE YELLOW ROBINS (both Plate 50); a "brown" group, including the JACKY WINTER and DUSKY ROBIN (both Plate 50); and an "other colors" group, including some that are black and white. In most species, the sexes look alike; the main exception is the red robins, in which females are brownish.

The *Australian babblers* are a small group of highly social, noisy, active birds that forage chiefly on the ground for insects. The family, Pomatostomidae, has five species, four of which occur in Australia (three are endemic and one is shared with New Guinea). They resemble the Eurasian babblers somewhat in behavior and appearance, but the two groups are not closely related. Australian babblers are medium-sized birds (18 to 29 cm, 7 to 11.5 in) with longish, down-curved bills. They are brown with boldly patterned white and brown faces and white-tipped tails. There are just two species of *logrunners*, family Orthonychidae, and both occur in Australia only in eastern wet forests; one also occurs in New Guinea. These are chunky, ground-dwelling, mid-sized songbirds (17 to 28 cm, 7 to 11 in), mostly brown and white, with short bills and largish feet. Another name for the LOGRUNNER (Plate 51) is Spine-tailed Logrunner, after the "spines," or short pieces of bare feather shafts, that protrude from the end of the tail in both logrunners. The other logrunner is known as the CHOWCHILLA, because some of its calls sound like this word.

Natural History

Ecology and Behavior

Australian robins occur mainly in forests and woodlands. A few larger species (*scrub-robins*) forage on the ground, but the great majority sit on tree branches or other perches, often with their tails moving up and down or side to side and flicking their wings, watching for potential prey. When a likely meal (chiefly insects and other invertebrates) is spotted, the bird flies gracefully down, grabs the prey from the ground or other surface, then returns back to its perch to feast. One group (genus *Microeca*), the most flycatcher-like of the family, spends a lot of time flying, chasing, and grabbing insects on the wing; there are three *Microeca* flycatchers in Australia, including the Jacky Winter. Some robins, in pairs, maintain year-round territories; others spend non-breeding periods in moving flocks of insectivorous birds.

Australian babblers spend their days in small groups of up to a dozen related individuals, and even sleep together in domed stick "dormitories" that they build in trees. These groups are fairly sedentary and defend communal territories. They forage on the ground, picking up bugs but also pushing their pointed bills into the soil to dig for insect larvae. They also search lower parts of tree trunks, branches, and shrubs for food. Although eating mostly insects, they are considered omnivorous, also snacking on spiders, tiny frogs and reptiles, crustaceans, and even some seeds and fruit. Babblers fly quickly, low to the ground, from place to place, or run ("bounce") from danger. Logrunners are noisy rainforest birds that live on territories in permanent communal groups of typically five or six. They use their large feet to scratch and scrape the ground for insects, crustaceans, and other forest-floor invertebrates. They fly little, foraging and escaping danger mostly via rapid running and hopping.

Breeding

Australian robins are generally monogamous breeders, both the male and female defending a territory in which they nest. The female usually builds the nest and incubates the 1 to 3 eggs for 13 to 18 days, but in some, such as the Jacky Winter, the male also incubates. Both sexes feed nestlings, which fledge in 10 to 18 days. Nests are small, shallow, cup-shaped affairs, placed among a tree's small branches or in a fork. Babblers breed communally, the dominant male and female doing the actual reproducing, the other members of the group (mostly young from previous nests) helping to feed the incubating female and then the developing nestlings and fledglings. The breeding pair builds the domed stick nest in a tree. The female alone incubates the 2 to 4 eggs for 16 to 23 days, and young fledge after about 3 weeks in the nest. Logrunners breed in pairs or communal groups. The female builds the domed nest of sticks and moss on the ground or in low vegetation and she incubates the 1 to 2 eggs. Males, with or without other members of the communal group, assist with feeding young.

Status

Most of the Australian robins are common or abundant birds. The GREY-HEADED ROBIN (Plate 50) has only a small distribution in the rainforests of northeastern Queensland, so they may be vulnerable in the future. The subspecies of the SCARLET ROBIN that occurs only on Norfolk Island is considered vulnerable—

habitat clearance and introduced predators are the reasons. The GREY-CROWNED BABBLER (Plate 51) has experienced population declines in several regions of Australia and is now classified as endangered in Victoria and South Australia.

Profiles
Flame Robin, *Petroica phoenicea*, Plate 50a
Jacky Winter, *Microeca fascinans*, Plate 50b
Eastern Yellow Robin, *Eopsaltria australis*, Plate 50c
Dusky Robin, *Melanodryas vittata*, Plate 50d
Pale-yellow Robin, *Tregellasia capito*, Plate 50e
Grey-headed Robin, *Heteromyias albispecularis*, Plate 50f
Logrunner, *Orthonyx temminckii*, Plate 51a
Grey-crowned Babbler, *Pomatostomus temporalis*, Plate 51b

24. Whipbirds, Whistlers, and Sittella

The three groups of small to mid-sized insect-eating songbirds described here include family Cinclosomatidae (totaling fifteen species distributed mainly in Australia and New Guinea, eight in Australia), which contains the *whipbirds* and *quail-thrushes*. The EASTERN WHIPBIRD (Plate 51), one of the two whipbirds, is the source of one of the most striking, characteristic sounds of eastern Australia's wet forests, a brief, very loud call that resembles a crack of a whip; you will know it as soon as you hear it. Whipbirds, mid-sized (to 30 cm, 12 in) and crested, are olive-brownish with black-and-white heads. Australia's four quail-thrushes, including the SPOTTED QUAIL-THRUSH (Plate 51), 18 to 28 cm (7 to 11 in) long, are boldly patterned in brown and grey and black and white.

Family Pachycephalidae contains about 47 species of *whistlers, shrike-thrushes, shrike-tits,* and *bellbirds,* distributed throughout Australia, New Guinea, many Pacific islands, and parts of Southeast Asia; 14 species occur in Australia. Known collectively as "whistlers" or "thickheads," these birds, which inhabit most areas with trees, are small to mid-sized (14 to 26 cm, 5.5 to 10 in), with robust bodies, thick, rounded heads, and thickish, strong bills. Some have bills with down-curved tips, like shrikes; hence the names shrike-thrushes and shrike-tits. Most of these birds (some whistlers and the shrike-thrushes and bellbirds) are outfitted in dull greys and browns, whereas others (shrike-tits, some whistlers) are boldly marked with bright yellows and black and white. Male and female thickheads generally look slightly different, females being duller.

The VARIED SITTELLA (Plate 51) is Australia's only member of the small family Neosittidae, which includes a total of three species of *sittellas* (the others in New Guinea); the group is closely related to the whistlers. Sittellas are small birds dwelling in tree trunks and branches. They are grey-brown and black and white, with longish, slim, slightly upturned bills, short tails, and yellow legs.

Natural History

Ecology and Behavior
Eastern Whipbirds occupy Australia's eastern wet forests and coastal scrubs. They forage on or near the ground for insects and insect larvae. Remaining year-round in mated pairs on territories 5 to 10 ha (12 to 24 ac) in area, the male and female call back and forth to each other in brief duets as they forage in dense forest, to advertise their territory and to keep track of each other; the male give the loud

"whipcrack" call, and the female answers with some brief, softer calls of her own. Quail-thrushes, fairly secretive birds, live on the forest floor in pairs or small groups.

Whistlers forage mainly for insects and insect larvae on tree trunks and branches (sometimes stripping pieces of bark away to look underneath), in tree foliage, and in some species, on the ground. Some larger species, such as the shrike-thrushes, also eat bird eggs and even small birds. Many of the whistlers are solitary during non-breeding periods, but others apparently occupy year-round territories in pairs; some, such as the shrike-tits and CRESTED BELLBIRD, often travel around in small family groups. Sittellas, also known as "treerunners," climb among a tree's trunk and branches, foraging for bugs; they probe in cracks and crevices and use their bills to flake off pieces of bark, looking for hidden insects and other small invertebrates. They usually traverse woodlands in communal groups of three to twelve or more. The groups are very social, the members huddling together when perched on tree branches and often preening each other.

Breeding

Whipbirds breed in monogamous pairs. The nest is a bulky cup of woven twigs placed in a shrub or thicket. The female incubates usually 2 eggs for about 17 days, while the male feeds her. Both sexes feed the young. At 10 to 11 days old, the nestlings hop out of the nest. These fledglings hide in the undergrowth for about a week, while the parents bring them food, until they can fly.

Whistlers are monogamous breeders, except for the shrike-tits, which breed in communal groups. Nests are usually coarse cups of twigs and bark placed in a tree fork or crevice. Both sexes carry out all or most nesting duties. One to 4 eggs are incubated for 14 to 18 days; young fledge after 10 to 15 days in the nest.

Sitellas breed communally, with the dominant male and female reproducing, the others in the group helping with nest construction and feeding the young. The breeding female alone incubates the 2 or 3 eggs for 18 to 20 days in the deep-cup nest that is placed in a tree fork. Young fledge when about 3 weeks old.

Notes

The Crested Bellbird, known especially for the the male's loud, far-carrying, liquid-noted song (rendered often as "pan-pan pallella"), has an unusual nest-decorating habit: it squeezes hairy caterpillars ("bushworms") to incapacitate them, then, for reasons known only to the bellbird, hangs them from the rim of the nest.

Status

Most species in the whipbird, whistler, and sittella groups are common and secure. A few species are threatened in some parts of their ranges owing to destruction of their woodland habitats. The WESTERN WHIPBIRD, which occurs now only in several small, fragmented populations over southern Australia, is considered vulnerable in South Australia and endangered in Western Australia. The Spotted Quail-thrush is endangered in South Australia, and the RED-LORED WHISTLER is endangered in New South Wales.

Profiles

Eastern Whipbird, *Psophodes olivaceus*, Plate 51c
Spotted Quail-thrush, *Cinclosoma punctatum*, Plate 51d
Varied Sittella, *Daphoenositta chrysoptera*, Plate 51e
Golden Whistler, *Pachycephala pectoralis*, Plate 52a
Crested Shrike-tit, *Falcunculus frontatus*, Plate 52b

Rufous Whistler, *Pachycephala rufiventris*, Plate 52c
Little Shrike-thrush, *Colluricincla megarhyncha*, Plate 52d
Grey Shrike-thrush, *Colluricincla harmonica*, Plate 52e

25. Flycatchers, Monarchs, Fantails, Magpie-larks, and Drongos

One of the dirty little secrets of Australian ornithology is the presence of numerous species of common black-and-white roadside songbirds that are sufficiently similar in appearance to drive the newly arrived novice birdwatcher bonkers. Two of these super-abundant black and white birds of settled areas, parks, and roadsides, the MAGPIE-LARK (Plate 55) and WILLIE WAGTAIL (Plate 53), are included in family Dicruridae, which encompasses Australia's *flycatchers* and others known as *monarchs, fantails,* and the SPANGLED DRONGO (Plate 54). (The other confusingly similar black-and-white birds are butcherbirds and the Australian magpie; both p. 178.) Most of these *dicrurids* are forest and woodland birds that feed by employing the classic flycatching technique: they perch motionless (or with tail moving) on branches, fences, or telephone wires, then dart out ("sally") in short, swift flights to snatch from the air insects foolhardy enough to enter their field of vision; they then return time and again to the same perch to repeat the process. Because of this behavior, the group can be considered "Australia's sallying insectivores." The family has about 140 member species distributed around Africa, Southeast Asia, and the Australian region. Nineteen species occur in Australia, mainly five flycatchers, six monarchs, five fantails, the drongo and the Magpie-lark. Dicrurids are small to mid-sized (most 14 to 21 cm, 5.5 to 8 in), with smallish but broad ridged bills that facilitate insect catching; most also have small whiskers around the bill (*rictal bristles*) that presumably help funnel flying bugs into the mouth. Tails are generally relatively long, to aid in highly maneuverable flight; the mid-sized drongo (to 32 cm, 12.5 in) has a conspicuously long, forked, upturned tail. (Drongos are a mostly Old World tropics group, about 20 species occuring in Africa and Asia.) Most, because they make their livings flying, have small, weak feet; a notable exception is the longer-legged, slender-billed Magpie-lark, which forages on the ground. Dicrurids are mostly clad in contrasting patterns of grey, reddish brown or reddish orange, or black and white. Many species exhibit strong *sexual dimorphism*—males and females look different.

Natural History

Ecology and Behavior

Flycatchers, monarchs, and fantails are usually spotted foraging either solitarily or in small family groups; the Magpie-lark, post-breeding, often gathers in small semi-nomadic flocks. Some (the flycatchers) tend to vibrate their tails while perched, as they search the atmosphere for flying insects. Others (fantails and some monarchs) move or fan their tails as they move through shrubs and foliage, hunting dinner; the tail movements may help flush insects from hiding places. Although "flycatching" is the feeding technique used most often in the group, other methods are employed. Some, such as the drongo, also take insects from foliage; some monarchs hop over tree trunks and branches in search of bugs; the Magpie-lark forages on damp ground and even in shallow fresh water for insects, earthworms, and mollusks; and Willie Wagtail, plentiful in urban and suburban areas, pursues insects, especially butterflies, on or near the ground. About half the dicrurid species are migratory, moving northwards after breeding to other parts of Australia, some to New Guinea, in search of food. Willie Wagtails are fairly sedentary. All of these birds breed in monogamous pairs, establishing breeding-season or year-round territories that are often aggressively defended from other members of the same species. Magpie-lark territories, for instance, have been measured to cover about 8 to 10 ha (20 to 25 ac). Willie Wagtails are celebrated for their aggressiveness, often chasing much larger birds, such as kookaburras, from their territories.

Breeding

In these birds, both males and females usually participate in all aspects of nesting: helping to build nests, incubate eggs, and feed and brood young. Flycatchers, monarchs, and fantails build cup-shaped nests of grasses and/or other vegetation, often held togther with spider-webbing or mud, and placed on a tree branch. Willie Wagtails build a small grass cup in a tree; 2 to 4 eggs are incubated for 2 weeks, and young fledge 2 weeks post-hatching. Magpie-larks construct on a tree branch a bowl of fibrous vegetation bound with mud; 3 to 5 eggs are incubated for about 17 days; young fledge at about 20 days old. Drongos have saucer-shaped nests that contain 3 to 5 eggs.

Notes

Willie Wagtail's name, as you might expect, arises with the bird's movements; when active or at rest, these birds almost constantly sway their bodies and wag their tails. A common name for the Magpie-lark is "peewee," after one of its commonest calls. In Australia, a person who is considered a jerk is sometimes called a "drongo"—perhaps alluding to the bird's seemingly ridiculous aerial maneuvers (during which, it is, of course, actually catching its food).

Status

Most of the Australian birds in this group are very common; none are currently threatened. Two drongoes of the Comoros Islands region, the GRAND COMORO DRONGO and the MAYOTTE DRONGO, are endangered.

Profiles

Leaden Flycatcher, *Myiagra rubecula,* Plate 53a
Black-faced Monarch, *Monarcha melanopsis,* Plate 53b
Grey Fantail, *Rhipidura fuliginosa,* Plate 53c
Restless Flycatcher, *Myiagra inquieta,* Plate 53d
Willie Wagtail, *Rhipidura leucophrys,* Plate 53e
Spangled Drongo, *Dicrurus bracteatus,* Plate 54b
Magpie-lark, *Grallina cyanoleuca,* Plate 55c

26. Cuckoo-shrikes, Trillers, Orioles, and Figbird

Cuckoo-shrikes and *orioles* are two groups of medium-sized, slender, attractive birds that, often conspicuously, patrol the canopy of forests and woodlands in search of insects and fruit. If you bring binoculars to Australia, you will see these arboreal birds. The two groups are closely related. The cuckoo-shrike family, Campephagidae (about 70 species spread over Africa, Asia, and the Australian region; seven in Australia), includes two Australian species known as *trillers* (after their metallic, chattering, trilling vocalizations) and the CICADABIRD, also named for its calls. Cuckoo-shrikes are sleek birds, 18 to 33 cm (7 to 13 in) in length, with longish tapered wings and tails, small feet, and shortish, broad, slightly down-curved bills. They tend to be grey with black and/or white markings; in some, females are browner and more streaked or barred. Neither cuckoos nor shrikes, the group is named for its general form and plumage (cuckoo-like) and bill (shrike-like). Family Oriolidae contains 25 species distributed over Africa, Eurasia, and the Australian region; Australia's three species are two orioles and the mostly frugivo-rous FIGBIRD (Plate 54). (This Old World oriole group is not to be confused with the New World orioles, which are included in the family of New World blackbirds, Icteridae). The Australian orioles are slender, 25 to 30 cm (10 to 12 in) long, with straight, robust, slightly down-curved bills that, in males, are often pinkish or red-dish orange (but dark in the Figbird). Plumages are usually brightly colored in greenish yellow, green, or gold, and black, often with lengthwise streaks; females typically are duller and browner.

Natural History

Ecology and Behavior
Cuckoo-shrikes forage solitarily, in pairs, or in small groups, mostly high within tree foliage but sometimes on the ground; one species, the GROUND CUCKOO-SHRIKE, is often seen on the ground in groups. Cuckoo-shrikes are primarily insectivores, also taking other small invertebrates and, usually, some berries and soft fruit. Caterpillars, particularly the hairy ones, are favorite foods of some species. They often forage by perching on a branch, looking around, and then pouncing on detected prey. Cuckoo-shrikes will also interrupt their usual graceful, undulating flights from tree canopy to tree canopy to chase and snatch from the air flying insects. Most species that occur in the southern part of the country, after breeding, are migratory or nomadic, moving to find adequate food supplies. Oriole ecology is similar to that of the cuckoo-shrikes in many respects. Orioles fly grace-fully, with undulating flight, from tree to tree, looking for bugs and fruit. The Figbird is heavily dependent on fruit, much of its diet consiting of figs and other similar fruits; but it also eats insects. OLIVE-BACKED (Plate 54) and YELLOW ORI-OLES tend to forage solitarily or in small groups of two or three, but Figbirds are strongly gregarious, usually seen in small flocks. As with the cuckoo-shrikes, the orioles are migratory or nomadic when not breeding.

Breeding
Cuckoo-shrikes are monogamous, but most appear to be cooperative breeders—*helpers*, presumably related to the breeding pair, assist with feeding young in the nest and after they fledge. Cuckoo-shrikes build small, shallow nests of vegeta-tion, bound with spider-webbing, on tree branches or in tree forks; sometimes they take over nests abandoned by other species. In most species, the sexes share nesting duties, but in some, only the female incubates. One to 5 eggs are incu-bated for 20 to 22 days (14 days in the trillers, which are smaller birds); young fledge when 25 to 28 days old (12 to 14 days in trillers). Orioles are monogamous breeders, building rough, baggy cup-shaped nests of plant fibers that are sus-pended from tree branches and hidden by foliage. Both sexes of Figbird perform nesting duties; in Australia's two oriole species, the female alone incubates. Two to 4 eggs are incubated for 17 to 18 days; young fledge at about 16 days of age.

Notes
Many cuckoo-shrikes, especially the larger species, have an unusual, unexplained habit: after landing on a tree branch, they open and then quickly fold their wings,

often several times. Males during courtship displays also open and fold their wings multiple times. People responsible for naming birds obviously had a difficult time with this group: within the (misleadingly named) cuckoo-shrike family, in addition to trillers, are birds called grey-birds, caterpillar-shrikes, flycatcher-shrikes, and wood-shrikes. Orioles, it seems, were an easier group to deal with: "oriole" is from the Latin aureolus, which means yellow or golden; the group is named for the common, widespread (Eurasia, Africa), bright yellow GOLDEN ORIOLE.

Status

Australia's cuckoo-shrikes and orioles are common birds and are not threatened. The BARRED CUCKOO-SHRIKE is considered vulnerable in New South Wales, as is the WHITE-BELLIED CUCKOO-SHRIKE in South Australia. The Ground Cuckoo-shrike is fairly rare in Queensland and Victoria. The REUNION CUCKOO-SHRIKE, of Réunion Island in the Indian Ocean is endangered, as is the Philippines' ISABELA ORIOLE.

Profiles

White-winged Triller, *Lalage sueurii*, Plate 53f
Black-faced Cuckoo-shrike, *Coracina novaehollandiae*, Plate 54a
Olive-backed Oriole, *Oriolus sagittatus*, Plate 54c
Figbird, *Sphecotheres viridis*, Plate 54d

27. Butcherbirds, Magpies, and Currawongs

Australia has a number of species of common, frequently seen birds with black-and-white-patterned plumages. Because they exhibit variations on the common black-and-white theme, they can be difficult to distinguish, especially for first-time visitors to the country. Most of these mid- to large-sized songbirds are included in family Artamidae (about 25 species spread over southern Asia and the Australian and Pacific island regions; 15 in Australia). (Other black-and-white birds that are seen often are the Magpie-lark and Willie Wagtail; p. 175.) In Australia, the group is represented by *butcherbirds, currawongs,* and the AUSTRALIAN MAGPIE (Plate 55; the woodswallows, p. 158, are now usually included in this family as well). The magpie can be considered a type of butcherbird. These highly successful birds share more than a "pied," or bi-color, plumage pattern; they are chiefly birds of forests and woodlands, and, to varying degrees, they are predatory—on larger insects but also on small vertebrates.

Butcherbirds (five Australian species), the smallest of the group at 24 to 44 cm (9.5 to 17 in), are outfitted in black, white, and grey (but juveniles tend to be brown); one, the BLACK BUTCHERBIRD, is all black. They have relatively large, straight, robust bills used to capture, kill, and dismember their prey. The three currawongs, all endemic to Australia, are large (to 50 cm, 20 in), mostly black or grey, with white wing and tail patches. They have long tails and long, straight bills with a sharp, hooked point. They resemble crows but are more slender and have yellow eyes. Australian Magpies, black and white, to 44 cm (17 in), have robust bills they use to dig in the soil for food and short tails presumably designed so that they don't scrape the earth when the birds are foraging on the ground. The magpie ranges over most of Australia and there are various geographic sub-species (races) that differ chiefly in the color of their back, which is variously white, black, or grey (which further confuses the correct identification of

Australia's gang of black-and-white birds). Males and females in this group of species generally look alike.

Natural History

Ecology and Behavior

Butcherbirds, usually seen alone, are predators who live in wet and dry forests and woodlands; in southern Australia they are also common in agricultural districts. They generally perch a few meters above the ground and scan for prey that includes large insects, crustaceans, small reptiles and mammals, and birds, especially young ones, up to the size of small doves. They pounce on the prey, kill it with their powerful bills, and then either wedge it into a tree fork or cranny or (less often) impale it on a thorn or other sharp object. Thus immobilized, the prey can be easily torn at, dismembered, and eaten, or, alternatively, left alone ("cached") to be consumed later. In this "butchering" behavior these birds are similar to the Old World shrikes, which are also sometimes called butcherbirds. At least some butcherbirds live on permanent territories, in small family groups of three to five.

Currawongs are omnivorous and occupy all types of forests and woodlands. They have what could be called a "crow-like" niche. They forage in all parts of trees, including on the trunk and on fallen logs, and on the ground. They look chiefly for insects but also take many small vertebrates. They also attack fruit in orchards, eat wild berries, and are not above scavenging in garbage dumps. Currawongs are mostly sedentary birds, although one, the PIED CURRAWONG (Plate 55), is known for forming into large flocks that roam over wide areas in search of abundant insect food during nonbreeding periods. At the start of the breeding season, territories are established in which pairs will nest and raise young. Australian Magpies, essentially butcherbirds that forage on the ground, occur mainly in small territorial groups of from 3 to 20 members or so, in all types of open habitats, including open forests but also agricultural areas and cities and towns. Territories, held all year and defended by the group, range from 2 to over 30 ha (5 to 74 ac). The social dynamics of the groups are complex, but usually there is a dominant pair, or a dominant male and multiple females, and a set of subordinates, which are usually offspring of or otherwise related to the head pair. The birds roost together at night, then fly to fields in the morning to start the day's foraging for insects. They walk over the ground searching, dig into the soil with their bills, and even look under cattle droppings.

Ecological Interactions

Within a species of currawong or butcherbird, male bills are usually a bit larger than female bills. It is thought that this is an example of *niche separation:* having bills of different sizes allows the two sexes to search for and consume prey of slightly different average sizes, thereby reducing competition between the sexes for food.

Breeding

Butcherbirds (and currawongs) build large, coarse, cup-shaped nests of sticks, lined with grass, high in tree forks. Butcherbirds tend to breed in monogamous pairs, but in many, only the female builds the nest and incubates the 2 to 5 eggs for 20 to 23 days. Nestlings fledge at about 4 weeks of age. The Australian Magpie female builds the nest and incubates the 1 to 6 eggs for 20 days; she also feeds the nestlings, usually until they fledge in 4 weeks, when other adults in her group start to lend a hand (bill). Butcherbirds, including the magpie, have reputations as aggressive defenders of their nests; they will swoop at people who get too close, and even hit them. Currawongs breed in isolated pairs. Two to 4 eggs are incubated by the female alone for about 20 days; both sexes feed the young, which fledge when a month old.

Notes

Currawongs are also called crow-shrikes and bell-magpies; the GREY CURRAWONG is also called "squeaker," after one of its calls. The word "currawong" supposedly sounds like one of the calls of the Pied Currawong. The Grey Butcherbird in Tasmania is also known, for some reason, as the Tasmanian Jackass.

Status

None of the Australian butcherbirds or currawongs are threatened.

Profiles

Pied Butcherbird, *Cracticus nigrogularis*, Plate 55a
Grey Butcherbird, *Cracticus torquatus*, Plate 55b
Australian Magpie, *Gymnorhina tibicen*, Plate 55d
Pied Currawong, *Strepera graculina*, Plate 55e
Grey Currawong, *Strepera versicolor*, Plate 55f

28. Crows, Ravens, Riflebirds (Birds of Paradise), Chough, and Apostlebird

Crows and *ravens* are members of the Corvidae, a passerine family of a hundred or so species that occurs just about everywhere in the world—or, as ecologists would say, *corvid* distribution is *cosmopolitan*. Corvids are known for their adaptability and for their seeming intelligence; in several ways, the group is considered by ornithologists to be the most highly developed of birds. The group includes the crows, ravens, *magpies*, and *jays*. Members of the family range in length from 20 to 71 cm (8 to 28 in), many near the higher end—large for passerine birds. Corvids have stout, fairly long bills, robust legs, and strong, largish feet. Many corvids, especially crows, ravens, *rooks*, and *jackdaws*, are all or mostly black. The COMMON RAVEN, all black, ranges over most of the northern hemisphere and is the largest passerine bird. Five corvids, all very similar in appearance even though three are called ravens and two, crows, are native to Australia. They are all large (48 to 52 cm, 19 to 20.5 in) and glossy black; most locals call all of them "crows," and birdwatchers usually tell them apart by their behavior. (A sixth corvid, a black-and-grey crow, has been introduced over small areas of southern Australia.)

The *birds of paradise* family (Paradisaeidae, mostly distributed in New Guinea) is comprised of about 43 species of mid-sized (in Australia, 25 to 30 cm, 10 to 12 in) tropical wet-forest birds that are celebrated for two aspects of their biology: the fantastic and bizarre plumages some of them possess—tremendously long tail feathers and sometimes head plumes—and the breeding displays males give to attract and convince females to mate with them. Birds of paradise are related to corvids and to bowerbirds (p. 183). Australia has only four species that, compared with many of New Guinea's representatives, are not very ornate. Three are known as *riflebirds* (no one knows precisely why), and have long, down-curved bills. Males are glossy black with patches of blue and green iridescence, particularly on the head and chest; females are brownish. The PARADISE (Plate 56) and VICTORIA'S RIFLEBIRDS are Australian endemics; the MAGNIFICENT RIFLEBIRD and TRUMPET MANUCODE, a glossy black, rather plain, starling-like member of the group with a short bill, are shared with New Guinea.

The APOSTLEBIRD and WHITE-WINGED CHOUGH (both Plate 56) are the only two members of the endemic Australian family Corcoracidae. The family is related to the corvids, and the two species are vaguely crow-like in appearance. They are dull-plumaged birds that live in communal groups (usually 5 to 15 individuals) on year-round territories; they roost and nest in trees but forage on the ground for insects and other small invertebrates, some small vertebrates, and seeds. Nests are mud cups (hence the family's common name, "mudnesters") placed on tree branches, and all members of a group help with nesting and raising young.

Natural History

Ecology and Behavior

Bright and versatile, corvids are quick to take advantage of new food sources and to find food in agricultural and other human-altered environments. Crows use their feet to hold food down while tearing it with their bills. Hiding food for later consumption, *caching*, is practiced widely by the group. Most corvids are fairly omnivorous, taking bird eggs and nestlings, carrion, insects, and fruits and nuts; visits to garbage dumps also yield meals. The AUSTRALIAN RAVEN (Plate 56) specializes in animal food (live insects, dead mammals, and birds), and the TORRESIAN CROW is known to take a lot of grain and other plant material, but both have varied diets. Corvids are usually quite social, often living in family groups, and sometimes foraging and roosting in mixed-species groups. Often the family group maintains and defends a year-round territory on which it forages, roosts, and breeds. Young and nonbreeding adults may form nomadic flocks.

Riflebirds are arboreal eaters of fruits, berries, and insects. They usually fly from fruiting tree to fruiting tree, staying in the higher canopy, and often hanging at odd angles to reach tasty morsels. They will also fly down to feed on tree trunks, stumps, and fallen logs. They use their long, strong bill to turn over bark and dig into dead wood in search of bugs, and to push deeply into fruits. In most species, males seem to hold territories year round, feeding and eventually displaying for females within these territories.

Breeding

Australia's crows and ravens are monogamous; some tend to nest alone, while others nests in loose colonies. Nests, constructed by both sexes, are large, bulky, and bowl-shaped, built of sticks, and placed usually in trees. The female alone incubates the 3 to 6 eggs for 17 to 20 days (the male hunts and brings her food). Either both sexes feed the nestlings or the female alone does it, with food brought by the male, for 29 to 43 days until fledging.

Riflebirds are "promiscuous" breeders. During breeding seasons, males spend most of each day (whenever they are not feeding) at display sites, usually a horizontal branch high in a large tree. They vocalize and display to attract the attention of passing females. Male display patterns are species typical, but the displays usually involve moving the head up and down, stretching the neck, rhythmically swaying the body, hopping side-to-side, and extending the wings. When a female approaches, a male's antics increase in intensity and he may encircle the female with his outstretched wings and "dance" around her. When she is satisfied, presumably of the male's good genetic make-up, if not his sincerity, the two mate. The female then leaves to nest on her own. The male returns to his mate-attraction displays and will mate with as many females as he can attract. The female builds a bulky bowl nest of dried leaves, twigs, ferns, and rootlets high in a tree or in a vegetation tangle, lays 1 to 3 eggs (often 2), and incubates them for 15 to 17 days; young fledge after 3 to 4 weeks in the nest.

Notes

Although considered by many to be among the most intelligent of birds, and by ornithologists as among the most highly evolved, corvid folklore is rife with tales of crows and ravens as symbols of ill omen. This undoubtedly traces to the group's frequently all-black plumage and habit of eating carrion, both sinister traits. Ravens, in particular, have long been associated in many northern cultures with evil or death, although these large, powerful birds also figure more benignly in Nordic and Middle Eastern mythology. Several groups of indigenous peoples of northwestern North America consider the Common Raven sacred and sometimes, indeed, as a god. The Australian Raven, Australia's largest corvid, has a reputation among ranchers as a predator of young lambs, but it is doubtful these birds actually kill lambs; most are probably only eating already dead animals.

Birds of paradise in New Guinea were, and still are, important parts of the cultures of many indigenous groups. Early European visitors to New Guinea found that many birds of paradise were venerated, their long plumes considered prizes and even as indications of wealth (this is not to say that these birds were not hunted regularly for food—they were). Some very long plumes were stored carefully and exhibited only during important ceremonial events. Other plumes were, and still are, used often for headdresses and body decoration (a feather through a nostril hole being a common local accoutrement). Various species of these birds were considered by some groups to be involved with the spirit world and so were not hunted, or were not hunted in sacred places, such as particular tree groves.

Status

Most corvids are common or very common birds. Some adjust well to people's activities, indeed often expanding their ranges when they can feed on agricultural crops. In fact, only a few corvids worldwide are threatened; the two most endangered are Pacific island species, the HAWAIIAN CROW and the MARIANA CROW. Australia's FOREST RAVEN, very simliar to the widely distributed Australian Raven but with a small range mostly in Tasmania and southern Victoria, is fairly rare and may be declining in the northern part of its range, in northeast New South Wales.

Australia's birds of paradise, the riflebirds and manucode, are currently secure, but they all have relatively small ranges in the wet forests of northeast Queenland (or, in the case of the Paradise Riflebird, southeastern Queensland and northeastern New South Wales), forests that have been increasingly degraded and cleared for agriculture. Some Paradise and Victoria's Riflebirds are killed by orchardists for attacking fruit crops. Many members of the family in New Guinea are vulnerable or threatened. The spectacular feathers of some of these birds led them to be killed almost indiscriminantly in the past (for instance, it is known that hundreds of thousands of birds of paradise skins were exported from New Guinea from 1900 to 1910, chiefly for feathers to decorate hats in Asia, Europe, and America). Today they are still targeted in parts of New Guinea for food and trade, and their habitats there are increasingly destroyed. On paper, at least, all birds of paradise are officially and absolutely protected in Australia, Indonesia (Irian Jaya), and Papua New Guinea, and by the CITES agreements.

Profiles

Paradise Riflebird, *Ptiloris paradiseus,* Plate 56a

Australian Raven, *Corvus coronoides*, Plate 56b
Torresian Crow, *Corvus orru*, Plate 56c
White-winged Chough, *Corcorax melanorhamphos*, Plate 56d
Apostlebird, *Struthidea cinerea*, Plate 56e

29. Bowerbirds

If you were to listen in on the excited dinnertable conversation at one of the eco-lodges near Lamington or Daintree National Parks and hear that a "bower" was located that day, secreted in the forest not far off a main trail, you might wonder just what these nature enthusiasts were talking about. Bowers, which are elaborate courtship structures, and the birds that make them are among the preeminent attractions of Australia to birders, watchers of TV nature documentaries, and other curious naturalists. The basic story is this: male *bowerbirds*, sometimes spectacularly colored, actually build bowers on their territories to attract females and convince them to mate. Some, for instance, erect walls of twigs that are stuck into the ground, walls that form a structure that resembles an actor's stage or a marriage bower. The walls may be "painted" by the male with his saliva, colored with compounds such as charcoal or leaf juices, and he may place around the bower small objects, both natural and artificial, that he has collected to impress females and enhance his courtship displays. With his bower constructed (or spruced up, if he is using an old one), a male vocalizes and cavorts to attract passing females. A female detects a male, approaches, evaluates his bower and his active, antic courtship displays and, if convinced that he is a high-quality individual, mates. In some ways, this interaction can be viewed as the male bowerbird using sophisticated "tools" to get what he wants; the comparison to human behavior (men tempting mates with structures built on real estate and offering them collected objects, including, perhaps, attractively colored rocks) has been made more than a few times.

There are only nineteen bowerbird species (family Ptilonorhynchidae). Ten occur in Australia; eight are endemic and two are shared with New Guinea (where the remaining species in the family are situated). A few Australian species have broad distributions, such as the WESTERN BOWERBIRD and very similar SPOT-TED BOWERBIRD, but most have small ranges in the wet forests of the eastern part of the country, and four occur only in the Cape York Peninsula and/or in the Cairns region. Bowerbirds are medium-sized to fairly large passerines (21 to 38 cm, 8 to 15 in), chunky, with shortish wings, tails, and legs; bills are short, heavy, and, in some, slightly down-curved or hooked. Some of these birds are stunningly beautiful, the male REGENT BOWERBIRD (Plate 57), for example, being among Australia's true jewels; having one of these bright, glossy black and yellow birds come near you to nibble on fruit put out at feeders at some eco-lodges is, for many, one of a trip's highlights. Males of drably colored bowerbirds, such as GREAT BOWERBIRDS (Plate 57) and Western Bowerbirds, usually have a bright patch of their plumage that they exhibit to females during courting displays—these two species have pink feathers on their necks that are erected into crests during displays. Females in certain species are plainly colored, mostly brown and streaked, but in others the sexes look alike. Two bright green bowerbirds that differ behaviorally from other members of the family are known as *catbirds* (for their feline-like yowling).

Natural History

Ecology and Behavior

Bowerbirds are mostly denizens of rainforests and other wet forests, but a few species live in drier habitats, including open woodlands and grassland. They forage in trees at all levels and on the ground. Diets tend mostly toward fruit and berries, but other plant materials such as leaves and shoots are also eaten (especially during winter, when fruit is often less available). They also take insects and other small invertebrates such as spiders, millipedes, and earthworms, and perhaps the odd small frog. In one study, diets of wet forest species contained only about 10% animal food. The TOOTH-BILLED BOWERBIRD (Plate 57) eats a lot of leaves. Most bowerbird males maintain exclusive territories, in the center of which they build their bowers. Their territories are sometimes part of a larger clan territory (the clan consisting of 10 to 20 individuals that defend a fairly large area), which may include 20 or more bowers and display sites. Many bowerbirds, such as the SATIN BOWERBIRD (Plate 57), form small communal flocks after breeding, sometimes raiding fruit orchards; other species appear to be solitary during nonbreeding periods. Catbirds, which are not bower builders and which breed monogamously, establish and maintain classical territories in which they forage, roost, and nest. A breeding pair may occupy their territory year round. The catbird diet is the same as for other bowerbirds—mostly fruit (catbirds especially like figs), and some insects and leaves/shoots. Catbirds have a reputation for killing the nestlings of other birds to eat and to feed to their own young.

Breeding

Bowerbirds that build bowers are divided into two types. *Maypole builders* construct single or twin towers of sticks; *avenue builders* make walled avenues of sticks, with cleared areas, or *platforms*, at both ends. There is a clear relationship between bower complexity and male plumage: the brighter the plumage, the simpler the bower. All bower builders decorate their bowers with collected objects placed on the ground. The types of objects collected, and their colors, are species specific. The males appear to collect things that more or less match, or amplify, their plumage colors. The beautiful black-and-yellow male Regent Bowerbird constructs a simple avenue bower of twigs planted upright in the soil, usually hidden in a vegetation tangle. The parallel bower walls, 6 to 9 cm (2.5 to 3.5 in) apart, are about 20 cm (8 in) long and 30 cm (12 in) high. The bower is usually painted a yellowish color, for which the male uses his saliva mixed with plant juices. The avenue between the walls is decorated with blackish and yellowish brown objects such as berries, small stones, snail shells, leaves, and even rodent droppings. Male Satin Bowerbirds, which are a lustrous deep blue-black, also build simple, two-walled avenue bowers of sticks, usually painted blackish with saliva mixed with charcoal; the walls are always oriented in a north–south direction. Males adorn the bower platforms with blue objects, which are fairly rare in these forests: berries, feathers, flowers, and these days, bottle caps, pen caps, and plastic cigarette lighters. Research shows that the more blue objects a male has, the more matings he obtains. In Australia, only the GOLDEN BOWERBIRD, endemic to the Cairns region of northeast Queensland, is a maypole builder, constructing twin towers.

Most bowerbirds are promiscuous breeders; after mating at a bower, a female goes off and nests by herself while males continue to advertise at their bowers, attempting to attract and mate with many females each breeding season. The female builds a rough, loose cup of twigs in a tree or vegetation tangle, lays 1 to 3 eggs, incubates them for 18 to 22 days, and feeds her nestlings for about 3 weeks, until they fledge. Catbirds are monogamous, the sexes sharing most but not all nesting duties. They build a large, bulky, deep-cup nest of twigs and leaves in a tree. The female alone incubates the 1 to 3 eggs for 24 days; nestlings, fed by both parents, fledge when about 20 days old.

Notes

Owing to their incredible bower construction and associated mating behavior, some biologists and naturalists consider bowerbirds to be among the most advanced of birds. On the other hand, perhaps bower construction should not be regarded as such a marvelous feat. After all, the behavior probably evolved from nest-building, which most birds do, often in amazingly elaborate ways. Similarly, gripping objects in the bill while displaying to females, as male bowerbirds will do, is practiced by some other birds; even males "painting" bowers with their saliva can be thought of as directing movements and energy that they would have used to feed young (if they were another species) into another direction.

Male Satin Bowerbirds, which prize blue objects and collect them at their bowers, are known to steal them from each other. This behavior makes one wonder about female mate choice: if a female evaluates two males and their bowers that are near each other, and one has many blue objects and one has few, does she choose to mate with the male with more objects because he is a superior collector, or because he is a better thief? In either case, she presumably hopes her male offspring, through genetic inheritance, will have a similarly highly developed trait and so be a successful breeder. It is also possible that females are actually judging males indirectly on their foraging prowess (a better collector indicating a good forager) or dominance level (a thief able to keep stolen goods indicating a dominant male).

Status

None of Australia's bowerbirds are currently considered threatened, although many of them are confined to the wet forests of eastern Queensland and New South Wales—forests that are increasingly cleared or degraded. The Spotted Bowerbird, very closely related to and resembling the Western Bowerbird, is endangered in Victoria and South Australia, where it is now very rare, but it is not threatened in other parts of its range. At least two species are vulnerable in New Guinea (IUCN Red List): ARCHBOLD'S and FIRE-MANED BOWERBIRDS.

Profiles

Tooth-billed Bowerbird, *Scenopoeetes dentirostris,* Plate 57a
Green Catbird, *Ailuroedus crassirostris,* Plate 57b
Regent Bowerbird, *Sericulus chrysocephalus,* Plate 57c
Satin Bowerbird, *Ptilonorhynchus violaceus,* Plate 57d
Great Bowerbird, *Chlamydera nuchalis,* Plate 57e

30. Larks, Pipits, and Sunbirds

Treated here are three very plain brown ground birds that eat seeds and bugs and one very distinctively colored bird of trees and shrubs that feeds largely on nectar. The SINGING BUSHLARK (Plate 58) and SKYLARK (Plate 58; also called Eurasian Skylark and Common Skylark), are Australia's two members of the *lark* family, Alaudidae, an almost entirely Old World group of about 90 species (one species, the HORNED LARK, occurs over much of North America). Larks are smallish

(12.5 to 19 cm, 5 to 7.5 in) ground-dwelling, open-country birds, with small, sparrow-like bills and longish legs, outfitted in dull brown and buff-streaked plumages that allow them to melt well into their grassland habitats. Male and female larks usually look alike. RICHARD'S PIPIT (Plate 58; also called Australian Pipit) is one of about 45 species of *pipits*, family Motacillidae, which occur on every continent save Antarctica; only Richard's inhabits Australia. Pipits, like larks, are smallish (Richard's is about 18 cm, 7 in, long), slim, ground-dwelling birds of grasslands and other open spaces. They are brown and streaked and have slender bills. Both larks and pipits have long toes and especially long hind claws (toenails) that furnish additional support as they stroll about the ground. The YELLOW-BELLIED SUNBIRD (Plate 59), a very common (within its coastal northern Queensland range), very pretty bird, with a long down-curved bill designed to probe and penetrate into flower parts to get at nectar, is Australia's sole representative of the family Nectariniidae (about 120 species distributed over Africa, Asia, and the Australian region). The males of this very small species (11 cm, 4.5 in) are striking, olive above, bright yellow below, with a glittering violet-blue throat and chest; females lack the blue-black patch.

Natural History

Ecology and Behavior

Skylarks and Singing Bushlarks are ground-dwelling birds of open fields, grasslands, and roadsides. They mostly stay rooted on the ground, and they walk or run rather than hop. In flight, they alternate jerky undulations with bouts of gliding. They eat insects and other small invertebrates, and seeds and other plant materials. Richard's Pipit walks and runs through the grass, picking up and sometimes chasing insects and other invertebrates, and will also eat seeds. Pipit flight is fast and undulating. These larks and the pipit are often seen in small to mid-sized groups (10 to 30 or more individuals being common), except when breeding. The Yellow-bellied Sunbird, a bird of wet forest margins, mangroves, vegetation along watercourses, agricultural areas, and settled areas/gardens, is often seen foraging alone; when Yellow-bellied Sunbirds meet at popular feeding places, they are usually aggressive toward each other. They fit their long, slender bills into tubular flowers to get at nectar at the bottom; their long tongue is used to pull nectar into the mouth by a combination of suction and capillary action. With large flowers, they tear petals away or use the bill to rip through the bottoms of petals to get at nectar. They also use the fine, pointed bill to probe into tight corners for spiders and insects (an all-nectar diet lacking, of course, in protein), and they pluck spiders from their webs. Sunbirds forage at all levels of the forest, from canopy to flowers near the ground. Even though they can be thought of as the "ecological equivalents" of the New World's hummingbirds (that is, they are very small nectar feeders, like hummingbirds), they do not hover at flowers; rather, they flit about the foliage, stopping and perching each time they feed.

Breeding

Larks are usually monogamous. Males are known for their aerial, acrobatic courtship display flights, during which they often utter long streams of melodious vocalizations. The female alone builds the nest, a rough cup of grass and other plant materials on the ground, and incubates the 2 to 5 eggs for 11 to 14 days. Both sexes feed the chicks for 9 to 10 days until fledging; chicks fledge before they can fly. Richard's Pipit is monogamous. The female incubates the 2 to

4 eggs for about 2 weeks in a shallow grass cup that is built in a depression in the ground. Both sexes feed the nestlings for two weeks, until fledging. Yellow-bellied Sunbirds are monogamous. A pair breeds on an exclusive territory that the male defends while the female builds the domed, hanging nest of plant fiber and spider webbing, and incubates the 2 or 3 eggs for about 2 weeks. Both sexes feed nestlings for 14 to 19 days until they fledge.

Notes
The Skylark was introduced to Australia from the UK during the mid-1800s, probably because settlers in southeast Australia wanted this familiar bird with its melodious songs around their homes. For similar reasons, skylarks are now naturalized citizens of such other far-flung places as New Zealand and Hawaii. Richard's Pipit is the world's most wide-ranging pipit, ocurring in Africa, Eurasia, Australia, and New Zealand.

Status
Most larks and pipits worldwide are common, successful birds. About eight species within the lark family are considered threatened or endangered, most of them African inhabitants. Perhaps only one pipit is now endangered (IUCN Red List): South America's OCHRE-BREASTED PIPIT. Australia's single sunbird is secure. A few of Africa's sunbird species are considered vulnerable, and Indonesia's ELEGANT SUNBIRD is endangered (IUCN Red List).

Profiles
Skylark, *Alauda arvensis,* Plate 58a
Singing Bushlark, *Mirafra javanica,* Plate 58b
Richard's Pipit, *Anthus novaeseelandiae,* Plate 58c
Yellow-bellied Sunbird, *Nectarinia jugularis,* Plate 59c

31. Estrildid Finches (Grassfinches)

Estrildid finches, or grassfinches, are small, common birds mainly of Australia's grassy, brushy open-country habitats. Their classification is controversial, but we can consider them members of an Old World family, Estrildidae, which contains about 130 species of small or very small seed-eating birds of southern Asia, sub-Saharan Africa, and the Australia and New Guinea regions; some are known as *mannikins* or *waxbills,* the latter because they have red, waxy-looking bills. About twenty species occur broadly over Australia. Many are drably marked in shades of brown, perhaps with barring patterns, but some have large bold patches of black and/or white and others are quite colorful (especially northern Australia's GOULDIAN FINCH, with green back, purple chest, yellow belly, and red, blue, and black head). Patches of red are common, particularly on the head, rump, or upper tail; many species have white dots on their sides. Bills of some species appear disproportionately large for such tiny birds—the big, powerful bills are required to handle and crush seeds, the staple of their diet. Members of one group (genus *Lonchura*), usually slightly heavier-looking than others and perhaps overall the most dully colored of the family, are generally called mannikins (the African and New Guinean/Australian species) or *munias* (Asian species); the former name, inevitably, causes these birds to be confused with the *manakins,* a South American group of small, colorful songbirds. Australian estrildid finches vary in length from 10 to 16 cm (4 to 6 in). The sexes look alike in some species, different in others.

Natural History

Ecology and Behavior

Estrildid finches are mainly birds of open and semi-open habitats—grasslands, agricultural areas, brush and scrublands, forest edges, and clearings; however, some dwell in open woodlands, such as the DIAMOND FIRETAIL (Plate 59), and even dense forests. Most are seed-eaters (but two African species eat ants), with grass seeds, collected from the ground or pulled from grass stalks, being the primary diet item; during breeding seasons many species switch to a diet comprised at least partially of insects. Estrildid finches are often monogamous breeders, a male and a female maintaining a stable pair-bond for one or more breeding seasons; some may mate for life. Perhaps the group's outstanding feature is the extreme gregariousness of the estrildid lifestyle. Various species either flock all year (in Australia, often in groups of 5 to over 50 individuals), breed in colonies when the reproductive urge hits, or flock together after pairs nest solitarily. Large numbers of individuals spend the entire day together, feeding, drinking, bathing, and roosting in flocks; during rests, they often preen each other.

Breeding

Most estrildid finches build untidy domed or spherical nests of grass and other vegetation that they place in shrubs, trees, or sometimes on the gound in tall, dense grass. Both sexes construct the nest (the male usually doing more shopping for and delivering materials, the female doing the actual building). The sexes take turns incubating the 3 to 8 eggs for 2 to 3 weeks, and both parents regurgitate food to nourish the nestlings for 2 to 3 weeks until they fledge. Fledgings, out of the nest, are fed by parents for another week or two before they are fully independent.

Notes

When estrildid finch flocks swell into the thousands, they can become significant agricultural pests. Species such as the NUTMEG MANNIKIN, which is native to Asia but has been introduced to various other parts of the world including eastern Australia, harm crops in their native lands and sometimes in their new homes as well. In Hawaii, the introduced Nutmeg Mannikin was largely responsible for eliminating rice as an agricultural crop in those islands.

Status

Estrildid finches are some of the world's most popular cage birds and some areas in which they are heavily hunted and trapped for the pet trade have experienced significant population declines. But conservation of estrildid finches mainly concerns conservation of their habitats; the destruction and alteration of natural habitats, mostly for crop farming and ranching, is generally agreed to be the prime threat to their populations. At least three estrildid species are listed as endangered by international conservation agencies, including one each in Fiji and the Philippines, and Australia's striking Gouldian Finch, which has experienced steep declines in its populations since the 1970s; Australia considers this finch endangered in Western Australia and threatened in the Northern Territory. The YELLOW-RUMPED MANNIKIN, likewise, is threatened in the Northern Territory, and the STAR FINCH is fairly rare in parts of its range, considered endangered in Queensland, and extinct in New South Wales.

Profiles
Double-barred Finch, *Taeniopygia bichenovii*, Plate 58d
Black-throated Finch, *Poephila cincta*, Plate 58e
Red-browed Finch, *Neochmia temporalis*, Plate 58f
Chestnut-breasted Mannikin, *Lonchura castaneothorax*, Plate 59a
Diamond Firetail, *Stagonopleura guttata*, Plate 59b

32. Old World Warblers and White-eyes

A few species of very common, nondescript, small insectivorous birds are Australian members of two large avian families. Being small birds that often flit about in tall grass, shrubs, or tree foliage, they mainly will be of interest to keen birders. The CLAMOROUS REED-WARBLER (Plate 59), GOLDEN-HEADED CISTICOLA ("si-STICK-ola"; Plate 59), and RUFOUS SONGLARK (Plate 60) are members of a huge assemblage (about 400 species) of tiny or small, usually inconspicuously marked brown birds, mainly arboreal insect-eaters with small, slender, pointed bills, known as the *Old World warblers* (family Sylviidae); most species occur in Africa and Asia, with nine in Australia. Old World warbler sexes often look alike or almost alike. The SILVEREYE (Plate 59), a tiny grey and yellowish green bird that occupies most habitats over eastern and southern Australia, is a representative of the *white-eye* family, Zosteropidae. The family includes about 85 species of small greenish birds with small, slightly down-curved, pointed bills and (usually highly conspicuous) white eye-rings composed of fine silvery white feathers. Males and females look alike. White-eyes are distributed over Africa, Asia, Australia (three species), and New Guinea.

Natural History

Ecology and Behavior
Clamorous Reed-warblers, Golden-headed Cisticolas, and Rufous Songlarks are usually seen in scrubby/high grass areas and thickets, grasslands, croplands, shrubs, and wetland vegetation. They eat mainly insects, which they pull off foliage, but also some seeds and other plant materials. Silvereyes are birds of forests, woodlands, forest edges, orchards, and gardens. They eat insects and spiders, fruit such as berries, and sometimes nectar from flowers. They are fast-moving birds, alighting in a tree, searching leaves for bugs, probing into crevices for spiders, then moving on to another tree. During non-breeding periods, both Old World warblers and white-eyes are often in small flocks; many of these species are migratory.

Breeding
During breeding periods, Old World warblers and white-eyes normally defend small territories in monogamous pairs. The warblers construct deep cup-like nests woven from vegetation and placed usually in grass, reeds, or a shrub. Two to 5 eggs are incubated for 12 to 15 days; chicks fledge after 11 to 16 days in the nest. White-eyes build cup-shaped nests of grasses, other vegetation, and spider webbing, suspended in a shrub or tree. Two to 4 eggs are incubated for 10 to 13 days; nestlings fledge after 9 to 13 days in the nest.

Status
Australia's Old World warblers and white-eyes are abundant birds, but a few populations, particularly some that are restricted to small islands, are in trouble. One,

the WHITE-CHESTED WHITE-EYE, endemic to Norfolk Island, with no confirmed sightings since about 1980, is CITES Appendix I listed; the Silvereye is vulnerable on Lord Howe Island. The IUCN Red List contains about 20 white-eye species listed as vulnerable or endangered, with about half of them being critically endangered. Flocks of Silvereyes are so common and destructive of fruit in parts of Australia that they are thought of as orchard and vineyard pests.

Profiles

Clamorous Reed-warbler, *Acrocephalus stentoreus,* Plate 59d
Golden-headed Cisticola, *Cisticola exilis,* Plate 59e
Rufous Songlark, *Cincloramphus mathewsi,* Plate 60b
Silvereye, *Zosterops lateralis,* Plate 59f

33. Thrushes, Starlings, Mynas, and Bulbuls

Included here briefly are a few miscellaneous, rather plain, medium-sized brown and black songbirds. Although they are not glamorously attired, they are nonetheless very common, frequently seen, and some of them at least have interesting backgrounds. The BASSIAN THRUSH and COMMON BLACKBIRD (both Plate 60) are included in the *thrush* family, Turdidae (sometimes combined with the Old World flycatchers into family Muscicapidae). The family has more than 300 species, which inhabit most terrestrial regions of the world and include some of the most familiar park and garden birds. Thrushes, usually a bit plumpish with straight bills, as a group are tremendously successful, especially when they have adapted to living near humans and benefiting from their environmental modifications. On five continents (but not Australia), thrushes are among the most common and recognizable native garden birds, including North America's AMERICAN ROBIN and Europe's REDWING and Common Blackbird. Australia boasts only four species, two of which, the SONG THRUSH and Common Blackbird, were introduced from Europe during the 1800s.

Considered by most locals to be a pest, the COMMON MYNA (Plate 60), introduced to Australia from Southeast Asia during the 1860s and later, and now common around eastern urban areas, is actually a beautiful bird that North Americans and Europeans will appreciate for its novelty. The chocolate brown mynas, seen in trees and on roads, are members of the *starling* family, Sturnidae, an Old World group of about 110 species that usually occupy all habitats in regions in which they occur. Most of the family consists of sturdily built brown or blackish birds, many with patches of iridescence in their plumage, but some starlings are brilliantly colored. They are mainly arboreal birds, but some, such as the Common Myna and COMMON STARLING (or European Starling, Plate 60), are also at home on the ground. Male and female mynas and starlings usually look alike.

The RED-WHISKERED BULBUL (Plate 51) is a striking-looking alien species, introduced to Australia from Asia during the 1880s. The *bulbul* family, Pycnonotidae, consists of about 120 species of mostly tropical forest-dwelling birds, distributed by nature throughout Africa and southern Asia. But people, through intentional or accidental (escaped cage birds) introduction, have spread bulbuls far and wide, so that there are now established breeding populations in such far-flung locations as New Zealand, the US mainland (Florida), Hawaii, and other Pacific island groups, in addition to Australia. Bulbuls are usually crested, small to mid-sized songbirds with slender, often slightly down-curved bills and longish tails. Most are dully turned out in subdued greys, browns, or greens, but some have small bright patches; the sexes look alike.

Natural History

Ecology and Behavior

Among the thrushes are species that employ a variety of feeding methods and that take several different food types. Many eat fruits; some are primarily insectivorous; and most are at least moderately omnivorous. Although arboreal birds, many thrushes frequently forage on the ground for insects, other arthropods, and, a particular favorite, delicious earthworms. These birds are residents of many kinds of habitats—forest edges, clearings, and other open sites such as shrub areas and grasslands, gardens, parks, suburban lawns, and agricultural lands. Australia's two native thrushes, the Bassian and RUSSET-TAILED THRUSHES, are primarily forest- and woodland-dwellers. Many thrushes are quite social, spending their time during the nonbreeding season in flocks of the same species, feeding and roosting together. Common Mynas are seen, often in mated pairs, in urban and agricultural areas. Common Starlings, more often seen in flocks, are also birds of settled and agricultural districts. Mynas and starlings spend a lot of their time on the ground, walking rather than hopping, looking for insects and other things to eat; they are considered fairly omnivorous. The Red-whiskered Bulbul, in its Australian range (mostly limited to the Sydney region), is a bird of gardens and parks; it eats insects and fruit.

Breeding

Thrushes breed monogamously, the male and female together defending exclusive territories during the breeding season; pairs may associate year round. Nests, usually built by the female and placed in tree branches, shrubs, or crevices, are cup-shaped, made of grass, moss, and like materials, and often lined with mud. Usually 2 or 3 eggs are incubated by the female only for 12 to 14 days. Young are fed by both parents for 12 to 15 days prior to their fledging. The Common Myna and Common Starling nest in cavities and are especially partial to holes in trees or cliff cavities, but will also place nests in holes in buildings. Males and females usually share in most of the nesting duties, although in the myna, only the female incubates the eggs. The METALLIC STARLING (Plate 60) nests in dense colonies, often with the nests of many pairs hanging from branches of the same tall rainforest tree.

Notes

It is not the Common Myna that imitates human speech quite well; that dubious achievement is accomplished by the HILL MYNA, *Gracula religiosa*, also native to India and Southeast Asia.

Status

Australia's native thrushes are secure, although a small, isolated population of the Bassian Thrush, in South Australia, is quite small. Mynas, as well as other members of the starling family, are often very common birds within their native ranges. One Australian species, the TASMAN STARLING, restricted to some islands off Australia's eastern coast, apparently became extinct during the early 1900s. Most bulbul species are common birds.

Profiles

Bassian Thrush, *Zoothera lunulata*, Plate 60a
Common Blackbird, *Turdus merula*, Plate 60c

Metallic Starling, *Aplonis metallica,* Plate 60d
Common Starling, *Sturnus vulgaris,* Plate 60e
Common Myna, *Acridotheres tristis,* Plate 60f
Red-whiskered Bulbul, *Pycnonotus jocosus,* Plate 51f

Environmental Close-up 4:
Nectar and Nectar-eaters

An interesting facet of Australian ecology and wildlife is the relatively large number of species that depend on nectar for their main food. For example, and most obviously, the largest single group of Australian passerine birds, with about 70 species, is family Meliphagidae, the honeyeaters (p. 168). Other Australian bird nectar specialists are the six species of lorikeets (p. 150) and one sunbird (p. 186). Among the mammals, about ten marsupial species regularly feed on nectar, and Australia has the only non-gliding mammal that eats only nectar and pollen, the tiny Honey Possum of southwestern Australia. About 25 species of Australian marsupials are known to visit flowers at least occasionally to feed on nectar and/or pollen, as are some of Australia's bats.

The reasons for the large incidence of *nectarivory* in Australia are not really known, but ecologists have their suspicions. The main underlying reason may be Australia's naturally nutrient-poor soils. When plants are in nutrient-rich soil, with plenty of available phosphorous, nitrogen, and potassium, they can combine these nutrients with carbon (which they take from the air as carbon dioxide and, using the sun's energy—photosynthesis—and water, form into small glucose molecules and then into large starch molecules) and use the resulting compounds for growth and maintenance. But when in nutrient-poor soil, such as where soil phosphorous is scarce (as it is over much of Australia except in the very east), plants cannot grow huge amounts of new tissue. Instead, they produce large amounts of carbon-containing substances (carbohydrates) that do not require phosphorous—such as sap and nectar, the latter being mostly a solution of water and sugars such as glucose, fructose, and sucrose.

Over millions of years, birds and other animals in Australia have come to specialize on the super-abundant nectar as a food source. This specialization has had broad consequences for nectar-eating wildlife, for the trees and other plants that produce the nectar, and even for people. Nectar in Australia is such a plentiful, constantly available and reliable food that birds that exploited nectar came to be dominant in many regions—and this is not the case on the other continents, where insect-eating birds usually predominate. But in Australia, thanks to high nectar availability, the honeyeaters are the most diverse, conspicuous, and (perhaps) abundant songbirds—in some regions, a 1 ha (2.5 ac) area can have ten different honeyeater species. In fact, in some habitats in which there are high numbers of honeyeaters—many eucalypt woodlands, for instance—there usually seems to be a dearth of other kinds of birds, and ecologists suspect that it is the abundance of honeyeaters themselves that depress the populations of other birds. They may do this in two main ways. The honeyeaters occasionally eat insects for protein—their nectar diet is essentially protein-free—but they only need small numbers of insects. Therefore they can inhabit places with low insect densities, places in which insectivorous birds may not be able to find enough food; in addition, the large numbers of honeyeaters can further depress insect populations, keeping insectivorous birds away. (Many larger honeyeaters, in addition to nectar and insects, also eat fruit and berries.) Also, honeyeaters are fairly large songbirds with reputations for aggressiveness—they are known to drive many other kinds of birds away from their territories—both nectar-eaters and insect-eaters. This kind of dominance of nectar-eating birds over insect-eaters has not been observed elsewhere in the world. (Of course, the other main group of nectarivorous birds is the New World's hummingbirds, which are tiny; honeyeaters weigh 8 to 180 g (0.3 to 6.5 oz), with an average weight of 37 g (1.3 oz); hummingbirds average 5 g (0.2 oz).)

A main ecological consequence of Australia's bird nectarivory is that, relative to other continents such as North America and Europe, few Australia land birds are migratory (p. 118). Trees and other plants flower and put out nectar all year, so the nectar-eaters don't need to make long, regular seasonal movements in search of food (but some make smaller, nomadic movements, changing areas to find active nectar sources). Another consequence is that some stages of breeding tend to be longer in many Australian birds than in birds elsewhere, such as longer egg incubation and longer periods before nestlings are independent of their parents. One reason is that a diet mainly of nectar and fruit, with only limited amounts of protein-rich insects, does not provide enough protein for rapid development.

Many smaller Australian mammals also visit flowers to eat nectar and pollen (dust-like reproductive spores), particularly small arboreal marsupials such as gliders (p. 220). They get abundant energy from the nectar and probably fulfill their protein needs with pollen. Also, some of these mammals seek out other carbohydrate-rich liquid food from trees—sap and oozing resins—and sometimes even make small cuts in trees to induce the flow of these viscous fluids.

Because so many birds in Australia visit flowers for nectar, it is not surprising that many Australian plants use birds, not insects, as main pollinators. Estimates are that at least 1,000 Australian plants (including most of the native tree and shrub flora) are pollinated at least partially by birds. In fact, the plants probably compete for birds' attention by exuding as much nectar as they can; some kinds of plants are known to put up to twice as much energy into nectar production as they put into seeds. This is a worthwhile effort for the plants, because birds are reliable, efficient pollinators—they travel far, are active in all kinds of weather (insects are not), and pollen sticks well to feathers. Many bird-pollinated plant groups actually place their flowers on or near the ground, permitting birds to stand on the ground to feed (and pick up pollen on their feathers for transport to other flowers of the same species—pollination).

Nectar (and other non-vegetative, carbohydrate-rich plant substances) is so abundant and conspicuous in many Australian habitats that people also noticed and collected it. Nectar was harvested directly by some Aboriginal people, and another, related substance known as *lerp* was also collected as a food source. Lerp is the sugary protective coating that certain kinds of plant bugs (psyllids; order Homoptera) form over themselves after feeding on plant fluids; these plant bugs are especially common on eucalypts. Aboriginal people used lerp as a food source, and under the best conditions could harvest up to 23 kg (50 lb) of lerp per day. (Many honeyeaters also feed on lerp. In fact, in some cases it has been discovered that honeyeaters that were thought to be searching on trees for insects are actually foraging for lerp and other sugary plant/insect "exudates"—*honeydew,* a sugary solution some small insects such as aphids produce after sucking plant juices, and *manna,* sugary granules on damaged eucalypt leaves.)

Chapter 10

MAMMALS

- *Introduction*
- *General Characteristics of Mammals*
- *Classification of Mammals*
- *Australian Mammals*
- *Seeing Mammals in Australia*
- *Family Profiles*
  - *1. Monotremes—Platypus and Echidna*
  - *2. Carnivorous Marsupials—Devil, Quolls, and Relatives*
  - *3. Bandicoots and Bilby*
  - *4. Koala*
  - *5. Wombats*
  - *6. Possums*
  - *7. Gliders*
  - *8. Potoroos, Bettongs, and Rat-kangaroos*
  - *9. Kangaroos, Wallabies, and Pademelons*
  - *10. Bats, the Flying Mammals*
  - *11. Rodents and Rabbits*
  - *12. Dingo and Fox*
  - *13. Marine Mammals*

Introduction

Leafing through this book, the reader will have noticed the pictures and profiles of many more birds than mammals. This may at first seem discriminatory, especially because people themselves are mammals and, owing to that direct kinship, are probably keenly interested and motivated to see and learn about mammals. Are not mammals as good as birds? Why not include more of them? There are several reasons for the discrepancy—good biological reasons. One is that the total number of mammal species worldwide, and the number in any region, is less than the number of birds. In fact, there are in total only about 4,600 mammal species, compared to 9,700 birds, and the relative difference is reflected in the fauna of Australia (300 mammals vs. 740 birds). But the more compelling reason not to include more mammals in a book on commonly sighted wildlife is that even in regions sporting high degrees of mammalian diversity, mammals are relatively rarely seen—especially by short-term visitors. Most mammals lack that basic protection from predators that birds possess, the power of flight. Consequently, mammals are considered delicious fare by any number of predatory beasts (eaten in good numbers by reptiles, birds, other mammals, and even the odd amphibian); most are active nocturnally, or, if day-active, are highly secretive. Birds often show themselves with abandon; most mammals do not. Exceptions are those mammals that are beyond the pale of predation—huge mammals and fierce ones. But there are no elephants in Australia, nor prides of lions. Australia does possess some fairly large native grazing land mammals that are conspicuous—kangaroos and wallabies (the largest ones standing nearly 2 m, 6.5 ft, tall). But these are a special case because they have few predators (aside from people), and grazing animals, especially relatively large ones that stay in groups, can often be conspicuous but still be relatively safe.

A final reason for not including more mammals is that of the roughly 110 mammal species that occur in eastern Australia but are not illustrated in this book (about 80 are shown), the great majority are bats, rodents, and rodent-like marsupials, for the most part small nocturnal animals that, even if spotted, are very difficult for anyone other than experts to identify to species.

Mammals are, of course, extremely important to travellers to Australia. After all, Australia is the land of monotreme and marsupial mammals—of kangaroos and koalas, wombats and bandicoots, platypuses and echidnas; because of these unique species, Australia has the distinction of being one of only a few travel destinations worldwide that many people visit specifically with the idea of seeing certain mammals. Therefore, in this book, mammals, even if most are rarely seen, are treated in fairly good number and detail.

General Characteristics of Mammals

If birds are feathered vertebrates, mammals are hairy ones. The group first arose, so fossils tell us, approximately 245 million years ago, splitting off from primitive reptiles during the late Triassic Period of the Mesozoic Era before the birds did the same. Four main traits distinguish almost all mammals and confer upon them great advantage over other types of animals; these traits allowed mammals in the past to prosper and spread and continue to this day to benefit them: hair on their bodies, which insulates them from cold and otherwise protects from environmental stresses; milk production for the young, freeing mothers from having to search for specific foods for their offspring; the bearing of live young instead of eggs, allowing breeding females to be mobile and hence safer than if they had to sit on eggs for several weeks; and advanced brains, with obvious enhancing effects on many aspects of animal lives.

Mammals are quite variable in size and form, many being highly adapted—changed through evolution—to specialized habitats and lifestyles: bats specialized to fly, deer and antelope specialized to run, kangaroos and jumping mice specialized to hop and jump, gophers and moles specialized to burrow, marine mammals specialized for their aquatic world. The smallest mammals are the shrews, tiny insect-eaters that weigh as little as 2.5 g (a tenth of an ounce). The largest are the whales, weighing in at up to 160,000 kg (350,000 lb, half the weight of a loaded Boeing 747)—as far as anyone knows, the largest animals ever.

Classification of Mammals

Mammals are divided into three major groups, primarily according to reproductive methods: the *monotremes*, or egg layers; the *marsupials*, or pouched mammals; and the *eutherians*, or placental mammals. The Australia/New Guinea region is the only place on Earth where the three types occur together.

Monotremes. The monotremes are an ancient group that actually lays eggs and still retains some other reptile-like characteristics. Only three species survive, the Platypus and two species of spiny anteaters; they are fairly common inhabitants of Australia (the Platypus and one Spiny Anteater) and New Guinea (the other spiny anteater).

Marsupials. The marsupials give birth to live young that are relatively undeveloped but that have strong arms. When born, the young crawl along mom's fur into her *pouch*, where they find milk supplies and finish their development. There are about 260 marsupial species, including kangaroos, koalas, wombats, gliders, bandicoots, possums, and opossums; they are limited in distribution to the Australia/New Guinea region and to South and Central America (where one group, the opossums, is fairly diverse, and one species, the road-accident-prone Virginia Opossum, has extended its range northwards into many parts of the US).

Eutherians. The majority of mammal species, 95% of them, are eutherians, the *true*, or *placental*, mammals. These animals are distinguished from the other groups by having a well-developed *placenta*, which connects a mother to her developing offspring, allowing for long internal development. (Some marsupials, such as the bandicoots, also have fairly well-developed placentas.) This trait, which allows embryos to develop to a fairly mature form in safety and for the female to be mobile until birth, has allowed the placental mammals to be rather successful, becoming, in effect, the dominant vertebrates on land for millions of years (except, of course, in Australia and New Guinea, where marsupials rule). The placental mammals include those with which most people are very familiar: rodents, rabbits, cats, dogs, bats, primates, elephants, horses, whales—everything from house mice to ecotravellers.

The 4,630 species of living mammals are divided into about 25 orders and 130 families. Approximately 300 species occur in Australia, about 190 of them within the region covered by this book. About 80% of Australia's 300 mammals are endemic.

Australian Mammals

Generally, Australia has fewer kinds of mammals than other sections of the world of equivalent area. In fact, Australia's native mammal fauna is comprised of only four orders—the monotremes, marsupials, bats, and rodents—whereas the other five occupied continents have seven to ten orders. Australia's monotremes are hugely interesting as biological curiosities and for what they tell us of mammal evolution, but with only a couple of species surviving, they are, ecologically, insignificant. (To all the Platypus lovers out there: I apologize for this blasphemy—please don't send scathing letters or e-mails!) And Australia's native (bats, rodents) and introduced (rabbits, cats, dingos, foxes, pigs, goats, deer, horses, donkeys, some rodents) placentals, while important to the Aussie ecology and economy, are largely similar to or the same as species elsewhere. It is the third mammalian group, the marsupials, at which Australia excels—two-thirds (173 of 260–270) of all living marsupial species occur in the Australia/New Guinea region—and it is this group that will receive the most attention in this chapter.

What kinds of animals are these marsupials? The short answer is: all kinds. They are highly variable in their forms and ecologies—just like the placental mammals. There are three major ecological groupings: the "meat-eaters" —carnivores and insectivores such as quolls and dunnarts (p. 206); the omnivores/insectivores—mostly the bandicoots (p. 210); and the plant-eaters, such as kangaroos and possums (pp. 217, 224). Mixed in with these groups are a host of totally unique types of mammals, each represented by only one or a few species, and each of which is difficult to imagine without seeing a picture. Here are just a few: (1) The NUMBAT, the only member of its own family (Myrmecobiidae), is a small (500 g, 1 lb) reddish brown marsupial with white crosswise stripes on its rear half, a long, bushy tail that it often carries erect, and a long, sharply pointed snout; they eat termites, and are now restricted to a few small regions in the southwestern corner of Western Australia. (2) The teddy-bear-like KOALA (Plate 63) of eastern Australia is also the only member of its own family (Phascolarctidae); with its appealing face (black nose, button eyes, funny ears) and furry, small body (4 to 15 kg, 9 to 33 lb), these tree-living marsupials are known worldwide as symbols of Australia and as rather supreme ecological specialists—they eat only the leaves of *Eucalyptus* trees (p. 19). (3) The MARSUPIAL MOLE, the only member of family Notoryctidae, is totally different than all other marsupials—so different that experts have not yet agreed on its classification—but the females have a pouch, so it is agreed, at least, that they are definitely marsupials. The mole is small (50 to 70 g, 2 to 3 oz), covered with usually light-colored fur, and lives most of its life underground (and is, in fact, blind). Moles eat insects and insect larvae, and, although they are rarely seen, they occur in desert areas over a broad swath of western Australia. (4) The three species of wombats (Plate 63), family Vombatidae, are mid-sized (20 to 39 kg, 44 to 85 lb), stocky brownish marsupials that spend their days in large, self-dug burrow systems and emerge in the night coolness to forage for grasses, sedges and roots. Wombats occur in various parts of eastern and southern Australia.

Some Australian marsupials are specialized for *folivory* (leaf-eating). Australia is unusual in having some arboreal mammals that are almost entirely dependent on leaves—koalas, tree-kangaroos, and some possums. This specialization probably developed because of the general scarcity of fruit in many Australian forests and the year-round availability of leaves in evergreen eucalypt forests; additionally, new leaves, which are more palatable, are often produced by eucalypts during much of the year.

One interesting facet of the Australian marsupials is that they are often pointed out as a strong, convincing case that demonstrates a phenomenon known as *convergent evolution*. Two unrelated species or groups are *convergent* when they come to resemble each other in one or more ways (in form, physiology, or behavior) because they are both evolutionarily adapting to the same type of environmental circumstances. For instance, think of the convergence in shape of sharks and porpoises—one a primitive type of fish, the other an advanced mammal that evolved from land mammals that were not fish-like in shape. Both sharks and porpoises are shaped as they are because their ancestors adapted to the needs of efficient underwater locomotion. Another example: There are two species of grassland birds of wholly different bird families—one, the Eastern Meadowlark, occurs in the Americas, and the other, the Yellow-throated Longclaw, is African. The scary thing is that these two unrelated birds look almost exactly alike—they are small, streaked, brownish birds with bright yellow underparts and similar black markings. Both species adapted to living in similar grassland habitats, and so found that having a camouflaging streaked brown back (for hiding on the brown ground), a bright yellow front (for being conspicuous when they want to be), and black markings (perhaps for communication with other members of their species) were highly useful characteristics. There are many examples of convergence between marsupial and placental mammals, but the five most cited are (1) the recently extinct TASMANIAN TIGER (Tasmanian Wolf; p. 205), which closely resembled in form (body shape and other attributes) a placental wolf or dog, such as the northern hemisphere's Gray Wolf; (2) the Marsupial Mole, which looks and functions very much like placental moles (which are all burrowing insectivores) and which, in fact, closely resembles Africa's Golden Mole—in size, shape, tiny tail, and kind and color of fur; (3) the close similarities in form and gliding behavior of Australia's gliders (p. 220) and the flying squirrels (rodents) of Asia and North America; (4) the similarities between Australia's cat-like carnivores, the quolls (p. 206; genus *Dasyurus*) and smaller cats, such as South America's Ocelot; and (5) similarities in form and behavior between fossorial herbivores such as Australia's wombats (p. 215) and North America's marmots, such as the Groundhog (genus *Marmota*).

One question about marsupials of great interest to mammalogists with an evolutionary bent: if, as fossils prove, marsupial and placental mammals existed together over wide areas in the distant past (for millions of years, starting from the Mesozoic Era's early Cretaceous or Late Jurassic period), why did the placentals survive and prosper in most places while the marsupials died out? Or, put another way, why were placentals the better competitors in what were essentially the great mammal wars of the late Mesozoic Era? For instance, fossils indicate that marsupials occurred in North America before placental mammals joined them, but that by the late Cretaceous period, marsupials had declined and placentals flourished—this is why Canada is rife with placental mammals but utterly lacking in marsupials. Similarly in South America, large groups of marsupials, such as entire families of carnivores, disappeared after placental mammals, including carnivores, invaded in great numbers from North America when a land bridge formed between the two continents. There are several reasons placentals may have been the more successful group, and so came to dominate most of the continents: (1) Placental young are safer within the mother for longer periods and born in a more developed state, so perhaps, on average, more of their young survive; also, placentals seem to be able to breed more rapidly than marsupials. (2) The part of the mammal brain associated with more complex behavior, the cerebral cortex, develops faster in placental young and grows larger than in marsupials—so perhaps in some ways placentals are "smarter" than marsupials. (3) Some kinds of advanced social and spacing behavior, well developed in placentals, are lacking or rare in marsupials—behaviors such as territoriality, social groups with long-standing dominance hierarchies, and group-rearing of young. (4) Likewise, some anti-predator behaviors of placentals are lacking in marsupials—coordinated action of herds, cooperative defense of young, sustained high-speed running escape. (5) Marsupials never "diversified" into as many species as did placentals. They never utilized all of the "lifestyles" available to them; for instance, they never expanded their reach into the air and water, as did the placentals. The marsupials never developed limbs modified as wings, fins, or flippers, and there never were marsupial counterparts to bats or to whales and dolphins, seals and sea lions. (6) Marsupials never exploited some highly nourishing and plentiful food sources that many placental mammals exploit: flying insects (the primary diet of many bats) and marine plankton (the food of the great whales) (Vaughan, et al. 1998).

Please note: it is not that placental mammals are "better" than marsupials: it is just that the two groups differed in the traits they brought to ecological competition, and, under the environmental conditions prevailing when then two groups occurred together, the placental mammals were more successful breeders, so their kind came to populate the continents and to dominate. Under another set of ecological circumstances, the marsupials may have "won." The likely reason that placental mammals never came to dominate in Australia has to do with plate tectonics and the shifting of the continents. When the Australian land mass separated from the other continents that it was attached to (Antarctica and South America, about 45 million years ago), only marsupials and monotremes occupied it. By the time the first placental mammals reached Australia (about 20 milllion years later, when bats and rodents from Asia arrived as the Australian continent moved close enough to Indonesia), the marsupials had become a diverse lot and successfully occupied most of the usual mammal "niches."

Seeing Mammals in Australia

No doubt about it, mammals are tough to see. One can go for weeks in eastern Australia and, if in the wrong places at the wrong times, see very few of them. A lot of luck is involved—a small bunch of wallabies happens to cross the trail a bit ahead of you. Or, as you are driving, you see a group of larger kangaroos in late afternoon, lounging in rangeland or grazing along a roadside. Or you will be out birdwatching along a gravel road in the pre-dawn greyness and a small mammal will stroll slowly out of the forest, cross the road, and walk back into the forest on the other side. I offer three pieces of general mammal-spotting advice. First, if you have time and are patient, in late afternoon or early evening stake out a likely looking spot near a pond, stream, or watering hole, be quiet, and wait to see what approaches. Second, try taking strolls very early in the morning; at this time, many nocturnal mammals are quickly scurrying to their day shelters. Third, although only for the stout-hearted, try searching with a flashlight at night around national park campgrounds, forest lodges, or resorts. After scanning the ground (for safety's sake as well as for mammals), shine the light toward the middle regions of trees, and look for bright, shiny eyes reflecting the light. You will certainly stumble across some kind of mammal or another; then it is simply a matter of whether you scare them more than they scare you.

Seeing kangaroos and Koalas is of paramount interest to people who journey to Australia to see wildlife; the first of these is easy, the second a bit harder. Anyone who spends a modest or moderate amount of time driving around eastern Australia, visiting parks, and/or hiking, will see kangaroos of various sizes and species (wallabies, pademelons, and proper kangaroos). They hop rapidly across roads and trails, graze in fields, and loll about roadside picnic areas and campgrounds. People dearly want to see Koalas, and because searching for wild ones high in trees can be arduous, many resort to visiting commercial establishments that exhibit captive Koalas and often let tourists touch or even hold more well-behaved individuals (wild Koalas can be mean and they have large sharp claws!). Koalas can also be seen in wildlife parks/zoos, such as the Ballarat Wildlife Park, west of Melbourne, which has kangaroos of various species lounging around the grounds and many Aussie marsupials, including difficult-to-see species such as wombats and Tasmanian Devils in enclosures. But Koalas are fairly common in some parts of eastern Australia, and, with a bit of persistent searching, can be found. Phillip Island, south of Melbourne, is known for its large, healthy Koala population. (Koalas have even been taken from here, as well as from nearby French Island, for translocation to other parts of Australia that have few Koalas.) Several national parks in eastern Australia that sport large expanses of relatively undisturbed *Eucaplytus* woodlands harbor good numbers of Koalas—for example, Brisbane Ranges National Park, west of Melbourne: park your car there, hike the trails, look upward occasionally, and eventually, you should see a Koala.

The true travelling connoisseur of mammalian fauna will not want to leave Australia without searching for wild montremes—Platypuses and Echidnas; the latter is usually easier to find than the former. Echidnas are common animals, and you can see them almost anywhere at any time—even simply waddling along a roadside. Platypuses, associated with fresh water, occur patchily only over the eastern parts of Queensland and New South Wales, the southern part of Victoria, and Tasmania; they are most often seen in or along lakes, ponds, and waterways in very late afternoon or at dusk.

Rounding out Beletsky's Big Five of Australian mammals are wombats. The Common Wombat (Plate 63), which occurs over parts of New South Wales and Victoria and in Tasmania, is difficult to see. Nocturnal, it inhabits forested, mountainous regions, and is often seen by people only at night, in car headlights, or as roadkill the next morning; otherwise wombats are sometimes seen at dawn or dusk, or during night searches.

Possums, such as the Mountain Brushtail Possum (Plate 65), are usually strictly nocturnal, but some are seen at forest lodges at night when fruit or other food is put out to attract them—for instance, at O'Reilly's Guest House at Lamington National Park, near Brisbane.

If you're in Tasmania, the big mammalian attraction is the Tasmanian Devil (Plate 61), a small, carnivorous marsupial with a wonderful name. But these dark, smallish, dog-like animals are mainly nocturnal and mostly solitary, so they are difficult to see; occasionally one is spied hurrying along a forested path at dawn or dusk.

For the region covered by this book, mammal diversity decreases from north to south (from tropical to temperate Aussie regions). The most bio-diverse region of the country for mammals is the "Wet Tropics" rainforest section of northern Queensland, where fully 36% of Australia's mammal species occur, including 30% of its marsupials, 58% of its bats, and 25% of its rodents.

Family Profiles

1. Monotremes—Platypus and Echidna

Literally remnants of a long ago age, the surviving monotremes can be considered among the world's most special vertebrate animals. They are definitely mammals, warm-blooded, covered with a furry pelt of hair, and feeding their infants on mammalian milk that oozes from mammary glands. But they retain some reptilian traits, chiefly their egg-laying reproduction and certain skeletal characteristics, that provide obvious living evidence of the evolutionary link between reptiles and mammals. The mammals, fossils tell us, branched off from primitive reptiles perhaps 245 million years ago. The few present-day monotremes—three species left over from what once must have been a large group that flourished over millions of years and then died out—are particularly of interest because they tell us what some of the early, primitive mammals may have looked like and how they may have behaved and functioned. The living monotremes are truly "living fossils," having survived to the present time only by the slightest element of chance. Because of their obvious dual mammal/reptile nature, an aura of "missing link" surrounds these curious species. The Australian monotremes survived probably because the most modern and successful mammals, the placentals, did not reach the Australia/New Guinea region until relatively recently, so they did not compete with the remaining few monotemes. Such competiton would likely have resulted in the monotremes' complete demise. Note that marsupial and placental mammals did not necessarily evolve directly from monotremes; they were likely separate evolutionary lines.

In addition to egg-laying, other distinctive monotreme traits are a bird-like skull, absence of teeth (except in youngsters), a long snout, or *rostrum*, covered by a leathery sheath, and a reptilian limb structure that makes sustained running difficult. Monotremes are also characterized by having a *cloaca*, a single opening at the rear of the animal through which reproductive, digestive, and excretory materials enter and exit the animal—a trait shared with reptiles and birds, but not with marsupial or placental mammals. In fact, "monotreme" means "single hole"—a reference to the cloaca.

The most famous monotreme, known by reputation to Aussies and others alike, is the PLATYPUS (or Duck-billed Platypus; Plate 61), an unmistakable, small, brown-furred, flattened, mostly aquatic mammal with a black duck-like bill. The only member of its own family (Ornithorhynchidae), it occurs over the eastern parts of Queensland and New South Wales, the southern part of Victoria, and in Tasmania, in both lowland and highland areas. Less widely known, and in a separate family (Tachyglossidae), are the two species of *echidnas*, or *spiny anteaters:* the SHORT-BEAKED ECHIDNA (Plate 61), which occurs throughout Australia and sparsely in parts of New Guinea, and the LONG-BEAKED ECHIDNA, which is found only in New Guinea.

Natural History

Ecology and Behavior

Platypuses are solitary animals that come together usually only to mate; however, in good habitat, many individuals may live within the same small area, using the same lake or stretch of river, for example. They spend their active hours mostly foraging in the water and their inactive hours in deep burrows (to over 10 m, 33 ft, long) they excavate in riverbanks or lake shores. Platypuses swim smoothly and quietly through the water, using their flat tail for propulsion—much like a beaver. To feed, they dive and, using their highly sensitive bill, probe and sift for food in the mud or gravel on the lake or river bottom. They eat a variety of items, including aquatic adult and larval insects, worms, crustaceans, small fish and tadpoles, and probably some plant materials. Platypuses are mostly active at dusk, night, or dawn, but may be out and about at any time of day. In the wild they apparently live ten to twelve years.

The Short-beaked Echidna is a solitary animal that occurs in almost all of Australia's terrestrial habitats, albeit sparsely in some. They are not territorial, but occupy overlapping *home ranges,* the area over which an individual roams and forages; males and females meet only to mate. Echidnas eat ants and termites. They push over rocks and ground debris looking for ant and termite nests, and also use their powerful front limbs (with stout claws) to dig into the ground for insect nests and to tear apart the large, hardened termite nests that dot the Australian landscape. When the insects' nest chambers are exposed, the Echidna darts its very long tongue into the swarming bugs, which adhere to the tongue's sticky mucous-like saliva and are then drawn back into the Echidna's mouth. Echidnas can be active at any time of day, but in hot desert regions they are mostly nocturnal. When not active, Echidnas rest in ground holes, in rock crevices or caves, in hollow logs, or under shrubs. In some colder places, such as mountainous areas that get snow, Echidnas "hibernate"—they enter a sleep-like state of *torpor*—to save energy; their metabolic rate slows and their body temperature drops to almost match that of the environment. The sharp, very hard spines distributed densely over the Echidna's back and sides are obvious defensive weapons: when approached or attacked, an Echidna curls into a ball if on hard ground, spines outward; or, if on soft soil, quickly digs downward, leaving its spines pointing upward out of the dirt to face a predator—and soon the entire animal disappears into the soil. Predation of these porcupine-like mammals is infrequent; dingos probably try to eat some of them.

Breeding

Platypuses start their breeding in August through October, depending on location. Males and females court by swimming together, sometimes in circles, sometimes chasing, the male often gripping the female's tail in his bill. After mating, the female digs a breeding burrow and lines a deep nest chamber in it with grass or leaves. About 2 weeks after mating, she lays 1 to 3 (usually 2) eggs in the nest, and then incubates them against her belly. The young hatch out (cutting their way out of the eggs with a hard "egg tooth" at the tip of their bill) after 1 to

2 weeks. They are only about 1 cm (a half inch) long when born. They get their first hair at 7 weeks; their eyes first open at 9 weeks. The female provides the young milk for 4 to 5 months—they lap the milk from the abdominal fur over the mammary glands. They remain in the breeding burrow during this period, the female leaving at intervals to forage.

Echidna breeding begins in July or August, males approaching females to mate, then departing. The female digs a breeding burrow and lays a single soft-shell egg there about 2 weeks after mating. The egg goes into a small pouch that develops at this time on the female's abdomen. The female incubates the egg in the pouch for 7 to 10 days, and the young that hatches remains in the pouch for 3 months or so, feeding on milk dispensed in the pouch from the mother's mammary glands. Spines first develop at 50 to 80 days of age. The female spends a lot of time in the breeding burrow but leaves at intervals to forage. Young are weaned from mom's milk at about 5 months old.

Notes

When the first Platypus (a dried specimen) was brought to Europe (England) around 1800, biologists there believed it was a fake, that it was actually the bill and feet of a duck-like bird cleverly attached to a strange, unknown mammal—an attempt to perpetrate a hoax on the scientific establishment. Even when it eventually proved to be a "real" animal, and its egg-laying nature was found out, the conventional wisdom for many decades was that the beast was more likely a "furred reptile" than an actual mammal.

Male Platypuses have venom glands located in their thighs that lead to a sharp, hollow spur on the ankle. The reason for this weapon's existence is not known (a defense against predators? A breeding-season weapon of use during male-male contests over females?), but what is known is that the spur can inflict a very painful wound in humans and even kill smaller animals (dogs, cats).

An Aboriginal legend that explains why the Platypus is a solitary animal concerns the confusion people of all cultures exposed to it have had over the biological identity of the species. It is said that a terrible storm in the distant past struck the country. Birds flew away to safety, and reptiles and mammals hid in caves to avoid the lightning, thunder, and torrential rains. When the storm passed, the animals emerged to find all the Platypuses drowned—they had been too slow to escape the floodwaters. Years passed and no Platypuses lived. Then, one day, Platypus tracks were sighted. The birds, reptiles, mammals, and fish gathered and spoke excitedly of welcoming the Platypus back into the community. But they all wanted to claim the Platypus as their own kind, and they argued. The birds said the Platypus laid eggs, so it was a bird. The reptiles said they also laid eggs, and claimed close kinship. Mammals said the Platypus was furred, as they were. Fish pointed out that the Platypus was often underwater, a fish trait if ever there was one. When the Platypus appeared, to settle the argument, he told the gathered animals that he was kin to all, and to none; and that is why the Platypus is a solitary animal (A. W. Reed 1998).

The Echidna family name, Tachyglossidae, which means "fast tongue," refers to the speed with which Echidnas flip their tongues in and out of their beaks—to over 90 times per minute.

Status

Australia's monotremes, although low in species diversity, are not currently threatened—both are fairly common animals. The Platypus is usually considered "potentially vulnerable" because of its limited, patchy distribution throughout its current range and because it is so specialized to live in and adjacent to lakes and waterways. Its water-associated lifestyle makes it very susceptible to shoreline habitat deterioration or destruction (riverbank disturbance, dam construction, etc.) and to water pollution from industry and agriculture. Such threats are thought to be responsible for the elimination of the platypus from the state of South Australia in the recent past. Platypuses are protected from hunting (they were killed in the past for their furry pelts), and mortality from natural predators is relatively low. Short-beaked Echidnas are common, abundant animals in many regions of Australia. New Guinea's Long-beaked Echidna is endangered.

Profiles

Platypus, *Ornithorhynchus anatinus*, Plate 61a
Short-beaked Echidna, *Tachyglossus aculeatus*, Plate 61b

Marsupials

Australia, of course, is the land of marsupials. These pouched mammals are doubtless Australia's most recognized emblems. It is probably correct to say that for the great majority of people worldwide who first learn of Australia, they simultaneously learn of its most famous residents—kangaroos. It is also fair to say that kangaroos and other marsupials, such as koalas, are uppermost in the minds (and on top of the viewing wish lists) of almost all first-time visitors to Australia who are interested in wildlife. Given the strong association between marsupials and Australia, and the fact that these mammals are pretty much the universal symbol for Australia (kangaroo silhouettes even appearing on most of the huge, flying metallic tubes that ferry overseas tourists to the island continent), we can even imagine that at the committee meeting during which the name "Australia" was chosen for the country, "Marsupiala" was a close runner-up in the voting.

When most of us think of Australian marsupials, we tend to think of herbivorous animals—kangaroos and koalas, for instance. But actually, there are all kinds, just as in the placental mammals, including insectivores and even carnivores such as quolls, dunnarts, and devils (the Tasmanian Devil, that is). The carnivore group until recently included a largish dog-like marsupial known as the Tasmanian Tiger, Tasmanian Wolf, or Thylacine (after its genus, *Thylacinus*). This mammal, essentially a "marsupial wolf," was brownish, 1 to 1.3 m (3 to 4 ft) long, weighed up to 35 kg (77 lb), and had a dog-like head and dark crosswise bands or stripes on its back and hindquarters. Originally abundant across Australia, the Thylacine hunted at night in pairs or solitarily, taking mostly kangaroos and wallabies. They apparently lost out in ecological competition with the Dingo (Plate 73), the placental dog that arrived in Australia within the last 4,000 years, and disappeared from the mainland within the last few thousand years. The Thylacine's final refuge, on Tasmania, became inhospitable when European settlers began ranching sheep, and the marsupial predator was intensively hunted and killed. The population plummeted, perhaps exacerbated by disease. The last wild Thylacine was captured in the early 1930s, and the last one in captivity died in 1936 at the Hobart Zoo; despite occasional, unverifiable reports of sightings in Tasmania, the Tasmanian Tiger is now most probably extinct.

Marsupials arose and diverged evolutionarily from other mammal groups perhaps 115 to 130 million year ago, during the Cretaceous Period; they probably developed first in South America. Some ancient marsupials were huge animals—for example, the Miocene- and Pliocene-age *Diprotodon*, a rhino-sized wombat lookalike, and giant kangaroos (such as *Procoptodon goliath*) that stood up to 3 m (10 ft) tall. (If you spend time in Sydney, be sure to stop by the fine Australian Museum to see some striking re-creations of these mega-marsupials.) Marsupials today range in size from the tiny, mouse-like Long-tailed Planigale, at 4 g (0.14 oz), to the Eastern Grey Kangaroo (Plate 67) and Red Kangaroo, which range up to a length of 2 m (6.5 ft) and weigh up to 90 kg (200 lb). The approximately 260 species of living marsupials are divided into 12 to 19 families (depending on whose classification scheme you want to follow) and about 75 genera; about 150 species occur in Australia.

The main thing that sets marsupials apart from other mammals, of course, is their mode of reproduction: the young, barely embryos, are born comparatively very early in a very undeveloped state; they crawl along the mother's fur and climb into her abdominal pouch (technically, the *marsupium*, Latin for "pouch"), where nipples and milk supplies are available and development continues. Red and Eastern Grey Kangaroos, for instance, are born about 35 days after conception, and the embryo that emerges from the female's reproductive tract weighs only about 1 g (1/30 of an ounce). Possums (p. 217) can weigh as little as 0.2 g (1/100 ounce) when born. American opossums give birth only 2 weeks after mating. After the embryonic marsupial completes its climbing act and finds a nipple, the nipple swells inside its mouth, essentially attaching it to the mother for a month or two (the youngster is called a "pouch embryo" during this time). When the young finally leave mom's pouch, they weigh about the same as would a newly born placental mammal of the same general species size.

Many marsupials are now threatened in Australia, and several species became extinct during the twentieth century. Habitat destruction and the usurpation of wild habitats for ranching and farming are the main threats to these animals. Australia's peculiarly poor record with respect to mammal conservation is detailed briefly in Chapter 5.

2. Carnivorous Marsupials—Devil, Quolls, and Relatives

The carnivorous marsupials comprise a successful family (Dayuridae) of tiny to mid-sized mammals that inhabit all regions of Australia and New Guinea, but are especially diverse in Australia's desert areas. *Dasyurids* range from tiny, shrew-like animals that weigh as little as 2 to 5 g (0.07 to 0.18 oz) and subsist on bugs and worms to the stocky, dog-like TASMANIAN DEVIL (Plate 61), which scavenges and hunts vertebrate prey and weighs as much as 9 kg (20 lb). Most dasyurids as adults are brownish or greyish and weigh less than 100 g (3.5 oz); males are usually larger than females. Many of the dasyurids are rather mouse- or rat-like in appearance, with long snouts, and the small ones usually have large ears and pointed snouts. Long, well-furred tails that are never prehensile are characteristic of the group. Many species either lack a pouch entirely or have a poorly developed one. These animals have needle-like incisor teeth and large, sharp-edged canines used to grasp and rip insects, worms, or small vertebrates; they typically capture their prey by stealth and surprise pounce rather than long chases. They are mostly nocturnal; some are arboreal, some terrestrial, and some are both. There are about 65 species of dasyurids, about 52 of which live in Australia; about 15 occur in this book's coverage area.

The Tasmanian Devil, the largest of the carnivorous marsupials, is now confined to Tasmania but once flourished on the Australian mainland. It is a short, dog-like mammal with large head and powerful jaws, black with white markings. The four species of Australian *quolls* (grouped with the Tasmanian Devil in subfamily Dasyurinae) are fairly large, cat-like dasyurids, easily identified by their characteristic white spots. The eight Australian *antechinuses* ("ant-eh-KINE-isses"; subfamily Phascogalinae) are small, grey or brown, mouse-like, mainly forest-dwelling dasyurids that weigh between 16 and 178 g (0.6 to 6 oz). They are terrestrial and arboreal animals with feet specialized for running. There are two Australian species of *phascogales*, which are a kind of antechinus; they are arboreal and squirrel-like; the larger one, which is widespread, weighs up to 230 g (8 oz). *Dunnarts* are small, terrestrial, mouse-like animals (commonly called "marsupial mice," as are the antechinuses), most of which weigh between 15 and 25 g (0.5 to 1 oz), but they range up to 70 g (2.5 oz). Their feet are adapted for hopping. Australia has 19 species. *Planigales* are very small, terrestrial, mouse-like dasyurids, often good climbers, that sometimes spend time underground; brown or grey, they range in weight from 5 to 22 g (0.2 to 0.8 oz). There are 4 Australian species, the LONG-TAILED PLANIGALE of northern Australia being among the world's smallest mammals, weighing regularly about 4 g (0.14 oz) and being about 6 cm (2.5 in) long, excluding tail.

Natural History

Ecology and Behavior

Tasmanian Devils are nocturnal and *crepuscular* (active at dawn and dusk) carnivores and scavengers. They usually hunt solitarily, covering ground with a strange, rocking gait. Typical home ranges, the area in which an individual lives and seeks food, vary from 8 to 20 sq km (3 to 8 sq mi), and a devil can travel 10 or more km (6 mi) per night in search of food. During the day these carnivores rest in burrows, crevices, or hollow logs. Despite their fierce reputation (based on the fact that they are relatively large carnivores with strong jaws and sharp teeth and were thought to be major predators of sheep), they are fairly shy animals. They eat whatever animals they can find that are small enough for them to take: insects, birds, some fish, barnyard poultry, but mostly smaller mammals: possums, wallabies, even wombats. A large part of their nutrition apparently comes from scavenging dead animals—and groups of devils are sometimes seen around carcasses of larger ranch animals. Devils are most abundant in drier forest regions of Tasmania, but can be found in most wooded areas.

Quolls are the largest marsupial carnivores on the Australia mainland, the SPOT-TAILED QUOLL (Plate 61) being the largest one. Their social and spacing systems are not well-known, but males in some species may defend territories and/or females during breeding seasons. They hunt animals but also scavenge for carrion and, at times, consume fruit and other plant materials. Insects are a large part of the diet of many species, but larger quolls take more vertebrate prey, including antechinuses, rats, rabbits, bandicoots, and even, in the case of the Spot-tailed Quoll, small wallabies. They kill prey by biting heads or necks. Quolls are mainly nocturnal, but sometimes can be seen hunting by daylight. They inhabit mostly wooded regions, but some species range widely, including into scrub and agricultural areas.

Relatively little is known of the ecology and behavior of many of the other, smaller, dasyurids. Antechinuses are mainly nocturnal and crepuscular hunters of insects. Some are terrestrial, some partly arboreal, and some both. They inhabit mainly forests, but some species occur in a wide range of habitat types. In addition to insects such as beetles and roaches, and larval insects such as grubs, some species eat a lot of spiders, centipedes, and worms; some species take small lizards, birds, and mice; and some species occasionally snack on fruit or flowers. Antechinuses, and perhaps many other small dasyurids, characteristically eat only the insides of small birds and small mammals, turning the skin inside out as they do so and leaving the everted skins behind when the meal is finished. Dunnarts are mostly small and nocturnally active, eating almost exclusively insects, spiders, and very small vertebrates such as tiny skinks. During the day they shelter in nests of grasses and leaves placed in hollow logs or thick vegetation. They inhabit a wide variety of habitat types, including forests, shrubland, grassland, and agricultural areas. In at least one species that was researched, dunnarts had small home ranges, those of males overlapping with other males, but those of females being non-overlapping with those of other females—that is, the females appeared to have exclusive territories. At least some dunnarts, such as the FAT-TAILED DUNNART (Plate 62), can store energy in the form of fat tissue in their tails—so tails swell when food is abundant and shrink in winter, when food is scarce. Some dunnart species are known to be able to enter into a state of reduced activity and reduced metabolic rate (*torpor*) when little food is available and/or cold weather makes a high metabolic rate untenable. Planigales are nocturnal ground-based predators of insects and other small arthropods, as well as small lizards and the odd tiny mammal.

Ecological Interactions

Being a female antechinus, in this writer's opinion, is better than being a male. In at least some of the species, including BROWN and YELLOW-FOOTED ANTECHINUSES (Plate 62), males breed once at about a year old and then die; females survive to raise the kids and perhaps breed again the next year. After all the males die, it is interesting to note, the entire population of a given species consists of females—pregnant females, thankfully, or the species would quickly come to an end. It happens like this: males (usually born in September) reach reproductive maturity by July; leading up to the August breeding season, males become increasingly aggressive with each other, as they compete for access to females. Stress hormones in their bodies, such as corticosterone, are at high levels, and this leads to reduced feeding and compromised immune systems, but allows for sustained mating. After mating, which is itself stressful in that it can last for six to twelve hours, males lose weight, develop sicknesses such as intestinal ulcers, and die within two weeks. The eco-evolutionary term for such male die-off after a single breeding effort is *semelparity* (one reproductive event per lifetime, otherwise known as "Big Bang" reproduction; the opposite term, for species such as eco-travellers that pursue multiple breeding events per lifetime, is *iteroparity*). Semelparous breeding is thought to have evolved in the antechinuses' case because these small mammals, given their ecological circumstances, don't have the time to breed twice in one year, and they are so unsure of survival to the next year that it is to their reproductive advantage to make one large breeding effort in their lifetime. Other examples of semelparous organisms are Pacific salmon, octopus and many other invertebrates, and annual plants.

Breeding

Tasmanian Devils mate usually in March or April; gestation is about 30 days. The female gives birth in a den in a hollow log or rock crevice. One to 4 young successfully crawl to the mother's pouch (a relatively well-developed pouch) after being born and attach to teats (of which there are only 4). After about 4 months in the pouch, the fully furred young emerge, often in August, and are left alone in the den when the mother forages. They are fully independent at 9 or 10 months old, and sexually mature at 2 years. Devils in the wild can live 6 to 7 years.

Most dasyurids, like the devil, are promiscuous breeders—no long-term pair bonds are formed. Males in many species apparently vocalize during breeding seasons to locate females; females respond when they are receptive to mating. After mating, male and female separate; in some species, males die soon after mating (see earlier). Females of various species nest in hollow logs, tree trunks, burrows, rock crevices, in thick grass clumps, and even in old bird nests lined with leaves. Gestation varies from about 2 to 6 weeks. Often, more young are born (often 8 or more, up to 20) than there are teats to suckle from; the only survivors are those emerging young that make it to the mother's pouch area and successfully attach to a teat. (Many of these marsupials have only a rudimentary pouch—really just a flap of skin around the teats; some, such as phascogales, lack any kind of pouch.) Young are suckled for 2 to 5 months. After leaving the pouch, young dasyurids either are left in the nest when the mother goes on foraging trips, or they cling to her fur and go along for the ride. Most dasyurids are sexually mature at 9 to 12 months old.

Notes

Quolls, sometimes called Australia's "native cats," apparently picked up this moniker because early European settlers called them "native polecats," a common name they used for weasels (which are also carnivores) back home; over time, the name shortened to "native cats." As mentioned above, many of the very small carnivorous marsupials were (and sometimes still are) called collectively "marsupial mice" by early Australian biologists—but this was before they were studied and found to be carnivorous (and not plant- and seed-eaters, as are most mice).

The Yellow-footed Antechinus is the best-known of the antechinus group, owing to its broad distribution in eastern Australia (where the humans are dense on the ground) and its common occupation of gardens and even houses. One of Australia's foremost mammalogists states, "Its nervous and cheeky disposition usually makes it a welcome and amusing visitor but its tendencies to pilfer from the kitchen and to build nests inside television sets and lounge chairs sometimes make it a nuisance" (R. Strahan 1995).

Status

Several dasyurids are threatened or endangered, mostly owing to destruction of their native habitats and to competition with introduced placental mammals such as dingos and foxes. The Tasmanian Devil was extirpated on the Australian mainland, possibly due to competition with dingos; now, however, it is a fairly common and abundant resident over parts of its final refuge, Tasmania. EASTERN QUOLLS, likewise, once roamed widely in the southeastern portion of the mainland, but are now restricted to Tasmania; competion with foxes, among other possible causes, likely led to their reduced range. WESTERN QUOLLS and the MULGARA have had their ranges much reduced in recent times, but causes are unclear. A tiny, mouse-like dasyurid known as the SOUTHERN DIBBLER, with small populations remaining in extreme southwestern Australia, is threatened, as is the RED-TAILED PHASCOGALE in the same region. Five species of dunnarts are threatened, and two of them, the LONG-TAILED DUNNART of central and western Australia and the SANDHILL DUNNART of south-central Australia, are CITES Appendix I listed as endangered. The Thylacine, or Tasmanian Wolf (p. 205), is also listed in CITES Appendix I, but is presumed extinct.

Profiles

Spot-tailed Quoll, *Dasyurus maculatus*, Plate 61c
Eastern Quoll, *Dasyurus viverrinus*, Plate 61d
Tasmanian Devil, *Sarcophilus harrisii*, Plate 61e
Yellow-footed Antechinus, *Antechinus flavipes*, Plate 62a
Brown Antechinus, *Antechinus stuartii*, Plate 62b
Dusky Antechinus, *Antechinus swainsonii*, Plate 62b
Brush-tailed Phascogale, *Phascogale tapoatafa*, Plate 62c
Common Planigale, *Planigale maculata*, Plate 62d
Fat-tailed Dunnart, *Sminthopsis crassicaudata*, Plate 62e
Common Dunnart, *Sminthopsis murina*, Plate 62f

3. Bandicoots and Bilby

Bandicoots are rat-like marsupials, rabbit-sized and smaller, that make their living using their short, powerful, clawed forelimbs to dig into the soil in search of insects and other foods. They are known especially for possessing a fairly advanced placenta and for a high reproductive rate—perhaps the highest among the marsupials. There are about 18 species of living bandicoots (including the BILBY), 8 of them in Australia and about 10 in the New Guinea region (2 species, the NORTHERN BROWN and RUFOUS SPINY BANDICOOTS, both Plate 63, occur in both Australia and New Guinea). All of Australia's bandicoots but one, and the Bilby, are currently placed in family Peramelidae; the Rufous Spiny Bandicoot (a bit different skeletally) is in a separate family, Peroryctidae, along with many of the New Guinea species; however, the entire group's classification is controversial.

Bandicoots are fairly slender animals with compact bodies, short necks, and pointed heads with long, tapered snouts. Their rear limbs (elongated for running) are larger than their forelimbs, and this unevenness contributes to an often bounding, or "bunny-hop," gait when moving slowly (but they can gallop along when they want to move fast). The main toes of the forelimbs have flattened claws for digging (other toes are reduced in size or absent). They have small to mid-sized ears and short, nonprehensile tails. Their hair is stiff and coarse, and they mostly come in greys and browns, with some having golden brown or cinnamon tinges; some species characteristically have crosswise bands on their rumps. In the bigger species, males can be significantly larger than females. The Bilby, a bluish grey desert-dweller, differs from others in the bandicoot group by being long-legged, long-tailed, and long-eared, with soft, silky hair.

Natural History

Ecology and Behavior
Bandicoots are terrestrial and *fossorial*, mostly solitary, and active mainly at night. They spend the daylight hours in a burrow or nest in the ground or grass. Emerging at night, they forage for their meals by digging holes in the soil with their powerful, clawed forelimbs and probing into the holes with their elongated noses; small, conical holes in the ground are evidence of recent bandicoot activity. They are known primarily as insectivores, but field studies show that they are actually omnivores—taking not just insects and their larvae but earthworms and other non-insect invertebrates, seeds, roots, fruit, succulent parts of plants, and even some small vertebrates such as baby rodents. Most bandicoots apparently spend much of the year alone, males and females coming together only to mate.

They occupy home ranges (the area in which an individual lives and seeks food) of usually 0.5 to 5 ha (1.2 to 13 ac), depending on species, with males having larger home ranges than females. Usually these areas are not defended from other individuals of the same species—that is, they overlap and are not strict territories; but when population densities make it economically beneficial, some bandicoots, such as the SOUTHERN BROWN BANDICOOT, may defend exclusive territories.

Breeding

Bandicoots have a type of placenta (as does the koala) that is similar is many ways to that possessed by placental mammals—the embryos are attached to the mother's uterine wall and nutrition passes from the mother to her embryos across membranes—but the bandicoot system is not as efficient in moving nutrients and other materials as the one employed by the placental mammals. Bandicoots have brief gestation periods—as little as 12.5 days in the Northern Brown and LONG-NOSED BANDICOOTS (Plate 63)—in fact, some of the briefest pregnancies known among mammals. Young are born when they weigh only abut 2 g (0.07 oz) and are only 1 cm (0.4 in) long. They crawl to mom's pouch and stay there for about 50 days; they are weaned about 10 to 14 days after leaving the pouch. Female bandicoots captured with pouch young usually have 2 to 4 of them, but the range is 1 to 7. Bandicoots are reproductively mature at between 3 and 6 months, and probably live more than 3 years in the wild. Bandicoot nests are often depressions in the ground covered with vegetation and ground litter.

Notes

Bandicoots in Australia were so named because they resembled the large rat-like rodents native to India, Southeast Asia, and Malaysia that are called "bandicoot rats." Some believe that the reason they have not been re-named (now that their different, marsupial nature is known) is "a lack of public interest in, or affection for, these (rat-like) marsupials; indeed, 'bandicoot' remains a derogatory term in the Australian vernacular" (R. Strahan in J. H. Seebeck 1990).

Status

Bandicoots in Australia, particularly those species of arid and semi-arid areas, have been suffering drastic declines in recent time. The main causes are probably two-fold: the use of the bandicoots' habitats for grazing of cattle and sheep (and rabbits), which causes habitat quality to decline, and the introduction of predators such as foxes and cats. Three Aussie species are recently extinct: the LESSER BILBY of the central deserts probably died out completely in the 1960s; the PIG-FOOTED BANDICOOT, which once occurred over large parts of central and southern Australia, survived until sometime between 1920 and 1950; and the DESERT BANDICOOT of central Australia died out probably in the 1940s. Several of the group are now considered threatened or endangered. The Bilby (CITES Appendix I listed) once occurred over large regions of central Australia, but is now restricted to small remnant patches of its former range. The WESTERN BARRED BANDICOOT (CITES Appendix I) once occupied many regions of southern and western Australia but is now restricted to two small islands (a nature reserve) off the western coast. Likewise, the GOLDEN BANDICOOT, once widespread in central and northern Australia, is now restricted to small patches of the north and northwest. And the EASTERN BARRED BANDICOOT, once common over parts of southern Victoria and Tasmania, is now probably restricted to Tasmania.

Profiles

Northern Brown Bandicoot, *Isodon macrourus*, Plate 63c
Long-nosed Bandicoot, *Perameles nasuta*, Plate 63d
Rufous Spiny Bandicoot, *Echymipera rufescens*, Plate 63e

4. Koalas

KOALAS (Plate 63) are cute—almost too cute to write about. But because I know that many users of this book will be intensely interested in these "living teddy bears," I'll devote a few paragraphs to them. For visitors to Australia from areas of the world where the stuffed animal toys known as teddy bears are common childhood icons, coming across a wild, free-ranging Koala (or coming face-to-face with one in a zoo or a Koala "farm") is a very interesting encounter—for many, perhaps one of the most gripping experiences of a trip. First of all, just what are Koalas? They are rather unique mammals, members of the marsupial order Diprotodontia, classed together with wombats, possums, and kangaroos. Their closest living relatives are the wombats, and wombats and the Koala together form subfamily Vombatiformes; Phascolarctidae, the Koala's family, contains but one species. The Koala, which occurs only in Australia, has a broad but patchy distribution in the east, inhabiting dry forests with smooth-barked eucalypt trees in tropical and temperate areas of central and southeastern Queensland, and in temperate eastern New South Wales, eastern and southern Victoria, and bits of southeastern South Australia. It occurs on both sides of the Great Dividing Range, below about 600 m (2,000 ft) elevation.

Koalas are medium-sized, stocky mammals, with dense grey or greyish brown fur. Their round face, big, round, fluffy ears, forward-facing eyes, and black nose make them appear vulnerable and particularly appealing to humans. They have relatively long limbs but only a stump of a tail. Their hands have sharp claws and opposable digits, which help them climb and move about their arboreal homes; their feet, likewise, have an opposable digit that aids in climbing tree trunks and branches. Koalas range up to about 80 cm (32 in) in length and 13 kg (29 lb) in weight, individuals in the cooler southern parts of their range being larger (and darker) than individuals in warmer northern areas. Males are larger than females in the same area (up to 50% heavier) and have a more prominent, bulging nose.

Natural History

Ecology and Behavior

Koalas are supreme arboreal *folivores* (leaf-eaters). Most of their lives are spent solitarily in trees, resting and eating. A typical Koala day runs something like this: 19 to 21 hours resting in a fork of a tree, followed by, starting at dusk, 3 to 5 hours of eating eucalyptus leaves. A few minutes may be spent travelling around the branches and canopy of a single tree and perhaps traversing the ground to move to another feeding tree (eucalypt woodlands characteristically have trees spaced fairly far apart, so moving from tree to tree in the canopy in often impossible). Koalas, high specialized gourmets, eat only leaves of eucalypt trees, and then only the leaves of certain species (in total about 35 of the 600 or so eucalypt species are eaten). In the southern part of their range they prefer Manna Gum, Swamp Gum, and Blue Gum (Plate C3); in the north, Red Gum and Grey Gum, among others. In any one area, most Koalas prefer 1 or 2 eucalypt species, although others are available; the preferred species usually grow in fertile soils along drainage lines, and it is thought that leaves of these species contain larger amounts of some necessary Koala nutrient. Each adult consumes between 0.5 and 1 kg (1 to 2 lb) of leaves per night. All of their water usually comes from dew they drink from tree leaves and from "metabolic water" that results from leaf digestion. Koalas have home ranges (the area in which they live and seek food) that vary, depending on local Koala density, from 1.5 to 3.5 ha (3.7 to 8.5 ac) for males and from 0.5 to 1 ha (1 to 2.5 ac) for females. In high-density areas, home ranges may overlap—that is, they are not exclusive to each individual. Koala social behavior in the wild is not well-known, but dominant males will chase smaller, subordinate males if and when they meet, and they apparently fight at times, because captured males often have battle scars. Males also sometimes apparently search out other Koalas, climb into their trees, and engage in male–male aggressive interactions or in male–female interactions. But Koalas descend to the ground regularly only to move between feeding trees, perhaps once a day or less. It is during these times that Koalas are most vulnerable to predation (dogs, dingos) and to people (automobiles). Large snakes and large birds of prey may kill some Koalas in trees.

Ecological Interactions

Koala survival being dependent on leaves, and fairly toxic leaves at that, it is not surprising that the little marsupials have numerous specialized digestive and other adaptations to deal with their diet of pure eucalyptus. Plant leaves, and eucalypt ones in particular, are a poor-quality, low-energy food source. They are difficult to digest, high in fiber (tough cellulose cell walls), low in protein, and loaded with compounds (up to 11% of these leaves' dry matter are *phenolics*, or volatile oils) that are toxic to most mammals. To counteract these problems, Koalas: (1) eat a lot of leaves (0.5 to 1 kg, 1 to 2 lb, per 24-hour period) because they only get a small amount of energy from each one; (2) tend to select younger leaves because they usually have lower concentrations of phenolic compounds; (3) chew the leaves well with ridged teeth and strong jaw muscles to physically break down some of the plant cell walls, thereby allowing digestion of the cells' contents; (4) have very long digestive tracts—the longer the tract, the more time it takes food to move through it, and so the more time the animal has to absorb nutrients from the food; (5) have livers that can inactivate the various potentially toxic compounds found in eucalypt leaf cells and cause them to be excreted; (6) are very low-energy animals; they don't waste much energy, usually moving slowly and deliberately and being essentially inactive for 19 to 21 hours per day.

As with other animals, including termites, that depend on tough plant materials for their nutrition, digestion in Koalas is aided by symbiotic microorganisms in their digestive system (in this case, especially in an organ known as the *caecum*, a largish pouch between the small and large intestine). In this mutualistic interaction, the bacteria get food (the cellulose in the eucalypt plant cell walls) and safe living accommodation, and the Koalas get increased nutrition and energy after the bacteria break down cell walls, releasing cell contents for digestion, and metabolize some of the cell contents in a fermentation process. A problem with the system is that Koalas are not born with the internal helpers—they must acquire them after birth. Young Koalas do this in an unattractive manner, by eating their mother's fecal material, special soft droppings, known as *pap*, probably produced in the mother's ceacum for just this purpose. Only after eating pap can young Koalas be weaned from milk to a leaf diet. Some other mammals behave similarly: some rodents and rabbits excrete soft feces that contain partially digested plant material, which they then eat (called *coprophagy*) so they can absorb more nutrients from it. After their intestinal microbes have fermented the material during the first go-round, a second, harder type of feces is then excreted, which is not eaten. (The Koala's essential gut bacteria present a problem to koala management: many Koalas are infected with the bacterial disease chlamydiosis, which damages eyes and urinary and reproductive tracts, leading to infertility. Unfortunately, antibiotics that might kill the *Chlamydia* bacteria would likely also kill the Koala's essential gut bacteria.)

So the Koala's dietary specialization on eucalyptus leaves was accomplished only with a number of significant behavioral and physiological adaptations. On the other hand, one can see the great advantages to the Koalas: eucalypt trees were plentiful during the Koala's evolution (and still are, comprising 90% of Australia's forest trees), and given the poor quality of eucalypt leaves as food, other animals tend to avoid them—there is little or no competition for this food resource.

Breeding
Koalas are polygynous breeders, with one male having several mates in a breeding season. They breed in spring and summer (October though February). Males advertise at night for receptive females by making loud bellowing sounds that can be heard 1 km (a half-mile) away. Mating occurs in trees, and then the female raises the young herself. Usually only 1 young (rarely 2) is born (in December or Janaury) after gestation of 34 to 36 days. The embryo, weighing only 1 g (0.03 oz) or so, crawls to mom's pouch and remains there for about 6 months. The young leaves the pouch permanently at 7 months, travels on the mother's back for another 3 or 4 months, and is independent at 11 to 12 months. Females remain in their birth areas, beginning to breed at age 2; males disperse (sometimes many km) from their birth areas when they are 2 or 3 and, although they are reproductively mature at age 2, most begin breeding when they are 4 years old. Males live typically 12 to 15 years, females up to 18 years.

Notes
One Aboriginal legend tells why Koalas have no tail: In the distant past, when the Koala had a splendid tail, a severe drought hit the forest. The other forest animals, thirsty, noticed that Koala seemed well sated with water. They suspected he had a secret source of water, and they sent Lyrebird to follow Koala and spy on him. Sure enough, Lyrebird saw Koala hanging upside down in a tree, lapping up water that had collected in a fork of branches. Suspecting that the tree might be filled with water, but unable to access it, Lyrebird found a firestick and set fire to the tree. The tree exploded, releasing water that all the forest animals could drink. But the fire singed Lyrebird's feathers, causing the brown markings we see today, and, unfortunately, incinerated Koala's tail. (A. W. Reed 1998)

Koalas can be smelled some distance away, and they smell, not surprisingly, of the eucalyptus oils of the leaves they eat.

Status
Koalas were once more numerous and widespread. They are still fairly widespread, but their distribution is fragmented. In the distant past, Koalas were killed for

food in trees by Aboriginal people and on the ground by dingos. European settlers killed millions of them for their fur during the 1800s and early 1900s. By the 1930s their populations had dwindled and they were threatened with extinction. Laws to protect them (hunting them was banned in various states between 1898 and 1927), along with intensive management programs, reversed their decline, and good populations now occur in areas that still have Koalas. In some areas, where their eucalyptus food trees are abundant and predators few, Koala populations increase dramatically, causing problems—too many Koalas in a small area, extensive damage to their food trees, road hazards. In fact, although many Australians very much like Koalas, some dislike them because they feel that Koalas are now too protected and "cuddled." The main sources of mortality for today's Koalas, aside from old age, are forest fires, habitat destruction, disease, and automobiles. In some populations, nearly 50% of Koalas surveyed suffer from a *Chlamydia* bacterial disease (chlamydiosis); biologists are working on vaccines. Up to 60% of the 4,000 Koalas estimated to die each year are hit by cars at night as they cross roads. Koalas are sometimes taken from areas of high Koala density (areas that are *Chlamydia*-free and where, owing to their large populations, they are depleting their food resources) and translocated to new areas that lack Koalas but that harbored them in the past. For instance, Koalas have been transplanted from French Island and Phillip Island (with their healthy, *Chlamydia*-free populations) to mainland Victoria since 1923; more than 10,000 animals were moved by 1988. Some of these translocations are successful, but some of the Koalas catch *Chlamydia* in their new locations and sicken or die, and many have trouble adjusting to their new surroundings.

Profiles

Koala, *Phascolarctos cinereus*, Plate 63a

5. Wombats

Why do you need to know what *wombats* are? One good reason: in some frequently visted regions of Australia, their silhouettes appear often on road signs (as deer silhouettes appear on North American road signs), and if you don't know what a wombat is, how are you to interpret the signs? Another reason: if locals refer to you as a "muddle-headed wombat," you will want to know to what degree you're being insulted. Wombats are terrestrial grazing herbivores that resemble small bears or large rodents. They are mainly nocturnal, spending the daylight hours below ground in networks of tunnels they dig with their short, powerful limbs and long, broad, strong claws. Wombats are members of the marsupial order Diprotodontia, classed together with Koalas, possums, and kangaroos. Their closest living relative is the Koala, and wombats and the Koala together form subfamily Vombatiformes. Vombatidae, the wombat's family, contains three species, all Aussie endemics: the COMMON WOMBAT (Plate 63), a widely distributed species of Australia's southeastern forests; the SOUTHERN HAIRY-NOSED WOMBAT, a common but patchily distributed animal restricted to semi-arid areas of extreme southern parts of Western Australia and South Australia; and the NORTHERN HAIRY-NOSED WOMBAT, a rare and endangered species that occurs now only in one small area of grassland/woodland in central-eastern Queensland (see below).

Wombats are stocky brown or brownish grey animals, up to about a meter (3.3 ft) long and 25 cm (10 in) high, that weigh 20 to 40 kg (44 to 88 lb). They have small eyes (with poor vision), rodent-like faces, flattened heads (used to compact the walls of their burrows and push logs and vegetation out of the way), and thick bodies. They share several traits with Koalas: a very short, almost imperceptible tail; a pouch, with two teats, that opens toward the rear of the animal; a very long intestine that aids digestion of high-fiber, low-nutrition plant materials; and a black button nose. Wombat males and females look alike.

Natural History

Ecology and Behavior

The Common Wombat is the species most often studied, so most of the information here concerns it. Wombats, in some ways, resemble rodents (especially large rodents such as the northern hemisphere marmots), and have a rodent-like ecological niche. They eat only vegetation (and perhaps some fungi): mostly sturdy native grasses but also herbs, mosses, and some roots and bark. To cut and rip this food, they have one pair of incisor teeth on the upper jaw and one pair in the lower; these teeth, which wear down as the animals use them, grow continually throughout life, as in rodents. The incisors cut the wombat's food and then the cheek teeth (molars) are used to grind and macerate. Wombats are nocturnal, sleeping, resting, and hiding in burrows. They emerge typically at dusk to begin the night's foraging, then return to a burrow by dawn, having covered up to 3 km (1.8 mi) during the evening's search for good food. In cold weather, some wombats also forage by day. Although usually slow-moving, wombats can cover ground quickly when necessary, and some have been clocked at 40 kph (25 mph) over short distances. When threatened, wombats tend to run for burrows or hide in hollow logs; eagles, dingos, and, in Tasmania, Tasmanian Devils, are their enemies.

Wombat burrow systems have been investigated closely (aided by the ability of small, thin researchers to actually descend into burrows). These burrows are up to 30 m (100 ft) long, 2 m (6 ft) deep, and 50 cm (20 in) wide, often with several entrances, side tunnels, and multiple rest chambers lined with vegetation. They are placed in flat ground, under rocky areas, or in slopes. Usually a wombat has several burrows—smaller ones, perhaps 2 to 5 m (6.5 to 16 ft) long, used for quick rest or refuge, and larger main burrows used for daytime sleeping. An individual burrow can be used for many years by several generations of wombats. Spending a large portion of their lives underground is helpful to wombats because they need expend relatively little energy on temperature regulation: burrows are always cool during hot days and passingly warm on frigid days.

Wombats have home ranges from 5 to 23 ha (12 to 55 ac) in size. Although home ranges overlap among individuals, each wombat might have a specific favored feeding area that it aggressively defends from others. These animals are mainly solitary, but when two males meet, for instance, fights can ensue if one of the males does not move away; they tend to bite each others' ears or hindquarters. However, a degree of sociality exists: during a night's roaming, an individual often visits several burrows and so meets other wombats, and more than one wombat may inhabit a large burrow system during the day. Also, several wombats may construct burrows in the same general area, forming a "colony" and facilitating social interactions.

Breeding

Wombats may breed at any time of year. After mating, the sexes separate and the female gives birth and raises the young on her own. Gestation is about 30 days.

The single young (rarely 2), only 1.5 cm (a half-inch) long at birth, crawls to the pouch and stays there for 6 to 7 months before beginning to make forays out of the pouch and around the burrow. Permanently out of the pouch at 9 to 10 months old, the young then remains with the mother for a few more months before moving out on its own. Wombats reach sexual maturity at 2 to 3 years, and live in the wild for 5 to 10 years (over 20 years in zoos).

Notes

The word "wombat" originated with the Aboriginal word for the animal, "wombach." Early European settlers tended to call these mammals "badgers," after medium-sized burrowing mammals from back home. *Vombatus ursinus*, the Latin name for the Common Wombat, means "bear-like wombat." Much larger wombats lived in Australia up to about 10,000 years ago; one, known as *Phascolonus*, weighed in at about 100 kg (220 lb).

Status

All three wombat species now have much reduced ranges as a result of habitat loss, habitat fragmentation, predation by introduced species such as dingos, competition for food grasses by grazing livestock, persecution by farmers and ranchers, and wombat–automobile collisions. All wombats are now protected, to varying degrees, in the states in which they occur. Farmers sometimes kill wombats because their tunnel systems can collapse under the weight of cattle or cars, causing chaos, and because they damage fences used to keep rabbits out of range and crop areas. The Northern Hairy-nosed Wombat, highly endangered and CITES Appendix I listed, survives only in the highly protected site of Queensland's Epping Forest National Park; the population size varied during the 1990s from 60 to about 80 individuals. Dingos occasionally still take some of these wombats. The biggest threats today to wombats are continued forest clearing and car accidents.

Profiles

Common Wombat, *Vombatus ursinus*, Plate 63b

6. Possums

Possum is the name given to a variety of small to medium-sized, mostly forest-dwelling nocturnal marsupials that move about in trees; they have strongly *prehensile* tails and opposable digits on feet and sometimes hands to help them grasp branches and clamber about their arboreal domains in search of plant matter or insect foods. The four families that contain possums are grouped together in order Diprotodontia, along with the koalas, wombats, gliders, and kangaroos; almost all possums are restricted to the Australia/New Guinea region (one species, the BEAR CUSCUS, occurs on the Indonesian island of Sulawesi). Possums range in size from the tiny LITTLE PYGMY-POSSUM of Tasmania and small bits of the mainland, which weighs usually a bit less than 10 g (0.3 oz), to the 5 kg (11 lb) COMMON SPOTTED CUSCUS (Plate 64).

Family Phalangeridae includes the *cuscuses* (a type of possum) and *brushtail possums*. These are medium-sized mammals of forests and woodlands that are usually arboreal, eating leaves and other plant materials. They have short, flat faces, forward-facing eyes, long, sharp, curved claws on their hands for tree climbing, and areas of bare skin on their tails; cuscuses, or *phalangers*, typically have large, roundish heads. There are about twenty species in the family; five occur in

Australia, four within the coverage area of this book. The cuscuses and brushtails are perhaps the most widely distributed of the families of marsupials in the Australian/New Guinea region. Family Burramyidae, with five species of *pygmy-possums* (all of which occur in Australia and one of which also occurs in New Guinea; four occur within the coverage area of this book), contains the smallest possums—arboreal insect-eaters with long, slender tails that inhabit a variety of habitat types. Family Petauridae contains some of the *gliders* (p. 220) and four or five species of possums, most of which are black-and-white striped (and therefore often skunk-like in appearance) and confined to the New Guinea region; two occur in Australia, both in the coverage area of this book, but only one of these, the STRIPED POSSUM (Plate 65) of Queensland's northeast, is common. *Petaurid* possums have long, densely furred tails and an exceptionally long, clawed fourth finger on each hand. Finally, family Pseudocheiridae, containing the *ringtail possums* (along with one of the gliders), includes about sixteen species, most of which occur in New Guinea; seven occur in Australia, five within the coverage area of this book. These possums have long, thin, short-furred tails, usually about the same length as their heads and bodies together.

Natural History

Ecology and Behavior

Cuscuses and brushtail possums are largely herbivorous, eating leaves (especially the brushtails) but also fruits, flowers, buds, and some bark (eggs, invertebrate animals, and even birds may also be taken at times by some species; some are known to eat meat in captivity). They inhabit forests and woodlands, moving about trees slowly and deliberately, seeking preferred food items. Relatively little is known of their social and spacing systems, but some species, such as the COMMON BRUSHTAIL POSSUM (Plate 65), maintain exclusive territories within their home ranges, with the private domains of individuals being marked with chemicals from skin scent glands that are located on various parts of their anatomies. Home ranges can vary from about 0.5 to 8 ha (1.2 to 20 ac), depending on species, sex, and habitat type. Pygmy-possums are tiny, fast-moving, agile tree climbers that move around their shrubland, heathland, and eucalypt forest habitats in search of their main food, flower nectar; they also take the odd insect for protein, and some soft fruits when nectar is less available. These usually solitary marsupials generally have home ranges of a hectare (2.5 ac) or less; but home ranges overlap, and cases of 100 or more individuals per hectare have been recorded. In winter, all the pygmy-possums, when food is unavailable or insufficent to meet their energy demands, have the ability to enter a state of *torpor*—to reduce their metabolisms and internal temperatures, go to sleep, and awake when food is again plentiful. The MOUNTAIN PYGMY-POSSUM, which lives at colder, high elevations in the Great Dividing Range in southern New South Wales and northeastern Victoria, actually hibernates for six months or so each winter.

The Striped Possum is a fast-moving tree dweller in the rainforests and adjacent woodlands of Queensland's northeast. It searches tree trunks, limbs, and fallen logs for grubs and other wood-boring insects, using its sharp incisors to tear into wood and its long tongue and elongated fourth fingers to probe into holes and crevices and grab the hapless bugs; they also occasionally nibble on leaves, fruit, and small vertebrates. Relatively little is known about their social behavior. Ringtail possums are highly specialized arboreal *folivores*, or leaf-eaters; they also take some flower blossoms and fruit. Like the pygmy-possums and Striped Possums, these animals are usually night-active, quiet, and secretive, so are relatively rarely seen. Predators of possums include large snakes, such as pythons, dingos, cats, foxes, and even quolls; owls and smaller snakes can take the smaller species, such as pygmy-possums.

Ecological Interactions
Ringtail possums practice *coprophagy*—they eat their own droppings—as an adaptation to deal with a diet composed primarily of leaves. Leaves are difficult to digest (green plant material is made of cells surrounded by tough cellulose cell walls) and get nutrients from. Ringtails have sharp molars that they use to grind their leafy meals, breaking many of the cell walls, releasing cell contents to be more easily digested. They have a large *caecum*, a compartment off the intestine, that holds microorganisms that digest cellulose, making more nutrients available to be absorbed by the possum digestive tract. Finally, ringtails eat their soft feces, which consists of partially digested plant matter and comes once a day from the caecum; in this way, they have a "second go-round," a second chance to digest and absorb nutrients from their food after their gut microorganisms have worked on it. A second, harder type of feces is then excreted, which is not eaten.

Breeding
Brushtail possums and cuscuses usually nest in tree cavities or hollow logs. Females mature sexually at 1 to 3 years of age, and breed once or twice a year. Only 1 young at a time is produced by brushtails; cuscuses usually have 1 or 2 young. Gestation is 15 to 18 days, and young remain in the mother's pouch for 4 to 8 months. After another 6 to 24 months in the birth area, young individuals disperse to find living and breeding sites of their own. Pygmy-possums become sexually mature at 4 to 6 months old and live only about 4 years. Females, nesting in tree hollows, often give birth to 4 to 6 young per litter, and breed usually twice a year. After gestations of 13 to 16 days, young remain in the mother's pouch for 25 to 30 days and are weaned when about 2 months old. Ringtail possums are usually solitary, but males court females for extended periods of a month or more before mating occurs. Litter size is generally 1 or 2 young. After 3 to 4 months in the pouch, young ride on the mothers back for several weeks when she forages. In the COMMON RINGTAIL POSSUM (Plate 65), males have been observed sometimes to help females with the kids, carrying the young on their backs.

Notes
A cuscus may have been the first marsupial in the Australian region to be recorded by Europeans. In a manuscript written in the 1540s, a Portuguese official wrote (probably describing the NORTHERN COMMON CUSCUS of the Moluccan Islands):

> Some animals resemble ferrets, only a little bigger. They are called *kusus*. They have a long tail with which they hang from trees in which they live continuously.... on their belly they have a pocket.... as soon as they give birth to a young one they grow it inside there at a nipple.... the people eat (these animals) like rabbits, seasoned with spices.

The round heads and forward-facing eyes of cuscuses caused some early European explorers of the region to believe these marsupial tree-dwellers were actually monkeys.

The Common Brushtail Possum was introduced from Australia to New Zealand during a 70- or 80-year period beginning in the 1840s, with the idea of creating a fur industry. The possums prospered and multiplied, indeed fostering a fur business, but the possums are now considered a significant ecological problem: the New Zealand tree leaves they feed on lack the natural plant defense chemicals that many Australian trees have, and so the possums have easy, abundant food; their populations grow dense, and the result is heavily damaged or killed trees—stripped of their leaves by marauding packs of possums.

Status

Some possums are killed as pests (brushtail possums damage plantation trees such as pines and sometimes harm crops such as bananas and pecans) and others for their fur. Pelts of the Common Brushtail Possum, sometimes in the millions per year, have been exported from Australia for more than a century. In New Guinea, possums are hunted for food (and can often be seen for sale at village markets). As a result of this persecution, as well as habitat loss and some increased predation by introduced predators such as cats and foxes, a few species of possums are threatened. New Guinea's BLACK SPOTTED CUSCUS is considered endangered by some (CITES Appendix II listed), and Australia's WESTERN RINGTAIL POSSUM and Mountain Pygmy-possum are vulnerable. LEADBEATER'S POSSUM, in family Petauridae along with the Striped Possum, is now endangered. It was thought extinct by the early 1900s but was rediscovered in 1961; it lives now only in parts of Victoria's high-elevation cool forests.

Profiles

Common Spotted Cuscus, *Spilocuscus maculatus,* Plate 64d
Eastern Pygmy-possum, *Cercartetus nanus,* Plate 65a
Striped Possum, *Dactylopsila trivirgata,* Plate 65b
Common Ringtail Possum, *Pseudocheirus peregrinus*, Plate 65c
Daintree River Ringtail Possum, *Pseudochirulus cinereus*, Plate 65d
Mountain Brushtail Possum, *Trichosurus caninus*, Plate 65e
Common Brushtail Possum, *Trichosurus vulpecula,* Plate 65f

7. Gliders

Gliders are tiny to medium-sized nocturnal marsupials that live in trees, consuming mainly insects and/or plant matter. They are members of three different families, but they are readily grouped together as gliders owing to a shared, highly unusual anatomical feature: a thin membrane of furry skin stretched between arm and leg that allows for gliding through the air for distances up to 100 m (330 ft), from high up in one tree to, usually, the base of another—an adaptation clearly suited to rapid locomotion and traversing distances in an tree-restricted world. In this trait, the gliders closely resemble the placental mammals known as *flying squirrels* that occur in Asia and North America (an obvious example of convergent evolution; p. 199). The three families that contain gliders are grouped together in order Diprotodontia, along with the Koala, wombats, possums, and kangaroos; all gliders are restricted to the Australia/New Guinea region. Gliders range in size from the tiny FEATHERTAIL GLIDER (Plate 64), at only about 8 cm (3 in) long and 12 to 14 g (0.5 oz), to the 1.5 kg (3.3 lb) GREATER GLIDER (Plate 64); both of these species range over large areas of eastern Australia.

Gliders are grey or brown squirrel-like animals, usually with largish ears. Family Petauridae contains seven species of gliders (and a few species of possums), four of which occur in Australia (such as YELLOW-BELLIED and SUGAR GLIDERS, both Plate 64). Gliders in this family are known as *wrist-winged gliders* because their gliding membranes extend from ankle to wrist, thus being longer and more extensive than the membranes of other gliders. Family Pseudocheiridae, which contains the sixteen species of ringtail possums (p. 218), also includes one glider, the Greater Glider; its gliding membrane extends from ankle to elbow. Finally, family Acrobatidae contains one Australian species, the Feathertail Glider. This glider's membrane extends from elbow to knee. Enhancing the Feathertail's soaring ability is a tail with long stiff hairs on each side that apparently acts somewhat like a bird's flight feathers, provding extra control surfaces for maneuverability while airborne. Male and female gliders are usually of similar size.

Natural History

Ecology and Behavior
Typically, gliders spend the daylight hours resting in tree hollows, then emerge at night to feed. They move to feeding areas by making a series of gliding flights, or *volplaning*. They leap into the air from high up on a tree, spreading their gliding membranes as they do so, and aim for the bottom reaches of a tree trunk 25 to 100 m (80 to 330 ft) away, depending on species (large species gliding farther). Changing the curvature of their membranes and moving the tail about as a rudder allows the gliders to alter direction while in flight. At the last moment, a glider pulls up and lands on all four feet against a tree trunk. Gliders are usually very active and agile in trees, with prehensile tails to assist them in hanging from branches or, at least, bracing themselves against branches. Glider diets vary: Yellow-bellied and Sugar Gliders eat mainly insects and spiders when they are available in large numbers (finding them often under loose bark), and some blossoms and nectar, but, especially in winter, switch to plant materials such as tree sap and gum from eucalypts and acacias. These gliders use their teeth to gouge and tear bark from tree trunks or branches, then eat the sugary sap that oozes from the wound. When the sap slows or stops, they open the wound again or make a new one—some trees have hundreds of glider incisions. The Greater Glider, the largest of Australia's gliders, feeds almost entirely on eucalypt leaves, generally on only two or three species in any given area. Like other mammals that feed largely on nutrient-poor, difficult-to-digest leaves, the greater glider has many metabolic and digestive adaptations—a low metabolic rate that requires little energy to maintain, a long digestive tract to absorb nutrients that are extractable from leaves, and intestinal microorganisms that assist in digesting plant material and making leaf nutrients more available for absorption. Feathertail Gliders eat insects and also use their brush-tipped tongue to gather plant nectar. Many of the smaller gliders live in small groups of up to twenty, huddling together in tree hollows or nests during cold weather; some, perhaps all, can enter a state of torpor during winter, when food is less available—reducing their metabolisms and internal temperatures, going to sleep, and awaking when food is again plentiful. Some gliders, such as the Yellow-bellied, are territorial, at least in some populations; most are not. Predators on small gliders include birds such as kookaburras, currawongs, and owls, mammals such as bats and cats, and large lizards (goannas). Larger gliders, particularly if they descend to the ground, are taken by foxes and dingos; large owls can take even large gliders from trees.

Ecological Interactions
Several glider species, such as Yellow-bellied, Sugar, and Feathertail Gliders, are specialized to feed on tree-flower nectar, as are pygmy-possums (p. 218) and many other Australian animals. The importance of nectar to the ecology of Australian animal and plant communities is an area of intense researcher interest (see Close-up, p. 192).

Breeding
Most glider breeding takes place from April through September. Gliders nest in tree hollows or other enclosed spots, old bird nests, or, in the case of Feathertail Gliders, in spherical leaf nests lined with fresh leaves and perhaps feathers. Yellow-bellied Gliders nest in pairs, Sugar Gliders in small groups of related individuals. Yellow-bellied and Sugar Gliders have 1 or 2 young that stay in-pouch for 2.5 to 3.5 months; after emerging, they are suckled in the den/nest for another 40 days or so, then begin to leave the den to forage with their mother. Greater Gliders nest in tree hollows. The male and female share the den until the single young leaves the pouch; young are then left alone in the den or carried on the mother's back while she forages. Young are independent at 9 months old and sexually mature at 2 years. Female Feathertails have 1 or 2 litters per year of 3 or 4 young each. The youngsters are pouch-ridden for about 2 months and are weaned about a month after first emerging from the pouch. Several glider species are known to live 5 to 7 years in the wild.

Notes

For the Yellow-bellied Glider, trees that have been tapped to yield sap for food also serve as social gathering spots—places where the gliders living in a given area meet each other at night and interact—for purposes both peaceful and aggressive. The dominant male of a group of gliders each night usually visits all currently tapped trees within its home range, interacting with other gliders that may be present at each tree. Non-resident gliders (ones that are not members of the group that lives in the area and that tapped the tree) caught visiting tapped trees are chased away.

Status

Gliders depend on trees for survival, so their status is often tied to forest management: where large tracts of forest remain undisturbed, most gliders do well; where forests are cleared or fragmented, glider populations can plunge. A few gliders, such as the Sugar Glider, a very common animal, seem to do well even in small forest fragments and in narrow forest strips farmers and ranchers leave between grazing land patches or croplands. But the Yellow-bellied Glider, which needs large stands of trees for its high-sap diet, has seen its numbers dwindle over some areas of its range. The MAHOGANY GLIDER, a wrist-winged glider, occurs only over a small area of northeastern coastal Queensland and is strongly threatened by continued forest clearing there. The Greater Glider needs tracts of undisturbed forest to prosper, so it is increasingly vulnerable. The Feathertail Glider, an abundant, widespread species, is not currently threatened; however, its need for mature forests, at a time when such forests are increasingly under development pressure, means that it is a species to watch.

Profiles

Sugar Glider, *Petaurus breviceps,* Plate 64a
Yellow-bellied Glider, *Petaurus australis,* Plate 64b
Greater Glider, *Peta uroides volans,* Plate 64c
Feathertail Glider, *Acrobates pygmaeus,* Plate 64e

8. Potoroos, Bettongs, and Rat-kangaroos

Potoroos, bettongs, and *rat-kangaroos* comprise a family of what are considered relatively primitive marsupials, at least when compared to their cousins, the kangaroos and wallabies. Primitive characteristics of the family, Potoroidae, include a somewhat prehensile tail and large upper canine teeth. *Potoroids* are restricted to Australia. Currently there exists a single species of rat-kangaroo, two potoroos, and five bettongs. These are generally small brownish marsupials that weigh between 530 g and 3 kg (1.2 to 6.6 lb), with either long, slender heads (rat-kangaroos, potoroos) or short, broad heads (bettongs).

Natural History

Ecology and Behavior
Potoroids are mainly terrestrial and often difficult to see (even the day-active ones) because they tend to stay in areas of thick shrubs or other dense cover, or quickly scoot into such habitat when alarmed. They are mainly nocturnal, but some, such as the MUSKY RAT-KANGAROO and LONG-NOSED POTOROO (both Plate 66), are also active during some daylight hours (especially the rat-kangaroo). These animals are usually solitary, but are sometimes seen in small feeding groups, such as around a tree that has dropped a lot of fruit to the forest floor. Potoroids may not need to drink (obtaining all or almost all of the water they need from their food) but they do eat. Rat-kangaroos, considered omnivores, eat mostly fruit but also seeds, fungi, and insects. Bettongs eat herbs, grasses, flowers, seeds, roots, and tubers, and some have been seen devouring dead, beached fish. Potoroos dig small holes in the ground, searching for roots, bulbs, tubers, underground fungi, and insects and insect larvae.

Breeding
An interesting facet of potoroid breeding behavior is that they collect plant material (grass, leaves) for their nests in their mouths and hands, then carry it to the nest site coiled in their tails. Nests are placed on or near the ground, for example in tree buttresses or vine tangles, or against a tree or large grass clump; some bettongs may nest in burrows. Rat-kangaroos and bettongs begin breeding when they are 1 year old, potoroos when they are 2. Gestation is usually 3 to 4 weeks. Female rat-kangaroos and bettongs raise 1 at a time, potoroos often 2 or 3. Young rat-kangaroos and bettongs remain in their mom's pouch for about 4 months, potoroos for 5 months.

Status

Some potoroids are fairly secure, such as the RUFOUS BETTONG (Plate 66), but the group as a whole is not currently very successful, especially when compared to their close relatives, the kangaroos and wallabies. Almost all the surviving potoroids occur now only over very small ranges, usually remnants of their historical ranges. People's habitat alterations, as well as the introduction of fierce food competitors (such as rabbits) and of predators such as foxes, certainly have contributed to the potoroids' decline. During the past 200 years, two of nine known species became extinct, and four are now considered endangered: LONG-FOOTED POTOROO (which occurs over small bits of eastern Victoria); BRUSH-TAILED BETTONG (southwestern Australia); NORTHERN BETTONG (northeast Queensland); and BURROWING BETTONG (islands off Western Australia).

Profiles

Musky Rat-kangaroo, *Hypsiprymnodon moschatus*, Plate 66a
Rufous Bettong, *Aepyprymnus rufescens*, Plate 66c
Long-nosed Potoroo, *Potorous tridactylus*, Plate 66d

9. Kangaroos, Wallabies, and Pademelons

Kangaroos are living symbols of Australia and certainly the first type of animal that comes to mind when people worldwide think of Australia. Kangaroos (and *wallabies* and *pademelons*, which are names given to smaller kangaroos) are the "ecological replacements" for the grazing hoofed mammals on continents that for the most part lack marsupials: the deer, antelope, and bison in North America, the deer, antelope, and buffalo in Eurasia, and the antelope, gazelles, and zebras in Africa. (Wallabies and pademelons are the ecological equivalents of small, placental grazers, such as rabbits.)

Aside from general ecology and behavior, which will be described briefly below, the main thing ecotravellers should know about kangaroos is that since European colonization of Australia, some kangaroos, particularly larger species, have done exceedingly well, to the point that they are hugely abundant and now even troublesome, and some, particularly smaller species in central and western arid and semi-arid regions, have fared very poorly. Large kangaroos have plenty to eat and few or no natural predators now, so their populations thrive; various states have kangaroo management plans under which licensed hunters shoot designated "problem" species (see Status, below). Many smaller species in arid, open areas have suffered stunning declines in their ranges and population sizes for various reasons (see Ecological Interactions, p. 226).

Kangaroos comprise the marsupial family Macropodidae, which means "big feet." This, of course, refers to the general body form of almost all kangaroos: they are (except for *tree-kangaroos*) stout mammals with large, powerful hindlimbs and long feet (with large fourth toes), small forelimbs, and long, thick tails that they use for balance as they hop around their terrestrial habitats. The 55 or so species of *macropods* (about 38 currently exist in Australia) can be split into five groups:

1. "typical" kangaroos, wallaroos, and wallabies (genus *Macropus*) and the SWAMP WALLABY (Plate 68; 13 Australian species total);
2. rock-wallabies (15 species) and pademelons (3 species);
3. nailtail wallabies (2 species) and hare-wallabies (2 species);
4. tree-kangaroos (2 species);
5. forest wallabies (restricted to the New Guinea region).

Macropods range in size from the very small MONJON (a small rock-wallaby also called a "rock weasel") that occurs over a small pocket of northwestern Australia, at about 1 kg (2.2 lb), to the broadly distributed RED KANGAROO, which weighs up to 85 kg (187 lb). Australia's five large, common kangaroos are the EASTERN GREY (Plate 67), WESTERN GREY, and Red Kangaroos, the COMMON WALLAROO (or "Euro," Plate 67), and the ANTILOPINE WALLAROO (Plate 67). Most kangaroos have deer-like faces and they generally come in various shades of marsupial brown and grey, some with a reddish or orangish tinge.

Some kangaroos (or 'roos, as they are known locally), wallabies, and pademelons are presently very common and conspicuous animals in eastern Australia, and if you travel outside of major cities, you are sure to see some of them. As for the various names of kangaroos, well, it's all very confusing, but in general: *wallabies* are kangaroos that as adults weigh less than 20 kg (44 lb); *wallaroos* (also called *hill kangaroos*) are kangaroos that are usually found in steep, hilly areas, stony rises, and escarpments (whereas kangaroos proper prefer flat or gently rolling terrain); and *rock-wallabies* prefer rocky areas (and are known for their often brighter, flashier markings, relative to the other groups).

Natural History

Ecology and Behavior

Kangaroos are Australia's dominant form of wildlife. Their success is probably related to their diet specialization on fibrous plant material—chiefly grasses—found on the ground. This food source is super-abundant but not available to many kinds of animals because its high cellulose content makes it very difficult to digest. However, kangaroos have several adaptations that permit them to thrive on grasses and other tough plant materials. For instance, to deal with the tough, abrasive nature of grasses and twigs, kangaroos (like elephants) have molar teeth that are serially replaced during life. Molars erupt in slow succession and move forward in the jaw with increasing age; the old molars in the center of the jaw, worn down by grinding food every day, eventually fall out. Also, like other mammals that graze on grasses (or eat leaves, like the Koala), kangaroos have intestinal helpers—bacteria that, through a fermentation process, aid digestion of tough plant tissue. Kangaroos are *grazers* (of grasses, herbs, and similar plants) or *browsers* (of leaves and twigs from trees and shrubs that they reach from the ground) or both. Some typical diets: the Eastern Grey Kangaroo eats mainly grasses and forbs (grass-like plants); the SWAMP WALLABY eats pieces of shrubs and bushes, tree seedlings, and pasture grasses; and the BRUSH-TAILED ROCK-WALLABY (Plate 69) eats grasses and forbs, browses a bit, and also picks up seeds, fruit, and flowers.

Kangaroos occupy most of Australia's habitats, from wet forests to desert; the majority of species occur in open forest, woodland, and/or grassland. They are well adapted for life in very arid areas, such as the desert grasslands that span most of the interior of the Australian continent; some species, for instance, can survive on as little as two or three liters (quarts) of water per week, obtaining most of their water from the foods they digest. The TAMMAR WALLABY of extreme southern Australia can drink sea water.

Kangaroos' most famous trait, aside from their pouch, is their method of locomotion. They jump, or "hop," (technically termed *saltation*, which means leaping, jumping, or dancing) and are the most well known hopping mammals. Characteristics associated with fast, efficient saltation are a stocky body with the center of gravity shifted to the rear, an elongated tail (which helps shift center of gravity rearwards), a short neck (the result of shortened neck vertebrae), elongated ankles, feet, and toes, and reduced forelimbs. The long, thin, not very flexible kangaroo tail serves as a third limb while hopping. Large species sometimes move slowly on all four limbs, with the tail acting as a fifth (a *pentapedal* gait). The tail also helps form a stable "tripod" with the hindlimbs, allowing kangaroos to stand vertically for fighting or looking for danger. Large kangaroos can hop along for sustained periods at about 40 kph (25 mph) and faster, up to about 70 kph (43 mph), for brief periods; they sometimes leap 3 m (10 ft) into the air and can cover a distance of 9 m (30 ft) per hop. When trying to escape danger, small kangaroos combine hopping quickly with erratic leaps and changing directions many times in a zig-zag pattern; this behavior might save some from dingos, but is a problem for the 'roos on paved roads, where their feet slip on the slick surface as cars approach. Saltation is an energy-efficient mode of locomotion; researchers estimate that to maintain a given speed, a kangaroo uses less energy than would a running dog or horse of the same weight.

The social behavior of kangaroos is not well known for many species. In general, it appears similar in many respects to the social behavior of the grazing, hoofed placental mammals, such as African antelopes—and varies just as widely, from solitary to highly gregarious. Usually smaller species are more solitary (thought to be the relatively primitive condition), and larger species more social—the larger wallabies, kangaroos, and most of the wallaroos all form permanent or semi-permanent groups. Body size, activity time, habitat types, and diet apparently influence group size. The small RED-NECKED PADEMELON (4 to 7 kg, 9 to 15 lb; Plate 69), a nocturnal shrub-eater, is often observed to be alone (although small feeding groups form where there is a lot of food), and it has overlapping home ranges that average about 14 ha (35 ac). Larger kangaroos, such as the Eastern Grey Kangaroo and Red Kangaroo, WHIPTAIL WALLABY (Plate 67), and Antilopine Wallaroo, which range from 10 to 60 kg (22 to 132 lb), are mainly grass-eaters, are more often active during at least some daylight hours, and are usually found in groups of 2 to 10 individuals. In some such species these smaller groups may also be subgroups that sometimes coalesce with other small groups into large aggregations. Home ranges for larger kangaroos, such as the Common Wallaroo and Red Kangaroo, are on the order of 50 sq km (20 sq mi). Rock-wallabies are usually found in colonies of between 10 and 100 individuals, the size of the colony depending on such factors as the extent of the rocky area that supports the colony and food availability in the area. No macropod species is thought to be territorial—their food resources are not economically defensible.

Tree-kangaroos, which in Australia occupy only a small coastal rainforest section of northeastern Queensland, are especially interesting because it is thought that they evolved from terrestrial kangaroos, which in turn are descended from primitive arboreal marsupials; in other words, millions of years ago the group left the trees, then later returned. Tree-kangaroos still resemble terrestrial kangaroos, and although certainly at home in their arboreal world, they still look a little out of place in trees and move about them a bit clumsily. Biologists believe that they are a fairly successful group only because of a relative absence of predators (mostly limited to large pythons in trees and dingos when they descend to the ground) and of comparably sized competitors in the trees. Tree-kangaroos are nocturnal and feed on leaves and fruit.

Ecological Interactions

Kangaroos' predominant ecological interaction with other animal species is the relationship they have with people. The ways in which people have altered the Australian continent during the past 200 years have profoundly affected kangaroo populations. Smaller kangaroos have suffered population declines in response to hunting; to heavy predation by introduced predators such as foxes and cats; to strong competition for food from introduced herbivores such as sheep, goats, pigs, and rabbits; to habitat alteration associated with cattle and sheep ranching; and, especially in eastern rainforest regions, to habitat destruction. Larger kangaroos certainly have experienced some declines from hunting, but because they suffer little natural predation and because their food is often super-abundant, their populations are usually stable or increasing. Some of these big kangaroos almost certainly have larger populations alive today than there were at the time of European colonization. The reasons are obvious: people have cleared huge areas of forest and woodland to create grazing pastures for their sheep and cattle, and these new grazing lands are essentially identical to the preferred grazing habitat for large kangaroos. In addition, to water their livestock in Australia's huge, arid center, people have tapped into underground water to create thousands of waterholes in areas that previously lacked open water, so kangaroos can now occupy regions that in the past were barred to them.

As for interactions with species other than people, you might ask whether the large, abundant, native, wild grazers (kangaroos) compete with or interact with the very abundant, non-native, domesticated grazers such as sheep. That is, if large kangaroos and sheep eat the same things and occur at the same grazing sites, do they interact, perhaps aggressively, as they "compete" for food? Across southern Australia in any given year there might be about 120 million sheep and 15 million large kangaroos. However, studies have shown there is little behavioral interaction between sheep and 'roos, for a number of reasons: diets are a bit different (sheep and 'roos often prefer different grass types), social behavior differs (sheep in huge flocks, 'roos in small groups), and activity times differ (sheep forage in mornings and during the day; 'roos in late afternoon and during the night).

Breeding

Reproduction in most kangaroos can occur at any time of year, but often is timed so that young leave the pouch at a season of good food availability. Kangaroos are sexually mature at about a year old in smaller species, to 2 or 3 years old in larger species. Breeding is promiscuous—males compete for access to females and, after mating, males play no additional roles in reproduction. Larger, more dominant males in a group aggressively try to monopolize receptive females, and male–male fights can occur. Courtship, during which a male stays near a female coming into heat, generally lasts 1 to 3 days. Gestation is 25 to 36 days (28 to 30 days in pademelons, 33 days in Red Kangaroos, 34 in some wallbies, 36 in Eastern Greys). Usually one young is born (occasionally twins), weighing less than 1 g (0.03 oz). It crawls into the mother's pouch and attaches to 1 of the 4 nipples. Pouch young are called "joeys." Young of various species spend 5 to 11 months in the pouch, but start leaving the pouch for brief periods before taking leave permanently. For instance, Red Kangaroo joeys start leaving the pouch at about 6 months old, but hop back in to sleep, travel, or to avoid danger. Even after permanently leaving the pouch, young still poke their head into mom's pouch for another 2 to 6 months to suckle. After leaving the pouch, young remain near their mothers until they are sexually mature.

Notes

It's not something you think much about, but some kangaroos have been taken from Australia and introduced to other regions of the world, where self-perpetuating populations now exist. Several islands off New Zealand's coasts now have thriving kangaroo populations. RED-NECKED WALLABIES (Plate 68) occur on New Zealand's main south island and also in two small areas of England. The Brush-tailed Rock-wallaby (Plate 69) maintains a foreign outpost on Oahu in the Hawaiian Islands. The present population, probably numbering fewer than 200 individuals, is descended from a single pair, which escaped captivity in 1916. They found the vegetation around the cliffs and rocky slopes of the Kalihi Valley, near Honolulu, to their liking, and have been there ever since, living in rock crevices and caves. As long as this wallaby population remains small and causes little ecological damage, Hawaiian wildlife managers seem content to leave the marsupials alone—especially because the species is considered threatened in Australia (and endangered in Victoria).

One Aboriginal legend tells how kangaroos got their long tail. In the distant past, when many animals still looked like people, Kangaroo and Wombat, former friends, had a fight over sleeping arrangements. The cause of the fight is rather murky, but it is thought that Wombat had a house but was reluctant to let Kangaroo, who was house-less, shelter there from the rain. Kangaroo hit Wombat on the head with a rock (which flattened Wombat's head, explaining why wombats look today as they do); Wombat retaliated by throwing a long spear at Kangaroo, which lodged in his lower back. Kangaroo could not remove the spear, and it became his tail.

Not suprisingly, the behavior of most species of tree-kangaroos, which are nocturnal and arboreal and live in some remote regions, is not well known (at least to Western science). I'll never forget an American graduate student that I met in Papua New Guinea. She was beginning her doctoral field research there, alone, and was adamant that she wanted to spend a few years studying the behavior of tree-kangaroos. To reach her high-elevation forest study site she had to fly in a tiny airplane to a remote airstrip in the mountains and then hike for three days.

Status

Most kangaroos are currently secure, but at least four wallaby species have become extinct since European colonization of Australia, and four or five others are currently considered endangered—some restricted now to very small portions of their former ranges or even to tiny offshore islands. The IUCN Red List includes about six threatened or endangered species, including RUFOUS (Plate 66) and BANDED HARE-WALLABIES, BRIDLED NAILTAIL WALLABY, and BRUSH-TAILED, BLACK-FOOTED, and PROSERPINE ROCK-WALLABIES. About six others are considered vulnerable. Large macropods thrive in Australia's enormous regions of livestock ranches and are considered by many to be agricultural pests. In the past, in efforts to reduce populations of these large 'roos, bounties were paid for their scalps; as long as there have been people on the Australian continent, these 'roos have been hunted for meat and their hides. Today, larger kangaroos are intensively managed by state wildlife departments, their numbers culled (via shooting) by licensed hunters when populations become too large; the meat and skins are sold commercially. In Queensland, for instance, four species are mainly subject to these measures: Eastern Grey and Red Kangaroos, Common Wallaroos, and Whiptail Wallabies.

Profiles

Lumholtz's Tree-kangaroo, *Dendrolagus lumholtzi*, Plate 66b
Spectacled Hare-wallaby, *Lagorchestes conspicillatus*, Plate 66e
Antilopine Wallaroo, *Macropus antilopinus*, Plate 67a
Black-striped Wallaby, *Macropus dorsalis*, Plate 67b
Eastern Grey Kangaroo, *Macropus giganteus*, Plate 67c
Whiptail Wallaby, *Macropus parryi*, Plate 67d
Common Wallaroo (Euro), *Macropus robustus*, Plate 67e
Red-necked Wallaby, *Macropus rufogriseus*, Plate 68a
Northern Nailtail Wallaby, *Onychogalea unguifera*, Plate 68b

Swamp Wallaby, *Wallabia bicolor,* Plate 68c
Allied Rock-wallaby, *Petrogale assimilis,* Plate 68d
Herbert's Rock-wallaby, *Petrogale herberti,* Plate 68e
Unadorned Rock-wallaby, *Petrogale inornata,* Plate 69a
Brush-tailed Rock-wallaby, *Petrogale penicillata,* Plate 69b
Tasmanian Pademelon, *Thylogale billardierii,* Plate 69c
Red-legged Pademelon, *Thylogale stigmatica,* Plate 69d
Red-necked Pademelon, *Thylogale thetis,* Plate 69e

Placental Mammals

10. Bats, the Flying Mammals

Bats are flying mammals that occupy the night. Like birds, they engage in sustained, powered flight—the only mammals to do so. Many bats navigate the night atmosphere chiefly by "sonar," or *echolocation:* broadcasting ultrasonic sounds—extremely high-pitched chirps and clicks—and then gaining information about their environment by "reading" the echos. Because of these characteristics, bats are quite alien to people's primate sensibilities; precisely because their lives are so very different from our own, they are increasingly of interest to us. In the past, of course, bats' exotic nocturnal behavior engendered in most societies not ecological curiosity, but fear and superstition.

Bats have true wings, consisting of thin, strong, highly elastic membranes that extend from the sides of the body and legs to cover and be supported by the elongated fingers of the arms. (The name of the order of bats, Chiroptera, refers to the wings: *chiro,* meaning hand, and *ptera,* wing.) Other distinctive anatomical features include bodies covered with silky, longish hair; toes with sharp, curved claws that allow the bats to hang upside down and are used by some to catch food; scent glands that produce strong, musky odors; and, in many, very odd-shaped folds of skin on their noses (*nose-leaves*) and prominent ears that aid in echolocation. Like birds, bats' bodies have been modified through evolution to conform to the needs of energy-demanding flight: they have relatively large hearts, low body weights, and fast metabolisms.

Bats are widely distributed, inhabiting most of the world's tropical and temperate regions, excepting some oceanic islands. With a total of about a thousand species, bats are second in diversity among mammals only to rodents. There are two main types of bats: Megachiropterans ("megabats"; about 175 species total), most of which are large and feed on fruit, plant juices, nectar and/or pollen; and Microchiropterans ("microbats"), which tend to be small and feed mainly on insects (but some feed on small vertebrates, even other bats, some on fish, and a few, the vampire bats, on blood). About 65 bat species occur in Australia, 11 of which are megabats. The most famous megabats are the *flying-foxes,* which occur in Africa, Asia, and the Australian region. Australia's 6 flying-foxes range in size from the LITTLE RED FLYING-FOX (Plate 70), at 300 to 600 g (0.7 to 1.3 lb), to the GREY-HEADED FLYING-FOX (Plate 70), which weighs up to 1 kg (2.2 lb) and has a wingspan up to 1.5 m (4.9 ft). Flying-foxes have fox-like faces with large eyes and generally lack tails; males tend to be larger than females. Australia's 55 or so microbats range in size from the tiny LESSER LONG-EARED BAT (Plate 71), at only 10 g (0.3 oz), to the GHOST BAT (Plate 70), at 150 g (5 oz).

Natural History

Ecology and Behavior

Ecologically, bats can be thought of as nighttime equivalents of birds. Most microbats, and all but one of Australia's, specialize on insects. They use their sonar not just to navigate but to detect insects, which they catch on the wing, pick off leaves, or scoop off the ground. Bats use several methods to catch flying insects. Small insects may be captured directly in the mouth; some bats use their wings as nets and spoons to trap insects and pull them to their mouth; and others scoop bugs into the fold of skin membrane that connects their tail and legs, then somersault in mid-air to move the catch to their mouth. Small bugs are eaten immediately on the wing, while larger ones, such as large beetles, are taken to a perch and dismembered. The GHOST BAT is different. It's a large bat and hunts visually, using its large eyes to detect animal prey, usually on the ground. Large insects as well as frogs, lizards, birds, small mammals such as rodents, and small bats are taken.

Bats spend the daylight hours in *day roosts*, usually tree cavities, shady sides of trees, caves, rock crevices, or in buildings or under bridges. For most species, the normal resting position in a roost is hanging by their feet, head downwards, which makes taking flight as easy as letting go and spreading their wings. Many bats leave roosts around dusk, then move to foraging sites at various distances from the roost. Night activity patterns vary, perhaps serving to reduce food competition among species. Some tend to fly and forage intensely in the early evening, become less active in the middle of the night, then resume intense foraging near dawn; others are relatively inactive early in the evening, but more active later on. Many bats are highly social animals, roosting and often foraging in groups.

Flying-foxes are usually highly gregarious, associating in colonies from a few to (in some regions of the world) a million or more. One Australian flying-fox, the Grey-headed, which occurs over coastal regions of central and southern Queensland, New South Wales, and Victoria, has been studied intensively. These flying-foxes roost during the day in large "camps," or colonies, in trees amid dense vegetation in gullies or valleys, and usually near water. Often two or three species of flying-foxes inhabit the same camp. As night falls, flying-foxes leave camp and fly to feeding areas, generally less than 15 km (9 mi) away, but some travel up to 50 km (30 mi). They eat mostly tree blossoms (such as eucalypt and fig blossoms) but also fruit. At dusk in coastal northern Australia, you can often see flying-foxes leaving their colonies and heading out for a night's foraging; if you camp in a tent near water, you will often hear flying-foxes overhead at night, their large wings making "wup-wup-wup" sounds like a helicopter.

Relatively little is known about which predators prey on Australian bats. However, the list certainly includes snakes, owls, hawks, and mammals such as cats and even other bats.

Ecological Interactions

Bats eat a variety of insects and some of the prey species have responded evolutionarily to this predation. For instance, several groups of moth species can sense the ultrasonic chirps of some echolocating insectivorous bats; when they do, they react immediately by flying erratically or diving down into vegetation, decreasing the success of the foraging bats. Some moths even make their own clicking sounds, which apparently confuse the bats, causing them to break off approaches. The interaction of bats and their prey animals is an active field of animal behavior research because the predators and the prey have both developed varieties of tactics to try to outmaneuver or outwit the other.

Bats are beneficial to forests. Many tropical trees and other plants have bats, instead of bees or birds, as their main pollinators. These species generally have flowers that open at night and are white, making them easy for bats to find. They also give off a pungent aroma that bats can home in on. Nectar-feeding bats use long tongues to poke into flowers to feed on nectar—a sugary solution—and pollen. As a bat brushes against a flower, pollen adheres to its body and is then carried to other plants of the same species, where it falls and leads to cross-pollination. Fruit-eating bats such as flying-foxes, owing to their high numbers, are important seed dispersers, helping to regenerate forests by transporting and dropping fruit seeds onto the forest floor.

Breeding
Bat mating systems are diverse, various species employing monogamy (one male and one female breed together), polygyny (one male and several females), and promiscuity (males and females both mate with more than one individual); the breeding behavior of many species has yet to be studied in detail. For the Grey-headed Flying-fox (and at least some of the other flying-foxes), mating and giving birth occur at camps (day roosts). Mating apparently can occur at any time of year, but most births take place in October and November. Gestation is about 6 months. A single young is born and is then carried by the mother (clinging to her chest) for a month or so when she forages. After that, she leaves the youngster at the camp and suckles it when she returns from her nightly feeding trips. After they are weaned (when each is about 5 months old), a colony's young congregate together in the camp in a creche, or "nursery tree." Ghost Bats, which roost in caves and rock crevices, mate usually in July or August and give birth to a single young about 3 months later. Young are left in the day roost while mothers forage, and prey animals are taken back to the roost to feed them. When they can fly well, juvenile Ghost Bats accompany their mothers and learn to hunt.

Notes
Flying-foxes are not shy about where they roost—they often occupy trees in town squares (such as in some towns in Papua New Guinea), and they are even familiar sights hanging about during the day near the tops of large, isolated trees in the Royal Botanic Gardens of both Sydney and Melbourne.

Bats are appreciated by knowledgeable people for their insect-eating ways. Individual bats can snap up thousands of small, pesky bugs per night. Owing to this facility, bats in the past were brought from mainland areas and released on some oceanic islands that lacked bats but that had hordes of annoying insects, such as mosquitos; only some of these introductions were "successful," with the released bats establishing self-propagating populations.

Bats have frightened people for a long time. The result, of course, is that there is a large body of folklore that portrays bats as evil, associated with or incarnations of death, devils, witches, or vampires. Undeniably, it was bats' alien lives—their activity in the darkness, flying ability, and strange form—and people's ignorance of them, that were the sources of these myriad superstitions. Many cultures worldwide have evil bat legends, from Australia to Japan and the Philippines, Europe, the Middle East, and Central and South America.

Status

Determining the status of bat populations is difficult because of their nocturnal behavior and habit of roosting in places that are hard to census. Because many bats worldwide roost in hollow trees, deforestation is obviously a primary threat. Further, many bat populations in temperate regions are known to be declining and under continued threat by a number of agricultural, forestry, and architectural practices. Traditional roost sites have been lost on large scales by mining and quarrying, by the destruction of old buildings, and by changing architectural styles that eliminate many building overhangs and church belfries, for instance. Many forestry practices advocate the removal of the hollow, dead trees that frequently provide bats with roosting space. Additionally, farm pesticides are ingested by insects, which are then eaten by bats, leading to death or reduced reproductive success.

Most Australian bats appear to be secure and, indeed, some of them are very abundant. One species, the DUSKY, or PERCY ISLAND, FLYING-FOX, has become extinct in recent times—only one skin of this animal survives, collected during the 1800s on Percy Island off Queensland's east coast. The Ghost Bat is known to have once ranged over half of Australia, but is now restricted to a smaller (though still large) area that spans much of northern Australia. Reasons for the contraction of its range and for its present patchy distribution are not known, so many consider it a vulnerable species. Its habit of roosting in caves, mines, and quarries suggests that people have disturbed these sites, and that their developments and industries have played a role in this bat's decline. Flying-foxes sometimes feed on fruit crops and because of this, they are sometimes killed in large numbers by farmers. Some flying-fox species, particularly those on some Pacific Ocean islands, are threatened or endangered (several are CITES Appendix I listed) because of destruction of their forest habitat, local hunting for food, and hunting for commercial trade. On Guam, for instance, flying-foxes and other fruit bats are considered delicacies, so huge numbers of these bats during the 1970s and 1980s were killed on other islands, frozen, and shipped to Guam.

Profiles

Black Flying-fox, *Pteropus alecto*, Plate 70a
Grey-headed Flying-fox, *Pteropus poliocephalus*, Plate 70b
Little Red Flying-fox, *Pteropus scapulatus*, Plate 70c
Ghost bat, *Macroderma gigas*, Plate 70d
Yellow-bellied Sheathtail Bat, *Saccolaimus flaviventris*, Plate 70e
Eastern Horseshoe Bat, *Rhinolophus megaphyllus*, Plate 71a
Common Bentwing Bat, *Miniopterus schreibersii*, Plate 71b
Lesser Long-eared Bat, *Nyctophilus geoffroyi*, Plate 71c
Gould's Wattled Bat, *Chalinolobus gouldii*, Plate 71d
Large-footed Myotis, *Myotis adversus*, Plate 71e

11. Rodents and Rabbits

Ecotravellers discover among *rodents* an ecological paradox: although by far the most diverse and successful of the mammals, rodents are, often with a few obvious exceptions in any region, relatively inconspicuous and rarely encountered. The number of living rodent species globally is about 2,000, more than 40% of the approximately 4,600 known mammalian species. Probably in every region of the world save Antarctica (where they do not occur), rodents—including the mice, rats, squirrels, chipmunks, marmots, gophers, beavers, and porcupines—are the most abundant land mammals. More individual rodents are estimated to be alive at any one time than individuals of all other types of mammals combined. Rodents' near-invisibility to people derives from the facts that most rodents are very small, most are secretive or nocturnal, and many live out their lives in subterranean burrows. That most rodents are rarely encountered, of course, many people do not consider much of a hardship.

Rodent ecological success is likely related to their efficient, specialized teeth and associated jaw muscles and to their broad, nearly omnivorous diets. Rodents are characterized by having four large incisor teeth, one pair front-and-center in the upper jaw, one pair in the lower (other teeth, separated from the incisors, are located farther back in the mouth). With these strong, sharp, chisel-like front teeth, rodents gnaw (*rodent* is from the Latin *rodere*, to gnaw), cut, and slice vegetation, fruit, and nuts; kill and eat small animals; dig burrows; and even, in the case of beavers, imitate lumberjacks.

Australia has about 65 species of native rodents; all are restricted in their distributions to the Australia/New Guinea region. All are members of the largest family of rodents, Muridae (the rats, mice, voles, lemmings, gerbils, and hamsters; about 1,100 species worldwide). The 65 species are divided by experts into "old endemics," which arose with ancestors that arrived in Australia many millions of years ago from Indonesia via New Guinea; and "new endemics"—Australia's true rats (genus *Rattus*), whose ancestors arrived more recently, just a few million years ago, from New Guinea. In addition, three introduced *murid* rodents, spread by people, have colonized large parts of Australia (as they have much of the world): the BLACK RAT (also called Roof Rat, House Rat) and BROWN RAT (Norway Rat, Lab Rat), confined mainly to wetter, coastal regions, and the HOUSE MOUSE, found essentially everywhere.

Most of the world's rodents are small mouse-like or rat-like mammals that weigh less than 1 kg (2.2 lb); they range, however, from tiny pygmy mice that weigh only a few grams to South America's pig-like CAPYBARA, behemoths at up to 50 kg (110 lb). Murid rodents are usually clad in various shades of grey or brown, but some are partly white or all black. Most of Australia's rodents are mouse- or rat-sized. Because rodents are not often observed, and because most traveller interest in Australian mammals is for marsupials, only a few common representative rodents are detailed here. The GIANT WHITE-TAILED RAT (Plate 72), one of Australia's largest rodents, a tree dweller, occurs over parts of tropical northern Queensland; the FAWN-FOOTED MELOMYS (Plate 72), of coastal Queensland and northeast New South Wales, is a representative of a large group of tropical tree rats of the Australian/New Guinea region; the WATER RAT (Plate 72) of northern and eastern Australia, largely carnivorous, is also unusual in that it has water-repellent fur and spends much of its time in fresh water; and the BUSH RAT (Plate 72) represents about seven species of common, native Australian ground rats.

Rabbits, even though they look a bit like rodents, are in a separate order, the Lagamorpha. The group is differentiated from rodents by having four instead of two front incisor teeth on the upper jaw, large hind legs, and long ears. About 70 species of rabbits (and *hares*; see Breeding, below) are distributed over most of the world's large land masses. Only two species occur in Australia. The RABBIT and BROWN HARE (both Plate 73) were introduced after European colonization and the Rabbit especially has caused enormous environmental damage.

Natural History

Ecology and Behavior

Giant White-tailed Rats, restricted to forests, swamps, and mangrove areas, are nocturnal, spending daylight hours in a burrow or treehole. They are omnivorous, at night climbing trees and searching the ground for fruits, nuts, seeds, fungi, and bird eggs, and occasionally taking small vertebrates such as frogs and lizards. The Fawn-footed Melomys, also nocturnal and a tree climber, occupies forests with a good ground cover of leaf litter and fallen logs. It makes leaf nests in trees, emerging at night to forage for fruits, leaves, and other plant materials. Water Rats, unlike most other Australian rodents, are frequently active by day and especially around sunset. They live near water (fresh, brackish, and ocean) and enjoy a partly aquatic life—taking most of their food while in the water. They have waterproof fur and swim in search of aquatic insects, fish, crustaceans, frogs, and even taking small water birds. Bush rats, although quite abundant in some forest, woodland, and scrub areas, are not often seen because they are nocturnal, often in burrows, and even when above ground they tend to stick to thick cover. They have a varied diet, taking fruit, seeds, and fungi, but they are especially fond of insects. Predators of Australia's rodents are hawks and owls, quolls, dingos, foxes, and feral cats.

The Brown (or European) Hare, a large lagamorph, was introduced to Australia by British settlers who wanted to hunt it as they did back home. It is confined mainly to eastern Australia (does not occur in Western Australia, Northern Territory, or over most parts of South Australia), and is generally restricted to grazing lands and croplands. Nocturnal, the hare emerges from its hiding places (it does not burrow) at dusk and forages on grasses and forbs; it also gnaws tree bark. The smaller Rabbit (or EUROPEAN RABBIT) was introduced to southeastern Australia during the 1850s and has now colonized much of the continent (being absent only from the tropical north). It mostly occupies grasslands and agricultural districts in arid regions, remaining near watercourses and irrigated areas. Rabbits live in burrows, emerging to graze on grass; they also eat bark, leaves, and roots. Rabbit populations vary widely in size, declining dramatically when disease (see below), parasites, and predation are common, then increasing rapidly when conditions are more favorable. Predators on these lagamorphs include foxes, feral cats, dingos, eagles, and some snakes and monitor lizards.

Ecological Interactions

Introduction of Black and Brown Rats to Australia, as you might expect, certainly caused problems, but it was the introduction of the Rabbit (and to a much lesser extent, the Brown Hare) that caused major ecological damage. The prolific Rabbit spread quickly from Victoria, where just 25 individuals were released in the late 1850s. By 1900, hundreds of millions of rabbits occupied about 3 million sq km (1.58 million sq mi). Thousands of km of anti-rabbit fencing was installed to try to halt their advance to the north and west, but the burrowing rabbits could not be stopped. They now occur over all of mainland Australia south of the Tropic of Capricorn, and are still slowly spreading northwards. Rabbits harm soil by closely cropping grasses that protect soil, and undermine topsoil with their burrows (the social rabbits build burrows near one another and connect them, forming extensive *warrens*); soil erosion is a result. Rabbits also compete for food (they prefer the best green grasses) with grazing livestock, and damage trees and shrubs when they eat bark. After years of work, Australian researchers finally discovered a pox virus in South American rabbits that they thought could control the Australian rabbits without harming other animals. The mosquito-transmitted *myxomatosis* virus was released in Australia in 1950 and spread rapidly. Initially it killed about 99% of rabbits infected, but, through natural selection, the rabbit immune system has adapted to the disease, and the virus is no longer so effective. As of the mid-1990s, there were still an estimated 300 million rabbits in Australia. During the 1990s, reseachers began experimenting with new, genetically engineered rabbit viruses. One, which causes Rabbit Calicivirus Disease, in which rabbits die of hemorrhaging within two days of infection, has now killed millions of rabbits in southeast Australia.

One hugely beneficial aspect of rodents not appreciated by many people: burrowing is an aspect of rodent behavior that has significant ecological implications because of the sheer number of individuals that participate. When so many animals move soil around (rats and mice, especially), over several years the entire topsoil of an area is turned, keeping soil loose and aerated and therefore more suitable for plant growth.

Breeding

Rats, mice, and rabbits, of course, are prolific breeders. As with most small mammals that are subject to heavy predation, they reach breeding age quickly and have short pregnancies and, usually, large litters. The rodents treated here are sexually mature at 2 (Hopping-mouse) to 4 (Bush Rat) to 8 (Water Rat) months of age. Gestation varies among species from 32 to 38 days. Litter size is generally 2 to 5, and females of some species have over 5 litters per year. Young are weaned at 3 to 8 weeks, depending on the species, and are independent at 4 to 12 weeks. The very young of many Australian rodents can escape predators by holding on with their mouths to their mother's nipples and clinging to her as she flees danger.

The Brown Hare has litters of 1 to 5 (usually 2 or 3), and some females produce litters every 6 to 8 weeks. As in other hares, young are *precocial*—born in a fairly developed state, eyes open, fully furred, and nearly ready to move; they are weaned in 4 weeks. The young of rabbits, such as Australia's Rabbit, are *altricial*—born naked, eyes closed, fairly helpless. Their eyes open at about 10 days, and they first emerge from their burrows at about 3 weeks. Rabbit litters of 4 to 12 young are born after pregnancies of 30 days. Females can breed when 3 to 4 months old, and can have 7 litters per year.

Notes

Through the animals' constant gnawing, rodents' chisel-like incisors wear down rapidly. Fortunately for the rodents, their incisors, owing to some ingenious anatomy and physiology, continue to grow throughout their lives, unlike those of most other mammals.

Rats are a popular food in many parts of the world. For instance, some restaurants in southern China specialize in rat. "Mountain" rats, brought in to markets from the countryside and considered clean, are much preferred over "dirty" city rats. Common dishes include mountain rat soup, spicy and salty mountain rat, and simmered mountain rat with black beans.

Status

As with Australia's marsupials, many of its native rodents have not done well since European colonization. Alteration of natural habitats associated with sheep and cattle grazing is a likely contributor to their decline. The ranges of many species, especially those of the arid interior of the country, have contracted dramatically. At least 7 species have become extinct during the past 250 years, including 2 rats, 1 mouse, and 4 hopping-mice. About a dozen species are currently considered vulnerable or already threatened.

Profiles

Giant White-tailed Rat, *Uromys caudimaculatus*, Plate 72a
Water Rat, *Hydromys chrysogaster*, Plate 72b
Fawn-footed Melomys, *Melomys cervinipes*, Plate 72c
Bush Rat, *Rattus fuscipes*, Plate 72d
Rabbit, *Oryctolagus cuniculus*, Plate 73c
Brown Hare, *Lepus capensis*, Plate 73d

12. Dingo and Fox

Carnivores (order Carnivora) are the ferocious mammals—the cat that sleeps on your pillow, the dog that takes table scraps from your hand—that are specialized to kill and eat other vertebrate animals. They are primarily ground dwellers and have teeth customized to grasp, rip, and tear flesh—witness their large, cone-shaped canines. Most are meat-eaters, but many are at least somewhat omnivorous, taking fruits and other plant materials. Only two carnivore families have representatives in Australia: *felids* (cats) and *canids* (dogs). Other carnivores, such as bears and weasels, are absent. The only cats in Australia are feral domestic cats; they are a problem because they kill native wildlife (birds, reptiles, and small mammals), but they will not be detailed here. Australia's two dogs, however, are of more interest. The DINGO (Plate 73) is a medium-sized dog, generally brownish/yellowish ("ginger") but sometimes black or white. It evolved probably from an Asian wolf, was brought to Australia by people 3,500 to 4,000 years ago (perhaps via Indonesia or New Guinea), and is now considered to be the same species as the domestic dog and the widely distributed Grey Wolf. It ranges throughout mainland Australia but is scarce in some areas. The RED FOX (also called simply Fox; Plate 73), was introduced from Europe into southern Victoria for sport reasons during the mid-nineteenth century. Within fifty years (by 1920) it ranged over most of the southern (temperate) half of Australia, and still does today. Its rapid spread was assisted by the simultaneous spread of good prey, the hare and rabbit (p. 233), and by human persecution of Dingos (which can both eat and compete with foxes). The Fox is reddish brown and much smaller than the Dingo, and it causes problems as an unwanted predator.

Natural History

Ecology and Behavior

Dingos are active day or night, hunting alone or in small packs. They eat whatever animals they can find and kill, including insects, lizards, birds such as geese, and mammals of all kinds: echidnas, wombats, wallabies, kangaroos (when hunting in packs), possums, baby sheep and cattle, and rodents; they will also eat carrion. The social unit is the pack, and even when individuals or smaller groups are temporarily separated, they keep in contact with howls (they do not bark like dogs). Packs move over average home ranges of about 30 to 40 sq km (12 to 15 sq mi). Red Foxes, like the Dingo, occupy just about all habitat types within their range. They are nocturnal, spending the daylight hours resting in an underground den, a thicket, or a hollow log. At night, solitarily (or in family groups during the breeding season), they hunt animals of all kinds: insects, birds, rabbits, rodents, wallabies and other small marsupials, and young sheep; they also eat carrion and scavenge livestock afterbirths and human garbage. Hunting territories roamed by a fox family group might range from 2 to 5 sq km (0.8 to 2 sq mi). Predatory foxes are believed to have strongly contributed to the serious declines of many of Australia's native marsupials, including some species of wallabies, rock-wallabies and the Numbat (p. 198).

Ecological Interactions
Dingos, via predation and competition, probably contributed to the elimination of the Tasmanian Devil and the Thylacine (also called Tasmanian Tiger; p. xxx) on the Australian mainland. Dingos never made it to Tasmania, so the Thylacine survived there through the 1930s, and the Tasmanian Devil survives there today. When ranchers in central and western Australia erected fences around their huge grazing regions to keep Dingos from cattle and sheep, they inadvertently affected kangaroo and wallaby populations; the large marsupials, freed from Dingo predation, increased dramatically, damaging grazing areas.

Breeding
Dingos tend to mate from April to June, giving birth in underground dens after pregnancies of about 63 days. Litters range from 1 to 10 young, and average 5. Young are independent of their mother at 3 to 4 months, and live up to about 10 years in the wild. Red Foxes give birth in dens mostly in July through November, after pregnancies of about 52 days; litter size ranges from 1 to 8, with 4 or 5 being the average. Young are weaned at 6 to 7 weeks old, and disperse from their birth area at 6 to 9 months.

Notes
One Aboriginal legend tells the origin of the Dingo: Once a great hunter named Pungalung, who lived near Ayers Rock, went on a long journey. Far from home he discovered a culture of mice-women. These creatures, half mouse, half woman, had no men in their societies. When Pungalung dared to tell and show the mice-women what men are and what they do, they became afraid and angry, grew bigger, and turned into Dingos, chasing Pungalung away. (A. W. Reed 1998)

Status
Dingos have survived well even though they were, and still are in some places, persecuted by people. Occasional Dingo attacks on people lead some to conclude that they are a public menace. Dingos, domestic dogs, and the Grey Wolf are actually "races" of the same species, and they can all interbreed and produce viable, fertile offspring. What is happening is that domestic dogs and Dingos are breeding together, producing hybrids (which often have a dark stripe down the mid-back), and it is thought that currently a third to a half of Dingos are actually hybrids; some researchers project that within 50 to 100 years, no pure-bred Dingos will exist—and the Dingo, as a distinct race, or subspecies, of dog, will be extinct. Queensland's Fraser Island, isolated from the mainland and domestic dogs, is known for its fairly pure-bred Dingo strain—there are about 200 Dingos on the island. Red Foxes are abundant in Australia, even though they are persecuted as "vermin" and hunted for their furry skins.

Profiles
Dingo, *Canis lupus dingo,* Plate 73a
Red Fox, *Vulpes vulpes,* Plate 73b

13. Marine Mammals

Four kinds of large marine mammals, the DUGONG (Plate 74), *seals, dolphins,* and *whales,* occur in eastern Australia's coastal waters and are seen fairly frequently. The Dugong, or Sea Cow, is a heavy-bodied, slow-moving marine mammal that inhabits shallow tropical and sub-tropical waters of the Indian and western Pacific Oceans, especially in calm, sheltered areas. The Dugong is one of four species that comprise the order Sirenia (the other three species, similar to the Dugong, are known as *manatees,* and are found in Africa, Central and South America, and the Caribbean). The group is actually related more closely to elephants than to the whales and dolphins or to the seals and walruses (which they vaguely resemble). Dugongs are large, grey, cylindrical animals, tapered at the front and back. The hands are modified into flippers and the tail is a single, divided, dolphin-like fluke, or paddle. They have thick, rough, mostly hairless skin, with some bristles near the mouth. Some grow to 3.3 m (10.8 ft) long and weigh up to 420 kg (925 lb).

Seals are familiar marine mammals with front and back legs modified as flippers and noses adapted to balance large beach balls. The seal order, Pinnipedia, is divided into three families, the *true* or *earless seals* (family Phocidae), the *walruses* (family Odobenidae), and the *eared seals* (family Otariidae). *Pinnipeds* probably evolved from terrestrial mammals such as the weasels and bears (order Carnivora), and still leave the water for resting and breeding. Most seal species occur in the Arctic and Antarctic regions, but several are common along Australia's southeastern coast. However, only a few are seen regularly by ecotravellers, and two of these, both eared seals, are profiled here. Eared seals, such as *fur seals* and *sea lions,* have small external ears and powerful front flippers that help with propulsion during swimming (whereas earless seals have ears that are simply holes on each side of the head, and front legs that are held to their sides as their hind flippers propel them through the water). Fur seals are distinguished, fittingly, by their layer of dense, short fur (*underfur*) under the sleek, longer, outer covering layer of *guard hair,* and by their relatively pointed snout (relative to most sea lions). Four of the world's 9 fur seal species occur in Australian waters (2 are profiled here), and they range from 1 to 2.5 m (3.3 to 8.2 ft) in length and from 40 to 350 kg (88 to 770 lb) in weight. Males are usually bigger than females, sometimes up to four or five times as heavy.

The approximately 75 species of *dolphins, porpoises,* and *whales* belong to order Cetacea, and almost all of them are found only in the world's oceans (there are a few species of freshwater dolphins). *Cetaceans* never leave the water and generally come to the surface only to breathe. Their hind legs have been lost through evolution (they evolved from terrestrial mammals with legs) and their front legs modified into paddle-like flippers. Their tails have become broad and flattened into paddles called *flukes.* A single or double nostril, called a *blowhole,* is on top of the head. Up to a third of an individual's weight consists of a thick layer of fat (*blubber*) lying under the hairless skin. Although cetacean eyes are relatively small, hearing is well developed.

Whether a given cetacean species is called a whale or a dolphin has to do with length: whales generally are at least 4.5 to 6 m (15 to 20 ft) long, while dolphins and porpoises are smaller. The differences between dolphins and porposies? Dolphins have a beak-type nose and mouth, a backwards-curving dorsal fin, and sharp, pointed teeth; porpoises are more blunt-nosed with a triangular dorsal fin and blunt teeth. Cetaceans are often divided into two broad categories. One group of large whale species, the *baleen whales,* have mouths that look like immense car radiator grills, filled with long, vertical, brownish strands of baleen, or *whalebone.* The BLUE WHALE, probably the largest animal that has ever lived, is a baleen whale. Blue Whales, fairly regular in Australian waters but rarely seen, grow to over 30 m (100 ft) in length and 160 tons in weight. The other group, known as the *toothed whales,* includes a few whales and all the porpoises and dolphins; they have mouths with teeth and not baleen.

Three commonly seen dolphins (family Delphinidae) in Australian waters are the SPINNER, COMMON, and PACIFIC BOTTLE-NOSED DOLPHINS (Plates 74, 75), all members of groups that are distributed throughout the world's warm-water seas. These dolphins are cigar-shaped, long and thin, and tapered at the ends. They have smooth, hairless skin and prominent beaks and dorsal fins, and range in length from about 2 m (6.5 ft; Spinner) to 3.5 m (11.5 ft; Bottled-nosed). The INDO-PACIFIC HUMPBACK DOLPHIN (Plate 75), also family Delphinidae, can look a bit different, with its dorsal fin sometimes perched on top of a hump on its mid-back (but humpback dolphins in Australian waters often lack much of a hump); it ranges up to about 3 m (10 ft) in length. (The largest member of the dolphin family is the KILLER WHALE, *Orcinus orca,* occasionally seen around Australia; males grow to 9.5 m (31 ft) long, and weigh as much as 8 tons.)

Whales profiled here are the relatively small MINKE WHALE (to about 10 m, 33 ft, in length) and the HUMPBACK WHALE (to 16 m, 52 ft; both Plate 75). Minke Whales are fairly common (so common that some countries still insist on hunting them; see below). But it is the Humpback Whale that is usually the top species on most whale-watchers' wish lists. The front flippers (or *pectoral fins*) of the Humpback are huge (as long as a third of the body length), white, and wing-like. (In fact, the Humpback's genus, *Megaptera,* means "large wing," referring to these flippers.) The dorsal fin is small, like a shark's. It is placed two-thirds of the way back on the body and mounted on a fleshy pedestal, a trait that distinguishes it from all other baleen whales. When a Humpback initiates a deep dive (*sounds*), its large scalloped flukes (the entire tail can be 4.5 m, 15 ft, across) come well up off the water's surface to expose the underside of the flukes, which are mottled white and black, a pattern so variable and personalized that scientists use it to reliably recognize and track individuals.

Natural History

Ecology and Behavior

Dugongs are seen alone or, more usually, in groups (mostly in small groups, but larger groups, up to a hundred or more, in places where they are undisturbed). They feed during both day and night, preferring calm, shallow, warm waters such as in bays, channels, coastal lagoons, and around some islands and reefs. In areas of the world where they are still hunted, Dugongs may come near shore to feed only at night. They eat mainly seagrasses, some algae, and, occasionally, the odd marine invertebrate, such as mussels. Predation of Dugongs is not frequent, but sharks, large marine crocodiles, and Killer Whales are known to attack them.

Although definitely marine mammals, fur seals spend a considerable proportion of their lives ashore, usually for breeding and resting. They feed underwater by pursuing fish, squid, octopus, lobster, crabs, and other invertebrates. The NEW ZEALAND FUR SEAL (Plate 74) has also been observed taking Little Penguins. Seals are superb underwater swimmers, diving easily to over 200 m (650 ft) to chase fish schools and probe the bottom for dinner.

Because Bottle-nosed Dolphins were the first to be kept in captivity for long periods (they are the species often seen in aquarium shows and achieved fame in the entertainment industry under their stage name, "Flipper"), and because they are often found close to shore and so are easily observed, more is known of their biology than of other species. Although sometimes found as solitary animals, these dolphins usually stay in groups, sometimes of up to a thousand or more. Large groups apparently consist of many smaller groups of about 2 to 6 individuals, which usually are quite stable in membership for several years. There are dominance hierarchies within groups, the largest male usually being top dolphin. Large pods are believed to aid the dolphins in searching for and catching food, and to decrease the likelihood of the dolphins themselves becoming food for such enemies as large sharks. They eat primarily fish and squid, which they catch by making shallow dives into the water. They are fast swimmers, routinely jumping clear of the water when feeding or travelling. Dolphins use sounds as well as visual displays and touching to signal each other underwater; they also use high frequency sound (mostly clicking and popping sounds—*echolocation*) for underwater navigation and to locate prey. Dolphins are considered highly intelligent and sometimes develop close affinities with people. Bottle-nosed Dolphins mature at about 6 years of age and live to be 25 years old. They feed at depths of up to 600 m (2,000 ft) and eat a wide variety of food, from bottom-dwelling fish, eels, small sharks, and crabs, to tuna.

Humpback Whales migrate to feed in polar waters and return to equatorial waters to breed. Calves have no blubber, so they must remain in warmer waters until they have fed sufficiently to put on a layer of fatty insulation for the cold polar waters. Humpbacks are usually found in family groups of 3 or 4 individuals. Greatly paradoxical is that the baleen whales, behemoths so large they can only be measured in tons and tens of meters, feed mainly on planktonic crustaceans, small shrimp-like animals barely 5 to 10 cm (2 to 4 in) long. They swim through food-rich layers of water, especially in polar regions, with their mouths wide open. Then they close their mouths and use their immense tongues (some weighing four tons) to push water out through their 300 or so baleen plates, straining the small shrimp that stay in the mouth and are swallowed in a monumental gulp. Humpbacks also feed on fish and squid. Humpbacks produce some of the most complex and fascinating songs of any animal. Each geographic group has its own song, or *dialect*, that all the individuals there copy and use, but the songs change from year to year. When given in the right layer of water—the appropriate depth and temperature—these songs can travel hundreds of kilometers. Because they apparently can communicate over very long distances, Humpbacks' social interactions—including mate attraction, group behavior, and territorial behavior—may be quite complex and difficult for us to understand. Humpbacks also frequently jump completely out of the water (*breaching*), usually in an arching back flip. This behavior may be associated with mate attraction and courtship or it may be to knock off parasitic barnacles that grow on the whales' skin.

Breeding

Dugongs first breed at 9 to 15 years old, generally when they reach about 2.4 m

(7.9 ft) in length. Mating takes place in May through November. A single young is born, usually in September through April, after a gestation of 13 to 14 months. Birth occurs in very shallow water, where the female and her newborn are more protected from predators such as sharks. The youngster stays with its mother for 18 to 24 months and may live up to 70 years.

New Zealand and AUSTRALIAN FUR SEALS (Plate 74), like many seals and sea lions, are polygynous breeders. Large males stake out and defend territories on gently sloping beaches or rocky coastlines (often on offshore islands), and either acquire and defend harems of females with which they mate (New Zealand Fur Seal) or simply mate with females that visit the territory (Australian Fur Seal). Because there are always more males than territories to defend, a large proportion of the males are left without territories and so without females to mate with. These unattached males form *bachelor herds* that spend time together hauled out on more inaccessible beaches. Sexual maturity occurs at 4 to 5 years, but most males do not breed until they are big, strong, and aggressive enough to establish or take over a territory—usually when they are 8 to 13 years old. Females mate a few days after giving birth. The embryo is dormant in the uterus for 3 to 4 months, then it implants on the uterus wall and continues its development, coming to term in another 8 to 9 months. Birth of the single pup occurs on the beach. Females leave their young to forage at sea, returning every few days to nurse; young are weaned at about a year old.

Dolphins usually produce a single young after pregnancies of about 12 months. When born, dolphins are about a meter (3 ft) long. The mating systems of dolphins in the wild are not well known, for the obvious reason that it is difficult to observe underwater courtship and mating behaviors; also complicating observation is that males and female look much alike. Pacific Bottle-nosed Dolphins mate near the surface, and their courtship involves elaborate stroking, nuzzling, and posturing. Birth is often attended by several female "midwives," which help nudge the newborn to the surface for its first breath. The calf accompanies its mother for about 2 years.

Humpback Whales reach sexual maturity at 9 to 10 years old, when they are about 12 m (40 ft) long. Courtship is in shallow waters near the equator and involves a lot of splashing, churning, and breaching. Gestation is about a year and calves, born in winter, nurse for an additional year. Minke Whales reach sexual maturity at about 6 years old, when they are roughly 7 m (23 ft) long. Gestation is 10 months, and young are suckled for 6 months.

Notes

Dolphins' intelligence and friendliness toward people have inspired artists and authors for thousands of years. Images of dolphins appear frequently on artwork and coins from at least 3,500 years ago, and from both ancient Greece and Rome. Aristotle, 2,300 years ago, noted that dolphins were mammals, not fish, and remarked on their intelligence and gentle personalities. Many other ancient writings tell stories of close relationships between people and dolphins. These animals are considered the only group aside from humans that regularly assists members of other species that are in distress. There have been many reports of dolphins supporting on the water's surface injured members of their own and other dolphin species, as well as helping people in the same way.

Many dolphins will approach moving sea vessels to "ride" the bow pressure wave (the wave produced at the front of the boat as it slices through the water).

They sometimes persist in "hitchhiking" in this way for twenty minutes or more, jostling and competing with each other for the best spots—where, owing to the water's motion, they need exert little energy to swim; they are essentially taking a free ride.

Status

The Dugong's most significant enemy is people. Dugongs are still hunted in Australia (some Aboriginal hunting is legal, and there is also illegal poaching) and other parts of their range. Dugongs are hit by boats and get entangled in fishing nets. They suffer from water pollution and their underwater seagrass food is damaged or killed by pollution and by land erosion that floods seagrass meadows with silt. Dugongs are protected in Australia in some marine reserves, such as the Great Barrier Reef Marine Park, and Australia's Dugongs are not currently endangered (but the Dugong is CITES I listed for the non-Australian parts of its range). The Dugong is considered vulnerable in Queensland and possibly threatened in the Northern Territory. Because of their extremely fine, thick pelts, most species of fur seals were nearly wiped out by hunters in the nineteenth and early part of the twentieth century. Only through a decline in the fur market and aggressive conservation efforts were they saved. All fur seals are CITES Appendix II listed.

Likewise, all marine dolphins are CITES Appendix II listed as species not currently threatened but certainly vulnerable if protective measures are not taken. Common Dolphins are among the dolphins most frequently caught accidentally in the nets of tuna fisherman, and hundreds of thousands have been killed in this way. Dolphins in some regions of the world are also sometimes killed by fishermen who consider them to be competitors for valuable fish, or to be used as bait—for instance, for crab fishing.

Many whale species were hunted almost to extinction during a 200-year period that ended in the early 1960s, when international controls and sanctions were placed on commercial whaling. For instance, whales, particularly SPERM WHALES, were heavily hunted in Pacific waters. Whales were killed by the thousands for the thin, transparent oil stored in a reservoir in the forward part of their heads, which was used in lamps. Sperm Whales also produce *ambergris*, a terrible-smelling black residue found in the intestines, which was used in making expensive perfumes. As late as 1963, more than 30,000 Sperm Whales were killed in a single year. However, this species, now under international protection as endangered (CITES Appendix I), has been recovering (population estimates range up to a half-million). Likewise, the Humpback Whale (CITES Appendix I), with a worldwide population now of perhaps 10,000, seems to be doing well. Blue Whales (CITES Appendix I), however, have not yet recovered from commercial whaling and have disappeared over much of their former range; worldwide population may be less than a thousand. Only a few countries (Japan, Norway, Iceland) continue to hunt whales (often Minke Whales) but they also pressure others to rescind international rules against whaling or otherwise get around the rules.

Profiles

Dugong, *Dugong dugon*, Plate 74a
New Zealand Fur Seal, *Arctocephalus forsteri*, Plate 74b
Australian Fur Seal, *Arctocephalus pusillus*, Plate 74c
Common Dolphin, *Delphinus delphis*, Plate 74d
Spinner Dolphin, *Stenella longirostris*, Plate 74e
Pacific Bottle-nosed Dolphin, *Tursiops truncatus*, Plate 75a

Indo-Pacific Humpback Dolphin, *Sousa chinensis,* Plate 75b
Minke Whale, *Balaenoptera acutorostrata,* Plate 75c
Humpback Whale, *Megaptera novaeangliae,* Plate 75d

Chapter 11

UNDERWATER AUSTRALIA

by Dr. Richard Francis

- *Introduction*
- *Reef Habitats*
- *Invertebrate Life*
- *Vertebrate Life*
- *Final Remarks*

Introduction

It is now widely known that the Great Barrier Reef (GBR) can be seen from the moon, and it is this distinction, perhaps more than any other, that has captured the popular imagination. But the size of the GBR, impressive as it is, is somewhat beside the point both from a biological perspective and that of the knowledgeable ecotraveller. This biggest of barrier reef systems provides the conditions that sustain an incredible abundance and variety of living things. We come to experience this spectacle. We come to experience the marine equivalent of a tropical rainforest.

The GBR is part of a vast biogeographic region known as the tropical Indo-Pacific; in fact, the GBR constitutes the southern portion of its central axis, which extends northward through New Guinea and the Philippines to southern Japan. The Indo-Pacific province extends westward into the Indian Ocean, from Madagascar to the Red Sea; and eastward through Melanesia (New Guinea region, Solomon Islands, etc.), Micronesia (Palau, Guam, Wake Island, etc.), and Polynesia (Tahiti, Samoa, Hawaii, etc.). The Hawaiian Islands form the easternmost outpost of Polynesia and hence of the entire tropical Indo-Pacific. There are only three other biogeographic provinces that harbor coral reefs: (1) the tropical eastern Pacific; (2) the tropical eastern Atlantic; and (3) the tropical western Atlantic (the Caribbean), none of which have the high biodiversity of the Indo-Pacific region.

The tropical Indo-Pacific region is the center of distribution and point of evolutionary origin of far more families of marine tropical animals—ranging from corals to fish—than the other tropical marine provinces. Within this province itself, the major center of distribution for marine families, and hence the region of greatest biodiversity, is the triangle extending roughly from New Guinea to the Philippines and then westward through Indonesia. Moving eastward from there—

through Melanesia, Micronesia, and finally Polynesia—we find a decreasing gradient of biodiversity. So, for example, there are fewer species of coral and coral reef fish on a typical reef in Micronesia than the GBR, and fewer still on a Polynesian reef.

Reef Habitats

The Great Barrier Reef is not a single thing, but a collection of thousands of individual reefs populating northeastern Australia's continental shelf. There is much variation among these reef communities. In order to acquire even a modest appreciation of the biodiversity of the GBR, you would need to visit hundreds, even thousands of these component reefs, and at various times of the day and year. For most of us, of course, our explorations will be more limited. So I will focus more on the biodiversity within, rather than among, reefs. Nevertheless, a few words about the variation among reefs are in order. On the largest spatial scale, there are marked regional differences within the GBR. For example, some species that occur in the southern portion of the reef do not occur in the northern portion, and vice versa. In general, the more northerly reefs are richer (contain more species) than the southerly reefs, primarily because they are closer to the epicenter of origin for most families of tropical reef animals and the reefs with the greatest biodiversity on earth. The southern portion of the reef, however, contains more species endemic to the GBR, species that evolved on the GBR and remain confined to the GBR.

There is also large-scale variation over the east-west axis of the GBR. The westernmost reefs, those closest to the mainland, are the most protected from wave action and storm damage, but they are more subject to adverse continental influences, especially near river mouths. The rivers bring to the reefs all manner of land-born pollutants, notably pesticides and organic waste products. But perhaps most fundamentally, the river runoff contains copious particulate material (soil, silt) that increases turbidity and hence reduces light penetration. Corals derive most of their nutrients from symbiotic algae. The algae, in turn, require sunlight for photosynthesis. For this reason, all else being equal, the clearer the water, the greater the coral growth. So in general, the conditions for coral growth are less ideal on the more turbid inner reefs than on the outer reefs. Nevertheless, a number of species, including Rainford's Butterflyfish (Plate 78), prefer the calm water of inner reefs and avoid the rougher and stormier outer reefs. On the other hand, the outer reefs contain many species not found on the inner reefs. The Meyer's Butterflyfish (Plate 78), for example, prefers the clear water and rich coral of the outer reef areas. Large predatory fish, including sharks, are also more common on the outer reefs. Moreover, the outer reef slopes provide an opportunity to view a number of large pelagic (open ocean) species, including jacks, tuna, and even marlin.

Much of the variation among reefs is over a much smaller scale. For most reef dwellers, each reef or reef patch is more like an island than part of a single whole; reef islands that superficially resemble each other can have a completely different character, even when they are quite close to one another. You may find a pair of Emperor Angelfish (Plate 81) on one reef, but search in vain for these fish on a seemingly identical adjacent reef. Such inter-reef variation is usually the result of either random differences in animal distributions (the Emperor Angelfish colonized one reef but never made it to the other) or in historical events that affected one reef but not the next one. It is because of this sort of small-scale geographic variation that even small reefs are increasingly accorded their own proper names.

Even single reefs often consist of distinct regions that support different communities of critters. It is for this reason that particular dive-sites on a reef get named. Moray Eels may be common on one part of the reef but virtually absent from another. And at yet a smaller scale, each dive-site provides a multitude of distinct environments, or *micro-habitats,* enough to support an awesome variety of reef creatures. It is for this reason that a diver will return to the same site over and over again. You simply cannot begin to appreciate the diversity of living things at a given dive-site until you have experienced it many times and in different seasons.

You will also need to see the reef at night, not just during the daylight hours. When the sun goes down, a completely different cast of characters emerges. Such "shift" changes occur on land as well, but they are much more gradual and less dramatic than similar transitions on the reef, where in as little as fifteen minutes the daytime contingent disappears and the creatures of the night emerge. As the anemones retract, the basket stars unfurl; as the Blacktip Reef Sharks (Plate 106) retreat to their shelters, the Whitetip Reef Sharks (Plate 106) emerge from theirs. Many wrasses bury themselves in the sand, while the parrotfish construct a giant mucous cocoon to sleep in. Crevices that harbor squirrelfish and soldierfish by day are taken over by surgeonfish and butterflyfish as the light wanes. The myriad damselfish are seemingly absorbed by the coral.

The diversity of living things you will see on even a single visit to a particular reef can be overwhelming. In order to make some sense of this variety, it helps to focus first on learning to distinguish some of the more common types of animals, for example, what makes a crab a crab and a shrimp a shrimp. Then, work your way down to the species level. With respect to the fish, it helps to first focus at the family level, on what makes a parrotfish a parrotfish, a wrasse a wrasse, or a butterflyfish a butterflyfish. Then, once you have learned these fish types, look for the diversity within them. Notice that most butterflyfish tend to have yellow, black, and white coloration, but some don't. Among the yellow, black, and white butterflyfish, notice the differences in the patterning of these colors as well as the similarities. At this point you will be able to distinguish different species of butterflyfish. But that is just the beginning. The really fun part comes from noticing such things as the similarities and differences in the way these different butterflyfish species behave, what they eat, how their snout length is associated with their diet, and where they are most likely to be found.

In the remainder of this chapter I will focus on some of the more important families of coral reef fish, but first a few words about the animals that are the foundation of the reef. The foundation of any coral reef is, of course, coral—not just any coral, but a kind of coral known as *hard coral.* Hard coral is hard because the soft coral creature secretes a crater of calcium carbonate, within which it resides. These stony secretions accrete and grow along with the coral colony, upward and outward, with each succeeding generation. There are over 200 kinds of hard coral on the GBR, many that cannot be distinguished by the untutored eye. But anyone can quickly learn some of the more common hard coral types because of basic differences in growth patterns and/or colony size, which result in characteristic colony shapes. A brain coral (*Leptoria,* Plate 108), for example, is easy to distinguish from a branching coral (*Acropora*, Plate 108). You will soon begin to notice as well the differences in the environments in which you find different types of coral. *Acropora* corals, for example, prefer protected areas. You will notice as well that the same species of *Acropora* coral is quite variable. They tend to be more deeply branched in protected areas than in exposed areas. Corals in general vary in size and shape, which depend largely on where they are located on the reef. Notice too, for example, that the Humbug Damselfish (Plate 83) and Reticulated Dascyllus (Plate 83) are always found in *Acropora* heads growing in protected areas, because only the deeply branched heads found there can afford them the protection they need. This is just one of many close associations between reef creatures and corals.

Invertebrate Life

The majority of reef inhabitants are not fish but an extremely varied assortment of animals that are collectively referred to as *invertebrates*. The corals themselves are the most prominent invertebrates and they come in myriad colors and shapes. There are actually several groups of corals, of which the hard corals comprise only one. Among the common types of hard coral in the GBR are the *Pocillopora* (Plate 108), which tend to form dense heads that look like cauliflowers. *Porites* (Plate 108) are encrusting corals that form domes or mounds of various sorts. Corals of the genus *Fungia* (Plate 108) are named for their mushroom shapes, and those of the genus *Leptoria* (Plate 108) are often referred to as brain corals. The *Acropora* corals, as described above, are branching corals.

There are several species of *fire coral* (Plate 107), so named because of the skin irritation they cause when touched. *Hydroids* are feather-like creatures. The soft corals include the *sea fans* (Plate 107), *gorgonians* (Plate 107), and *leather corals*. The *sea anemones* (Plate 107) are coral cousins, which along with *jellyfish* (Plate 109) comprise the vast group of invertebrates known as *cnidarians*. All cnidarians possess stinging elements known as *nematocysts*, with which they capture prey and ward off predators. One group of damselfish, called *anemonefish* (Plate 85), have evolved a close symbiotic relationship with certain anemones, and are able to take advantage of the anemones' stinging elements for their own protection.

The *sponges* (Plate 107) are among the most primitive multicellular animals. They add much of the color to the reef environments and provide homes for many reef inhabitants. Some form large barrel-like structures, others form amorphous mats, and still others look like incredibly colorful puffs of velvet.

The so-called *flatworms*, such as *Pseudoceros dimidiatus* (Plate 109), are among the most beautiful reef inhabitants. They are sometime confused with nudibranchs (see below) but they are not even closely related. *Polychaete worms*, also called marine worms, (such as *Pherecardia striata*, Plate 109), including feather dusters (such as the Christmas Tree Worm, Plate 109) and tube worms, are another important element in the reef community.

The *mollusks* comprise perhaps the largest marine group. The *gastropods* (*snails* and *slugs*) are particularly bountiful (Plates 109, 110, 111). These include, in addition to the *cone shells, cowries, olives, tritons, volutes, helmets, turbans, limpets,* and *sea hares,* the incredibly gorgeous *nudibranchs,* or *sea slugs* (Plates 111, 112). The Spanish Dancer (Plate 112), which comes in varying shades of red, is one of the largest and most commonly seen. It is named for the flamenco-like undulations it makes while swimming. The observant diver will spy a number of other beautiful nudibranchs as well. Another important group of mollusks includes the *cockles, clams, scallops,* and *oysters.* These so-called *bivalves* (Plate 112) can be found under sand or attached to rocks. Also belonging to this phylum are the *squids* (Plate 112) and *octopuses* (Plate 112), collectively referred to as *cephalopods.* These are among the most intelligent creatures in the sea and well worth looking for.

The phylum Arthropoda includes many inhabitants of both land and sea. The largest group of marine arthropods are called *crustaceans.* This group includes all the *shrimp* (Plate 113) and *crabs,* as well as *lobsters* (Plate 113). These can be further subdivided into several families each. Among the more interesting shrimp species are those that serve as *cleaners,* several of which are illustrated in the plates. They set up cleaning stations in much the same way as the cleaner wrasses (Plate 88; see below).

Finally, the *echinoderms* comprise a large and diverse phylum of marine animals, the most famous of which are the *sea stars* (Plates 113, 114). Another large group consists of *sea urchins* (Plate 114) and their relatives the *sand dollars.* The *sea cucumbers* (Plate 114) are perhaps the oddest members of this group. They look like caterpillars on steroids.

Vertebrate Life

Surgeonfish (family Acanthuridae)

This family is well represented in the GBR and includes both the beautiful BLUE TANG (Plate 99) and the very common BROWN SURGEONFISH (Plate 98). Surgeonfish are so called because of their scalpel-like projections at the base of the tail, which they use to slash at other fish. They are primarily algae grazers and they have exceptionally long intestines that are essential for the digestion of this food. Members of one subgroup of surgeonfish are referred to as *unicornfish.* Among the most spectacular reef inhabitants, unicornfish are named for the projections extending forward from their heads. The BLUESPINE UNICORNFISH (Plate 99) is typical; the horn-like projections give it a somewhat sinister look.

The MOORISH IDOL (Plate 100) is on everyone's list of the top five most gorgeous reef creatures. This species is closely related to surgeonfish but comprises its own distinct family. You will usually find these beauties in pairs or small groups, probing the nooks and crannies with their long snouts. Notice how much more deliberately they move compared to the more skittish surgeonfish. Their grace only enhances their spectacular coloration.

Rabbitfish (family Siganidae)

Rabbitfish (Plate 100), which are often referred to as "spinefeet" in Australia, are also closely related to surgeonfish. They generally have ovoid, compressed bodies and small mouths. They feed primarily on benthic (bottom-dwelling) algae and seaweed, but some species also feed on benthic invertebrates. Their spines are venomous and can inflict painful—though not life-threatening—wounds to the unwary diver.

Butterflyfish (family Chaetodontidae)

Butterflyfish (Plates 76 to 80) are among the most celebrated reef inhabitants. Their graceful movements and striking color patterns have long delighted aquarists and divers alike. They have deep, highly compressed bodies, narrow snouts, and very small mouths. Some butterflyfish feed on live coral polyps, for which activity their narrow snouts are ideally suited. In FORCEPSFISH (also called LONGNOSE BUT-TERFLYFISH, Plate 79) the snout extends into needle-shaped pincers, ideal for probing the reef's recesses. Most butterflyfish, especially the larger species, can be found in mated pairs. Interestingly, they pair up as juveniles, long before they become sexually mature. It is suspected that during the early part of the association, if they both happen to be of the same sex, one or the other member of the pair will change sex. Alternatively, both may have the capacity to mature as males or females, so they must decide this matter among themselves. Once paired, they remain paired for life—which can exceed twenty years—with a degree of fidelity unrivaled among mammals. One species, RAINFORD'S BUTTERFLYFISH (Plate 78), is endemic to the GBR.

Angelfish (family Pomacanthidae)
These beauties are closely related to the butterflyfish. They too have deeply compressed bodies and small mouths. They can be distinguished from butterflyfish, however, by their prominent cheek spine. Most are territorial, but there is marked variation in diet. The EMPEROR ANGELFISH (Plate 81) and other members of its genus feed primarily on sponges, while BICOLOR ANGELFISH (Plate 80) eat only algae and detritus. Many, and perhaps most, angelfish, undergo sex change. They begin life as females; those that live long enough to attain a large size then change into males. This is referred to as *protogynous* (female first) *sex change.*

Damselfish (family Pomacentridae)
These small fish comprise another important component of the reef community. They are not nearly as colorful as the butterflyfish or angelfish, but behaviorally they are among the most interesting reef inhabitants. Those species that feed on benthic algae, such as the AUSTRALIAN GREGORY (Plate 85), are highly territorial. Among the most pugnacious reef inhabitants, they strike out at any fish that dares enter their territories, even much larger surgeonfish and butterflyfish. When in the breeding mode they will even attack divers.

Unlike most reef fish, damselfish lay their eggs on the substrate. They then carefully guard them against marauding wrasses and surgeonfish for one to two weeks. The males tend the eggs. When the larvae hatch, they become planktonic but they enter the *plankton* (the ocean's huge population of tiny floating organisms) at a much more advanced state of development and for a shorter period of time than most reef fish. Since they have fairly short planktonic stages, damselfish tend to have smaller geographic ranges than, say, butterflyfish or surgeonfish.

Many damselfish, including the HUMBUG (Plate 83), are *protogynous sex changers*, beginning their lives as females and becoming males only after reaching a large size. One group of damselfish, called *anemonefish* (Plate 85), have evolved a close symbiotic relationship with certain anemones, and are able to take advantage of the anemones' stinging elements for their own protection. Anemonefish are *protandous* (male-to-female) *sex changers*. The largest fish in the anemone is always a female.

Wrasses (family Labridae)
This is one of the largest families of fish. Though they vary greatly in size, shape and habits, they all have a single, continuous dorsal fin and they tend to stay

close to the bottom. Many wrasses move in a distinctive jerky manner as they explore the substrate for food. They primarily use their pectoral fins to swim, using their tails only when rapid movement is required.

Many wrasse species undergo dramatic color changes as they mature, and this is often accompanied by a sex change as well. Formerly these different developmental stages were often mistakenly identified as distinct species. A convention has arisen in which the first color pattern in a sexually mature fish is referred to as the "initial phase," and the second color pattern as the "terminal phase." Some species, such as the YELLOWTAIL CORIS (Plate 87), have a distinct juvenile coloration as well. Juveniles of the aptly named ROCKMOVER WRASSE (Plate 89) mimic drifting algae and do not remotely resemble the adults in color or shape.

In some species, such as the CLEANER WRASSE (Plate 88) and ELEGANT CORIS, all of the initial phase fish are females. In these species the color change is accompanied by sex change to male (protogynous sex change). In other species, such as the MOON WRASSE (Plate 89), the initial phase fish may be either male or female. Some initial phase males eventually undergo a color change to become terminal phase males. In addition, some females subsequently undergo both a color change and a sex change to become terminal phase males. The two male types in these "diandric" species exhibit completely different reproductive behavior. The terminal phase males defend a territory to which they attract females with their vigorous courtship displays. The much smaller initial phase males, however, use their female-like appearance to get close to the courting couple, which they then shower with their own sperm—a deceitfully effective way for a small male to compete with its larger counterparts. In addition, initial phase males sometimes form marauding gangs that overwhelm the territorial defense of the terminal phase males.

All wrasses are brimming with personality and fascinating to watch. One of the most famous in this regard is the Cleaner Wrasse (Plate 88). The male Cleaner Wrasse stakes out a territory to which he attracts several females to form a harem. His territory attracts more than mates, however; it attracts his *clients* as well, which include such large predatory fish as jacks and snappers. They come here in order to have their external parasites removed and the Cleaner Wrasses are happy to oblige, systematically probing the clients' surfaces and, in what looks initially like suicide, inside the mouth as well. The cleaner completely disappears into the maw of larger fish, often emerging through the gills. When one client is done, the next fish, which has been patiently waiting in the queue, steps up for his ministrations. *Cleaning stations*, as these territories are called, can usually be found in fairly prominent locations on the reef, such as around outcrops. They are well worth seeking out. Some other wrasse species, in addition to the Cleaner Wrasse, also act as cleaners.

Parrotfish (family Scaridae)

Parrotfish are closely related to the wrasses and share their complex life histories, including the color and sex changes. Parrotfish are distinguished by their beak, formed by the fusion of several front teeth. Further back in the mouth are powerful molars formed of bony plates, the lower convex, the upper concave. They put both their beak and pharyngeal molars to good use in first removing and then grinding chunks of hard coral in order to extract the algae. The sounds they make in the process are quite audible underwater. Parrotfish manage to digest their food without the aid of a stomach. Instead they have an exceptionally long intestine. When the coral residue reaches the end of the line (intestine), the parrotfish excretes it in wispy clouds of fine sand, destined someday for one of the GBR's famous beaches.

The initial phase fish form aggregations that seem to swarm over the reef with the rising tide, taking their bites of coral on the move. The terminal phase males, however, tend to be highly territorial. In general, the terminal phase parrotfish are brightly colored, while the initial phase fish (both female and male) are some shade of red or brown, and often mottled.

Gobies (family Gobeidae)

Gobies comprise the largest fish family and they are particularly abundant in tropical marine environments. Because of their diminutive size, gobies are generally overlooked by snorkelers and all but the more observant divers. They are, however, fascinating creatures. Like damselfish, they lay eggs on the substrate that are tended by the father. The YELLOW SHRIMP GOBY (Plate 96) has a fascinating relationship with an Alpheid Shrimp. The fish lives in the shrimp's burrow; in return the goby keeps a lookout for predators while the none-too-keen-sighted shrimp goes about its life. At the first sign of danger the goby darts into the burrow along with the alerted shrimp. This is a nice example of inter-species symbiosis of the sort known as mutualism (p. 60): "if you scratch my back, I'll scratch yours."

Blennies (family Blenniidae)

This is another large family of small ground-hugging fish. Like the gobies, blennies lay eggs on the substrate that the male tends. They are highly territorial and pugnacious. Blennies have scaleless elongate bodies; the head is typically blunt with fleshy tentacles, or *cirri*, on the upper surface, and the dorsal fin extends along the entire body. The mouth is generally low on the head and replete with numerous slender teeth. Most are herbivorous, but the so-called *fang*, which are named for their large canine teeth, feed on the scales and flesh of live fish. One of these, the MIMIC BLENNY (Plate 95), secures its meals by mimicking the Cleaner Wrasse (Plate 88), enabling it to get close to unsuspecting large fish, which it then rudely robs of fin or scales. The MIDAS BLENNY (Plate 95) mimics a species of fairy basslet for less sinister ends. Its close relative, the GREAT BARRIER REEF BLENNY (Plate 95), is endemic to the GBR.

Triggerfish (family Balistidae)

The name triggerfish derives from a mechanism by which these fish erect their stout first dorsal spine by means of the movement of the second dorsal spine. Presumably this helps discourage would-be predators. Triggerfish swim by undulating the dorsal and anal fins. They have somewhat compressed bodies and long tapering snouts equipped with chisel-like teeth that they employ while feeding on a variety of hard-shelled benthic animals, including crabs, mollusks, and sea urchins. Female triggerfish also deploy their teeth while guarding their eggs. Divers should take care not to swim too close to some of the larger triggers, such as the TITAN TRIGGERFISH (Plate 100), while the fish are so engaged; they can inflict a nasty wound.

Puffers (family Tetradontidae) and Porcupinefish (family Diodontidae)

No survey of reef fish would be complete without mentioning these two closely related groups of unique reef fish. Puffers (Plate 102) are so-called because of their ability to inflate themselves in the presence of predators. Porcupinefish (Plate 103) add to this defense mechanism an array of spines that are erected in the process. When they are inflated, the pectoral fins, with which they propel themselves, become ineffective, so they tend to list and roll in a comical manner. Though comical looking, both groups should be treated with respect—especially the larger individuals—because they can inflict a nasty bite. Like the triggerfish, puffers and porcupinefish feed on invertebrates with hard exoskeletons. The puffers tend to be diurnal, but the larger-eyed porcupinefish are nocturnal.

Groupers (family Serranidae)

This family contains some of the most important reef predators. Groupers prey primarily on other fish and crustaceans but they are not at all finicky. The larger species are often referred to in Australia as *cod* or *rockcod* and many are important food fish. A number of these have been implicated in *ciguatera poisoning*, especially the Coral Trouts (genus *Plectropomus*). Some species, including the POTATO COD (Plate 91), achieve truly massive sizes and are among the largest fish on the reef. The family includes a number of diminutive species as well, including the basslets of the subfamily Anthiinae. Fairy basslets (genus *Pseudanthias*), such as SCALEFIN, REDFIN, and PURPLE ANTHIAS (Plates 90, 91), are spectacularly beautiful fish that form large aggregations above the reefs. Many groupers and basslets are protogynous sex changers (p. 249).

Sharks and Rays

Several shark species can be found on or around the reefs. Of these, the BLACK-TIP REEF SHARK (Plate 106) is most likely to be encountered by day in shallow water. These slender and sleek creatures are quite timid but they have been known to bite the legs of wading humans. WHITETIP REEF SHARKS (Plate 106) are nocturnal, but can be found in the caves where they rest during the day. The SCALLOPED HAMMERHEAD (Plate 106) is more of an open-water species that you are most likely to see off reef walls. TIGER SHARKS are rarely seen but they represent the greatest threat to divers. It is extremely rare, however, for an encounter with a Tiger Shark to result in an attack. The SILVERTIP SHARK (Plate 106) and GREY REEF SHARK (Plate 106) should also be treated with respect.

Of the rays, the SPOTTED EAGLE RAY (Plate 105) is the most commonly seen. These enchanting animals often perform acrobatics underwater and above. I have noticed that they seem particularly prone to leap out of the water when they are in pairs but I don't know what to make of this. MANTA RAYS (Plate 105) are among the most impressive and awe-inspiring creatures on land or sea. A group of mantas, gracefully winging their way through the water—with their entourages of *remoras* (smaller fish that have commensal relationships with sharks and rays; p. 60)—is a sight you will remember for the rest of your life.

Final Remarks

Don't just be dazzled. The reefs reward those who can appreciate the subtle as well as the dramatic. When you enter the water you will encounter an environment that differs dramatically from that of your everyday life. Let yourself be dazzled, but also seek to look beyond the surface spectacle. When you enter the water, schools of fusiliers and fairy basslets will first attract your attention, and closer to the reef, butterflyfish and damselfish will catch your interest. As you explore further, you will encounter surgeonfish, angelfish, and rabbitfish. You will need to look much closer to find the anemonefish—which never stray far from the shelter of their anemones—or the sweetlips and groupers. Once you have familiarized yourself with these more obvious reef denizens, begin to look for the more hidden and obscure inhabitants, the squirrelfish under the ledges, the puffers and porcupine-fish. And, for a real challenge, try to find some of the small gobies in the reef's nooks and crannies. When you are good at finding gobies, you can consider yourself a true reef connoisseur.

REFERENCES AND ADDITIONAL READING

Below is a list of the most comprehensive and authoritative references for Australian natural history—the main sources used to compile the information in this book, and the sources you should seek out and read if you desire further information on the subjects they treat.

Berra, T. M. 1999. *A Natural History of Australia*. San Diego, California: Academic Press.

Boag, D. 1982. *The Kingfisher*. Poole, UK: Blandford Press.

Bryden, M., H. Marsh, and P. Shaughnessy. 1998. *Dugongs, Whales, Dolphins and Seals: A Guide to the Sea Mammals of Australasia*. St. Leonards, New South Wales: Allen & Unwin.

Burgman, M. A., and D. B. Lindenmayer. 1998. *Conservation Biology for the Australian Environment*. Chipping Norton, New South Wales: Surrey Beatty.

Churchill, S. 1998. *Australian Bats*. Sydney: New Holland Publishers.

Cogger, H. G. 2000. *Reptiles and Amphibians of Australia*. 6th ed. Frenchs Forest, New South Wales: Reed New Holland.

Cronin, L. 1991. *Key Guide to Australian Mammals*. Kew, Victoria: Reed Books.

Duellman W., and L. Trueb. 1994. *Biology of Amphibians*. Baltimore, Maryland: Johns Hopkins University Press.

Garnett, S. 1993. *Threatened and Extinct Birds of Australia*. Royal Australasian Ornithologists Union, Report 82.

Gosliner, T. M., D. W. Behrens, and G. C. Williams. 1996. *Coral Reef Animals of the Indo-Pacific*. Monterey, California: Sea Challengers.

Kuiter, R. E. 1999. *Guide to Sea Fishes of Australia*. Sydney: New Holland Publishers.

MacDonald, D., ed. 1984. *Encyclopedia of Mammals*. New York: Facts on File Publications.

Menkhorst, P. W., ed. 1996. *Mammals of Victoria*. Melbourne: Oxford University Press.

Pizzey, G., and F. Knight. 1997. *A Field Guide to the Birds of Australia*. Sydney: HarperCollins Publishers.

Randall, J. E., G. R. Allen, and R. C. Steene. 1990. *Fishes of the Great Barrier Reef and Coral Sea*. Honolulu: University of Hawaii Press.

Reed, A. W. 1998. *Aboriginal Legends—Animal Tales*. Sydney: Reed New Holland.

Reeves, R. R., B. S. Stewart, and S. Leatherwood. 1992. *The Sierra Club Handbook of Seals and Sirenians*. San Francisco: Sierra Club Books.

Schodde, R., and I. J. Mason. 1999. *The Directory of Australian Birds*. I. Passerines. Collingwood, Victoria: CSIRO Publishing.

Schodde, R., and S. C. Tidemann, eds. 1986. *Reader's Digest Complete Book of Australian Birds*. Surry Hills, New South Wales: Reader's Digest (Australia) Ltd.

Seebeck, J. H. et al., eds. 1990. *Bandicoots and Bilbies*. Chipping Norton, New South Wales: Surrey Beatty and Sons.

Simpson, K., and N. Day. 1996. *The Princeton Field Guide to the Birds of Australia,* 5th ed. Princeton: Princeton University Press.

Stanger, M., M. Clayton, R. Schodde, J. Wombey, and I. Mason. 1998. *CSIRO List of Australian Vertebrates: A Reference with Conservation Status.* Collingwood, Victoria: CSIRO Publishing.

Strahan, R., ed. 1995. *Mammals of Australia*. Washington, DC: Smithsonian Institution Press.

Swan, G. 1995. *A Photographic Guide to Snakes and Other Reptiles of Australia.* Sanibel Island, Florida: Ralph Curtis Books.

Taylor, J. M. 1984. *The Oxford Guide to Mammals of Australia*. Melbourne: Oxford University Press.

Tyler, M. J. 1984. *There's a Frog in My Stomach*. Sydney: Angus and Robertson.

Tyler, M. J. 1992. *Encyclopedia of Australian Animals: Frogs*. Sydney: Angus and Robertson.

Tyler, M. J. 1999. *Australian Frogs: a Natural History*. Ithaca, NY: Cornell University Press.

Vaughan, T. A., J. Ryan, and N. Czaplewski. 1998. *Mammalogy*. Orlando, Florida: Harcourt Brace.

Waller, G., ed. 1996. *SeaLife: A Complete Guide to the Marine Environment.* Washington, DC: Smithsonian Institution Press.

HABITAT PHOTOS

1. Rocky trail at Royal National Park, just south of Sydney (New South Wales).

2. Cliffs along trail at Blue Mountains National Park on a misty, dark day (New South Wales).

3. Hacking River from Kangaroo Creek Trail, Royal National Park (New South Wales).

4. Southern section of Ben Boyd National Park, along Coastal Walk (New South Wales).

5. Fire track at Kosciusko National Park (New South Wales).

6. Fire track through coastal forest on a drizzly morning, Bundjalung National Park (New South Wales).

7. Off Johnson's Beach, Myall Lakes National Park (New South Wales).

8. Jeep track trail, Myall Lakes National Park (New South Wales).

9. Moss-covered trees in higher-elevation beech forest at New England National Park (New South Wales).

10. Treeferns at Tarra-Bulga National Park (Victoria).

11. Sandy trails through eucalypt forest at Brisbane Ranges National Park (Victoria).

12. Along trail to Sealer's Cover, Wilsons Promontory National Park (Victoria).

13. Stream crossing, Box Circuit Trail, Lamington National Park (Queensland).

14. Typical southeastern Australia ranch grazing land, Kiewa Valley, near Gundowring (Victoria).

15. Along Big Walk Trail, Mt. Buffalo National Park (Victoria).

16. Roadside open eucalypt forest with termite mounds, Lakefield National Park (Queensland).

17. Crocodile warning sign and foolhardy birdwatcher at Hanushs Waterhole, Lakefield National Park (Queensland).

18. Night Paddock Lagoon, Mungkan Kaanju National Park (Queensland).

19. Billabong (stagnant water hole) at Kakadu National Park (Northern Territory).

20. Coinda ("Yellow Waters") area of flooded forest, floodplain of South Alligator River, Kakadu National Park (Northern Territory).

21. Rocky outliers along trail to Gubara Plunge Pools, Kakadu National Park (Northern Territory).

22. Open moorland at 1,070 m (3,500 ft) elevation, from Dobson Road, Mt. Field National Park (Tasmania).

23. Coastal view at Freycinet National Park (Tasmania).

24. Beautiful Lake Dobson, Mt. Field National Park (Tasmania).

IDENTIFICATION PLATES

Plant Plates A–K
Animal Plates 1–114

Abbreviations on the Identification Plates are as follows:

M	male	B	breeding plumage
F	female	NB	non-breeding plumage
A	adult	D	dark form
IM	immature	L	light form

The species pictured on any one plate are not necessarily to scale.

Explanation of Symbols Used in the Plate Section

HABITAT SYMBOLS

= Rainforest (also called closed forest, monsoon forest).

= Open forest and woodland (includes most eucalypt forests; also called sclerophyll forest).

= Shrubland (generally with shrubs up to 4 m, 13 ft, high).

= Heathland (open areas of evergreen shrubs usually less than 2 m, 6.5 ft, high; occurs over some coastal lowlands and in subalpine and alpine areas).

= Open habitats: grassland, pastures, savannah (grassland with scattered trees and shrubs), gardens, roadsides, rocky cliffs. Species found in these habitats prefer very open areas.

= Freshwater. For species typically found in or near lakes, dams (ponds), reservoirs, streams, rivers, marshes, swamps, billabongs (stagnant pools in beds of seasonal streams).

= Saltwater. For species usually found in or near the ocean, ocean beaches, or mangroves.

REGIONS (see Map 2, p. 27):

CYP = The Cape York Peninsula, which is the northern tip of Queensland
TRQ = Tropical Queensland; coastal and inland northern parts of the state
TEQ = Temperate Queensland; inland southern parts of the state
NSW = New South Wales
VIC = Victoria
TAS = Tasmania

Plate A

family Myrtaceae

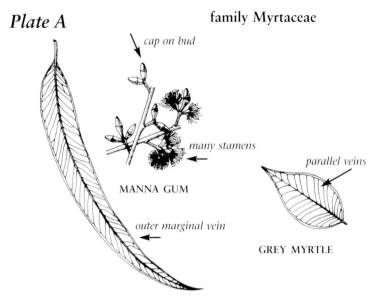

cap on bud

many stamens

MANNA GUM

parallel veins

outer marginal vein

GREY MYRTLE

Plate A1

Distinguishing characteristics of family Myrtaceae. A bud and flower of Manna Gum (*Eucalyptus viminalis*), a eucalypt species found in Victoria and Tasmania, showing the cap on the bud that falls off to expose a mass of stamens around a cup. The leaves of Manna Gum and the rainforest tree Grey Myrtle (*Backhousia myrtifolia*) both show the parallel veins joining an outer marginal vein.

family Proteaceae

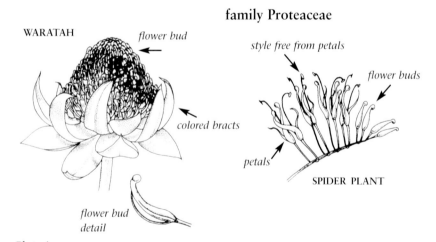

WARATAH

flower bud

style free from petals

flower buds

colored bracts

petals

SPIDER PLANT

flower bud detail

Plate A2

Distinguishing characteristics of family Proteaceae. The family is highly variable in leaf shape and growth, but the flowers for most species show a characteristic form. Waratah (*Telopea speciosissima*) is a spectacular example, but the delicate inflorescence (a structure made up of several flowers) of species such as the Spider Plant (*Grevillea linearifolia*) is the more common sight.

Plate B   family Epacridaceae

DAPHNE HEATH

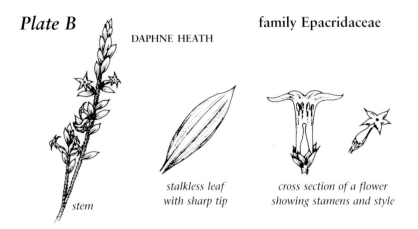

stem

stalkless leaf
with sharp tip

cross section of a flower
showing stamens and style

Plate B1

Distinguishing characteristics of family Epacridaceae. Most plants in the group, like Daphne Heath (*Brachlyoma daphnoides*), are small shrubs with almost stalkless leaves that are often heart-shaped. Tubular white flowers showing a star-shaped lobe usually cover the shrub when it is in flower.

family Fabaceae

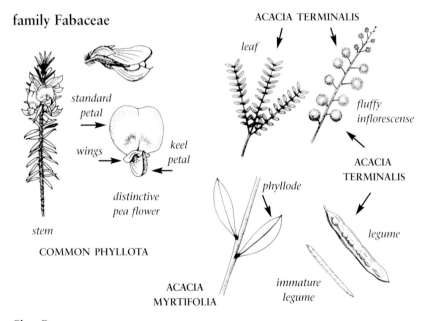

ACACIA TERMINALIS

leaf

standard
petal

wings

keel
petal

distinctive
pea flower

stem

COMMON PHYLLOTA

fluffy
inflorescense

ACACIA
TERMINALIS

phyllode

legume

ACACIA
MYRTIFOLIA

immature
legume

Plate B2

Distinguishing characteristics of family Fabaceae. Both peas and wattles have distinctive flowers and all produce a pod (legume). The flowers of most of the peas, such as Common Phyllota (*Phyllota phylicoides*), have petals in a distinct form as shown. For wattles, leaves can either be a leaflike stem (phyllode), as in *Acacia myrtifolia*, or a compound leaf, such as in *Acacia terminalis*. Flowers of all wattles are in fluffy inflorescences (a structure made up of several flowers).

Plate C1

Spotted Gum

Corymbia (Eucalyptus) maculata

(family Myrtaceae)

Extending from southern New South Wales to Bundaberg, Queensland, this tree is distinguished by a mottled trunk caused by irregular shedding of the bark. It often forms tall open forests along coastal regions.

Plate C2

Red Bloodwood

Eucalyptus gummifera

(family Myrtaceae)

Along coastal areas from eastern Victoria through to southern Queensland, this tree is characterized by a rough bark in small squares, often with a red gum substance exuding from wounds. The large urn-shaped fruit shows it is closely related to spotted gums.

Plate C3

Sydney Blue Gum

Eucalyptus saligna

(family Myrtaceae)

On moist slopes with richer soils, tall white-green stems that extend beyond a dense moist understory often indicate blue gum forests. This smooth barked tree has a "sock" of persistent rough bark around the base. It occurs from Batemans Bay (New South Wales) to Queensland.

Plate C4

Smooth-barked Apple

Angophora costata

(family Myrtaceae)

A distinctive tree with smooth, bright orange or pink bark, often twisted and gnarled in regions around Sydney. The leaves are bright green and occur opposite each other along the stems, a characteristic that separates angophoras from the other closely related eucalypt groups, genus *Eucalyptus* and genus *Corymbia*.

Plate C 273

Eucalypts

C1 Spotted Gum,
Corymbia (Eucalyptus) maculata

C2 Red Bloodwood,
Eucalyptus gummifera

C3 Sydney Blue Gum,
Eucalyptus saligna

C4 Smooth-barked Apple,
Angophora Costata

Plate D1
Yellow Tea-tree
Leptospermum polygalifolium
(family Myrtaceae)
A shrub 2 to 4 m (6.5 to 13 ft) high that is widespread throughout New South Wales and Queensland in damp sandy soils. It produces creamy-white flowers with green centers, and the leaves have conspicuous oil glands.

Plate D2
Paper-bark
Melaleuca linariifolia
(family Myrtaceae)
Paper-barks (there are several species) occur in swamps, producing feathery white inflorescences that cover these dense shrubs or small trees. This particular species is widespread in New South Wales from the coast to the mountains.

Plate D3
Tick Bush
Kunzea ambigua
(family Myrtaceae)
While found only occasionally in coastal areas of Victoria, this shrub is common throughout coastal New South Wales and is frequently seen on roadsides and in disturbed areas.

Plate D4
Black She-oak
Allocasuarina littoralis
(family Casuarinaceae)
This species of she-oak can be found in most habitats and is frequently seen in eucalypt forests and scrubs, often near the coast, from Tasmania to Queensland. The jointed cylindrical branches and cone fruits are distinctive of all she-oaks.

Tall Shrubs and Trees

D1 Yellow Tea-tree,
Leptospermum flavescens

D2 Paper-bark,
Melaleuca linariifolia

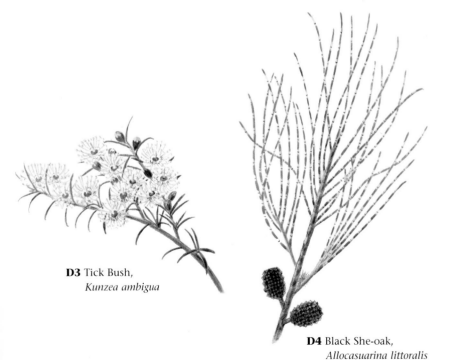

D3 Tick Bush,
Kunzea ambigua

D4 Black She-oak,
Allocasuarina littoralis

Plate E1
Old Man Banksia
Banksia serrata
(family Proteaceae)
The gnarled and twisted trunk of this tree, with large, tough, serrated leaves, is a common sight in open eucalypt woodlands from Tasmania to Queensland. The inflorescences produced in winter are large, yellow with abundant nectar, and are followed by cones with large velvety capsules.

Plate E2
Coast Banksia
Banksia integrifolia
(family Proteaceae)
This banksia is a common sight on sand dunes behind beaches from Melbourne to Fraser Island (Queensland). The yellow inflorescences are relatively small and the leaves have a striking silver underside.

Plate E3
Broad-leaved Hakea
Hakea dactyloides
(family Proteaceae)
While some hakea produce sharp, needle-shaped leaves, this tall shrub has broader leaves. A distinctive large, woody fruit that is warty follows small white flowers along the stems. This species occurs from New South Wales to Queensland.

Plate E4
Northern Christmas Bell
Blandfordia grandiflora
(family Blandfordiaceae)
Christmas bells are found in wet scrubs and produce a spike of flowers that rises above the low foliage of the heath. This species is found on the north coast of New South Wales and Queensland and produces the largest flowers.

Woodlands and Heaths

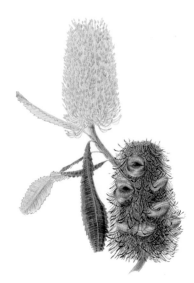

E1 Old Man Banksia,
Banksia serrata

E2 Coast Banksia,
Banksia integrifolia

E3 Broad-leaved Hakea,
Hakea dactyloides

E4 Northern Christmas Bell,
Blandfordia grandiflora

Plate F1
Common Heath
Epacris impressa
(family Epacridaceae)
This species is common in scrubs in Victoria and Tasmania. It is unusual in that the flowers vary from white to a bright red.

Plate F2
Lance Beard-heath
Leucopogon lanceolatus
(family Epacridaceae)
One of many epacrids found in eucalypt forests and scrubs. Densely hairy flowers distinguish the genus. This species has larger leaves than many species and occurs from Tasmania to Queensland. The plant's tasty red fruits are eaten by many birds.

Plate F3
Common Correa
Correa reflexa
(family Rutaceae)
A small shrub with heart-shaped leaves that are covered with brown hairs. The drooping tubular flowers are either yellow-green or red with yellow tips. It occurs from Tasmania to Queensland.

Plate F4
Slender Rice-flower
Pimelea linifolia
(family Thymelaceae)
This plant's slender white flowers in spherical inflorescences are a common sight in the understory of eucalypt forests from Tasmania to Queensland.

Woodlands and Heaths

F1 Common Heath,
Epacris impressa

F2 Lance Beard-heath,
Leucopogon lanceolatus

F3 Common Correa,
Correa reflexa

F4 Slender Rice-flower,
Pimelea linifolia

Plate G1

Coast Rosemary
Westringia fruticosa
(family Lamiaceae)
This common compact shrub is frequently planted along coastal areas because it is hardy and has attractive white flowers. Often there are flowers year-round.

Plate G2

Dusky Coral-pea
Kennedia rubicunda
(family Fabaceae)
While most peas are yellow or purple, this climber has large red flowers and leaves composed of three leaflets. It is common in many habitats from Victoria to Queensland.

Plate G3

Eggs and Bacon
Dillwynia floribunda
(family Fabaceae)
A widespread shrub that grows to 1 m (3.3 ft) high, it's found along the coast in New South Wales. During spring the clustered flowers are striking in the understory of dry woodlands north and south of Sydney. There are many species that look similar.

Plate G4

Austral Grass Tree
Xanthorrhoea australis
(family Xanthorrhoeaceae)
Grass trees are hard to distinguish and only flower after fire. The tall inflorescence is sometimes dripping with nectar and is visited by birds, mammals, and insects.

Woodlands and Heaths

G1 Coast Rosemary,
Westringia fruticosa

G2 Dusky Coral-pea,
Kennedia rubicunda

G3 Eggs and Bacon,
Dillwynia floribunda

G4 Austral Grass Tree,
Xanthorrhoea australis

Plate H1
Myrtle Beech
Nothofagus cunninghamii
(family Fagaceae)
This tree dominates cool closed forests in Victoria and Tasmania. Another beech, *Nothofagus moorei*, with larger leaves, occurs in northern New South Wales at high altitudes.

Plate H2
Lilly-pilly
Acmena smithii
(family Myrtaceae)
From Sydney to northern Queensland, the pink, finely grained bark of this tree makes it distinct within temperate closed forests. Leaves show the drip tip typical of rainforest leaves.

Plate H3
Coachwood
Ceratopetalum apetalum
(family Cunoniaceae)
The "bump" at the base of the toothed leaf is characteristic of this common tree species in temperate closed forests in New South Wales. The bark is pale grey with spots of darker coloring, with raised rings.

Plate H4
Sassafras
Doryphora sassafras
(family Monimiaceae)
Together with Coachwood and Lilly-pilly, this tree species dominates temperate closed forests in New South Wales. The leaves are strongly aromatic when crushed and are broader than the toothed leaves of the Coachwood.

Forests and Temperate Rainforests

H2 Lilly-pilly,
Acmena smithii

H1 Myrtle Beech,
Nothofagus cunninghamii

H3 Coachwood,
Ceratopetalum apetalum

H4 Sassafras,
Doryphora sassafras

Plate I1
Sweet Pittopsorum
Pittosporum undulatum
(family Pittosporaceae)
Occurring from Victoria to Gympie (Queensland), this tall shrub frequently occurs on disturbed edges of rainforests and moist gullies. In some places it is so common that it is considered a weed. The flowers are very fragrant, forming white clusters that are followed by yellow capsules containing dark seeds with a bright orange covering.

Plate I2
Blueberry Ash
Elaeocarpus reticularis
(family Elaeocarpaceae)
This ash is a shrub that grows to 30 m (100 ft) high and has attractive white bell flowers followed by blue-purple fruits through winter. It occurs on rainforest edges from Tasmania to southern Queensland.

Plate I3
Cheese Tree
Glochidion ferdinandi
(family Euphorbiaceae)
A large bushy tree frequently defoliated in late summer by insects, occuring on rainforest edges and creeks. The fruit resembles a large cheese or pumpkin that opens to reveal a number of black seeds covered by a bright red aril (a fleshy attachment to seeds).

Plate I4
Cabbage Tree
Livistona australis
(family Arecaceae)
A common tree along creeks and in wetter areas within closed forests from Victoria to Fraser Island, Queensland. Many black fruits occur in clusters in late summer.

Plate I 285

Temperate and Subtropical Rainforests

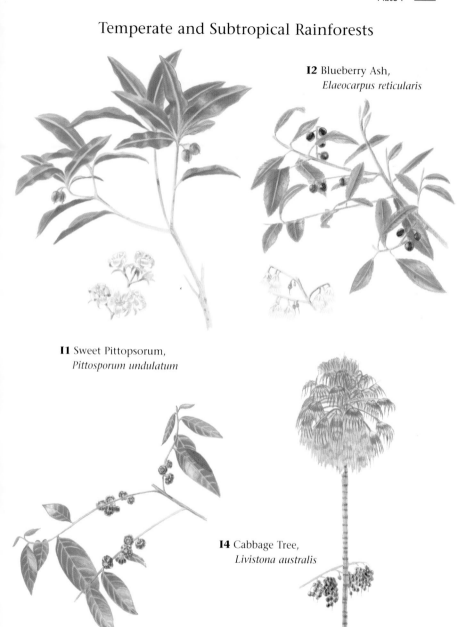

I2 Blueberry Ash,
Elaeocarpus reticularis

I1 Sweet Pittopsorum,
Pittosporum undulatum

I4 Cabbage Tree,
Livistona australis

I3 Cheese Tree,
Glochidion ferdinandi

Plate J1
Bangalow Palm
Archontophoenix cunninghamiana
(family Arecaceae)
This feather-leaved palm occurs in damp areas along creeks and swamps from Batemans Bay (New South Wales) to northern Queensland. Its leaves differ in shape from the Cabbage Tree (Plate I4). The fruits are bright red and clustered in drooping heads.

Plate J2
White Booyong
Heritiera trifoliolatum
(family Sterculiaceae)
A large tree with coppery-colored foliage that occurs from northern New South Wales to Gladstone, Queensland. The leaves have three leaflets and the seeds are winged. This species dominates lowland closed forests while a similar species, Black Booyong (*Argyrodendron actinophyllum*) occurs in poor soils and at high altitudes from central New South Wales to Gympie, Queensland.

Plate J3
Yellow Carabeen
Sloanea woolsii
(family Elaeocarpaceae)
This large tree is characteristic of subtropical closed forests from central New South Wales to central Queensland. The leaves have a swollen stalk at both ends, with small tufts of hair where the veins join the midrib on the leaves. The fruit is a brown hairy capsule containing seeds covered with an orange aril (a fleshy attachment to seeds).

Plate J4
Giant Stinging Tree
Dendrocnide excelsa
(family Urticaceae)
This tree, as well as two related species, causes a painful sting if the hairs on the leaves and stems are touched. The leaves are bright green, frequently with holes from beetle attack. All species commonly occur in gaps within closed forests.

Subtropical and Tropical Rainforests

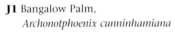

J2 White Booyong,
Argyrodendron trifoliolatum

J1 Bangalow Palm,
Archonotphoenix cunninhamiana

J4 Giant Stinging Tree,
Dendocnide excelsa

J3 Yellow Carabeen,
Sloanea woolsii

Plate K1
Hoop Pine
Araucaria cunninghamii
(family Araucariaceae)
One of the few native conifers in Australia, this large tree is an emergent in closed forests on poorer soils north from northern New South Wales. Leaves are small points crowded along green branches.

Plate K2
Black Bean
Castanospermum australe
(family Fabaceae)
A large tree, often found near water in closed forests in northern New South Wales and Queensland. The yellow-orange pea flowers occur in large clusters and are followed by a very large pod (about 20 cm, 8 in, long) that encloses up to 5 seeds. The dark green leaves are also large and compound (with many leaflets).

Plate K3
Firewheel Tree
Stenocarpus sinuatus
(family Proteaceae)
Occurring from northern New South Wales to Cairns, this tree is spectacular in flower. The conspicuous red wheel-like inflorescences (structures made up of several flowers) contrast against the dark green foliage. With the flowers typical of this family, the species is easy to identify.

Plate K4
Bumpy Satinash
Syzigium cormiflorum
(family Myrtaceae)
Flowers and fruits are produced in great numbers along the old trunks and big branches of this tree. It is found from Townsville north in both lowland and highland closed forests.

Tropical Closed Forest

K2 Black Bean,
Castanospermum asutrale

K1 Hoop Pine,
Araucaria cunninghamii

K3 Firewheel Tree,
Stenocarpus sinuatus

K4 Bumpy Satinash
Syzigium cormiflorum

Plate 1a
Common Froglet
(also called Brown Froglet, Eastern Froglet)
Crinia signifera
ID: A small frog, extremely variable in color, ranging from grey to almost black; the skin may be smooth, warty, or with folds along the body. The belly is blotched with black and white; fingers and toes are not webbed; to 3 cm (1.2 in).

HABITAT: Almost all habitats from the ranges to the coast; found beneath rocks, vegetation, and debris at the edges of creeks, ponds, swamps, and areas of seepage.

REGIONS: TRQ, TEQ, NSW, VIC, TAS

Plate 1b
Brown Toadlet
(also called Bibron's Toadlet)
Pseudophryne bibronii
ID: A small brown frog with darker flecks and sometimes reddish spots; there is often a yellow spot on the vent and at the base of each arm; the belly is distinctively marked with black and white marbling; fingers and toes are not webbed; to 3 cm (1.2 in).

HABITAT: Forests, heathlands, or grasslands where there are damp conditions; shelters in leaf litter, grass clumps, or burrows.

REGIONS: TRQ, TEQ, NSW, VIC, TAS

Plate 1c
Corroboree Frog
Pseudophryne corroboree
ID: A bright yellow or greenish yellow frog with black stripes along the body; it looks as though it has been enameled and cannot be mistaken for anything else; fingers and toes are not webbed; to 3 cm (1.2 in).

HABITAT: Found in the southern Alps above 1,000 m (3,300 ft), in grassy marshlands, sphagnum bogs, and woodlands.

REGIONS: NSW

Plate 1d
Southern Toadlet
(also called Orange-throated Toadlet)
Pseudophryne semimarmorata
ID: Dark brown to olive green with distinct warts on the back; the throat is tan or orange and the belly is black and white; fingers and toes are not webbed; to 3 cm (1.2 in).

HABITAT: Forests, woodlands, heaths, and grasslands; found in damp areas under litter, logs, or rocks.

REGIONS: VIC, TAS

Plate 1e
Hip Pocket Frog
(also called Pouched Frog, Marsupial Frog)
Assa darlingtoni
ID: A small frog, red-brown to grey, with darker markings that often form V's on the back; the sides are dark grey to black; fingers and toes are not webbed; to 2.5 cm (1 in).

HABITAT: Antarctic beech forests and rainforests in mountainous areas.

REGIONS: TEQ, NSW

Plate I 291

a Common Froglet

b Brown Toadlet

c Corroboree Frog

d Southern Toadlet

e Hip Pocket Frog

Plate 2a

Striped Marsh Frog
(also called Brown Frog, Brown-striped Frog)
Limnodynastes peronii

ID: A larger frog, light brown to grey-brown with darker brown stripes; sometimes there is a pale stripe running down the back; a pale stripe runs from below the eye to the base of the arm; fingers and toes are not webbed; to 7 cm (2.75 in)

HABITAT: Found in ponds and swamps in open, grassy areas; also turns up in suburban fish ponds and swimming pools. One of the most common frogs along the east coast.

REGIONS: CYP, TRQ, TEQ, NSW, VIC, TAS

Plate 2b

Spotted Marsh Frog
Limnodynastes tasmaniensis

ID: A smallish to mid-sized frog, pale grey to brown or dull green with irregular olive green or brown spots; there is often a pale stripe down the middle of the back; a pale stripe runs from below the eye to the base of the arm; fingers are not webbed but there is slight webbing on the toes; to 4.5 cm (1.8 in).

HABITAT: Swampy grass country close to streams or ponds; also in disturbed woodlands and grasslands, and in roadside ditches.

REGIONS: TRQ, TEQ, NSW, VIC, TAS

Plate 2c

Ornate Burrowing Frog
Limnodynastes ornatus

ID: A stout, mid-sized frog, variable in color, light or dark grey to brown with darker blotches; there is often a large pale patch on the back behind the eyes; fingers are not webbed but there is slight webbing on the toes; to 4.5 cm (1.8 in).

HABITAT: From wet forests near the coast to arid woodlands; a burrowing frog found in grasslands and open forests.

REGIONS: CYP, TRQ, TEQ, NSW

Plate 2d

Eastern Banjo Frog
(also called Four-bob Frog, Eastern Pobblebonk)
Limnodynastes dumerilii

ID: A mid-sized to large frog with a rough warty skin, brown to grey with pale mottled markings along the sides; a cream to yellow streak runs from below the eye towards the arm, and there is a very obvious enlarged gland on the hind limbs; the fingers are not webbed but there is slight webbing on the toes; to 7.5 cm (3 in).

HABITAT: Found in a wide range of habitats from rainforests to roadside ditches; common after rain.

REGIONS: TEQ, NSW, VIC, TAS

Plate 2e

Giant Burrowing Frog
(also called Owl Frog)
Heleioporus australiacus

ID: A large frog, dark brown to grey, with yellow or cream spots along the sides; the skin is warty and there is a short yellow stripe on the upper lip behind the eye; fingers are not webbed but the toes are slightly webbed; to 10 cm (4 in).

HABITAT: Found in open forests and coastal heaths; most common in the sandstone areas of the Sydney region.

REGIONS: NSW, VIC

NOTE: Considered vulnerable in New South Wales and Victoria.

Plate 2 293

a Striped Marsh Frog

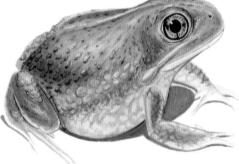

b Spotted Marsh Frog

c Ornate Burrowing Frog

d Eastern Banjo Frog

e Giant Burrowing Frog

Plate 3a

Great Barred Frog
(also called Giant Barred Frog)
Mixophyes fasciolatus

ID: A large, long-legged frog, tan to brown with darker scattered markings; the legs are distinctively barred; there is a dark stripe from the snout through the eye and over the eardrum, and the sides are spotted; fingers are not webbed but the toes are partly webbed; to 8 cm (3 in).

HABITAT: Found in the coastal ranges in rainforests and wet open forests, where it occurs close to permanent running water.

REGIONS: TRQ, TEQ, NSW

Plate 3b

Striped Burrowing Frog
Litoria alboguttata

ID: Brown to olive green with darker blotches and usually a pale stripe down the middle of the back; a dark streak from the snout through the eye and onto the sides; warts and ridges of skin on the back; fingers are not webbed but the toes are half webbed; to 8 cm (3 in).

HABITAT: Found around temporary pools and flooded clay pans in grasslands and woodlands.

REGIONS: CYP, TRQ, TEQ, NSW

Plate 3c

Green and Golden Bell Frog
Litoria aurea

ID: Variable in color, usually patterns of green and bronze-gold; some individuals may be all green or all gold; blue coloration in the groin and on the thighs; there is a cream stripe edged with black below that runs from the nostril through the eye to the groin; fingers are not webbed but the toes are three-quarters webbed; to 8 cm (3 in).

HABITAT: Found around permanent swamps and ponds with rushes and other vegetation at the water's edge.

REGIONS: NSW, VIC

NOTE: Considered endangered in New South Wales.

Plate 3d

Green Tree Frog
Litoria caerulea

ID: A large bulky green frog that sometimes has a few white spots, particularly on the sides; yellow on the back of the thighs; the fingers are about one-third webbed and the toes are three-quarters webbed; to 10 cm (4 in).

HABITAT: Temperate to tropical forests and woodlands; found in trees and rocky areas near streams and swamps; also around houses.

REGIONS: CYP, TRQ, TEQ, NSW

Plate 3 **295**

a Great Barred Frog

b Striped Burrowing Frog

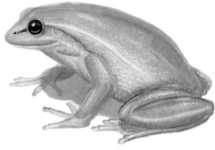

c Green and Golden Bell Frog

d Green Tree Frog

Plate 5a
Wood Frog
(also called Water Frog)
Rana daemeli
ID: A large frog with well-developed limbs and a pointed triangular head; pale to dark brown with a few darker flecks; distinctive fold of skin along the back from behind the eye to the hind limbs; fingers not webbed and toes fully webbed; to 8 cm (3 in).

HABITAT: Found in vegetation around permanent streams and pools; basks during the day but is very wary.

REGIONS: CYP

Plate 5b
Peron's Tree Frog
(also called Emerald-spotted Tree Frog)
Litoria peronii
ID: Grey to fawn or dark brown with small, scattered, bright green spots; the groin and thighs are yellow with a black marbling; fingers are half-webbed and the toes are fully webbed; to 6.5 cm (2.5 in).

HABITAT: Found in a variety of habitats, from forested areas to open grasslands and suburban areas; it utilizes waterholes, ponds, temporary ponds, or ditches.

REGIONS: TRQ, TEQ, NSW, VIC

Plate 5c
Ornate Frog
Cophixalus ornatus
ID: A small frog, highly variable in color; ranges from pale fawn to dark brown with darker flecks; there is sometimes a pale stripe down the middle of the back, and a black streak behind the eye; often a dark bar with a pale edge between the eyes; the fingers and toes are not webbed; to 3 cm (1.2 in).

HABITAT: Found in rainforests from sea level to the ranges.

REGIONS: CYP, TRQ

Plate 5d
Cane Toad
(also called Giant Toad, Marine Toad)
Bufo marinus
ID: Large, ranging in color from grey to pale or dark brown; there are many warts on the back and the skin is rough, with large glands (parotoid) behind the head; protruding eyes with thick warty eyelids; fingers are not webbed and the toes are fully webbed; to 20 cm (8 in).

HABITAT: Open woodlands, low grasslands, suburban gardens, and roadside ditches.

REGIONS: CYP, TRQ, TEQ, NSW

Plate 5e
Blackish Blind Snake
(also called Worm Snake, Blind Snake)
Ramphotyphlops nigrescens
ID: Pink-brown to almost black, with a cream to pink belly; the head is blunt and not distinct from the neck, and the eyes are reduced to dark spots; it has a short tail ending in a point; there is usually a black spot on either side of the vent; to 75 cm (30 in) but averages 25 cm (10 in).

HABITAT: Occurs from the coast to the ranges in open woodlands, heaths, shrublands, and dry or wet open forests, where it shelters under flat rocks and logs or inside rotten stumps.

REGIONS: TEQ, NSW, VIC

Plate 5 **299**

a Wood Frog

b Peron's Tree Frog

c Ornate Frog

d Cane Toad

e Blackish Blind Snake

Plate 6a

Carpet Python
Morelia spilota variegata

ID: A mid-sized python, pale to dark brown with lighter blotches or bands that are darker at the edges; there are a number of color variations, some of which have been recognized as subspecies; they differ in background color and in the shape, color, and placement of blotches; to 4 m (13 ft) but averages 2 m (6.6 ft).

HABITAT: Occurs in timbered or rocky areas, where it shelters in tree hollows, rock crevices, and hollow logs; it is also well known for taking up residence in outbuildings or the roofs of houses; nocturnal, but may be seen basking or moving about during the day.

REGIONS: CYP, TRQ, TEQ, NSW, VIC

Plate 6b

Diamond Python
Morelia spilota spilota

ID: A mid-sized python, black with small yellow or cream spots on most scales; some spots are arranged in the form of blotches along the length of the body; to 4 m (13 ft) but averages 2 m (6.6 ft).

HABITAT: Rainforests and timbered areas, and commonly in suburban areas; this is the most southerly of the pythons and is found along the coast and ranges; nocturnal and arboreal, but may be found basking during the day.

REGIONS: NSW, VIC

Plate 6c

Black-headed Python
Aspidites melanocephalus

ID: A mid-sized python with a glossy black head and neck; the body is cream to light brown with dark brown crossbands; to 3 m (10 ft) but averages 1.5 m (5 ft).

HABITAT: Found in woodlands, shrublands, and grasslands, where it shelters in burrows, hollow logs, or grass hummocks; a terrestrial python that lacks the heat sensitive pits on the lips that are found on most Australian pythons.

REGIONS: CYP, TRQ, TEQ

Plate 6d

Water Python
Liasis fuscus

ID: A mid-sized python, dark brown with whitish lips and throat; the belly is yellow and this color extends onto the sides; the skin is shiny and can have an iridescent sheen; to 3 m (10 ft) but averages 2 m (6.6 ft).

HABITAT: Found near watercourses in woodlands and rocky areas where it shelters in burrows, crevices, or under vegetation; it may be found underwater among vegetation at the edges of waterholes.

REGIONS: CYP, TRQ, TEQ

Plate 6e

Amethystine Python
(also called Scrub Python, Amethyst Python)
Morelia amethistina

ID: Largest of the Australian pythons, it has a slender body, fawn to brown above, with numerous dark brown or black variegated markings; the scales have an iridescent sheen that gives rise to one of its common names; to 6 m (19.5 ft) but averages 3 m (10 ft).

HABITAT: Found in the tropical lowlands, slopes, and ranges in both rainforests and drier forests; arboreal and nocturnal.

REGIONS: CYP, TRQ

Plate 6 **301**

a Carpet Python

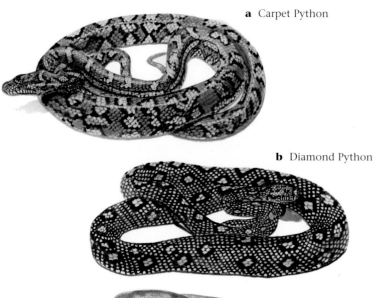

b Diamond Python

c Black-headed Python

d Water Python

e Amethystine Python

Plate 7a

Eastern Small-blotched Python
(also called Eastern Children's Python,
Spotted Python)
Antaresia maculosus

ID: A small to mid-sized python with a fawn to
light brown body covered with dark brown
blotches, usually ragged-edged; the head is light
brown with darker flecks; to 1 m (3.3 ft) but
averages 75 cm (30 in).

HABITAT: Wet coastal forests, dry woodlands,
and grassland savannahs; often associated with
stony hills and outcrops; nocturnal and partly
arboreal.

REGIONS: CYP, TRQ, TEQ, NSW

Plate 7b

Brown Tree Snake
(also called Eastern Brown Tree
Snake)
Boiga irregularis

ID: A mid-sized snake with a very broad head,
prominent eyes, and a thin neck; brown to reddish
brown with darker blotches that form narrow
bands across the body; the belly is usually salmon
colored; to 2 m but averages 1.2 m.

HABITAT: Rainforest edges, wet and dry
sclerophyll forests, coastal heathlands, and
mangroves; nocturnal and arboreal. CAUTION:
Venomous but not dangerous.

REGIONS: CYP, TRQ, TEQ, NSW

Plate 7c

Green Tree Snake
(also called Tree Snake, Golden Tree
Snake)
Dendrelaphis punctulata

ID: A slender, mid-sized snake with large eyes; there
is considerable geographic variation in color, but it is
often olive green with yellow on the under-sides; it
can also be dark brown, black, blue, or golden
yellow; to 1.8 m (5.9 ft) but averages 1 m (3.3 ft).

HABITAT: Woodlands, forests, and heathlands,
usually next to watercourses; active during the
day; arboreal.

REGIONS: CYP, TRQ, TEQ

Plate 7d

Keelback
(also called Freshwater Snake, Grass
Snake)
Tropidonophis mairii

ID: A smallish snake with strongly keeled scales
that give rise to its common name; grey, brown,
olive, or reddish to black, often with narrow
darker crossbands; to 1 m (3.3 ft) but averages 50
cm (20 in).

HABITAT: Lowlands through to the ranges, in the
vicinity of streams, swamps, or lagoons where
there is ample cover such as grasses, reeds, or
similar vegetation; terrestrial; partly aquatic.

REGIONS: CYP, TRQ, TEQ, NSW

Plate 7e

Southern Death Adder
(also called Common Death Adder,
Death Adder)
Acanthophis antarcticus

ID: A bulky, mid-sized snake with a broad
triangular head, narrow neck, and bulky body; it
has a thin tail ending in a spine; grey to reddish
brown in color, usually with indistinct crossbands;
white-edged scales form prominent bars on the
lips; to 1 m (3.3 ft) but averages 40 cm (16 in).

HABITAT: Plains, slopes, and lower ranges; wet
open forests, woodlands, heathlands, and
shrublands; sedentary, burrowing into leaf litter or
sandy soil; active during the day but also moves
about at night. CAUTION: Dangerously venomous!

REGIONS: TRQ, TEQ, NSW

Plate 7 **303**

a Eastern Small-blotched Python

b Brown Tree Snake

c Green Tree Snake

d Keelback

e Southern Death Adder

Plate 8a
Highland Copperhead
Austrelaps ramsayi
ID: A mid-sized snake that is greyish brown to black, the snout usually paler; it is orange-red on the lower sides fading to cream on the belly; there is a conspicuous white edging to the scales of the upper lips; to 1.5 m (4.9 ft) but averages 1.2 m (4 ft).

HABITAT: Found in the cooler areas of the Great Dividing Range where it occurs around streams and swamps; often associated with areas of dense tussock grass. CAUTION: Dangerously venomous!

REGIONS: NSW, VIC

Plate 8b
Lowland Copperhead
Austrelaps superbus
ID: Mid-sized, this snake is reddish brown or dark grey to blackish brown; the lower sides are usually orange-red and the belly is cream to grey; the young often have a dark band across the nape and a dark stripe down the middle of the back; to 1.4 m (4.6 ft) but averages 1.2 m (4 ft).

HABITAT: Found in the vicinity of swamps and watercourses in woodlands, heathlands, and tussock grasslands; it shelters beneath fallen timber, in burrows, or in dense tussock clumps. CAUTION: Dangerously venomous!

REGIONS: VIC, TAS

Plate 8c
Western Brown Snake
Pseudonaja nuchalis
ID: This mid-sized snake has a slender body and a small head; it is extremely variable in color and can range from olive grey to dark brown or orange-brown; some have a black head and nape, others broad dark crossbands, others a reticulated pattern formed by dark-edged scales, and yet others have a series of dark scales on the nape that often form a chevron; to 1.5 m (4.9 ft) but averages 1.2 m (4 ft).

HABITAT: Occurs in more arid and semi-arid habitats and vegetation types where it shelters in burrows and soil cracks or beneath fallen timber. CAUTION: Dangerously venomous!

REGIONS: CYP, TRQ

Plate 8d
Eastern Brown Snake
Pseudonaja textilis
ID: A large slender snake that varies from light tan to almost black; there are usually no markings on the body but occasionally banded specimens may be seen; in some areas juveniles are boldly banded; the belly is cream with orange or grey blotches; to 2.5 m (8.2 ft) but averages 1.5 m (4.9 ft).

HABITAT: The most commonly seen snake in eastern Australia, it is mainly found in open woodlands and grazing lands; day-active; shelters in burrows and crevices or under rubbish. CAUTION: Dangerously venomous!

REGIONS: CYP, TRQ, TEQ, NSW, VIC

Plate 8e
Stephen's Banded Snake
Hoplocephalus stephensii
ID: Dark brown to black with a series of light, narrow crossbands; the lips are barred with black and cream and the head is brown to black with cream blotches behind the eyes and on the nape; to 1.2 m (4 ft) but averages 65 cm (26 in).

HABITAT: Arboreal and nocturnal, this snake is found along rainforest edges or in open forests where it shelters in trees and rocky outcrops. CAUTION: Venomous; a bite may require treatment.

REGIONS: TRQ, TEQ, NSW

Plate 8 305

a Highland Copperhead

b Lowland Copperhead

c Western Brown Snake

d Eastern Brown Snake

e Stephen's Banded Snake

Plate 9a

Black Tiger Snake
(also called Tasmanian Tiger Snake)
Notechis ater
ID: Although called Black Tiger Snake, this robust snake shows considerable color variation and can be black or dark brown to tan or yellow; sometimes there are lighter or darker crossbands; the belly is light to dark grey; to 1.8 m (6 ft) but averages 1.2 m (4 ft).

HABITAT: Found in woodlands, shrublands, and tussock grasslands where it shelters in burrows and tussock clumps. CAUTION: Dangerously venomous!

REGIONS: TAS

Plate 9b

Eastern Tiger Snake
Notechis scutatus
ID: A large, solid snake, olive grey to tan to dark brown, with or without yellowish crossbands that give it the "tigerish" appearance; the belly is cream, yellow, or grey; to 2 m (6.6 ft) but averages 1.2 m (4 ft).

HABITAT: Found in moist swampy areas on the coast and ranges where it occurs in a variety of habitats. CAUTION: Dangerously venomous!

REGIONS: TEQ, NSW, VIC

Plate 9c

Taipan
Oxyuranus scutellatus
ID: A large, slender snake, tan to dark brown; the head is long and usually paler than the body; the scales on the neck and at least the forebody are keeled; the belly is cream to yellow; to 3.5 m (11.5 ft) but averages 2 m (6.6 ft).

HABITAT: Occurs on the coastal plains and foothills where it is found in a variety of habitats including sugarcane fields; secretive and not frequently encountered; shelters in burrows, fallen timber, or ground debris. CAUTION: Dangerously venomous!

REGIONS: CYP, TRQ, TEQ, NSW

Plate 9d

Mulga Snake
(also called King Brown Snake)
Pseudechis australis
ID: A large, bulky snake, coppery brown, red-brown, or olive-brown to almost black; the scales sometimes have a darker edge, giving the snake a reticulated appearance; to 2.5 m (8.2 ft) but averages 1.5 m (4.9 ft).

HABITAT: Found in a wide range of habitats where it shelters in burrows and cracked soil. CAUTION: Dangerously venomous!

REGIONS: CYP, TRQ, TEQ

Plate 9e

Red-bellied Black Snake
Pseudechis porphyriacus
ID: A mid-sized snake, uniform glossy black with a red or pink belly; the belly color can be white in populations from tropical Queensland; the snout is often slightly paler; to 2.2 m (7.2 ft) but averages 1.5 m (4.9 ft).

HABITAT: Temperate to tropical slopes, ranges, and lowlands; coastal and inland in the vicinity of permanent watercourses, swamps, or lakes; day-active; most commonly encountered during warmer months basking or foraging near permanent water. CAUTION: Dangerously venomous!

REGIONS: TRQ, TEQ, NSW, VIC

Plate 9 307

a Black Tiger Snake

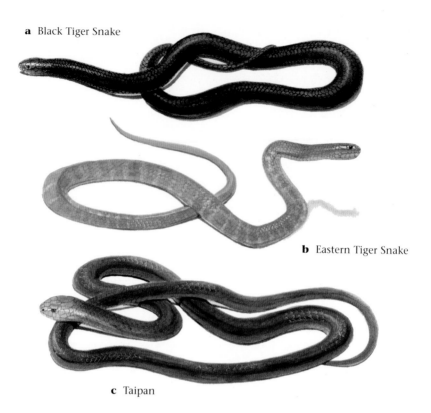

b Eastern Tiger Snake

c Taipan

d Mulga Snake

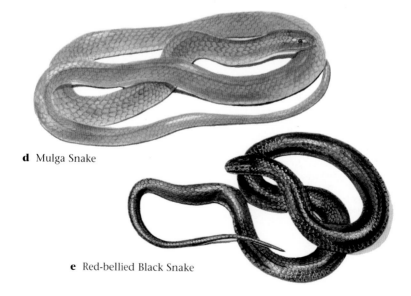

e Red-bellied Black Snake

Plate10a
Yellow-faced Whipsnake
Demansia psammophis
ID: A mid-sized, very slender snake with a dark, distinctive comma-shaped marking edged in cream around the eye; the body is grey to olive-brown, often with a slight reddish flush; to 1.2 m (4 ft) but averages 80 cm (31 in).

HABITAT: Day-active and fast-moving, this snake is found in the lowlands and ranges where it occurs in most habitat types. CAUTION: Venomous, but not regarded as dangerous.

REGIONS: CYP, TRQ, TEQ, NSW

Plate 10b
White-lipped Snake
Drysdalia coronoides
ID: A small snake, grey to dark brown with a white streak running from the snout along the lips to the neck; this stripe is edged above with black; the belly is cream, yellow, or pink; to 50 cm (20 in) but averages 40 cm (16 in).

HABITAT: The most cold-adapted of Australian snakes, this species is found from the Australian Alps down to the coast; it is day-active and occurs in woodlands, shrublands, and tussock grasslands. CAUTION: Venomous, but not regarded as dangerous.

REGIONS: NSW, VIC, TAS

Plate 10c
Marsh Snake
Hemiaspis signata
ID: A small snake, brown or dark grey to black, with two cream stripes on the head, one from the eye to the neck and the second on the upper lip; the belly is dark grey to blackish but occasional specimens have a salmon-colored belly; to 90 cm (35 in) but averages 60 cm (24 in).

HABITAT: Found from the coast to the ranges; it occurs close to water in woodlands, shrublands, and tussock grasslands. CAUTION: Venomous, but not regarded as dangerous.

REGIONS: TRQ, TEQ, NSW

Plate10d
Coral Snake
Simoselaps australis
ID: A small snake with a pink to red body that has numerous dark-edged cream bands; there is a broad black band across the head and nape, and the snout is shovel-shaped; to 50 cm (20 in) but averages 30 cm (12 in).

HABITAT: A nocturnal, burrowing snake found in sandy plains and slopes. It occurs in woodlands and shrublands where it shelters under logs or in stumps. CAUTION: Venomous, but not regarded as dangerous.

REGIONS: TRQ, TEQ, NSW

Plate 10e
Bandy-bandy
Vermicella annulata
ID: A small snake with the entire body banded in distinct black and white rings that usually extend onto or across the belly; to 75 cm (30 in) but averages 60 cm 24 in).

HABITAT: A nocturnal, burrowing species found on slopes and plains in open forests and woodlands, shrublands, and grasslands. CAUTION: Venomous, but not regarded as dangerous.

REGIONS: CYP, TRQ, TEQ, NSW, VIC

Plate 10　309

a Yellow-faced Whipsnake

b White-lipped Snake

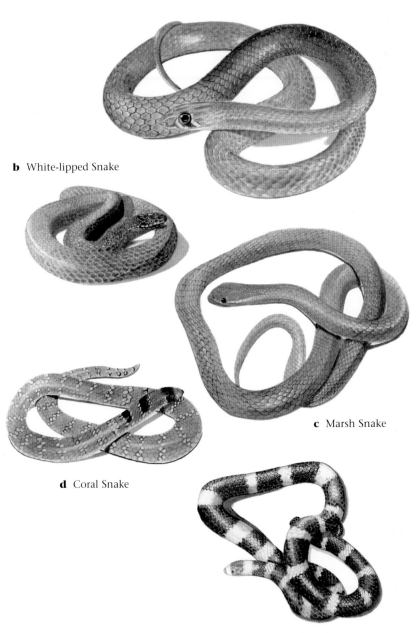

c Marsh Snake

d Coral Snake

e Bandy-bandy

Plate 11a
Stokes' Sea Snake
Astrotia stokesii
ID: Sea snake with a large head and bulky body; cream to almost black in color, usually with darker crossbands and spots; the scales on the belly are small and paired, and on adults they form a distinctive keel; to 2 m (6.6 ft) but averages 1.2 m (4 ft).

HABITAT: Found in coastal waters and coral reefs around northern Australia, usually at depths of 10 to 20 m (33 to 66 ft). CAUTION: Dangerously venomous!

REGIONS: CYP, TRQ, TEQ, NSW

Plate 11b
Yellow-bellied Sea Snake
Pelamis platurus
ID: The head is long, narrow, and distinct from the neck in this very recognizable species; black or dark brown above with yellow or light tan lower sides and belly; flattened paddle-shaped tail; to 1 m (3.3 ft) but averages 70 cm (28 in).

HABITAT: In the open sea of the Pacific and Indian Oceans; this species is essentially a deep-water sea snake; some are washed up on beaches because of strong currents or storms. CAUTION: Dangerously venomous!

REGIONS: CYP, TRQ, TEQ, NSW, TAS

Plate 11c
Saltwater Crocodile
(also called Estuarine Crocodile)
Crocodylus porosus
ID: Grey to almost black, with some darker mottling; has a broad snout and a raised ridge running from in front of the eye to the center of the snout; to 7 m (23 ft) but averages 4 m (13 ft).

HABITAT: Tropical tidal rivers, estuaries, and swamps; in the wet season it will move into freshwater swamps; occasionally seen in the open sea. CAUTION: Extremely dangerous.

REGIONS: CYP, TRQ

NOTE: Considered vulnerable in Australia, CITES Appendix II listed.

Plate 11d
Freshwater Crocodile
Crocodylus johnstoni
ID: Grey to brown with regular dark markings, this crocodile has a long, slender, and relatively smooth snout; to 3 m (10 ft) but averages 2 m (6.6 ft).

HABITAT: Permanent freshwater swamps, rivers, and billabongs; also may be found in tidal waterways in places where the Saltwater Crocodile (11c) is absent.

REGIONS: CYP

NOTE: Considered vulnerable, CITES Appendix II listed.

Plate 11 **311**

a Stokes' Sea Snake

b Yellow-bellied Sea Snake

c Saltwater Crocodile

d Freshwater Crocodile

Plate 12a
Leathery Sea Turtle
(also called Leatherback Sea Turtle)
Dermochelys coriacea
ID: The largest of the marine turtles, it looks as though it is covered in hard black rubber; seven ridges run lengthwise, and the shell is sharply tapered at the rear; to 2.2 m (7.2 ft) but averages 1.8 m (6 ft).

HABITAT: Found in tropical and temperate seas, especially in the calmer waters of estuaries and bays.

REGIONS: CYP, TRQ, NSW

Plate 12b
Green Sea Turtle
Chelonia mydas
ID: Greenish above with brown or black markings; the scales on the side of the head have distinctive pale edges; cream-colored on the belly; one claw on each front flipper; hatchlings are black with white bellies; to 1.5 m (4.9 ft) but averages 1 m (3.3 ft).

HABITAT: Shallow, warm coastal waters, particularly along the Great Barrier Reef.

REGIONS: CYP, TRQ
NOTE: Endangered, CITES Appendix I listed.

Plate 12c
Hawksbill Sea Turtle
Eretmochelys imbricata
ID: Olive green to brown sea turtle with dark brown or black variegations; as common name suggests, the upper jaw of this turtle juts forward to form a beak; two claws on each front flipper; the carapace is serrated at the rear; to 1 m (3.3 ft) but averages 80 cm (32 in).

HABITAT: Found in tropical and warm temperate waters, particularly around coral reefs.

REGIONS: CYP, TRQ
NOTE: Endangered, CITES Appendix I listed.

Plate 12d
Eastern Snake-necked Turtle
Chelodina longicollis
ID: As the name suggests, this turtle has a long, snake-like neck with many pointed tubercles (lumps); brown to black, although often covered in mud or algae; the seams of the scales on the belly are edged in black; there are four claws on the front foot; to 25 cm (10 in) but averages 15 cm (6 in).

HABITAT: Inhabits swamps, billabongs, and farm dams (ponds); it prefers still or slow-moving water and may be found some distance from shore in search of a new body of water; it is capable of emitting an offensive smell from the musk glands if alarmed.

REGIONS: TRQ, TEQ, NSW, VIC

Plate 12e
Krefft's River Turtle
(also called Krefft's Short-necked Turtle)
Emydura krefftii
ID: Pale brown to blackish on top, with a bluish green belly; a yellow or blue-green stripe behind the eye; five claws on each front foot; to 25 cm (10 in) but averages 20 cm (8 in).

HABITAT: Large rivers and waterholes.

REGIONS: CYP, TRQ, TEQ

Plate 12 **313**

a Leathery Sea Turtle

b Green Sea Turtle

c Hawksbill Sea Turtle

d Eastern Snake-necked Turtle

e Krefft's River Turtle

Plate 13a

Marbled Southern Gecko

(also called Marbled Gecko)

Christinus marmoratus

ID: A mid-sized gecko, grey to light brown with darker brown or black reticulations across the head and body; juveniles often have a row of yellow or orange spots down the tail; to 7 cm (2.75 in) plus tail.

HABITAT: The most southerly of the Australian geckos, generally found in moister, cooler areas where it shelters under bark or in crevices of standing trees; it also uses rock crevices for shelter.

REGIONS: NSW, VIC

Plate 13b

Eastern Stone Gecko
(also called Stone Gecko)

Diplodactylus vittatus

ID: A smallish gecko, brown with a pale grey or cream zig-zag stripe down the middle of the back; this pale stripe merges into the similarly colored top of the head; small, light spots are scattered along the sides; to 5 cm (2 in) plus tail.

HABITAT: A ground-dwelling gecko that occurs in moister forests to arid shrublands; shelters during the day under stones and logs or in rotting timber.

REGIONS: TRQ, TEQ, NSW, VIC

Plate 13c

Bynoe's Prickly Gecko

Heteronotia binoei

ID: A mid-sized gecko with numerous keeled scales on the body and tail (which give rise to the term "prickly" gecko); brown with a pattern of black and pale bands that are very distinct in some populations; to 5 cm (2 in) plus tail.

HABITAT: Found in most habitats within its range; this ground-dwelling gecko shelters under ground debris and fallen timber or in rock crevices.

REGIONS: CYP, TRQ, TEQ, NSW

Plate 13d

Southern Leaf-tailed Gecko

(also called Broad-tailed Gecko)

Phyllurus platurus

ID: A large gecko with a flattened appearance and long spindly legs; grey to dark red-brown, mottled with darker flecks; many low, pointed tubercles (lumps) on the body and on original tails (regenerated tails are smooth; see p. xxx); to 8 cm (3 in) plus tail.

HABITAT: A rock-dwelling gecko found in sandstone areas, where it shelters in caves, crevices, and overhangs; in suburban areas it will often move into garages or basements.

REGIONS: NSW

Plate 13e

Barking Gecko
(also called Thick-tailed Gecko)

Underwoodisaurus milii

ID: A large gecko, dark purple-black or dark red-brown with cream to yellow spots forming bands across the body, more pronounced on the head and neck; the head is large and the tail is carrot-shaped, with several bands of white spots; to 8 cm (3 in) plus tail.

HABITAT: Usually rocky country with woodlands or shrublands.

REGIONS: TEQ, NSW, VIC

Plate 13 **315**

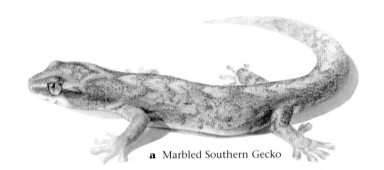

a Marbled Southern Gecko

b Eastern Stone Gecko

c Bynoe's Prickly Gecko

d Southern Leaf-tailed Gecko

e Barking Gecko

Plate 14a

Burton's Snake-lizard
Lialis burtonis

ID: This lizard has a very distinctive wedge-shaped head; the color is extremely variable, cream to deep brown, either plain or with stripes and/or blotches; the tail is as long as or longer than the body and there is a small flap (vestige of a hindlimb) on either side of the vent; to 30 cm (12 in) plus tail.

HABITAT: Found on the coast and ranges in most habitats; it usually shelters in grass clumps, under dense bushes, or in ground litter; active during the day and at night.

REGIONS: CYP, TRQ, TEQ, NSW

Plate 14b

Southern Scaly-foot
Pygopus lepidopodus

ID: A large legless lizard, grey to reddish brown, either with no markings or with a series of black dashes in rows down the body; the body scales are keeled and not at all glossy; the tail is twice the length of the body and there is a large hindlimb flap; to 25 cm (10 in) plus tail.

HABITAT: Found from the coastal dunes to the forests of the ranges.

REGIONS: TRQ, TEQ, NSW, VIC

Plate 14c

Sand Goanna
(also called Racehorse Goanna, Bungarra)
Varanus gouldii

ID: A mid-sized goanna, cream to brown with lighter and darker spots that form irregular bands across the body; a black stripe behind the eye; the tail is banded except for the tip, which is cream or yellow; to 1.6 m (5.3 ft) but averages 1.2 m (4 ft).

HABITAT: Day-active, this goanna prefers sandy areas in woodlands, shrublands, or grasslands; it shelters in burrows and will quickly make for one if disturbed.

REGIONS: CYP, TRQ, TEQ, NSW

Plate 14d

Lace Monitor
Varanus varius

ID: A large goanna, grey to dull blue-black with scattered cream or yellow markings that tend to form bands across the body and limbs; the tail is banded in blue-black and cream; one distinctive form has broad yellow and black bands along the body and tail; to 2 m (6.6 ft) but averages 1.5 m (4.9 ft).

HABITAT: An arboreal lizard that also forages on the ground, it occurs in the forests and tall woodlands of the coast and ranges.

REGIONS: TRQ, TEQ, NSW, VIC

Plate 14 **317**

a Burton's Snake-lizard

b Southern Scaly-foot

c Sand Goanna

d Lace Monitor

Plate 15 (*See also*: Dragons, p. 97)

Plate 15a
Jacky Lizard
Amphibolurus muricatus
ID: A mid-sized dragon, grey to pale brown with a series of lighter patches along the back that sometimes merge to form two stripes down the middle of the back; the inside of the mouth is yellow; body scales are keeled and there are numerous pointed tubercles (lumps) on the sides and limbs; a series of enlarged scales down the middle of the back form a crest from the head to the tail; to 35 cm (14 in) but averages 25 cm (10 in).

HABITAT: A semi-arboreal dragon that occurs in coastal heaths and woodlands.

REGIONS: TRQ, TEQ, NSW, VIC

Plate 15b
Frilled Lizard
Chlamydosaurus kingii
ID: A large dragon, grey to reddish brown with a pattern of darker markings that make it quite inconspicuous when lying on a tree branch; the frill is normally only extended when the lizard feels threatened; it will then often run off on its hind legs to the nearest tree; to 90 cm (35 in) but averages 75 cm (30 in).

HABITAT: Day-active and mainly arboreal; occurs in tropical to warm temperate woodlands; also occurs in Papua New Guinea.

REGIONS: CYP, TRQ, TEQ

Plate 15c
Eastern Water Dragon
Physignathus lesueurii
ID: A large dragon with a crest of enlarged spiny scales from the nape to the tail; grey to olive green with blackish crossbars; there is often a broad black stripe from the eye through the ear to the neck; the throat and belly are often flushed with red or olive green; to 90 cm (35 in) but averages 60 cm (24 in).

HABITAT: Occurs along the coast and adjacent ranges; a day-active and semi-aquatic lizard found in tree- and scrub-lined watercourses.

REGIONS: CYP, TRQ, TEQ, NSW, VIC

Plate 15d
Eastern Bearded Dragon
Pogona barbata
ID: A large dragon with a large triangular head; well-developed beard with numerous enlarged spines across the throat; grey, yellowish brown, or red-brown with a grey belly that has scattered darker circles; the inside of the mouth is yellow; to 55 cm (22 in) but averages 40 cm (16 in).

HABITAT: Day-active and semi-arboreal, these dragons are often encountered basking on roads or perched on nearby fence posts; they occur in open forests and woodlands.

REGIONS: TRQ, TEQ, NSW

Plate 15 319

a Jacky Lizard

b Frilled Lizard

c Eastern Water Dragon

d Eastern Bearded Dragon

Plate 16a
Shaded-litter Rainbow Skink
(also called Striped Rainbow Skink)
Carlia munda
ID: A small lizard, grey to dark brown with flecks of white, pale brown, and black; there is a thin white stripe from the lips to at least the forelimb; breeding males have a bluish throat and red sides; four fingers and five toes; to 4.5 cm (1.8 in) plus tail.

HABITAT: Found from the coastal dunes to the ranges; occurs in grasslands, shrublands, and woodlands.

REGIONS: CYP, TRQ, TEQ

Plate 16b
Southern Rainbow Skink
Carlia tetradactyla
ID: A small lizard, deep brown with white spots or dashes in three to four rows; the sides are orange, and in breeding males the lower sides are blue-green; four fingers and five toes; to 5 cm (2 in) plus tail.

HABITAT: Tussock grasslands along the lower ranges; occurs around rocky outcrops.

REGIONS: TEQ, NSW, VIC

Plate 16c
Fence Skink
(also called Wall Lizard)
Cryptoblepharus virgatus
ID: This small lizard has a flattened body and a distinct cream or white stripe along each side of the back, bordered by a broad black stripe; overall, the body can be silver-grey to brown to almost black; to 4.5 cm (1.8 in) plus tail.

HABITAT: Usually arboreal and found in open woodlands and shrublands; also utilizes rock outcrops and walls. Common on fences and buildings.

REGIONS: CYP, TRQ, TEQ, NSW, VIC

Plate 16d
Robust Ctenotus
Ctenotus robustus
ID: A mid-sized, robust lizard, fawn to brown in color with a pale stripe along each side of the back; there is a broad black stripe, edged with white, down the middle of the back; to 12 cm (5 in) plus tail.

HABITAT: Open woodlands, shrublands, or grasslands where there is thick ground cover.

REGIONS: CYP, TRQ, TEQ, NSW, VIC

Plate 16e
Coppertail
Ctenotus taeniolatus
ID: A small lizard, brown with a black stripe, edged in white, down the middle of the back; several black and white stripes along the sides; the tail is a conspicuous orange or reddish brown; to 8 cm (3 in) plus tail.

HABITAT: Occurs from coastal heaths to the ranges, usually in rocky areas where there is loose surface rock and sandy soil.

REGIONS: TRQ, TEQ, NSW, VIC

Plate 16 321

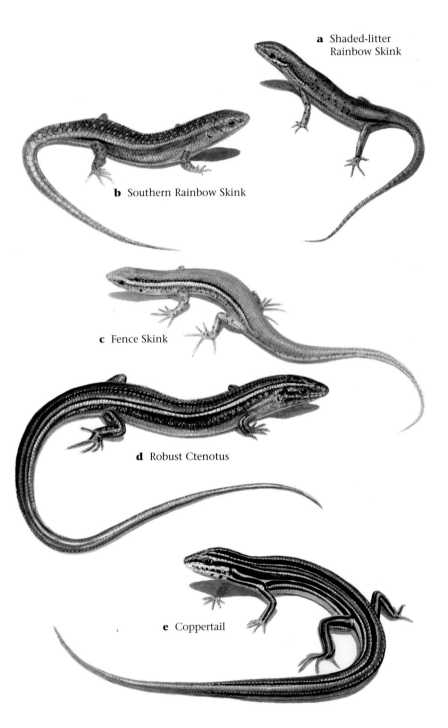

a Shaded-litter Rainbow Skink

b Southern Rainbow Skink

c Fence Skink

d Robust Ctenotus

e Coppertail

Plate 17a
Major Skink
Egernia frerei
ID: A large lizard that ranges in color from light to dark brown; a darker streak on each scale forms narrow lines from neck to tail; some may have pale spots on the sides; lips are cream with a brown bar; to 20 cm (8 in) plus tail.

HABITAT: Day-active but shy, this lizard is usually observed basking in sunlight at the edge of forest clearings. When disturbed, it quickly retreats into dense ground cover.

REGIONS: CYP, TRQ, TEQ, NSW

Plate 17b
Cunningham's Skink
(also called Cunningham's Spiny-tailed Skink)
Egernia cunninghami
ID: A large, robust lizard with scales on the back and sides that are keeled with a single sharp spine; variable in color, ranging from light brown to black; some populations have no patterning while others have patterns of dark brown and cream spots; belly is pink to orange; to 20 cm (8in) plus tail.

HABITAT: Occurs in rock outcrops from the coast through to the ranges; some populations in the northern parts of its range utilize hollows and cracks in dead trees.

REGIONS: TEQ, NSW, VIC

Plate 17c
Land Mullet
Egernia major
ID: A large, bulky lizard, highly polished black or dark brown; juveniles have white spots along the sides that disappear as the animal grows; to 30 cm (12 in) plus tail.

HABITAT: Day-active but shy, it basks in forest clearings but always close to cover; occurs in rainforests and wetter open forests.

REGIONS: TRQ, TEQ, NSW

Plate 17d
Tree Skink
Egernia striolata
ID: A mid-sized lizard with a somewhat flattened head and body; scales are not glossy and are slightly rough, dark brown to grey with scattered pale flecks; there is a broad lighter band along the top of the sides and a dark band below this; the white lips are edged with brown and the belly is yellow to orange; to 12 cm (4.5 in) plus tail.

HABITAT: Usually arboreal and found in cracks and hollows or under the bark of dead trees; in some areas this species is rock-dwelling, sheltering in crevices or under rock slabs on outcrops.

REGIONS: TRQ, TEQ, NSW, VIC

Plate 17e
White's Skink
(also called White's Rock Skink)
Egernia whitii
ID: A mid-sized lizard, grey-brown to red-brown with no markings or with two wide, dark stripes down the back, each stripe enclosing a series of creamy spots; the sides have patches of black and scattered white spots; to 10 cm (4 in) plus tail.

HABITAT: A day-active species that lives in burrow systems beneath rocks, often in family groups. Occurs in both lowland and alpine habitats.

REGIONS: TEQ, NSW, VIC, TAS

Plate 17 **323**

a Major Skink

b Cunningham's Skink

c Land Mullet

d Tree Skink

e White's Skink

Plate 18a
Warm-temperature Water Skink
Eulamprus heatwolei
ID: A mid-sized skink, coppery brown with numerous black flecks on the head and scattered black flecks on the body; a pale stripe runs from above the eye to the forelimb; upper sides are black with cream spots and the lower sides are cream with black flecks; belly is cream with black blotches on the throat and chin; to 10 cm (4 in) plus tail.

HABITAT: Usually associated with watercourses or seepages; in the southern part of its range it occurs on the coastal plains, while further north it is found in the ranges.

REGIONS: NSW, VIC

Plate 18b
Eastern Water Skink
(also called Golden Water Skink, Water Skink)
Eulamprus quoyii
ID: A mid-sized lizard, golden olive-brown with scattered dark flecks and a pale, narrow stripe from the eye along the side of the back to the tail; the upper sides are black with cream or yellow spots, and the belly is white to yellow, often mottled with grey or black flecks; to 11 cm (4.3 in) plus tail.

HABITAT: Found on the coast and ranges where it occurs near permanent water courses; day-active.

REGIONS: TRQ, TEQ, NSW

Plate 18c
Bar-sided Forest Skink
Eulamprus tenuis
ID: This mid-sized skink is fawn-grey to deep brown with scattered dark blotches that form a variegated pattern; upper sides are dark brown, broken into blotches, and the lower sides are cream with darker markings; to 8 cm (3 in) plus tail.

HABITAT: Found in the ranges and lowlands where it occurs in rainforests and other moist habitats; normally active early morning and late afternoon.

REGIONS: TRQ, TEQ, NSW

Plate 18d
Grass Skink
(also called Dark-flecked Garden Sunskink)
Lampropholis delicata
ID: A small lizard, dark grey-brown to deep brown with an occasional narrow, darker stripe down the middle of the back and some dark flecks; the upper sides are dark brown; to 4.5 cm (1.8 in) plus tail.

HABITAT: Found from the coast to the ranges in moist habitats; day-active.

REGIONS: TRQ, TEQ, NSW, VIC, TAS

Plate 18e
Garden Skink
(also called Pale-flecked Garden Sunskink)
Lampropholis guichenoti
ID: A small skink, grey-brown to coppery-brown, usually with a dark stripe down the middle of the back; normally has scatterings of paler and darker scales on the body; a dark brown stripe with a pale edge runs from the nostril through the eye and along the sides to the base of the tail; to 4.5 cm (1.8 in) plus tail.

HABITAT: Found from the coast to the ranges in woodlands, heaths, and grasslands; also common in suburban gardens; day-active.

REGIONS: TEQ, NSW, VIC

Plate 18 **325**

a Warm-temperature Water Skink

b Eastern Water Skink

c Bar-sided Forest Skink

d Grass Skink

e Garden Skink

Plate 19a
Tussock Cool Skink
Pseudemoia entrecasteauxii
ID: A small lizard, light brown to olive-brown with a darker stripe down the middle of the back and a pale stripe along the upper part of each flank; upper flanks are brown with a whitish stripe running from the ear to the tail; the stripe becomes flushed with red or orange in mature males; to 5.5 cm (2.2 in) plus tail.

HABITAT: Cool woodlands and tussock grasslands; often seen in large numbers basking on tussocks and in litter; day-active.

REGIONS: NSW, VIC, TAS

Plate 19b
Weasel Skink
(also called Weasel Shadeskink)
Saproscincus mustelina
ID: A small lizard with a distinctive creamy white stripe at the back corner of each eye and usually an orange to red stripe above the hind limbs and onto the tail; russet brown in color with scattered pale flecks and white to yellow underneath; to 5 cm (2 in) plus tail.

HABITAT: Prefers dense ground cover in moist, semi-shaded areas; occurs along the coast and in the Great Dividing Range; day-active.

REGIONS: NSW, VIC

Plate 19c
Pink-tongued Skink
Hemisphaeriodon gerrardii
ID: A large lizard with a broad, angular head, slender body, and long, prehensile tail; juveniles have a bright blue tongue that usually changes to pink as they mature; silver-grey to light brown in color with black or brown crossbands that are sometimes indistinct; some have no crossbands; to 20 cm (8 in) plus tail.

HABITAT: Found along the coast and ranges usually in rainforests or wet open forests, although it will also utilize the moist areas of other forests; semi-arboreal; forages at dusk and early evening.

REGIONS: TRQ, TEQ, NSW

Plate 19d
Blotched Bluetongue
Tiliqua nigrolutea
ID: A large lizard with a broad, triangular head and a stout body; it has short limbs, a short tail, and a blue tongue; dark brown to black in color with a series of large yellow to pink blotches; to 30 cm (12 in) plus tail.

HABITAT: Lowland slopes and ranges in woodlands, heaths, and grasslands; day-active.

REGIONS: NSW, VIC, TAS

Plate 19e
Common Bluetongue
(also called Eastern Bluetongue)
Tiliqua scincoides
ID: One of the world's largest skinks, with a triangular head, stout body, and blue tongue; silver-grey to yellow-brown in color with a series of dark brown to black crossbars; often has a wide black streak from the eye to the ear; northern populations are brown with paler bars that are often broken up; to 35 cm (14 in) plus tail.

HABITAT: Found from the coast to the ranges to the grasslands of the interior. Common in suburban gardens; day-active.

REGIONS: CYP, TRQ, TEQ, NSW, VIC

Plate 19f
Shingleback
(also called Sleepy Lizard, Boggi, Stumpy Lizard)
Trachydosaurus rugosus
ID: Unmistakable large lizard with large pine-cone-like scales, short rounded tail, large angular head, and blue tongue; red-brown to black in color, with or without cream or yellow spots; to 25 cm (10 in) plus tail.

HABITAT: Found west of the ranges in most habitats; commonly seen on roads particularly in spring; day-active.

REGIONS: TEQ, NSW, VIC

Plate 19　**327**

a Tussock Cool Skink

b Weasel Skink

c Pink-tongued Skink

d Blotched Bluetongue

e Common Bluetongue

f Shingleback

Plate 20a

Southern Cassowary
Casuarius casuarius

ID: Huge, ostrich-like, shaggy black bird; blue head with horny helmet, or "casque;" two reddish wattles hang down from front of neck; to 1.8 m (5.9 ft) tall, females a bit larger than males.

HABITAT: Tropical rainforests, especially in and around clearings and near watercourses; often solitary, but also in pairs or small groups. CAUTION: If approached, may kick and cause injury.

REGIONS: CYP, TRQ

NOTE: The Cape York Peninsula population of this species is vulnerable; the more southerly Queensland population, around Cairns, is endangered.

Plate 20b

Emu
Dromaius novaehollandiae

ID: Huge, shaggy, ostrich-like bird; brown, grey-brown, or blackish with blue or whitish skin showing on head and throat; blackish feathers on head, neck; to 2 m (6.5 ft), females a bit larger than males. CAUTION: If approached, may kick and cause injury.

HABITAT: Woodlands, heathlands, grasslands, scrublands, and agricultural areas; usually in pairs or small groups.

REGIONS: CYP, TRQ, TEQ, NSW, VIC

Plate 20c

Orange-footed Scrubfowl
Megapodius reinwardt

ID: Large chicken-like ground bird with crested head, brown above, grey below, with orange legs and feet; 40 to 50 cm (16 to 20 in).

HABITAT: Coastal rainforests and beach scrub areas; in pairs or small groups.

REGIONS: CYP, TRQ

Plate 20d

Australian Brush-turkey
Alectura lathami

ID: Large, black, chicken-like ground bird with bare red head and neck; yellow wattle hangs from neck, more prominent in males; side-to-side flattened tail; to 70 cm (28 in).

HABITAT: Tropical and temperate rainforests and some drier forests and scrublands; solitary, in pairs, or in small groups.

REGIONS: CYP, TRQ, TEQ, NSW

Plate 20e

Brown Quail
Coturnix ypsilophora

ID: Small brownish/tan/grey chicken-like ground bird, heavily streaked; small, dark V-shaped bands on chest, short black bill, and dark "ear-spot;" to 21 cm (8 in).

HABITAT: Grasslands, savannahs, pastures and other agricultural areas, and swampy regions; solitary, in pairs, or in small groups; day- and dusk-active.

REGIONS: CYP, TRQ, TEQ, NSW, VIC, TAS

Plate 20 329

a Southern Cassowary

b Emu

c Orange-footed Scrubfowl

d Australian Brush-turkey

e Brown Quail

Plate 21a
Magpie Goose
Anseranas semipalmata
ID: Large black and white goose with black, nobbed head and black neck; narrow, hooked, reddish or yellowish bill; orangish legs; male to 92 cm (36 in); female to 82 cm (32 in); wingspan to 1.7 m (5.6 ft).

HABITAT: Wetlands, including swamps, ponds with marsh vegetation, wet grasslands, and river floodplains; often in large groups.

REGIONS: CYP, TRQ, TEQ, NSW

Plate 21b
Black Swan
Cygnus atratus
ID: Large black water bird with red bill and white wingtips, most visible in flight; black legs; male to 1.4 m (4.6 ft); female to 1.2 m (3.9 ft); wingspan to 2 m (6.5 ft).

HABITAT: Open stretches of fresh and salt water, estuaries, swamps, lakes, flooded pastures and fields, and mudflats; solitary to large groups.

REGIONS: CYP, TRQ, TEQ, NSW, VIC, TAS

Plate 21c
Australian Shelduck
(also called Mountain Duck)
Tadorna tadornoides
ID: Largish black duck with brownish chest, white ring around neck; female has white eye-ring and white at base of bill; wing has white and green patches, most visible in flight; to 72 cm (28 in), females a bit smaller; wingspan to 1.3 m (4.3 ft).

HABITAT: Open stretches of shallow fresh or brackish water, marshes, and agricultural areas; occasionally in open woodlands or on the ocean; in pairs or groups.

REGIONS: NSW, VIC, TAS

Plate 21d
Cape Barren Goose
Cereopsis novaehollandiae
ID: Large grey goose with black tail and reddish legs, short black bill mostly covered with yellowish or greenish cere (naked skin at base of bill), white crown; to 1 m (3.3 ft).

HABITAT: Chiefly seen in agricultural areas— pastures and fields—and also along shores of lakes, ponds, and swamps; breeds on offshore islands; usually in groups.

REGIONS: VIC, TAS

Plate 21e
Australian Wood Duck
(also called Maned Duck)
Chenonetta jubata
ID: Mid-sized, grey, goose-like duck with dark head and black stripes on back, speckled breast, and a small dark bill; male has difficult-to-see dark "mane" of longish feathers on back of neck; female has lighter brown head and light eye stripes; to 56 cm (22 in); wingspan to 80 cm (31 in).

HABITAT: Lakes, ponds, swamps, bays, coastal areas; dry, wet, or flooded pastures and grasslands; open woodlands, often in trees near water; in pairs or flocks.

REGIONS: CYP, TRQ, TEQ, NSW, VIC, TAS

Plate 21f
Plumed Whistling-Duck
Dendrocygna eytoni
ID: Mid-sized brownish duck with reddish brown sides and long whitish/creamy flank feathers (plumes) that sweep upwards along back; pinkish bill and legs; to 60 cm (24 in), females a bit smaller; wingspan to 90 cm (35 in).

HABITAT: Grasslands, pastures and other agricultural areas; ponds and other wetlands, mangroves, and river flood plains; in small to large groups.

REGIONS: CYP, TRQ, TEQ, NSW, VIC

Plate 21 **331**

a Magpie Goose

F

M

b Black Swan

d Cape Barren Goose

c Australian Shelduck

e Australian Wood Duck

f Plumed Whistling-Duck

Plate 22 (*See also*: Ducks and Grebes, p. 129; Penguins, p. 127)

Plate 22a
Pacific Black Duck
Anas superciliosa
ID: Largish dark brown duck with black and white striped head; green, bluish, or purplish patch on top of wing, visible in flight; olive-grey or yellow-green legs and feet; to 61 cm (24 in); wingspan to 93 cm (37 in).

HABITAT: Open water with associated vegetation—ponds, lakes, pools, including in city parks, swamps, and mudflats; in pairs or groups.

REGIONS: CYP, TRQ, TEQ, NSW, VIC, TAS

Plate 22b
Grey Teal
Anas gracilis
ID: Mid-sized greyish brown duck with white throat and around base of bill, green and white patches on top of wing are visible in flight; to 48 cm (19 in); wingspan to 67 cm (26 in).

HABITAT: Most water habitats; in pairs or groups.

REGIONS: CYP, TRQ, TEQ, NSW, VIC, TAS

Plate 22c
Chestnut Teal
Anas casatanea
ID: Mid-sized brownish duck with red eyes; male has green head, reddish brown chest, black rump; female is more greyish brown, lacks male's bright colors, and is similar to Grey Teal (but lacks white throat area); to 46 cm (18 in).

HABITAT: Coastal marshes and swamps, mudflats, estuaries, and lakes; in pairs or groups.

REGIONS: TRQ, TEQ, NSW, VIC, TAS

Plate 22d
Hardhead
(also called White-eyed Duck)
Aythya australis
ID: Largish brown duck with large white wing patches visible in flight; male has white eyes and black bill with light tip; female is lighter brown than the male, with dark eyes and blue-grey bill; to 55 cm (22 in); wingspan to 70 cm (28 in).

HABITAT: Wetlands of all types, marshes, swamps, lakes, and ponds, but usually prefers deep, open water with emergent vegetation; solitary, in pairs, or in groups; dives.

REGIONS: CYP, TRQ, TEQ, NSW, VIC, TAS

Plate 22e
Australasian Grebe
Tachybaptus novaehollandiae
ID: Small brownish/greyish duck-like water bird with straight, dark bill with light tip; black head with reddish brown stripe, yellow patch on face; in winter (nonbreeding) plumage, top of head is dark, bottom of head and throat is white, bill is grey-brown; to 27 cm (10.5 in).

HABITAT: Fresh water—ponds, lakes, and other wetlands; often in small groups; dives.

REGIONS: CYP, TRQ, TEQ, NSW, VIC, TAS

Plate 22f
Little Penguin
(also called Fairy Penguin)
Eudyptula minor
ID: Cute little penguin, black to bluish grey above, white below; 40 to 45 cm (16 to 18 in).

HABITAT: Beaches and up to 300 m (1,000 ft) inland from the ocean, mostly on sandy or rocky islands; feeds at sea; usually solitary.

REGIONS: NSW, VIC, TAS

Plate 22 333

a Pacific Black Duck

b Grey Teal

c Chestnut Teal

M, B

F

d Hardhead

M

B

e Australasian Grebe

f Little Penguin

Plate 23a
Wedge-tailed Shearwater
(also called Muttonbird)
Puffinus pacificus
ID: Mid-sized seabird with wedge-shaped tail, light or flesh-colored legs, and greyish bill with down-curved dark tip; the dark form is dark above, greyish below, with lighter throat and chest; light form is dark above, light below; to 46 cm (18 in); wingspan to 1.1 m (42 in).

HABITAT: Pelagic (and sometimes coastal) seabird; rarely comes to land except to nest in burrows on small islands, including many in the Great Barrier Reef.

REGIONS: CYP, TRQ, NSW

Plate 23b
Short-tailed Shearwater
(also called Muttonbird)
Puffinus tenuirostris
ID: Mid-sized brown-black or sooty grey seabird with lighter throat and short, rounded tail; small light mark around/under eye; narrow, dark bill and dark feet; some with light patches under wings, visible in flight; to 42 cm (16.5 in); wingspan to 90 cm (35.5 in).

HABITAT: Pelagic (and sometimes coastal) seabird; rarely comes to land except to nest in burrows on small offshore islands.

REGIONS: NSW, VIC, TAS

Plate 23c
Wilson's Storm-Petrel
Oceanites oceanicus
ID: Small sooty brown/black seabird with white rump and pale grey bar/crescent on top of each wing, visible in flight; black, squarish tail; short, dark bill; to 19 cm (7.5 in); wingspan to 42 cm (16.5 in).

HABITAT: Pelagic seabird; rarely near land except to nest in burrows or rock crevices on Antarctic or sub-Antarctic islands; feeds over ocean, hovering, often with legs patting or breaking the water's surface.

REGIONS: TRQ, NSW, VIC, TAS

Plate 23d
Lesser Frigatebird
Fregata ariel
ID: Large black seabird with long, narrow, pointed wings and long forked tail; male with reddish throat patch (seen only during breeding displays) and long grey bill with down-curved tip; thin white line from under body to under wing, visible in flight; female with white breast that extends as partial collar on neck, pinkish or grey bill, reddish eye-ring; to 81 cm (32 in); wingspan to 1.9 m (6.2 ft).

HABITAT: Found around seashores; often seen soaring high over coastal areas and islands; breeds on islands off northeastern Australia.

REGIONS: CYP, TRQ, NSW

Plate 23e
Australian Pelican
Pelecanus conspicillatus
ID: Very large white seabird with black on wings and tail, huge bill (to 50 cm, 19.5 in, long in males; to 40 cm, 15.5 in, in females) with pinkish bill pouch; to 1.8 m (5.9 ft), males larger than females; wingspan to 2.6 m (8.5 ft).

HABITAT: Fresh and salt water, coastal and inland; prefers shallow areas of large bodies of water; usually in flocks; flies in groups, in lines, or in V-formations.

REGIONS: CYP, TRQ, TEQ, NSW, VIC, TAS

Plate 23 **335**

a Wedge-tailed Shearwater

b Short-tailed Shearwater

L

D

D

c Wilson's Storm-Petrel

M

d Lesser Frigatebird

F

B

e Australian Pelican

Plate 24a
Australasian Gannet
Morus serrator
ID: Large white seabird with creamy/yellowish head, black patches on wings and tail, greyish pointed bill, vertical black line on throat, and black legs; to 92 cm (36 in); wingspan to 2 m (6.5 ft).

HABITAT: Coastal; found along seashores and bays.

REGIONS: TRQ, NSW, VIC, TAS

Plate 24b
Darter
Anhinga melanogaster
ID: Large waterbird with long, sharply pointed bill and rounded black tail; male black or dark grey with white stripe from face to side of neck; female grey or grey-brown with whitish underparts; to 94 cm (37 in); wingspan to 1.2 m (3.9 ft).

HABITAT: Fresh and salt water—lakes, ponds, rivers, swamps, and sometimes coastal bays and estuaries; usually prefers shallow areas.

REGIONS: CYP, TRQ, TEQ, NSW, VIC

Plate 24c
Brown Booby
Sula leucogaster
ID: A mid-sized seabird with brown back, brown neck, white belly, and grey/bluish (male) or yellowish (female) cone-shaped, sharply pointed bill; greenish or yellowish feet and pointed wings; youngsters with pale brownish belly; to 76 cm (30 in); wingspan to 1.4 m (4.5 ft).

HABITAT: Oceans, both in- and off-shore; sometimes coastal, in harbors, bays, and estuaries; often seen around islands in the Great Barrier Reef.

REGIONS: CYP, TRQ, NSW

Plate 24d
Great Cormorant
Phalacrocorax carbo
ID: Largish black waterbird with white patch on face and thigh (during breeding season), bare yellow skin on face and throat, dark narrow bill with down-curved tip; 70 to 90 cm (28 to 35 in); wingspan to 1.5 m (5 ft); largest Australian cormorant.

HABITAT: Fresh and salt water; usually prefers larger lakes, rivers, reservoirs, and along coasts in bays and estuaries; solitary or in groups.

REGIONS: CYP, TRQ, TEQ, NSW, VIC, TAS

Plate 24e
Little Black Cormorant
Phalacrocorax sulcirostris
ID: Mid-sized black waterbird (often with a greenish sheen), slender, dark/greyish bill with down-curved tip, dark facial skin; to 64 cm (25 in); wingspan to 1 m (3.3 ft).

HABITAT: Fresh and salt water; lakes, ponds, rivers, reservoirs, and, less often, along coasts in mangroves, bays, and estuaries; often in groups.

REGIONS: CYP, TRQ, TEQ, NSW, VIC, TAS

Plate 24f
Little Pied Cormorant
Phalacrocorax melanoleucos
ID: Mid-sized black waterbird with white face and underparts, black and white neck, relatively short, yellowish bill with down-curved tip; during breeding, black head feathers may form crest; to 62 cm (24 in); wingspan to 90 cm (35 in); the smallest Australian cormorant.

HABITAT: Fresh and salt water; lakes, ponds, rivers, reservoirs, and along coasts in bays, estuaries, and around islands; solitary or in groups.

REGIONS: CYP, TRQ, TEQ, NSW, VIC, TAS

Plate 24 **337**

a Australasian Gannet

b Darter

c Brown Booby

d Great Cormorant

e Little Black Cormorant

f Little Pied Cormorant

Plate 25a
White-faced Heron
Egretta novaehollandiae
ID: Largish grey bird with white face, dark bill, and yellowish legs; wings darker grey than underparts; to 69 cm (27 in); wingspan to 1 m (3.3 ft).

HABITAT: Fresh water and saltwater wetlands—lakes, ponds, marshes, wet pastures and grasslands, mudflats, and shorelines; solitary or in groups.

REGIONS: CYP, TRQ, TEQ, NSW, VIC, TAS

Plate 25b
Eastern Reef Egret
Egretta sacra
ID: Largish waterbird with long, thickish bill; dark form (shown) is dark grey with white vertical stripe on throat, greyish to yellowish bill and legs; light form is white with yellowish bill and yellowish grey legs; immature dark form (shown) is brownish grey; immature light form is white; to 68 cm (27 in); wingspan to 1 m (3.3 ft).

HABITAT: Shallow coastal waters—shorelines, reefs, beaches, mangroves, mudflats, estuaries, and tidal rivers; solitary or in small groups.

REGIONS: CYP, TRQ, TEQ, NSW, VIC

Plate 25c
White-necked Heron
Ardea pacifica
ID: Large waterbird with blackish grey back and wings, white head and neck with dark spots on front of neck, and grey or grey-brown streaked underparts. Small white patch on shoulder part of wing, blackish/greyish bill and legs, dark red plumes on back during breeding; immature has more spots on neck; to 75 to 105 cm (30 to 41 in); wingspan to 1.6 m (5.2 ft).

HABITAT: Freshwater wetlands—shallow ponds, pools, flooded pastures, and grasslands; solitary or in groups.

REGIONS: CYP, TRQ, TEQ, NSW, VIC, TAS

Plate 25d
Pied Heron
Ardea picata
ID: Mid-sized bluish grey waterbird with white throat/neck, dark or black crested head, and yellow bill and legs; 43 to 55 cm (17 to 22 in).

HABITAT: Coastal wetlands, including lakes, ponds, lagoons, swamps, tidal rivers, mudflats, mangroves, and also garbage dumps; solitary or in groups.

REGIONS: CYP, TRQ

Plate 25e
Cattle Egret
Ardea ibis
ID: Mid-sized white bird with large head, thickish neck, yellow bill, and yellowish or dark legs; during breeding, head, chest, and back turn a yellowish buff or orangish buff color, and bill and legs are reddish or orangish; immature bird is white with yellowish bill; 50 cm (20 in); wingspan to 91 cm (3 ft).

HABITAT: Pastures, agricultural areas, freshwater wetlands, and garbage dumps; usually in groups, often in association with grazing mammals.

REGIONS: CYP, TRQ, TEQ, NSW, VIC, TAS

Plate 25f
Little Egret
Egretta garzetta
ID: Largish white waterbird with dark or black bill, yellow or orangish facial skin, and dark legs; two long head plumes during breeding; 55 to 65 cm (22 to 26 in); wingspan to 1 m (3.3 ft).

HABITAT: Fresh water and saltwater wetlands—ponds, marshes, mudflats, and mangroves; solitary or in small groups.

REGIONS: CYP, TRQ, TEQ, NSW, VIC, TAS

Plate 25 **339**

a White-faced Heron

b Eastern Reef Egret

IM

A

IM

d Pied Heron

c White-necked Heron

A

B

NB

e Cattle Egret

f Little Egret

Plate 26a
Rufous Night-heron
Nycticorax caledonicus

ID: Large reddish brown waterbird with short neck, black crown, white underparts, and black bill; immature similar, but with white spots on back and dark streaks on underparts; to 65 cm (26 in); wingspan to 1.1 m (3.6 ft).

HABITAT: Fresh or brackish water, usually along forested margins of lakes, pools, rivers, streams, estuaries, and swamps; also wet meadows and flooded grasslands, saltmarshes, and on small offshore islands; usually in small groups.

REGIONS: CYP, TRQ, TEQ, NSW, VIC, TAS

Plate 26b
Great Egret
Ardea alba

ID: Large white waterbird with yellow facial skin and yellowish bill, often with dark tip, and dark or black legs; breeding birds have black bills, long, white, lacy plumes along back and, at times, greenish facial skin; 80 to 104 cm (31 to 41 in); wingspan to 1.6 m (5.2 ft).

HABITAT: Freshwater wetlands—shallow parts of rivers, lakes, ponds, estuaries, and mudflats; solitary or in groups.

REGIONS: CYP, TRQ, TEQ, NSW, VIC, TAS

Plate 26c
Australian White Ibis
(also called Sacred Ibis)
Threskiornis molucca

ID: Large white (often dirty white) waterbird with black head and long black bill; when standing, some wing feathers give appearance of black "tail"; wings have black tips visible in flight; to 76 cm (30 in); wingspan to 1.2 m (3.9 ft). (The Glossy Ibis, *Plegadis falcinellus*, is smaller and brown or purplish brown. The Straw-necked Ibis, *Threskiornis spinicollis*, has dark, iridescent upperparts with a white neck and underparts.)

HABITAT: Inland wetlands, especially swamps, but also pastures, gardens, garbage dumps, mudflats, mangroves, and coastal lagoons; solitary or in groups.

REGIONS: CYP, TRQ, TEQ, NSW, VIC, TAS

Plate 26d
Royal Spoonbill
Platalea regia

ID: Large white waterbird with large, black, spoon-shaped bill and black legs; during breeding, has yellow patch above eye, red mark on forehead, and white head plumes; to 80 cm (31 in); wingspan to 1.2 m (3.9 ft). (The Yellow-billed Spoonbill is white with yellowish bill and legs.)

HABITAT: Fresh and saltwater wetlands—ponds, flooded pastures, billabongs, mangroves, mudflats, estuaries, and saltmarshes; solitary or in groups.

REGIONS: CYP, TRQ, TEQ, NSW, VIC, TAS

Plate 26e
Black-necked Stork
(also called Jabiru)
Ephippiorhynchus asiaticus

ID: Very large white waterbird with glossy, greenish black head and neck, huge black bill, black wing patches and tail, and reddish legs; to 1.3 m (4.3 ft); wingspan to 2 m (6.5 ft).

HABITAT: Coastal and subcoastal wetlands—lakes, ponds, pools, mangroves, mudflats, and also open woodlands; solitary, in pairs, or in groups.

REGIONS: CYP, TRQ, TEQ, NSW

Plate 26f
Brolga
Grus rubicunda

ID: Very large grey bird with grey crown, red head with grey "ear" patch, blackish chin pouch ("dewlap"), and dark legs; to 1.4 m (4.6 ft); wingspan to 2.3 m (7.5 ft). (The Sarus Crane, *Grus antigone*, of northern Queensland is similar, but also has red on neck, reddish legs, and lacks dewlap.)

HABITAT: Coastal and subcoastal freshwater wetlands, mostly swamps; also grasslands, pastures, and croplands; in pairs or groups.

REGIONS: CYP, TRQ, TEQ, NSW, VIC

Plate 26 341

a Rufous Night-heron

b Great Egret

c Australian
White Ibis

IM

d Royal Spoonbill

B

F Brolga

e Black-necked Stork

Plate 27a
Osprey
Pandion haliaetus
ID: Large brownish bird with white head, dark stripe through eye, grey legs; wing in flight has backward "bend"; underside of wing is white with darker stripes and markings; to 65 cm (26 in), with males a bit smaller; wingspan to 1.7 m (5.5 ft).

HABITAT: Mostly coastal and up larger rivers; also on and around islands; seen flying or perched in trees near water; usually solitary or in pairs.

REGIONS: CYP, TEQ, NSW

Plate 27b
Black-shouldered Kite
Elanus axillaris
ID: Mid-sized grey hawk with white head and chest, black wing patch, and black eye mark (extending from in front of to behind the eye); to 38 cm (15 in), with males a bit smaller; wingspan to 94 cm (37 in). (The Letter-winged Kite, *Elanus scriptus*, is very similar to the Black-shouldered Kite, but its black eye mark extends only in front of the eye.)

HABITAT: Open woodlands and grasslands with trees, coastal areas, and agricultural districts; solitary or in small groups.

REGIONS: CYP, TRQ, TEQ, NSW, VIC

Plate 27c
Black Kite
Milvus migrans
ID: Largish dark brown hawk with pale head, dark eye mark, and lighter brown wing patch; longish, forked tail; underside of wing and tail have light bars; immature is a bit paler, with more streaks and spots; to 58 cm (23 in), males a bit smaller; wingspan to 1.3 m (4.3 ft).

HABITAT: Grasslands and savannahs, woodlands, trees along watercourses, coastal areas, and garbage dumps; often in groups.

REGIONS: CYP, TRQ, TEQ, NSW, VIC, TAS

Plate 27d
Whistling Kite
Haliastur sphenurus
ID: Largish brown hawk with darker brown wings and black flight feathers; underside of wing shows conspicuous black patches in flight; body has light streakin; longish, rounded, pale brown tail; immature has more conspicuous light streaks and spots; to 59 cm (23 in), males a bit smaller; wingspan to 1.3 m (4.3 ft).

HABITAT: Open woodlands, often near water, wetland areas, and seashores; solitary or in small groups.

REGIONS: CYP, TRQ, TEQ, NSW, VIC, TAS

Plate 27e
Brahminy Kite
Haliastur indus
ID: Largish brown hawk with white head and chest, rounded tail with white tip; in flight, underside of wing is black-tipped; to 51 cm (20 in), males a bit smaller; wingspan to 1.2 m (3.9 ft).

HABITAT: Primarily coastal and around islands— beaches, estuaries and up rivers, mudflats, mangroves, and harbors; solitary, in pairs, or in small groups.

REGIONS: CYP, TRQ, NSW

Plate 27 343

b Black-shouldered Kite

a Osprey

A

d Whistling Kite

IM

c Black Kite

e Brahminy Kite

Plate 28a
Brown Goshawk
Accipiter fasciatus
ID: Large grey-brown hawk with reddish brown ring encircling neck, reddish brown underparts with fine white horizontal bars, and yellowish legs; in flight, underside of wing is brown in front, light/greyish behind; immature is brown above, brown and white striped below; to 56+ cm (22+ in), males a bit smaller; wingspan to 96 cm (3.2 ft).

HABITAT: Open forests, woodlands, and other areas with trees, including parks and gardens; also scrub and agricultural areas; solitary or in pairs.

REGIONS: CYP, TRQ, TEQ, NSW, VIC, TAS

Plate 28b
White-bellied Sea-Eagle
Haliaeetus leucogaster
ID: Very large white raptor with grey back and wings, white tail, and whitish legs; in flight, underside of wing is white in front, dark behind; immature is brownish white with greyish brown wings; to 85 cm (33 in), males a bit smaller; wingspan to 2.1 m (6.9 ft).

HABITAT: Coastal areas, inland rivers, and lakes; solitary, in pairs, or in small groups.

REGIONS: CYP, TRQ, TEQ, NSW, VIC, TAS

Plate 28c
Wedge-tailed Eagle
Aquila audax
ID: Very large dark brown to blackish raptor with pale brown band on wing; in flight, underside of wing is dark brown with whitish line at mid-wing; long, dark, wedge-shaped tail; feathered legs; to 104 cm (3.4 ft), males a bit smaller; wingspan to 2.2 m (7.2 ft).

HABITAT: Open forests and woodlands, grasslands, and scrub areas; often in trees along watercourses and lake shores; solitary, in pairs, or in small groups.

REGIONS: CYP, TRQ, TEQ, NSW, VIC, TAS

Plate 28d
Brown Falcon
Falco berigora
ID: Large raptor with light and dark cheek patches, light throat, and greyish legs; light form is reddish brown above, whitish below, with brown feathers over upper legs; dark form is uniformly brown; to 51 cm (20 in), males a bit smaller; wingspan to 1.2 m (3.9 ft).

HABITAT: Open woodlands, grasslands, agricultural districts, and roadsides; usually solitary or in pairs.

REGIONS: CYP, TRQ, TEQ, NSW, VIC, TAS

Plate 28e
Nankeen Kestrel
Falco cenchroides
ID: Small reddish brown raptor with black eye mark, dark grey bill, light underparts with dark streaks, dark wingtips, and yellow legs; male has grey head, grey tail with black bar; to 35 cm (14 in), males a bit smaller; wingspan to 80 cm (31 in).

HABITAT: Most open habitats—grasslands, agricultural areas, roadsides, beach areas, and some open woodlands; solitary, in pairs, or in small groups.

REGIONS: CYP, TRQ, TEQ, NSW, VIC, TAS

Plate 28 **345**

a Brown Goshawk

IM

F

b White-bellied Sea-Eagle

IM

A

c Wedge-tailed Eagle

D

M

L

F

e Nankeen Kestrel

d Brown Falcon

Plate 29 (*See also*: Marsh and Stream Birds, p. 130)

Plate 29a
Buff-banded Rail
Gallirallus philippensis
ID: Small brown-olive waterbird; grey chest with reddish brown band; remainder of underparts finely barred black and white; white line above eye, reddish brown stripe through eye to neck; reddish brown bill; immature is duller and lacks reddish brown markings; to 33 cm (13 in).

HABITAT: Coastal marshes, swamps, wet pastures, and other wetlands; agricultural areas, gardens, scrubby woodlands, and heathlands; solitary, in pairs, or in small groups.

REGIONS: CYP, TRQ, TEQ, NSW, VIC

Plate 29b
Purple Swamphen
Porphyrio porphyrio
ID: Striking, mid-sized, black wading bird with bluish head, neck, and chest; red bill and forehead "shield"; reddish legs; to 48 cm (19 in).

HABITAT: Marshes, swamps, and streams, and along lake and pond shores; often in small groups.

REGIONS: CYP, TRQ, TEQ, NSW, VIC, TAS

Plate 29c
Tasmanian Native-hen
Gallinula mortierii
ID: Mid-sized, olive-brown, chicken-like bird with dark tail held erect, grey underparts, white patch on side, yellowish bill, and grey legs; to 48 cm (19 in).

HABITAT: Grassy areas usually near water, agricultural areas, and roadsides; solitary, in pairs, or in groups; flightless.

REGIONS: TAS

Plate 29d
Dusky Moorhen
Gallinula tenebrosa
ID: Smallish grey waterbird with brown wings and rump, red bill with yellow tip, red forehead "shield," dark tail, reddish and olive legs; to 38 cm (15 in).

HABITAT: Freshwater wetlands—marshes, swamps, and lakes; in pairs or small groups.

REGIONS: CYP, TRQ, TEQ, NSW, VIC, TAS

Plate 29e
Eurasian Coot
Fulica atra
ID: Smallish grey waterbird with darker grey head, white bill and forehead "shield," red eyes, grey legs; to 39 cm (15 in).

HABITAT: All kinds of wetlands; in pairs or groups, sometimes large flocks.

REGIONS: CYP, TRQ, TEQ, NSW, VIC, TAS

Plate 29f
Comb-crested Jacana
Irediparra gallinacea
ID: Small brown waterbird with white face and neck, yellowish or reddish bill with dark tip, red "comb" on head, black chest band, white belly, dull green legs, and very long green toes; to 26 cm (10 in), with males a bit smaller.

HABITAT: Swamps, lakes, ponds, billabongs, and lagoons, as long as there is floating vegetation to walk on; solitary, in pairs, or in small groups.

REGIONS: CYP, TRQ, TEQ, NSW

Plate 29 **347**

a Buff-banded Rail

b Purple Swamphen

c Tasmanian Native-hen

d Dusky Moorhen

e Eurasian Coot

f Comb-crested Jacana

Plate 30a
Bush Stone-curlew
(also called Bush Thick-knee)
Burhinus grallarius
ID: Largish, brown-grey, streaked wading bird found on land; whitish forehead, stripe above eye, throat, and underparts; dark line runs from below to behind the large yellowish eye; light shoulder patch; to 58 cm (23 in); wingspan to 1 m (3.3 ft).

HABITAT: Open woodlands, grasslands, coastal scrub areas, golf courses, roadsides, and settled regions; solitary, in pairs, or in small groups.

REGIONS: CYP, TRO, TEO, NSW, VIC

Plate 30b
Australian Bustard
Ardeotis australis
ID: Large brown ground bird with greyish white neck and underparts; male has black crown and chest band; female has brownish crown; to 1.2 m (3.9 ft), females a bit smaller; wingspan to 2.2 m (7.2 ft).

HABITAT: Grasslands, grassy woodlands, scrublands, and some crop areas; solitary, in pairs, or in small groups.

REGIONS: CYP, TRO, TEO

Plate 30c
Eastern Curlew
Numenius madagascariensis
ID: Large brown- and black-streaked wading bird with lighter belly, very long down-curved bill, the lower part of which is pinkish at base, darker at end; to 66 cm (26 in); wingspan to 1.1 m (3.6 ft).

HABITAT: Coastal—sandy beaches, mudflats, estuaries, and mangroves; sometimes lake shores and wet grasslands; solitary or in groups of various sizes; migrant that breeds in Asia.

REGIONS: CYP, TRO, NSW, VIC, TAS

Plate 30d
Black-winged Stilt
Himantopus himantopus
ID: Mid-sized, slender white marsh bird with black wings, back, and back of neck; long, reddish legs; long, thin, straight black bill; to 39 cm (15 in).

HABITAT: Fresh and saltwater marshes, swamps, estuaries, mudflats, lake shores, and ponds; in pairs or small groups.

REGIONS: CYP, TRO, TEO, NSW, VIC, TAS

Plate 30e
Masked Lapwing
Vanellus miles
ID: Mid-sized wading bird, brown above, white below, with conspicuous yellow facial wattles; black on top of head and, in some regions, on side of neck and chest; pale yellow bill, dark reddish legs, and dark-tipped spur on shoulder, often not noticeable; to 38 cm (15 in); wingspan to 85 cm (33 in).

HABITAT: Grasslands, pastures, mudflats, beaches, and parks in settled areas; in pairs or groups.

REGIONS: CYP, TRO, TEO, NSW, VIC, TAS

Plate 30 **349**

a Bush Stone-curlew

b Australian Bustard

c Eastern Curlew

d Black-winged Stilt

e Masked Lapwing

Plate 31a
Red-necked Stint
Calidris ruficolis

ID: Very small grey or grey-brown shorebird with whitish underparts; dark line through eye, pale stripe above eye; black legs; shortish black bill; in breeding plumage, head, neck, and chest are reddish brown; to 16 cm (6 in).

HABITAT: Beaches, mudflats, saltwater and freshwater wetlands, both coastal and inland; in small or large groups; migrant that breeds in Asia.

REGIONS: CYP, TRQ, TEQ, NSW, VIC, TAS

Plate 31b
Bar-tailed Godwit
Limosa lapponica

ID: Largish, grey-brown, mottled and barred shorebird with very long, slightly upturned bill with dark tip; dark legs; male in breeding plumage has reddish head, neck, and underparts; to 45 cm (18 in).

HABITAT: Coastal mudflats and estuaries; sometimes along inland lake shores and flooded grassy areas; usually in small to large groups; migrant that breeds in Asia.

REGIONS: CYP, TRQ, NSW, VIC, TAS

Plate 31c
Sharp-tailed Sandpiper
Calidris acuminata

ID: Small greyish or brownish shorebird with whitish underparts and dark streaks on breast and sides; reddish brown crown; dark line through eye, light line above eye; straight or slightly down-curved black bill; yellow-olive legs; in breeding plumage, back is mottled reddish brown and black; to 22 cm (8.5 in).

HABITAT: Mudflats, marshes, mangroves, various wetlands, pastures, and croplands, both coastal and inland; migrant that breeds in Asia.

REGIONS: CYP, TRQ, TEQ, NSW, VIC, TAS

Plate 31d
Pacific Golden Plover
Pluvialis fulva

ID: Mid-sized, slender, long-legged shorebird; mottled brown and golden above, lighter below; whitish or buffy line above eye; shortish black bill; dark legs; to 26 cm (10 in).

HABITAT: Mudflats, beaches, estuaries, and mangroves; also fields, agricultural areas, lawns, parks, meadows, and sometimes in inland areas; solitary or in small groups; migrant that breeds in Asia.

REGIONS: CYP, TRQ, NSW, VIC, TAS

Plate 31e
Red-capped Plover
Charadrius ruficapillus

ID: Very small grey-brown shorebird with white face and underparts; dark eye-stripe; black bill and legs; white line on wing seen in flight; in breeding plumage, crown and back of neck are reddish with black markings; to 16 cm (6 in).

HABITAT: Beaches, mudflats, and saltwater and freshwater wetlands, both coastal and inland; solitary, in pairs, or in groups.

REGIONS: CYP, TRQ, TEQ, NSW, VIC, TAS

Plate 31f
Black-fronted Dotterel
Elseyornis melanops

ID: Very small brown shorebird with white throat and belly; black forehead, eye-stripe, and chest bar in V shape; reddish brown shoulder bar; red bill with dark tip; pinkish legs; to 17 cm (6.5 in).

HABITAT: Freshwater wetlands—lake shores, ponds, rivers, and mudflats; occasionally in coastal saltwater areas; solitary, in pairs, or in small groups.

REGIONS: CYP, TRQ, TEQ, NSW, VIC, TAS

Plate 31   **351**

a Red-necked Stint

NB

c Sharp-tailed Sandpiper

b Bar-tailed Godwit

NB

NB

NB

e Red-capped Plover

NB

d Pacific Golden Plover

B

f Black-fronted Dotterel

Plate 32a

Pied Oystercatcher
Haematopus longirostris
ID: Largish black wading bird with white belly; long, straight, reddish bill; red eye and eye-ring and pinkish legs; to 50 cm (20 in).

HABITAT: Coastal beaches, mudflats, estuaries, and islands; solitary, in pairs, or in groups.

REGIONS: CYP, TRQ, NSW, VIC, TAS

Plate 32b

Pacific Gull
Larus pacificus
ID: Large white gull with blackish wings; white rear edge on wings, seen mainly in flight; white tail with black bar; large yellow bill with reddish tip; light eye; yellow legs; immature is pale brown with yellowish or horn-colored bill with dark tip, grey-brown legs; to 64 cm (25 in); wingspan to 1.5 m (4.9 ft).

HABITAT: Coastal areas, offshore islands, and sometimes around garbage dumps; solitary, in pairs, or in small groups.

REGIONS: NSW, VIC, TAS

Plate 32c

Silver Gull
Larus novaehollandiae
ID: Mid-sized white gull with grey back and wings; red bill and legs; black wingtips, seen especially in flight; white tail; light eye; immature with brown mottled back and wings, yellowish brown bill with dark tip, brownish legs; older immatures ("sub-adults"; shown) are less brown and have reddish bills, legs; to 45 cm (18 in); wingspan to 94 cm (37 in).

HABITAT: Coastal and inland, near water; also in town parks, gardens, and garbage dumps; usually in groups.

REGIONS: CYP, TRQ, TEQ, NSW, VIC, TAS

Plate 32d

Roseate Tern
Sterna dougallii
ID: Smallish tern, grey above, pink-tinged white below, with black cap and back of neck; bill is usually blackish with red base but varies, and is sometimes all red with dark tip; red legs; in flight, white underneath (new feathers pinkish) with long white tail streamers; to 38 cm (15 in); wingspan to 80 cm (31 in).

HABITAT: Usually seen in offshore waters and around islands, but sometimes coastal; solitary or in small groups.

REGIONS: CYP, TRQ

Plate 32e

Crested Tern
(also called Greater Crested Tern)
Sterna bergii
ID: Mid-sized tern, grey above, white below, with black bushy cap and legs; yellowish or yellow-orange bill; nonbreeding plumage is less black on head; to 50 cm (19.5 in); wingspan to 1.1 m (3.6 ft).

HABITAT: Coastal and offshore waters; some lakes and larger rivers; solitary or in groups.

REGIONS: CYP, TRQ, NSW, VIC, TAS

Plate 32 **353**

a Pied Oystercatcher

IM

b Pacific Gull

A

IM

A

d Roseate Tern

B

c Silver Gull

e Crested Tern

B

NB

Plate 33a
Sooty Tern
Sterna fuscata
ID: Mid-sized tern, dark/blackish above, white below, with forked tail; white forehead, black stripe through eye; straight, pointed, black bill; to 44 cm (17 in); wingspan to 94 cm (37 in).

HABITAT: Offshore waters and oceanic islands; usually in groups.

REGIONS: CYP, TRQ, NSW, VIC

Plate 33b
Common Tern
Sterna hirundo
ID: Smallish tern, grey above, white below, with white forehead and black cap; dark shoulder bar seen when perched; forked tail; black bill; black or orangish legs; in breeding plumage, black head cap extends to forehead, underparts are greyish, and white tail, edged in black, has long trailing streamers; to 38 cm (15 in); wingspan to 80 cm (31 in).

HABITAT: Mainly offshore waters, but also coastal—beaches, bays, estuaries—and sometimes freshwater wetlands, or lakes near the coast; solitary or in small groups; migrant that breeds in Asia.

REGIONS: CYP, TRQ, NSW, VIC

Plate 33c
Whiskered Tern
(also called Marsh Tern)
Chlidonias hybridus
ID: Small tern, grey above, white below; white forehead, black streaked cap, blackish or dark reddish bill and legs; in breeding plumage with solid black cap, black forehead, dark grey chest/belly, dark red bill; to 28 cm (11 in); wingspan to 70 cm (28 in).

HABITAT: Fresh water and saltwater wetlands, including marshes, lakes, ponds, and estuaries; usually in small to mid-sized groups.

REGIONS: CYP, TRQ, TEQ, NSW, VIC

Plate 33d
Common Noddy
(also called Brown Noddy)
Anous stolidus
ID: Mid-sized brown seabird with dark brown wings and a long, dark, narrow tail; light head cap; narrow black mark or line between eye and long, straight black bill; black legs; to 44 cm (17 in); wingspan to 85 cm (33 in).

HABITAT: Open seas, shorelines, and reefs around offshore and oceanic islands; in groups; nest on islands in trees, shrubs, or on the ground.

REGIONS: CYP, TRQ

Plate 33e
Black Noddy
(also called White-capped Noddy)
Anous minutus
ID: Smallish sooty black seabird with long, dark, narrow forked tail; light head cap; slender, straight, black bill; legs usually dark brown, but orangish/yellowish in some populations or in some seasons; to 37 cm (14.5 in); wingspan to 68 cm (27 in).

HABITAT: Open seas and shorelines of offshore and oceanic islands; in groups; nest in trees on islands.

REGIONS: CYP, TRQ

Plate 33 **355**

a Sooty Tern

b Common Tern

NB

IM

A

c Whiskered Tern

d Common Noddy

e Black Noddy

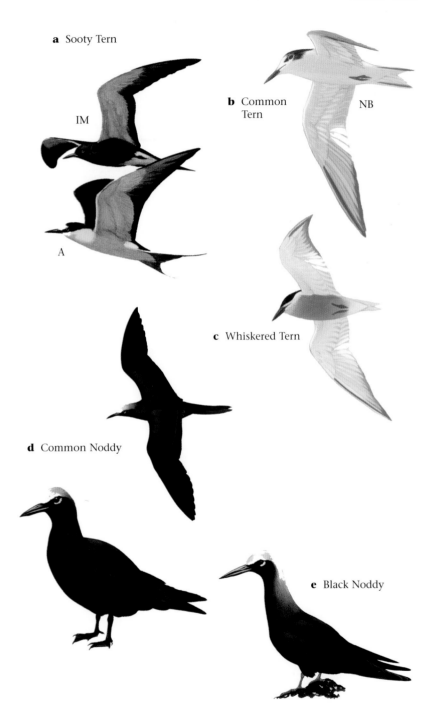

Plate 34a

Spotted Turtle-Dove
(also called Spotted Dove)
Streptopelia chinensis
ID: Mid-sized greyish/brownish dove with rosy or pinkish grey chest and belly; black patch on neck with white spots; to 31 cm (12 in).

HABITAT: Open and semi-open areas; open woodlands, forest clearings and edges, scrub areas, cultivated areas, parks, gardens, and urban areas; arborial or terrestrial. Introduced; native to southern Asia.

REGIONS: TRQ, NSW, VIC, TAS

Plate 34b

Brown Cuckoo-Dove
(also called Brown Pigeon)
Macropygia amboinensis
ID: Largish, brown, long-tailed pigeon, darker above, lighter below; male especially with iridescent sheen on back of neck; female mottled on throat and chest; to 44 cm (17 in).

HABITAT: Rainforests, especially around edges, and thickets; in pairs or small groups.

REGIONS: CYP, TRQ, NSW

Plate 34c

Emerald Dove
(also called Emerald Ground-Dove)
Chalcophaps indica
ID: Smallish brown or pinkish brown pigeon with green wings; two light bars across back; orangish bill and legs; male with white shoulder patch; to 28 cm (11 in).

HABITAT: Rainforests, especially at edges, wetter open forests, mangroves, costal heathlands, and scrub areas; solitary, in pairs, or in small groups.

REGIONS: CYP, TRQ, NSW

Plate 34d

Peaceful Dove
(also called Zebra Dove)
Geopelia striata
ID: Small brownish grey dove with dark barring; bluish face/throat in some areas; bluish skin around eye; reddish legs; to 21 cm (8 in).

HABITAT: Open, dry areas including lightly forested sites, woodlands, dry scrublands, agricultural sites, and other peopled areas—town parks, gardens, city streets; terrestrial; in pairs or groups.

REGIONS: CYP, TRQ, TEQ, NSW, VIC

Plate 34e

Common Bronzewing
Phaps chalcoptera
ID: Mid-sized brown or greyish pigeon with scaled pattern on back and wings; male with yellowish/buffy forehead and dark purplish or brownish crown, pinkish grey chest; female duller, with grey forehead; to 36 cm (14 in).

HABITAT: Woodlands, heaths, and scrub areas; arboreal or terrestrial; in pairs or small groups.

REGIONS: TRQ, TEQ, NSW, VIC, TAS

Plate 34 357

a Spotted Turtle-Dove

b Brown Cuckoo-Dove

c Emerald Dove

d Peaceful Dove

e Common Bronzewing

Plate 35a
Rose-crowned Fruit-Dove
Ptilinopus regina
ID: Small dull green pigeon with reddish crown; yellow line separates crown from greyish head; orangish belly; yellow tail tip; immature is mostly green with yellowish belly; to 25 cm (10 in). (The Superb Fruit-Dove, *Ptilinopus superbus*, a similar, coastal rainforest species, has a red/purplish crown, large orange neck collar, conspicuous dark/blackish chest band, and whitish underparts.)

HABITAT: Rainforests, open forests, mangroves, and fruit trees; solitary, in pairs, or in small groups.

REGIONS: CYP, TRQ, NSW

Plate 35b
Crested Pigeon
Ocyphaps lophotes
ID: Mid-sized grey pigeon with conspicuous black crest; reddish eye-ring and legs; white and black bars on wings; greenish wing patch; dark tail tipped white; to 34 cm (13 in).

HABITAT: Wooded grassy areas, agricultural districts, roadsides, along watercourses, and in settled areas; solitary, in pairs, or in groups.

REGIONS: TRQ, TEQ, NSW, VIC

Plate 35c
Wompoo Fruit-Dove
Ptilinopus magnificus
ID: Large, long-tailed green pigeon with grey head, purplish chest, yellow belly, and yellow/gold wing bar; to 45 cm (18 in).

HABITAT: Rainforests, some adjacent open forests, and fruit trees; solitary, in pairs, or in small groups.

REGIONS: CYP, TRQ, NSW

Plate 35d
Pied Imperial-Pigeon
(also called Torresian Imperial-Pigeon)
Ducula bicolor
ID: Large white pigeon with white and black wings, white and black tail, pale yellowish bill, grey/bluish legs; to 44 cm (17 in).

HABITAT: Coastal rainforests, some adjacent open forests, coastal scrub areas, mangroves, and islands; solitary or in groups.

REGIONS: CYP, TRQ

Plate 35e
Topknot Pigeon
Lopholaimus antarcticus
ID: Large grey pigeon with odd grey and brown crest; dark grey/blackish wings; dark tail with light bar; reddish bill, eye, and legs; to 46 cm (18 in).

HABITAT: Rainforests, some adjacent open forests, and fruit trees; usually in groups.

REGIONS: CYP, TRQ, NSW

Plate 35f
Wonga Pigeon
Leucosarcia melanoleuca
ID: Largish grey pigeon with white forehead; large white V-shaped breast marking; white underparts with black spots; reddish legs; to 42 cm (16 in).

HABITAT: Rainforests, open forests, scrub areas, agricultural districts, and roadsides; solitary, in pairs, or in small groups.

REGIONS: TRQ, TEQ, NSW, VIC

Plate 35　359

a Rose-crowned Fruit-Dove

IM

A

b Crested Pigeon

c Wompoo Fruit-Dove

d Pied Imperial-Pigeon

e Topknot Pigeon

f Wonga Pigeon

Plate 36a

Red-tailed Black-Cockatoo
Calyptorhynchus banksii
ID: Large black parrot with large helmet-like crest and large bill; male with blackish bill, red patch on tail; female with lighter bill, yellow spotting on body, and orangish tail panels; to 65 cm (25.5 in), female a bit smaller.

HABITAT: Open forests and woodlands, scrublands, and grasslands; often along watercourses; in pairs or small to very large groups.

REGIONS: CYP, TRQ, TEQ, NSW

Plate 36b

Palm Cockatoo
(also called Great Black Cockatoo)
Probosciger aterrimus
ID: Large dark grey or black parrot with huge grey bill, long crest, and pinkish or red naked skin on cheek; to 62 cm (24.5 in), female a bit smaller.

HABITAT: Rainforests and adjacent open forests, often along watercourses; solitary, in pairs, or in small groups.

REGIONS: CYP

NOTE: Endangered, CITES Appendix I listed

Plate 36c

Yellow-tailed Black-Cockatoo
Calyptorhynchus funereus
ID: Large black parrot with yellow ear patch, yellow panels in tail; male with blackish bill and reddish eye-ring; female with lighter bill and grey eye-ring; to 62 cm (24.5 in).

HABITAT: Rainforests, open forests and woodlands, heathlands, and scrublands; usually in pairs or small groups.

REGIONS: TRQ, TEQ, NSW, VIC, TAS

Plate 36d

Sulphur-crested Cockatoo
Cacatua galerita
ID: Large white parrot with blackish bill, conspicuous yellow crest; yellowish tinge under wings and tail; to 52 cm (20.5 in).

HABITAT: Rainforests, open forests, agricultural areas, and around human settlements; often along watercourses; usually in small to large groups.

REGIONS: CYP, TRQ, TEQ, NSW, VIC, TAS

Plate 36e

Galah
Cacatua roseicapilla
ID: Mid-sized parrot, grey above, pinkish or reddish below; light crest on reddish head; male eye is brown, female eye is red; to 36 cm (14 in).

HABITAT: Open woodlands, shrublands, grasslands, along watercourses, agricultural areas, and around human settlements; in pairs or small to large groups.

REGIONS: CYP, TRQ, TEQ, NSW, VIC, TAS

Plate 36f

Gang-gang Cockatoo
Callocephalon fimbriatum
ID: Mid-sized dark grey parrot with light feather edges; male has red-crested head; female has grey-crested head; to 37 cm (14.5 in).

HABITAT: Open forests and woodlands, scrublands, agricultural areas, and around human settlements; in pairs or groups.

REGIONS: NSW, VIC

Plate 36 **361**

c Yellow-tailed
Black-Cockatoo

a Red-tailed
Black-Cockatoo

F

M

b Palm
Cockatoo

F

M

f Gang-gang
Cockatoo

e Galah

d Sulphur-crested
Cockatoo

Plate 37a
Rainbow Lorikeet
Trichoglossus haematodus
ID: Smallish multicolored parrot with blue head, green back and wings, yellow-green collar, red-orange chest, blue belly, and red bill; to 32 cm (12.5 in).

HABITAT: Rainforests, open forests and woodlands, heathlands, scrublands, agricultural areas, and around human settlements; in pairs or groups.

REGIONS: CYP, TRQ, TEQ, NSW, VIC

Plate 37b
Scaly-breasted Lorikeet
Trichoglossus chlorolepidotus
ID: Small green parrot with yellow scaly marking on neck and underparts; red bill; orangish/reddish under wings, seen in flight; to 24 cm (9.5 in).

HABITAT: Open forests and woodlands, and around human settlements; in pairs or groups.

REGIONS: CYP, TRQ, TEQ, NSW, VIC

Plate 37c
Musk Lorikeet
Glossopsitta concinna
ID: Small green parrot with red forehead and ear patch; yellowish patch near shoulder; black bill with reddish tip; to 23 cm (9 in).

HABITAT: Open forests and woodlands, agricultural areas, and around human settlements; in pairs or groups.

REGIONS: TRQ, NSW, VIC, TAS

Plate 37d
Purple-crowned Lorikeet
Glossopsitta porphyrocephala
ID: Very small green parrot with orangish forehead, purple crown, yellowish ear patch, pale blue chest, black bill; red patch under wing, seen in flight; to 17 cm (6.5 in).

HABITAT: Open forests and woodlands, agricultural areas, and around human settlements; usually in groups, often with other lorikeet species.

REGIONS: NSW, VIC

Plate 37e
Australian King-Parrot
Alisterus scapularis
ID: Male is mid-sized red parrot with green wings and lighter green wingbar; blue rump; dark tail; bill reddish above, dark below. Female is green with red belly and reddish grey or grey bill. To 43 cm (17 in).

HABITAT: Rainforests, open forests and adjacent agricultural areas, along watercourses, and around human settlements; in pairs or small groups.

REGIONS: TRQ, TEQ, NSW, VIC

Plate 37 363

a Rainbow Lorikeet

b Scaly-breasted Lorikeet

c Musk Lorikeet

d Purple-crowned Lorikeet

M

F

e Australian King-Parrot

Plate 38a
Crimson Rosella
Platycercus elegans
ID: Smallish to mid-sized red parrot with blue cheek, shoulder patch, and tail; black scaled pattern on back and onto wings; whitish bill; immature is olive green with reddish forehead, throat, and under tail; to 36 cm (14 in).

HABITAT: Rainforests, open forests and woodlands, agricultural areas, roadsides, and around human settlements; in pairs or small groups.

REGIONS: TRQ, NSW, VIC

Plate 38b
Red-winged Parrot
Aprosmictus erythropterus
ID: Smallish green parrot with red shoulder patch, bluish lower back, and orange-red bill; male has light green head and body, dark green wings, back, and tail; female is pale green, duller, with less red in wing; to 32 cm (12.5 in).

HABITAT: Open forests, grassy woodlands, adjacent agricultural areas, shrublands, and trees along watercourses; in pairs or small groups.

REGIONS: CYP, TRQ, TEQ

Plate 38c
Eastern Rosella
Platycercus eximius
ID: Smallish parrot with red head and chest, yellow back with black scaling, yellow/pale green lower breast and belly; red patch under tail; white cheek, blue-edged dark tail; to 32 cm (12.5 in).

HABITAT: Open forests and woodlands, grasslands, agricultural areas, roadsides, and around human settlements; in pairs or small groups.

REGIONS: TRQ, NSW, VIC, TAS

Plate 38d
Pale-headed Rosella
Platycercus adscitus
ID: Smallish parrot with yellow or whitish head; white and blue cheek patches; black and white scaled back; light blue underparts or just lower breast and belly; red patch under tail; to 31 cm (12 in).

HABITAT: Open forests and woodlands, scrublands, agricultural areas, roadsides, and around human settlements; in pairs or small groups.

REGIONS: CYP, TRQ, TEQ, NSW

Plate 38e
Swift Parrot
Lathamus discolor
ID: Small green parrot with red forehead and throat; blue crown and sometimes a subtle bluish cheek patch; brownish yellow bill; dark reddish tail; red patches under wings and tail, seen in flight; to 25 cm (10 in).

HABITAT: Open forests and woodlands, agricultural areas, and around human settlements; usually in small groups.

REGIONS: TEQ, NSW, VIC, TAS

Plate 38f
Red-rumped Parrot
Psephotus haematonotus
ID: Male is smallish green parrot with yellowish shoulder patch and belly, red rump; female is olive green or grey-green with lighter underparts; blue patch on wing; green rump. To 28 cm (11 in).

HABITAT: Open forests and woodlands, grasslands, agricultural areas, roadsides, and around human settlements; in pairs or groups.

REGIONS: TRQ, TEQ, NSW, VIC

Plate 38 365

a Crimson Rosella

A

IM

b Red-winged Parrot

c Eastern Rosella

d Pale-headed Rosella

e Swift Parrot

F

M

f Red-rumped Parrot

Plate 39a
Shining Bronze-Cuckoo
Chrysococcyx lucidus
ID: Smallish, metallic greenish above, white and bronze-brown/greenish striped below; brown cap; to 18 cm (7 in).

HABITAT: Rainforests, open forests and woodlands, and gardens; solitary or in small groups; migrant that breeds in Australia, winters in New Guinea area.

REGIONS: CYP, TRQ, TEQ, NSW, VIC, TAS

Plate 39b
Fan-tailed Cuckoo
Cacomantis flabelliformis
ID: Mid-sized, dark grey above, with greyish throat and buffy, pale brown, or reddish brown chest/belly; dark, wedge-shaped tail with white markings on feathers; yellowish eye-ring; to 27 cm (10.5 in).

HABITAT: Rainforests, open forests and woodlands (often along watercourses), roadsides, mangroves, and orchards; solitary or in pairs.

REGIONS: CYP, TRQ, TEQ, NSW, VIC, TAS

Plate 39c
Brush Cuckoo
Cacomantis variolosus
ID: Mid-sized, grey-brown above, with pale grey throat and buffy or pale reddish brown chest/belly; grey eye-ring; white-tipped squarish tail; to 25 cm (10 in).

HABITAT: Rainforests, open forests and woodlands, scrub areas with trees, roadsides, mangroves, and trees along watercourses; solitary, in pairs, or in small groups.

REGIONS: CYP, TRQ, TEQ, NSW, VIC

Plate 39d
Common Koel
Eudynamys scolopacea
ID: Large, with red eye and greyish or cream bill; male is glossy black with bluish tinge; female is brown with white spots above, light with dark bars below; black cap, dark throat stripe. To 46 cm (18 in).

HABITAT: Rainforest margins, open forests and woodlands, trees along watercourses and in agricultural areas, and parks; solitary, in pairs, or in small groups; migrant that breeds in Australia, winters in New Guinea/Indonesia.

REGIONS: CYP, TRQ, TEQ, NSW

Plate 39e
Channel-billed Cuckoo
Scythrops novaehollandiae
ID: Very large, with huge, straw-colored, slightly down-curved bill; grey above, light/whitish below; red skin around eye; white-tipped tail; to 66 cm (26 in).

HABITAT: Rainforests, open forests and woodlands, trees along watercourses and in agricultural areas, and roadsides; solitary, in pairs, or in small groups; migrant that breeds in New Guinea/Indonesia.

REGIONS: CYP, TRQ, TEQ, NSW

Plate 39f
Pheasant Coucal
Centropus phasianinus
ID: Large ground bird with blackish head/chest, brown back/wings with lighter streaks; black bill; red eye; in nonbreeding plumage, brown streaked head/chest, lighter bill; to 70 cm (27.5 in), female a bit larger.

HABITAT: Grasslands, scrub areas, heathlands, cane fields, and roadsides; solitary or in pairs.

REGIONS: CYP, TRQ, TEQ, NSW

Plate 39 **367**

a Shining Bronze-Cuckoo

b Fan-tailed Cuckoo

c Brush Cuckoo

d Common Koel

F

M

e Channel-billed Cuckoo

NB

B

f Pheasant Coucal

Plate 40a
Barn Owl
Tyto alba
ID: Mid-sized owl with heart-shaped face; tawny/brownish or greyish above with spots, light below with dark spots; dark eyes; pale bill; to 40 cm (16 in), female a bit larger.

HABITAT: Open forests and woodlands, forest edges, grasslands, and agricultural districts; solitary or in pairs; nocturnal.

REGIONS: CYP, TRQ, TEQ, NSW, VIC, TAS

Plate 40b
Southern Boobook
Ninox novaeseelandiae
ID: Smallish brown owl with light spots on wings; underparts brown with light streaks or mottling; green-yellow eyes surrounded by dark patches (facial mask); in northeast Queensland, overall dark reddish brown with only faint light streaking below; to 36 cm (14 in), female a bit larger.

HABITAT: Rainforests, open forests and woodlands, scrub areas, agricultural districts, orchards, and gardens; solitary, in pairs, or in small groups; nocturnal.

REGIONS: CYP, TRQ, TEQ, NSW, VIC, TAS

Plate 40c
Barking Owl
Ninox connivens
ID: Mid-sized owl, brown or grey with white spots on wings; underparts white with dark streaks; large yellow eyes without surrounding dark facial mask; to 44 cm (17 in), male a bit larger.

HABITAT: Open forests and woodlands, scrub areas, and trees near watercourses; solitary or in pairs; nocturnal.

REGIONS: CYP, TRQ, TEQ, NSW, VIC

Plate 40d
Tawny Frogmouth
Podargus strigoides
ID: Large grey bird, streaked and mottled, darker above, lighter below; large head; wide, heavy bill; male darker, female often with brownish highlights; to 53 cm (21 in); much larger in the southeast; male a bit larger.

HABITAT: Rainforest edges, open forests and woodlands, trees along watercourses, roadsides, and parks; in pairs and small groups; dusk- and night-active.

REGIONS: CYP, TRQ, TEQ, NSW, VIC, TAS

Plate 40e
Australian Owlet-nightjar
Aegotheles cristatus
ID: Smallish grey owl-like bird with tiny black bill; dark stripes on head; long, finely barred, grey tail; pink feet; whiskers on face; northern individuals are lighter, and there is also a form with a reddish brown tinge; to 25 cm (10 in).

HABITAT: Rainforest edges, open forests and woodlands, scrub areas, and trees along watercourses; solitary or in pairs; nocturnal.

REGIONS: CYP, TRQ, TEQ, NSW, VIC, TAS

Plate 40f
White-throated Nightjar
Eurostopodus mystacalis
ID: Mid-sized dark grey bird with fine mottling, spots, and bars; long, pointed wings; dark throat with white band; white spots on wings, seen in flight; black bill; to 37 cm (14.5 in), female a bit larger.

HABITAT: Open forests, woodlands, and heathlands; solitary or in pairs; nocturnal; often roosts by day on the ground.

REGIONS: CYP, TRQ, TEQ, NSW, VIC

Plate 40 369

a Barn Owl

c Barking Owl

b Southern Boobook

d Tawny Frogmouth

F

M

e Australian Owlet-nightjar

f White-throated Nightjar

Plate 41a
White-throated Needletail
Hirundapus caudacutus
ID: Large dark swift (largest in Australia) with white forehead, throat, and under tail; short dark tail ends with short, needle-like projections; to 21 cm (8 in).

HABITAT: Over forests and woodlands, lakes, and settled and agricultural areas; often along coasts and in mountain areas; in groups; migrant that breeds in Asia.

REGIONS: CYP, TRQ, TEQ, NSW, VIC, TAS

Plate 41b
White-rumped Swiftlet
Collocalia spodiopygius
ID: Small dark grey or grey-brown swift with light grey rump; long black wings; forked black tail; to 11.5 cm (4.5 in).

HABITAT: Over rainforests, coastal ranges, beaches, and islands; in groups.

REGIONS: CYP, TRQ

Plate 41c
Welcome Swallow
Hirundo neoxena
ID: Small and slight, blue-black above, light greyish below, with reddish brown forehead and throat; black bar through eye; deeply forked tail; to 15 cm (6 in). (The migratory Barn Swallow, *Hirundo rustica*, which winters in northern Australia, is very similar, but has a black chest band.)

HABITAT: Many, including open forests and woodlands, grasslands, wetlands, and coastal and settled areas; solitary, in pairs, or in groups.

REGIONS: CYP, TRQ, TEQ, NSW, VIC, TAS

Plate 41d
White-backed Swallow
Cheramoeca leucosternus
ID: Small, slight, black and white bird with deeply forked tail; white throat, chest, and back; brownish white crown; to 15 cm (6 in).

HABITAT: Open, drier, inland sites, including woodlands and fields, sandy areas and dunes, along watercourses, and lakes; in groups.

REGIONS: TRQ, TEQ, NSW, VIC

Plate 41e
Fairy Martin
Hirundo ariel
ID: Small and slight, with blue-black back, dusky greyish or brownish wings, and slightly forked tail; reddish brown head; white streaks on back of neck, dark streaks on throat; white rump and underparts; to 13 cm (5 in).

HABITAT: Open areas near water or wetlands, around cliffs, caves, culverts, and bridges; in groups.

REGIONS: CYP, TRQ, TEQ, NSW, VIC, TAS

Plate 41f
Tree Martin
Hirundo nigricans
ID: Small, slight blue-black bird with brownish/dusky wings and slightly forked tail; reddish brown/buffy forehead, black crown; whitish rump and underparts; to 13 cm (5 in).

HABITAT: Open woodlands and other sites with large trees, usually near water or wetlands; in groups.

REGIONS: CYP, TRQ, TEQ, NSW, VIC, TAS

Plate 41 **371**

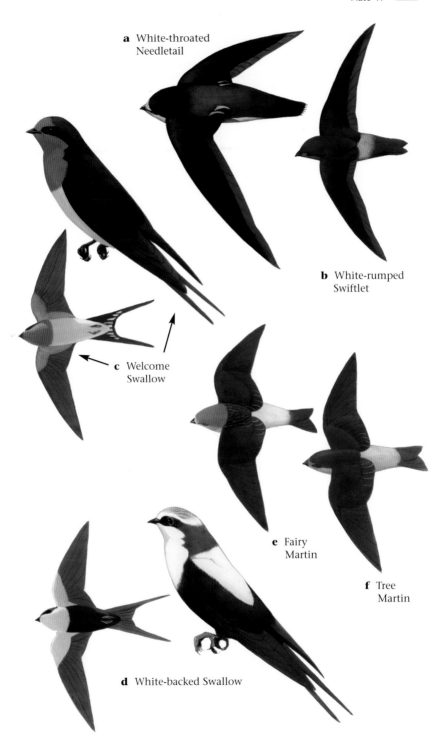

a White-throated Needletail

b White-rumped Swiftlet

c Welcome Swallow

e Fairy Martin

f Tree Martin

d White-backed Swallow

Plate 42a
Laughing Kookaburra
Dacelo novaeguineae
ID: Large kingfisher with massive bill dark above, light below; light head with dark eye-stripe; brownish or blackish back and wings, whitish neck, chest, and belly; blue patch/mottling on wing; to 46 cm (18 in).

HABITAT: Open forests and woodlands, trees along watercourses, agricultural areas, and parks; solitary, in pairs, or in small groups.

REGIONS: CYP, TRQ, TEQ, NSW, VIC, TAS

Plate 42b
Azure Kingfisher
Alcedo azurea
ID: Small, beautiful, deep blue kingfisher with long black bill; light mark in front of eye; light throat/chest, reddish brown belly; red feet; to 19 cm (7.5 in).

HABITAT: Along forested rivers, creeks, rainforest streams, lakes, swamps, and mangroves; solitary or in pairs.

REGIONS: CYP, TRQ, TEQ, NSW, VIC, TAS

Plate 42c
Buff-breasted Paradise-Kingfisher
Tanysiptera sylvia
ID: Stunning smallish kingfisher with very large orange-red bill; deep blue and black above, buffy or pale reddish brown below; white rump and long white tail plumes; to 35 cm (14 in), including tail.

HABITAT: Lowland rainforests and scrubby riversides; solitary or in pairs; migrant that winters in New Guinea.

REGIONS: CYP, TRQ

Plate 42d
Forest Kingfisher
Todiramphus macleayii
ID: Smallish blue and white kingfisher with white spot in front of eye and black eye-stripe; white patch on wing, seen in flight; male has white band around neck; to 22 cm (8.5 in).

HABITAT: Open forests and woodlands, wooded swamps, trees along watercourses, mangroves, and agricultural areas; solitary or in pairs.

REGIONS: CYP, TRQ, NSW

Plate 42e
Blue-winged Kookaburra
Dacelo leachii
ID: Large kingfisher with massive bill dark above, light below; whitish head with dark streaks; wings mostly blue, rump blue; male has blue tail, female has reddish brown tail; to 40 cm (16 in).

HABITAT: Open forests and woodlands, trees along watercourses, and agricultural areas; solitary, in pairs, or in small groups.

REGIONS: CYP, TRQ, TEQ

Plate 42f
Sacred Kingfisher
Todiramphus sanctus
ID: Smallish kingfisher with greenish head and back, blue wings and tail; buffy/whitish underparts; small light spot in front of eye; black eye-stripe; to 23 cm (9 in).

HABITAT: Open forests and woodlands, mangroves, along river and lake shores, coastal areas, and parks; solitary, in pairs, or in small groups.

REGIONS: CYP, TRQ, TEQ, NSW, VIC, TAS

Plate 42 **373**

a Laughing Kookaburra

b Azure Kingfisher

c Buff-breasted Paradise-Kingfisher

d Forest Kingfisher

e Blue-winged Kookaburra

f Sacred Kingfisher

Plate 43a
Dollarbird
Eurystomus orientalis
ID: Mid-sized bluish or greenish blue bird with brown head and blue throat; reddish bill, eye-ring, and legs; shortish dark-tipped tail; "dollar-sized" light mark on wing, seen in flight; to 30 cm (12 in).

HABITAT: Rainforests, open forests and woodlands, especially around forest edges, trees along watercourses, and agricultural areas; solitary, in pairs, or in small groups.

REGIONS: CYP, TRQ, TEQ, NSW, VIC

Plate 43b
Rainbow Bee-eater
Merops ornatus
ID: Smallish brightly colored bird with long, thin, black, slightly down-curved bill and black eye-stripe; greenish and blue overall; tawny crown; yellow throat with black band; dark tail with extra-long center feather shafts; to 26 cm (10 in) including long tail.

HABITAT: Rainforests, open forests and woodlands, roadsides and other open areas, mangroves, and beaches; in pairs or groups.

REGIONS: CYP, TRQ, TEQ, NSW, VIC

Plate 43c
Noisy Pitta
Pitta versicolor
ID: Mid-size, chunky, colorful bird; green above, buffy/yellowish below; brown and black head; blue shoulder patches and rump; reddish under short tail; to 20 cm (8 in).

HABITAT: Rainforests and adjacent open forests; ground-dwelling; solitary or in pairs.

REGIONS: CYP, TRQ, NSW

Plate 43d
Superb Lyrebird
Menura novaehollandiae
ID: Large songbird, brown above, grey below; long legs; male with extremely long, filamentous tail feathers; female a bit smaller, with shorter, plainer tail; male to 1 m (3.3 ft), including tail to 60 cm (2 ft); female to 86 cm (34 in), including shorter tail. (Albert's Lyrebird, *Menura alberti*, which occurs only in the small border area where New South Wales meets Queensland, is similar, but a bit smaller and more reddish brown above and below.)

HABITAT: Rainforests and wetter open forests of costal regions and the Great Dividing Range; ground-dwelling; solitary, in pairs, or in small groups.

REGIONS: TRQ, NSW, VIC, TAS

Plate 43e
White-throated Treecreeper
Cormobates leucophaeus
ID: Mid-sized brown or olive-brown songbird with white throat/chest, dark streaked or mottled belly; longish, thin, slightly down-curved bill; female with small orange spot on neck; to 17 cm (6.5 in).

HABITAT: Rainforests, open forests and woodlands, and trees along watercourses; solitary, in pairs, or in small groups.

REGIONS: TRQ, TEQ, NSW, VIC

Plate 43f
Brown Treecreeper
Climacteris picumnus
ID: Mid-sized brown or dark brown songbird, often with greyish head; buffy underparts with streaked belly; light stripe above eye, fine dark stripe through eye; male with small black markings on upper breast, female with similar reddish brown markings; to 18 cm (7 in).

HABITAT: Open forests and woodlands, especially at forest edges, and trees along watercourses; solitary, in pairs, or in small groups.

REGIONS: CYP, TRQ, TEQ, NSW, VIC

Plate 43 375

a Dollarbird

b Rainbow Bee-eater

c Noisy Pitta

d Superb Lyrebird

e White-throated Treecreeper

f Brown Treecreeper

Plate 44a
Superb Fairy-wren
Malurus cyaneus

ID: Small brown songbird with whitish/greyish underparts; long, dark tail typically held upright; male in breeding plumage (shown) has bright blue and black head and back; female has reddish brown bill and eye-ring; to 15 cm (6 in).

HABITAT: Open forests and woodlands, thickets, swamplands, heathlands, coastal areas, roadsides, parks, and gardens; in pairs or small groups, often on the ground.

REGIONS: TRQ, TEQ, NSW, VIC, TAS

Plate 44b
Variegated Fairy-wren
Malurus lamberti

ID: Small brown songbird with whitish underparts; long blue tail typically held upright; male in breeding plumage (shown) has bright blue crown, eye patch, and back patch, black thoat/chest, reddish brown shoulder patch; female is brown or brown-grey with tan bill, reddish brown eye-ring, and, in some western regions, bluish grey head/back; to 15 cm (6 in).

HABITAT: Open forests and woodlands, forest edges, heathlands, shrublands, thickets, parks, gardens, and rocky escarpments; in pairs or small groups.

REGIONS: TRQ, TEQ, NSW, VIC

Plate 44c
Red-backed Fairy-wren
Malurus melanocephalus

ID: Small songbird with long tail typically held upright; male is black or dark brown with red back and black bill; female is grey-brown or pale brown above, whitish below, with light brown bill; to 13 cm (5 in).

HABITAT: Grassy areas associated with woodlands, dense undergrowth, thickets, and swamps; in pairs or small groups.

REGIONS: CYP, TRQ, TEQ, NSW

Plate 44d
Spotted Pardalote
Pardalotus punctatus

ID: Very small songbird; black on top with white spots, white eye-stripe, reddish rump; male has yellow throat/chest; female is a bit duller, whitish or pale brown below; to 10 cm (4 in).

HABITAT: Open forests and woodlands, scrubby areas, along watercourses, and parks; solitary, in pairs, or in small groups.

REGIONS: TRQ, TEQ, NSW, VIC, TAS

Plate 44e
Striated Pardalote
Pardalotus striatus

ID: Very small songbird; olive-grey with black crown (sometimes with white streaks) and eye-stripe; light stripe above eye starts with yellowish mark; red or yellow spot on white-streaked blackish wing; to 11.5 cm (4.5 in).

HABITAT: Rainforests, open forests and woodlands, scrubby areas, mangroves, and roadsides; in pairs and small groups.

REGIONS: CYP, TRQ, TEQ, NSW, VIC, TAS

Plate 44f
White-throated Gerygone
Gerygone olivacea

ID: Very small songbird; olive-greyish or grey-brown with white throat, yellow chest/belly; white spot on forehead, red eye; dark tail with white mark near tip; to 11 cm (4.3 in).

HABITAT: Open forests and woodlands, trees along watercourses, and scrubby areas; prefers higher foliage; solitary or in pairs.

REGIONS: CYP, TRQ, TEQ, NSW, VIC

Plate 44 377

a Superb Fairy-wren

M, B

F

b Variegated Fairy-wren

M, B

F

d Spotted Pardalote

M

F

c Red-backed Fairy-wren

e Striated Pardalote

f White-throated Gerygone

Plate 45a
Brown Gerygone
Gerygone mouki
ID: Very small songbird; brown or olive-grey with conspicuous light stripe above eye; greyish cheek; dark tail with white tip; to 11 cm (4.3 in).

HABITAT: Rainforests, open forests, and mangroves; in pairs or small groups.

REGIONS: CYP, TRQ, NSW, VIC

Plate 45b
Yellow-throated Scrubwren
Sericornis citreogularis
ID: Small olive-brown songbird; yellowish throat/upper chest; wide black (male) or brown (female) stripe through eye, narrow light stripe above eye; to 15 cm (6 in).

HABITAT: On the ground or in shrubbery in rainforests, open forests, and woodlands, usually in densely vegetated areas; solitary or in pairs.

REGIONS: CYP, TRQ, NSW

Plate 45c
White-browed Scrubwren
Sericornis frontalis
ID: Small olive-brown or cinnamon-brown songbird; whitish throat; cream or buffy-grey underparts; wide dark stripe through eye, light stripe above and below eye; reddish brown rump; to 14 cm (5.5 in).

HABITAT: Open forests and woodlands, scrubby areas, heathlands, and parks, usually in dense vegetation; in pairs or small groups.

REGIONS: CYP, TRQ, TEQ, NSW, VIC

Plate 45d
Brown Thornbill
Acanthiza pusilla
ID: Very small brown or olive-brown songbird; reddish brown forehead; red eye; grey throat/chest with dark streaks; yellowish white or tawny belly; tail with blackish band; to 10.5 cm (4 in).

HABITAT: In dense undergrowth in rainforests, open forests and woodlands, vegetation along watercourses, scrub areas, mangroves, and parks; solitary, in pairs, or in small groups.

REGIONS: TRQ, NSW, VIC, TAS

Plate 45e
Yellow-rumped Thornbill
Acanthiza chrysorrhoa
ID: Very small olive-grey songbird; black forehead with white spots; white stripe above eye, dark stripe through eye; yellow rump and pale yellow underparts; to 12.5 cm (5 in).

HABITAT: Open forests and woodlands, scrublands, parklands, especially in grassy areas, and agricultural districts; in pairs or groups.

REGIONS: TRQ, TEQ, NSW, VIC, TAS

Plate 45f
Yellow Thornbill
(also called Little Thornbill)
Acanthiza nana
ID: Very small songbird, olive-green above, yellow below; greyish cheek area with streaks; brown tail with dark bar near end; to 10 cm (4 in).

HABITAT: Drier open forests and woodlands, trees along watercourses, orchards, and parks; solitary, in pairs, or in small groups.

REGIONS: TRQ, TEQ, NSW, VIC

Plate 45 **379**

a Brown Gerygone

b Yellow-throated Scrubwren

c White-browed Scrubwren

d Brown Thornbill

e Yellow-rumped Thornbill

f Yellow Thornbill

Plate 46a
Red Wattlebird
Anthochaera carnunculata
ID: Largish grey-brown songbird with light streaks; blackish crown, red eye, yellow belly, pinkish legs; reddish wattle hangs from cheek; to 36 cm (14 in).

HABITAT: Open forests and woodlands, scrub areas, heathlands, orchards, parks, and gardens; solitary, in pairs, and in groups.

REGIONS: TRQ, NSW, VIC

Plate 46b
Little Wattlebird
(also called Brush Wattlebird)
Anthochaera chrysoptera
ID: Mid-sized grey-brown or olive-brown songbird, lighter underneath, with fine silvery streaks; lower part of face is whitish; dark throat and legs, reddish brown patch on wing, seen in flight; to 32 cm (12.5 in).

HABITAT: Open forests and woodlands, scrub areas, heathlands, parks, and gardens; solitary, in pairs, and in groups.

REGIONS: TRQ, NSW, VIC, TAS

Plate 46c
Noisy Friarbird
Philemon corniculatus
ID: Largish grey songbird with bare black head; black knob on large bill; slight brownish stripe over red eye; silvery-white frilly feathers on upper chest; grey tail with narrow white tip; to 36 cm (14 in).

HABITAT: Open forests and woodlands, scrub areas, trees along watercourses, orchards, parks, and gardens; solitary, in pairs, or in small groups.

REGIONS: CYP, TRQ, TEQ, NSW, VIC

Plate 46d
Little Friarbird
Philemon citreogulari
ID: Mid-sized songbird, brown or grey-brown above, pale grey below; bluish black or blue-grey facial skin; large down-curved bill; light band behind neck; white hair-like feathers on chest; to 29 cm (11.5 in).

HABITAT: Open forests and woodlands, orchards, parks, and gardens; solitary, in pairs, or in small groups.

REGIONS: CYP, TRQ, TEQ, NSW, VIC

Plate 46e
Blue-faced Honeyeater
Entomyzon cyanotis
ID: Mid-sized songbird, olive-yellow or yellowish green above, white below; black head and throat; blue skin around light eye, with white stripe behind it; to 32 cm (12.5 in).

HABITAT: Open forests and woodlands, scrub areas, trees along watercourses, orchards, parks, and gardens; in pairs or groups.

REGIONS: CYP, TRQ, TEQ, NSW, VIC

Plate 46f
Lewin's Honeyeater
Meliphaga lewinii
ID: Mid-sized olive green songbird with darker head; large yellowish (often crescent-shaped) mark behind eye and narrow yellowish stripe under eye; robust black bill; to 22 cm (8.5 in). (Two other species in the Cape York Peninsula region, Yellow-spotted and Graceful Honeyeaters, look very similar but are a bit smaller, with finer bills.)

HABITAT: Rainforests, wetter open forests, scrublands, heathlands, mangroves, agricultural areas, and gardens; solitary or in pairs.

REGIONS: CYP, TRQ, TEQ, NSW, VIC

Plate 46 **381**

a Red Wattlebird

b Little Wattlebird

c Noisy Friarbird

d Little Friarbird

e Blue-faced Honeyeater

f Lewin's Honeyeater

Plate 47a
Bell Miner
Manorina melanophrys
ID: Mid-sized olive green songbird with yellow/orangish bill and legs; black forehead and side of throat; patch of red skin behind eye; to 20 cm (8 in).

HABITAT: Temperate rainforests and open forests, often along watercourses; in pairs or groups.

REGIONS: TRQ, NSW, VIC

Plate 47b
Noisy Miner
Manorina melanocephala
ID: Mid-sized grey songbird, paler below, with yellowish green tint on wings and tail; white forehead; black crown and cheek; patch of yellow skin behind eye; yellow bill; to 28 cm (11 in).

HABITAT: Open forests and woodlands, often along watercourses, shrublands, heathlands, roadsides, parks, and gardens; in groups.

REGIONS: CYP, TRQ, TEQ, NSW, VIC, TAS

Plate 47c
Bridled Honeyeater
Lichenostomus frenatus
ID: Mid-sized dark brown songbird with blackish head; yellowish/light stripe from bill to under eye; streaky white patch behind eye; greyish patch on side of neck; black bill with yellow base; to 22 cm (8.5 in).

HABITAT: Rainforests and wetter open forests, often along watercourses; solitary, in pairs, or in small groups.

REGIONS: CYP

Plate 47d
Yellow-faced Honeyeater
Lichenostomus chrysops
ID: Smallish or mid-sized grey-brown songbird, paler below; wide yellowish stripe under eye with black stripes above and below it; small light mark behind eye; to 18 cm (7 in).

HABITAT: Open forests and woodlands, scrublands, heathlands, and mangroves; solitary and in pairs.

REGIONS: CYP, TRQ, TEQ, NSW, VIC

Plate 47e
Varied Honeyeater
Lichenostomus versicolor
ID: Mid-sized grey-brown songbird; yellow underparts with brown streaks; wide black stripe through eye; white stripe/patch on side of neck; to 21 cm (8 in). (The Mangrove Honeyeater, *Lichenostomus fasciogularis*, endemic to the coasts of Tropical Queensland and northern New South Wales, is similar but has a brown-scalloped yellowish throat and grey-brown streaky chest/belly.)

HABITAT: Mangroves, coastal scrubby areas, and nearby woodlands; solitary, in pairs, or in small groups.

REGIONS: CYP

Plate 47 **383**

a Bell Miner

b Noisy Miner

c Bridled Honeyeater

d Yellow-faced Honeyeater

e Varied Honeyeater

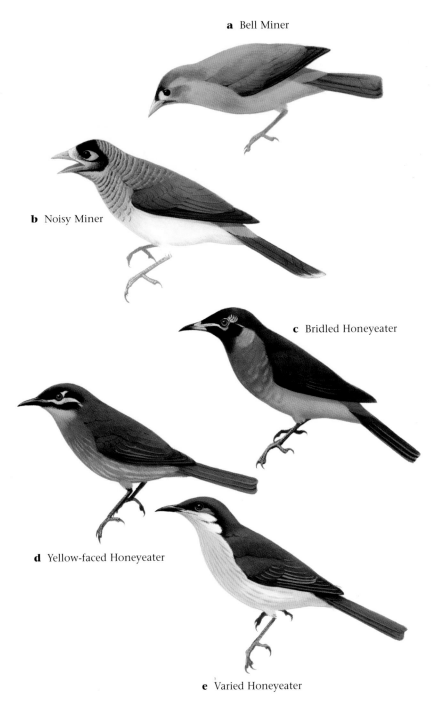

Plate 48a
White-eared Honeyeater
Lichenostomus leucotis
ID: Mid-sized olive green songbird with black face/throat; grey crown; white ear patch; yellowish green underparts; to 22 cm (8.5 in).

HABITAT: Open forests and woodlands, shrublands, heaths, and scrubby areas, especially along watercourses; solitary or in pairs.

REGIONS: TRQ, TEQ, NSW, VIC

Plate 48b
Fuscous Honeyeater
Lichenostomus fuscus
ID: Smallish olive-brown songbird, lighter below; darker patch around eye; yellow mark on neck; black eye-ring and bill during breeding (shown) or eye-ring and base of bill yellowish; to 17 cm (6.5 in).

HABITAT: Open forests and woodlands, heaths, scrubby areas, and trees along watercourses; in pairs or groups.

REGIONS: TRQ, NSW, VIC

Plate 48c
White-plumed Honeyeater
Lichenostomus penicillatus
ID: Smallish olive-grey songbird with yellow head, lighter belly; white bar on neck with slight blackish bar above it; to 17 cm (6.5 in).

HABITAT: Open forests and woodlands, heaths, trees along watercourses, parks, and gardens; solitary, in pairs, or in small groups.

REGIONS: TEQ, NSW, VIC

Plate 48d
White-naped Honeyeater
Melithreptus lunatus
ID: Small olive-green or brownish green songbird with black head and chin; white below; slight white band behind head; reddish crescent of skin above eye; to 15 cm (6 in). (The White-throated Honeyeater, *Melithreptus albogularis*, is very similar but has a white chin, bolder white band behind head, and bluish white crescent above the eye.)

HABITAT: Open forests and woodlands, parks, and gardens; in small groups.

REGIONS: TRQ, TEQ, NSW, VIC

Plate 48e
Brown Honeyeater
Lichmera indistincta
ID: Small brown or olive-brown songbird with longish, black, down-curved bill; light mark behind eye; yellow-tinted wing and tail feathers; to 15 cm (6 in).

HABITAT: Open forests and woodlands, mangroves, heahthands, scrublands, trees along watercourses, parks, and gardens; solitary, in pairs, or in groups.

REGIONS: CYP, TRQ, TEQ, NSW

Plate 48 385

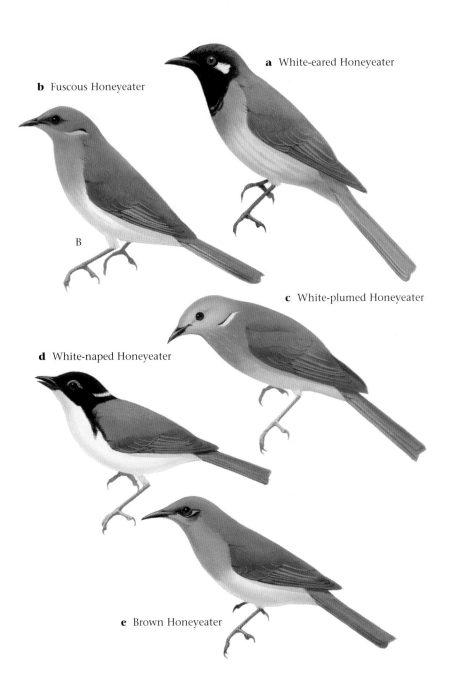

a White-eared Honeyeater

b Fuscous Honeyeater

B

c White-plumed Honeyeater

d White-naped Honeyeater

e Brown Honeyeater

Plate 49a
Eastern Spinebill
Acanthorhynchus tenuirostris
ID: Smallish songbird with long, thin, down-curved bill; dark above, tawny/buffy below, with dark crown and red eye; black crescent at shoulder; dark patch on white throat; black tail with white edges; to 16 cm (6.3 in).

HABITAT: Open forests and woodlands, heahthands, shrublands, and gardens; solitary or in pairs.

REGIONS: CYP, TRQ, TEQ, NSW, VIC, TAS

Plate 49b
New Holland Honeyeater
Phylidonyris novaehollandiae
ID: Mid-sized black and white songbird with yellow wing patch; white eye; white eyebrow starts above eye (in the very similar White-cheeked Honeyeater, *Phylidonyris nigra*, white eyebrow starts before eye, near bill); to 19 cm (7.5 in).

HABITAT: Open forests and woodlands, coastal heahthands and scrub areas, parks, and gardens; solitary or in groups.

REGIONS: TRQ, NSW, VIC, TAS

Plate 49c
Banded Honeyeater
Certhionyx pectoralis
ID: Small blackish songbird; underparts white with black chest band; white rump; black, slightly down-curved bill; immature is brown instead of black, and yellowish patch on face; to 14 cm (5.5 in).

HABITAT: Open forests and woodlands, mangroves, vegetation along watercourses, and coastal scrub areas; in pairs or small groups.

REGIONS: CYP, TRQ

Plate 49d
Scarlet Honeyeater
Myzomela sanguinolenta
ID: Very small songbird with black, down-curved bill; male is red with black wings, tail, and eyestripe, and grey belly; female is brownish, darker above, lighter below, with reddish tinge on forehead and chin; to 11 cm (4.3 in). (The Red-headed Honeyeater, *Myzomela erythrocephala*, of CYP, is similar, but the male is mostly black, including the back, with red head and rump.)

HABITAT: Rainforests, open forests and woodlands, mangroves, heathlands, vegetation along watercourses, and gardens; solitary, in pairs, or in small groups.

REGIONS: CYP, TRQ, NSW, VIC

Plate 49e
White-fronted Chat
Epthianura albifrons
ID: Small grey or grey-brown songbird with slim, sharp, black bill and light eye; male with white face and underparts, black band from behind head to across chest; female is paler, with brown crown, light line between bill and eye, and brown chest band; to 13 cm (5 in).

HABITAT: Open areas, including grasslands, heaths, low vegetation, marshes, and agricultural areas; in pairs or groups.

REGIONS: NSW, VIC, TAS

Plate 49 387

a Eastern Spinebill

b New Holland Honeyeater

c Banded Honeyeater

d Scarlet Honeyeater

M

F

F

M

e White-fronted Chat

Plate 50a
Flame Robin
Petroica phoenicea
ID: Male is small, dark grey songbird with red underparts, small white mark above bill, white wing patches, and white-edged dark tail; female is brownish (lighter below) with darker wings with white bars; to 14 cm (5.5 in). (The Scarlet Robin, *Petroica multicolor*, is similar, but the male has a black throat and larger white patch above bill.)

HABITAT: Open forests and woodlands, scrubby areas, agricultural sites, and parks; in pairs or groups.

REGIONS: TRQ, NSW, VIC, TAS

Plate 50b
Jacky Winter
Microeca fascinans
ID: Small songbird, grey-brown above, lighter (greyish or whitish) below; darker wings with white edges; narrow dark stripe though eye, light stripe above eye; dark tail with white outer feathers; small black bill; to 14 cm (5.5 in).

HABITAT: Open woodlands, vegetation along watercourses, scrub areas, agricultural sites, and roadsides; solitary or in pairs.

REGIONS: CYP, TRQ, TEQ, NSW, VIC

Plate 50c
Eastern Yellow Robin
Eopsaltria australis
ID: Small songbird, grey above, yellow below; yellowish or olive lower back and rump; light grey or whitish chin; to 16 cm (6 in).

HABITAT: Rainforests, open forests and woodlands, scrubby areas, thickets, and gardens; solitary, in pairs, or in small groups.

REGIONS: CYP, TRQ, TEQ, NSW, VIC

Plate 50d
Dusky Robin
Melanodryas vittata
ID: Smallish brown, grey-brown, or olive-brown songbird with darker wings that have inconspicuous light edging/markings; dark stripe through eye; small black bill; to 17 cm (6.5 in).

HABITAT: Open forests and woodlands, scrubby areas and gardens with trees; solitary, in pairs, or in groups.

REGIONS: TAS

Plate 50e
Pale-yellow Robin
Tregellasia capito
ID: Small songbird, olive green above, yellowish below; grey or olive-grey head; white throat; in the northern part of its range, near Cairns and Cooktown, it is whitish between bill and eye (shown); in the south, buffy between bill and eye; to 13.5 cm (5.5 in).

HABITAT: Rainforests; solitary, in pairs, or in small groups.

REGIONS: CYP, TRQ, NSW

Plate 50f
Grey-headed Robin
Heteromyias albispecularis
ID: Mid-sized songbird, olive-brown above, whitish below, with grey crown and reddish brown rump; white line behind and/or below eye; dark wings with light wing bars; black bill with light tip; pinkish legs; to 18 cm (7 in).

HABITAT: Rainforests, usually in higher-elevation areas; solitary, in pairs, or in small groups.

REGIONS: CYP

Plate 50 **389**

a Flame Robin

b Jacky Winter

d Dusky Robin

c Eastern Yellow Robin

f Grey-headed Robin

e Pale-yellow Robin

Plate 51a

Logrunner
Orthonyx temminckii

ID: Mid-sized brown or reddish brown songbird with black mottling above, lighter or whitish below, grey face, small black bill; male with white throat/chest bordered by broad black stripe; female with orangish throat/chest; to 20 cm (8 in).

HABITAT: Rainforests, on the ground; in pairs or small groups.

REGIONS: TRQ, NSW

Plate 51b

Grey-crowned Babbler
Pomatostomus temporalis

ID: Mid-sized songbird, greyish brown or blackish brown above; whitish throat/upper chest; brown or reddish brown lower chest/belly; grey on top of head; broad white stripe above pale yellow eye, dark stripe through eye; long, down-curved black bill; to 29 cm (11.5 in).

HABITAT: Open forests and woodlands, scrubby areas, roadsides, and agricultural areas with trees; in small groups.

REGIONS: CYP, TRQ, TEQ, NSW, VIC

Plate 51c

Eastern Whipbird
Psophodes olivaceus

ID: Mid-sized dark-crested songbird with smallish, black, slightly down-curved bill; male is dark olive-green with black head/chest and large white cheek patch; female is brownish with light, inconspicuous cheek patch; to 30 cm (12 in).

HABITAT: Rainforests and wetter open forests, trees along watercourses, and coastal scrubby areas; in pairs or small groups, usually on/near the ground.

REGIONS: CYP, TRQ, NSW, VIC

Plate 51d

Spotted Quail-thrush
Cinclosoma punctatum

ID: Mid-sized songbird, brown and black mottled/streaked above, with grey chest, smallish black bill, pinkish legs; male with black face/throat, white patch on side of throat, white stripe above eye; female with buffy/whitish stripe above eye, buffy/orangish patch on side of throat; to 28 cm (11 in).

HABITAT: Open forests and woodlands, usually in drier areas; in pairs or small groups.

REGIONS: TRQ, TEQ, NSW, VIC, TAS

Plate 51e

Varied Sittella
Daphoenositta chrysoptera

ID: Small grey-brown or brownish songbird, lighter or white below, sometimes with dark streaks; black or grey head (white in some western regions); bill yellowish at base, dark at tip; yellowish legs; male with white throat, female with dark throat; to 12.5 cm (5 in).

HABITAT: Open forests and woodlands, scrub areas, parks, and gardens; in small or large groups.

REGIONS: CYP, TRQ, TEQ, NSW, VIC

Plate 51f

Red-whiskered Bulbul
Pycnonotus jocosus

ID: Mid-sized, dark-crested, brownish songbird with white throat and cheek patch; red patch behind eye; red under tail; to 21 cm (8 in).

HABITAT: Settled areas: parks, gardens, suburban and urban areas; some agricultural sites, woodlands, and scrub areas. Introduced; native to southern Asia.

REGIONS: NSW, VIC

Plate 51 **391**

F

M

a Logrunner

b Grey-crowned Babbler

c Eastern Whipbird

F

M

F

M

d Spotted Quail-thrush

e Varied Sittella

F

M

f Red-whiskered Bulbul

Plate 52 (See also: Whistlers, p. 173)

Plate 52a
Golden Whistler
Pachycephala pectoralis
ID: Smallish songbird; male has black head, white throat, yellow ring around neck, olive-grey back, dark wings and tail; female is brownish grey above, lighter below, with a pale wing bar and sometimes a yellowish area under tail; to 18 cm (7 in).

HABITAT: Rainforests, open forests and woodlands, scrub areas and coastal vegetation, mangroves, parks, and gardens; solitary, in pairs, or in mixed-species groups.

REGIONS: CYP, TRQ, TEQ, NSW, VIC, TAS

Plate 52b
Crested Shrike-tit
Falcunculus frontatus
ID: Mid-sized crested songbird with black and white head; olive green above, yellow below; robust black bill; male with black throat, female with olive-green throat; to 19 cm (7.5 in).

HABITAT: Rainforests, open forests and woodlands, scrub areas, trees along watercourses, parks, and gardens; in pairs or small groups.

REGIONS: TRQ, TEQ, NSW, VIC

Plate 52c
Rufous Whistler
Pachycephala rufiventris
ID: Smallish songbird; male is grey above, reddish brown below, with broad black stripe through eye and down to chest, white throat; female is olive-grey or brownish grey above, buffy with darker streaks below, with whitish throat; to 17.5 cm (7 in).

HABITAT: Open forests, woodlands, and scrub areas; solitary, in pairs, or in mixed-species groups.

REGIONS: CYP, TRQ, TEQ, NSW, VIC

Plate 52d
Little Shrike-thrush
Colluricincla megarhyncha
ID: Smallish songbird, olive-brown above with lighter head, reddish brown below with slightly streaked chest and whitish throat; light brown/pinkish bill; to 19 cm (7.5 in).

HABITAT: Rainforests, coastal open forests, swamp areas, and mangroves; solitary or in pairs.

REGIONS: CYP, TRQ, NSW

Plate 52e
Grey Shrike-thrush
Colluricincla harmonica
ID: Mid-sized songbird, grey above with olive-brown back, lighter grey below; dark grey wings and tail; light patch between eye and bill; female with slight whitish eye-ring; to 25 cm (10 in).

HABITAT: Open forests and woodlands, scrub areas, vegetation along watercourses, parks, and gardens; solitary, in pairs, or in small groups.

REGIONS: CYP, TRQ, TEQ, NSW, VIC, TAS

Plate 52   393

a Golden Whistler

b Crested Shrike-tit

M

F

c Rufous Whistler

F

M

d Little Shrike-thrush

e Grey Shrike-thrush

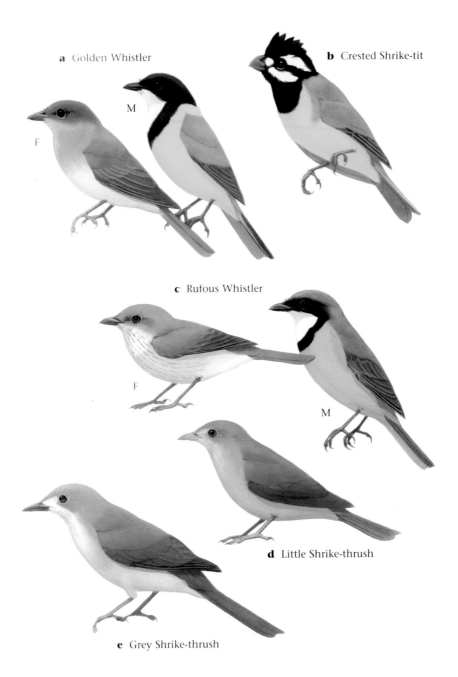

Plate 53a
Leaden Flycatcher
Myiagra rubecula
ID: Smallish songbird with black and blue bill, small crest (often not erected); male is blue-grey above with white belly; female is dull grey above with orangish upper chest, whitish belly; to 16.5 cm (6.5 in). (The Satin Flycatcher, *Myiagra cyanoleuca*, is very similar, but male is darker, almost black.)

HABITAT: Open forests and woodlands, vegetation along watercourses, and mangroves; solitary or in pairs.

REGIONS: CYP, TRQ, TEQ, NSW, VIC, TAS

Plate 53b
Black-faced Monarch
Monarcha melanopsis
ID: Mid-sized songbird, grey or bluish grey above, with black forehead and throat; grey upper chest, reddish brown lower chest and belly; grey or bluish grey bill; to 19 cm (7.5 in). (The Black-winged Monarch, *Monarcha frater*, of the Cape York Peninsula, is similar but with black wings and tail; the Spectacled Monarch, *Monarcha trivirgatus*, of the eastern coast is also similar, but with more black on the face, surrounding the eyes.)

HABITAT: Rainforests, open forests and woodlands, and coastal scrub areas; solitary or in pairs.

REGIONS: CYP, TRQ, NSW, VIC

Plate 53c
Grey Fantail
Rhipidura fuliginosa
ID: Smallish songbird, grey above with white eyebrow; white throat, greyish upper chest, whitish or buffy lower chest/belly; two narrow, pale wingbars; to 17 cm (6.5 in).

HABITAT: Rainforests, open forests and woodlands, mangroves, scrub areas, parks, and gardens; solitary, in pairs, or in small groups.

REGIONS: CYP, TRQ, TEQ, NSW, VIC, TAS

Plate 53d
Restless Flycatcher
Myiagra inquieta
ID: Mid-sized songbird, blue-black above, with slightly duller, browner wings; white below, often with buffy tinge on upper chest; small crest (often not erected); to 21 cm (8.3 in).

HABITAT: Open forests and woodlands, trees along watercourses, agricultural areas, parks, and gardens; solitary, in pairs, or in small groups.

REGIONS: CYP, TRQ, TEQ, NSW, VIC

Plate 53e
Willie Wagtail
Rhipidura leucophrys
ID: Mid-sized terrestrial songbird; black above with white eyebrow; faint white flecks at side of mouth; small black bill; white lower chest/belly; to 22 cm (8.5 in).

HABITAT: Most habitats except dense wet forests; solitary, in pairs, or in small groups.

REGIONS: CYP, TRQ, TEQ, NSW, VIC, TAS

Plate 53f
White-winged Triller
Lalage sueurii
ID: Male is mid-sized songbird, black above, white below, with black and white wings, grey rump (in nonbreeding plumage, with brown crown and back, dark stripe through eye, and lighter stripe above eye); female is brown above, with dark stripe through eye, lighter stripe above eye, brownish chest; to 19 cm (7.5 in).

HABITAT: Open forests and woodlands, scrubby open areas, and vegetation along watercourses; solitary, in pairs, or in groups.

REGIONS: CYP, TRQ, TEQ, NSW, VIC, TAS

Plate 53 **395**

a Leaden Flycatcher

b Black-faced Monarch

F

M

d Restless Flycatcher

c Grey Fantail

e Willie Wagtail

F

M

f White-winged Triller

Plate 54a

Black-faced Cuckoo-shrike
Coracina novaehollandiae

ID: Largish grey or bluish grey songbird with black face/throat; whitish or pale grey below; tail with white tip; to 35 cm (14 in).

HABITAT: Rainforests, open forests and woodlands, trees along watercourses, scrub areas, parks, gardens, and roadsides; solitary, in pairs, or in small groups.

REGIONS: CYP, TRQ, TEQ, NSW, VIC, TAS

Plate 54b

Spangled Drongo
Dicrurus bracteatus

ID: Mid-sized black songbird with inconspicuous light spots on head, neck, and chest; long forked, flaring tail; robust black bill; red eye; to 32 cm (12.5 in), female a bit smaller. (The Metallic Starling, Plate 60d, is similar, but has a pointed tail.)

HABITAT: Rainforest edges, open forests and woodlands, mangroves, agricultural areas, parks, gardens, and roadsides; solitary, in pairs, or in groups.

REGIONS: CYP, TRQ, TEQ, NSW

Plate 54c

Olive-backed Oriole
Oriolus sagittatus

ID: Mid-sized songbird, olive green and streaked above, with brownish wings; whitish below with heavy dark streaking; dark tail with white tip; large orangish bill; red eye; to 28 cm (11 in). (The Yellow Oriole, *Oriolus flavocinctus*, of the Cape York Peninsula is similar, but yellow-olive or yellow-green all over.)

HABITAT: Rainforests, open forests and woodlands, trees along watercourses, scrub areas, parks, and gardens; solitary, in pairs, or in groups.

REGIONS: CYP, TRQ, TEQ, NSW, VIC

Plate 54d

Figbird
Sphecotheres viridis

ID: Male is mid-sized songbird, yellowish green above, with black head, grey neck/throat/upper chest, whitish belly, red skin around eye; male in Cape York Peninsula has yellow throat/chest; female is olive-brown, heavily streaked, with greyish or bluish skin around eye; to 29 cm (11.5 in).

HABITAT: Rainforests, open forests and woodlands, trees along watercourses, mangroves, parks, gardens, and roadsides; solitary, in pairs, or in groups.

REGIONS: CYP, TRQ, TEQ, NSW

Plate 54e

Dusky Woodswallow
Artamus cyanopterus

ID: Mid-sized brown songbird with grey wings with white edge; black area between bill and eye; grey-blue bill with black tip; black tail with white tip; to 18 cm (7 in).

HABITAT: Open forests and woodlands, scrub areas, and roadsides; in pairs or groups.

REGIONS: TRQ, TEQ, NSW, VIC, TAS

Plate 54f

White-breasted Woodswallow
Artamus leucorynchus

ID: Mid-sized songbird, brownish grey above with white chest, belly, and rump; all-dark tail; grey-blue bill with black tip; to 18 cm (7 in).

HABITAT: Rainforests, open forests and woodlands, trees near water, and mangroves; in pairs or groups.

REGIONS: CYP, TRQ, TEQ, NSW, VIC

Plate 54 **397**

a Black-faced Cuckoo-shrike

b Spangled Drongo

c Olive-backed Oriole

d Figbird

M

F

e Dusky Woodswallow

f White-breasted Woodswallow

Plate 55a
Pied Butcherbird
Cracticus nigrogularis
ID: Large songbird with black head and upper chest, white and black back, white rump and lower chest/belly; black wing with white markings; black tail with white lower edges; robust bluish grey bill with black hooked tip; immature is brown and whitish; to 36 cm (14 in).

HABITAT: Woodlands, scrub areas, agricultural districts, parks, gardens, and roadsides; solitary, in pairs, or in groups.

REGIONS: CYP, TRQ, TEQ, NSW, VIC

Plate 55b
Grey Butcherbird
Cracticus torquatus
ID: Largish songbird with black head, grey back, blackish wings with white streak; white collar, whitish or greyish chest/belly; white-tipped dark tail; robust bluish grey bill with black hooked tip; immature is brown and whitish; to 30 cm (12 in).

HABITAT: Rainforest edges, open forests and woodlands, scrub areas, agricultural districts, parks, gardens, and roadsides; solitary, in pairs, or in small groups.

REGIONS: CYP, TRQ, TEQ, NSW, VIC, TAS

Plate 55c
Magpie-lark
Grallina cyanoleuca
ID: Mid-sized black and white songbird with white bill; male with white stripe over eye, black throat/upper chest; female with white forehead and throat; to 29 cm (11.5 in)

HABITAT: Open habitats with trees, roadsides; in pairs or small groups.

REGIONS: CYP, TRQ, TEQ, NSW, VIC

Plate 55d
Australian Magpie
Gymnorhina tibicen
ID: Large black and white songbird, all black below with greyish/whitish bill; male with black head and back separated by wide white patch in back of neck (in some regions, including Victoria area, entire back is whitish), white rump and wing patch; female with grey back; to 44 cm (17 in).

HABITAT: Open forests and woodlands, and other open habitats with trees: agricultural areas, roadsides, parks, and gardens; usually in small groups.

REGIONS: CYP, TRQ, TEQ, NSW, VIC, TAS

Plate 55e
Pied Currawong
Strepera graculina
ID: Large black songbird with white patch on wing, white-tipped tail, and white under tail; robust black, hooked bill; yellowish eyes; to 50 cm (20 in), females a bit smaller.

HABITAT: Open forests and woodlands, scrub areas, agricultural regions, and settled areas; solitary, in pairs, or in groups.

REGIONS: CYP, TRQ, TEQ, NSW, VIC

Plate 55f
Grey Currawong
Strepera versicolor
ID: Large grey songbird with white patch on wing (seen mostly in flight), white-tipped tail, and white under-tail area; robust black, non-hooked bill; yellowish eyes; to 50 cm (20 in), females a bit smaller.

HABITAT: Open forests and woodlands, heathlands, scrub areas, agricultural regions, roadsides, and settled areas; solitary, in pairs, or in groups.

REGIONS: NSW, VIC, TAS

Plate 55 **399**

b Grey Butcherbird

a Pied Butcherbird

c Magpie-lark

F

M

d Australian Magpie

e Pied Currawong

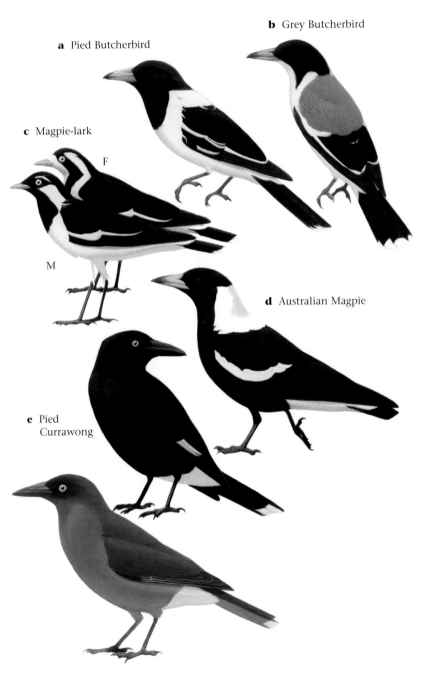

f Grey Currawong

Plate 56a

Paradise Riflebird
Ptiloris paradiseus

ID: Largish songbird with very long, down-curved, black bill; male is black with iridescent greenish/bluish crown and throat/chest; female is olive-brown above with whitish stripe above eye, buffy white below with brown markings; to 30 cm (12 in). (The Magnificent Riflebird, *Ptiloris magnificus*, of the northern CYP, is similar but the male has a narrow greenish band across its chest; Victoria's Riflebird, *Ptiloris victoriae*, is also similar but a bit smaller, and occurs only in the Cooktown-Cairns-Townsville region.)

HABITAT: Rainforests and adjacent open forests; solitary or in pairs.

REGIONS: TRQ, NSW

Plate 56b

Australian Raven
Corvus coronoides

ID: Large black bird with robust black bill; shaggy feathers fall from throat; white eye; to 53 cm (21 in). (Two other, very similar raven species are the Forest Raven, *Corvus tasmanicus*, which occurs in TAS, southern VIC and a bit of NSW, and the Little Raven, *Corvus mellori*, which occurs over most of VIC and NSW).

HABITAT: All except rainforests; common in agricultural and settled areas; in pairs or groups.

REGIONS: TRQ, TEQ, NSW, VIC

Plate 56c

Torresian Crow
Corvus orru

ID: Large black bird with robust black bill; white eye; to 53 cm (21 in), but usually a bit smaller than the Australian Raven.

HABITAT: Rainforest edges and most other habitats, including agricultural and settled areas; in pairs or small groups.

REGIONS: CYP, TRQ, TEQ, NSW

Plate 56d

White-winged Chough
Corcorax melanorhamphos

ID: Large black songbird with large white patch on wing, seen mostly in flight; long, black, down-curved bill; red eye; to 46 cm (18 in).

HABITAT: Dry forests and woodlands, scrub areas, trees along watercourses, and agricultural and some settled areas; in small groups.

REGIONS: TRQ, TEQ, NSW, VIC

Plate 56e

Apostlebird
Struthidea cinerea

ID: Large grey songbird with lighter streaking, brown wings, black tail, and shortish, robust black bill; to 33 cm (13 in).

HABITAT: Dry forests and woodlands, scrub areas, trees along watercourses and roads, and some agricultural and settled areas; in small groups.

REGIONS: CYP, TRQ, TEQ, NSW, VIC

Plate 56 401

a Paradise Riflebird

M

F

c Torresian Crow

b Australian Raven

d White-winged Chough

e Apostlebird

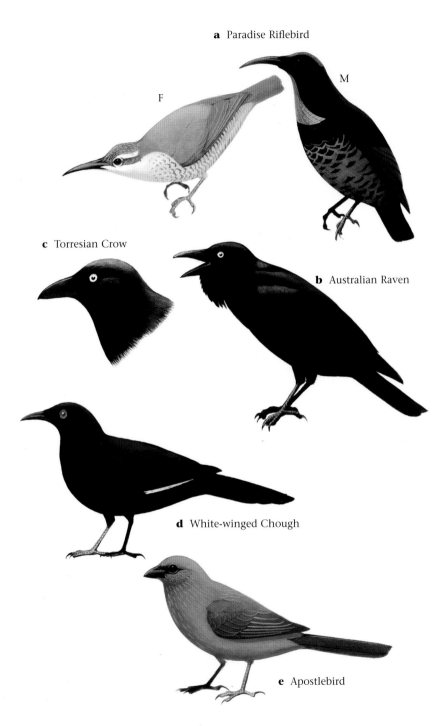

Plate 57a

Tooth-billed Bowerbird
(also called Tooth-billed Catbird)
Scenopoeetes dentirostris
ID: Mid-sized, stocky, olive-brown bird, lighter and heavily streaked below, with light eye-ring and brownish bill; to 27 cm (10.5 in).

HABITAT: Rainforests; solitary or in small groups.

REGIONS: CYP, TRQ

Plate 57b

Green Catbird
Ailuroedus crassirostris
ID: Mid-sized green bird with darker head, whitish bill and eye-ring, reddish eye; to 32 cm (12.5 in). (The similar Spotted Catbird, *Ailuroedus melanotis*, occurs in the Cairns and CYP regions.)

HABITAT: Rainforests and adjacent agricultural areas and trees along watercourses; in pairs or small groups.

REGIONS: TRQ, NSW

Plate 57c

Regent Bowerbird
Sericulus chrysocephalus
ID: Male is mid-sized, striking yellow and black with pale bill; female is mottled olive-brown with black patches on throat and back of neck, blackish bill; to 28 cm (11 in).

HABITAT: Rainforests and adjacent zones, scrub areas, orchards, and gardens; solitary or in groups.

REGIONS: TRQ, TEQ, NSW

Plate 57d

Satin Bowerbird
Ptilonorhynchus violaceus
ID: Male is mid-sized glossy blue-black with light bill and legs, shortish tail; female is olive green above, light below with brown scallop pattern; brownish wings and tail, brown bill; blue eyes; to 33 cm (13 in).

HABITAT: Rainforests and adjacent areas, some open forests, and woodlands; solitary or IN groups.

REGIONS: TRQ, NSW, VIC

Plate 57e

Great Bowerbird
Chlamydera nuchalis
ID: Mid-sized grey or grey-brown bird with darker back, wings, and tail, and robust, slightly down-curved bill; male with pinkish/lilac crest (often folded down) on back of neck; female usually a bit smaller and often lacks crest; to 38 cm (15 in).

HABITAT: Open forests and woodlands, scrubby areas, thickets, trees along watercourses, parks, and gardens; solitary or in small groups.

REGIONS: CYP, TRQ, TEQ

Plate 57 **403**

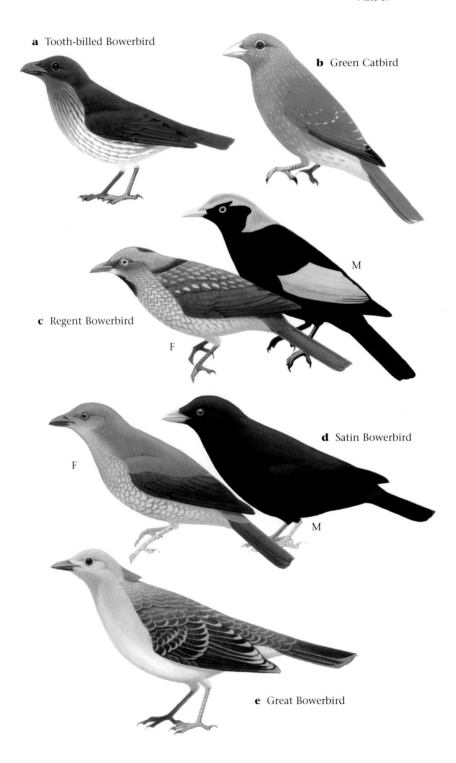

a Tooth-billed Bowerbird

b Green Catbird

M

c Regent Bowerbird

F

d Satin Bowerbird

F

M

e Great Bowerbird

Plate 58a
Skylark
Alauda arvensis
ID: Small to mid-sized brownish streaked songbird; light chest with brown streaks, whitish belly; usually inconspicuous crest; white tail edges seen in flight; smallish, pointed, buffy bill; to 19 cm (7.5 in).

HABITAT: Grasslands, scrub areas, agricultural districts, roadsides, and coastal dunes; solitary, in pairs, or in small groups. Introduced; native to Europe.

REGIONS: NSW, VIC, TAS

Plate 58b
Singing Bushlark
Mirafra javanica
ID: Small songbird, pale brown, reddish brown or dark brown, heavily streaked above; lighter below with dark spots, streaks, or mottling on chest; light stripe above eye; short, blunt bill, brown above, lighter below; to 15 cm (6 in).

HABITAT: Grasslands, open woodlands, scrub areas, and agricultural districts; solitary or in groups.

REGIONS: CYP, TRQ, TEQ, NSW, VIC

Plate 58c
Richard's Pipit
Anthus novaeseelandiae
ID: Smallish brown bird with darker streaks; whitish below with dark spots/streaks on chest; light stripe above eye; slender bill and long legs are flesh-colored; longish white-edged tail; to 18 cm (7 in).

HABITAT: Grasslands, open woodlands, agricultural districts, roadsides, and coastal dunes; solitary or in pairs.

REGIONS: CYP, TRQ, TEQ, NSW, VIC, TAS

Plate 58d
Double-barred Finch
Taeniopygia bichenovii
ID: Very small songbird, brownish or brown-grey above, white below, with two black bars; white face; blackish wings with light spots; black tail; bluish grey or grey bill, grey legs; to 11 cm (4.3 in).

HABITAT: Open forests and woodlands, grasslands, scrub areas, vegetation along watercourses, agricultural areas, parks, and gardens; in pairs or groups.

REGIONS: CYP, TRQ, TEQ, NSW, VIC

Plate 58e
Black-throated Finch
Poephila cincta
ID: Very small songbird, fawn-brown to olive-brown with blue-grey head and black throat/upper chest, tail, and bill; some with white rump, some black; reddish legs; to 11 cm (4.3 in).

HABITAT: Open forests, woodlands, and scrub areas, often near water; in pairs or groups.

REGIONS: CYP, TRQ, TEQ, NSW

Plate 58f
Red-browed Finch
Neochmia temporalis
ID: Small olive green songbird, grey below, with red eye-stripe, bill, and rump; black tail; to 12 cm (4.75 in).

HABITAT: Open forests and woodlands (especially open, grassy parts), scrub areas, heaths, mangroves, agricultural areas, roadsides, parks, and gardens; in pairs or groups.

REGIONS: CYP, TRQ, TEQ, NSW, VIC

Plate 58 **405**

a Skylark

b Singing Bushlark

d Double-barred Finch

c Richard's Pipit

e Black-throated Finch

f Red-browed Finch

Plate 59a
Chestnut-breasted Mannikin
Lonchura castaneothorax
ID: Small brown songbird with black face/throat, black chest band, and white belly; silver or blue-grey bill; female paler than male; to 12 cm (4.75 in).

HABITAT: Swamp and marsh vegetation, mangroves, coastal heaths, and roadsides; in pairs or groups.

REGIONS: CYP, TRQ, TEQ, NSW

Plate 59b
Diamond Firetail
Stagonopleura guttata
ID: Small songbird with brown back/wings, grey head; white underneath with black chest band with white spots; black eye-patch; reddish bill; to 13 cm (5 in).

HABITAT: Open forests and woodlands (especially open, grassy parts), scrub areas; in pairs or groups.

REGIONS: TRQ, TEQ, NSW, VIC

Plate 59c
Yellow-bellied Sunbird
(also called Olive-backed Sunbird)
Nectarinia jugularis
ID: Small songbird, olive above, yellow below, with very long, slender, down-curved bill and black tail with light tip; male only with blue-black throat/upper chest; to 12 cm (4.75 in).

HABITAT: Rainforest edges, vegetation along watercourses, mangroves, agricultural areas, parks, and gardens; solitary, in pairs, or in small groups.

REGIONS: CYP, TRQ

Plate 59d
Clamorous Reed-Warbler
Acrocephalus stentoreus
ID: Small brown songbird, darker above, very light below, with whitish/cream throat; light stripe above eye; slender bill dark above, lighter below; to 17 cm (6.5 in).

HABITAT: Reed vegetation in marshes, swamps, and vegetation along watercourses and gardens; in pairs or groups.

REGIONS: CYP, TRQ, TEQ, NSW, VIC, TAS

Plate 59e
Golden-headed Cisticola
Cisticola exilis
ID: Male is very small, brownish/gold, lighter below, with black streaked wings, shortish dark tail with light tip; slender bill dark above, lighter below; female's head has black streaks (as does the male's during nonbreeding season); to 11 cm (4.3 in).

HABITAT: Grasslands, marsh vegetation, shrublands, agricultural areas, and roadsides; in pairs or groups.

REGIONS: CYP, TRQ, TEQ, NSW, VIC

Plate 59f
Silvereye
Zosterops lateralis
ID: Small greenish songbird with grey back and chest, greenish or yellowish throat, brown/buffy sides; conspicuous white eye-ring; small dark bill; to 12 cm (4.75 in).

HABITAT: Most terrestrial habitats, including agricultural areas, parks, and gardens; in pairs or groups.

REGIONS: CYP, TRQ, TEQ, NSW, VIC, TAS

Plate 59 **407**

a Chestnut-breasted Mannikin

b Diamond Firetail

c Yellow-bellied Sunbird

M

F

d Clamorous Reed-Warbler

M

F

e Golden-headed Cisticola

f Silvereye

Plate 60a
Bassian Thrush
(also called White's Thrush)
Zoothera lunulata
ID: Mid-sized brown songbird with dark scale pattern; whitish below, also with scale pattern; light eye-ring and patch between eye and bill; brown bill; black and white bars under wing, seen in flight; to 29 cm (11.5 in).

HABITAT: Rainforests, open forests and woodlands, and forests along watercourses; usually on the ground; solitary, in pairs, or in small groups.

REGIONS: TRQ, NSW, VIC, TAS

Plate 60b
Rufous Songlark
Cincloramphus mathewsi
ID: Small, brown, streaked songbird, lighter to whitish below, with reddish brown rump and upper tail; dark lower tail; light stripe above eye; bill is black (male) or brownish (female); to 19 cm (7.5 in), male larger than female.

HABITAT: Grassy woodlands, scrub areas, and parks; solitary, in pairs, or in groups.

REGIONS: CYP, TRQ, TEQ, NSW, VIC

Plate 60c
Common Blackbird
Turdus merula
ID: Male is mid-sized, dull black with orange/yellowish bill and eye-ring; female is dark brown above, a bit lighter below, with whitish throat, light brown/yelowish bill; to 26 cm (10 in).

HABITAT: Open forest and woodlands, scrub areas, along watercourses, agricultural areas; parks, and gardens; solitary or in pairs. Introduced; native to Europe.

REGIONS: NSW, VIC, TAS

Plate 60d
Metallic Starling
(also called Shining Starling)
Aplonis metallica
ID: Mid-sized black songbird with green and purple iridescence; red eye; robust black bill; long pointed tail; immature has white underparts with dark streaks; to 24 cm (9.5 in).

HABITAT: Rainforest and adjacent woodlands, mangroves, and gardens; in small to large groups.

REGIONS: CYP, TRQ

Plate 60e
Common Starling
Sturnus vulgaris
ID: Mid-sized blackish songbird with green and purple iridescence; in some seasons with brownish, buffy, and white specks; shortish tail; bill yellowish or black (in winter); to 23 cm (9 in).

HABITAT: Open woodlands, scrub areas, cities, towns, agriculural areas, roadsides, beaches, parks, and gardens; usually in groups. Introduced; native to Eurasia.

REGIONS: TRQ, TEQ, NSW, VIC, TAS

Plate 60f
Common Myna
Acridotheres tristis
ID: Mid-sized, plump, chocolate brown songbird with black head; white wing patches seen in flight; black tail with light tip; yellow bill, legs, and patch behind eye; to 25 cm (10 in).

HABITAT: Agricultural sites, urban areas, and roadsides; in pairs or groups. Introduced; native to southern Asia.

REGIONS: TRQ, NSW, VIC

Plate 60 409

a Bassian Thrush

b Rufous Songlark

c Common Blackbird

M

F

d Metallic Starling

IM

e Common Starling

A

f Common Myna

Plate 61a
Platypus
(also called Duck-billed Platypus)
Ornithorhynchus anatinus
ID: Small, streamlined aquatic/amphibious mammal; dense brown fur with woolly underfur covers entire body except duck-like bill and feet; no visible ears; 40 to 55 cm (16 to 22 in) including tail; 700 to 2200 g (1.5 to 4.8 lb); males larger than females; the only duck-billed mammal in the world.

HABITAT: Mostly aquatic; found in and around lakes, ponds, rivers, and streams in many habitat types within its range (seaboard of Queensland, New South Wales, and Victoria, including both sides of Great Dividing Range, and in Tasmania); solitary; usually dusk- and dawn-active, but may be active at any time.

REGIONS: TRQ, TEQ, NSW, VIC, TAS

Plate 61b
Short-beaked Echidna
(also called Spiny Anteater)
Tachyglossus aculeatus
ID: Small brown or blackish animal with a slender, beak-like snout and long, sharp, sturdy spines; in cooler regions, such as Tasmania, hairs may be long enough to completely cover the spines; you will know it when you see it; 30 to 45 cm (12 to 18 in); 2.5 to 6.5 kg (5.5 to 14 lb).

HABITAT: Almost all terrestrial habitats, on the ground; solitary; nocturnal in hot deserts, dusk- and dawn-active in other places, but may be seen at any time.

REGIONS: CYP, TRQ, TEQ, NSW, VIC, TAS

Plate 61c
Spot-tailed Quoll
(also called Tiger Cat, Spot-tailed Native Cat)
Dasyurus maculatus
ID: Mid-sized rodent-like animal with pointed snout, shortish ears, brown or reddish brown coloring above, lighter below; white spots on body and tail; the largest marsupial carnivore on the mainland, with males larger than females; 35 to 76 cm (14 to 30 in), plus tail 34 to 55 cm (13 to 21 in); to 7 kg (15 lb).

HABITAT: Mainly in open forests and woodlands, but sometimes in rainforests and coastal heaths; terrestrial and arboreal; usually nocturnal but sometimes forages by day; solitary.

REGIONS: CYP, TRQ, NSW, VIC, TAS

NOTE: Considered vulnerable in New South Wales and Victoria.

Plate 61d
Eastern Quoll
(also called Eastern Native Cat)
Dasyurus viverrinus
ID: Mid-sized, rodent-like animal with pointed snout, mid-sized ears, brown or black coloring above, lighter below; white spots on body (but not on tail); males larger than females; 28 to 45 cm (11 to 18 in), plus tail 17 to 28 cm (6 to 11 in); 0.7 to 2 kg (1.5 to 4.4 lb).

HABITAT: Open dry forests, heathlands, scrub and pasture areas on Tasmania only and some nearby offshore islands; terrestrial and arboreal; nocturnal; solitary.

REGIONS: TAS

NOTE: Considered vulnerable.

Plate 61e
Tasmanian Devil
Sarcophilus harrisii
ID: Mid-sized, stocky, with blunt snout and round, short ears; black with a few white markings, usually one on chest; 57 to 65 cm (22 to 26 in), plus tail 24 to 26 cm (9 to 10 in); 6 to 10 kg (13.2 to 22 lb).

HABITAT: Common in many northern, eastern, and central areas of Tasmania where livestock rangeland provides carrion, but can be seen almost anywhere in the state; terrestrial; nocturnal; often solitary.

REGIONS: TAS

Plate 61　411

a Platypus

b Short-beaked Echidna

c Spot-tailed Quoll

d Eastern Quoll

e Tasmanian Devil

Plate 62a
Yellow-footed Antechinus
(also called Yellow-footed Marsupial Mouse)
Antechinus flavipes
ID: Small, rodent-like, with grey head and orange-brown back, sides, and feet; more orangy in northern part of range, more brownish in southern reaches; light eye-rings; dark-tipped tail; males larger than females; 8.5 to 16.5 cm (3.5 to 6.5 in), plus tail 6.5 to 15 cm (2.5 to 6 in); 20 to 80 g (1 to 3 oz).

HABITAT: Rainforests, dry open forests, and woodlands, as well as more open sites, including suburban gardens; terrestrial and often arboreal; night- and sometimes day-active; solitary.

REGIONS: TRQ, TEQ, NSW, VIC

Plate 62b
Dusky Antechinus
(also called Dusky Marsupial Mouse)
Antechinus swainsonii
ID: Small and rodent-like with small ears, greyish brown or brownish black coloring, often with grizzled appearance; males larger than females; 9 to 20 cm (3.5 to 8 in), plus tail 7.5 to 12 cm (3 to 5 in); 35 to 80 g (1 to 3 oz). (The Brown Antechinus, *Antechinus stuartii*, which occurs in wet and dry forests over small areas of coastal tropical Queensland and eastern New South Wales, is a bit smaller than the Dusky Antechinus, greyish brown, and usually has a tail as long as its body.)

HABITAT: Varied, including wet open forests, woodlands, and heathlands; common in alpine heaths; terrestrial (juveniles also arboreal); day- and night-active; solitary.

REGIONS: TRQ, NSW, VIC, TAS

Plate 62c
Brush-tailed Phascogale
Phascogale tapoatafa
ID: Small and rodent-like with large, unfurred ears, grey or grizzled grey coloring above, light below; large brush-like tail; males larger than females; 15 to 26 cm (6 to 10 in), plus tail 16 to 23 cm (6 to 9 in); 100 to 300 g (3.5 to 11 oz).

HABITAT: Drier open forests; mostly arboreal but also terrestrial; night-active; solitary.

REGIONS: CYP, TRQ, TEQ, NSW, VIC

NOTE: Considered vulnerable in New South Wales.

Plate 62d
Common Planigale
(also called Pygmy Marsupial Mouse)
Planigale maculata
ID: Tiny, rodent-like, with flattened head and whitish chin/throat; reddish brown, cinnamon, or greyish coloring with white spots above; lighter below; males larger than females; 7 to 10 cm (3 to 4 in), plus tail 6 to 9.5 cm (2.5 to 4 in); 6 to 22 g (0.2 to 1 oz).

HABITAT: Rainforests, open forests, and some grasslands, as well as marshlands and some rocky areas; terrestrial; nocturnal; often solitary.

REGIONS: CYP, TRQ, TEQ, NSW

Plate 62e
Fat-tailed Dunnart
(also called Fat-tailed Marsupial Mouse)
Sminthopsis crassicaudata
ID: Tiny, rodent-like, with large ears and eyes, pointed snout; brown above, white below; head and body together are longer than the tail, which is usually swollen at the base; males a bit larger than females; 6 to 9 cm (2.4 to 3.5 in), plus tail 4 to 7 cm (1.5 to 2.7 in); 10 to 20 g (0.3 to 0.7 oz).

HABITAT: Open forests, woodlands, heathlands, and some shrubland and grassland areas; terrestrial; nocturnal; usually solitary.

REGIONS: TEQ, NSW, VIC

Plate 62f
Common Dunnart
(also called Common Marsupial Mouse)
Sminthopsis murina
ID: Tiny, rodent-like, grey above, whitish below, with large ears, large eyes, and pointed snout; tail about as long as body and not enlarged at base; males a bit larger than females; 6.5 to 10.5 cm (2.5 to 4 in), plus tail 7 to 10 cm (2.8 to 4 in); 10 to 30 g (0.3 to 1 oz).

HABITAT: Dry forests, woodlands, and heathlands; terrestrial; nocturnal; usually solitary.

REGIONS: TRQ, NSW, VIC

Plate 62 **413**

a Yellow-footed Antechinus

Brown Antechinus

b Dusky Antechinus

c Brush-tailed Phascogale

d Common Planigale

e Fat-tailed Dunnart

f Common Dunnart

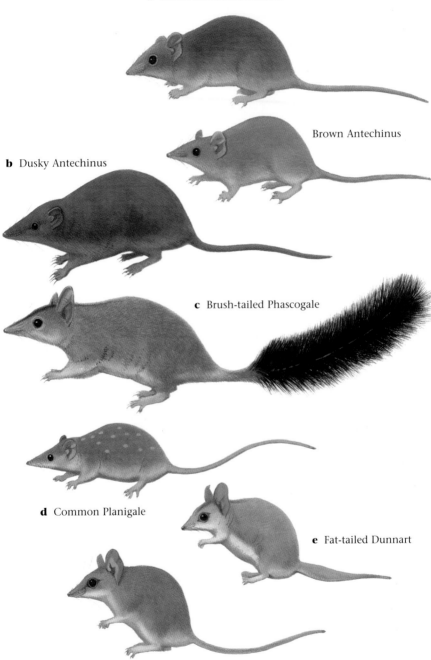

Plate 63a

Koala
(also called Native Bear, Monkey Bear)
Phascolarctos cinereus

ID: I won't waste ink here describing Koalas in detail; if you see a teddy bear sitting in a tree, you've found one; to 80 cm (32 in) long; to 13 kg (29 lb); smaller, lighter-colored (pale grey) in warmer Queensland; larger, darker (grey-brown) in cooler New South Wales and Victoria.

HABITAT: Dry eucalypt forests below 600 m (2,000 ft) with smooth-barked eucalypt trees; central and southeastern Queensland, eastern New South Wales, and eastern and southern Victoria on both sides of the Great Dividing Range; arboreal, nocturnal, but often spotted by day nestled in the fork of a tree.

REGIONS: TRQ, TEQ, NSW, VIC

NOTE: Considered vulnerable in New South Wales.

Plate 63b

Common Wombat
(also called Forest Wombat)
Vombatus ursinus

ID: Largish, thick-bodied, and rodent-like with short limbs, long claws, and stubby tail; grizzled brown, brown-grey, beige, or, rarely, blackish; to 1 m (3.3 ft); 25 cm (10 in) high; 20 to 40 kg (44 to 88 lb).

HABITAT: Mainly wetter eucalypt forests and adjacent grasslands/grazing lands from southeast Queensland along the Great Dividing Range to southwest Victoria; some occur in coastal grasslands; also Tasmania and Flinders Island; terrestrial and fossorial (burrowing); dusk- and night-active; solitary.

REGIONS: TEQ, NSW, VIC, TAS

Plate 63c

Northern Brown Bandicoot
(also called Brindled Bandicoot)
Isodon macrourus

ID: Small, rodent-like, with long snout and short, rounded ears; grizzled brown or brown-black above, whitish below; 30 to 47 cm (12 to 18 in), plus tail 8 to 21 cm (3 to 8 in); 0.5 to 3.1 kg (1 to 7 lb).

HABITAT: Prefers areas with good ground cover, such as dense grasses or shrubs, both in and around open forests/woodlands and more open habitats; terrestrial; nocturnal; solitary.

REGIONS: CYP, TRQ, TEQ, NSW

Plate 63d

Long-nosed Bandicoot
Perameles nasuta

ID: Small, rodent-like, with very long snout and long, pointed ears; grey-brown above, whitish below; 31 to 42 cm (12 to 16 in), plus tail 12 to 15 cm (5 to 6 in); 0.8 to 1.1 kg (1.8 to 2.4 lb).

HABITAT: Wet and dry forests and woodlands, with and without dense ground cover; terrestrial; nocturnal; solitary; digs conical holes in forest floor, suburban lawns, and gardens.

REGIONS: CYP, TRQ, TEQ, NSW, VIC

Plate 63e

Rufous Spiny Bandicoot
Echymipera rufescens

ID: Small, rodent-like, with long, blunt snout; spiny fur blackish or grizzled with reddish brown on back and rump; short, black, almost hairless tail; 30 to 40 cm (12 to 16 in), plus tail 7 to 10 cm (3 to 4 in); 0.5 to 2 kg (1 to 4.5 lb).

HABITAT: Rainforests and adjacent grassy and open woodlands; often in rocky areas near watercourses; terrestrial; nocturnal; solitary.

REGIONS: CYP

Plate 63 **415**

a Koala

b Common Wombat

c Northern Brown Bandicoot

d Long-nosed Bandicoot

e Rufous Spiny Bandicoot

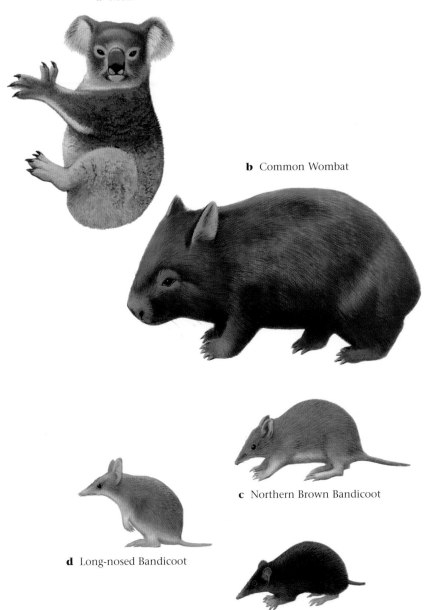

Plate 64a
Sugar Glider
(also called Sugar Squirrel, Lesser Glider)
Petaurus breviceps
ID: Small, squirrel-like; light grey to brownish grey above, pale grey to creamy white below; distinct dark stripe along mid-back; 15 to 21 cm (6 to 8 in), plus tail 16 to 21 cm (6 to 8 in); 100 to 170 g (3.6 to 6 oz). (Note: the Squirrel Glider, *Petaurus norfolcensis*, occurs in many of the same areas; it is a bit larger than Sugar Glider, with a longer, more pointed face and bushier tail.)

HABITAT: All types of forests and woodlands; arboreal; nocturnal (often leaves day shelter at dusk); usually in small groups.

REGIONS: CYP, TRQ, TEQ, NSW, VIC, TAS

Plate 64b
Yellow-bellied Glider
(also called Fluffy Glider)
Petaurus australis
ID: Mid-sized, squirrel-like; grey or grey-brown above, whitish to orangish below with a distinct dark stripe along mid-back, dark stripe on thigh; ears large and hairless; tail about 1.5 times as long as body; 27 to 32 cm (10.5 to 12.5 in), plus tail 42 to 48 cm (16.5 to 19 in); 450 to 700 g (1 to 1.5 lb).

HABITAT: Wet and dry open forests and woodlands; arboreal; nocturnal (often leaves day shelter at dusk); often in small groups.

REGIONS: TRQ, TEQ, NSW, VIC

NOTE: This species is considered vulnerable in New South Wales and northern Queensland.

Plate 64c
Greater Glider
(also called Dusky Glider, Squirrel)
Petauroides volans
ID: Mid-sized (cat-sized), with large, rounded, furred ears; variable coloring, brown, black-brown, grey, or cream above, whitish below; very long, furry tail; 35 to 45 cm (14 to 18 in), plus tail 45 to 60 cm (18 to 24 in); 0.9 to 1.8 kg (2 to 4 lb). The largest gliding marsupial.

HABITAT: Treetops of eucalypt woodlands, most commonly in higher-elevation areas; arboreal; nocturnal; solitary.

REGIONS: TRQ, TEQ, NSW, VIC

Plate 64d
Common Spotted Cuscus
(also called Phalanger)
Spilocuscus maculatus
ID: Mid-sized, densely-furred, with shortish snout; small ears almost invisible; male grey with light spots above, whitsh below; female often uniformly grey, sometimes with lighter rump; 35 to 45 cm (14 to 18 in), plus tail 45 to 60 cm (18 to 24 in); 0.9 to 1.8 kg (2 to 4 lb).

HABITAT: Rainforests and adjacent open forests, plus some mangrove areas; arboreal; nocturnal (but sometimes day-active); solitary.

REGIONS: CYP

Plate 64e
Feathertail Glider
(also called Pygmy Glider, Flying Mouse)
Acrobates pygmaeus
ID: Tiny (mouse-sized); grey or greyish brown above, whitish below; long, feather-like tail; short, fast glides; 6 to 8 cm (2.5 to 3 in), plus tail 7 to 8 cm (2.8 to 3 in); 10 to 15 g (0.3 to 0.5 oz). The smallest gliding mammal.

HABITAT: All forest types and woodlands; arboreal; nocturnal; in small groups.

REGIONS: CYP, TRQ, TEQ, NSW, VIC

Plate 64 417

a Sugar Glider

b Yellow-bellied Glider

c Greater Glider

d Common Spotted Cuscus

e Feathertail Glider

Plate 65 (*See also*: Possums, p. 217)

Plate 65a

Eastern Pygmy-possum
(also called Possum Mouse)
Cercartetus nanus

ID: Very small, mouse-like, with smallish round ears; grey, fawn, brownish, or olive-brown above, whitish or pale grey below; tail as long as body; 8 to 11 cm (3 to 4 in), plus tail 7 to 10 cm (2.5 to 4 in); 20 to 45 g (0.7 to 1.6 oz).

HABITAT: Wet open forests, eucalypt forests, some rainforests; also heathlands and shrublands with trees; arboreal; nocturnal; solitary.

REGIONS: TRQ, NSW, VIC, TAS

Plate 65b

Striped Possum
(also called Striped Phalanger)
Dactylopsila trivirgata

ID: Medium-sized, squirrel-like, black-and-white striped; fourth finger very long; 24 to 27 cm (9.5 to 10.5 in), plus tail 31 to 34 cm (12 to 13 in); 250 to 530 g (0.5 to 1.2 lb).

HABITAT: Tropical rainforests and adjacent woodlands, plus some coastal scrub areas; arboreal; nocturnal; solitary.

REGIONS: CYP, TRQ

Plate 65c

Common Ringtail Possum
(also called Rufous Ringtail)
Pseudocheirus peregrinus

ID: Mid-sized, rodent-like; grey to blackish above, sometimes with reddish brown tinge, white to reddish brown below; short ears with white patch underneath; short-furred, tapered tail with white tip; 30 to 38 cm (12 to 15 in), plus tail 30 to 35 cm (12 to 14 in); 0.65 to 1.1 kg (1.4 to 2.4 lb).

HABITAT: Rainforests, open forests, and woodlands, usually with dense understory vegetation, generally in wetter regions; arboreal; nocturnal; solitary or in small family groups.

REGIONS: CYP, TRQ, TEQ, NSW, VIC, TAS

Plate 65d

Daintree River Ringtail Possum
Pseudochirulus cinereus

ID: Medium-sized, small-eared, with tapered, white-tipped tail; brown, light brown or carmel above, whitish below; dark stripe on head and often continuing along mid-back; males a bit larger; 33 to 37 cm (13 to 14.5 in), plus tail 32 to 39 cm (12.5 to 15 in); 0.7 to 1.5 kg (1.5 to 3.3 lb).

HABITAT: Rainforests above 400 m (1,300 ft) in northeastern Queensland; mainly arboreal but occasionally on the ground; nocturnal; solitary.

REGIONS: TRQ

Plate 65e

Mountain Brushtail Possum
Trichosurus caninus

ID: Medium-sized, with shortish, rounded ears; dark grey, silver grey, or amber-brown above, whitish below; blackish, bushy, tapered tail; 40 to 48 cm (16 to 19 in), plus tail 32 to 42 cm (13 to 17 in); 2.5 to 4.5 kg (5.5 to 10 lb).

HABITAT: Rainforests and adjacent open forests, moist forest gullies/valleys, mostly along Great Dividing Range; mainly arboreal but sometimes on the ground; nocturnal; solitary or in pairs.

REGIONS: TRQ, NSW, VIC

Plate 65f

Common Brushtail Possum
(also called Silver-grey Possum)
Trichosurus vulpecula

ID: Medium-sized with long ears and blackish facial markings; silver grey or reddish brown above (or blackish, especially in the southeast and Tasmania), whitish to reddish brown below; black bushy or sparsely haired tail; 40 to 48 cm (16 to 19 in), plus tail 32 to 42 cm (13 to 17 in); 2.5 to 4.5 kg (5.5 to 10 lb).

HABITAT: Rainforests, open forests, and woodlands; mainly arboreal but sometimes on the ground; nocturnal; solitary.

REGIONS: CYP, TRQ, TEQ, NSW, VIC, TAS

Plate 65 419

a Eastern Pygmy-possum

b Striped Possum

c Common Ringtail Possum

d Daintree River Ringtail Possum

e Mountain Brushtail Possum

f Common Brushtail Possum

Plate 66a

Musky Rat-kangaroo
Hypsiprymnodon moschatus

ID: Small, brown, with grey-brown head and scaly, naked-looking tail; 5 toes on hindfoot (others in this group and "true" kangaroos have 4); bounding gait; 20 to 27 cm (8 to 10.5 in), plus tail 12 to 17 cm (5 to 6.5 in); 400 to 700 g (0.8 to 1.5 lb).

HABITAT: Some rainforest areas of northeastern Queensland (from about Ingham in the south to near Cooktown in the north); terrestrial but also in fallen trees; day- or night-active; solitary.

REGIONS: TRQ

Plate 66b

Lumholtz's Tree-kangaroo
(also called Tree-climber)
Dendrolagus lumholtzi

ID: Large, dark brown, with light band across forehead and down each side of face (the similar Bennet's Tree-kangaroo, whose range lies to the north of Lumholtz's, lacks these light bands); very long tail is light at base and very dark at end; 52 to 65 cm (20.5 to 25.5 in), plus tail 65 to 75 cm (25.5 to 29.5 in); 5.1 to 8.6 kg (11 to 19 lb).

HABITAT: Some mountainous rainforest areas of northeastern Queensland (from about Kirrama in the south to Mt. Spurgeon in the north); arboreal and terrestrial; solitary.

REGIONS: TRQ

NOTE: Rare; CITES Appendix II listed.

Plate 66c

Rufous Bettong
(also called Rufous Rat-kangaroo)
Aepyprymnus rufescens

ID: Mid-sized, greyish with reddish brown tinge, lighter below; long claws on forelimbs; tail is hairy and tapered; faint light stripe on hip; 37 to 39 cm (14.5 to 15.5 in), plus tail 34 to 40 cm (13.5 to 16 in); 1 to 3.5 kg (2.2 to 7.7 lb). (Note: the similar Tasmanian Bettong occurs in eastern Tasmania.)

HABITAT: Wet and dry open forests, usually with grassy ground cover; terrestrial; nocturnal; solitary or in small groups.

REGIONS: TRQ, TEQ, NSW, VIC

NOTE: Considered vulnerable in New South Wales.

Plate 66d

Long-nosed Potoroo
(also called Long-nosed Rat-kangaroo)
Potorous tridactylus

ID: Small, rat-like, with pointed snout; brown or greyish brown above, lighter below; short, rounded ears, very short hindlimbs, naked skin from nose onto snout; 32 to 40 cm (12.5 to 16 in), plus tail 18 to 26 cm (7 to 10 in); 660 to 1640 g (1.5 to 3.6 lb).

HABITAT: Moist and dry open forests and heathlands of coastal regions, in areas with dense ground cover (in Queensland, occurs in extreme southeast corner only); terrestrial; nocturnal but sometimes active in late afternoon; solitary or in small family groups.

REGIONS: TRQ, NSW, VIC, TAS

NOTE: Considered vulnerable in New South Wales.

Plate 66e

Spectacled Hare-wallaby
Lagorchestes conspicillatus

ID: Small, stocky wallaby, brown or greyish brown above, whitish below, with orange around eyes; light stripe on hip; 40 to 47 cm (16 to 18.5 in), plus tail 37 to 39 cm (14.5 to 15.5 in); 1.6 to 4.5 kg (3.5 to 10 lb).

HABITAT: Grasslands and grassy areas of open forest, woodlands, and shrublands; most often found in livestock grazing areas; terrestrial; nocturnal; solitary but occasionally in small groups.

REGIONS: CYP, TRQ

Plate 66 **421**

a Musky Rat-kangaroo

b Lumholtz's Tree-kangaroo

c Rufous Bettong

d Long-nosed Potoroo

e Spectacled Hare-wallaby

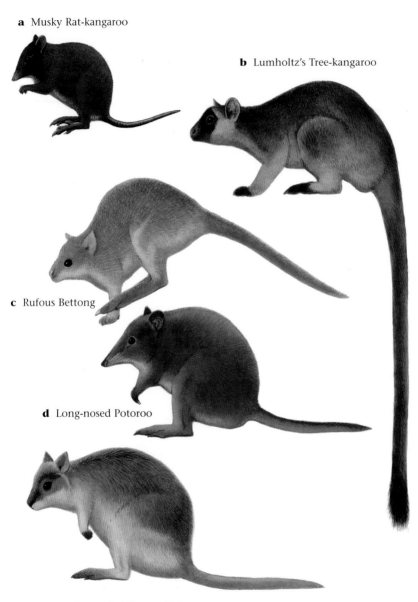

Plate 67a
Antilopine Wallaroo
(also called Antelope Kangaroo)
Macropus antilopinus
ID: Large, reddish tan or light brown with lighter or whitish underparts; tips of hands and feet black; pale lower jaw; some females all grey or with grey head and neck; to 1.2 m (4 ft), plus tail to 90 cm (3 ft); to 49 kg (108 lb); males much larger than females.

HABITAT: Tropical open forests with grassy floor and savannah-like areas; usually in flat or rolling landscapes, but sometimes in hilly regions; usually more active in late afternoon and night (especially in hot weather); solitary or small groups.

REGIONS: CYP

Plate 67b
Black-striped Wallaby
(also called Scrub Wallaby)
Macropus dorsalis
ID: Mid-sized, light brown, greyish brown or reddish brown, with conspicuous dark stripe along mid-back and lighter or whitish underparts; white patch below eye; horizontal light stripe on thigh; to 82 cm (2.7 ft), plus tail to 83 cm (2.7 ft); to 20 kg (44 lb); males much larger than females.

HABITAT: Areas with thick shrub cover including at rainforest edges, open forests with dense shrubs, scrub areas, and thickets; active late afternoon and night; in small groups.

REGIONS: TRQ, TEQ, NSW

NOTE: Considered endangered in New South Wales.

Plate 67c
Eastern Grey Kangaroo
(also called Black-faced Kangaroo)
Macropus giganteus
ID: Large, robust, light to dark grey with paler underparts; dark hands, feet, and tail tip; hairy snout; female often with white chest; to 1.3 m (4.3 ft), plus tail to 1.1 m (3.6 ft); to 75 kg (165 lb); males much larger than females.

HABITAT: Drier open forests, woodlands, and scrub areas; active late afternoon and night; in small groups.

REGIONS: CYP, TRQ, TEQ, NSW, VIC, TAS

Plate 67d
Whiptail Wallaby
(also called Pretty-face Wallaby)
Macropus parryi
ID: Mid-sized, slender, brownish grey (or light grey in winter) with whitish underparts, dark brown forehead, brown and white ears, white stripe along lip, light brown stripe down neck, and white hip stripe; some with dark-tipped tail; to 95 cm (3 ft), plus tail to 1 m (3.3 ft); to 26 kg (57 lb); males larger than females.

HABITAT: Open forests with grassy floors, usually in rolling or hilly terrain; active mainly in early morning and late afternoon; in small and mid-sized groups.

REGIONS: TRQ, TEQ, NSW

Plate 67e
Common Wallaroo (Euro)
(also called Hill Kangaroo)
Macropus robustus
ID: Large, dark grey and blackish to reddish brown, with shaggy, coarse hair; lighter underparts; some males with reddish brown stripe across shoulders; nose bare and black; short, thick tail; to 1.1 m (3.6 ft), plus tail to 90 cm (3 ft); to 60 kg (132 lb); males larger than females.

HABITAT: Varied, but always in or around rocky areas, caves, escarpments, or rock ledges, where it shelters during heat of day; nocturnal; solitary or in small groups.

REGIONS: CYP, TRQ, TEQ, NSW, VIC

Plate 67 **423**

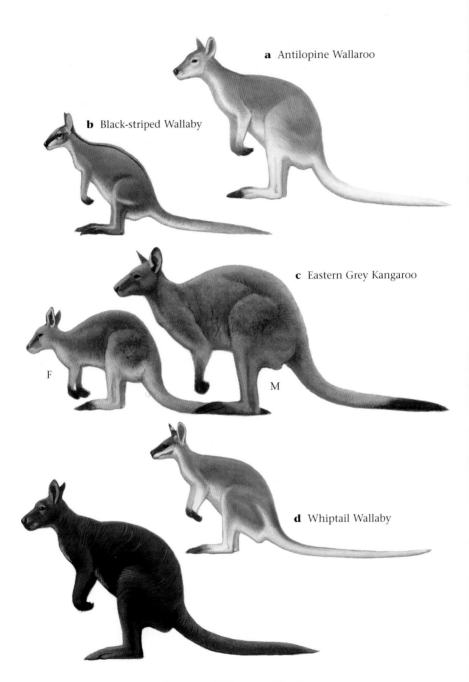

a Antilopine Wallaroo

b Black-striped Wallaby

c Eastern Grey Kangaroo

F

M

d Whiptail Wallaby

e Common Wallaroo or "Euro"

Plate 68a

Red-necked Wallaby
(also called Brush Walllaby)
Macropus rufogriseus

ID: Mid-sized, brown, reddish brown, or grizzled grey (dark grey in Tasmania) with reddish brown neck and shoulders, whitish or grey underparts, light stripe on lip, black snout, hands, and feet; tail with bushy tip; females usually paler than males; to 90 cm (3 ft), plus tail to 88 cm (2.9 ft); to 26 kg (57 lb); males larger than females.

HABITAT: Coastal heathlands, open forests, and woodlands, usually with dense shrub/grass floor; active late afternoon and night; solitary or in small groups.

REGIONS: TRQ, TEQ, NSW, VIC, TAS

Plate 68b

Northern Nailtail Wallaby
Onychogalea unguifera

ID: Smallish, light brown or tan, with dark stripe along mid-back and onto tail, faint dark stripe often on shoulder, light stripe on side and thigh; squarish snout; tail end dark and bushy, with hidden nail at tip; to 70 cm (2.3 ft), plus tail to 73 cm (2.4 ft); to 9 kg (20 lb); males larger than females.

HABITAT: Open woodlands with grassy floors, shrublands, grasslands with scattered trees or shrubs; nocturnal; solitary or feeding in groups of 2 to 4.

REGIONS: CYP

Plate 68c

Swamp Wallaby
(also called Black Wallaby)
Wallabia bicolor

ID: Mid-sized, dark brown or blackish with reddish brown, orangish, or yellowish brown underparts; light cheek stripe; dark hands, feet, and, often, tail (tip sometimes whitish); to 85 cm (2.8 ft), plus tail to 86 cm (2.8 ft); to 22 kg (48 lb); males larger than females.

HABITAT: Rainforests, open forests with dense shrub/grass floor, and heathlands; active day or night; solitary or in feeding groups of 2 or 3.

REGIONS: CYP, TRQ, TEQ, NSW, VIC

Plate 68d

Allied Rock-wallaby
Petrogale assimilis

ID: Small, dark brown to grey-brown, with lighter underparts, forearms, parts of legs, and base of tail; light cheek stripe (some also with dark stripe on head); dark hands and feet; tail very dark at end, with brushy tip; to 59 cm (1.9 ft), plus tail to 55 cm (1.8 ft); to 5 kg (11 lb); males larger than females.

HABITAT: Rocky areas of wet and dry forests, over parts of northeast Queensland and some offshore islands; usually nocturnal; in small colonies.

REGIONS: TRQ, TEQ

Plate 68e

Herbert's Rock-wallaby
Petrogale herberti

ID: Small, grey-brown with darker head and shoulders, lighter underparts, faint light cheek stripe, dark stripe from forehead to mid-back; outside of ears dark at base, faint white side stripe, dark hands, forearms, and feet; tail darkens toward end; to 61 cm (2 ft), plus tail to 66 cm (2.2 ft); to 6.8 kg (15 lb); males larger than females.

HABITAT: Rocky areas with caves and crevices in rainforest valleys, wet and dry open forests, and woodlands; usually nocturnal; in small to mid-sized colonies.

REGIONS: TRQ, TEQ

Plate 68 **425**

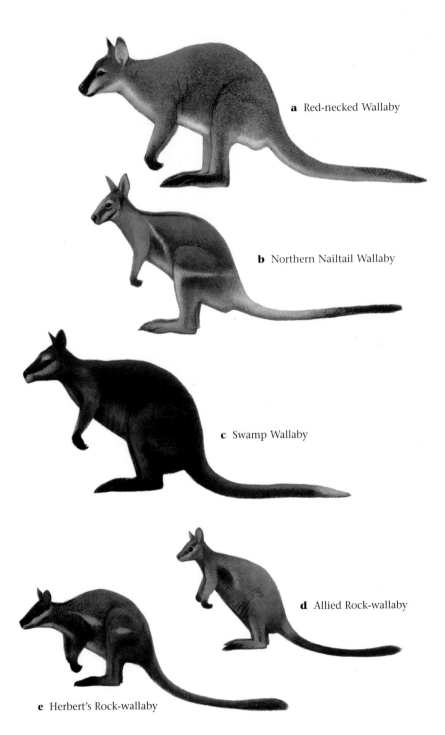

a Red-necked Wallaby

b Northern Nailtail Wallaby

c Swamp Wallaby

d Allied Rock-wallaby

e Herbert's Rock-wallaby

Plate 69a

Unadorned Rock-wallaby
(also called Plain Rock-wallaby)
Petrogale inornata
ID: Small, grey, grey brown, or brownish (coloring varies with the coloring of their rocky homes), with lighter underparts, forearms, and at tail base; some with light cheek stripe and/or dark stripe along mid-back; long tail darkens from base to slightly bushy tip; to 57 cm (1.8 ft), plus tail to 64 cm (2.1 ft); to 5.6 kg (12 lb); males larger than females.

HABITAT: Rocky, hilly areas in forested regions of central coastal Queensland, north of Rockhampton and south of Townsville; nocturnal; in small colonies.

REGIONS: TRQ

Plate 69b

Brush-tailed Rock-wallaby
Petrogale penicillata
ID: Smallish, brown, with lighter or whitish underparts, reddish brown rump; some with greyish shoulders; light cheek stripe, dark stripe on top of head, ears black outside, light inside; very dark hands and feet; tail darkens from base to very brushy tip; to 59 cm (1.9 ft), plus tail to 70 cm (2.3 ft); to 10 kg (22 lb); males larger than females.

HABITAT: Steep rocky sites with caves and ledges in open forests and woodlands, some rainforest gullies/valleys, and more open areas with rocky outcroppings; nocturnal; solitary or in small groups.

REGIONS: TRQ, NSW, VIC

NOTE: Considered vulnerable in Queensland and New South Wales; endangered in Victoria.

Plate 69c

Tasmanian Pademelon
(also called Red-bellied Pademelon)
Thylogale billardierii
ID: Smallish and stocky, dark brown or grey-brown with lighter, often reddish brown underparts; thickish short tail; to 62 cm (2 ft), plus tail to 48 cm (1.6 ft); to 10 kg (22 lb); males larger than females; the only pademelon in Tasmania.

HABITAT: Coastal and higher-elevation forests with or near extensive grassy areas; nocturnal; usually in small groups.

REGIONS: TAS

Plate 69d

Red-legged Pademelon
Thylogale stigmatica
ID: Small, brown or grey-brown (darker overall in rainforests), with lighter underparts, reddish brown cheeks, forearms/shoulders, and thighs; thickish short tail; to 54 cm (1.8 ft), plus tail to 47 cm (1.5 ft); to 6.9 kg (15 lb); males larger than females.

HABITAT: Densely-vegetated sites in rainforests, open wet forests, and some scrubby thicket areas; nocturnal; solitary or in small feeding groups.

REGIONS: CYP, TRQ, NSW

NOTE: Considered vulnerable in New South Wales.

Plate 69e

Red-necked Pademelon
(also called Pademelon Wallaby)
Thylogale thetis
ID: Small, brownish grey, with lighter or whitish underparts; reddish brown neck and shoulders; short, thickish tail; to 62 cm (2 ft), plus tail to 51 cm (1.7 ft); to 9 kg (20 lb); males larger than females.

HABITAT: Dense rainforests, open wet forests, and forest edges (especially bordering grassy areas) in the southeast corner of Queensland and eastern New South Wales; active day or night; solitary or in small feeding groups.

REGIONS: TRQ, NSW

Plate 69 427

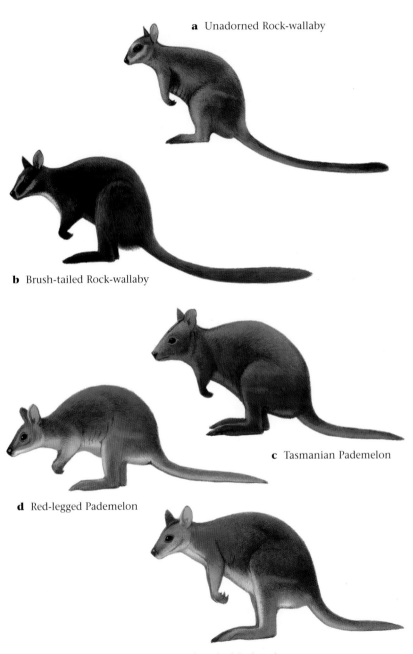

a Unadorned Rock-wallaby

b Brush-tailed Rock-wallaby

c Tasmanian Pademelon

d Red-legged Pademelon

e Red-necked Pademelon

Plate 70a
Black Flying-fox
(also called Black Fruit Bat)
Pteropus alecto
ID: Large bat covered with short black hair, sometimes with "frosted" belly; often reddish brown at back of neck; some with faint brown eye-rings; head and body length to 26 cm (10 in); wingspan to 1.5 m (4.9 ft); 600 to 850 g (1.3 to 1.9 lb).

HABITAT: Coastal rainforests, mangrove forests; day roosts in trees on mangrove islands, in swamps and along estuaries, often mixed with other flying fox species; nocturnal; colonial; eats fruit and blossoms.

REGIONS: CYP, TRQ, NSW

NOTE: Considered vulnerable in New South Wales.

Plate 70b
Grey-headed Flying-fox
(also called Grey-headed Fruit Bat)
Pteropus poliocephalus
ID: Large bat covered with dense shaggy hair; grey or whitish head, grey back; reddish brown or reddish yellow around neck; head and body length to 29 cm (11.5 in); wingspan to 1.5 m (4.9 ft); 600 to 1000 g (1.3 to 2.2 lb).

HABITAT: Rainforests and wet open forests; day roosts in trees with dense canopies, near water, often in gullies or valleys and often mixed with other flying fox species; some nomadic; nocturnal; colonial; eats fruit and blossoms.

REGIONS: TRQ, NSW, VIC

Plate 70c
Little Red Flying-fox
(also called Collared Flying Fox)
Pteropus scapulatus
ID: Large bat (but smallest of Australia's common flying foxes), reddish brown or light brown, sometimes with grey head; some with yellowish or orangish patch on neck and shoulders; reddish brown wings; head and body length to 21 cm (8 in); 300 to 600 g (0.6 to 1.3 lb).

HABITAT: Rainforests, open forests, swamps, and open shrubby areas; roosts in trees in forests, woodlands, and mangroves, usually near water; eats mainly tree and shrub blossoms.

REGIONS: CYP, TRQ, TEQ, NSW, VIC

Plate 70d
Ghost Bat
(also called False Vampire Bat)
Macroderma gigas
ID: Large bat, grey or light brown above, lighter below; inland individuals can be very pale or whitish ("ghost-like"); long ears joined at base; large eyes; long noseleaf; no tail; head and body length to 14 cm (5.5 in); wingspan to 70 cm (28 in); to 170 g (6 oz).

HABITAT: Rainforests, open forests, savannah-like areas, and grasslands; roosts in caves, rock crevices, or abandoned mines, alone or in groups of a few individuals to hundreds; nocturnal; colonial; eats small vertebrates, insects, and spiders.

REGIONS: CYP, TRQ, TEQ

NOTE: Considered rare in Queensland, possibly threatened in Northern Territory.

Plate 70e
Yellow-bellied Sheathtail Bat
(also called Yellow-bellied Freetail Bat)
Saccolaimus flaviventris
ID: Mid-sized bat with shiny black back, yellow or whitish belly, and sharply pointed snout; head and body length to 9 cm (3.5 in); to 60 g (2 oz).

HABITAT: Varied, from rainforests to shrublands, grasslands, and deserts; roosts in tree holes and crevices; solitary or in small groups of up to 10; nocturnal; eats insects, mainly beetles.

REGIONS: CYP, TRQ, TEQ, NSW, VIC

NOTE: Considered vulnerable in New South Wales.

Plate 70 429

a Black Flying-fox

b Grey-headed Flying-fox

c Little Red Flying-fox

d Ghost Bat

e Yellow-bellied Sheathtail Bat

Plate 71a
Eastern Horseshoe Bat
Rhinolophus megaphyllus
ID: Small bat with greyish brown back, lighter belly; often reddish brown in Queensland; large noseleaf, horseshoe-shaped on bottom; head and body length to 5.8 cm (2 in); wingspan to 30 cm (12 in); to 14 g (0.5 oz).

HABITAT: Rainforests, open forests, woodlands, and coastal scrublands; roosts usually in small colonies in caves, rock piles, road culverts, or old buildings; nocturnal; eats small insects, mainly moths.

REGIONS: CYP, TRQ, NSW, VIC

Plate 71b
Common Bentwing Bat
(also called Schreiber's Long-tailed Bat)
Miniopterus schreibersii
ID: Small bat with blackish, dark brown, or reddish brown back, ligher belly; short snout, domed head, short, rounded ears; head and body length to 6 cm (2.5 in); wingspan to 36 cm (14 in); to 19 g (0.7 oz).

HABITAT: Rainforests, open forests, woodlands, and grasslands; roosts in small to large colonies in caves, old mines, road culverts, or old buildings; eats small insects, mainly moths.

REGIONS: CYP, TRQ, NSW, VIC

NOTE: Considered vulnerable in New South Wales.

Plate 71c
Lesser Long-eared Bat
(also called Geoffroy's Long-eared Bat)
Nyctophilus geoffroyi
ID: Small bat with grey or greyish brown back, lighter belly; large, long ears joined at base; noseleaf; high ridge on snout; head and body length to 5 cm (2 in); wingspan to 27.5 cm (11 in); to 14 g (0.5 oz).

HABITAT: All, including urban areas; roosts in crevices, tree holes, under bark, or in buildings, alone or in small groups; nocturnal; eats insects.

REGIONS: TRQ, TEQ, NSW, VIC, TAS

Plate 71d
Gould's Wattled Bat
(also called Gould's Lobe-lipped Bat)
Chalinolobus gouldii
ID: Mid-sized bat with brown back and belly, darker, blackish head and shoulders; short snout; short, broad ears; flap of skin (wattle) at corner of mouth; head and body length to 7.5 cm (3 in); wingspan to 33 cm (13 in); to 19 g (0.7 oz).

HABITAT: All, including urban and alpine areas; roosts in trees (in holes, crevices, among leaves) and in buildings, alone (males) or in small groups (females); nocturnal; eats insects, especially moths.

REGIONS: TRQ, TEQ, NSW, VIC, TAS

Plate 71e
Large-footed Myotis
(also called Large-footed Mouse-eared Bat)
Myotis adversus
ID: Small bat with grey, greyish brown, or reddish brown back, lighter belly; long ears, large feet; head and body length to 5.5 cm (2 in); wingspan to 29 cm (11.5 in); to 15 g (0.5 oz).

HABITAT: Most wooded habitats near water; roosts in caves, tree holes, road culverts, or under bridges, in small to mid-sized (a few hundred) groups; nocturnal; hunts over water for insects and occasional tiny fish.

REGIONS: CYP, TRQ, NSW, VIC

Plate 71 431

a Eastern Horseshoe Bat

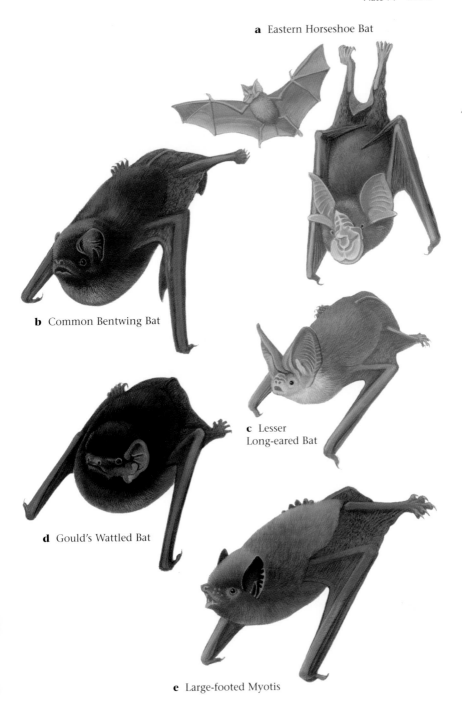

b Common Bentwing Bat

c Lesser Long-eared Bat

d Gould's Wattled Bat

e Large-footed Myotis

Plate 72a

Giant White-tailed Rat

(also called Giant Rat, White-tailed Rat)

Uromys caudimaculatus

ID: Large rat, greyish brown with whitish underparts, small ears, long whiskers, light-colored feet; long, naked, scaly, non-prehensile tail with dark base and white end; to 36 cm (14 in), plus tail to 36 cm (14 in); to 900 g (2 lb); one of Australia's largest rodents.

HABITAT: Rainforests and adjacent wet open forests; arboreal but also on the ground; nocturnal; solitary.

REGIONS: CYP, TRQ

Plate 72b

Water Rat

(also called Beaver Rat)

Hydromys chrysogaster

ID: Large rat, usually very dark above, whitish to orangish below; small ears; densely-furred thick tail dark, often with whitish tip; hindfeet partly webbed; to 36 cm (14 in), plus tail to 33 cm (13 in); to 1.3 kg (2.8 lb).

HABITAT: Near fresh, brackish, and saltwater—around lakes and watercourses, mangroves, rocky coastlines, and ocean beaches; terrestrial, fossorial (burrowing), and aquatic; active day or night; solitary.

REGIONS: CYP, TRQ, TEQ, NSW, VIC, TAS

Plate 72c

Fawn-footed Melomys

(also called Large Khaki Rat)

Melomys cervinipes

ID: Mid-sized rodent, reddish brown to orangish brown with grey or whitish underparts and light brown feet; long, brown, naked, scaly tail usually longer than body; to 20 cm (8 in), plus tail to 36 cm (14 in); to 110 g (4 oz).

HABITAT: Coastal rainforests, mangroves, wet open forests with dense ground cover, leaf litter, and allen logs; arboreal and terrestrial; nocturnal; solitary.

REGIONS: CYP, TRQ, NSW

Plate 72d

Bush Rat

(also called Western Swamp Rat)

Rattus fuscipes

ID: Mid-sized rodent, brownish with lighter underparts; large rounded ears; hindfeet usually darker than forefeet; long, sparsely furred tail with rings of scales, usually shorter than the body; to 21 cm (8 in), plus tail to 20 cm (8 in); to 225 g (8 oz).

HABITAT: Coastal rainforests, open forests, sub-alpine woodlands with dense ground cover, and coastal scrub areas; terrestrial and fossorial (burrowing); nocturnal; solitary.

REGIONS: CYP, TRQ, NSW, VIC

Plate 72 **433**

a Giant White-tailed Rat

b Water Rat

c Fawn-footed Melomys

d Bush Rat

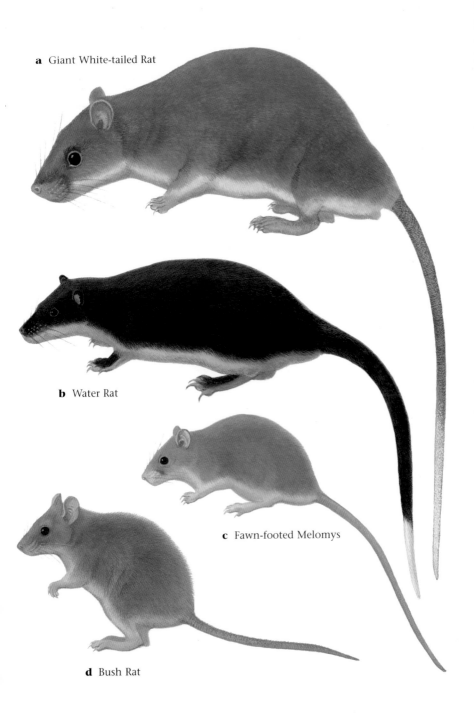

Plate 73a
Dingo
(also called Australian Native Dog)
Canis lupus dingo
ID: Mid-sized dog, usually sandy yellow or orangish brown but sometimes black and brown or white; often has white patches on chest, feet, and/or tail tip; bushy tail; to 1 m (3.3 ft), plus tail to 38 cm (15 in); to 23 kg (50 lb).

HABITAT: All habitats; terrestrial; active day or night; solitary or in small groups.

REGIONS: CYP, TRQ, TEQ, NSW, VIC

Plate 73b
Red Fox
(also called Fox, European Red Fox)
Vulpes vulpes
ID: Small, dog-like, reddish brown with whitish or grey underparts; light patch often on snout; dark patches often on feet and tail; to 74 cm (29 in), plus tail to 45 cm (18 in); to 8 kg (18 lb); males often larger than females.

HABITAT: All habitats; terrestrial; nocturnal; solitary or in small family groups.

REGIONS: TRQ, TEQ, NSW, VIC

Plate 73c
Rabbit
(also called European Rabbit)
Oryctolagus cuniculus
ID: Small rabbit, brown, with large ears the same color as body; small tail, usually with light and dark parts; to 41 cm (16 in); to 2.4 kg (5.3 lb).

HABITAT: Grasslands and most other habitats from sea level to 1,600 m (5,300 ft), as long as there is grass to graze on; usually near water in arid areas; terrestrial or fossorial (in burrows); day- or night-active; in groups.

REGIONS: TRQ, TEQ, NSW, VIC

Plate 73d
Brown Hare
(also called European Hare, Jackrabbit)
Lepus capensis
ID: Largish rabbit, brown or reddish brown with whitish underparts, reddish brown chest and legs; very long ears with black tips; small tail usually black on top; to 64 cm (25 in), plus tail to 9 cm (3.5 in); to 5 kg (11 lb).

HABITAT: Primarily agricultural and grazing lands but also grasslands and even forests and woodlands when there is a grassy floor; terrestrial; nocturnal; usually solitary.

REGIONS: TRQ, TEQ, NSW, VIC, TAS

Plate 73 **435**

a Dingo

b Red Fox

c Rabbit

d Brown Hare

Plate 74a

Dugong
(also called Sea Cow)
Dugong dugon
ID: Very large, hairless, grey or brown sea mammal, usually lighter or whitish below; broad upper lip with whiskers; small eyes; paddle-like front limbs; male with protruding, tusk-like, upper incisor teeth; to 3 m (10 ft); to 400 kg (880 lb).

HABITAT: Warmer, shallow coastal waters, usually in areas with sea grasses (which it eats); usually in groups.

REGIONS: CYP, TRQ, NSW

NOTE: CITES II listed for Australia, CITES I listed in the remainder of its range.

Plate 74b

New Zealand Fur Seal
Arctocephalus forsteri
ID: Mid-sized sea mammal with small external ears, long whitish whiskers; dark grey or brownish above, usually lighter below (females especially usually lighter on chest); male with thick fur (mane) on neck and often with lighter fur on pointed snout; males to 2.5 m (8.2 ft), 180 kg (400 lb); females to 1.5 m (5 ft), 60 kg (130 lb).

HABITAT: Along Australia's south and southeast coast; breeds on rocky islands.

REGIONS: NSW, VIC, TAS

Plate 74c

Australian Fur Seal
(also called Tasmanian Fur Seal)
Arctocephalus pusillus
ID: Largish sea mammal with visible external ears, long whiskers; male brown or brownish grey with pointed snout and thick fur (mane) on neck; female light brown or grey with light brown, cream, or yellowish throat; males to 2.3 m (7.5 ft), 350 kg (770 lb); females to 1.7 m (5.6 ft), 110 kg (240 lb).

HABITAT: Along Australia's southeast coast; breeds on rocky islands only in Bass Strait.

REGIONS: NSW, VIC, TAS

Plate 74d

Common Dolphin
Delphinus delphis
ID: Smaller dark brown or blackish dolphin with grey sides and often white and cream-colored or yellowish side stripes; light belly; long, prominent beak; large dorsal fin (to 40 cm, 16 in, high); 1.5 to 2.5 m (5 to 8 ft).

HABITAT: Coastal and offshore areas around Australia.

REGIONS: CYP, TRQ, NSW, VIC, TAS

Plate 74e

Spinner Dolphin
Stenella longirostris
ID: Sleek grey dolphin, often with dark grey back, lighter grey sides, and whitish belly; pronounced slender beak; no spots on body; grey flippers and flukes; often a dark eye-stripe; dorsal fin, sometimes curved forward instead of rearward, about 25 cm (10 in) high; 1.7 to 2.1 m (5.5 to 7 ft).

HABITAT: Coastal and offshore areas; in small to medium-sized schools; leaps from water and spins.

REGIONS: CYP, TRQ, NSW, VIC, TAS

Plate 74 437

a Dugong

b New Zealand Fur Seal

c Australian Fur Seal

d Common Dolphin

e Spinner Dolphin

Plate 75a
Pacific Bottle-nosed Dolphin
Tursiops truncatus
ID: Light grey, dark grey, or slate-blue dolphin with pronounced beak; flippers and flukes often darker; belly often lighter, whitish or pinkish; curved line of mouth resembles a smile; dorsal fin about 25 cm (10 in) high; 2 to 3.5 m (6.5 to 11.5 ft).

HABITAT: Coastal and offshore areas; often leaps out of water; in small to medium-sized schools; sometimes mixes with Humpback Whales (75d).

REGIONS: CYP, TRQ, NSW, VIC, TAS

Plate 75b
Indo-Pacific Humpback Dolphin
Sousa chinensis
ID: Mid-sized whitish or greyish dolphin often with darker spots; long beak; short, stocky flippers; dorsal fin often on top of a hump (especially noticeable in some older animals, but many individuals in Australian waters lack the conspicuous hump); 2 to 3 m (6.5 to 10 ft).

HABITAT: Warm, shallow coastal areas and inland into estuaries, rivers, and mangrove swamps; in small groups.

REGIONS: CYP, TRQ

NOTE: All humpback dolphins considered endangered, CITES Appendix I listed.

Plate 75c
Minke Whale
Balaenoptera acutorostrata
ID: Smallish, shiny-black baleen whale with pointed head and sickle-shaped dorsal fin well behind middle of back; pale band across long flippers; to 10 m (33 ft).

HABITAT: Coastal and offshore waters.

REGIONS: CYP, TRQ, NSW, VIC, TAS

NOTE: Endangered, CITES Appendix I listed.

Plate 75d
Humpback Whale
Megaptera novaeangliae
ID: Huge blackish whale with lighter or whitish belly; long whitish flippers with scalloped or knobby edges, to a third of body length; small dorsal fin; wart-like knobs on head; lower jaw with large lump; to 16 m (52 ft).

HABITAT: Coastal and offshore waters; often seen in small groups (2 to 8 whales); often breaches (jumps from water) and spyhops (pushes head out of water and rotates it, looking around).

REGIONS: TRQ, NSW, VIC, TAS

NOTE: Endangered, CITES Appendix I listed.

Plate 75 **439**

a Pacific Bottle-nosed Dolphin

b Indo-Pacific Humpback Dolphin

c Minke Whale

d Humpback Whale

Fish Text by Richard Francis

Lengths given for fish are "standard lengths," the distance from the front of the mouth to the point where the tail appears to join the body; that is, tails are not included in the measurement.

Plate 76a
Tiera Batfish
Platax tiera
Adults have discus-shaped bodies with steeply sloped foreheads. Also look for the black blotch at the base of the pectoral fin. Juveniles have extremely long dorsal and anal fins, the back portions of which are black. (to 60 cm, 24 in)

Plate 76b
Golden-striped Butterflyfish
Chaetodon aureofasciatus
This butterflyfish is common inside the barrier reef. The body is pale yellow with dusky sides. A darker yellow-orange bar runs through the eye. (to 12.5 cm, 5 in)

Plate 76c
Triangular Butterflyfish
Chaetodon baronessa
This butterflyfish has a different body shape than most. It is adorned with alternating narrow bars of cream and dusky purple that angle toward the tail and reinforce its generally "triangular" form. There are also three dark bars on the head; the middle one runs through the eye. (to 15 cm, 6 in)

Plate 76d
Threadfin Butterflyfish
Chaetodon auriga
This species is common inside the barrier reef in protected, shallow reefs. It is one of the more omnivorous members of the family, feeding on algae, marine worms, small crustaceans, and even coral polyps. The background color is white in front and yellow toward the tail. Two series of dark stripes extend at right angles from each other and diagonally. A dark stripe extends through the eye, and there is a characteristic black spot toward the rear of the dorsal fin, from which extends a filament-like projection. (to 20 cm, 8 in)

Plate 76e
Bennett's Butterflyfish
Chaetodon bennetti
Most commonly found in pairs on outer reefs, this butterflyfish is almost entirely a lemon yellow color, save for a black eyestripe, a black eyespot at midbody, and two thin blue bands on the lower body. (to 18 cm, 7 in)

Plate 76f
Speckled Butterflyfish
Chaetodon citrinellus
Also known as the Citron Butterflyfish, this relatively small species prefers shallow reefs in which there is little coral growth. Look for somewhat irregular rows of small dark spots over a very pale yellow background. Also note the black eyestripe. (to 11 cm, 4.5 in)

Plate 76 441

a Tiera Batfish

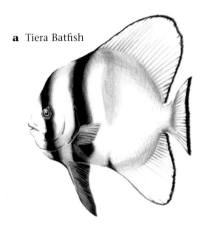

b Golden-striped Butterflyfish

c Triangular Butterflyfish

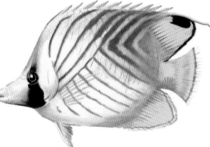

d Threadfin Butterflyfish

e Bennett's Butterflyfish

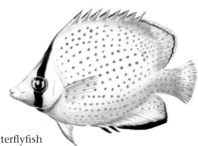

f Speckled Butterflyfish

Plate 77a
Saddled Butterflyfish
Chaetodon ephippium
Another highly omnivorous butterflyfish, and
highly monogamous as well, this species is named
for the black area on the rear portion of its upper
body, which is bordered by a broad white band.
(to 23 cm, 9 in)

Plate 77b
Dusky Butterflyfish
Chaetodon flavirostris
The body of this species is black, its fins and
forehead yellow. It has a fairly diverse diet, which
includes algae, coral, and benthic (bottom-
dwelling) invertebrates. (to 20 cm, 8 in)

Plate 77c
Lined Butterflyfish
Chaetodon lineolatus
The largest member of the family, this species
prefers coral-rich areas, where it dines on polyps
as well as anemones. It is white with thin, vertical
black lines, a prominent black eyestripe, and a
bright yellow posterior with a black swath. A pair
of these beauties is a breathtaking sight. (to 30
cm, 12 in)

Plate 77d
Spotnape Butterflyfish
Chaetodon oxycephalus
This species can be distinguished from the very
similar Lined Butterflyfish (Plate 77c) by the black
spot on its forehead. It feeds on coral and
anemones. (to 25 cm, 10 in)

Plate 77e
Raccoon Butterflyfish
Chaetodon lunula
The common name derives from the black
raccoon-like mask. The rest of the body is
generally dusky greenish brown, tending toward
yellow below. Though monogamous, it is more
likely to be found in small groups than many other
butterflyfish. (to 20 cm, 8 in)

Plate 77f
Blackback Butterflyfish
Chaetodon melanotus
This species frequents areas with ample coral,
which constitutes its main food source. The body
is white with many thin, diagonal black bands. The
fins and snout are bright yellow, and a black stripe
runs through the eyes. Note also the black band
on the caudal peduncle (the narrow part of the
fish where the tail appears to join the body), by
means of which this species can be distinguished
from the very similar Spot-tail Butterflyfish
(*Chaetodon ocellicaudus*), which has a black tail
spot instead. (to 15 cm, 6 in)

Plate 77 443

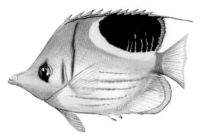

a Saddled Butterflyfish

b Dusky Butterflyfish

c Lined Butterflyfish

d Spotnape Butterflyfish

e Raccoon Butterflyfish

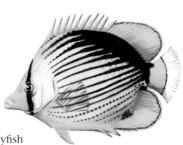

d Blackback Butterflyfish

Plate 78a
Meyer's Butterflyfish
Chaetodon meyeri
This is one of the more spectacular members of
this family of eye-catching fish. The body is bluish
white with prominent oblique black bands. These
bands continue through the yellow fins, and they
are outlined in yellow in the head region. This fish
feeds primarily on coral polyps, so it prefers
coral-rich areas. (to 18 cm, 7 in)

Plate 78b
Ornate Butterflyfish
Chaetodon ornatissimus
The head of this species is very much like that of
the Meyer's Butterflyfish (Plate 78a). The body is
white with diagonal orange bands. It prefers
coral-rich areas, where it dines primarily on coral
polyps. (to 19 cm, 7.5 in)

Plate 78c
Bluespot Butterflyfish
Chaetodon plebius
This butterflyfish can be distinguished from all
others by the ovoid blue swatch on its upper body.
Note also the black eyestripe (outlined with blue)
and black eyespot near the tail. This species
feeds primarily on coral polyps. (to 13 cm, 5 in)

Plate 78d
Spot-banded Butterflyfish
Chaetodon punctatofasciatus
You will find this butterflyfish in pairs on outer reef
slopes. The body is orangish tan with vertical
rows of dark spots that coalesce into bands on
the upper body. Note also the orange eyestripe
and the white band, outlined in black, extending
from the tail to the anal fin. The Dot-and-dash
Butterflyfish (*Chaetodon pelewensis*) is quite
similar, but the rows of spots are oblique, and the
white band is replaced by an orange one. (to 11
cm, 4.5 in)

Plate 78e
Rainford's Butterflyfish
Chaetodon rainfordi
This butterflyfish is endemic to the Great Barrier
Reef. It prefers shallow protected areas near the
coastline, often where there is little coral growth.
It feeds primarily on algae and benthic
invertebrates. It is more teardrop-shaped than
ovoid. The body is lemon yellow, with bands of
darker yellow and bluish. (to 15 cm, 6 in)

Plate 78f
Reticulated Butterflyfish
Chaetodon reticulatus
You are not likely to confuse this species with any
other butterflyfish. Behind the pronounced black
eyestripe there is a broad band of light blue-grey
that extends through the dorsal fin. Behind this is a
checkerboard pattern extending to the tail. This is
another highly monogamous species in which pair
members rarely stray far from one another. It can
be found foraging for coral polyps on coral-rich
regions of outer reefs. (to 20 cm, 8 in)

Plate 78 445

a Meyer's Butterflyfish

b Ornate Butterflyfish

c Bluespot Butterflyfish

d Spot-banded Butterflyfish

e Rainford's Butterflyfish

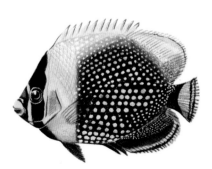

f Reticulated Butterflyfish

Plate 79a
Chevron Butterflyfish
Chaetodon trifascialis
This species is named for the chevron-shaped
black lines over the white background color. Note
also the black eyestripe and black tail outlined
with yellow. The dorsal and anal fins are also less
rounded than in most butterflyfishes, giving it a
distinctive profile. This species feeds solely on
live corals, and maintains feeding territories
around the more productive areas, which it
ardently defends. (to 18 cm, 7 in)

Plate 79b
Redfin Butterflyfish
Chaetodon trifasciatus
This beauty, which is also known as the Oval
Butterflyfish, can be found in pairs in protected
coral-rich areas. The body is cream-colored with
purple horizontal stripes. A black bar, flanked by
yellow, runs through the eyes. The common name
derives from an orange band near the rear of the
anal fin. (to 15 cm, 6 in)

Plate 79c
Pacific Double-saddled Butterflyfish
Chaetodon ulietensis
This denizen of coral-rich areas can be found
foraging in pairs. The body is mostly white, but the
posterior portion is bright yellow. There are two
prominent dark patches on the upper body, from
which the common name derives. Note also the
black bar through the eye and the thin, vertical
black stripes. (to 15 cm, 6 in)

Plate 79d
Teardrop Butterflyfish
Chaetodon unimaculatus
This omnivorous species is common on outer
reefs. Look for the prominent black spot on the
back, broad black eyestripe, and narrow black
stripe extending through the posterior portions of
the dorsal and anal fins. (to 20 cm, 8 in)

Plate 79e
Beaked Coralfish
Chelmon rostratus
This butterflyfish is common in shallow, near-shore
portions of the inner reef. The background color is
white, but this is transected by three orange bars,
the rearmost of which has a prominent black spot
near the base of the anal fin. Another much thinner
yellow-orange bar extends through the eye. Note
also the forceps-like snout. (to 20 cm, 8 in)

Plate 79f
Forcepsfish
Forcipiger flavissimus
This distinctive butterflyfish uses its long snout to
extract a variety of foodstuffs, including the tube
feet of sea urchins and other echinoderms. The
body is lemon yellow, while the head is black
above and bluish white below. Note also the small
black spot on the anal fin near the base of the tail.
The very similar Longnose Butterflyfish
(*Forcipiger longirostris*), which is less common,
can be distinguished by its much longer snout. (to
22 cm, 8.5 in)

Plate 79 447

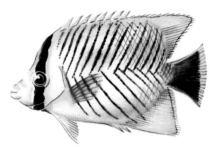

a Chevron Butterflyfish

b Redfin Butterflyfish

c Pacific Double-saddled Butterflyfish

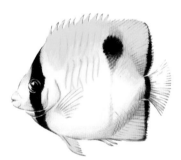

d Teardrop Butterflyfish

e Beaked Coralfish

f Forcepsfish

Plate 80a
Pyramid Butterflyfish
Hemitaurichthys polylepis
The feeding habits of this butterflyfish are quite different from those of the other family members illustrated here; it forages in large schools for plankton (the ocean's huge population of tiny floating organisms) in the water column. It is named for the pyramid-shaped white area on its body, which is surrounded by yellow. (to 18 cm, 7 in)

Plate 80b
Longfin Bannerfish
Heniochus acuminatus
Bannerfishes are named for their elongate dorsal fins. Of the several species that occur on the reef, this is the one with the longest banner. The body is white with two broad black bands. Note also the yellow on the pectoral fins, the tail fin, and the rear portion of the dorsal fin. (to 25 cm, 10 in)

Plate 80c
Ocellated Coralfish
Parachaetodon ocellatus
This diamond-shaped butterflyfish frequents sandy areas inside the northern portion of the barrier reef. Its body is white with vertical bronze-colored bars, including one through the eye. (to 18 cm, 7 in)

Plate 80d
Three-spot Angelfish
Apolemichthys trimaculatus
This angelfish can be distinguished by its bright yellow coloration and electric-blue lips. Note also the black and white bands on the anal fin. Look for it on outer reef slopes. (to 25 cm, 10 in)

Plate 80e
Bicolor Angelfish
Centropyge bicolor
The front half of the body is generally golden yellow, except for the blue band that extends from the forehead through the eyes; the rear half is dark blue, and the tail is yellow. Members of this genus feed primarily on algae and bottom detritus. (to 15 cm, 6 in)

Plate 80f
Conspicuous Angelfish
Chaetodontoplus conspicullatus
This species is endemic to the southern portion of the Great Barrier Reef and Coral Sea. It can be easily identified by its blue-grey body, yellow face, and yellow and black tail. Note also the blue ring around the eye and the thin blue lines on the cheek. (to 25 cm, 10 in)

Plate 80 449

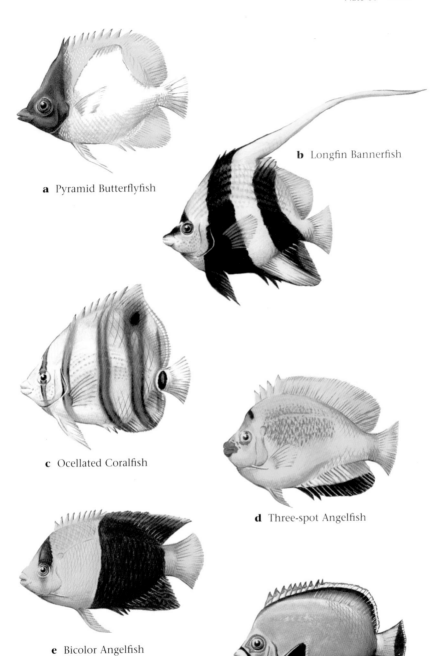

a Pyramid Butterflyfish

b Longfin Bannerfish

c Ocellated Coralfish

d Three-spot Angelfish

e Bicolor Angelfish

f Conspicuous Angelfish

Plate 81a
Scribbled Angelfish
Chaetodontoplus duboulayi
This angelfish prefers shallow coastal reefs. In contrast to most angelfish, the sexes look somewhat different. The background color in both is black, but females have yellow speckling on their sides, while males have numerous thin blue lines. In both sexes, there is a broad black band through the eye, on either side of which is a yellow band. Behind the eye is a conspicuous white patch. The dorsal and anal fins have electric-blue lines, as well as a blue margin. (to 25 cm, 10 in)

Plate 81b
Queensland Angelfish
Chaetodontoplus meredithi
As the common name implies, this is a Great Barrier Reef endemic. It can be found inside the barrier, especially near the coastline. The body is black, the face light blue, and the tail yellow. There are also yellow areas on top of the head and on the throat. (to 25 cm, 10 in)

Plate 81c
Emperor Angelfish
Pomacanthus imperator
This is one of the largest angelfish and perhaps the most beautiful. It undergoes a striking color change during the transition from juvenile to adult. Juveniles are black with irregular blue and white lines, while the adults have very distinctive yellow stripes on a blue background. This species prefers coral-rich areas, where it can be found near caves and overhangs. (to 38 cm, 15 in)

Plate 81d
Semicircle Angelfish
Pomacanthus semicirculatus
This is another large angelfish that undergoes a dramatic color change. Juveniles are black with alternating blue and white stripes that curve toward the tail. In adults, the head is blue-grey while the body is dusky brown to grey and adorned with blue spots. Note also the filamentous projections from the dorsal and anal fins and the blue margin on the posterior body and tail fin. (to 38 cm, 15 in)

Plate 81e
Yellowmask Angelfish
Pomacanthus xanthometapon
This species has a distinctive beard-like blue region around the cheeks and mouth; above and below is the yellow mask. The tail is also yellow. Note the black spot at the rear of the anal fin. Like the Emperor and Semicircle Angelfish (Plates 81c, 81d), it feeds primarily on sponges. (to 38 cm, 15 in)

Plate 81f
Regal Angelfish
Pygoplites diacanthus
This beauty is also a sponge-eater. It can be identified by its distinctive body coloration, which consists of alternating bands of white, black, and gold. (to 26 cm, 10 in)

Plate 81 451

a Scribbled Angelfish

b Queensland Angelfish

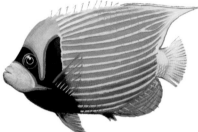

c Emperor Angelfish

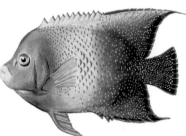

d Semicircle Angelfish

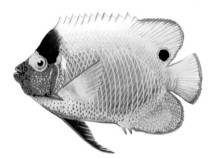

e Yellowmask Angelfish

f Regal Angelfish

Plate 82a
Scissor-tail Sergeant
Abudefduf sexfasciatus
The sergeants are fairly drab-looking damselfish with lots of personality, especially during the breeding season. Six species occur on the Great Barrier Reef. This species closely resembles the Indo-Pacific Sergeant (*Abudefduf vaigiensis*), but can be distinguished from it by the distinct black stripes on each lobe of the caudal fin. (to 17 cm, 6.5 in)

Plate 82b
Spiny Chromis
Acanthochromis polyacanthus
Most damselfish exhibit parental care to some degree, but it is most highly developed in this species, the only one without a pelagic (open-ocean) larval stage. Once hatched, the young remain with the parents and feed on mucous from their bodies. Spiny Chromis coloration varies widely, from whitish grey to almost black. The tail is deeply forked. (to 14 cm, 5.5 in)

Plate 82c
Golden Damsel
Amblyglyphidodon aureus
The bright yellow coloration distinguishes this species from other deep-bodied damsels. It prefers the drop-offs of reefs adjacent to deep water. (to 12 cm, 4.5 in)

Plate 82d
Half-and-half Chromis
Chromis iomelas
There are a number of species from this genus in the area, all of which feed on current-borne plankton, in contrast to most other damselfish. This species can be readily identified by its body coloration, which is black in front and white in the rear half of the body. The Bicolor Chromis (*Chromis margaritifer*) is also black and white, but the white portion of the body is much smaller. (to 7 cm, 3 in)

Plate 82e
Barrier Reef Chromis
Chromis nitida
This is one of a number of barrier reef fishes that are common in the southern region but rare or absent in the northern region. A black stripe runs from the snout through the eye to the tip of the dorsal fin, above which the body is olive green, and below which it is white. Note also the black streaks on the tail and anal fins. (to 12 cm, 5 in)

Plate 82f
Blue-green Chromis
Chromis viridis
This damselfish forms large aggregations above coral heads ("bommies" in Australian), a dazzling sight. The body coloration is pale blue-green and appears iridescent in the right light. The similarly colored Black-axil Chromis (*Chromis atripectoralis*) is larger and has a distinct black area at the base of the pectoral fin. (to 9 cm, 3.5 in)

Plate 82 **453**

a Scissor-tail Sergeant

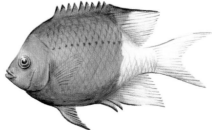

b Spiny Chromis

c Golden Damsel

d Half-and-half Chromis

e Barrier Reef Chromis

f Blue-green Chromis

Plate 83a
Dark-fin Chromis
Chromis atripes
This little damsel is very common in the outermost reefs. Its body is tan, the fins translucent except for black margins. Note also the black spot at the base of the pectoral fins and the small black band in the middle of the eye. (to 7 cm, 3 in)

Plate 83b
Blue Devil
Chrysiptera cyanea
Members of this damselfish genus are often called "demoiselles," but this one gets a much catchier name. The body coloration is bright blue with scattered small white speckles. Males have an orange area on the rear half of the tail fin that is lacking in females. This species is common in the northern reef region but does not occur in the Coral Sea. (to 8.5 cm, 3.5 in)

Plate 83c
Yellowfin Damsel
Chrysiptera flavipinnis
This distinctive damselfish has a bright blue body with a yellow back. (to 8.5 cm, 3.5 in)

Plate 83d
South Seas Demoiselle
Chrysiptera taupou
This damsel has a beautiful body to go along with its romantic common name. Most of the body is bright blue with scattered white spots; the belly is bright yellow. Males also have yellow tails and dorsal fins, but in females these structures are translucent. (to 8.5 cm, 3.5 in)

Plate 83e
Humbug Damselfish
Dascyllus aruanus
You are most likely to find this handsome creature in groups of 10 to 50 over heads of Acropora corals (Plate 108), into which they will disappear if you approach too closely. The body is white with three broad, vertical black bands, the frontmost of which runs through the eyes. The similar Black-tailed Dascyllus (*Dascyllus melanurus*) has a black, rather than all-white, tail. The Threeband Demoiselle (*Chrysiptera tricincta*) also has very similar coloration, but its eyeband does not run through the mouth as in the Humbug, and it prefers sandy areas rather than coral. The Humbug Damselfish and other members of this genus are known sex changers (female to male; p. 249). (to 8.5 cm, 3.5 in)

Plate 83f
Reticulated Dascyllus
Dascyllus reticulatus
This damselfish also hangs out around coral heads. The body is a tan color with a black bar at the level of the pectoral fin base, and a less distinct one near the tail. (to 9 cm, 3.5 in)

Plate 83 455

a Dark-fin Chromis

b Blue Devil

c Yellowfin Damsel

d South Seas Demoiselle

e Humbug Damselfish

f Reticulated Dascyllus

Plate 84a
Three-spot Dascyllus
Dascyllus trimaculatus
This damsel has a charcoal-colored body with black accents at the scale margins. The three spots, which are white, are easiest to see in the juveniles; the one on the head always disappears in the adults. (to 13 cm, 5 in)

Plate 84b
Black-vent Damsel
Dischistodus melanotus
This damsel is white with a greenish brown area over its upper body and head, as well as a dark spot at the base of the anal fin. Juveniles are brown in the front half of the body and white in the back half. They also have a white bar behind the head, as well as an eyespot in the middle of the dorsal fin. (to 16 cm, 6.5 in)

Plate 84c
Australian Damsel
Pomacentrus australis
This little beauty is endemic to the Great Barrier Reef, but is most common in the southern portion. Its body coloration is a deep purplish blue, lightening toward the belly. (to 9 cm, 3.5 in)

Plate 84d
Neon Damsel
Pomacentrus coelestis
Large aggregations of these little damsels are a dazzling sight. Their body color is mostly sky-blue, with variable yellow areas near the belly, as well as on the anal and tail fins. The common name reflects the fact that under certain lighting conditions they seem to glow. Look for them over areas of coral rubble. (to 10 cm, 4 in)

Plate 84e
Lemon Damsel
Pomacentrus moluccensis
The bright yellow coloration distinguishes this damsel from all others. (to 7.5 cm, 3 in)

Plate 84f
Blue Damsel
Pomacentrus pavo
The body coloration of this damsel is more blue-green than blue, and larger fish are often adorned with darker streaks on the body scales as well as light markings on the head and upper body. It prefers isolated coral patches in sandy lagoons. (to 11 cm, 4.5 in)

Plate 84 **457**

a Three-spot Dascyllus

b Black-vent Damsel

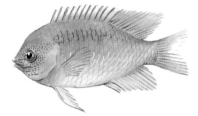

c Australian Damsel

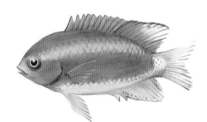

d Neon Damsel

e Lemon Damsel

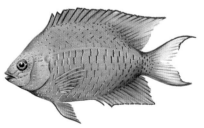

f Blue Damsel

Plate 85a
Australian Gregory
Stegastes apicalis
This robust damsel prefers inner reefs close to
shore. It is endemic to the Great Barrier Reef
region and the eastern Australian coast to the
south. It is very dark brown, almost black, with a
yellow margin on the dorsal fin and upper lobe of
the tail fin. (to 14 cm, 5.5 in)

Plate 85b
Barrier Reef Anemonefish
Amphiprion akindynos
Anemonefish are famous for their commensal
associations (p. 60) with seemingly inhospitable
anemones. This species is a relative generalist,
because it is associates with four distinct
anemone species. The body is brownish orange
with two dramatic white bands. Note also the
white tail. The similar-looking Orange-fin
Anemonefish (*Amphiprion chrysopterus*) is much
less common in northeastern Australian waters.
(to 12 cm, 4.5 in)

Plate 85c
Red-and-black Anemonefish
Amphiprion melanopus
Also called the Black Anemonefish, the coloration
of this species varies somewhat geographically.
The body is generally a deep red-orange with a
large black region on the sides. It generally has a
dramatic white bar behind the eye, though fish
from the Coral Sea often lack the stripe. This
species prefers to associate with the colonial
anemone *Entacmaea quadricolor*. (to 12 cm, 4.5 in)

Plate 85d
Clown Anemonefish
Amphiprion percula
This delightful fish is one of the most
photographed species in the sea. The body is
bright orange with three broad white bands
trimmed in black. It can be found in the company
of two anemone species, *Stichodactylus gigantae*
and *Heteractis magnifica*. (to 8 cm, 3 in)

Plate 85e
Pink Anemonefish
Amphiprion perideraion
The common name of this anemonefish derives
from the pinkish orange body coloration. The color
is accentuated by a vertical white bar behind the
eye and another white bar that runs the length of
the body along the dorsal surface, including the
dorsal fin. This species associates only with the
anemone *Heteractis magnifica*. (to 10 cm, 4 in)

Plate 85f
Spine-cheek Anemonefish
Premnas biaculeatus
Though it belongs to a completely different genus
than the other anemonefish, this species is also
intimately associated with anemones. Females are
larger than males in all anemonefish, but in this
species the size difference is especially dramatic.
The sexes also differ in coloration, the males
being more deeply and brightly colored. The body
coloration ranges from scarlet to reddish brown,
with two or three vertical white bars. It associates
primarily with the anemone *Entacmaea
quadricolor*. (to 16 cm, 6.5 in)

Plate 85 459

a Australian Gregory

b Barrier Reef Anemonefish

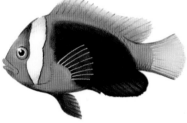

c Red-and-black Anemonefish

d Clown Anemonefish

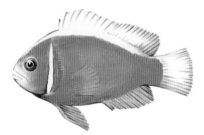

e Pink Anemonefish

f Spine-cheek Anemonefish

Plate 86a
Flame Hawkfish
Neocirrhites armatus
Hawkfish are a family of small lie-in-wait predators. They spend all their time on the substrate, so they have dispensed with air bladders (the organs with which most fish regulate their buoyancy) altogether. This species hangs out in the branches of coral, waiting for its prey. It is perhaps the most strikingly colored of hawkfish. The body is bright red with a dark brown band running below the dorsal fin. Note also the brown patch around the eyes. (to 9 cm, 3.5 in)

Plate 86b
Longnose Hawkfish
Oxycirrhites typus
This hawkfish can be readily distinguished by its elongate, forceps-like snout. The background coloration is white and is overlaid with reddish crosshatch markings. It can often be seen perched on the surface of soft corals, and it is more likely to move up into the water column than other hawkfish. (to 13 cm, 5 in)

Plate 86c
Arc-eye Hawkfish
Paracirrhites arcatus
This hawkfish occurs in two color phases, one with a red background and a prominent white band, the other a dark greenish brown. Both color varieties have a neon line arcing from below to above the eye. (to 14 cm, 5.5 in)

Plate 86d
Spotted Wrasse
Anampses meleagrides
As in many wrasses, the males and females look markedly different, a phenomenon known as sexual dimorphism. Females are dark brown, almost black, with parallel rows of white spots, one on each body scale, and a bright yellow tail. Males are reddish brown with a bright orange tail adorned with blue spots. The head is covered with irregular blue lines and the stomach has rows of blue streaks. Note also the white crescent and blue band on the tail. (to 21 cm, 8.5 in)

Plate 86e
Blackfin Hogfish
Bodianus loxozonus
Hogfish are a group of relatively large predatory wrasses that frequently prey on other fish. This species can be identified by the large black area near the tail. The rest of the body is red above the midline and white below, with rows of orange stripes in the white region that break up at the head. The head is also white. (to 40 cm, 16 in)

Plate 86f
Humphead Maori Wrasse
Cheilinus undulatus
All members of this genus are large by wrasse standards, but this species is huge by the standards of any fish. It preys on a variety of benthic (bottom-dwelling) animals including sea urchins, mollusks, crabs, and other crustaceans. The common name comes from the prominent bulbous protuberance on the head. Despite its immense size, it is quite shy. (to 2.3 m, 7.6 ft)

Plate 86 461

a Flame Hawkfish

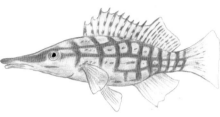

b Longnose Hawkfish

c Arc-eye Hawkfish

d Spotted Wrasse

e Blackfin Hogfish

f Humphead Maori Wrasse

Plate 87a
Harlequin Tuskfish
Choerodon fasciatus
Tuskfish are so called because of their protruding canines. This beautiful species is a favorite of photographers and aquarists alike. The body is white with eight or nine vertical orangish red bars edged in blue. The white areas tend to become duskier with age. It preys on a variety of benthic (bottom-dwelling) animals, including marine worms, mollusks, and crustaceans. (to 30 cm, 12 in)

Plate 87b
Exquisite Wrasse
Cirrhilabrus exquisitus
The terminal phase males (p. 250) are truly exquisite; the females and initial phase males (p. 250) are much less so, but such is true of most wrasses. All members of this species have a characteristic oval spot at the base of the tail, below which a blue line extends forward. Another blue line extends from the corner of the mouth to the gill cover, and another from behind the eye. Terminal phase males have red coloration on their fins and belly. Note also the blue fin spots. (to 12 cm, 4.5 in)

Plate 87c
Yellowtail Coris
Coris gaimard
In this wrasse, the sexes look fairly similar, but juveniles and adults look so different that they were at one time thought to be two different species. Juveniles are red with large white blotches outlined in black. Adults have an olive green coloration with small blue spots that increase in density toward the tail. The caudal fin is bright yellow. Note also the light green bands on the head. (to 40 cm, 16 in)

Plate 87d
Slingjaw Wrasse
Epibulus insidiator
This wrasse has a mouth large enough for a snapper, which is not at all typical of wrasses. It is atypical in another way as well: some of the females are more colorful than the males. Females are either a drab dark brown or a striking bright yellow, whereas the males have olive green bodies, becoming yellow toward the back, and a white head with a dark line extending through the eye. (to 35 cm, 14 in)

Plate 87e
Bird Wrasse
Gomphosus varius
This wrasse can be easily identified by its elongate mouth, which evidently someone thought was birdlike. Females are brown, tending toward white on the belly and head; males are bright blue-green. (to 32 cm, 12.5 in)

Plate 87f
Tailspot Wrasse
Halichoeres melanurus
Females of this wrasse have alternating yellow and blue stripes along the length of the body, a large black spot ringed with blue on the dorsal fin, and a smaller one at the base of the tail. Males have green bodies that darken toward the tail and pinkish orange stripes on the head. The tail fin is blue with red bands. Note also the yellow area at the base of the pectoral fins. (to 10.5 cm, 4 in)

Plate 87 463

a Harlequin Tuskfish

b Exquisite Wrasse

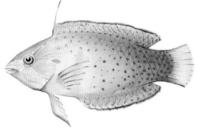

c Yellowtail Coris

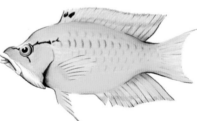

d Slingjaw Wrasse

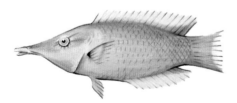

e Bird Wrasse

f Tailspot Wrasse

Plate 88a
Ornate Wrasse
Halichoeres ornatissimus
Both sexes in this species are light red with a
green spot on each scale and green stripes on the
head. Females have a black spot on the dorsal fin.
This common wrasse roots around on substrates
for crustaceans and mollusks. (to 15 cm, 6 in)

Plate 88b
Ringwrasse
Hologymnosus annulatus
Ringwrasses have distinctive tapering snouts.
Initial phase fish (mostly females; p. 250) are a
dusky olive brown; the tail has a white region
toward the tip. Terminal phase males (p. 250) are
green with purplish red bars; the head is purple
with blue-green bands and the tail is blue with a
green crescent toward its end. This species feeds
primarily on small fish. (to 40 cm, 16 in)

Plate 88c
Pastel Ringwrasse
Hologymnosus doliatus
Initial phase fish (mostly females; p. 250) are
bluish grey with brown bars; there is a small dark
blue spot on the gill cover. Terminal phase males
(p. 250) are light blue-green with a pale saddle in
the pectoral region that is bordered by dark bluish
purple. (to 50 cm, 20 in)

Plate 88d
Bicolor Cleaner Wrasse
Labroides bicolor
Most members of this genus specialize as
cleaners (p. 250), deriving their sustenance from
the ectoparasites of larger fish. This species is
less bound to traditional cleaning stations (p. 250)
than other cleaner wrasses. Females are grey
with a black lateral stripe that becomes pale
yellow as it approaches the tail. Males are black
in the front half and yellow to white toward the
tail. (to 14 cm, 5.5 in)

Plate 88e
Cleaner Wrasse
Labroides dimidiatus
This cleaner sticks close to traditional cleaning
stations, where its client fish assemble for its
services (p. 250). Females are black with a bright
blue stripe on the back and head. Males are light
blue, tending to pale yellow, with a black stripe
running from the snout to the end of the tail. (to
11.5 cm, 4.5 in)

Plate 88f
Blackspotted Wrasse
Macropharyngodon meleagris
This species gets its common name from the
initial phase fish (p. 250), which has irregular
black spots over the entire body. Terminal phase
males (p. 250) have an orangish red background
color with a green spot edged in blue on each
scale; the head has green markings. There is also
a black spot in the shoulder area. (to 15 cm, 6 in)

Plate 88 465

a Ornate Wrasse

b Ringwrasse

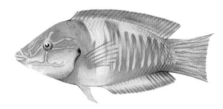

c Pastel Ringwrasse

d Bicolor Cleaner Wrasse

e Cleaner Wrasse

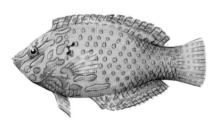

f Blackspotted Wrasse

Plate 89a
Rockmover Wrasse
Novacaulicthys taeniourus
This wrasse gets its name from its habit of overturning and moving surprisingly large rocks in its quest for benthic (bottom-dwelling) invertebrates such as worms, urchins, mollusks, and crustaceans. All adults are dark brown with a white spot on each scale; the head is whitish grey with dark lines radiating from the eye. The tail is white in front and black at the back. Juveniles are uncanny mimics of drifting red algae. (to 30 cm, 12 in)

Plate 89b
Bluelined Wrasse
Stethojulis bandanensis
This is a very active, shallow-water wrasse. The initial phase is grey with tiny white dots on the upper body and a bright red spot above the base of the pectoral fin. The terminal phase is green on the upper body and pale blue below, the two regions separated by a thin blue line. A crescent-shaped red area lies above the pectoral fin. Of the four blue lines on the head, the topmost extends the length of the dorsal fin. (to 12.5 cm, 5 in)

Plate 89c
Moon Wrasse
Thalassoma lunare
This is another very active wrasse; it feeds on small fish and benthic invertebrates. The initial phase (p. 250) is green with vertical red dashes on each scale and irregular rose-colored bands on the head; there is also a rose band on each lobe of the tail. The terminal phase (male; p. 250) is similar, but more purplish blue throughout. (to 25 cm, 10 in)

Plate 89d
Sunset Wrasse
Thalassoma lutescens
This wrasse prefers benthic shrimp and crabs. The initial phase (male and female; p. 250) is greenish yellow with very faint, light reddish orange lines on the head. The terminal phase (male; p. 250) has a rose pink coloration on the head with irregular curving green lines. Behind the head, the body is blue, tending to green toward the tail, which is yellow with a blue-edged rose band on each lobe. (to 25 cm, 10 in)

Plate 89e
Fivefinger Razorfish
Xyrichthys pentadactylus
Razorfishes have characteristically steep head profiles. They prefer sandy bottoms, into which they dive when threatened. Females of this species are light grey with a black spot at midbody; most of the body scales have a light red dot. Males have a series of dark red spots behind the eye and lack the red dots on the scales. (to 25 cm, 10 in)

Plate 89f
Bumphead Parrotfish
Bolbometapon muricatum
This is the largest parrotfish species on the reef, but it is wary and difficult to approach. Named for the bulbous protuberance on top of its head, it feeds on both algae and live coral. All adults (male and female) are greenish blue. Juveniles are greenish brown with five vertical arrays of small white spots. (to 1.2 m, 3.9 ft)

Plate 89 467

a Rockmover Wrasse

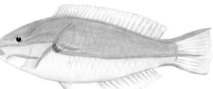

b Bluelined Wrasse

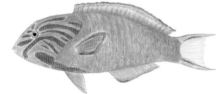

c Moon Wrasse

d Sunset Wrasse

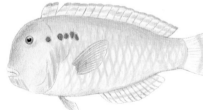

e Fivefinger Razorfish

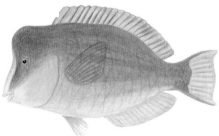

f Bumphead Parrotfish

Plate 90a
Stareye Parrotfish
Calatomus carolinus
The initial phase is mottled pinkish grey and brown. The terminal phase males (p. 250) are blue-green with pink scale margins and irregular pink bands radiating from the eye. (to 50 cm, 20 in)

Plate 90b
Bicolor Parrotfish
Cetoscarus bicolor
The initial phase (p. 250) of this parrotfish is dusky reddish brown with a pale back; the scales on the side of the body are black with white margins. Terminal phase males (p. 250) are green with pink scale margins; the head and front of the body are covered with pink spots. The juveniles look like members of a completely different species. Most of the body is white, as is the snout, while an orange saddle covers most of the head. Note also the orange-rimmed black area on the dorsal fin. (to 80 cm, 32 in)

Plate 90c
Bleeker's Parrotfish
Scarus bleekeri
The initial phase (p. 250) is dark brown with a yellow tail; broad, light bands are often present on the upper body. The terminal phase (male; p. 250) is blue-green with a pink bar on each body scale, and there is a green-edged yellow area on the cheek and blue-green bands on the chin. (to 30 cm, 12 in)

Plate 90d
Bluebarred Parrotfish
Scarus ghobban
Also called the Blue-chin Parrotfish, this species prefers lagoons with shallow reefs and sandy areas. The initial phase (p. 250) is yellow to green with light blue areas. The terminal phase (male; p. 250) is mostly yellow, becoming green on top. The scale margins are salmon pink and there are two distinct blue bands on the chin. (to 80 cm, 32 in)

Plate 90e
Scalefin Anthias
Pseudanthias squamipinnis
This is the most common member of the genus on shallow reefs. Males and females have markedly different coloration. Females are deep yellow throughout, while males are lavender to fuschia with magenta fins and a long projection from the front of the dorsal fin. These fish, and probably other members of the genus, undergo socially regulated sex changes (p. 250). (to 15 cm, 6 in)

Plate 90f
Redfin Anthias
Pseudanthias dispar
This beauty is one of the more shallow-water anthias sea basses. It occurs at depths frequented by snorkelers as well as divers. The body is orange-yellow above and pale lavender below. The dorsal fin is bright red and the pelvic fins have long threadlike projections in males. (to 10 cm, 4 in)

Plate 90 **469**

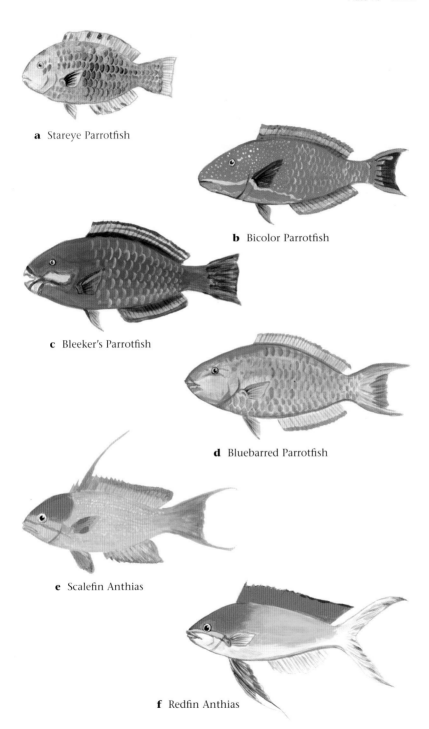

a Stareye Parrotfish

b Bicolor Parrotfish

c Bleeker's Parrotfish

d Bluebarred Parrotfish

e Scalefin Anthias

f Redfin Anthias

Plate 91a
Purple Anthias
Pseudanthias tuka
You can find aggregations of this beauty on outer reef slopes in fairly shallow water. The body is purple in both sexes, but males have a yellow area on the chin while females have a yellow band below the dorsal fin and yellow bands on each lobe of the tail. The similar Amethyst Anthias (*Pseudanthias pascalus*), which also occurs on the reef, is purple throughout. (to 12 cm, 4.5 in)

Plate 91b
Peacock Rockcod
Cephalopholis argus
There are a number of grouper species of this genus in the Great Barrier Reef, but this is one of the more distinctively colored. It feeds mainly on other fishes. Highly prized as a food fish, it has been implicated in ciguatera poisoning. Its coloration is olive green to brown, with numerous dark-edged blue spots throughout; there are five or six pale bars on the rear half of the body. (to 40 cm, 16 in)

Plate 91c
Coral Cod
Cephalopholis miniata
This grouper prefers coral-rich, clear water environments. It feeds mainly on small fish, but will also take an occasional crustacean. It is usually some shade of red with numerous bright blue spots throughout. (to 41 cm, 16 in)

Plate 91d
Barramundi Cod
Cromileptes altivelis
This rather oddly shaped grouper prefers silty reef areas, often in quite shallow water. It is a highly prized food fish, which may explain why it is so shy and retiring. It can be identified readily by its white color and numerous black spots. (to 65 cm, 26 in)

Plate 91e
Queensland Grouper
Epinephelus lancelotus
Also called the Giant Grouper, this is the largest fish found on the reef itself. It feeds on a variety of animals, particularly Spiny Lobsters (Plate 113e). The coloration is dark grey to brown; juveniles have bars of brown and yellow. (to 2.7 m, 8.9 ft; to 400 kg, 880 lb)

Plate 91f
Potato Cod
Epinephelus tukula
This is another giant predator, but one that is much less wary than the Queensland Grouper (Plate 91e). It will readily approach divers, especially when it can expect handouts, as at the famous Cod Hole (a famous dive site, north of Port Douglas/Mossman). The coloration is greyish brown with large, dark brown spots. (to 2 m, 6.6 ft; to 100 kg, 220 lb)

Plate 91 **471**

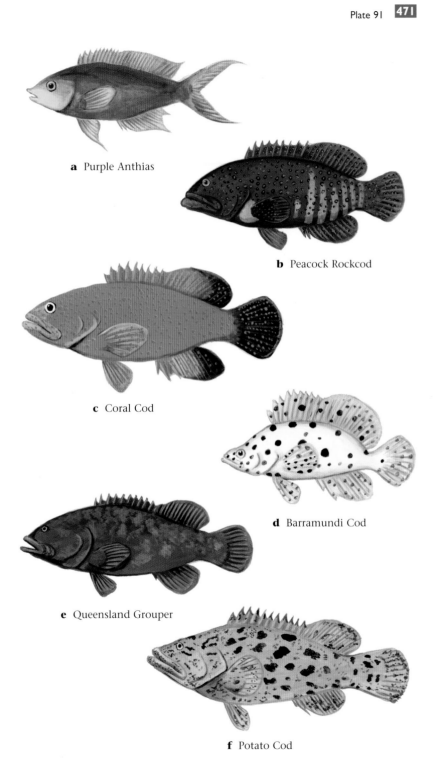

a Purple Anthias

b Peacock Rockcod

c Coral Cod

d Barramundi Cod

e Queensland Grouper

f Potato Cod

Plate 92a
Chinese Footballer
Plectropomus laevis
This large grouper is a highly prized food fish, but it is one of the species most likely to be involved in ciguatera poisoning. It comes in two colorations: the light form is white with several broad, brown bars and yellow fins, while the dark form is reddish brown with numerous blue spots and less distinct bars. (to 1 m, 3.3 ft)

Plate 92b
Coral Trout
Plectropomus leopardus
This is one of the most common groupers on the Great Barrier Reef, another highly coveted food fish that can cause ciguatera poisoning. The coloration is variable, ranging from tan to reddish brown with many tiny blue spots. (to 80 cm, 32 in)

Plate 92c
Coronation Trout
Variola louti
Like members of the genus *Plectropomus* (Plate 92a, 92b), this grouper feeds primarily on reef fish. It is good to eat and has been implicated in ciguatera poisoning. The tail has a distinctive lyre shape (as does the similar Lyretail Trout, *Variola albimarginata*). The coloration varies from red to brown, with numerous small spots of blue, pink, or lavender. (to 80 cm, 32 in)

Plate 92d
Royal Dottyback
Pseudochromis paccagnellae
Dottybacks are small, colorful, wrasse-shaped fish that reside in the cracks and crevices of coral reefs. This species is a particular favorite of marine aquarists. The front half of the body is bright purple, the rear half bright yellow. (to 7 cm, 3 in)

Plate 92e
Girdled Cardinalfish
Archamia zosterophora
The cardinalfish family is one of the largest families of coral reef fish, but they are often overlooked because they are small and nocturnal. All cardinalfish have two dorsal fins. They eat various sorts of zooplankton on their nocturnal forays. Cardinalfish have a unique (by marine fish standards) form of brood care: upon fertilization the male takes the eggs in his mouth and broods them there for up to several weeks, during which he does not feed. This species prefers to reside in Acropora corals (Plate 108), where it hides among the branches by day. It is somewhat transparent, with two orange bars behind the eye and a broad brown bar below the second dorsal fin. (to 8 cm, 3 in)

Plate 92f
Coral Cardinalfish
Sphaeramia nematoptera
This distinctive reef denizen resides in branching corals in calm, shallow water. The two dorsal fins are large, as are the anal and pelvic fins. The front part of the body is yellow-brown, behind which is a dark brown band extending through the first dorsal and pelvic fins; behind this bar, the body is white with brown spots. (to 8 cm, 3 in)

Plate 92 473

a Chinese Footballer

b Coral Trout

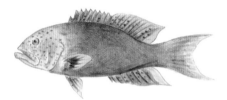

c Coronation Trout

d Royal Dottyback

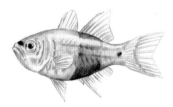

e Girdled Cardinalfish

f Coral Cardinalfish

Plate 93a
Giant Trevally
Caranx ignobilis
Trevallys, or jacks, are large predatory fishes of the midwater zone. They can often be found on reef margins, especially near drop-offs on outer reefs. This species is most likely to be found coursing over reef tops. It is silvery grey to black above and paler below. (to 1.7 m, 5.6 ft)

Plate 93b
Bigeye Trevally
Caranx sexfasciatus
Named for its large eyes, this species is more fusiform (torpedo-shaped) than the Giant Trevally (Plate 93a). It is bluish green above, shading to silver below. This is a nocturnal species that is found in large schools by day, often near reef escarpments. (to 80 cm, 32 in)

Plate 93c
Red Snapper
Lutjanus bohar
Snappers are among the prime offenders in ciguatera poisoning, and this species in particular cannot be sold for meat in Australia, though it is a highly prized food fish elsewhere. Also called the Red Bass in Australia, it is quite bold and will readily approach divers. It has a reddish tint throughout. (to 80 cm, 32 in)

Plate 93d
Blackspot Snapper
Lutjanus fulviflamma
This is a common mid-sized snapper that can be found on fairly shallow reefs. It is grey-brown with yellow fins and several yellow lateral stripes; there is a prominent black spot on each side. (to 35 cm, 14 in)

Plate 93e
Yellow-margined Seaperch
Lutjanus fulvus
This is a common mid-sized snapper. It is generally tan to silvery yellow, with yellow pectoral, pelvic and anal fins; the dorsal fin and tail are deep reddish brown. (to 40 cm, 16 in)

Plate 93f
Bluestripe Seaperch
Lutjanus kasmira
This nocturnal predator can be found in stationary schools by day. The head and belly are white, but the rest of the body and fins are yellow; there are four bright blue stripes on each side. (to 35 cm, 14 in)

Plate 93 475

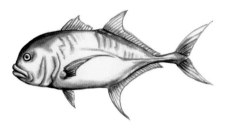

a Giant Trevally

b Bigeye Trevally

c Red Snapper

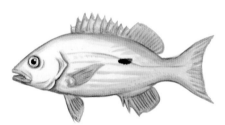

d Blackspot Snapper

e Yellow-margined Seaperch

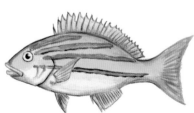

f Bluestripe Seaperch

Plate 94a
Red Emperor
Lutjanus sebae
This snapper prefers shallow, calm water such as lagoons, where there are coral patches surrounded by sandy areas. Adults are dark red to pink. Juveniles are white with three broad, reddish brown bars, the frontmost of which runs through the eye. (to 60 cm, 24 in)

Plate 94b
Sailfin Snapper
Symphorichthys spilurus
This is the most strikingly colored reef snapper. The body is yellow with numerous bright blue stripes. There is a black eyespot near the base of the tail, and two brown bands in front, one through the eye. There are several filamentous projections from the rear of the dorsal fin. (to 60 cm, 24 in)

Plate 94c
Many-spotted Sweetlips
Plectorhinchus chaetodontoides
The group of fish known as grunts are called sweetlips in Australia, apparently in reference to their kissable-seeming mouth margins. This species is white with many brown spots. Juveniles, however, are light brown with large, dark-edged white spots. This coloration mimics a toxic nudibranch, and the imitation is reinforced by seemingly spastic whole-body movements. (to 60 cm, 24 in)

Plate 94d
Diagonal-banded Sweetlips
Plectorhinchus goldmanni
Schools of this grunt are among the more spectacular reef sights. The body is white with numerous diagonal black bands; the fins, as well as those sweet lips themselves, are yellow. (to 50 cm, 20 in)

Plate 94e
Orange-striped Emperor
Lethrinus obsoletus
Emperors are predatory fish closely related to grunts (sweetlips) and snappers. They are generally nocturnal, resting by day in shady areas, often assuming a mottled coloration. The larger species are highly valued as food fishes. This is one of the more common emperors on coral reefs. It is greenish grey, with an orange stripe extending from the pectoral fin to the tail. (to 40 cm, 16 in)

Plate 94f
Yellowfin Goatfish
Mulloidichthys vanicolensis
Goatfishes can often be recognized by their catfish-like barbels (not visible in this illustration), chemosensory organs that allow them to taste their surroundings in a quest for benthic (bottom-dwelling) prey. Most are nocturnal, but they can be found out in the open, often in groups, by day. This species is silvery white, with yellow fins and a yellow lateral stripe. (to 38 cm, 15 in)

Plate 94 **477**

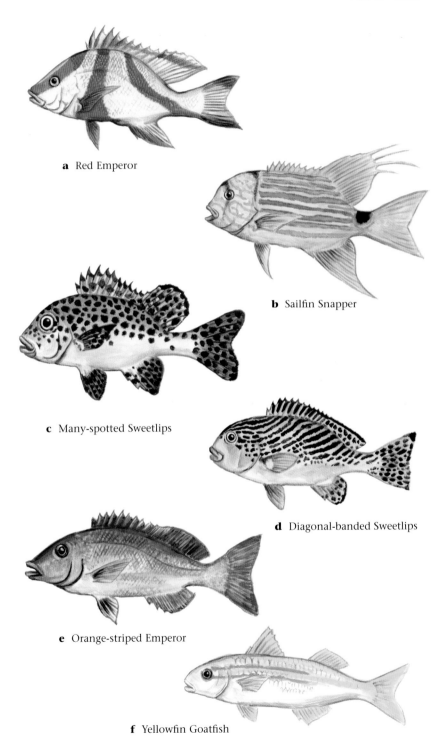

a Red Emperor

b Sailfin Snapper

c Many-spotted Sweetlips

d Diagonal-banded Sweetlips

e Orange-striped Emperor

f Yellowfin Goatfish

Plate 95a
Goldsaddle Goatfish
Parupeneus cyclostomus
This goatfish differs from most in that it preys primarily on other fishes. It comes in two color varieties, a yellow form and a dark form. It is the dark form that has the golden saddle on the back near the base of the tail. (to 50 cm, 20 in)

Plate 95b
Manybar Goatfish
Parupeneus multifasciatus
The background coloration of this goatfish is variable, ranging from grey to reddish brown. There are several dark bars on the body and a black patch behind the eye. (to 30 cm, 12 in)

Plate 95c
Mimic Blenny
Aspidontus taeniatus
This is one of the fang blennies, so called because of their impressive canines. This one mimics the Cleaner Wrasse (Plate 88e) in both coloration and behavior, allowing it to approach a client fish (p. 250); but instead of plucking ectoparasites off its surface, the Mimic Blenny takes a chunk of fin or flesh, the removal of which is much less appreciated. The body is elongate, with a broad black stripe extending from the tail that becomes narrower toward the nose; below the stripe is white tending to bluish toward the tail. (to 11.5 cm, 4.5 in)

Plate 95d
Midas Blenny
Ecsenius midas
Named for its yellow coloration, this blenny schools with the Scalefin Anthias (Plate 90e) and is thought to be its mimic. There is a second, dark blue color phase that does not associate with the Scalefin Anthias. (to 13 cm, 5 in)

Plate 95e
Great Barrier Reef Blenny
Ecsenius stictus
This bug-eyed blenny is endemic to the Great Barrier Reef. It is grey with several rows of brownish spots on the front half of the body; there is a Y-shaped black mark at the base of the pectoral fin and a black line below the gill cover. (to 6 cm, 2.5 in)

Plate 95f
Mandarinfish
Synchiropus splendidus
This goby can be readily identified by its distinctive coloration of green bands over an orange background. It is avidly sought by fishermen to sell to the exotic aquarium fish trade. (to 6 cm, 2.5 in)

Plate 95 **479**

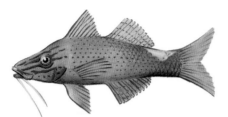

a Goldsaddle Goatfish

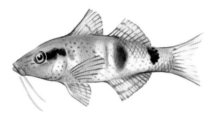

b Manybar Goatfish

c Mimic Blenny

d Midas Blenny

e Great Barrier Reef Blenny

f Mandarinfish

Plate 96a
Old Glory
Amblygobius rainfordi
This goby is green with five blue-edged red stripes running the length of the body. There are also five white spots along the base of the dorsal fin, as well as a black eyespot on the second dorsal fin and another at the base of the tail. (to 6.5 cm, 2.5 in)

Plate 96b
Yellow Shrimp Goby
Cryptocentrus cinctus
Shrimp gobies are so called because of their habit of consorting with some types of shrimp. This association, which is mutualistic in its benefits, extends to inhabiting the same burrow. This shrimp goby comes in two distinct color varieties, one yellowish orange and one white. Both have four or five dusky bars on the body and small blue or white spots on the head. (to 7.5 cm, 3 in)

Plate 96c
Spikefin Goby
Discordipinna griessinger
A distinctive orange projection from the front of the first dorsal fin makes this goby easy to identify. The body color is white with an orangish brown band on the lower body. The fins are orange, and the second dorsal and upper tail fin are adorned with dark brown spots. (to 2.5 cm, 1 in)

Plate 96d
Fourbar Goby
Gobiodon citrinus
This goby lives among the branches of Acropora corals (Plate 108). It is bright yellow with two blue lines below the eye and two longer ones behind. It produces a toxic mucous. (to 6.5 cm, 2.5 in)

Plate 96e
Redhead Goby
Paragobiodon echinocephalus
Another goby that lives in live corals, this species has a red-orange head with many fine bristles. The rest of the body and fins are black. (to 3.5 cm, 1.5 in)

Plate 96f
Silverlined Mudskipper
Periopthalmus argentilineatus
Mudskippers, which live on mudflats in mangroves, have distinctive protruding eyes and are extremely pugnacious; their territorial disputes are legendary. This is one of five species that occur in the Great Barrier Reef region. It is mottled brown and dark brown with a white belly. There is a distinct black band, edged in white, on the dorsal fins. (to 12 cm, 4.5 in)

Plate 96 **481**

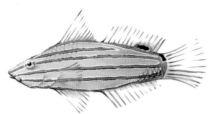

a Old Glory

b Yellow Shrimp Goby

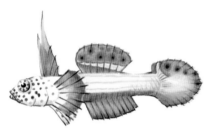

c Spikefin Goby

d Fourbar Goby

e Redhead Goby

f Silverlined Mudskipper

Plate 97a
Twinspot Goby
Signigobius biocellatus
The spots for which this fish is named are eyespots, one on each dorsal fin. The rest of the body is a mottled pinkish tan and brown. The anal and pelvic fins are black with blue spots. Some think this species mimics a crab, but if so, the illusion is meant only for the low-resolution eyes of crabs. (to 6.5 cm, 2.5 in)

Plate 97b
Sixspot Goby
Valencienna sexguttata
This goby burrows in sand underneath rocks. It is egg-white all over with six small (and hard to see) blue spots on the cheeks. (to 14 cm, 5.5 in)

Plate 97c
Fire Dartfish
Nemateleotris magnifica
Dartfish, also called firefishes or fire gobies, are closely related to the gobies but distinct enough to warrant their own family. This species is one of the most beautiful fish in the ocean. The body is white in front, becoming purple toward the tail. The elongate front portion of the dorsal fin is white to pale yellow and projects upward; the median fins (the dorsal, anal, and caudal fins) are red, becoming darker toward the tail. These fishes are wary and never stray far from their burrows, into which they retreat at the slightest provocation. They are highly prized by aquarists. (to 8 cm, 3 in)

Plate 97d
Whitefin Surgeonfish
Acanthurus albiperctoralis
This surgeonfish feeds on zooplankton near drop-offs, usually in small groups. It is black throughout, except for the outer part of the pectoral fins, which are white. (to 33 cm, 13 in)

Plate 97e
Ringtail Surgeonfish
Acanthurus blochii
You are more likely to find this surgeonfish grazing for algae over sandy areas than on the reef itself. It has a dark greenish body with bluish purple median fins (the dorsal, anal, and caudal fins) and a white swatch at the base of the tail. Note also the yellow area behind the eye. (to 50 cm, 20 in)

Plate 97f
Whitespotted Surgeonfish
Acanthurus guttatus
Look for this surgeonfish in the surge zone, where it often forms small schools. The rearward portion of the body has white spots, while two vertical white stripes adorn the head region. This species is more deep-bodied than most surgeonfishes. (to 38 cm, 15 in)

Plate 97 483

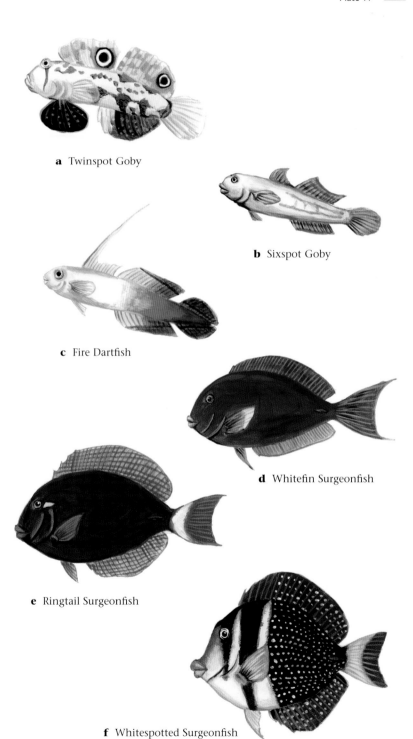

a Twinspot Goby

b Sixspot Goby

c Fire Dartfish

d Whitefin Surgeonfish

e Ringtail Surgeonfish

f Whitespotted Surgeonfish

Plate 98a
Striped Surgeonfish
Acanthurus lineatus
This very aggressive and territorial surgeonfish lives on the outer edges of reefs that are exposed to wave action. It is among the most strikingly colored members of the family. On the upper part of the body there are alternating yellow and black-edged blue bands; the belly area is lavender. (to 38 cm, 15 in)

Plate 98b
Whitecheek Surgeonfish
Acanthurus nigricans
Also called the Goldrim Surgeonfish, this fish prefers shallow water on rocky shores or exposed reefs. It is black with a white tail. A yellow margin rims the body below the dorsal and anal fins, and there is a yellow band near the end of the tail. Note also the white patch below the eye and the yellow over the spines. (to 21 cm, 8.5 in)

Plate 98c
Brown Surgeonfish
Acanthurus nigrofuscus
This rather drab surgeonfish is quite common on shallow reefs. The body is tan with lavender tones; there are yellow spots on the head, and black spots at the base of the dorsal and anal fins near the tail. (to 21 cm, 8.5 in)

Plate 98d
Orangeband Surgeonfish
Acanthurus olivaceus
This surgeonfish, which is one of the more distinctively colored ones, can be found in sandy areas near reefs. Its body is tan in front and dark brown toward the tail; a striking orange patch, outlined in purple, extends from behind the eye. Juveniles are bright yellow. (to 35 cm, 14 in)

Plate 98e
Mimic Surgeonfish
Acanthurus pyroferus
The body of this surgeonfish is dark brown; there is a diffuse orange patch around the base of the pectoral fins and a distinct, curving black band on the cheeks. The tail has a yellow margin. Juveniles are shaped like angelfish and are thought to mimic the Lemon Angelfish (*Centropyge flavissimus*), although the advantage they would derive thereby is not obvious. (to 25 cm, 10 in)

Plate 98f
Convict Surgeonfish
Acanthurus triostegus
This surgeonfish forms large aggregations that swarm over the reef, overwhelming territorial damselfish by their sheer numbers. The body is greenish grey with six vertical black bands. (to 26 cm, 10 in)

Plate 98 485

a Striped Surgeonfish

b Whitecheek Surgeonfish

c Brown Surgeonfish

d Orangeband Surgeonfish

e Mimic Surgeonfish

f Convict Surgeonfish

Plate 99a
Yellowfin Surgeonfish
Acanthurus xanthopterus
This is one of the largest surgeonfish, often found in sandy areas far from coral reefs. The body is purplish grey; there is a yellow area around the eye and on the pectoral fins. (to 56 cm, 22 in)

Plate 99b
Blue Tang
Paracanthurus hepatus
This beauty, which is also called the Palette Surgeonfish, prefers coral-rich areas in clear water with lots of current, especially on outer reefs. It is a brilliant blue, with a curving black patch and a bright yellow tail. (to 31 cm, 12 in)

Plate 99c
Sailfin Tang
Zebrasoma veliferum
This surgeonfish likes to be where the waves are breaking and churning things up. The body is adorned with alternating dark brown and white bars. When alarmed, it raises its large dorsal and anal fins, dramatically increasing its apparent size and altering its shape. (to 40 cm, 16 in)

Plate 99d
Orangespine Unicornfish
Naso lituratus
This fish seems like a caricature of artistic excess. There is no need to describe it; the illustration will suffice. (to 45 cm, 17.5 in)

Plate 99e
Humpnose Unicornfish
Naso tuberosus
One of the more bizarre-looking fish in the ocean, it gets its name from the large bulbous protuberance on the nose. There is also a distinct hump on the upper back. The coloration is silvery grey. (to 60 cm, 24 in)

Plate 99f
Bluespine Unicornfish
Naso unicornis
This unicornfish has the projections for which this group of surgeonfish derives its name. It feeds primarily on leafy algae such as sargassum and, somewhat surprisingly for such a large fish, it will enter very shallow water in search of it. It is named for its bright blue tail spines. (to 70 cm, 28 in)

Plate 99 487

a Yellowfin Surgeonfish

b Blue Tang

c Sailfin Tang

d Orangespine Unicornfish

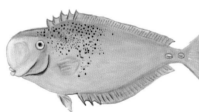

e Humpnose Unicornfish

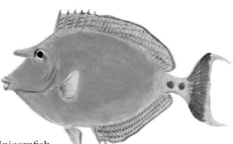

f Bluespine Unicornfish

Plate 100a
Moorish Idol
Zanclus cornutus
Perhaps the most extravagantly beautiful fish in the ocean, it cannot be mistaken for any other. It feeds primarily on sponges over a wide range of depths. (to 20 cm, 8 in)

Plate 100b
Coral Rabbitfish
Siganus corallinus
Rabbitfish are characterized by their venomous pelvic spines, which can inflict painful, but rarely fatal, injuries on the unwary human. This species is yellow with numerous blue dots over the entire body and head. The tail is forked. (to 28 cm, 11 in)

Plate 100c
Blue-lined Rabbitfish
Siganus puellus
This rabbitfish feeds on algae and sponges on shallow reefs. It usually occurs in pairs. The body is yellow with irregular blue lines and a distinct dark brown band through the eye. (to 38 cm, 15 in)

Plate 100d
Foxface
Siganus vulpinus
This rabbitfish is believed to pair for life. Most of the body is yellow. The head and face are white with a broad black band through the eye and a triangular black patch on the throat. (to 30 cm, 12 in)

Plate 100e
Orange-lined Triggerfish
Balistapus undulates
This triggerfish eats pretty much anything. The body, head and fins are green with orange lines. (to 30 cm, 12 in)

Plate 100f
Titan Triggerfish
Balistoides viridescens
This is the largest triggerfish, so it is aptly named. It is quite wary for its size, except for when the female is guarding eggs—when so occupied, she is extremely aggressive and will deliver nasty bites to any intruder, including divers. The body is dusky brown to green with a dark band through the eye, as well as dark bands on the median fins (the dorsal, anal, and caudal fins). (to 75 cm, 30 in)

Plate 100   489

a Moorish Idol

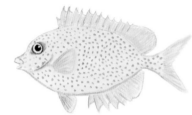

b Coral Rabbitfish

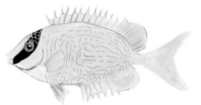

c Blue-lined Rabbitfish

d Foxface

e Orange-lined Triggerfish

f Titan Triggerfish

Plate 101a
Clown Triggerfish
Balistoides conspicillum
Also called the Black Triggerfish, this is a spectacularly colored animal that is highly sought by aquarists. It prefers outer reefs. The body is black with large white spots on the belly, a yellowish area on the back, a white band across the nose, and yellow margins below the dorsal and anal fins; note also the yellow mouth. (to 50 cm, 20 in)

Plate 101b
Yellow-spotted Triggerfish
Pseudobalistes fuscus
Divers should also respect these nesting females. The body is blue with numerous yellow spots. (to 55 cm, 22 in)

Plate 101c
Lagoon Triggerfish
Rhinecanthus aculeatus
Also called the Whitebanded Triggerfish, this species prefers reef flats in lagoons with sandy bottoms. The body is white with a large black region interrupted by four bluish white diagonal bands. There are thin blue lines around the eyes, a yellow area around the mouth, and a yellow line extending from the mouth. (to 25 cm, 10 in)

Plate 101d
Wedge-tail Triggerfish
Rhinecanthus rectangulus
Also called the Reef Triggerfish, this species likes outer reefs with lots of surging water. The head and lower body is white with a broad, diagonal black band extending from the eye; above this band the body is tan; there is another triangle of black at the base of the tail. Note also the blue lines around the eye and the blue patch on the upper lip, as well as the triangular yellow lines over the tan area of upper body. (to 25 cm, 10 in)

Plate 101e
Scimitar Triggerfish
Sufflamen bursa
Also called Lei Triggerfish (in Hawaii), it is white with two prominent yellow bands extending from the base of the pectoral fins, one through the eye and one behind. (to 24 cm, 9.5 in)

Plate 101f
Beaked Leatherjacket
Oxymonocanthus longirostris
What Australians call leatherjackets are often called filefish elsewhere. This species, also called the Longnose Leatherjacket or Longnose Filefish, feeds on live coral polyps. It is green with numerous orange spots. (to 9 cm, 3.5 in)

Plate 101　491

a Clown Triggerfish

b Yellow-spotted Triggerfish

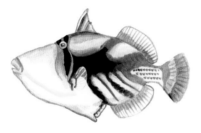

c Lagoon Triggerfish

d Wedge-tail Triggerfish

e Scimitar Triggerfish

f Beaked Leatherjacket

Plate 102a
Scrawled Leatherjacket
Aluterus scriptus
Also called the Scribbled Leatherjacket, Scribbled Filefish, and Scrawled Filefish, this species is quite omnivorous, feeding on algae, anemones, hydrozoans, and gorgonians, among other benthic (bottom-dwelling) items. The body is greyish green with irregular blue markings throughout, as well as small black spots. It has a rather droopy countenance. (to 75 cm, 30 in)

Plate 102b
Star Puffer
Arothron stellatus
This large puffer is white with numerous small black spots throughout, except for the belly region. Juveniles are orange with black spots. (to 90 cm, 35 in)

Plate 102c
Mimic Leatherjacket
Paraluteres prionurus
This fish is a precise mimic of the poisonous Black-saddle Toby (Plate 102g). It can be distinguished primarily by its two dorsal fins, the frontmost of which is lacking in the toby. (to 10 cm, 4 in)

Plate 102d
Thornback Cowfish
Lactoria fornasini
Cowfishes are named for the horn-like projections above their eyes. You are most likely to find this species in sand and weeds rather than coral. It is brown with irregular blue markings throughout. (to 15 cm, 6 in)

Plate 102e
Spotted Boxfish
Ostracion meleagris
This species is highly dimorphic. Females are black with numerous small white spots; males are black on top (with white spots) but blue elsewhere, with orangish brown spots. (to 18 cm, 7 in)

Plate 102f
Ambon Toby
Canthigaster amboinensis
This small puffer prefers shallow outer reefs near the surging water. It is generally brown on top, becoming white toward the belly; there are numerous blue lines on the head and blue spots on the body. Note also the numerous brown spots below the eye, and the more diffuse reddish brown spots on the side of the body. (to 14 cm, 5.5 in)

Plate 102g
Black-saddle Toby
Canthigaster valentini
This species is mimicked by the Mimic Leatherjacket (Plate 102c). It is quite common in shallow-water coral reefs, much more so than the mimic. The body is white with a broad brown bar on the head and three more on the body; it also has small light brown spots distributed throughout most of the body, a yellow tail, and blue lines radiating from the eyes. (to 9 cm, 3.5 in)

Plate 102 **493**

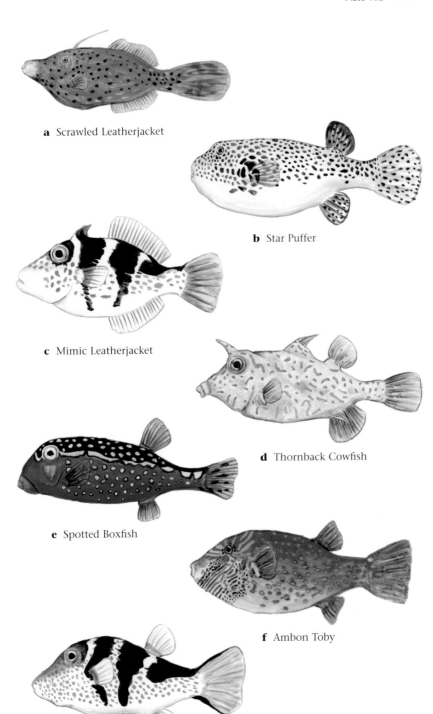

a Scrawled Leatherjacket

b Star Puffer

c Mimic Leatherjacket

d Thornback Cowfish

e Spotted Boxfish

f Ambon Toby

g Black-saddle Toby

Plate 103a
Porcupinefish
Diodon hystrix
Porcupinefish are puffers with spines. This
species frequents both coral and rocky reefs,
where it dines on mollusks, urchins, and crabs. It
is greyish brown, becoming white near the belly,
with small black spots throughout. (to 70 cm, 28 in)

Plate 103b
Crocodile Longtom
Tylosurus crocodilus
Also known as the Houndfish, this member of the
needlefish family hangs out near the surface,
waiting to devour any small fish that happens by.
It is extremely elongate, with a long, toothy beak.
The coloration is silver with a black keel at the
base of the tail, and a dark blue stripe along each
side. (to 1.3 m, 4.3 ft)

Plate 103c
Crown Toby
Canthigaster coronatus
Also called the Three-barred Toby, this species is
superficially similar to the Black-saddle Toby
(Plate 102g), but the body is larger and more
elongate; the eyes are also yellow-orange and
have more prominent, brighter blue lines radiating
from them. Note also the orange markings on the
lower sides and belly. (to 13.5 cm, 5.5 in)

Plate 103d
Bigscale Soldierfish
Myripristis berndti
Soldierfish (and squirrelfish) are large-eyed
nocturnal animals that hang out in reef crevices
and crannies by day. This species eats primarily
crustacean larvae in the plankton. The body is
pale pink to grey, the fin margins bright red; the
first dorsal fin is yellow. (to 30 cm, 12 in)

Plate 103e
Scarlet Soldierfish
Myripristis pralinia
The body of this soldierfish is red, tending toward
pink below. The pelvic fins are pink, but the rest
are red. (to 20 cm, 8 in)

Plate 103f
Spotfin Squirrelfish
Neoniphon sammara
Squirrelfish differ from soldierfish primarily in that
squirrelfish possess a venomous spine on the gill
cover. They also tend to eat adult crustaceans off
the bottom rather than larval crustaceans in the
plankton. This species is common on shallow,
protected reefs. The body is silver with lateral red
stripes. The first dorsal fin is red with white
margins; the rest of the fins, with the exception of
the pelvics, are yellow with red margins and the
pelvic fins are translucent. (to 30 cm, 12 in)

Plate 103g
Crown Squirrelfish
Sargocentron diadema
This is a common shallow-water reef fish. It is red
with several white lateral stripes on the body; the
dorsal fin is dark red to black. (to 13 cm, 5 in)

Plate 103 **495**

a Porcupinefish

b Crocodile Longtom

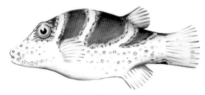

c Crown Toby

d Bigscale Soldierfish

e Scarlet Soldierfish

f Spotfin Squirrelfish

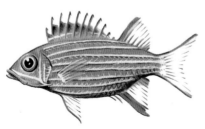

g Crown Squirrelfish

Plate 104a
Peppered Squirrelfish
Sargocentron punctatissimum
This species occurs in very shallow water, including tide pools. The body is silvery red with blue highlights and narrow red stripes; the spiny dorsal fin is red with a white spot on each membrane segment. (to 13 cm, 5 in)

Plate 104b
Turkeyfish
Pterois volitans
Also called the Red Firefish, Lionfish, or Zebrafish, this is the most spectacular member of the scorpionfish family found on the reef. The oversized fins have a feathery appearance, and the body and head have thick reddish brown bars, alternating with white bars and thinner red lines. As is true of all scorpionfishes, the dorsal, anal, and pelvic spines are highly venomous. (to 38 cm, 15 in)

Plate 104c
Trumpetfish
Aulostomus chinensis
Also called the Painted Flutemouth, this odd-shaped predator uses stealth to approach its prey (small fish), sometimes even hiding behind larger fish such as parrotfish. It also uses camouflage and can change color to match its surroundings. There are two color forms, brown and yellow. (to 80 cm, 32 in)

Plate 104d
Cornetfish
Fistularia commersomii
Also called the Smooth Flutemouth, this fish is similar to the Trumpetfish (Plate 104c) but much more slender. It is common on shallow reefs, where it is most active at night. (to 1.5 m, 4.9 ft)

Plate 104e
Starry Moray
Echidna nebulosa
This smallish moray, also known as the Snowflake Moray, is more likely to be found out and about during the daytime than other morays. It is white with two rows of large black blotches. (to 70 cm, 28 in)

Plate 104f
Yellowmargin Moray
Gymnothorax flavimarginatus
This common moray is one of the most easily tamed, even to the point of taking food from a diver's hand. It is brown with yellow mottling. The yellow fin margins for which it is named can only be seen when it is swimming. (to 1.2 m, 3.9 ft)

Plate 104 **497**

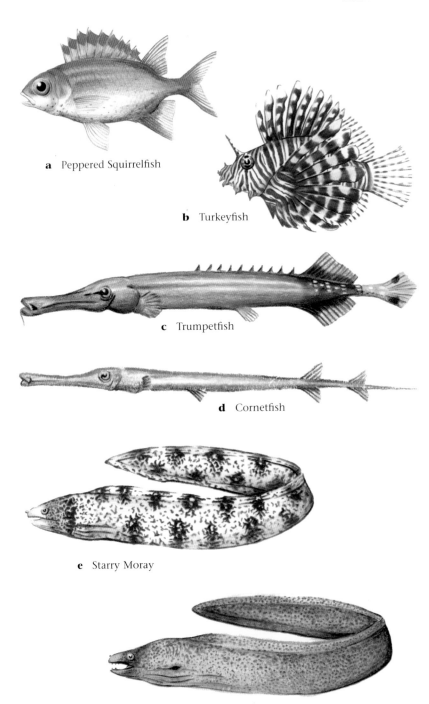

a Peppered Squirrelfish

b Turkeyfish

c Trumpetfish

d Cornetfish

e Starry Moray

f Yellowmargin Moray

Plate 105a
Whitemouth Moray
Gymnothorax meleagris
This common moray is dark brown with numerous small white spots. The mouth lining is bright white. (to 1 m, 3.3 ft)

Plate 105b
Giant Moray
Gymnothorax javanicus
This is the largest Pacific moray and it occurs in a variety of reef habitats in shallow water. It is light brown with irregular darker brown spots. (to 2.2 m, 7.2 ft)

Plate 105c
Undulated Moray
Gymnothorax undulatus
This is one of the most common morays, and one of the most aggressive toward divers. The body is yellowish with dense, irregular dark brown blotches. (to 1 m, 3.3 ft)

Plate 105d
Spotted Eagle Ray
Aetobatus narinari
Eagle rays are fairly common on inshore, shallow reefs. Like mantas, they have a penchant for leaping out of the water, for reasons that are not entirely clear. This species can be readily identified by the numerous white spots that cover its body. (to 2.5 m, 8.2 ft, wingtip to wingtip)

Plate 105e
Manta Ray
Manta biorostris
These gentle giants are among the largest of all rays and among the most awe-inspiring ocean creatures. Aside from their size and graceful swimming movements, mantas are famous for their spectacular leaps above the water surface. They are generally pelagic (open-ocean) but are often encountered by divers near coral reefs. Aside from their huge size, they can be recognized by the distinctive flaps in front of the eyes. (to 6.7 m, 22 ft, wingtip to wingtip; to 1800+ kg, 4000+ lb)

Plate 105f
Blue-spotted Stingray
Taeniura lymma
There are a number of stingray species in the area. They are named for their tail spines, which can deliver an extremely painful wound. Stingrays generally prefer shallow water over sandy bottoms, so human waders should be cautious. This species is frequently encountered on coral reefs, resting under ledges. It can be identified by the prominent blue spots that cover the entire body. (to 2.4 m, 7.9 ft, wingtip to wingtip)

Plate 105 **499**

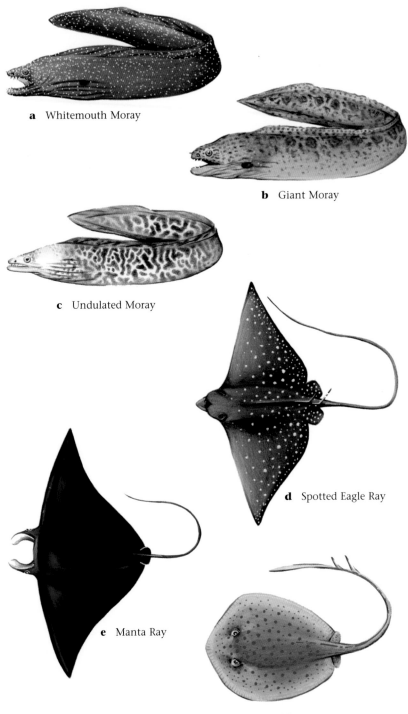

a Whitemouth Moray

b Giant Moray

c Undulated Moray

d Spotted Eagle Ray

e Manta Ray

f Blue-spotted Stingray

Plate 106a
Banded Wobbegong
Orectolobus ornatus
Wobbegongs have a distinctively flattened body shape and variegated, cryptic body coloration. They typically lay motionless on the bottom and prey on a variety of benthic (bottom-dwelling) animals. Though not aggressive, they will attack if stepped on, and they can deliver a nasty, sometimes even fatal, bite with their extremely sharp, fang-like teeth. This species is generally grey-brown with several dark brown bars on the body; the head is mottled in various shades of brown. (to 2.9 m, 9.5 ft)

Plate 106b
Silvertip Shark
Carcharhinus albimarginatus
This is one of the more common members of the requiem shark family (often referred to as whaler sharks in Australia; family Carcharhinidae) on the Great Barrier Reef. Requiem sharks are active swimmers and are responsible for about half of all reported shark attacks on humans. The young are born alive as miniature versions of the adults. Silvertips are common on outer reef slopes. The body is dark grey on top, shading to white toward the belly. It is named for the distinctive white tips on the first dorsal, pectoral, and tail fins. (to 3 m, 9.8 ft)

Plate 106c
Grey Reef Shark
Carcharhinus amblyrhyncos
This requiem shark (family Carcharhinidae) is common on outer reef slopes, generally in shallower water than the Silvertips (106b). It is the most prone to adopt the hunchbacked threat posture when agitated. This threat should be heeded, as these sharks are potentially dangerous, and most attacks occur when divers approach too closely. The body is greyish brown, shading to white at the belly; the tail fin has a distinctive black trailing edge. (to 2.6 m, 8.5 ft)

Plate 106d
Blacktip Reef Shark
Carcharhinus melanopterus
This is one of the most common sharks on shallow reefs. It is timid, but has been known to bite the feet of waders. The snout is fairly short and rounded. The body is grey-brown above and white below, and there is a distinct darker band extending into the white region, which runs from above the pectoral fin toward the tail. All of the fins have black near the tip, but the black area is especially pronounced on the first dorsal fin. (to 1.8 m, 5.9 ft)

Plate 106e
Whitetip Reef Shark
Triaenodon obesus
Though a bold and curious shark that often approaches divers, this species is considered harmless and has rarely been implicated in attacks. It is a nocturnal shallow-water shark that rests in caves and under ledges during the day. It is brownish above, tending toward yellowish white below. The tips of the dorsal fins and tail are white, but most noticeably on the first dorsal fin and upper tail fin. (to 2.1 m, 6.9 ft)

Plate 106f
Scalloped Hammerhead
Sphyrna lewini
Hammerheads are among the most readily recognizable fishes in the ocean. Their oddly shaped heads are thought to increase their sensory capacity (smell, pressure, vision) and/or maneuverability. This species is one of the largest members of the family. Though imposing, it is not aggressive. The head is somewhat concave. (to 4.2 m, 14 ft)

Plate 106 **501**

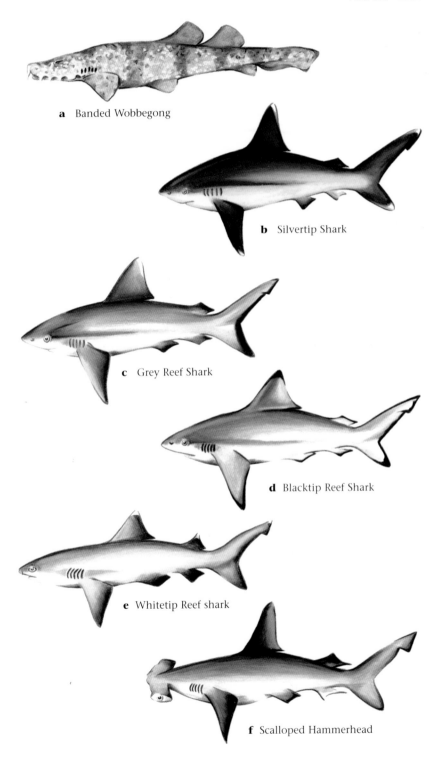

a Banded Wobbegong

b Silvertip Shark

c Grey Reef Shark

d Blacktip Reef Shark

e Whitetip Reef shark

f Scalloped Hammerhead

Plate 107a
Barrel Sponge
Xestospongia testudinaria
This huge sponge can be readily identified by its size alone. Look for various sorts of crustaceans inside the barrel, as well as the diverse animals that inhabit its deep ridges.

Plate 107b
Fire Coral
Millepora sp.
An encrusting, sometimes branching group of coral species that inflicts very nasty, burning stings when touched. They can cause welts and swelling in sensitive people, although the effect is usually of short duration.

Plate 107c
Glomerate Tree Coral
Dendronephthya sp.
This gorgonian, or soft coral, forms attractive, prickly, rounded colonies.

Plate 107d
Sea Fan
Semperina sp.
Sea fans form upright colonies in which their branches are are all in the same plane, or "dimension." Members of this genus are usually reddish brown with white branch tips.

Plate 107e
Magnificent Sea Anemone
Heteractis magnifica
This large anemone is a favorite of anenomefish and photographers alike. It prefers exposed areas with lots of current.

Plate 107f
Bulb Tentacle Sea Anemone
Entacmaea quadricolor
The tentacles of this anemone are bulbous. It is another favorite of anemonefish, but especially the Red-and-black Anemonefish, *Amphiprion melanopus* (Plate 85). Usually only the tentacles appear above the surface; the main part of the anemone lays hidden in crevices.

Plate 107g
Merten's Sea Anemone
Stichodactyla mertensi
Perhaps the world's largest anemone and a favorite of anemonefishes, this species can be distinguished by the convoluted disc margin.

Plate 107   503

a Barrel Sponge

b Fire Coral

c Glomerate Tree Coral

d Sea Fan

e Magnificent Sea Anemone

f Bulb Tentacle Sea Anemone

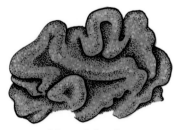

g Merten's Sea Anemone

Plate 108a
Pocillopora eydouxi
This coral species prefers areas with lots of water movement. It forms round heads with compact branches of uniform size.

Plate 108b
Acropora cerealis
This hard coral forms densely branched colonies with well-delineated individual polyp skeletons. The color is usually whitish, with pink or purplish tips. It is common on upper reef slopes.

Plate 108c
Acropora hyacinthus
This common coral forms flat, plate-like colonies on upper reef slopes and reef flats. The color is uniform and varies from green to tan.

Plate 108d
Porites cf. Lobata
This mounding coral forms lumpy, shallow domes. It prefers calm waters and can be particularly abundant in lagoons.

Plate 108e
Fungia sp.
Fungia is a mushroom-shaped coral with ridges radiating from the center.

Plate 108f
Brain Coral
Leptoria phrygia
Named for the cortex-like surface invaginations, this species can be found on reef slopes in clear water.

Plate 108g
Bushy Black Coral
Antipathes sp.
It's only black when it's dead; living coral is brownish-orange. *Antipathes* is very plant-like in appearance—bushy and densely branched.

Plate 108 **505**

a *Pocillopora eydouxi*

b *Acropora cerealis*

c *Acropora hyacinthus*

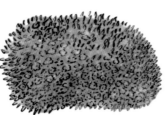

d *Porites cf. Lobata*

f Brain Coral

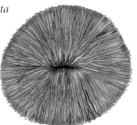

e *Fungia* sp.

g Bushy Black Coral

Plate 109a

Upside-Down Jellyfish
Cassiopea andromeda
Look for this jellyfish in calm water over sand. It hangs upside down in order to absorb the most sunlight for its symbiotic algae.

Plate 109b

Pseudoceros dimidiatus
The striking color of this flatworm suggests that, like nudibranchs (sea slugs), it is toxic. The most common form has wide yellow stripes alternating with wide black stripes. Also look for the orange margin.

Plate 109c

Pseudoceros ferrugineus
This flatworm beauty has a yellow margin; the body has shades of lavender and burgundy. The bright coloration indicates that it is toxic.

Plate 109d

Pherecardia striata
This species is a type of fireworm, which are known for their painful stings. It is covered with white hairy structures called setae, and if you get close enough you can see them—a series of thin pink and white stripes running longitudinally along the back.

Plate 109e

Christmas Tree Worm
Spirobranchus giganteus
This species is variable in color, but always has two spirals of tentacles; it lives in tubes on living coral.

Plate 109f

Horned Helmet
Cassia cornuta
This common helmet is also the largest. It feeds on echinoderms, including the notorious Crown-of-thorns (Plate 113h). Look for it on sand inside the outer barrier reefs.

Plate 109g

Moon Snail
Polinices mammilla
The glossy shell is white and so is the animal inside. The Moon Snail feeds on other mollusks. It can be found on sand or on mudflats in shallow water.

Plate 109 **507**

a Upside-down Jellyfish

b *Pseudoceros dimidiatus*

c *Pseudoceros ferrugineus*

d *Pherecardia striata*

e Christmas Tree Worm

f Horned Helmet

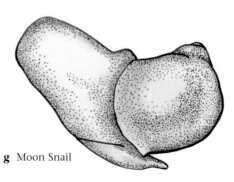

g Moon Snail

Plate 110a
Honey Cowrie
Cypraea helvola
A very common cowrie, this species is colored reddish brown with many white spots. It prefers shallow water.

Plate 110b
Mole Cowrie
Cypraea talpa
The shell is brown and gold banded; the mantle is black with many tiny white spots. Look for this cowrie underneath coral heads.

Plate 110c
Tiger Cowrie
Cypraea tigris
One of the larger cowries, this species frequents a number of habitats but is probably most common in coral rubble. It has a white shell with black spots. It is .

Plate 110d
Pacific Deer Cowrie
Cypraea vitellus
The shell of this cowrie is brown with white spots. The papillae (bumps) on the mantle are particularly large.

Plate 110e
Triton's Trumpet
Charonia tritonis
This is one of the largest sea snails and an important predator of the Crown-of-Thorns (Plate 113h). Look for it on sandy areas between reef patches.

Plate 110f
Pope's Miter
Mitra papalis
This large miter has orange spots on a cream-colored shell. Unlike most miters, this species prefers sandy habitats.

Plate 110g
Marble Cone
Conus marmoreus
Like many cones, this species has many triangular markings, but it has a darker shell than most other members of the genus. Cones are predators and this one prefers to eat other cone snails.

Plate 110 509

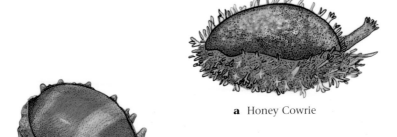

a Honey Cowrie

b Mole Cowrie

c Tiger Cowrie

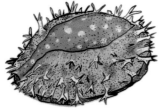

d Pacific Deer Cowrie

e Triton's Trumpet

f Pope's Miter

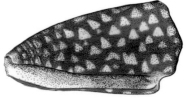

g Marble Cone

Plate 111a
Textile Cone
Conus textile
A favorite among shell collectors, this species is extremely venomous. The venom, which it uses to kill small fish, can also kill humans. It is most common in coral rubble in shallow water.

Plate 111b
Sundial
Architectonica perspectiva
This beautiful gastropod (the largest group of mollusks, which includes the snails, limpets, slugs, whelks, conchs, and sea slugs) has a characteristic coiled form. It likes sandy areas in shallow water.

Plate 111c
Netted Olive
Oliva reticulara
This attractive sea snail preys on other gastropods (the largest group of mollusks). Look for the orange area near the front of the shell's aperture.

Plate 111d
Chelidonura hirudinina
This delicate little nudibranch (sea slug) rewards close inspection. It is blue-green with black lines forming a "T" on the head. It prefers shallow water over sand or rocks.

Plate 111e
Elysia ornata
This sea slug (nudibranch) has a green body with orange and black margins.

Plate 111f
Umbraculum umbraculum
Look for this sea slug in tide pools or shallow reefs. It is bright orange with round white papillae (bumps) projecting from its back.

Plate 111g
Berthella martensi
This sea slug can literally come apart before your eyes. When disturbed it sheds all or part of its mantle, which consists of three parts. The color is quite variable.

Plate III 511

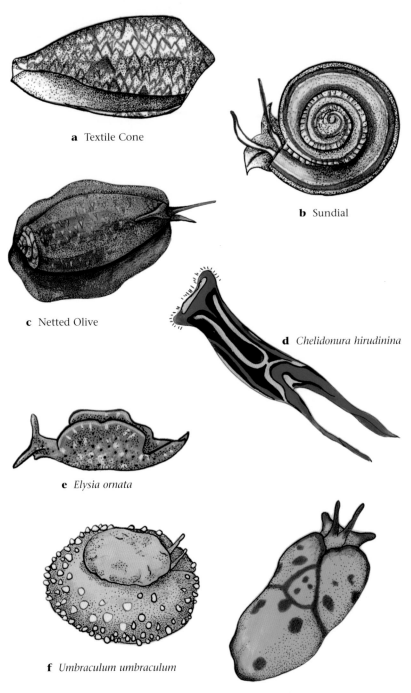

a Textile Cone

b Sundial

c Netted Olive

d *Chelidonura hirudinina*

e *Elysia ornata*

f *Umbraculum umbraculum*

g *Berthella martensi*

Plate 112a
Spanish Dancer
Hexabranchus sanguineus
This species is named for the undulating movements it makes while swimming through the water. It is the largest nudibranch (sea slug) in the world. It is always some shade of red.

Plate 112b
Phyllidiella pustulosa
This nudibranch (sea slug) has a black body with pink tubercles (bumps). It is one of the most common species of nudibranch throughout the Indo-Pacific.

Plate 112c
Common Pearl Oyster
Pinctada margaritafera
This bivalve attaches to coral rubble and rocks. It can be recognized by the jagged teeth around the aperture.

Plate 112d
Bigfin Reef Squid
Sepioteuthis lessoniana
This is the squid you are most likely to encounter on the reef, especially at its edges. The fins of this species extend much further down the mantle than in most squids. The color, as in most squids, is variable and changeable.

Plate 112e
Octopus cyanea
This is a relatively large octopus that is out and about during the day. It also prefers the relatively shallow water favored by snorkelers and scuba divers. Look for a black spot surrounded by a thin black ring at the base of the arm web.

Plate 112f
Blue-ringed Octopus
Hapalochlaena lunulata
This extremely venemous, though non-aggressive, creature is active in shallow reefs during daylight. The blue rings become more obvious when the octopus is agitated.

Plate 112g
Giant Clam
Tridacna gigas
This is the largest of the giant clams (genus Tridacna), reaching a length of up to 1.3 m (4.3 ft). Formerly common in offshore reefs, it is now rare over much of its range owing to overharvesting.

Plate 112h
Broadclub Cuttlefish
Sepia latimanus
This large cuttlefish is a quick (color) change artist. It is active during daylight on shallow reefs, where it can often be found in pairs. It can be quite curious.

Plate 112 **513**

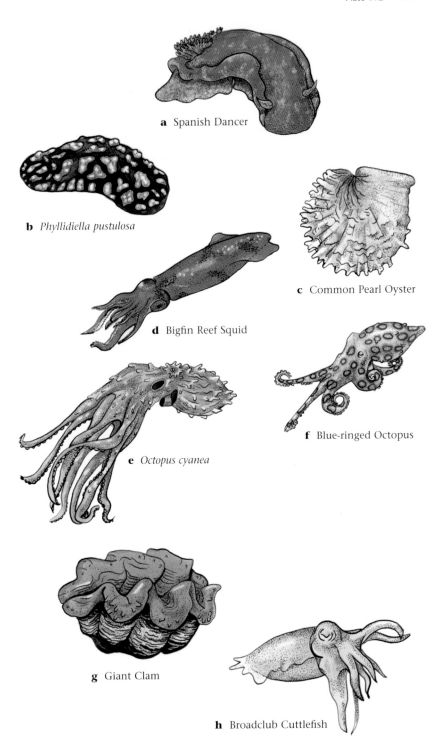

a Spanish Dancer

b *Phyllidiella pustulosa*

c Common Pearl Oyster

d Bigfin Reef Squid

e *Octopus cyanea*

f Blue-ringed Octopus

g Giant Clam

h Broadclub Cuttlefish

Plate 113a
Odontodactylus scyllarus
This mantis shrimp is a real beauty. It has a bright green body, blue head and eyes, and bright red appendages. It prefers sand and rubble and feeds at night on a variety of other crustaceans, mollusks, and worms.

Plate 113b
Banded Coral Shrimp
Stenopus hispidus
Cleaner shrimp are often strikingly colored, ostensibly to attract clients to their cleaning stations (p. 250). This species has a thin body with red and white bands extending to the claws. When a fish arrives at a cleaning station, the shrimp palpitates it with its antennae; this causes the fish to relax so that the shrimp can crawl all over its body, looking for ectoparasites.

Plate 113c
Bumblebee Shrimp
Gnathophyllum americanum
This blunt-headed shrimp has one large claw that is almost as long as its body and a shorter one on the other side, like a fiddler crab. Its body is white with black and brown bands.

Plate 113d
Harlequin Shrimp
Hymenocera picta
This shrimp can be easily identified by its bold markings—red, burgundy, or purple spots on a white body. It preys on starfish, which it consumes from the tip of the arm toward the central mouth. In this way it keeps the starfish alive for an extended period so that the shrimp can dine at its leisure.

Plate 113e
Spiny Lobster
Panulirus pencillatus
This is the most common spiny lobster and can be readily identified by the white spots on the back of the carapace.

Plate 113f
Linckia multiflora
This variably colored sea star is common on shallow reefs. It is usually mottled with red, blue, and yellow hues.

Plate 113g
Nardoa rosea
This sea star is endemic to the Great Barrier Reef, where it can be found in very shallow reefs. It can be identified by the prominent white and orange tubercles (bumps) on its surface.

Plate 113h
Crown-of-Thorns
Acanthaster planci
This notorious sea star is no longer considered quite the predatory demon it was once thought to be, but local population explosions of this species have resulted in the decimation of coral reefs. Its formidable spines make it easy to identify.

Plate 113 515

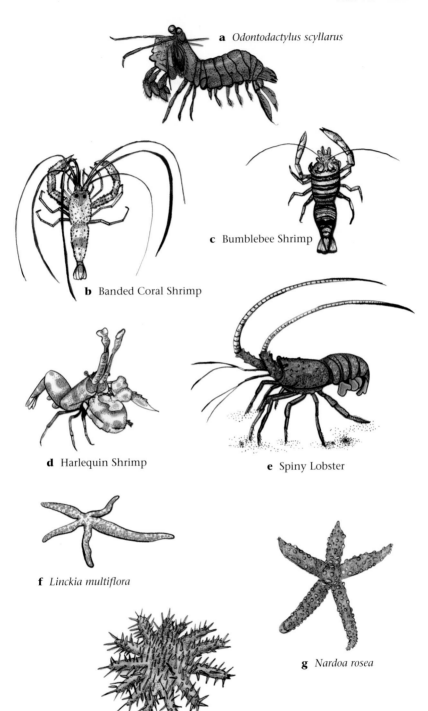

a *Odontodactylus scyllarus*

c Bumblebee Shrimp

b Banded Coral Shrimp

d Harlequin Shrimp

e Spiny Lobster

f *Linckia multiflora*

g *Nardoa rosea*

h Crown-of-Thorns

Plate 114a
Ophiothrix nereidina
This brittle star has a green disc and long spines.
It is active in shallow water.

Plate 114b
Echinothrix diadema
The spines of this urchin are closed at the tip and
pointed. They are also densely packed. This
urchin is more likely to be found out in the open
than most others.

Plate 114c
Tripneustes gratilla
This is one of the more common urchins. It prefers
calm, shallow water such as lagoons. It frequently
covers itself with debris, presumably for
camouflage. The color is quite variable, and the
spines are arranged in distinct bands.

Plate 114d
Echinometra mathaei
This is a stout-spined urchin. The spines tend to
be reddish with a white ring around the base of
each. It is found on very shallow reefs.

Plate 114e
Slate Pencil Urchin
Heterocentrotus mammillatus
The extremely thick blunt spines are what
distinguishes this sea urchin. The color is
extremely variable. It prefers shallow reefs; look
for it in crevices.

Plate 114f
Bohadschia paradoxa
This sea cucumber likes sandy habitats in shallow
water. One of the fatter species, it is brown with
fairly short papillae (bumps).

Plate 114g
Holothuria atra
This sausage-shaped sea cucumber is black, but
it often covers itself with sand. One of the most
common species, it sometimes forms
aggregations in shallow sandy areas.

Plate 114h
Stichopus chloronotus
This sea cucumber prefers coral rubble and rocky
areas. Its dark green body is adorned with long
black papillae (bumps) with orange tips.

Plate 114 517

a *Ophiothrix nereidina*

b *Echinothrix diadema*

c *Tripneustes gratilla*

d *Echinometra mathaei*

e Slate Pencil Urchin

f *Bohadschia paradoxa*

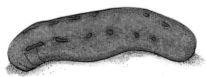

g *Holothuria atra*

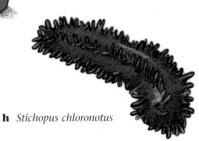

h *Stichopus chloronotus*

SPECIES INDEX

GENERAL INDEX

Explanation of Symbols Used in the Plate Section

HABITAT SYMBOLS

= Rainforest (also called closed forest, monsoon forest).

= Open forest and woodland (includes most eucalypt forests; also called sclerophyll forest).

= Shrubland (generally with shrubs up to 4 m, 13 ft, high).

= Heathland (open areas of evergreen shrubs usually less than 2 m, 6.5 ft, high; occurs over some coastal lowlands and in subalpine and alpine areas).

= Open habitats: grassland, pastures, savannah (grassland with scattered trees and shrubs), gardens, roadsides, rocky cliffs. Species found in these habitats prefer very open areas.

= Freshwater. For species typically found in or near lakes, dams (ponds), reservoirs, streams, rivers, marshes, swamps, billabongs (stagnant pools in beds of seasonal streams).

= Saltwater. For species usually found in or near the ocean, ocean beaches, or mangroves.

REGIONS (see Map 2, p. 27):

CYP = The Cape York Peninsula, which is the northern tip of Queensland
TRQ = Tropical Queensland; coastal and inland northern parts of the state
TEQ = Temperate Queensland; inland southern parts of the state
NSW = New South Wales
VIC = Victoria
TAS = Tasmania